Mass Communication Review Yearbook

Editorial Board

Mass Communication Review Yearbook

Volume 1

1980

G. Cleveland Wilhoit
Editor

Harold de Bock
Associate Editor

SAGE
PUBLICATIONS

For information address:

SAGE Publications, Inc.
275 South Beverly Drive
Beverly Hills, California 90212

SAGE Publications Ltd
28 Banner Street
London EC1Y 8QE, England

Printed in the United States of America

International Standard Book Number 0-8039-1186-6

International Standard Series Number 0196-8017

FIRST PRINTING

Contents

About the Editors

G. CLEVELAND WILHOIT is Professor of Journalism and Associate Director of the Bureau of Media Research at Indiana University. A member of the editorial board of *Journalism Quarterly*, he is also a member of the News Research Committee of the American Newspaper Publishers Association. Head of the Standing Committee on Research of the Association for Education in Journalism (AEJ), Wilhoit is a past-head of the Theory and Methodology Division of AEJ. He is also a member of the International Association of Mass Communication Researchers (IAMCR). Wilhoit has published in communication and political science journals and is a contributing author of *Hand-Book of Reporting Methods*. He is coauthor of *Newsroom Guide to Polls and Surveys* and *A Computerized Bibliography of Mass Communication Research, 1944-1964*. In 1975 Wilhoit was a visiting research fellow at the Audience Research Department, Netherlands Broadcasting Foundation. Wilhoit received his Ph.D. in mass communication research and political science at the University of North Carolina at Chapel Hill in 1967.

HAROLD de BOCK is Director of Audience Research at the Netherlands Broadcasting Foundation (NOS), Hilversum. He has published in mass communication research journals in Europe and the United States. He recently directed a major audience research project in the Netherlands Antilles. De Bock received his Kandidaats and Doctoraat degrees in political science and mass communications from the University of Amsterdam. He received the Ph.D. in mass communications from Indiana University in 1973. De Bock is a member of the International Association of Mass Communication Researchers.

Preface

A chief goal of this new Sage *Mass Communication Review Yearbook* series was to produce a series of volumes that is international in scope, concentrating particularly on mass communication research in America and Europe. The first task was establishment of a distinguished editorial board of scholars.

The international editorial board members, whose names are printed in the front matter of the *Yearbook*, have been extremely active in the development of this first volume. These scholars, from 13 countries, searched journals and unpublished sources for the best recent research in their areas.

Hundreds of articles and manuscripts were evaluated. A primary criterion for selection was the extent to which an article synthesized a particular area of inquiry or attempted to define the field in a provocative way. Other work that was representative of significant approaches or that addressed highly important communication problems was included.

This first volume reflects both the richness and the frequency of contemporary articles that synthesize and define the field. Future volumes will attempt to maintain a synthesizing focus, but both the form and content of subsequent volumes will, obviously, depend on trends and activity in the field. Some sections will change from year to year to reflect those directions. Each volume, though, will have sections dealing with theory, methodology, policy research, and political communication.

Editing a book that is as broad in scope and in geographic territory as this one is not easy. Harold de Bock, associate editor for Europe, has made the job of trans-Atlantic editing far less difficult, and I owe him a great deal. His facility with languages and knowledge of European work have been invaluable.

F. Gerald Kline, Director of the School of Journalism and Mass Communication at the University of Minnesota, developed the idea for this series (in concert with the publishers) and was also a great help in setting up the international editorial board and the procedures for editing the series.

David H. Weaver, Director of the Bureau of Media Research at Indiana University, provided both critical judgment and administrative support for this project. Frances Goins Wilhoit, head of the Indiana University journalism library, provided extensive bibliographic research for the volume.

Inez Woodley, administrative secretary of the Bureau of Media Research, combined her talents as an unusually good copy editor and fine secretary to become absolutely indispensable to the book. Jeff Black, a Bureau assistant, was a great help not only clerically but in keeping us sane with his unique sense of humor.

—G. Cleveland Wilhoit
Bloomington, Indiana

Introduction

G. Cleveland Wilhoit

With unprecedented international scholarly exchange, mass communication research has become a worldwide field. Establishment of research centers throughout the world has expanded the volume of investigation and study, and repeatedly we encounter the need for improved communication of these significant findings. *Communication Abstracts,* established in 1978 by Sage Publications, is a major advance for the field in quickly disseminating the results of individual studies.

Still lacking, though, is a medium for synthesizing the vast range of international research in mass communication on a regular basis. This *Yearbook* series is an attempt to provide some of the needed synthesis of bench mark developments and of important trends in the field.

Specifically, the *Yearbook* has two main objectives. The first is to publish annually in a single volume the most durable work in mass communication research. Articles that integrate ongoing work, that map new directions, or that represent a significant approach have priority.

Second, the book attempts to accelerate the growing communication between European and American scholars. A considerable portion of each *Yearbook* will contain European work that has not yet come to the widespread attention of an American scholarly audience.

For this volume, a distinguished editorial board of 38 scholars surveyed their fields of expertise for the best recent work and recommended hundreds of articles. From those recommendations, and from additional searches by the editors, 47 articles were chosen for publication.

Organized in eight sections, most of which will appear in the format of future editions, this volume contains both original and reprinted work. Several European pieces in the *Yearbook* are translated into English for the first time here.

There are many young scholars in the list of authors published here, but the roll is dominated by mature scholars who have published widely and contributed much to the field. Several pioneering leaders, such as Wilbur Schramm and Kurt Lang, have important articles here, suggesting that the field has reached a state of maturity sufficient to attract some of the best scholars for the entirety of their careers.

Vigorous intellectual questions bring out the best in any discipline. Much of the material in this book suggests the new decade will indeed mark a germinal period of the field's history. Great scholarly development is evidenced in the increasing level of collaboration and sometimes bitter debate between American and European scholars, and within each national group. Furthermore, there are indications that a historical perspective of ourselves and our research questions has emerged, deeply enriching the work we do.

MAJOR TRENDS IN THE FIELD

The several years' work reviewed and the material published in this first *Yearbook* indicate major trends in the field. The most significant, and one already alluded to, is the extent of international exchange. References in research articles are far likelier to have an international scope today than ten years ago, and the number of debates and conferences transcending national boundaries has grown dramatically.

Expanded international contacts have enriched the field in numerous ways; one of the most visible is in the fostering of lively debate about the purposes and theoretical bases of mass communication research. Some European scholars are harsh in their evaluation of American work, labeling it primarily "administrative" research influenced by the needs and objectives of the institutions of mass communication. Their own work, they argue, is "critical" and based on a clearer philosophy of society than is U.S. research.

While there is some truth to the Europeans' claim, a search for the best work throughout the world shows surprisingly greater similarity in theory, scope, and method of mass communication research than the debate would suggest. Uses and gratifications studies, cultural indicators research, content analyses of news bias, and agenda-setting-type studies—with assumptions similar to those found in American work—are conducted around the world.

A major difference, on the other hand, is apparent in the disciplinary identification of mass communication scholars. Europeans, at least the visible, vocal ones, often identify themselves as sociologists or social theorists, and they reject the idea of a communication theory that is discrete from social theory. Americans are far more eclectic than are Europeans, but have been influenced greatly by a social psychology mold. About thirty percent of all research published in U.S. journals has used experimental design to study media effects.[1] While it is clear that the American identification with social psychology as a model is lessening as the shift toward a media institutional research context is realized, many U.S. researchers still hold to the notion of a unified communication theory as a goal.

Both the European preoccupation with social theory and the American focus on social psychology and communication theory lead to an emulation of the traditional disciplinary forms of the social sciences. Such modeling on the traditional disciplines tends to cut us off from the humanistic, artistic, historical, and ethical moorings that are so important to the research on the institutional context of mass communication.

So, as the field moves toward a much greater concern about the development, control, support, and institutional context of mass communication, our scope of inquiry must be far broader than the social sciences. The arts, humanities, history, and the study of applied technology must all inform our inquiry.

A major development in recent mass communication research is a continuing shift in the conceptualization of effects research away from a preoccupation with attitude change, persuasion, and direct effects, toward such concerns as the role of mass media in political reasoning, knowledge acquisition, and agenda-setting. Corollary with this shift is a reanalysis of the "limited effects" interpretation, which typified much of the research at mid-century, to view suggesting longer-term, significant influences of mass media on socialization and social change.

The move to a longer-term, longitudinal view of the role of mass communication has been accompanied, if not preceded by, changes in methodology. Time-series studies, path analysis, cross-lagged correlation, and field designs are being applied more frequently. Multimethodological approaches are also more numerous than a decade ago.

A most dramatic change has been to link content analysis to survey work in major programs of research. Agenda-setting studies and cultural indicators research use the two methodologies to establish linkages between media and audience effects. Content analysis, particularly the quantitative approach, still has vocal critics, as we see in this volume, but its usefulness is obviously enhanced when it is combined with other methodologies.

Finally, accompanying the trend toward longitudinal, long-term studies in the field is an awareness that the institutions of mass communication should be focal points of research, placing those institutions in their societal context. Historically, in one of the least-studied areas of mass communication, the development, control, and support of mass media institutions, today are emerging as a dominant subject of concern throughout the world.[2]

SCOPE OF THE YEARBOOK

The last several years have marked a time of disquiet about the definition of the field and the purpose of its inquiry. As a result, an unusual number of integrative works have been produced, several of which appear here. The first section of the book, Theoretical Perspectives, underscores this concern, presenting some of the most penetrating analyses in the history of the field.

As research concerns shift toward longitudinal, long-term studies, research methodology has become more sophisticated. New strategies of research are suggested in Part II of the book.

Part III, Political Communication, contains major studies that synthesize a great deal of research on political knowledge and reasoning. Information-seeking from both individual and community levels is dealt with in Part IV.

A symposium of articles about cultural indicators research is presented in Part V. Dealing with crime and violence in the mass media, the articles represent a trans-Atlantic assessment of cultural indicators analysis.

Impact of Mass Communication: Television, Part VI, presents major integrative works which summarize and assess hundreds of studies on the effects of television. The articles range from a look at total societal effects to an analysis of the research on TV and children.

Part VII, International and Comparative Research, contains pioneering work on the question of news flow in Third World countries. Studies of the media system in China and the role of mass media in social change in modern Europe are also presented.

The final section deals with two scholarly debates on policy research in mass communication.

The remainder of this chapter summarizes and synthesizes the studies presented in this volume of the *Yearbook*.

PART I: THEORETICAL PERSPECTIVES

A common thread in many of the synthesizing works in Part I is the popular division of European and American work along the lines of critical research as opposed to administrative (noncritical) scholarship. That such a strict division is no longer valid, if it ever was, is suggested by the array of scholarship in this volume.

Jay G. Blumler, in the first article in this section, finds American work virtually unclassifiable, as compared to the typically critical work of Europeans. He sees European work as questioning some of the basic assumptions of liberal democratic philosophy, and he urges that American work move closer to the "institutional cutting edge" of policy research.

While the institutional priorities suggested by Blumler are well worth attention, his provocative piece does not consider a very sturdy historical-legal research tradition in the United States that has been just as critical of classical liberal assumptions as has European research. The work of the Hutchins Commission on Freedom of the Press, in the 1940s, and that of Fred Siebert and J. Edward Gerald, typify a critical tradition that has been very much alive in America.[3]

Kurt Lang, in the second piece in this book, argues that the empirical tradition of research in the United States (and it is only this tradition of which Europeans largely are aware) was anticipated (and certainly not rejected) in the works of major German classical sociologists such as Max Weber. Furthermore, Lang points out that broad social-political trends in the early and middle parts of this century were just as responsible for the "administrative" questions asked by American empirical researchers as were the market needs of the mass media.

Two young British researchers at the University of Leicester's Centre for Mass Communication draw a different bead on American work. Peter Golding and Graham Murdock reject the validity of seeking mass communication theory, a frequently cited goal in American work, and argue that the only task of research is to analyze the social processes through which mass media messages are produced and interpreted. The focus of mass communication research, in their view, is on the contextual pressures that shape media messages, as opposed to the messages themselves.

Golding and Murdock virtually ignore the question of how one researches the role of contextual pressures in shaping messages without also looking at what the messages say. They essentially reject any role for content analysis, including the type employed by George Gerbner and Larry Gross in a cultural indicators approach.

The basic sociological questions that excite Golding and Murdock are obviously important, and we need to be reminded of them constantly. On the other hand, Steven Chaffee's compelling look at some of the most important empirical work in the field clearly suggests American researchers are aware of the need for major new work on the media in the context of social units such as the family and the community. More importantly, Chaffee carefully crafts another of the common threads running through much of the work in this book, the eclipsing of the minimal effects interpretation and the emergence of new approaches that are sensitive to longitudinal and less direct effects of mass communication.

It is conceptually broadened hypotheses about media effects and methodological advances that Chaffee sees to be responsible for opening pathways to a more realistic assessment of mass communication impact. No doubt Chaffee is right about this, but Denis McQuail adds another dimension.

McQuail reminds us that the relationship of mass media to government and society is not static, and that with changing media relationships the effects themselves may change. His observation raises the question of whether media power in the major industrial societies may have increased since the early landmark studies of the 1940s, suggesting that the minimal effects interpretation might have been right for its time.

In calling for a media science, McQuail introduces another common thread of the work in this yearbook, the problems of the uneasy relationship among researchers, professional media people, and government. The relationship McQuail describes is similar to that of the journalist and public officials, one that ranges from cooperation to an adversarial stance. He clearly defines the field in terms similar to those advanced by David Weaver and Richard Gray in their contribution, and he rejects the idea that questions arising from a professional media context are uninteresting.

Weaver and Gray have sparked a spirited debate among American researchers with their chapter on the history and future of the field. Their analysis suggests that, in the American context, research priorities have been closely tied to research funding, even though the diversity of funding sources for mass communication was found to be much greater than that for sociology and psychology. The pattern, then, has been an increasing concentration of effects studies. Weaver and Gray argue that a major intellectual focus of the field ought to be the institutional setting of journalists and the social-intellectual climate in which they work.

The field of research in the Weaver and Gray article is defined much too narrowly for James W. Carey, who responds critically to the piece. For Carey, the intellectual history of communication takes a much wider, richer path, including Dewey, Lippmann, and many others. He is correct, of course, but Weaver and Gray also see the relevant intellectual roots as broad (hence their call for studies of broad social-intellectual impact on the journalist).

Another serious reservation held by Carey is a problem sensed by many of the authors in this volume, particularly in the policy section at the end of the book. That problem is the threat to the independence of the scholar who defines his or her turf around a professional-institutional field, a problem which Carey addresses even more directly in his critique of the Katz report in the last section of the *Yearbook*. Steven Chaffee's comments on the Weaver-Gray paper share Carey's reservation about the definition of the field, but he, like McQuail, is more comfortable than Carey with the institutional boundaries for research suggested by the paper.

In an essay about the "mass" in mass communication research, John Corner deals with the term that many apologize for and about which others are merely ambivalent. He argues that the utility of mass is its designation of the kind of system our research deals with, and he further says the term conveys well the notion that the communication experience mass media provide is different from other kinds of communication experience.

Taking a step back to a more macroscopic view of the field, Karl Erik Rosengren's concluding piece reviews a great many studies from mass communication and the sociology of knowledge. He argues that the central intellectual focus is the relationship between mass communication and social structure, a view largely shared by Golding and Murdock. Rosengren,though, argues that the basic problem is not so much with the questions that we have asked as with our methodology. He anticipates the issue of time in communication research, a problem dealt with in the next section on methodology.

PART II: RESEARCH STRATEGIES AND METHODOLOGY

The strengths and weaknesses of various research strategies in getting at substantive problems have also created intense attention and concern among mass communication scholars. This section contains five chapters dealing with major methodological problems.

Time is a crucial problem in mass communication research. The difficulty of assessing the role of media in society without appropriate time-series data was pointed out convincingly by Rosengren in his earlier article. McQuail also reminded us that the relative power positions of the media may shift with time, making time and history crucial for long-term understanding of media's role.

Philosophical conceptions of time and its uses in other fields of research set the background for the lead piece in this section in which F. Gerald Kline discusses the research design considerations of time. The social-psychological research tradition of the 1940s and 1950s used time causally in the experimental setting, but little was written about the timing of post measures. Kline points out that establishing causal links is only one of many problems involving time, and he suggests the crucial importance of time as a resource, as a social meaning, as a sequence, and as a quantitative relationship in research designs.

The outpouring of uses and gratifications studies in recent years has seemed to many to have produced a great deal more data than it has produced intriguing or useful findings. With the approach under attack from many quarters, Jay Blumler takes a major step in not only defending the gratifications strategy but in proposing how it may be more fruitfully applied. He argues cogently that there is no such thing as a uses and gratifications theory and that it is a misunderstanding to suspect that there ought to be one. The research *uses* of the gratifications approach are what matters, and Blumler suggests there are plenty of those. But its major use is for the testing of theoretical propositions against the sometimes hard realities of audience experience. Just because the audience is a bit obstinate and elusive to our data is no reason to give up on the approach.

Lee Becker pulls together four major sets of data to look at the reliability and validity of various gratifications measures. He shows that open-ended measures may not be sensitive to some gratifications which emerge from closed questions. His secondary analysis indicates that greater validity is obtained when gratifications measures are applied to a limited subject matter—politics, for example—than when they are applied to media content in general. The clearest finding, though, is that gratifications are not media-specific in the studies considered.

News bias research, one of the oldest concerns in the field, is not a very fashionable area of work, but it is of growing importance. As many societies of the world increasingly demand fairness or impartiality from their mass media, the research topic gains in social significance.

Broadcast law in Sweden requires impartiality in broadcast news. As a result of controversy about whether such regulation is successful, Swedish scholars have developed innovative ways to measure news bias. Rosengren summarizes various approaches.

Because news media must maintain credibility within their dominant cultures, Rosengren aruges that the news must be *partial* to some extent, partial to the basic values of the dominant culture in which it is written and reported. As a result, Rosengren attempts to synthesize the ideas of what he calls the objectivity, internatonal news flow, and credibility of research traditions. He finds that the *manifest* content of the media is not enough to address questions of reportorial bias. Study of the entire news process, and its social setting, is necessary.

The call for an institutional-organizational research perspective that appears so frequently in the works published here is superbly answered in the piece by Paul Hirsch. He not only examines the strengths and theoretical relationships of the occupational, organizational, and institutional models of research, but his analysis suggests it is a mistake to think of studies of news and entertainment as separate enterprises. They should be studied together in a macro-level approach in which the media are treated as culture processors, on terms somewhat similar to those called for in George Gerbner's rationale for cultural indicators studies. Hirsch's contribution is a theoretical-methodological strategy for organizing such inquiry. His work comes closer to offering a map of the institutional research territory than any we have had before.

PART III: POLITICAL COMMUNICATION

One of the most common criticisms of mass communication research over the years has been that it is disjointed and lacking context. Many of the synthesizing works presented in this volume go far toward giving a connectivity that has been missing. This is especially true of political communication, an area which has received considerable thought and synthesis over the years, particularly in political campaign communication.

The U.S. presidential campaign TV debates of 1976 were the subject of a large number of studies, which are masterfully analyzed and woven together by Steven Chaffee. Avoiding the traditional effects perspective, Chaffee looks at thirty studies to consider the usefulness of the debates to voters and to the political system. Chaffee's analysis indicates the TV debates were clearly useful. They provided issue information to a huge audience of American voters. Voting intentions of persons who were regular viewers of the series were more likely to be changed than were those of the casual watchers. Regular viewers were also least likely to be influenced by predispositional factors and were more likely to vote according to their perceptions of policy differences between themselves and the presidential candidates.

A reasonably positive picture of the utility of the televised debates shown in the Chaffee analysis is blurred a bit by the work of Peter Clarke and Eric Fredin. Using a large national sample involving 67 news markets in the United States, Clark and Fredin look at mass communication and political reasoning by prospective voters. For television their findings are dismal. Television use appears to be negatively related to having reasons to favor or oppose a U.S. senatorial candidate in 1974. On the other hand, newspaper use correlates positively with political reasoning. In addition, intermarket comparison shows that newspaper competition and diversity were related to public understanding of campaign issues.

In reconciling the disparity between what seems to be a useful role for TV debates and a negative role for television in senatorial campaign news, a crucial question is how much information is available about Senate campaigns. Admittedly, comparing presidential TV debates to senatorial campaign news is like comparing the Super Bowl to local TV sportscasts. One is a media event, attracting colossal audiences to a defined time slot. The other is much less predictable. Still, the differences noted between the Chaffee and the Clarke-Fredin findings may boil down to the amount of information actually available in televised news coverage of state political campaigns.

Just such a question is at the heart of Kent Asp's chapter about a civic crisis in 1977 as result of the proposed construction of an inner-city parking garage in Gothenburg, Sweden. Asp developed a content analysis scheme to measure the information value of the mass media coverage of the demonstrations and issues that emerged during the controversy. The scheme hinges on identifying a universe of possible arguments about the issue and then measuring the depth and breadth of their media coverage.

In general, Asp concluded that the mass media enable the protesting constituencies to block successfully the government-proposed parking garage. This was possible not only because the media legitimized the protest, but also because media coverage contributed to the poitical reasoning and debate which surrounded the demonstrations.

In addition, Asp found divergent information value among Swedish media. Morning newspapers had a higher information value about the controversy than did afternoon papers. Television news had less information value than did newspapers. Asp speculates that the television interviewing form may be more responsible for the differences than just the amounts of time spent in covering the controversy in the different media

Charles Atkin and Walter Gantz tackle another neglected area, the possible role of TV news in the political socialization of children. Using longitudinal questionnaire data from elementary-grade students, Atkin and Gantz find a positive relationship between viewing TV news and political knowledge among older children. A random subsample of parents were interviewed by telephone, enabling the authors to conclude also that parent-child discussion of news increases the likelihood that children will watch TV news. Cross-lagged correlation analysis shows TV news to be the predominant causal factor in political socialization of the older children.

In the final chapter in this section, David Weaver and Judith Buddenbaum analyze more than 100 uses and effects studies of television and newspapers. A majority, but not all, of the studies concerned political communication by these media. Although TV and newspapers appear to be functional complements on both knowledge and diversion, there is competition between them for the audience's diversionary time. In line with the work discussed in this section, Weaver and Buddenbaum's synthesis finds newspaper use to be more strongly associated with voting turnout and other political behavior than is television.

PART IV: INFORMATION-SEEKING

Information-seeking strategy is an area of study that places in relief the magnitude of mass communication research problems. Individual styles may be reasonably expected to influence information-seeking, but the universe of information available to seek is, at least in part, influenced by macro-social variables such as community. The magnitude of the problem is illustrated in the two chapters in this section.

A model of information-seeking is developed in the work by Lewis Donohew, Leonard Tipton, and Roger Haney. Living in the midst of a world center of horse-racing and horse farms, Donohew and his University of Kentucky colleagues devised an ingenious experiment dealing with horse-racing to explore information-seeking styles. Their experiment isolated four distinct styles of information-seeking. There were loners, formal seekers, risky seekers, and informal seekers. Formal seekers pursued a broad-based strategy and acquired more information than the other groups. Risky seekers used a very narrow strategy, depending on a few key sources. Loners and informal seekers seemed to divide on personality, with the informal seekers being more outgoing and interpersonal than the other groups.

Although the different styles appear unrelated to actual success in the experimental task of predicting winning horses, the possibility of differential quality of information gain and decision-making exists for the four styles. In addition, the model has implications for the study of mass media reporters as well as audience behavior.

Although it is quite a leap from studies of individual information-seeking to the study of information societies, the two levels are very much related. Despite widespread calls for such studies, few researchers have taken a macro-level, empirical perspective on mass communication. An exception is this work by C. N. Olien, G. A. Donohue, and P. J. Tichenor.

Data from nineteen Minnesota communities support the thesis that community structure and size tend to shape the mass media information available, the media choices, and the uses made of those media by the citizens. Community structure was clearly more highly correlated with media choice and use than was educational level. Olien, Donohue, and Tichenor conclude from their work that community structure is a principal element of media environment and information control.

PART V: CRIME AND VIOLENCE IN MASS COMMUNICATION

Of all the cultural indicators possible in mass communication, crime and violence seem to have been the most researched. In fact, the cultural indicators approach, associated most directly with the work of George Gerbner and Larry Gross, seems to be most frequently cited in terms of violence.

This part of the book presents a variety of perspectives about the major work of Gerbner and Gross on violence and crime in the content of television. While their chapter seems focused on media content alone, Gerbner and Gross, of course, see their work as much broader and more theoretical. They maintain that television is now the foremost vehicle of culture production and social control throughout most of the world.

Appropriately, Gerbner and Gross appear first with the tenth in their series of violence profiles. Far more than a profile, though, the work contends that the dismal picture of crime, violence, fear, and inequity pervading television is not so much an instigator of fear and violence as it is a demonstration of power. The TV portrait of mayhem and justified violence is a subtle means of social control. Through the ritual of television-watching by the clock and not by the program, enormous audiences see the rules of life, see who has power and who is weak, all according to the established power structure that is reflected by (that *is*) television.

Furthermore, the latest Gerbner-Gross report provides still more survey data (this time of adolescents) revealing that the perceptions of heavy TV viewers (those who watch a great deal of TV) about law enforcement procedures are dramatically different from the outlook of light viewers. Calling their survey work cultivation analysis, the Gerbner-Gross team concludes from it support for their thesis about the cultural power of TV.

Luc van Poecke, a Belgian scholar, applauds the theoretical implications of the Gerbner-Gross thesis about the cultural power of television, but his praise ends there. He argues that the content analysis scheme, preoccupied only with quantification of disconnected social acts, becomes the message. It is inadequate, he says, because it fails to tap the semiotic context of the messages. Classical content analysis is not equal to the theoretical task of studying mass communication as the production of ideology, concludes van Poecke.

Conceptions of violence are so closely related to both culture and time that research on the topic is extremely difficult. This difficulty and the validity and causality problems of experimentation lead James D. Halloran to dismiss most of the American work on media violence. The most serious problem in his view is that the questions are all wrong. Gerbner's work, though, is more to his liking. The cultural indicators approach is sensitive to what Halloran regards as the key question of whether televised violence is used to legitimize and maintain power and authority of established elites. He sees this as a far more realistic and serious question than the trivial results from experiments on individual modeling behavior or the instigation of aggression through frustration.

Horace Newcomb, a Texas scholar, is more in line with van Poecke's critique. He commends the innovative research done by Gerbner and Gross, but he questions the basic validity of the violence profile research. In Newcomb's view, the cultural indicators approach is couched in terms of a ritual model of culture studies, but it is the old, outmoded transportation model of communication that actually drives the research. The proof of this, he asserts, is the cultivation analysis of survey results. As it turns out, the work of Anthony Doob and Glen Macdonald, the last piece in this section, suggests that Newcomb may be right.

But Gerbner and Gross do not agree with Newcomb. In their rebuttal, they maintain that the survey data prove the validity of their cultural indicators analysis, particularly when comparing heavy and light viewers' perceptions of crime. Furthermore, they see their analysis as doing far more than a simple transportation model implies because they go a step further and demonstrate that the social sources of television content are rooted deeply in our societal structure.

There is agreement, then, that the cultivation analysis of the survey data is a vital link in the Gerbner-Gross cultural indicator theory. It is on this point that the two Canadian scholars, Doob and Macdonald, perform a replication of Gerbner's work. Doob and Macdonald collect survey data from carefully designated high and low-crime areas of Toronto. Replicating Gerbner and Gross' interview schedule (with additional questions of their own) dealing with perceptions of crime and the likelihood of becoming victims of crime, Doob and Macdonald find results similar to those of the Gerbner team. Heavy TV viewers exaggerate the likelihood of their being crime victims. However, when the actual incidence of crime in the respondents' neighborhoods was controlled for, there was *no* overall relationship between television viewing and fear of victimization. Gerbner and Gross have carefully controlled their analyses for a great range of socioeconomic variables, but the Doob and Macdonald findings obviously suggest the need to include incidence of crime as a variable.

In general, then, major criticisms of cultural indicators research may be alleviated through methodological improvements, in both the content analysis and the survey elements. Greater consideration of the dramatic or news content of the cultural indicators being coded and tighter controls on social environmental variables in the cultivation analysis are cleary needed in this important area of research.

PART VI: IMPACT OF
MASS COMMUNICATION: TELEVISION

Although all the authors in the preceding section question the validity of much of the traditional work on the effects of television, far more effort and money have supported that work than any other subfield. The 1978 publication by Columbia University Press of *Television and Human Behavior,* a synthesis of thousands of studies, has been widely noted. Here the senior author of that work distills much of the larger Rand Corporation report.

George Comstock points out that the conclusion of minimal effects has been mistakenly applied to television, primarily because of the failure to document a major independent impact of television on viewers. The perspective has now changed. Even though the independent effects of television appear small—because they are interlarded with a host of other factors—their social importance may be great, Comstock concludes.

Widespread popular speculation about the effects of *Roots,* an eight-part TV series about the origins and history of slavery in America, accompanied the broadcasts in January 1977. Kenneth K. Hur and John P. Robinson collected survey data about the program from a sample of Cleveland, Ohio, residents. *Time* magazine called *Roots* a "nightly Super Bowl," attracting the largest audience in the history of American television.[4] Hur and Robinson agree that it attracted huge audiences, but they doubt it had the impact popularly attributed to it. Their data show that selective exposure and selective perception limited the program's influence on white racial attitudes in the Cleveland sample.

The approach in Comstock's earlier piece, however, suggests possible alternate interpretations of the Hur-Robinson data. Apparently there is no measure of the salience and intensity of white viewers' attitudes toward the problem of racial equality in the United States, nor of blacks' attitudes on similar dimensions. If the considerable audience of white sympathetic to problems of racial inequality *before* the program saw the problem as more salient *after* the series, that could, indeed, be a very powerful effect. Hur and Robinson do speculate that the program may have had great impact on black viewers, which in the long run may result in far more than "minimal effects" on the society at large.

No subject involving mass media draws more controversy than television and children. The debate ranges from TV as a "plug-in drug" to the uncommon potential of television for prosocial learning.

In a very thorough review of a wealth of research and thought on children and television, Ellen Wartella questions the view that the young are passive sponges of TV. She maintains that children are *active* in cognizing their television worlds. Wartella concludes that there is a need for age-specific programming geared to the stages of child development. In addition, she contends that television, with appropriate parent-teacher intervention and supplementation, may be used to increase children's sophistication about advertising and media persuasion at an earlier age.

It is the experimental work on the topic of the effects of televised violence that has received top billing in much public discussion about the topic, at least before the work on cultural indicators became so widely discussed. F. Scott Andison has performed a unique analysis of 63 of the most important experimental studies on the topic since 1956. Andison reasons that the research shows that watching televised violence is related to subsequent aggression, but the more interesting results of his work relate to possible television effects on the experiments themselves. He speculates that the increasingly positive results (TV linked significantly to aggression) in the later years of experimentation may be related to the greater amounts of time spent with TV in those years. An alternate explanation he considers is improved methodology.

The impact of external social-psychological forces upon research on media violence and pornography is analyzed more fully by Thelma McCormack, a Canadian sociologist. McCormack reminds us that the experimental research in this area is only incidentally related to mass communication. Certainly, she says, the research has neither communication nor social theory underlying it.

McCormack's main charge, though, is that a clear sexist bias explains discrepant findings in violence and pornography. The experimental findings show that mass media violence leads to subsequent aggression but that pornography is innocuous. Such conclusions spring from a machismo orientation, a narcissistic pride in male sexual virility on the one hand and disquiet about homosexual overtones (males fighting males in boxing vignettes) on the other.

Removing media violence and pornography questions from the confines of psychology to the social world of conflict theory and reference group theory would, in McCormack's view, get at the true effects, which require social rather than biological explanations.

PART VII: INTERNATIONAL
AND COMPARATIVE RESEARCH

Intense international debate about world news flow and changing conceptions of national development have affected the direction of international and comparative research in recent years. Both these major themes are reflected in the work in this section.

In the lead article, Wilbur Schramm reports on new research that goes to the heart of the world debate about news flow. As visiting Aw Boon Haw Professor at the Chinese University of Hong Kong in 1977-1978, Schramm directed a team of researchers in a study of news circulation in Asia, with particular attention to the role of the international wire services.

The Asia wires of Reuters, Agence France-Presse, Associated Press and United Press International, and sixteen prestige Asian newspapers formed the major portion of the analysis. The research shows that Asian newspapers are essentially local, reflecting the interests and needs of their audiences. They devote about three-quarters of their news to their individual countries and show no greater interest in developmental news than do Western media.

Wire service coverage was fairly similar to the newspapers, with about half the wire news being about the Third World. As a whole, the patterns of coverage in the wires were similar to those in the newspapers, except that the dailies published a slightly higher proportion of crime and disaster news than did the wire services.

Coverage of "developmental" news (defined as "good" news about science, education, and commerce and the like) was sparse in both the wires and the newspapers. Schramm's chapter indicates that stories of a political nature were handled better than economic development stories, raising the question of whether the difference is a result of inadequate education in the area of economics, a nontraditional discipline for reporters.

In Schramm's research, development news from China was likelier to be used in Asian newspapers than such news from other countries, partly because China is obviously both important and interesting to other Asian countries. Some of the best work on China's communication system is now being conducted at the East-West Communication Institute at the University of Hawaii. Two articles from the Institute are reprinted here.

An outstanding China scholar, A. Doak Barnett, describes how the Chinese use very limited media technology to achieve great pervasiveness, penetration, and intensity of mass communication. Barnett details a highly centralized national communication system in which messages flow down through the Communist regime's major hierarchies of organization.

Great stress is given to interpersonal communication through oranizations in China. In addition, language changes have occurred as a result of the Chinese revolution which Barnett sees as enormously important in the transmisson of values. He calls for research on the role of communication in conflict resolution in China, in light of little apparent upward or lateral communication.

In the second piece dealing with communication in China, Godwin Chu describes some of the recent language changes. His analysis shows the deliberate, organized use of language to shift the traditional Chinese view of the universe as static to a view that it is controllable and conquerable. This is accomplished by replacing archaic terms of classical Chinese with colloquial phrases that contain strong action-oriented connotations.

Turning to Europe and television, the news coverage of foreign nations on Dutch television was analyzed by a team of researchers from the University of Amsterdam and the Audience Research Service of the Dutch Broadcasting Foundation. Eighty-five newscasts and public affairs programs from September 1975 and February 1976 were content analyzed.

Frans Bergsma, who directed the research team, attempts to test Galtung's complementarity hypothesis: The absence of some news values in a potential news event must be compensated for by other news values in order for it to receive news coverage. Little support was found for the Galtung hypothesis, but the study did find that socioculturally distant, less powerful, and poorer nations were treated more negatively in Dutch TV news than were richer, more similar cultures.

Longitudinal surveys, field experiments, and content analysis are used in Elisabeth Noelle-Neumann's chapter to address the role of mass media in social change in modern Europe. She looks closely at German journalists' opinions about various issues over the last decade and makes comparisons with both media content and public opinion over the same period.

Noelle-Neumann sees strong support for her hypothesis that under conditions of "media consonance" (consensus of coverage) the mass media are agents (or molders) of social change. Thus, her work clearly goes beyond the agenda-setting hypothesis to further document "a return to a concept of powerful media," a phrase Noelle-Neumann coined in 1973.

Ironically, as the media systems of developed societies begin to appear more powerful than the limited effects interpretation suggested, the conception of their role in developing societies has changed radically. World events and severe intellectual criticism have eclipsed the old paradigm of communication and national development, which implied a primarily one-way flow of messages from government development agencies to the people. The new paradigm of self-development, described in the chapter by Everett M. Rogers, suggests two main roles for mass communication: (1) answering requests for technical information by local constituencies and (2) disseminating information about the self-development accomplishments of local groups. Rogers concludes that the passing of the old paradigm is an example of a move to a more international behavioral science.

PART VIII: POLICY RESEARCH

Robust argument and some of the most strident published exchanges in the history of the field characterize the development of policy research in mass communication. Although the in-fighting may be unpleasant, it is a sign of a vibrant field.

Many of the issues raised in earlier sections emerge here, too. The definition of the field, the relation of its intellectual boundaries to the institutional setting of the professional journalist, the suggestion of a media science—all these strike at the heart of the policy research debate. The central issue, though, is the autonomy and independence of the researcher.

Both cases of policy research considered here are from Britain. British and American researchers comment on the cases in this section.

After fifteen months as a resident scholar with the British Broadcasting Company, Elihu Katz has proposed a program of policy research involving independent scholars and broadcasters. The aim is to improve media performance to meet the communication needs of society. He notes that British researchers, who are members of the same elites as broadcasters, are much closer to them than are their American colleagues. This social proximity gives British researchers an impact on public policy that is denied American researchers. In spite of this, Katz sees a need for more than this "common ground" between researchers and broadcasters. He argues that a "better shelter" is essential for cooperative research on institutional, audience, and societal questions.

In a response to the Katz proposal, James W. Carey argues that policy research is doomed to ambiguity because of the constant threat to the scholar's independence when working so closely with media institutions. Vital intellectual questions are unlikely to emerge from the cooperative setting proposed by Katz, and Carey argues that only compelling intellectual questions will attract the best minds to mass communication research.

James D. Halloran sees the statement of research priorities in the Katz report as both asociological and atheoretical, and he contends that the report is framed primarily in the broadcasters' terms of reference.

Herbert J. Gans is highly supportive of the Katz report, but he has suggestions for improving mass communication research generally. He argues that our work is too media-centered in that it often ignores the macro-social processes that surround mass communication.

Katz has the last word here with his comments on some of the arguments raised above. He contends that policy research can be intellectually challenging and that diverse financial support should be provided for the collaborative experiment he envisions.

In 1975 the major British political parties, the BBC, and the Independent Broadcasting Authority invited Jay G. Blumler, Michael Gurevitch, and Julian Ives to examine the strengths and problems of the British system of election broadcasting. The University of Leeds team conducted hundreds of interviews with experts and participants in the political campaign process. Content analysis of political coverage and secondary analysis of election surveys complemented elite interviews.

In their report *The Challenge of Election Broadcasting*, the Blumler team called for a series of programs called "Election Access," whereby the political parties would have unbridled party advocacy followed by broadcaster-controlled journalistic scrutiny. As a complement to this approach, broadcast news would be relieved of its obligations to provide precisely equal time and would assume a more journalistic, reportorial view of the campaign, reporting only what was, in the broadcaster's conception, newsworthy. Third, a "Campaign Review" program would periodically air the parties' reactions to the news.

In the chapter reprinted here from the Blumler team's report, the underlying assumptions of the team's research are outlined. Briefly, they assume that television has a formative influence on political campaigning and that there should be a clear division of labor between the televised political advocacy of the parties and journalistic scrutiny of the parties.

Nicholas Garnham writes a stinging review of the Blumler report, arguing that its recommendations were pro-broadcaster and likely to accelerate the decline of the political parties. Blumler and his colleagues cogently respond to the criticism and extend the debate to the crucial problem of policy research: To whom or what does the policy researcher owe allegiance? The answer, Blumler and Gurevitch assert, is that the researcher is loyal to a set of explicit principles, and not to individuals or media institutions.

CONCLUSION

When in the late 1930s Agnes Nieman left a bequest to Harvard University to raise the standards of American journalism, Harard's President James B. Conant was perplexed. He was doubtful that Harvard should be associated with journalism. "The last thing I should have thought of asking Santa Claus for was journalism," he is quoted as saying.[5]

In some ways, Conant's dilemma is still with us. Just how closely connected to the institutions of mass media should our research be, either intellectually or in terms of financial support?

The question, albeit in a variety of forms, is a theme that runs through many of the pieces in this *Yearbook*. It is a nagging question, and it is not resolved here. Perhaps it need not be resolved. Just as Harvard developed its distinguished program of Nieman Fellowships for journalists, so has mass communication research emerged as an eclectic and robust field. It is a field that is intellectually organized around an enormously attractive human activity, public communication. The interaction with professionals within mass media institutions, which is so important to the study of those media, will always be hazardous and controversial. But the work in this volume suggests that it is worth the risk.

CONTENT OF FUTURE VOLUMES

As this first volue of the *Yearbook* goes to press, some likely emphases of Volume 2 are apparent. Dozens of studies about international news flow are under way, generated by the Unesco resolutions and debate about the treatment of Third World countries in the world press. In addition, the World Administrative Radio Conference in Geneva in 1979 to consider radio spectrum allocation has produced considerable research on Third World communication systems. So Volume 2 is likely to include several studies along these lines.

A second notable emphasis of Volume 2 will be on communicator studies in an institutional setting, an area where much contemporary work is ongoing around the world. Last, agenda-setting research will be given solid theoretical assessment in Volume 2.

NOTES

1. Wayne A. Danielson and G. Cleveland Wilhoit, *A Computerized Bibliography of Mass Communication Research, 1944-1964* (New York: Magazine Publishers Association, 1967), p.xvii.

2. Danielson and Wilhoit, p. xix.

3. Commission on Freedom of the Press, *A Free and Responsible Press* (Chicago: University of Chicago Press, 1947). William E. Hocking, *Freedom of the Press: A Framework of Principle* (Chicago Press, 1947). Fred S. Siebert, Theodore Peterson, and Wilbur Schramm, *Four Theories of the Press* (Urbana: University of Illinois Press, 1963). J. Edward Gerald, *The Social Responsibility of the Press* (Minneapolis: University of Minnesota Press, 1963).

4. "Why 'Roots' Hit Home." *Time* (February 14, 1977): 69-71.

5. *Nieman Reports* (Winter 1979) 4: 2.

PART I

THEORETICAL PERSPECTIVES

Contrasts of European and American research objectives and theoretical orientations emerge in this first section. Some of the most outstanding scholars in the field attempt to define the purposes and scope of mass communication inquiry. While the perceived differences between the continents may be greater than the actual state of things, the evidence of serious intellectual exchange among mass communication scholars throughout the world is a very healthy sign.

The chapters in Part I suggest that the field's research questions are robust and of great social significance. It is apparent that the institutional setting of mass communication will be a major focus of future research and that the "minimal effects" interpretation of the middle part of the century has given way to fresh perspectives, new methodology, and a more vigorous academy of researchers.

In this Founders Lecture by Jay G. Blumler, honoring the memory of pioneer American researchers Chilton R. Bush and Ralph O. Nafziger, the philosophy and purposes of European and American work are compared. Blumler—who spoke to a packed audience of Association for Education in Journalism members at their Madison, Wisconsin, meeting in 1977—argues that American mass communication research is virtually unclassifiable, contrary to the common European criticism that is predominantly administrative research. On the other hand, he says, European work is cast in the form of critical research that questions the most basic assumptions of liberal democratic media philosophy. He says the major need of American work is to move toward the "institutional cutting edge" of policy research. Dr. Blumler is Director of the Centre for Television Research at the University of Leeds, England.

1

PURPOSES OF
MASS COMMUNICATIONS RESEARCH
A Transatlantic Perspective

Jay G. Blumler

*U.S. researchers are urged
to take initiative to bring
researchers and media leaders
closer together, thereby
increasing impact of research
on operations of media.*

► Overviews of work in progress in some portion of our field are commonly triangular in perspective. They comment, first, on the state of theoretical debate in the reviewed area, singling out those conceptual differences that shape its intellectual controversies; secondly, on the methodologies that guide various strategies of data collection, bearing the freight of our technical improvement hopes; and thirdly, on the emerging body of substantive findings, fixing the shifting boundary line between what we suppose we know and what we know we do not yet know.

In this talk my point of departure is rather different. It is as if I would direct attention to the *table* on which the triangle rests, a focus that comes naturally into view when strikingly divergent mass communications research styles of different countries—or Continents in our case—are contemplated. Such a transatlantic per-

spective tends to provoke questions about the *purposes* of our enterprise. Why may we engage in mass communications research? What are its social purposes? What are the chief alternative forms that answers to this question can take? Are they bound to polarize into two quite antithetical and irreconcilable positions—with one camp radically critical of the prevailing mass communications order, while the other willingly or unwittingly upholds it, and each fails to address the predominant preoccupations of the other? Is there no viable middle course of research purpose falling between such extremes? If there is, how might it be defined, and to what clarification and redirection of our energies might its pursuit call us?

► Should you ever cull the bibliographies for answers to these questions, you would not find many entries under the heading, "Mass Communications Research, Pur-

► The author is research director of the Centre for Television Research at the University of Leeds. This is the text of the first Founders' Lecture sponsored by the Theory and Methodology Division and the International Communications Division at the Annual Conference of the Association for Education in Journalism, Madison, Wisconsin, August 1977. The Founders' Lectures were instituted to honor the memory of Chilton R. Bush and Ralph O. Nafziger.

From Jay G. Blumler, "Purposes of Mass Communications Research: A Transatlantic Perspective," *Journalism Quarterly* 55 (Summer 1978) 219-230. Reprinted by permission.

poses of." But you *would* discover that a transatlantic contrast of scholarly approach prompted one of the few published confrontations over these matters, which was entered into in the early 1940s by Paul Lazarsfeld and Theodore Adorno, the former in an essay entitled, "Administrative and Critical Communications Research,"[1] the latter in an article entitled, "A Social Critique of Radio Music."[2] Both men had emigrated from Europe to the United States in the 1930s, Lazarsfeld eventually feeling very much at home here, Adorno never completely settling here. Both agreed that two models carved up the leading research purpose alternatives between them. Rare for individuals locked in quite fundamental dispute, they also agreed upon the essential features of these opposed models. Their discussion merits recall today, partly for its relevance to current developments in our field in Europe and the United States, partly for highlighting the seeds of polarization over the issues involved and partly for illustrating the difficulties of transcending the resulting differences.

According to Lazarsfeld and Adorno alike, the point of departure of *administrative research* was a perception of the mass media as neutral tools, capable of serving a wide range of purposes. Research in this so-called administrative vein takes as given the purposes of media users, or would-be users, and then collects information intended to promote the realization of those purposes. This might include studies of people's communication preferences, their exposure patterns and the various content forms made available to audiences, as well as studies of media impact under diverse conditions of presentation and reception. As Lazarsfeld defined this approach in a passage which is notable, perhaps, for the ambiguity it both contained and concealed:

Behind the idea of such research is the notion that modern media of communication are tools handled by people or agencies for given purposes. The purpose may be to sell goods, or to raise the intellectual standards of the population, or to secure an understanding of governmental policies, but in all cases, to someone who uses a medium for something, it is the task of research to make the tool better known and thus to facilitate its use.

For its part, *critical communications research* is skeptical of the very project of taking a single purpose and studying the means of its realization in isolation from the total historical situation in which such planning and activity takes place. Modern media of communication do far more to people than even those who administer them mean to do, and, from drives in the surrounding social fabric, they acquire a momentum all their own, leaving administrative agencies much less choice for independent action than they believe they enjoy. That is why critical communications research calls for study of what Lazarsfeld termed "the general role of our media of communication in the present system," yielding two other features of its approach in turn. First, it develops a broad general theory of the prevailing social trends of our time, locating communication organizations and processes within them. Lazarsfeld illustrated this tendency via the idea that centralized capitalism, needing to sell the goods it produces, develops a promotional culture, which engulfs the mass communications system at all levels and exposes audience members to manipulative forces, pushing them around like pawns on a chess board and depriving them of the spontaneity and dignity of autonomous human beings. Thus, the second main element of the critical mode is introduced; a sense of basic human values, which are continually denied and violated by existing economic, social and communication arrangements.

Adorno's essay chiefly adds to this definition a passionate demonstration of how an adherent of the critical standpoint would react to the suggestion that research should show how radio could bring good music to as many listeners as possible. Over the span of only a few pages, a

[1] Paul F. Lazarsfeld, "Administrative and Critical Communications Research," *Studies in Philosophy and Social Science,* Vol. 9, 1941. All citations from Lazarsfeld below are taken from this article.

[2] T.W. Adorno, "A Social Critique of Radio Music," *Kenyon Review,* 7: 208-217 (Spring 1945). All citations from Adorno below are taken from this article except where otherwise noted.

litany of critical agony after agony is piled up. You cannot study the attitudes of listeners on their own, Adorno argues, without considering how they reflect broader social behavior patterns, indeed how they are conditioned by the structure of society as a whole. In today's "society of commodities," he goes on, music itself has assumed a "commodity character," which radically alters both it and the listening experience. It gives rise to commodity listening, involving, for example, a tendency to listen to Beethoven's Fifth as if it were a set of quotations from Beethoven's Fifth. It fosters an indiscriminate and uncomprehending form of popular enthusiasm that misses the entire point of the composition. It is so promoted that "the listener virtually has no choice. Products are forced upon him. His freedom has ceased to exist." And it is packaged, universally and without qualification, in a standardized form. Adorno's wholesale relegation of mediated popular culture to a standardized dustbin is tellingly reflected in this sentence of quite unrelieved and undifferentiated condemnation: "And there is, above all, that whole sphere of music, whose life-blood is standardization: popular music, jazz, be it hot, sweet, or hybrid."

Lazarsfeld, a man of broad sympathies and ecumenical temperament, actually hoped that these approaches might complement each other and even be cultivated collaboratively in joint ventures. Such cooperation never materialized, however, presumably due to confusions and stumbling blocks on both sides of this research purpose divide.

Lazarsfeld erred mainly in conflating two sorts of purposes, which he brought under the single umbrella of administrative research as if they were essentially alike. He apparently saw no fundamental difference between research designed to promote media administrators' present goals, whatever they might be—such as selling more goods—and research designed to serve some broader social purpose, to which administrators might not be

committed, and to which they would therefore have first to be called—such as disseminating good music, drama or mature political information to the masses. Consequently, he drew no clear distinction between research in the service of media institutions' current objectives and research aimed to modify those objectives.

In Adorno's case, the confusions were yet more profound. They typify in an extreme form weaknesses that can still be found, though not so nakedly, in present-day takers of a critical stance. One concerns the curiously elastic role that is assigned to empirical fact-gathering in the critical system. This is simultaneously suppressed and accepted. It is suppressed because those who are caught up in the affairs of the empirical world typically misunderstand their own place in it: they are therefore lousy witnesses! Of listeners, Adorno said, for example, "We must try to understand them better than they understand themselves." Presumably that is why he forcibly stated in another writing that, "No continuum exists between critical theorems and the empirical procedures of natural science."[3] Yet he also acknowledged the legitimacy, even the necessity, for empirical enquiry. The paradox is soluble only by assigning to empirical work a firmly subordinate and guided role. The foundations of critical theory are rooted in self-evident truths about the nature of the social system and its connections with the communication system. The task of empirical enquiry, then, is largely to expose those links concretely and to show how the known social patterns impose themselves on, and operate within, the communication sphere in practice.

Another tension within the critical system stems from its Platonic, even Augustinian, outlook on the prevailing communication order. This severely limits its action implications, despite critical researchers' disdain for merely academic scholarship. On the one hand, there is an ideal world of social and communication relationships, in which man, if he inhabited it, could express and develop his humanity through cultural activity. But on

[3] T.W. Adorno, "Scientific Experiences of a European Scholar in America," in Donald Fleming and Bernard Bailyn (Eds.) *The Intellectual Migration* (Cambridge, Mass: Harvard University Press, 1969).

the other hand, media institutions are so socially constrained as to be incapable of belonging in any way to that ideal domain. The arrangements in force are as if cast down in a sphere of illusion and chimera, irretrievably cut off from direct access to all genuine human values, and so are doomed—even damned you might say—to pursue their own corrupt course. Lazarsfeld himself seemed keenly aware of the characteristic Platonism of this point of view, as this passage shows:

In order to understand clearly the idea of critical research, one must realize that it is being urged by men, who have the idea ever present before them, that what we need most is to do and think what we consider true, and not to adjust ourselves to the seemingly inescapable.

▶ Many research paths have been blazed, modified, erased and reopened in the third of a century that has passed since the time of the Lazarsfeld-Adorno debate. How do the terms in which they couched their conflicting alternatives appear in the light of research tendencies now prevalent in Europe and North America, respectively?

For Europe, the answer to such a question is more clear than what can be said about the American scene. Europe is undoubtedly providing a congenial proving ground for the development of much critically grounded mass communications inquiry at present. Not all European media scholars have adopted this model. Yet those who reject or look askance at it sometimes feel as if in a beleaguered and outmoded minority, while some of the most active and self-confident European academics belong to what is virtually, though with many internal distinctions and points of dispute of course, a critical research school.[4]

For summary purposes, four features of critically oriented European research deserve notice. First, macroscopic levels of enquiry are decidedly favoured. In his Inaugural Lecture of 1973, for example, Professor James Halloran, director of the Leicester University Centre for Mass Communication Research, argued the case for an extension of the field's research agenda in two directions, going beyond

what he regarded as its previously arid over-preoccupation with audience-level phenomena.[5] One thrust was toward what he termed "the factors that govern or influence what the media make available" for public consumption. These are only a selection of what could be provided and are not just a matter of chance. Hence, researchers should be "asking questions about the development of media institutions, their organization and structure, their patterns of membership, control, resources and technology, as well as studying the professional values and day-to-day operations of those working in the media." A related thrust of inquiry was toward the social environment surrounding mass media functioning. In Halloran's words, "What is made available by the media, and consequently what helps to shape attitudes and values, will be influenced by a whole series of economic, legal, political, professional and technological considerations. So, to understand the part played by the media in our society, we must study the whole communication process [within] those appropriate contexts."

Secondly, in modern versions of critical thought, the relationship between ideological conviction and empirical research remains essentially as it stood in Adorno's framework, though in practice the originally quite slim empirical chink that he allowed for has been much widened. The key to this feature of today's critical outlook is the idea that the mass media function essentially as agencies of social legitimation—as forces, that is, which reaffirm those ultimate value standards and beliefs, which in turn uphold the social and political status quo. Thus, one writer argues that, economically, the mass media are "a crucial element in the legitimation of capitalist society."[6] Others maintain that, socially, they encourage people to accept

---

[4] A useful source of writings reflecting the diverse tendencies is James Curran. Michael Gurevitch and Janet Wollacott (Eds.), *Mass Communication and Society* (London: Edward Arnold, 1977).

[5] James D. Halloran, "Mass Media and Society: The Challenge of Research," Inaugural Lecture. University of Leicester, October 1973. All citations from Halloran below are taken from this Lecture.

[6] Ralph Miliband, *The State in Capitalist Society*, (London: Weidenfield and Nicolson, 1969).

gross inequalities as if they were natural, inevitable or socially functional.[7] Yet another author contends that the mass media—and particularly broadcasting—support a certain form of political order, celebrating the virtues of pragmatism, compromise and moderated conflict, while giving favored access "to the accredited witnesses of society," such as top party leaders, local councilors, respected experts, accepted interest group spokesmen etc.[8] Many others maintain that in their coverage of a wide range of deviant phenomena—in portrayals, for example of family and sexual morality, pornography, drug-taking, rock music fans, political corruption and street demonstrations—the mass media convey a consensual impression of what society stands for in these fields, thereby acting primarily as agents of social control.[9]

Since so little of this fabric of interpretation is thought problematic, where exactly can its empirical chink be found? This is primarily focused on mediating mechanisms, on the interface between the social and political structure on the one side and characteristic media procedures and outputs on the other. As Murdock and Golding have explained, "It is not sufficient simply to assert that the mass media are part of the ideological apparatus of the state, it is also necessary to demonstrate how ideology is produced in concrete practice."[10] And as Peter Chibnall has added:

Marxist analysis only rarely operates at this level of concrete practice. It tends to ignore the kinds of routine operations, tacit assumptions, conceptual frameworks and occupational constraints which systematically shape the everyday production of knowledge.[11]

[7] Graham Murdock and Peter Golding, "Capitalism, Communication and Class Relations," in Curran, Gurevitch and Wollacott, op. cit.

[8] Stuart Hall, "Media Power: The Double Bind," *Journal of Communication*, 24: 19-26, (Autumn 1974).

[9] Stanley Cohen and Jock Young, *The Manufacture of News: Deviance, Social Problems and the Mass Media*, (London: Constable, 1973).

[10] Murdock and Golding, op. cit.

[11] Peter Chibnall, *Law-and-Order News*, (London: Tavistock, 1977).

[12] John Westergaard, "Power, Class and the Media," in Curran, Gurevitch and Wollacott, op. cit.

Consequently, in much of their current work, critical media sociologists strive to show, for example, how conventional news values, reporters' working routines, and professional norms of objectivity, impartiality and balance, favor established interests, already familiar spokesmen and orthodox understandings of social problems.

Thirdly much of the European critical literature is probing sharply at certain Achilles heels of liberal-democratic press ideology. The assumption that the news media can promote civic enlightenment to any significant degree is challenged by an insistent diagnosis of the pressures that deflect them from this task. In short, liberal-democratic press philosophy is dismissed as if blatantly out of touch with reality.

Such, for example, is the fate of the liberal stress on the *autonomy* of the news media and their freedom from influences emanating from other power centres. The *appearance* of such independence is preserved, it is said, only by respecting certain limits beyond which journalistic enquiry does not normally stray. But in any case, the ties binding media institutions to other power sources are patently obvious once they are mentioned. In some instances, partisan interests control newspapers. In many others, a market orientation severely limits the amount and kind of attention the press can pay to social issues. Even the vaunted impartiality of broadcasting is exercised in practice with a keen regard for the prevailing contours of established economic and political power.[12]

Another vital ingredient of liberal communication theory, which has attracted much critical fire, is its emphasis on a *diversity* of press output and viewpoint. Since no single philosophy, set of interests or body of decision-takers can be assumed to have a monopoly of wisdom on any question, liberalism expects the news media to give voice to those diverse ways of looking at social issues that a pluralistic society will generate. This will help the citizen in turn to make up his own mind on current problems by bringing to his attention rival ways of regarding and tackling them. Yet more often than not, critical media sociologists insist, journalism in the Western world projects a near-uniform impression of a given issue domain, its conditioning circumstances and its likely solutions, rather than a variegated one. At election time, for example, few differences can be found among the issue priorities projected by the various newspapers and network news programs. In the sphere of `industrial relations, according to a recent British study, "the different newspapers are generally reporting the same stories on each day in much the same way" and "trade unions are portrayed largely as organizations involved in conflict."[13] Hartmann and Husband have contended that most British news reports about race relations concentrate on stories of crime, actual or feared conflicts of ethnic interest, and tales of the overflow of colored immigration into the country.[14] In reporting crime news and other deviant behavior, several recently published works maintain, only a limited range of explanations—such as personal inadequacy, the agitation of trouble-makers or poor parental control— are disseminated at the expense of attention to more plausible but more socially challenging causative agents—poverty, slum conditions, a poor education and despair over a hopeless future.[15]

Fourthly, European critical researchers seem to be caught up in a double bind of their own making over the ultimate social purposes of their work. On the one hand, they do not want to be confined to ivory-tower academic quarters. Nordenstreng has cited "a tendency towards *policy orientation*" as one of two "global trends" affecting European mass communications research at present.[16] In his Inaugural Lecture Professor Halloran also affirmed that, "Our main interest is to contribute to an important debate—to add to a public body of information," though, he added, "with no strings attached," since the researcher's policy contributions must spring from what he termed "an independent critical stance." On the other hand, he and his colleagues find existing media institutions to be so comprehensively comprised by, and locked into, the prevailing power structure that they cannot plausibly hold out any hope for their improvement ·from within. Halloran manifests this tendency in the profound skepticism he directs at both professional ideologies and mass media policy and planning practices. Of the former, he asks, "Is it not time that the media were demystified, and that we began to question the restrictions and the possible tyranny of professionalism?" Of the latter, he notes that on more than one occassion, "media planning and policy ... have stemmed more from ignorance, prejudice and narrow vested interests than from knowledge, reason and concern about the public interest." Yet none of this is the fault of individuals. As Halloran concludes: "Deliberate lies, distortion, falsification or direct slanting are not the main issues. It is the unwitting bias inherent in the system as it currently operates that is important."

The response of the Annan Committee (established in 1974 to investigate the future of British broadcasting) to the testimony submitted to it by many critically minded researchers, sheds further light on these policy dilemmas. Its report describes how one researcher told it that the less edifying traits of journalistic news values were a "product of professional, historical, organizational, economic and political factors." Faced with such a cumulation to constraints, it would have been natural to conclude that, short of a social revolution, the electronic media could perform no differently, certainly no better than they do at present. Since few of the researchers drew that conclusion (or any other for that matter) from their testimony, the Annan Committee, in evident bafflement over what the researchers *were* exactly saying, had to draw out the possible policy implications for itself in this fascinating passage:

[13] Denis McQuail. *Analysis of Newspaper Content* Research Series 4, Royal Commission on the Press. (London: Her Majesty's Stationery Office, 1977).

[14] Paul Hartmann and Charles Husband. *Racism and the Mass Media* (London: Davis Poynter, 1974).

[15] Cohen and Young, op. cit.; Chibnall, op. cit.

[16] Kaarle Nordenstreng. "Recent Developments in European Communications Theory," in Heinz-Dietrich Fischer and John C. Merrill (Eds.). *International and Intercultural Communication* (New York: Hastings House, 1976).

Many of these arguments seemed to us unconvincing. They posited a state of affairs where every reporter is assumed to be a disembodied seraph free from any political influences within the State or within society. Or they seemed to suggest that broadcasters, as in totalitarian countries, should consistently disseminate some particular message or some political and social philosophy. Or that broadcasters should eschew the parliamentary democracy on which the country is based. We reject such notions.[17]

▶ But how shall we characterize the output of much American journalism research in light of the available models of academic purpose that have so far been presented? In preparation for this Lecture, I searched in vain through a number of recent issues of JOURNALISM QUARTERLY for materials to answer this question. Despite the tendency for many European critics of American research (Jeremy Tunstall is the latest example)[18] to depict it as faithfully following the administrative path first delineated by Lazarsfeld, the particular journal numbers I consulted had published very little work that I could classify as clearly administrative in intention. Admittedly, an occasional piece concluded on this type of note:

This life-style-related approach offers new insights for a 1) describing its present readers, 2) determining what content appeals to present readers and 3) identifying what content would appeal to groups not now in the newspaper's audience who might be attracted.[19]

But such administrative guidance was far more often the exception than the rule. It was even more difficult to find examples of research in the critical style, similar to what is proliferating in Europe at present, though I daresay I might have detected more specimens had the target of my search been the *Journal of Communications*.

[17] *Report of the Committee on the Future of Broadcasting* (London: Her Majesty's Stationery Office, 1977).

[18] Jeremy Tunstall, *The Media are American: Anglo-American Media in the World*, (London: Constable, 1977).

[19] Barbara E. Bryant, Frederick P. Currier and Andrew J. Morrison, "Relating Life Style Factors of Person to His Choice of a Newspaper," JOURNALISM QUARTERLY, 53: 74-79, (Spring, 1976).

[20] Morris Janowitz, "Professional Models in Journalism: the Gatekeeper and the Advocate," JOURNALISM QUARTERLY, 52: 618-626, 662, (Winter, 1975).

It is true that I identified two strands of work which stood out as more overtly normative than the rest. Yet even here I wondered whether I, the would-be classifier, was imposing normative intentions on authors who were themselves largely innocent of any such purposes. At any rate, one batch of research seemed to reflect an application of the characteristic American value of equality of opportunity to the communication sphere—opportunity to use the media for one's own purposes, as well as opportunity to be presented fairly and without undue distortion to others through media portrayals of one's group. In this camp I would place work on knowledge gaps, studies of the communication needs and habits of deprived minorities, such as the urban poor and the elderly, and content analyses of how the media portray such historically subordinate groups as women, blacks, other ethnic minorities, and even children. Yet another set of writings seemed to reflect expectations of mature journalistic performance, using conventional liberal-democratic standards as touchstones when examining media content, reporter ethics and even audience comprehension. In this camp, I would place much of what is published about election campaign communication, analyses of the amount, accuracy and other characteristics of press coverage of such domains as environmental news and social problems, as well as articles about the purposes, organization and content of the community press, and Janowitz' discussion of gatekeeper and advocate paradigms of journalists' professional roles.[20]

Otherwise—and particularly when contrasted with the current European thrust much American material seemed virtually unclassifiable in such purposive terms: its social commitments and anchorages were not clearly manifest. Unfairly, perhaps, the image formed in my mind of a huge, in many respects impressive, but nevertheless rather rambling, exposed and vulnerable giant. Yet even if this image is extreme, its plausibility should sound a salutary warning. It is, after all, a common theme of much foreign comment on American research that, as one author has recently put it, it is:

....ad hoc, piecemeal and ineffective .... totally lacking [in] any theoretical framework about the media and [their] relations to the wider society or about society itself .... it [tends] to analyse only one sort of effect, that on the individual, while other foci, such as effects on groups and social institutions are omitted ...and it is heedless of their crucial inter-linkage with other social institutions.[21]

Sweeping charges, but has anybody troubled to arm the giant with cudgels to wield in his defense against them? Has too little spadework been invested in clarifying the purposes of journalism research in this country? Does much American work, despite its unrivaled theoretical precision, methodological rigor, technical imagination and sophisticated data-handling, rest insecurely on rather untended and therefore shaky philosophical underpinnings?

If so, this source of weakness may be associated with several others. Let me briefly mention a few that struck me during my tour of the pages of JOURNALISM QUARTERLY. First, there is a curious hesitation to address in any sustained way those larger themes and controversies from which the real world of mass communications cannot be isolated. Is the modern mass communications system most appropriately regarded as a plural set of media outlets, serving the differential needs of a pluralist society, for example, or as a set of conformist institutions, more or less uniformly churning out the ingredients of a socially conservative consensus? How are the media functions of social control and social change promoted and intertwined? To what news-gathering and news-processing activities, if any, does the image of the media operating as merely to mirror an external social reality (fondly held by many media executives and professionals) correspond? How can such a passive image be squared with that more active agenda-setting perspective, which stands out as one of the most productive sources of journalism research to emerge from American academics in recent years?[22] It would be inaccurate to imply that such issues are

entirely neglected on this side of the Atlantic. Nevertheless, many published writings do convey the impression that their authors have been socialized to keep their eyes firmly down to the ground, and to subordinate references to such larger issues to the nuts-and-bolts tasks of specifying hypotheses, operationalizing variables, laying out quantification procedures and sifting the complexities of typically dusty empirical data.

Secondly, to European ears at least, the spirit of scholarly debate, especially between rival traditions, seems curiously muted. Of course it animates some book reviews and overview essays, but otherwise it is as if a stultifying spirit of live and let live encourages each scholar to plough his own furrow. He will report how his findings diverge from those of his fellows, and he will expect a searching scrutiny of the technical merits of his effort. But on the whole he is sheltered from any philosophically directed probing of his presuppositions. There are undoubtedly many exceptions to this generalization—for example in the way that certain political communication scholars in the late 1960s and early 1970s questioned the credentials of the limited effects model of mass media impact. Yet such attention to the underlying assumptions of diverse research tendencies is mainly reserved for critical turning-point moments in the discipline's development, instead of playing a continuing part in the process of knowing what one is doing and where one stands in response to fundamental challenges that can be leveled against it.

Thirdly, I noticed some imbalances of research attention that seemed difficult to justify. It is remarkable, for example, that so little heed is given to broadcast news and current affairs in a publication called JOURNALISM QUARTERLY. Large areas of the structure and workings of the broadcasting industry have seemingly

[21] Annabelle Sreberny-Mohammadi, "Television and its Effects: A Reconstruction of the Ditchley Conference," Communications and Development 1: 8-10, (Spring, 1977).

[22] For an update of research in this tradition, see Donald L. Shaw and Maxwell E. McCombs, The Emergence of American Political Issues: The Agenda-Setting Function of the Press (St. Paul: West Publishing Co., 1977).

escaped all but the cursory academic notice—how individual stations function as journalistic enterprises, the struggles for position within the system between the stations, networks and outside producers, the news programmes of the Public Broadcasting System, the impact on the industry of the pressures of numerous citizen groups, the attempted regulatory activity of the FCC, and relevant judicial doctrines. Although such topics occasionally surface in the literature—most frequently in the form of articles on communication law—on the whole, research into broadcast journalism is slighter and more irregular than its inherent importance warrants.[23]

In addition, there was little material that attempted to explore the interface between media organization and forces operative in the surrounding social system. Except for the impressively cumulative community-level research of Tichenor et al,[24] the links between media institutions and extra-media influences appear to have been little examined. We barely know even how to conceptualize them. So, precisely where European critical research is most self-confident—in exposing (admittedly one-sidedly) the societal constraints that circumscribe the news functions of the mass media in practice—its American counterpart is largely silent.

If such a lack exists, it may be connected, fourthly, with certain ideological dilemmas, which Americans engaged in journalism research have not yet managed to resolve. How, for example, can we remain true to liberal-democratic press values without romanticizing and falsifying the reality of press operations? Most of us probably accept as a valid ideal the notion of an editorially independent press, capable of exercising reportorial scrutiny over public affairs without undue sub-

[23] Richard M. Perloff, "Journalism Research: A 20-Year Perspective," JOURNALISM QUARTERLY, 53:123-126 (Spring, 1976).

[24] P.J. Tichenor, A.I. Nnaemeka, C.N. Olien and G.A. Donohue, "Community Pluralism and Perceptions of Television Content," JOURNALISM QUARTERLY, 54: 254-261, (Summer, 1977).

[25] Bruce N. Westley and Malcolm S. MacLean, Jr., "A Conceptual Model for Communications Research," JOURNALISM QUARTERLY, 34:31-38, (Spring, 1957).

servience to major power interests. But how can this belief be reconciled with the dependence of working journalists on a structured hierarchy of news sources for the bulk of the stories that eventually appear in the print and electronic media? Westley and MacLean's model of the inter-relations of sources (or advocates), media channel intermediaries, and audiences, so incisively productive in other respects, is surely misleading when applied to this particular problem.[25] Would-be advocate sources differ among themselves, not only in the potential audience-appeal of their messages (as the Westley-Maclean analysis implies) but also in sheer power, visibility and prestige. What is more, they arm themselves with public relations officials and strategies designed to exert pressure on media intermediaries to accept their material. What is still more, they enter into highly patterned, that is to say institutionalized and entrenched, inter-relationships with media personnel, which can have the effect of downgrading audience needs to a quite shadowy and tenuous, rather than a controlling, influence on the process as a whole. It is true that the independence ideal can be sustained in the face of such considerations by regarding instances of source-reporter accomodation as essentially unprofessional deviations—lapses into an atypical coziness that should be resisted by reaffirmation of the autonomy principle. Yet the forces responsible for much source-media accomodation appear to have too much sociological validity and staying power to make such a dismissive response entirely convincing. And if that is so, where exactly does the independence ideal of press status and functioning stand?

To pose another unresolved issue: How can we remain true to liberal-democratic press values without tamely accepting all that the press says and does in their name? The dilemma implied by this question springs from those features of press ideology which induce a supreme respect for First Amendment values and for the risks attendant on any authoritative intervention into press affairs. Consequently, we find it difficult to do other than accept Judge Gurfein's judgement: "A cantankerous press, an obstinate press, a ubiquitous press must be suffered by those in authority in order to preserve the even greater values of freedom of expression and the right of the people to know."[26] Yet a political philosophy equivalent of this version of press philosophy could surely be found only in something like the doctrine of the divine right of kings. Media power is not supposed to be shared: That's an infringement of editorial autonomy. It is not supposed to be controlled: That's censorship. It's not even supposed to be influenced: That's news management! But why should media personnel be exempt from Lord Acton's dictum that all power corrupts and absolute power corrupts absolutely? And if they are not exempt, who exactly is best fitted to guard the press guardians, as it were? It is difficult to evade the responsibility, which this line of thought seems to devolve on academic scholars, to undertake a judicious but penetrating analysis of press performance. Of course, effective criticism can emanate from other than academic circles. But the uninformed criticism of many sectors of public opinion can be too readily dismissed as narrowly "interested" and self-serving. In a sense only in which the mass media have to operate, while some of the more informed sources of criticism (e.g. politicians) can be too readily dismissed as narrowly "interested" and self-serving. In a sense only academic investigators can legitimately hold the press to account for how it is organized, how its relations to sources are conducted, how it covers vital news topics, how it interprets audience needs and how in practice it serves its readers, viewers and listeners.

► How shall we draw the far-flung threads of this discussion into a concluding focus? Can anything be done about the numerous dilemmas, gaps and areas of weak definition that I have claimed to notice in the record of American journalism research? If not, then the field of research models will probably be left, more of less by default, to a *professional-expert* orientation—according to which no exterior social purpose is postulated, and the function of scholarship is conceived largely in terms of the generation of theories, investigation techniques and findings which can be deployed in the service of a very wide range of purposes according to researcher taste, opportunity and the availability of funds. Such a model should not automatically be condemned. It has an integrity of its own. Its adherents will suffer fewer of those confused overlaps of scientific and civic role that can bedevil their more normatively minded colleagues. But it may also bias research output towards that which is most do-able, most able to attract financial support, most likely to yield publishable findings and most likely to advance investigators' careers.

If, however, the social purposes of journalism research are to be revitalized along different lines; if the field of press criticism is not to be abdicated to academics lacking any firm commitment to liberal-democratic principles; and if the ideological needs and doubts of our more thoughtful students are to be met; - then we should try to develop yet another research model, one that would stand between the old categories of administrative and critical research. Neither thoroughgoingly pragmatic, nor fiercely Platonic, it would be Aristotelian in spirit, meliorative in aim, and diagnostic and formative in approach. Imbued with a keen sense of the gap between the promise of press performance and its actuality, it would strive to produce findings enabling its extent to be gauged and encouraging policy makers to close it. Although it would not treat the needs of press institutions for market survival and prosperity as paramount, it would assume, until the lessons of experience dictated otherwise, that their personnel could be moved by more public-spirited goals. In Britian, such goals would be expressed in the language of "public service." In America, they might be derived instead from "the social responsibility theory of

---

[26] United States v. New York Times Co., 328 F. Supp. 324, 331 (S.D.N.Y. 1971). *aff'd.* 403 U.S. 713 (1971).

the press." It is salutary to recall in this connection that Theodore Peterson first proclaimed that "pure libertarian press theory is obsolescent," and a need for its replacement by social responsibility theory, as long as 20 years ago.[27] Yet we still lack a corresponding *social responsibility model* of the purposes of journalism research.

This is not the place to elaborate such a model in detail, but in order to give it qualities of coherence, realism and an institutional cutting edge, respectively, those interested in developing it might need to proceed along three priority paths.

For the sake of *coherence,* an attempt might at some stage have to be made to translate the meliorative research model into a broad-ranging program of proposed investigations. Although such a step might seem daunting and unlikely when contemplated in the abstract, what can be accomplished in this spirit has been impressively demonstrated by Elihu Katz' recent report for the BBC, *Social Research in Broadcasting: Proposals for Further Development.*[28] This outlined six areas of policy-relevant proposals, including the social impact of broadcasting; the nature of the audience, how it chooses, uses and processes programs; the management of creativity inside broadcasting organizations; and research into three forms of programming—for understanding reality, for entertainment and to uphold sub-group identities. Of course these categories reflect a unique fusion of the British cultural setting and Katz' personal priorities. But his work has confirmed the practicality of approaching an inter-connected set of research problems from a meliorative policy standpoint.

For the sake of *realism,* we need to undertake more studies of the interaction of communication sources with media personnel in a variety of news reporting areas, hopefully in this way giving research more to say about forces acting on the society-to-media interface. My own confidence in the value of such a tack was recently much strengthened by the outcome of a study I completed, with colleagues, of interaction between political party publicists and news and current affairs broadcasters during the two British General Elections of 1974.[29] Analytically, the study was enhanced by an opportunity to ascertain how the same process—the creation and dissemination of campaign messages—was approached by both kinds of communicators (as well as how they took account of each other in their calculations). In addition, our policy task of recommending some options for change in future election broadcasting arrangements was enriched by this two-sided perspective, since, as the enquiry proceeded, it became increasingly clear that we had to propose different forms of party-broadcaster interaction for past ways of meshing their contributions together, which over the years had acquired the force of entrenched precedents.

This experience has also suggested that we need to learn how to apply a pluralistic power model to analysis of source-media interaction in a variety of spheres. Such a project could involve many exciting steps. First, there would be analysis of the mainsprings of the different forms of power over each other that the two kinds of communicators can wield, and how each sort of communicator takes account of this. Yet a pluralist power model is not necessarily a *naked* power model. For on both sides, the available power will tend to be exercised in line with certain expectations about how it *should* be used, and the sources and character of those expectations will need to be charted in some detail. These would include expectations emanating from a given communicator's own peer group, from patterned inter-relationships he has entered into with the other sort of communicator and from perceptions of societal expectations of communication service as well. It is precisely into this complex

[27] Frederick S. Siebert, Theodore Peterson and Wilbur Schramm, *Four Theories of the Press,* (Urbana: University of Illinois Press, 1956).

[28] Elihu Katz, *Social Research on Broadcasting: Proposals for Further Development,* (London: British Broadcasting Corporation, 1977).

[29] Jay G. Blumler, Michael Gurevitch and Julian Ives, *The Challenge of Election Broadcasting* (Leeds: Centre for Television Research, 1977), mimeo.

that an input of research-based expectations can occasionally be fed by skillful policy-minded investigators. Next, we could consider the consequences of the prevailing power and expectation networks for message content and, ultimately, for the satisfaction or frustration of audience needs. Finally, we could consider how these structures of communicator power, guided by certain expectations, vary and shift across time, across news topic domains, across media and even across cultures.

For Americans, however, the most problematic of the three paths to tread is the one I labeled, "*institutional cutting edge.*" Meliorative research can thrive only in a setting where policy makers and researchers can talk together, learn to understand one another and come to influence each other.[30] The researcher must become sufficiently familiar with how the media operate to be able to frame proposals which are relevant to prevailing circumstances. But he must also have confidence that the media institutions are staffed by individuals who are open in some way to a public service appeal. In Britian the would-be policy researcher's problems of this sort are eased by the relatively definite institutionalization of public service expectations—in, for example, the Charter and Governors of the BBC, the Independent Broadcasting Act and the Members of the IBA, the Press Council and in those reviews of broadcasting and the press that are periodically conducted by officially appointed but in-dependent committees, of which the Annan Committee was the most recent example.

What precisely are their American counterparts? Although they do exist, in comparison they seem more diffuse, less powerful and less strategically situated. Citizens' groups, local media councils, public broadcasting stations, the service ethic of professionally trained journalists, and the FCC itself—all play a part in media betterment; yet taken together, they still convey the impression of a set of rather thin reeds—not broken but not exactly sturdy either.

On this front an outsider is ill-placed to advise. It might help, however, if research could more often be directed at some of these institutions themselves, providing case studies of their philosophies, methods of operation, sources of power, records of achievement and failure and patterns of strengths and limitations—partly in order to judge how their influence on media standards might be enhanced in the future. In addition, policy-minded researchers might look out for chances to contribute to any reviews of the workings of these bodies that may be initiated from time to time. From this standpoint, the current hearings into the Federal Communication Act of 1934, being held by the House of Representative Subcommittee on Communications, presents a rare opportunity that more researchers in this country should be seizing.

[30] Elihu Katz and Michael Gurevitch. *The Secularisation of Leisure.* (London: Faber and Faber, 1976).

Adherents to the Frankfurt "critical" school of European scholarship are stridently critical of the "positivist" empirical work in mass communication research. Kurt Lang, a pioneering sociologist of mass communication, tackles the debate head on. He argues that the empirical tradition was anticipated (and certainly not rejected) in the works of major German classical sociologists such as Max Weber. Furthermore, he points out that broad historical, social, and political trends of the early and middle parts of this century were just as responsible for the questions asked by empirical researchers as were the market needs of the mass media. Finally he argues that no responsible and competent communication researcher can ignore social structure and social trends nor avoid being "critical." Dr. Lang is professor of Sociology at the State University of New York at Stony Brook.

2

THE CRITICAL FUNCTIONS
OF EMPIRICAL
COMMUNICATION RESEARCH
Observations on
German-American Influences

Kurt Lang

Communication research may be new but it has been around long enough to have a history subject to distortion and myth making. One of these 'myths' seems to have a wide circulation among some younger scholars, at least in England. It is not so much that they are unaware of past work in the field but that their knowledge is selective and that therefore some schools are rejected on the basis of less than full information, possibly because not all studies are readily available. Some may be out of print or hard to locate.

In this paper I do not mean to review the history of communication research but only to concentrate on a few facts and cite some forgotten landmark studies so as to correct one distorted but influential interpretation of the empirical tradition. In that interpretation, which dates from the 1960s, what is good and progressive has its roots in the Marxist approach to media analysis; what is to be avoided as reactionary is the product of commercially-supported media research cultivated and exported from the USA. The picture, as I see it, is less clear-cut. If I pose the issue here in terms of American media research *vs.* the Frankfurt 'critical' school, it is only because this is the way it has been posed in questions and challenges thrown at me while visiting German and British universities this past year.

I would contend, and mean to support by reference to past developments, these propositions:

1. The empirical tradition in communication research is as much a German as an American phenomenon.
2. Its development through the 1930s and early 40s was as much a response to broad intellectual, social, and political interests as it was to the demands of media organizations operated for profit.
3. There is no *inherent* incompatability between the 'positivism' of administrative communication research and the critical approach associated with the Frankfurt School.

The origin of the empirical tradition

Late nineteenth century social thought in all the industrialized countries was greatly preoccupied with the role of the press in the formation of public opinion. In England this interest found expression in the writings of Bagehot, Maine, Bryce and Graham Wallas; in France, in the writings above all of Gabriel Tarde whose sociological

With permission from *Media, Culture and Society* 1 (January 1979) 83-96. Copyright by Academic Press Inc. (London) Ltd.

system based on laws of imitation is in some ways reminiscent of the far more super-ficial but widely known theories of Gustave LeBon. But it remained for Max Weber (1864–1920) to launch the first attempt to put the study of the press on a firm empirical basis. In his business report to the first meeting of the German Sociological Society (Deutsche Gesellschaft für Soziologie, 1910: 39–62), he proposed two co-operative study projects: the first on the sociology of the press (*Zeitungswesen*), the other on the sociology of voluntary associations.

The press project never got off the ground largely because—as Weber was to explain two years later (DGS, 1912)—of his own involvement in a legal suit about some press reports. Nevertheless, it is worth looking at the specific questions he proposed for study and the methods deemed appropriate for their investigation What gets into the paper? How does the character of the newspaper as a capitalist enterprise run for profit affect its treatment of the news? What differences are there between papers in the same country and between the press in different countries and what accounts for these differences? What are the effects, especially the long-term consequences, of a particular form of news presentation? Speaking rhetorically, he then asked, where can the data for such studies be found? The answer was simple: they were already largely available in newspaper content, so 'we will, to be quite clear, begin in a simple-minded way to measure with scissors and compass, how the content of the press has shifted quantitatively during the past generation, not least in the advertising section, in the feature pages, between cultural items and editorials, between editorials and news, between what is reported and what is not' (DGS, 1910: 52).

The proposal, in its entirety, indicates that Weber was anticipating, and certainly not rejecting, the kind of content analysis Harold D. Lasswell was later to develop for studies of propaganda (Lasswell, 1927). This is not to say that Weber thought of this proposed press study as more than a first step toward dealing with important and basic issues. Thus, rather than assuming the answer, he asked whether 'the growing concentration [of the press] gives it more power to shape public opinion to suit its own preferences or, the other way around, whether it increases the sensitivity of the individual enterprise to shifts in public opinion—as has been claimed but not unambiguously demonstrated' (DGS, 1910, 46 f.). This question is but a part of a broader set of questions he posed about the role of the press.

Other, not unsimilar, approaches to the study of the press were being suggested. One came from the American, Robert E. Park (1864–1944), whose interest in the press predated Weber's proposal. Under the influence of Franklin Ford at the University of Michigan, he was planning to publish an entirely new kind of newspaper which would contain 'thought news', meaning it would register movements of public opinion in much the same way traditional newspapers supplied stock market and other economic reports to indicate likely trends in consumer behavior. The venture failed, and after working on various daily newspapers as a reporter for some twelve years Park took an M.A. at Harvard, then went to Germany to study sociology under George Simmel and Wilhelm Windelband, taking his Ph.D. in Heidelberg in 1904. Park's well-known and seminal studies of the immigrant and foreign language press in America, published in the 1920s,[1] seem exactly the type of case study Weber was recommending as part of his larger project. Yet there is no indication that Park was even aware of Weber's proposal.

[1] The first of his papers on the subject was delivered at the National Conference of Social Work in 1920. See especially Park (1922).

There is an even more marked affinity between Park's approach and that of Ferdinand Toennies (1885–1936), another first-generation sociologist known for his socialist convictions. In his *Kritik der öffentlichen Meinung*, published in 1922, and in an article a year later, Toennies examined the nature of public opinion in a modern mass society,[2] much as Park had done in his Ph.D. thesis. Public opinion, Toennies argued, is not what one hears, or what one sees, or what one reads. All these are potentially misleading as indicators, especially what one reads. For, what is published reflects the liberal free-trade viewpoints of the capitalist owners. Toennies had in mind mainly editorial opinion but Park carried this line of reasoning a step farther by focusing not so much on editorial opinion but on the news itself, the demand for which has shifted power away from the editor and put it into the hands of reporters. To understand the nature and influence of the newspaper, so Park argues in two articles written in 1940 and 1941, we must above all understand the nature of news as distinct from historical knowledge. News consists of isolated events. Since knowledge of these events is not based on perception but on communication, nothing without attention value will ever become 'news'. But these events do more than provoke contagious excitement. If news is focused, attention is equally focused and public opinion comes to rest on the 'interpretations' of news as these develop throughout society.

Much of what Park and Toennies had to say about the press and public opinion was programmatic. Yet Park, in particular, had a remarkable talent for catalyzing concrete studies. One of the most perceptive of these, for which he wrote the introduction, was Helen M. Hughes' *News and the Human Interest Story* (Hughes, 1940), which related the characteristics and presumed requirements of readers to the presentation of news in different papers. This monograph pioneered a line of analysis that seems to have been 'rediscovered' during the past decade. I cite it here mainly to underline once again the links between media research and the mainstream of classical sociology as practised both in Germany and the United States.

The older 'new' media

Until the arrival of radio, the emergence of the full-length feature film, and growing concern over totalitarian propaganda, the study of mass communication meant mainly the study of the printed press. This changed as new media emerged and techniques appropriate to their study were developed. Not all these approaches and techniques originated in the United States.[3] Many were in fact imported and then developed to a new level of sophistication by a group of emigré scholars from Germany and Austria, most born around the turn of the century, who subsequently played leading roles in the field. Not that they worked alone or apart in their research.[4] I concentrate on certain of these only to indicate that the problems with which they concerned themselves and dealt empirically were relevant to those broad issues that critics of the American approach consider to be the monopoly of the Critical School, specifically of those members who returned to Frankfurt after World War II. The

[2] The first appeared under the imprint of the Springer-Verlag in Berlin. For the second see Toennies (1923).

[3] I cannot say for certain when and where the first survey of the radio audience was conducted, but the one by RAVAG (the Austrian radio organization) seems to be the precursor of the American ones. See Huth (1937).

[4] In addition to Lasswell, I should mention the work of Hadley Cantril, of Carl I. Hovland, and the series of studies on motion pictures sponsored by the Payne Foundation.

work I refer to below can hardly be called crassly empirical. The persons responsible for it had broad interests and a sense of social responsibility, which they shared with the best of their American colleagues.

A main influence was, of course, the Viennese born Paul F. Lazarsfeld (1900–1977). As a member of the socialist student group there, he had participated in a number of Booth-type social surveys on housing and (with Marie Jahoda) published a study of unemployed workers in Marienthal. He first came to the United States in 1933 on a Rockefeller Foundation Fellowship and was, from 1937 on, director of the Office of Radio Research, first at Princeton University and later at Columbia. His surveys on radio listening and communication behavior as well as his two panel studies of the media during American Presidential campaigns are too well known to necessitate any review.

Lazarsfeld's interest in media research was to a large degree methodological. The problems of pinpointing effects were for him the same whether the communication was intended to sway votes, sell a product, teach the virtues of citizenship, or combat racism. No matter what the objective, he approached his subject with great ingenuity, always intent on teasing from his data the precise elements of the situation in which the impact was maximized. That the effects he sought to document were broad-ranging is best documented in an article published in 1948 (Lazarsfeld, 1948). There he identified sixteen types of effects, based on the differentiation of four 'causal' influences and four different objects of influence. Causal influences were: exposure to a single message; exposure to a series of messages (e.g. a campaign or regular listening to news broadcasts); the presence of a given medium (e.g. television rather than print); and the socio-economic control structure of the mass media (e.g. private ownership supported by advertising rather than the various forms of public ownership and political control). Each of these can, in turn, act on a different object: a single individual; an aggregate of persons (such as an electorate); a social group; or the institutional structure of society. Effects to be studied then include the response of the individual, the distribution of individual responses, group response (such as the rise in morale when a group gains public recognition via the media) and institutional impact (for instance, 'high' culture being diluted by the pervasiveness of commercially marketed popular culture).

Lazarsfeld, in his own work, tended to concentrate on the effects of a series of messages, as in the campaign studies or on the effects of a medium, as he did in his studies on radio listening. Choosing to concentrate, as he did, on the distribution of individual responses (i.e. effect in terms of the distribution within some aggregate), for which the survey method was clearly the most appropriate instrument, he clearly excluded from his empirical enquiries the study of more basic and significant effects. He was, however, not unmindful of what he neglected. Studies on magazine literature, on popular music, on the daytime radio serial—all conducted by his students or co-workers—are testimony that he conceived the field as encompassing much more than his own work.

It is in a way ironic that the way Lazarsfeld approached the study of effects led many of his followers to downgrade the influence of the mass media of communication. The findings from *The People's Choice* and *Voting*, conducted in communities where neither political party had a media monopoly and both acted within a framework of overall consensus, should have occasioned little surprise.[5] But in the study of Decatur, Illinois, the specific objective was to trace the content of interpersonal communication

[5] For a critique of these studies, see Lang and Lang (1965).

back to the media, an objective that the late C. Wright Mills, the project director, told me in 1956, was negated by an inappropriate methodology. After lying around the Bureau of Applied Social Research for some years, the data were reanalyzed and published in *Personal Influence* by Katz and Lazarsfeld (1955). Its emphasis on the relative impotence of the mass media *vis-à-vis* interpersonal communication in day-to-day decision making did more than anything else, except perhaps the publication of *The Effects of the Mass Media* by Klapper (1960), to promote the theorem that mass communication had little or no effect.

Another influential figure was Kurt Lewin (1890–1947), who had taught psychology at the University of Berlin before emigrating to the United States in 1933. Today Lewin is best remembered for his development of group dynamics at the University of Iowa. That in 1945 he was able to move his entire team of researchers to the Massachusetts Institute of Technology testifies to the recognition his work had earned him by that time. Like Lazarsfeld, Lewin was not a Marxist but nevertheless had a keen interest in social problems and action research. While still in Germany, he had contributed an article on group psychology to a volume entitled *Krise der Psychologie-Psychologie der Krise*,[6] in which a group of psychologists—among them such renowned Marxists as Otto Rühle and Manes Sperber—tried to reconcile the findings of psychologists and the experiences of psychotherapists with the requirements for social reform. This was an interest Lewin never abandoned in his life-long effort to develop a topological psychology as a scientifically valid guide for changing social values.

In his studies, Lewin emphasized naturalist observation and concreteness. The forces that produced change had to be real. He paid particular attention to the social channels through which new ideas and practices penetrate group barriers and to the 'gatekeepers' who controlled the flow. During World War II, his theoretical interests became linked to the war-related effort to change American food habits so as not to discard as inedible certain nutritious foods abundantly available at the time. His studies of how particular foods reach the family table demonstrated that lectures by experts were far less effective than discussion among peers followed by a group decision (Lewin, 1942). The finding may appear trivial but, given its more general implications, it has found its way into communication literature. So, too, has the concept of gatekeeper. A student of Lewin's first observed how the gatekeeper function was performed by the night editor at a local radio station as he decided which of many bulletins reaching him should be discarded or retained for newscasts (White, 1950). To be sure, the concept of an individual gatekeeper has proved to be inappropriate in studying media organizations like the metropolitan newspaper, a television network or a wire service. The Lewinian model can nevertheless be applied to the total flow of content between the various levels and subgroups that interact within an organizational framework to produce mass communication content.

A third center of research activity merits our attention. This centered on the analysis of Nazi propaganda and involved scholars employed in various private, semi-official, and governmental capacities, particularly the Research Project on Totalitarian Communication at the New School for Social Research, the Foreign Broadcast Intelligence Service at the U.S. Office of War Information, and the War Communication Research Project at the Library of Congress directed by Harold D. Lasswell (1900–   ). Emigré scholars who knew both the language and the country played a major role in activities at all these centers.

[6] To the best of my recollection, this volume was privately published in Berlin in 1927.

Ernst Kris (1900–1957) had studied art history and also received psychoanalytical training. He had been a keeper at the Kunsthistorische Museum in Vienna before coming to Britain, where he worked for the BBC radio monitoring service during the first year of the war. Thereafter, he went to the United States to work with the Research Project on Totalitarian Communication, a foundation-supported activity that maintained close contact with various governmental agencies. In his postscript to *German Radio Propaganda*, Kris writes about destroying the myth of propaganda and replacing it with a better understanding of the limitations to and functions of propaganda. 'In no society', he wrote, 'can the persuasiveness of propaganda eliminate the impact of facts; all he [the propagandist] can do is to reinterpret them' (Kris and Speier, 1944). The remark echoes the earlier insight of Park.

Some of Kris' more general conclusions based on his wartime activity were developed in a joint article with Nathan Leites, one of Lasswell's collaborators (Kris and Leites, 1947). The article, heavy on psychoanalytic jargon, should nevertheless be regarded as a classic. The authors note three trends in propaganda content. Compared with the World War I output, World War II propaganda: (1) exhibited a higher degree of sobriety and was less highly emotionalized; (2) was less moralistic and more factual in tone; and (3) put a ceiling on gross divergences from ascertainable facts, consequently providing more information. These shifts marked an attempt to counter two rather pervasive tendencies likely to thwart the propagandist intent on mobilizing the masses. The first of these tendencies is a generalized distrust of propaganda and of the authority the propagandist represents, a distrust compounded by the individual's fear of his own suggestibility. Another is the tendency toward a withdrawal of participation (privatization), expressing the feeling that one does not understand complicated world issues and cannot determine one's own fate. It results from the increasing disparity between the power and influence of the self and that of organizations. Both tendencies merge in so far as scepticism serves the individual as a defense against involvement in larger issues.

The question then becomes to what extent the propagandist structures and defines reality (performs ego functions) or seeks to mobilize moral indignation (appeals to the superego). Kris and Leites state explicitly that any unsuccessful ego function endangers the positive relationship between the two and hence encourages a reversion to patterns of behavior known from childhood, such as projective distrust against those who should act as guides, generalized hostility, and withdrawal from participation. The 'democratic' propagandist seeks to counter these tendencies by structuring reality so it can be anticipated and so gain acceptance for himself as a model. 'Totalitarian' propaganda relies more heavily on superego appeals but these cease to work, except for fanatics, once the situation gets out of control, as during the Nazi defeat.

This Kris and Leites analysis did not appear until two years after the war in Europe ended. Its conclusions were, however, firmly grounded in various studies showing how Nazi propagandists tried to manipulate reality to serve their military and political goals. Emigré scholars had a big hand in these studies. The work of Siegfried Kracauer (1899–1966) on Nazi film and Hans Speier (1905–) on German radio news deserve special notice because both go beyond the purely descriptive level to provide broader insights into the communication of actuality.

Kracauer had already established a reputation in Germany as the regular Berlin correspondent to the features section of the liberal *Frankfurter Zeitung*. He had joined its editorial staff in the early 1920s after university studies in archeology and art history as well as in philosophy and the social sciences. Before arriving in the United States via France, he had published a book on white-collar employees in Germany. His study on the Nazi war film was conducted under a Rockefeller Fellowship. Speier had joined the faculty of the New School of Social Research in New York and, with Kris, became involved in the Research Project on Totalitarian Communication. Best known today for his work on war and international negotiations, his pre-emigration work includes two articles on the development of social theory from Hegel to Marx, both published in the highly prestigious *Archiv für Sozial-wissenschaft und Sozialpolitik*, as well as an article on working class mobility in which he analyzed some of the implications of the worker turning bourgeois.

It may be only a coincidence that both Kracauer and Speier wrote about the stratum of employees which provided a good deal of early support for the Nazis but they were certainly in close touch with each other while working on Nazi propaganda. They did not formally collaborate but their work—Kracauer's on war films and newsreels, Speier's on war news—follows a rather similar theme. That theme, as I read it, emphasizes the Nazi propagandist's efforts to maintain the impression of actuality, by presenting the physical and human world through pictorial representation and/or eyewitness accounts, while using the details to create a pseudo-reality supportive of the Nazi totalitarian political system.

For this purpose maps are an especially useful device because, as Speier puts it in his article on 'magic geography' (Speier, 1969a), they enable one to 'perceive visually relationships within a context' and have the capacity of making the suggested order appear 'natural'. A clearly propagandistic device in the Nazi war film was the use of flowing maps with moving borders to illustrate Germany's geographical encirclement. They could also be employed as a graphic display of Nazi power. The movement of arrows around a field is meant to evoke certain visceral reactions—of being entrapped, if the forces represented by the arrows are hostile, or of being in control, if they are friendly (Kracauer, 1947). The visual presentation tends to be without any historical context; the alleged suffering of the Germans because of encirclement remains an abstraction.

The propaganda intent behind these maps is clear but, in pressing the analysis beyond the obvious, we begin to understand how our image of the world is shaped by the mode of presentation in many more subtle ways. For one thing, the maps of every country express, consciously or not, a more or less ethnocentric viewpoint simply because one's own country is centrally located. Cartographers in Europe typically cut their world maps at a longitude different from that employed by American mapmakers. Moreover, as every cartographer knows, spherical space cannot be presented on a two-dimensional plane without some distortion—of size, of shape or of distance. For maps covering a small area, these distortions are minor but when maps depict relationships among the major land masses of the world, they become highly significant. Every map is based on some compromise. The traditionally favored Mercator projection preserves shape and direction but at the expense of size and distance. As Speier notes, the projection magnifies the areas farthest from the equator, giving a visual prominence to old nations in the northern latitudes far in excess of their actual size. Can one tell from such a map that the land mass of Brazil is larger by nearly 10% than that of continental United States minus sparsely-populated Alaska? Great Britain and Sweden also appear unduly large compared with India and Indonesia.

If maps are a time-honored representational device, battlefront reportage, using audio recordings, film footage and videotapes, is a relatively new communication technique through which the population can experience a war at a distance. I believe that in this respect the contrast between the First and the Second World War was actually greater than that between World War II and Vietnam. Be this as it may, both Speier and Kracauer emphasize how intent the Nazis were on preserving the actuality aspects in their coverage: 'The front reports [on radio] translate the remote and complicated war effort into terms of immediate and simple experience, but they do so at the expense of an adequate concept. While they describe detail realistically, they manipulate information by selecting the details they describe. The front reports are realistic, but their realism is, in a sense, inappropriate, as is our perception of a picture when we see it from a point too close' (Speier, 1969*b*).

The Nazi reports by wireless would reiterate 'we see . . . we hear'. They would also stress the number of front-line reporters killed. So, too, in their newsreels, the Nazis put a great premium on speed in processing. They allowed the pictures to 'speak for themselves' but never tired of reminding the audience that the films had indeed been shot at the front. To underline this point, they might deliberately include some photographically flawed picture sequences. The pictures themselves provided little information but only exemplified the message the Nazis intended to convey. Kracauer concluded that the Nazis 'practised a leftist montage technique in reverse order: they did not try to elicit reality from a meaningless arrangement of shots, but nipped in the bud any real meaning their candid-camera work might convey' (Kracauer, 1947: 297). Nazi reportage avoided as much as possible any portrayal of the suffering and death inseparably related to war. The film, *Victory in the West*, made up of newsreels, showed no human corpses but only a dead horse. Even more selective was the treatment of the home front. Civilians were rarely shown and then only as 'cheering crowds'. Kracauer contrasted the description of the Berlin crowds on 18 July 1940, after the fall of France, by William L. Shirer, an American reporter who was present, with the impression conveyed by the film sequence of the crowd behavior. Careful editing suggested a distinctly militant mood, but Shirer saw nothing but holiday crowds with nothing martial about them.

The last group of emigrés centered about Max Horkheimer (1895–1973) and his Institute for Social Research, founded at Frankfurt in 1930 and affiliated, from 1934 to 1948, with Columbia University in New York City. This group was distinctly Marxist in its orientation but later, while in New York, Horkheimer adopted the less controversial Critical label. While Horkheimer himself was never involved in any form of communication *research*, several of his associates, with interests in art, music and literature, turned to the examination of the more popular versions of these art forms.

One of these associates was Leo Lowenthal (1902–   ), who wrote on the sociology of literature in Horkheimer's *Zeitschrift für Sozialforschung*, for which he served as managing editor during its ten-year existence. After coming to America, his interest in the relation between literature and society led him to the analysis of biographies in popular magazines. This was not the sharp turn away from broad concerns to a pre-occupation with minutiae that it may appear. Biographies tend to personify social values, particularly when one contrasts the American tendency to reflect society and national life through the biography of some typical figure with the Nazi practise of reducing the individual to the representative of some collective entity more real than any person and his struggles could ever be. Lowenthal thus turned to looking at the occupations and characteristics of these popular biographies as a reflection of changing values (Lowenthal, 1943). Comparing biographies during the first decade of this century with those in the 1940s, he found a shift away from the heroes of production, as Lowenthal called them, to the idols of consumption. Persons whose careers were made in the entertainment world, light entertainment in particular, had come to predominate over the entrepreneurs in the serious world of business, industry, science, and so forth.

Does this finding sound familiar, even trite? If so, it is because the study found such resonance. It anticipated a number of far less empirically grounded analyses of American society as it emerged during the affluent post-war years. I mention, in particular, the characterological distinction between the inner-directed and other-directed types developed by David Riesman in *The Lonely Crowd*, the social criticism of the marketing personality by Erich Fromm in *Man for Himself*, and even to some extent the picture of *One-Dimensional Man* created by Herbert Marcuse. In so far as both Fromm and Marcuse once also had close ties to Horkheimer's Institute of Social Research, the affinity is hardly happenstance.

Nor should one overlook that much of the activity of the group around Horkheimer, like that of others during these years, was a reaction against the fascist threat to democracy. It was altogether natural that several of them should have entered the employ of the government or became involved in the war effort as outside consultants. What I do not want to leave unmentioned, however, is the participation of this group in the studies on prejudice and the fascist potential in America, financed by the American Jewish Committee (AJC) just after the war ended, some of which seem to have sunk into relative oblivion. One that merits resurrection is *Prophets of Deceit* by Lowenthal and Guterman (1947). Here the psychology of native American fascist agitators (the little would-be Hitlers)—what motivates them, their appeals to potential followers—was inferred from themes in their speeches and various tracts they distributed. Their study drew more directly on the formulations of Lasswell than on *Autorität und Familie*, a book by Horkheimer that joined structural and psycho-logical interpretations of fascism. This book did, however, provide the theoretical underpinning for what was not only by far the most expensive of these AJC-sponsored studies but the one with the greatest impact on American social science. That study was *The Authoritarian Personality*, co-authored by Theodor W. Adorno (1962–1969) and three psychologists, among them Marie Jahoda, who had been a close collaborator of Lazarsfeld (Adorno *et al.*, 1950). Adorno, as everyone probably knows, was an early associate of Horkheimer, who returned with him after the Second World War to Frankfurt.

The purpose of this investigation into the authoritarian personality was to identify the fascist potential or—in communication terms—the susceptibility of the target audience to fascist propaganda. The focus was on personality and family history by means of attitude scales, projective tests, and interviews. It was, in short, an empirical approach in the strict 'positivist' sense with all the derogatory connotations some attach to that label. The investigators developed scales to measure anti-semitism, ethnocentric prejudice generally, and an underlying authoritarian attitude. The last was called the F-scale, where F stands for fascism, but the items were deliberately worded to avoid any explicitly anti-semitic or Nazi content, but used statements designed to elicit expressions of fears about unconventionality, extrapunitiveness, thinking in in-group *vs.* out-group terms, and so forth. Having shown that the three scales correlated, the researchers concluded that anti-semitism was only part of a broader enthnocentric point of view and that this, in turn, expressed a more fundamental authoritarian disposition. Projective test results revealed that authoritarian (F-scale) scores were related to personality dispositions, thereby validating the underlying theory about the psychological roots of fascism.

But there were problems with the data, as there usually are when any research is intended to plough new ground. The population available for psychological testing was predominantly middle-class, and later studies showed this to be a more serious drawback than had been supposed. The correlations on which the main conclusion of *The Authoritarian Personality* was based did not hold among working-class subjects.[7] Notwithstanding these formidable shortcomings, the F-scale seems never to have been disavowed and for two decades remained the most widely used measure of the fascist disposition and was invoked to explain all kinds of behavior, political and otherwise. Although I doubt that Adorno was himself responsible for the study design, or its inevitable shortcomings, he did associate himself with it by contributing several theoretical chapters. These have not, as far as I have been able to ascertain, found their way into those volumes of his collected works, which have so far rolled off the presses in Germany. The omission does not diminish the impact the study had for a while on American social science.

The 'critical' foundations of communication research

If I have dwelled at some length on the study of authoritarianism, it is for two reasons. First, the experience shows that the empirical validation of a theory is always a tricky business and that those intent on developing their skills in this area ought not to be denigrated for the trying, as some followers of the Critical School are inclined to do. More important, the extent of Adorno's involvement, to the point of co-authorship, affords an opening for stating again my third contention: the incompatibility between the various streams of communication research was not nearly as sharp as those who mistake ideology for social science may want to believe. On the contrary, there were many points of contact, even collaboration between the circles I have treated separately, not to speak, of course, of various ties, each, including Adorno, formed with American research teams. Suffice it to cite one or two examples. Both Kracauer and Lowenthal at one time or another served as members of the Bureau of Applied Social Research directed by Lazarsfeld. Kurt Lewin, as well as several of Lazarsfeld's close associates, participated in various research sponsored by the American Jewish Committee. My next example is meant to caution especially against overdrawing the contrast between two extremes—between the 'positivism' ascribed to Paul Lazarsfeld and generally associated with America and the so-called critical approach of the Frankfurt School.

The first issue of *Studies in Philosophy and Social Science* (the successor and final volume of *Zeitschrift für Sozialforschung*, which ceased publication in 1941) sheds further light on the relationship between these supposed polarities. In the preface to the issue, Horkheimer expresses himself as 'particularly indebted to Paul F. Lazarsfeld who has taken the categories developed by us [the Critical School] in a totally different and highly abstract context, and attempted to present them in terms of concrete desiderata confronting today's social research' (*Studies in Philosophy and Social Science*, 1941). He goes on to speak of collaboration between his own institute and the research activities of Columbia University in producing the issue.

The contents of the issue are an interesting mix. It contains an article by Adorno

[7] See Herbert Hyman's critique in Lazarsfeld and Merton (1954).

on popular music, one by Lasswell on radio as an instrument for reducing personal insecurity, and still another by Charles A. Siepmann (formerly of the BBC) on the educational uses of radio. The only empirical piece, in the sense we understand it today, is by Herta Herzog (part of the Lazarsfeld circle), entitled 'On Borrowed Experience', her initial attempt to probe into the psychological functions ('uses and gratifications', if you wish) of daytime radio serials, which she later elaborated. Most revealing as to how the two supposedly divergent approaches fit together and even complement one another is the first article in the volume, 'Remarks on Administrative and Critical Communication Research' by Lazarsfeld (1941).

Administrative research, as Lazarsfeld defines it, is based on the 'idea that modern media of communication are tools handled by people or agencies for given purposes'. It centers on a more or less standardized set of problems, including the nature of the audience, the impact of the message content, and how the one affects the other. These things are not always obvious, and to gain an understanding of them requires empirically grounded knowledge. Such knowledge is also required if we are to understand 'the more general role of the media of communication in the present social system', a matter that rarely interests the sponsor or client of administrative research but is the central concern of Critical Theory. For this the purely administrative definition of a problem is usually too narrow. Research designed to answer a particular, even a practical purpose is often enriched and vitalized by the incorporation of perspectives derived from formulations by critical theorists about how general trends in society affect the way mass media function and, consequently, affect certain basic values. Lazarsfeld welcomes Critical Theory as a potentially vitalizing influence on administrative research.

Lest it be supposed that this view remains unreciprocated let us cite some comments Adorno made years after his return to Germany and long after he and Lazarsfeld had ceased to collaborate. In his *Thesen zur Kunstsoziologie* (see *Schriften*, 1977) he refers to the inappropriateness of conceptualizing the relation of art and society only as the extent of its diffusion through society. To do so, he contended, would be to substitute a methodological preference for empirical measurement for the real task of the sociology of art. The social effect of any art work is not determined solely by its reception by individuals. This cannot be ascertained without full consideration of the many mechanisms of dissemination, social control and authority 'as long recognized by empirical social research in America. Thus Paul F. Lazarsfeld, one of its most renowned representatives, included in his book *Radio Research 1941* two studies which explicitly deal with how such mass effects arise . . .' (*Schriften*, 1977, p. 367).

Adorno's reference is to studies of the music industry and of how songs are 'plugged'. The sociology of music in Germany, he continues, falls below the standard achieved by research in America in so far as it fails to give such problems the attention they deserve. '*I feel myself totally misunderstood if my publications on the sociology of music since my return from the emigration were to be interpreted as contrary to empirical social research.* Emphatically, I mean to underline that I consider these procedures not only important within their own sphere but also as appropriate' (*Schriften*, 1977, p. 368, my emphasis). It takes nothing more than common sense to realize that all data, including survey data, have to be seen and interpreted in their proper context, if they are to serve our understanding of society and not only provide intelligence for managerial decision.

A less ambiguous expression of basic agreement is scarcely possible, even though most of Adorno's writings seem clearly opposed to the Lazarsfeld viewpoint. This is, basically, because Lazarsfeld and the survey analysts take the radio listener, including the listener to popular music seriously, whereas Adorno exhibits a certain contempt for the listeners to popular music who do not understand, as he does, music as a 'language in itself'—who are not, in other words, musical connoisseurs with the sophistication that was Adorno's. These people, he wrote in the 1941 issue of *Studies in Philosophy and Social Science*, merely seek novelty (Adorno, 1941). They fail to make the kind of leisure time effort that alone can bring new and esthetically rewarding experience. It is, he adds, not the people themselves who are to blame for this failure but the boredom of their work. Still, given the circumstances, the social function of popular music is to provide catharsis and so help keep the masses in line.

Adorno has, of course, had a lot more to say about the linkage between class structure and music, but one cannot help wonder about the continental snobbery that shines through what he has to say. After all, none of the classical composers consciously addressed themselves only to a musically trained audience, which is itself a new concept, but wrote their scores for whoever cared to listen. I cannot resist comparing Adorno's aristocratic attitude with that of Raymond Williams, who argues that it is precisely because certain types of broadcasting programs—so-called serious music, being one of them—are associated by working class members with symbols of class that keeps them from making fuller use of these programs (Williams, 1966). His observation raises exactly the kind of issue that even the most narrowly conceived administrative research can shed some light on.

Here I am referring to the work of another German, Theodor Geiger (1891–1952), whose active socialism forced his emigration to Denmark in 1933. There, uninfluenced by developments in the United States, he interested himself in the sociological study of promotional activity and propaganda, writings available in Scandinavian languages. But there is a modest experiment, reported in the *Public Opinion Quarterly*, that suggests that the Danish public may actually have a more refined musical taste than it dares to believe (Geiger, 1950).

In an experiment carried out with the co-operation of Danish radio, the same 'classical' concert was scheduled for broadcast on two Saturdays three weeks apart but with different labels. During the first airing, the program was listed as 'popular music' and the works were played without comment; on the second Saturday, the same program of music was broadcast but listed as a 'classical' concert and accompanied by a discussion of some musical terms. Included were selections from Haydn, Schubert, Mozart, Beethoven and Mendelssohn-Bartholdy. Geiger tells us that the pieces were by no means 'ear-pleasing' but a bit on the heavy side.

Since the study was conducted in a one-station area, the size of the radio audience could be monitored by a device that recorded the amount of electrical disturbance created by the number of sets in use in two neighborhoods—one a predominantly middle-class suburb, the other a working-class district. According to this measure, the number who listened to the 'classical' concert was indeed far smaller than the number who listened to the 'popular' concert. More important, very few who listened to the music when labeled popular appeared to have tuned out. In neither neighborhood was there any marked drop-off in listening *during* the program. The audience at the end was nearly as large as it had been at the beginning, and the greatest decline came after the program had ended. Nor were there any phone calls to complain about the music, except for some musically sophisticated who recognized the music and could not understand why it had not been correctly identified. It would appear that the audience for classical music might be greater than it is, except that some people are put off by the musical terminology into thinking that the music is not for them but only for the better-educated. These findings, which tend to support Williams rather than Adorno, have obvious implications. If replicated, they would mandate certain changes in broadcasting policies.

I obviously cannot avoid, nor do I wish to, the argument that research on audiences, responses and effects only serves the manipulatory interests of the managers of the communication agencies, that information is power and only enhances the power they already have. This is an issue that defies a simple answer. We have to acknowledge that the use to which such findings are put, or whether they are used at all, is really a political problem over which a researcher usually has little control. This does not mean that the researcher can afford to be unmindful of the problem of usage or indifferent to it.

Researchers do not work in a political void, and their consultative and advisory roles allow them to exercise influence. They need not accept the narrow administration definition of the research problem but can educate the client or executive to be sensitive to its larger aspects, including the unanticipated effects of any given policy. In some cases, researchers may have no alternative but to refuse to do the research. But it is always possible to insist on one thing—at least when one functions in an academic environment or scientific institute—and that is that the findings be put in the public domain, accessible to all, no matter how embarrassing these may prove to some particular interest group, including the sponsor.

Finally, I find it impossible to understand how any responsible and competent communication researcher can carry on without taking structure and social trends into account. Much communication research by its nature focuses on barriers—barriers to understanding, distortions of reality, the uneven distribution of access and information, and so on. In the interest of gaining valid and meaningful knowledge—which is not the monopoly of any single tradition or school—we are all critical, with or without a capital 'C'.

Bibliography

ADORNO, T. W. (1941). On popular music, *Studies in Philosophy and Social Science*, vol. 9, no. 1, pp. 17–48

ADORNO, T. W. (1977). *Schriften*. Suhrkamp Verlag, Frankfurt a. Main, vol. 1, no. 10.

ADORNO, T. W. et al. (1950). *The Authoritarian Personality*, Harper, New York

DEUTSCHE GESELLSCHAFT FÜR SOZIOLOGIE, Geschäftsbericht (1910). In *Verhandlungen der deutschen Soziologentage*, vol. 1

DEUTSCHE GESELLSCHAFT FÜR SOZIOLOGIE, Geschäftsbericht (1912). In *Verhandlungen der deutschen Soziologentage*, vol. 2

GEIGER, T. (1950). A radio test of musical taste, *Public Opinion Quarterly*, vol. 14, pp. 36–48

HUGHES, H. M. (1940). *News and the Human Interest Story*, University of Chicago Press, Chicago

HUTH, A. (1937). *La radiodiffusion, puissance mondiale*, Paris, p. 511

KATZ, E. and LAZARSFELD, P. F. (1955). *Personal Influence*, The Free Press, New York

KLAPPER, J. T. (1960). *The Effects of the Mass Media*, The Free Press, New York

KRACAUER, S. (1947). *Propaganda and the Nazi War Film*, reprinted in *From Caligari to Hitler*, Princeton University Press, New Jersey, appendix

KRIS, E. and LEITES, N. (1947). Trends in twentieth century propaganda, *Psychoanalysis and the Social Sciences*, vol. 1, pp. 393–409

KRIS, E. and SPEIER, H. (1944). *German Radio Propaganda*, Oxford University Press, Oxford, p. 477

LANG, K. and LANG, G. E. (1965). Mass media and voting, reprinted in Bernard Berelson and Morris Janowitz, (eds), *Reader in Public Opinion and Communication*, 2nd edition, The Free Press, New York

LASSWELL, H. D. (1927). *Propaganda Techniques in the World War*, Kegan Paul, Trench, London

LAZARSFELD, P. F. (1941). Remarks on administrative and critical research, *Studies in Philosophy and Social Science*, vol. 9, pp. 2–16

LAZARSFELD, P. F. (1948). In *Current Trends in Social Psychology*, University of Pittsburgh Press, Pittsburgh

LAZARSFELD, P. F. and MERTON, R. K., (eds) (1954). *Studies in the Scope and Methods of 'The Authoritarian Personality'*, The Free Press, New York

LEWIN, K. (1942). In *Problems of Changing Food Habits*, National Research Council, Washington, DC

LOWENTHAL, L. (1943). Biographies in popular magazines, in Paul F. Lazarsfeld and Frank Stanton, (eds), *Radio Research, 1942–43*, Essential Books, Fairlawn, NJ

LOWENTHAL, L. and GUTERMAN, N. (1947). *Prophets of Deceit*, Harper, New York

PARK, R. E. (1922). *The Immigrant Press and Its Control*, Harper, New York

PARK, R. E. (1940). News as a form of knowledge: a chapter in the sociology of knowledge, *American Journal of Sociology*, vol. 45, pp. 669–686

PARK, R. E. (1941). News and the power of the press, *American Journal of Sociology*, vol. 46, pp. 1–11

SPEIER, H. (1969a). Magic geography, reprinted in *Social Order and the Risks of War*, MIT Technology Press, Cambridge, Mass., pp. 357 ff.

SPEIER, H. (1969b). Radio communication of war news in Germany, reprinted in *Social Order and the Risks of War*, MIT Technology Press, Cambridge, Mass., pp. 343–357

Studies in Philosophy and Social Science (1941). Vol. 9, no. 1

TOENNIES, F. (1923). Macht und Wert der öffentlichen Meinung, *Die Dioskuren; Jahrbuch für Geisteswissenschaften*, vol. 2, pp. 72–99

WHITE, D. M. (1950). The gatekeeper; a study in the selection of news, *Journalism Quarterly*, vol. 27, pp. 283–290

WILLIAMS, R. (1966). *Communications*, revised edition, Chatto & Windus, London, p. 95 f.

First presented to the Leicester, England, meeting of the International Association of Mass Communication Researchers in 1977, this article by Peter Golding and Graham Murdock rejects the validity of a communication or mass communication theory. The authors argue that the task of research is to analyze the social processes through which mass media messages are produced and interpreted, focusing on the contextual pressures that shape those messages, as opposed to the messages themselves. Dr. Golding is Research Officer and Dr. Murdock is Research Fellow at the Centre for Mass Communication Research, University of Leicester, England.

3

THEORIES OF COMMUNICATION AND THEORIES OF SOCIETY

Peter Golding and Graham Murdock

Mass communication research has grown into a vast academic enterprise. Our current conventions are testimony to its emergence as a fully fledged occupation, replete with the institutional apparatus of a mature discipline. University departments and schools of mass communications, journals devoted to communications, mass communications, human communication, and the media constantly spring up as the field grows, becomes specialised and differentiated. In our view this growth has become confused, and it is not surprising that the history of mass communications studies is punctuated by frequently expressed concern at the direction and shape scholarship in the field is taking. This concern has normally addressed two questions. First, there is the problem of defining the subject matter of study. Journals in the field often attempt to explain their existence by virtue of a set of common interests suggested by their title. The *Journal of Communication,* for example, is interested in "the study of communication theory, practice, and policy" and "significant problems and issues in communications." *Communication Research* is "concerned with the study of communication processes at all levels" especially "explication and testing of models that explain the processes and outcomes of communication." *Human Communication Research* "is devoted to advancing knowledge and understanding about human symbolic transactions"; and so on. Laudably cross disciplinary, awesomely broad in intellectual sweep, these concerns embrace a staggering and often unbounded range of interests and topics. In wondering at

From Peter Golding and Graham Murdock, "Theories of Communication and Theories of Society," *Communication Research* 5, 3 (July 1978) 339-356. Copyright 1978 by Sage Publications, Inc.

this heterogeneity, scholars have occasionally perceived a unity which can be made secure by constructing a single theory for the field. This view we believe to be false, and we will look carefully at it below.

The second question which has caused disquiet is not what to study, but how? Which methods are best able to cope with those aspects of human life we define as our concern? From which disciplinary base is it best to approach problems of mass communications? We wish to argue that these two frequently expressed misgivings have promoted a search for a false solution, a holy grail of unified theory and disciplinary order which represents a misleading objective. We will argue first that attempts of this kind are based in false assumptions about the power of theories of comunication and mass communications, and in confused linkages between the concepts of communications and culture. Second, we will suggest that we do not need a theory of mass communications but a theory of society to generate guiding propositions and research in the areas in which we are interested. In brief, we argue that the answer to the question "Where are we going and how do we get there?" is that we cannot get there from where we are.

THE CRITIQUE

In reviewing the many critiques of communication studies that have appeared over the years one theme emerges as central to all of them; the neglect of theory and the underdevelopment of a conceptual framework to guide research. This criticism comes from a number of directions. First there have been those commentators who note the apparently aimless refinement of research methods by researchers developing more and more sophisticated empirical techniques and statistical constructs, while seeming to lose sight of the broader implications of their research or its theoretical significance. Nordenstreng, critically appraising American mass communication research in 1968, concluded that "the field concentrates on being correct in the technical methods at the expense of being loose on the conceptual level" (Nordenstreng, 1968: 208).

The obsession with methods is diagnosed as symptomatic of a theoretical vacuum in which the paucity of ideas is masked by a dazzling display of empirical ingenuity.

A slightly different line of attack was taken by critics who noted not so much a lack of theory, but a lack of theorists. Berelson's famous and deliberately challenging post-mortem, delivered at the 1958 Conference of the American Association for Public Opinion Research, concluded that the field was exhausted, or in his own metaphor "as for communication research, the state is withering away" (Berelson, 1959: 1). He argued that the main reason was the desertion of the seminal thinkers to newer, more exciting, arenas, and he cites, in particular, Hovland, Lasswell, and Lazarsfeld, as well as the late Kurt Lewin. The resulting conceptual stagnation Berelson believed had prevented further development of existing lines of inquiry. This verdict did not go unchallenged, and spirited replies pointed out the important contributions of students of these major figures and the continuing vigour of many areas of communication studies. But the force of Berelson's verdict continued to trouble observers puzzled by the dearth of theory in the field.

In looking at the evolution of mass communications studies, a third line of argument traced the problem to the practical beginnings and pragmatic intentions of the discipline's forbears. The need of the American commercial radio industry to chart its audience, and the demands of war-time propaganda research were important determinants of the directions studies took. Hovland headed the research branch of the U.S. Army Information and Education Division. War-time food consumption patterns were the focus and stimulus to the communication studies of Lewin and his students, and of course the commissioned market research at the Bureau of Applied Social Research at Columbia produced many influential studies of media consumption in the New York area. The practical concerns with manipulation, effects, and influence were not without a theoretical yield, especially at the level of social psychology. But later observers came to see these interests as administratively rather than theoretically guided, and as inviting elaboration of quantitative techniques to measure effects rather than more general elucidation of communications theory. Not least among such observers, incidentally, was Lazarsfeld himself, the key figure at Columbia, who as early as 1941 was constrasting critical with administrative research (Lazarsfeld, 1972). The professional association of communications studies with schools of journalism was seen to enhance this concern with the quantification of effects and the lack of independent theorization (Brown, 1970; Gans, 1972).

Finally, theoretical retardment was related to the fragmentation of the field of study. Merton, for example, contrasted American mass communication research with European *wissensociologie.* In the former "the strong concern with empirical test leads prematurely to a curbing of imaginative hypotheses: the nose is held so close to the empirical grindstone that one cannot look up to see beyond the limits of the immediate task" (Merton, 1957: 443). Further, such research deals with separate problems in the short-term, applying an array of research techniques to the solution of pragmatic problems in market and military research as they arise, with little attempt to accumulate a body of relevant theory in an academic context. Others have noted how this scatter of interests guided by professional, commercial or political requirements has remained too diverse to respond to or promote a unity of theory.

In these different ways, then, mass communications studies have been attacked for theoretical immaturity. It is important, however, to put these evaluations in perspective. It is too often assumed that mass communications research has steadily advanced from conceptual infancy to its present fully fledged vigour. We are assumed to have spotted the gaps ignored by earlier pioneers and become more aware of the limitations of their vision. From a concentration on "with what effects?" we are deemed to have gradually moved on to the other links in Lasswell's famous paradigm. This optimistic view ignores two factors. First, critical awareness was not altogether absent among early researchers. In 1941, for example, Lazersfeld was arguing for critical communications research, and calling for analysis of organisations and control, and for a reformulation of effects and content studies in a broader social context (Lazarsfeld, 1972). The second, and related factor, is that mass communications, like other disciplines, has not had a linear development from the simple to the subtle, the limited to the comprehensive. If we historically situate the perspectives and interests that have successively dominated the field, we find not a sequence but a set of contending perspectives. The lack of theory, in other words, has been more apparent than real. Before looking at the implicit theories that did guide American mass communications research, we can note in passing two orientations that failed to gain a secure foothold. One was the traditions of European literary criticism and the sociology of knowledge, predominantly Marxist in approach, whose characteristics Merton's essay brought out so well. The second was the interest shown by sociology, particularly at Chicago, in journalism by such writers as Robert Park, himself for some years a reporter, Park's student, Helen Hughes, and later Chicago sociologists like Janowitz and the Langs. Significantly, however, these writers came to an interest in the media from broader based sociological concerns with crowd behaviour, urban ecology, or ethnic minorities. Thus, these were comparatively isolated studies and never developed as central to mass communication research. Indeed, it was the very fact that their roots were in broader sociological fields that prevented such a development.

In arguing that mass communications research was never lacking in theory, we are referring to the general guiding perspectives from which social structures were viewed by researchers, which led them to formulate problems and findings as they did. The first major perspective of this kind was the theory of mass society. Social structure was seen as an amorphous mass surmounted by a dominant elite. Inequality was conceived as organised around an uneven distribution of power, not of property, and the mass as inhabiting an urbanised, industrialised world in which primary social ties were weakened and individuals had become susceptible, manipulable, and "atomised." With this picture of urban America researchers concentrated on the vulnerability to elite manipulation of the masses by the new and powerful tools of the modern media. Many such researchers were themselves refugees from the formative and traumatic experience of such a situation in Nazi Germany, and translated this experience into their observation of America. Research concentrated first on propaganda, persuasion, attitude change; second on "mass culture" and the threat of brutalisation of high culture by the imposed mediocrity produced by commercial media for the masses.

The second such guiding theory implicit in mass communication research was functionalism, or in its political science form, pluralism. In the stable growth of postwar America, observers saw the good society in the making, a stable effective democracy in which major inequalities had been eradicated and the social structure could be seen as a series of parallel institutions, requiring possibly minor reform, but fundamentally in good order. For the sociologists functionalism led to the search for stabilising relationships between the institutions: the family, education, industry, religion, culture, and so on. For political scientists the quest was for the mechanisms of checks and balances by which competing centres of power were equalled out to provide the stable order and relative equality they saw around them. By the time Klapper came to write his influential summary of mass communications research in 1960 this perspective was predominant, and in his presidential address to the American Association for Public Opinion Research in 1963, he was able to assert the primacy of functionalism (Klapper, 1963). In investigating the functions of the media, researchers thus concentrated on the integrative effect of mass communications. Rather than consider cultural stratification, functionalists would seek the ways in which the media convey values from one generation to the next; that is, the media are conceived as a functional institution of socialisation, not as part of a legitimising apparatus in an egalitarian social order. In providing a functionalist textbook on mass communications, Wright explained that "Transmission of culture focusses on the communicating of information values and social norms from one generation to another" (Wright, 1959: 16).

The functionalist approach thus redefined "effects" studies, by starting from a social result—an integrated, nonstratified ordered, and stable society—and then querying how the media contributed to this result. It invited studies which, at a sociological level, investigated the media and institution x, y or z with no particular priority among them; while at a psychological level researchers sought the gratifications derived by individuals from media output.

Theories, then, were indeed to be found in mass communications research, but as implicit presuppositions rather than as explicit expositions. Dissatisfaction with this state of affairs led to the search for theory, a quest for a unifying body of ideas which would reclaim mass communications studies for academic respectability.

THE QUEST FOR A THEORY

The first such overarching framework was sought in a theory of communication. If all human relationships involved communication in some form, and the distinctive characteristic of human society was the centrality of symbolic interchange, then clearly, it was assumed, a theory of communication was the ideal location for propositions about mass communications in particular. The whole range of human action could be subsumed by it. As Lerner (1973: 541) has recently put it: "Since communication is an integral dimension of all social relations, studies of communications range, in the wise words of Edward Sapir, 'from the glance of a pair of lovers to debates in the League of Nations'." As an added attraction, mathematicians and cyberneticians were producing formulae which suggested parallels for the investigation of human behaviour. Grasping at clues distributed by linguists, mathematicians, and information theorists, scholars in media studies began to explore the idea of "communication theory." By 1973 Lin (pp. vii, 212) was writing confidently that communication research has gradually evolved into a major research discipline over the last 20 years" and that "human communication is becoming an integrated scientific discipline."

Several writers were more cautious, however, and pointed to the fallacious assumption of homogeneity entailed in taking the communications element in different spheres as subject to equivalent generalisations. Cherry, for example, wrote of his concern that

> an awareness of certain unity of a group of studies is growing, originally diverse and disconnected, but all related to our communicative activities. The movement is rapidly becoming "popular," so great is the desire for unification, and this popularity carries with it a certain danger. . . . Awareness of the universal nature of "communication" has existed for a very long time, in a somewhat vague and empirical way, but recently the mathematical developments which come under the heading of the "Theory of Communication" have brought matters to a head, and many there are who regard this work as a panacea. . . . *At the time of writing the various*

*aspects of communication . . . by no means form a unified study:
there is a certain common ground which shows promise of fertility,
nothing more* [1966: 2; emphasis in original].

The mere verbal accident of the concept of communication
appearing in so many diverse fields suggested a common ground,
whereas this was merely an artifact of the immense semantic
elasticity of the word. Even some enthusiasts have conceded the
lack of unity at the level of theory. Gordon, for example, author of
a book subtitled "considering a cross discipline," warns that

> [T]he only element that does, as a matter of fact, consistently
> distinguish studies in communication from other disciplines is
> subject matter, one of the weakest glues on the market today in the
> delineation of areas of human inquiry. . . . The subject matter of
> communication, taken alone, is therefore probably among the least
> productive—and possibly the most futile—starting point for the
> delineation of appropriate areas of inquiry into human interaction
> or the process it involves [1975: 45-46].

We certainly would not wish to argue against the obvious
desirability of cross-disciplinary intercourse and a flexibility of
subject matter. At the same time, however, it is important to
remain wary of going beyond the dissolution of existing intellectual boundaries to the construction of new ones in the false
belief that a new and better organising principle has been un-
earthed. As well as seducing constructors of curricula into
absurdly ambitious and formless amalgams of quite disparate
interests, communications theory has a more serious deficiency.
This weakness is the idealism inherent in the idea of communications as the stuff of human relations. This is most clearly expressed by Duncan, who, working in the symbolistic interactionist
tradition, argues that "We must return the study of man in society
to a study of communication, for how we communicate determines how we relate as human beings" (Duncan, 1968: 438).
Elsewhere he has argued that social hierarchy is determined by
the symbols we have available to us (see e.g., Duncan, 1967). This
view together with its popular variant expressed in the ubiquitous
formula that "it's a problem of communication," evacuates from
analysis the key problems of power and inequality in structural
relations without which social theory is barren.

The second, slightly more limited, attempt at theory construction has been the often expressed desire for a theory of mass communications. At the simplest level it has been identified with model construction, in which a few key concepts are connected by vague generalisations, normally expressed diagrammatically. How many chain diagrams linking sender-message-receiver have been presented as insightful theories, with the occasional addition of a loop going in the opposite direction called "feedback" as a sophisticated refinement? The more advanced of these "models" have a dotted line round the edge called "social context." Model building is not theory building, and banal sketches of this kind are not even adequate as models.

But, again, there are more serious weaknesses in the attempt to arrive at a theory of mass communication. Williams has castigated such a construct as "scraps of applied psychology and linguistics" (Williams, 1958: 301). But it is not merely the eclecticism of mass communication theory that is worrying but its inductive tendencies. Berelson, for example, has suggested that a theory will emerge "if we get a solid body of important empirical propositions documented on communication behaviour. When you put these together and, so to speak, add them up, that's it" (quoted in Nordenstreng, 1968: 210). Yet it was just such a directionless hunt for fragmented "findings" that prompted the search for theory in the first place. Expecting a theory of mass communications to emerge presupposes first that we know what we are looking for, second that we are not already working with the kind of implicit theory we have earlier described.

A theory of mass communication is further indicated by its mistaken location of the mass media at the centre of social life. Pool argues that we now have "societies organised around mass media systems" (Pool, 1965). Thus we can study whole societies by concentrating on their mass media. This is an obvious overstatement. Nonetheless, versions of this same vision have tempted eminent practitioners such as de Fleur (1966: xiii) to announce the emergence of mass communications studies, "as a new academic discipline in its own right." Media determinism, in its arbitrary allocation of an unwarranted and unsupportable significance to the subject matter at hand, distorts beyond reprieve a balanced view of social structure and process. As

Schramm (1959: 8-9) shrewdly noted, some years ago, in replying to Berelson: "We sometimes forget that communication research is a field, not a discipline. In the study of man it is one of the great crossroads where many pass but few tarry. . . . Therefore we must not look for the unique theory in communication which we are accustomed to see in disciplines." Similarly, McQuail has recently reminded us that the media are not the only organisations involved in the manufacture and distribution of values, nor are they independent of the forces exerted by other institutional spheres. As he notes (1972: 12), "If the media are more acted upon than acting, it has profound implications for the kinds of questions one asks." A theory of mass communications, whether in McLuhanesque or some other form, would present a picture of social structure incompatible with empirical reality, based more in the accidents of academic departmentalisation than on a coherent view of society.

A third attempt at a solution, the "cultural studies" approach, focuses on the general relations between the social order of a society and the totality of symbolic forms through which its meaning is explicated and expressed—in short its culture. Whilst they acknowledge the centrality of the mass media in relaying social meanings in modern societies therefore, supporters of this approach stress the need to situate the media in the context of the culture as a whole. Hence, in addition to analysing mass communications, cultural studies also deals with the traditional forms of symbolisation embedded in art, literature, and religion, and with everyday expressive forms such as conversation, clothing, and bodily gestures. In a field where people are still apt to regard contemporary culture as more or less synonymous with television programming, this contextualisation represents a considerable gain in breadth. As such it is to be welcomed. However, in approaching the analysis of culture, the cultural studies approach poses severe problems of method.

Proponents of cultural studies start from the incontestable fact that all cultural forms contain traces of the processes and assumptions involved in their creation and offer interpretive guidelines to would-be consumers. Hence, they argue, a careful analysis of particular artifacts "can yield evidence about the whole organisation within which it is embedded" (Williams, 1961: 46).

As Carey has pointed out, "This is a process of making large claims for small matters: studying particular plays, conversations, songs, dances . . . and gingerly reaching out to the full relations within a total way of life" (Carey, 1975: 190). Media artifacts are therefore regarded as texts, and the process of analysis consists of "reading off" the layers of social meaning they contain, and then extrapolating outwards to the social relations involved in their production and use. This basic approach has been developed in a number of different directions, and to do justice to this diversity would require at least another paper, if not a book. Here, we will offer some brief illustrations beginning with Burgelin's manifesto for a semiotic approach to mass communications.

For Burgelin, the study of mass communications is practically coextensive with the analysis of media messages. Certainly he sees the explication of the meanings relayed by the media as the "prime object of interest for research in this area" (Burgelin, 1972: 314). To accomplish this, he argues, it is necessary for the analyst "to take into account only the internal relations of the system, and exclude all those between the system and society" (1972: 314). Only after the structure of the message has been exhaustively mapped can the researcher begin to trace its relations to contexts of production and reception. However, this second stage is very much an afterthought, a secondary activity which relies primarily on inferences from the first stage supplemented by general contextual material. With rare exceptions, the kind of semiotic analysis proposed by Burgelin does not seek to analyse the processes of creation and consumption independently. The result is a highly asymmetric analysis in which an elaborate anatomy of symbolic forms sits alongside a schematic and incomplete account of social processes. So long as the primary aim is the explication of meaning, this imbalance does not matter too much. However, as soon as textural analysis is used as a basis for statements about social processes, severe problems of inference present themselves, as Roland Barthes' seminal essay, "Myth Today," illustrates.

The essay revolves around an analysis of a news photo of a Negro soldier saluting the French flag which Barthes argues signifies "that France is a great Empire . . . and that there is no better answer to the detractors of an alleged colonialism than the zeal shown by this Negro in serving his so-called oppressors" (Barthes, 1973: 116). It is one of an almost infinite series of press representations—"a nun hands a cup of tea to a bedridden Arab, a white schoolmaster teaches attentive piccaninnies"—all of which conceal the exploitation and racism of French imperialism and portray the empire as simultaneously natural and just. These images in turn are part of a wider system of symbolisation through which the ruling class conceals the brute facts of inequality and class domination and presents the existing social order as inevitable and full of opportunity. This dominant ideology permeates and determines every aspect of symbolisation. "Everything," Barthes argues, "our films, our pulp literature, our conversations, the cooking we dream of, the garments we wear is dependent on the representation which the bourgeoisie *has and makes us have* of the relations between man and the world" (Barthes, 1973: 140). By this point in the argument, however, a subtle sleight of hand has taken place. What began as an interpretation of particular cultural forms is suddenly being presented *as though* it were an analysis of the social dynamics of class domination. In point of fact it is nothing of the sort. While he offers a fruitful elaboration of Marx's famous dictum that "the ideas of the ruling class are the ruling ideas," Barthes certainly does not demonstrate how this ideological domination is created and sustained. To say that the mass media are saturated with bourgeois ideology is simply to pose a series of questions for investigation. To begin to answer them, however, it is necessary to go on to show how this hegemony is actually reproduced through the concrete activities of the media personnel and the interpretive procedures of consumers. This requires detailed and direct analysis of the social contexts of production and reception and their relations to the central institutions and processes of class societies. Extrapolations from cultural texts, no matter how subtle and elaborate, are no substitute.

Many prominent exponents of cultural studies have, however, recognised the difficulties inherent in the attempt to synthesise textual and social analyses and have attempted to work these problems through in their writings. Without doubt, the most interesting and influential of the recent attempts is to be found in the work of Raymond Williams.

More than anyone else, Williams has been responsible for putting cultural studies on the English academic map. For over twenty years he has worked away at the edges of adjacent disciplines looking for points of contact and cross-fertilization between literary criticism, sociology, social history, and latterly, Marxism. The promise of intellectual integration held out by this project is immensely attractive but at the same time problematic, as Williams himself is the first to recognise.

Since he starts by acknowledging that "Questions about forms in communications are also questions about institutions and about the organisation of social relationships" (Williams, 1974b: 23), he is immediately confronted with the problem of relating textual and social analysis, criticism, and sociology, and deciding on their relative priorities. In his earlier works, such as *The Long Revolution,* he attempted to side-step the issue by insisting that both types of analysis were equally indispensable. It was, he argued, "an error to suppose that social explanation is determining." Consequently, it was not a question of relating cultural forms to social formations, but of studying "their interrelations without any concession of priority to any one" (Williams, 1961: 45). Subsequently, however, his increasing commitment to a version of the Marxist model of base and superstructure has forced him to reassess this position. In particular, he has increasingly acknowledged that textual and sociological analyses are rooted in fundamentally opposed approaches to the study of culture and that eventually a choice must be made between the two. As he put it in a recent paper, "The true crisis of cultural theory, in our own time, is between the view of the work of art as object and the alternative view of art as a practice" (Wiliams, 1973: 15). Later on in the same paper, he endorses the latter, more sociological alternative. "We have," he argued, "to break from the notion of isolating the object and then discovering its components. On the contrary, we have to discover the nature of a practice and then its conditions" (Williams, 1973: 16). As he recognises, to adopt this approach is to recognise the primacy of social analysis and the prior need to ground this analysis in a coherent model of the overall social structure. In his recent book on television, for example, he strongly criticises conventional research approaches to mass communications for the self-enclosure and lack of articulation to broader social theories.

> To say that television is now a factor in socialisation, or that its controllers and communicators are exercising a particular social function, is *to say very little until the forms of the society* which determine any particular socialisation and which allocate the function of control and communication *have been precisely specified* [Williams, 1974a: 120; my emphasis].

Unfortunately, in his actual analysis he draws away from the implications of this critique. The result is the familiar asymmetry. The meat of the television book, for example, consists of a detailed analysis of the forms and flow of television programming sandwiched between a relatively brief account of the evolution of Britain's broadcasting structures and suggestions for their modification and change.

Hence, while we would support the general thrust of Williams' recent arguments, we would also insist on the need to follow their logic through into the practice of research. We begin, then, by preserving cultural studies' focus on the relation between culture and society while reversing its conventional priorities. In our view, the primary task of mass communications research is not to explore the meanings of media messages, but to analyse the social processes through which they are constructed and interpreted and the contexts and pressures that shape and constrain these constructions. To accomplish this we certainly require more adequate theories and conceptual schema, but they need to be themes of social structure and social process not themes of communications.

TOWARDS A RELEVANT THEORETICAL CONTEXT

To call for more social theory now is to enter an academic brawl in which there are almost as many contending theories on offer as there are combatants. Even so, having spent most of the paper criticising the efforts of others, we feel some obligation to at least suggest the basic outlines of an alternative. What follows is a bald sketch of an orientation which is still in the process of formation. It has emerged gradually out of our continuing attempt to grapple with the problems and potentialities presented by the various research projects that we have been involved in. More particularly, it represents an effort to develop an integrative framework capable of relating the various levels of the mass communications process, both to each other and to the central dimensions of social structure and social process.

Our basic departure point is the recognition that social relations within and between modern societies are radically, though variably, inegalitarian. And leading on from this our focus is on the relations between the unequal distribution of control over systems of communications and wider patterns of inequality in the distribution of wealth and power. In the context of the advanced societies of both East and West, this entails exploring the relations between communications systems and systems of economic and social stratification. In particular, it focuses attention on the relations between the mass media and the central axis of stratification—the class structure. At the broader level of the international system, our formulation focuses on the unequal exchanges between advanced and developing nations and on the various dimensions of imperialism.

These systems of internal and international stratification are by no means self-sustaining, however. On the contrary, they must be constantly maintained and reproduced. Hence our second main concern is with the processes of legitimation through which the prevailing structures of advantage and inequality are presented as natural and inevitable. This entails exploring the relations between communication systems and the other agencies through which disadvantaged groups are incorporated into the existing social order, and, in particular, education systems and other agencies involved in the distribution of social knowledge and cultural competence. These processes of incorporation and legitimation do not work in an entirely smooth and uninterrupted manner, however. On the contrary, gaps and contradictions are constantly appearing between what is supposed to be happening and what is actually taking place between what has been promised and what has been delivered. Into these cracks and fissures flow currents of criticism and movements of contestation. Our third and final starting point, then, is with the sources of social dissent and political struggle, and with the dialectical relations between challenge and incorporation.

Despite the fact that this approach is still both tentative and provisional, we would argue that it offers several advantages.

First, it provides a coherent framework within which to relate the various levels of the mass communications process to each other and to central dimensions of social structure and social process. As such, it provides a useful basis from which to begin constructing a comprehensive and integrated social analysis of mass communications systems. Second, by focusing on the relations between symbol systems and stratification, it not only opens up a series of important areas for further investigation but also directs attention to currents of social theory that have so far been largely untapped by mass communications researchers.

By now, however, some may be beginning to feel a little uneasy and may have begun to ask themselves whether this isn't just a cleverly concealed bid for the ascendency of sociology in general and our particular brand in particular. When it comes right down to it, aren't we simply saying that the only work worth doing in mass communications research is sociological analysis? The answer is no. Admittedly, it is a possible reading of our argument but it is a misreading all the same.

Although sociologists have been centrally concerned with the problems of stratification and social reproduction, they have not had the field entirely to themselves. Indeed, many people, ourselves included, would argue that many of the most fruitful contributions have come from elsewhere, from radical economics, from social history, from social psychology, and from Marxist scholarship and practice. What we are calling for, then, is not a commitment to the discipline of sociology as currently institutionalised within academia, but a commitment to the basic questions that provided its original impetus; questions about the relations between cultural systems and economics and social formations, questions about the dynamics of social and cultural reproduction, and questions about the sources of change and contestation. As Bernstein (1974: 158) has recently put it, our main task is to show how the prevailing distributions of property and power and the dominant principles of control "shape the structure of symbolic arrangements, how they enter into our experience as interpretative procedures and the conditions of their repetition and change." And to accomplish this successfully, we need to ground our work more solidly and consistently than we have done up until now in general social theory.

REFERENCES

BARTHES, R. (1973) Mythologies. London: Paladin Books.

BERELSON, B. (1959) "The state of communication research." Public Opinion Q. 23: 1-6.

BERNSTEIN, B. (1974) "Sociology and the sociology of education: a brief account," pp. 145-159 in J. Rex (ed.) Approaches to Sociology. London: Routledge & Kegan Paul.

BROWN, R. (1970) "Approaches to the historical development of mass media studies," pp. 41-57 in J. Tunstall (ed.) Media Sociology. London:Constable.

BURGELIN, O. (1972) "Structural analysis of mass communication," pp. 313-328 in D. McQuail (ed.) Sociology of Mass Communications. London: Penguin.

CAREY, J. W. (1975) "Communication and culture." Communication Research 2, 2 (April): 173-191.

de FLEUR, M. L. (1966) Theories of Mass Communication, New York: McKay.

CHERRY, C. (1966) On Human Communication. Cambridge: MIT Press.

DUNCAN, H. D. (1968) Communication and Social Order. New York: Oxford Univ. Press.

——— (1967) "The search for a social theory of communication in American sociology," in F.E.X. Dance (ed.) Human Communication Theory. New York: Holt, Rinehart & Winston.

GANS, H. J. (1972) "The famine in American mass communications research." Amer. J. of Sociology 77, 4 (January): 697-705.

GORDON, G. N. (1975) Communications and Media. New York: Hastings House.

KLAPPER, J. T. (1963) "Mass communication research: an old road resurveyed." Public Opinion Q. 27 (Winter): 515-527.

LAZARSFELD, P. F. (1972) "Administrative and critical communications re-search." Reprinted in P. F. Lazarsfeld, Qualitative Analysis. Boston: Allyn & Bacon.

LERNER, D. (1973) "Notes on communication and the nation state." Public Opinion Q. 37, 3: 541-549.

LIN, N. (1973) The Study of Human Communication. Indianapolis: Bobbs-Merrill.

McQUAIL, D. (1972) "Introduction," in D. McQuail (ed.) Sociology of Mass Com-munications. Hamondsworth: Penguin.

MERTON, R. K. (1957) "Wissensociologie and mass communications research," pp. 439-455 in R. K. Merton, Social Theory and Social Structure. New York: Free Press.

NORDENSTRENG, K. (1968) "Communications research in the United States." Gazette 14, 3: 207-216.

POOL, I.D.S. (1965) "Mass communication and political science," in L. W. Kindred (ed.) Communication Research and School Community Relations.

SCHRAMM, W. (1959) "Comments on Berelson." Public Opinion Q. 23.

WILLIAMS, R. (1974a) Television: Technology and Cultural Form. London: Fontana Books.

——— (1974b) "Communications as cultural science." J. of Communication 23, 4 (Summer): 17-25.

——— (1973) "Base and superstructure in Marxist cultural theory." New Left
   Rev. 82 (November/December): 3-16.
——— (1961) The Long Revolution. London: Chatto & Windus.
——— (1958) Culture and Society. London: Chatto & Windus.
WRIGHT, C. R. (1959) Mass Communication. New York: Random House.

*Peter Golding is Research Officer and Graham Murdock Research Fellow in
the Center for Mass Communication Research, University of Leicester. The
authors have a forthcoming book for Routledge & Kegan Paul,* Cultural
Capitalism: The Political Economy of Mass Communication.

Conceptually broadened hypotheses about media effects and methodological advances have pro-duced contemporary mass communication research that severely questions the view of minimal media impact that predominated our thinking in the middle of this century. In this compelling over-view, Steven H. Chaffee describes the major directions of nearly a half-century's empirical work and charts several new research directions. He argues for major new work on media in the context of social units such as the family and the community. Dr. Chaffee is Vilas Professor of Research in Journalism and Mass Communication at the University of Wisconsin—Madison.

4

MASS MEDIA EFFECTS
New Research Perspectives

Steven H. Chaffee

The great mass media industries of today developed as part of the in-dustrial revolution of the nineteenth century and the continuing technological revolution of the twentieth.[1] The United States mass press of the 1830s served the expanding population of a nation of businessmen, in which questions about the social value of a commer-cial enterprise scarcely had any place. The innovative muckraking magazines and the aggressive metropolitan newspapers that flowered in the 1890s were themselves instruments of reform, attacking "big business" enthusiastically enough to obscure the fact that they were part of it. Film and radio grew up in the self-indulgent era of commer-cialism that followed World War I, under the control of public-be-damned autocrats. But television has, almost from the beginning of its mass diffusion in the 1950s, found itself beset by a proliferating tangle of demands for public accountability. To an extent, these pressures have spilled over onto the earlier mass-communication industries, disturbing the complacency of once-remote media barons.

This recent historical shift toward media accountability is usually at-tributed to two major factors: the fact that broadcast media must be publicly regulated at least to the extent of allocating radio frequencies and television channels to particular local stations; and the widespread disenchantment with the massive institutions of American society that grew out of the extended depression of the 1930s.[2] A careful student of the current media-reform movement might well conclude that a

From Steven H. Chaffee, "Mass Media Effects: New Research Perspectives," *Communication Research—A Half-Century Appraisal*, Daniel Lerner and Lyle M. Nelson, eds., Honolulu: Univer-sity Press of Hawaii (1977) 210-241. Reprinted by permission.

third factor should be added to this brief list—the development of
social research on the effects of mass communication. The tools of
media-effects research are employed on all sides: by pressure groups to
document their special cases, by public agencies interested in propagating their campaigns via mass channels, and by the media themselves to improve the potency of their product. Those social scientists
who offer the conceptual and methodological skills for investigating
the social impact of mass communication find themselves in a seller's
market. They also find that their study of that impact is increasingly
used to modify the very thing they are investigating.

VARIETIES OF MEDIA EFFECTS

Even a cursory examination of the empirical research literature
reveals many concepts of possible effects—and indicators of "effectiveness"—of the mass media. A few simple distinctions will indicate the
multiplicity of approaches. First, we can separate effects that can be attributed to a medium because of its physical properties and the sheer
time a person devotes to it from effects that are traced to specific
content it transmits. Next a traditional division is made among the reception of information, the modification of behavior, and changes in
feelings, opinions, and intentions to act; these divisions are generally
labeled the cognitive, behavioral, and attitudinal (or affective)
categories of media effects. A third set of distinctions concerns the unit
of observation; an effect may manifest itself in the individual member
of the audience, in the interpersonal interaction between two (or a
few) audience members, or in the corporate activity of a larger social
system such as a community, a formal organization, or a nation. This
simple list, which includes one dichotomy (physical versus content-
specific effects) and two trichotomies (cognitive–behavioral–attitudinal and individual–interpersonal–system) produces an eighteen-cell
matrix ($2 \times 3 \times 3 = 18$). And, as shall be seen, several quite different
kinds of effects may be considered in some of those eighteen cells.

An examination of a random collection of studies of media effects,
or even of most summaries of that literature, would not give the impression of nearly as much variety as the preceeding paragraph suggests. A definite plurality, and quite probably a solid majority, of all
studies to date would fall into the one cell representing individual-
level content-specific attitudinal effects. The first major program of
studies, initiated during World War II by Carl Hovland, was almost
entirely built in this single model.[3] These studies were so well design-

ed and executed that they encouraged imitation and spin-offs. Not uncommonly today one may find citations of Hovland's work of several decades ago as the point of origin for current research, for example in such areas as source credibility, persuasibility, and the duration of effects.[4] But as the title of this paper implies, new research perspectives are being developed and pursued in the effects field. To a considerable extent they consist of explorations of some of the seventeen other cells in our 2 × 3 × 3 matrix.

EFFECTS OF THE MEDIA AS PHYSICAL AND TIME-CONSUMING ENTITIES

The production of mass media is a large and growing sector of the economy in the United States[5] and throughout most of the postindustrial world. Publication of daily newspapers rivals even the giant United States automobile industry in the value of industrial production.[6] The total payroll for the creation, fabrication, and distribution of newspapers, magazines, radio, hi-fi, television, and film represents a significant portion of the nation's work force. As with all mass-production industries, environmental costs arise. For instance, the newsprint for the thick newspapers that most Americans receive each day consumes a great deal of wood pulp from shrinking forests, and paper production is a major river-polluting industry. (Also, newsprint has been in chronic shortage worldwide for some years.) Another familiar example is the home television receiver, which draws a significant amount of electrical power some five hours each day in the typical household. The economic and environmental impact of the mass media on society has been little studied until very recently, and indeed has not ordinarily been considered part of "media effects" research at all—although it would seem to belong in any comprehensive cost-benefit analysis.

A second physical aspect is that the mass media introduce socially visible objects into people's immediate living environment. One's television set is a piece of furniture in the home; magazines are artfully arranged on coffee tables and books on shelves. These artifacts of mass communication need not be "consumed" for their content in order to serve socially expressive purposes. A person's perceived social status can be manipulated by conspicuous consumption of fashionable or approved media items—or by nonconsumption, as in the case of the self-styled intellectual who "wouldn't have a television set in the house." Many writers have made passing mention of this symbolic use of media consumption, but such usage has received little research attention.[7]

Time spent with mass media, on the other hand, has been a standard research topic. Surveys routinely include self-reported estimates of the hours a child spends watching television or the minutes an adult devotes to the newspaper in an average day. Somewhat curiously, these measures are usually treated as "cause" rather than "effect" variables. Watching television, to be sure, exposes the viewer to material that may have certain content-specific effects (see below). But the act of spending hours viewing is itself manifestly an effect of the existence of television. The key "effect" regards what the person has *not* been doing while watching television. In their comparison of "Teletown" and "Radiotown," two neighboring communities that differed mainly in that the second did not receive a television signal, Schramm, Lyle, and Parker addressed this very question; they were able to give fairly precise estimates of the reduction in play, sleep, reading, film attendance, and so forth, attributable to television.[8] Unfortunately the example set by this study has been followed more by direct replication than by extension into novel areas. Clues abound. When a football game is shown on television, attendance at the game is decreased; so, it appears, is the incidence of burglaries, at least when the telecast occurs at night. Water levels in community reservoirs reportedly drop suddenly during television's commercial breaks, due apparently to the simultaneous flushing of many toilets. City streets seem practically deserted during the telecasts of important football games. From such examples one gets the sense of a great deal of rescheduling of peoples' lives as a consequence of mass media. While this shifting of times to accommodate media schedules may seem trivial from the individual's viewpoint, thoughtful research might demonstrate that some of it is important for the functioning of the system as a whole.

A fourth general class of effects that are not content-specific has to do with the *dissipation* of feelings that lead a person to the media. Lyle and Hoffman[9] asked a sample of children and adolescents which of several activities (reading a book, watching television, listening to music, among others) they were likely to do under various psychological conditions (when you feel alone, when you are tired, when you are angry, and so on). While media use is presumably one effect of being, say, lonely or angry, the data imply also that the alleviation of this condition is the anticipated effect of the media activity. Also implicit is the assumption that the specific content encountered in the medium does not matter much; the responses indicate that each medium is sought under differing conditions *as a medium* rather than in search of a particular program or song or story. The "gratifications" served by the mass media as general entities have been commingled with those served by specific types of content in much research.[10] In the area of public-affairs information and news, recent data indicate that the effect that is sought is content-specific but not medium-specific.[11] A precise accounting of those effects that are sought in medium-specific fashion (without regard to content) has yet to be undertaken.

Another general effects question is that of feelings toward the media themselves. Many studies have been made of the relative credibility of different media and of the general evaluations of the media and of people who work in media industries. For instance, surveys have shown that newspaper reporters rank a bit below undertakers in job prestige norms; that most people say they get most of their news from television and would believe a television news report if it differed from one in a newspaper; and that parents and children are very eager to get television before it comes to a community—and very thankful for it once it arrives.[12] The origins of these and other attitudes about the media have not been studied in any detail, except for some data on demographic correlates.[13] Some of the causes of these attitudes toward the media will undoubtedly turn out to be content-specific, but others will not. For example, one reason parents welcome television is that it gets children out from underfoot, functioning in effect as a cheap babysitter. Institutionalized persons appreciate the sheer availability of media because in many cases they would otherwise have nothing to occupy their time. Negative feelings toward media are often expressed too, for various reasons. We have the conceptual and methodological tools to investigate these matters much more thoroughly.

CONTENT-SPECIFIC EFFECTS OF THE MEDIA

When people refer to "media effect," they ordinarily have in mind some particular type of content that is delivered via mass media, rather than general effects of "the media" as physical and time-consuming entities. Commonly, a distinction is made between content provided by our presentday media that would have been delivered by other means in their absence, and content that would not reach people *at all* but for the existence of media channels. But this division is more often a distinction than an important difference. Usually at stake is content that gets propagated in greater or lesser amounts, or to larger or smaller numbers of persons, because of the kind of media systems we have. For example, violent and pornographic scenes in drama date back to antiquity, although they seem to be employed with astonishing frequency by today's film and television writers. News about governmental activities, even though it may not be covered much more extensively than a few generations ago, reaches a wider citizenry now due to the dissemination capabilities of news magazines, wire services, newspapers, and television.

Changes in the methodology of media-effects research reflect the idea that media systems control the amount, rather than the kind, of communication in society. The early experimental model of Hovland lent itself to categorical statements about the effects of *presentation versus withholding* of a particular item of media content.[14] Today, one finds many studies of the effects attributable to *heavy versus light* exposure to a particular type of content; so many channels offer so many kinds of material that the concept of an experiment "control group" is practically impossible to operationalize for some of the most interesting categories of content.[15] Historically, we have shifted from the experiment to the field survey as the more widely applied method for hypothesis testing, although experimental tests are still preferred in content areas where they are feasible. Such a shift would seem to be retrogressive—it does indeed seem so to many—without new methods for drawing causal inferences from nonexperimental data.[16]

Information gain is obviously one criterion for the assessment of media effectiveness; for the most part, this criterion has seemed too obvious to be very interesting to most investigators. Knowledge has traditionally been treated as a less consequential outcome than either "attitudes" or "behavior" in weighing the impact of mass communication on society. And yet propagation of information is the way most media professionals, when asked, characterize what they are trying to accomplish. And, interestingly, informational outcomes are often cited by media audiences as their reason for spending time even with what appears on its face to be purely entertainment programming.[17] To the extent that these expressed motivations are valid indicators, they should lead to more attention to broadly informational media effects.[18]

Something of a recession, on the other hand, seems to be underway in the area of affective outcomes of mass communication. Attitudinal effects were once assumed to represent an intermediate in a fixed psychological process that led from the intake of raw information to the exhibition of corresponding overt behavior.[19] The current perspective is instead one in which behavior and information are often treated as important specific indicators of media effectiveness, without assuming that they derive their social meaning from a presumed connection with attitudes.

Behind this shift has been the gradual accumulation of evidence that the direction of causation linking attitudes to knowledge and behavior is ambiguous. Experiments have demonstrated that a change in a broad social attitude (racial prejudice) can produce *subsequent* changes in expressed information.[20] Cognitive dissonance theory proved to be a good predictor of attitude changes that *followed* forced compliance with a new behavioral standard.[21] Careful examinations of studies in which both attitudinal and behavioral changes have been induced show low correlations between the two, and remarkably few examples of directly parallel effects.[22]

This ambiguity does not necessarily indicate that attitudinal effects have been declared irrelevant and are no longer thought worth assessing. Rather, they have been put in their conceptual place. When favorable opinions themselves are desired, as in the case of an oil company's institutional advertising or of a one-issue candidate's antiabortion or antiracism campaign, affective reactions may well be more important criteria of effectiveness than is any knowledge gained, or concrete behavior. On the other hand, when one's goal is to sell soap or purchase automobiles, the overt behavior of product supersedes attitudes; a corporation does not especially care if its brand is more loved than others so long as it is purchased. Many informational campaigns are tied to longer range attitudinal or behavioral goals, so much so that Hyman and Sheatsley in their classic explanation of "why information campaigns fail" defined failure almost exclusively in affective-behavioral rather than in informational terms.[23] More recent investigators have set forth conditons under which information campaigns might succeed, but these hinge to a considerable extent on holding to information transmission as one's superordinate goal.[24]

A fair amount of information, sometimes called "mobilizing information," conveyed via mass media has direct implications for one's behavior without necessarily activating any intermediating affective response. For example, the television and theater logs in the daily newspaper are basically informational and are usually consulted by a person whose general behavioral intention has already been determined; only a bit of shaping is required to get the person to the right place at the right time. Other examples include the media weather report, which may control your decision to plan a picnic or to plant a garden on a particular day; the end paragraph of a news story, which tells you where and when a political event that you might otherwise have missed is to be held; or the obituary notice that informs you of the funeral arrangements for a long-time friend.

Two classes of behavior relevant to the question of media effects can be distinguished. First, things which people have always done one way or another are modified on the basis of media inputs. The other category consists of those activities in which one would not have engaged at all had it not been for the propagation of a new message that could only be brought via mass communication. The first of these groups of behavior is doubtless the more common, but the second is in many ways more intriguing to the student of media and society.

Most of the major behavioral outcomes which are thought to be modified by media content existed before our present media resources came into being. If a quantity of pornographic or violent material occurs on the screen, and even if it can be linked empirically to increase in sexual offenses or aggressive acts, the obvious fact remains that pre-electronic society experienced approximately the same range of problems with sex and violence as we do today. Television has brought presidential addresses "live," and the gore of distant wars only slightly delayed on film or tape, into our living rooms; but previous generations learned what their presidents had said and had vivid images of their wars, albeit the transmission took a bit longer, reached fewer people, and was probably subject to more distortion in the process.

An individual finds it difficult to conceive of new activities he or she engages in as made possible only by modern media. But studies that examine the behavior of many persons simultaneously and in concert have noted numerous examples of effects for which mass communication is a necessary, not just a sufficient, condition. One of the most vivid was the group hysteria in certain neighborhoods that was created by the Orson Welles "War of the Worlds" broadcast in 1938.[25] Most sociologists agree with the statement that it is not inconsequential that we are all able to laugh at the same joke at the same time.[26] Political scientists often view mass communication as a means of holding the society together while it undergoes change rather than as an activating agent for change in itself.[27] Unquestionably our present-day capacity for organized social action is greatly enhance by the means of communication open to us.

Students in introductory classes in mass communication are sometimes given a chance to compare their lives with and without media by being assigned to "abstain" from any media inputs for a period of several days. While hardly scientific, these exercises are often illuminating. The students report that they find some media inputs impossible to avoid, as in the case of billboards and Muzak; that they find others ingrained in necessary activities, such as radio music while driving, or magazines while waiting for a doctor's appointment; and that some media activities are essential to their present form of existence, such as studying textbooks for their classes. Occasionally a student even reports suffering "withdrawal symptoms" such as craving candy after several days without the habitual mass media.

Of all the activities that mass media make possible, perhaps the most important is the immediate broadcasting of information about an impending crisis or a current disaster situation. Schramm has commented that the national experience of grief and readjustment following the assassination of President John Kennedy in 1963 was eased greatly because it could be widely shared via the mass media.[28] Coleman has analyzed the "crisis" role of the media in terms of a series of phases in the development and resolution of a community conflict.[29] When a local issue such as fluoridation or school busing arises, the news media are sometimes slow in detecting and explaining it. As many parties take strongly opposed stands, outrageous statements are often made; much of this debate is communicated via informal discussion channels, where rumor and slander can flow unchecked. The media cannot expand their coverage beyond their relatively fixed capacity—only so many column inches of newspaper or minutes of newscast per day; and they have their rules about what is appropriate to publish, which may exclude unverified, libelous, or obscene statements. Coleman sees a community conflict as approaching resolution once it is brought under the control of media coverage, in which an attempt is made to separate truth from falsehood and to check hyperbolic statements against one another.

The role of the mass media in handling more chronic sources of community conflict has been addressed in a series of empirical studies by Tichenor, Donohue, and Olien.[30] They find newspaper editors in small towns working to avoid the appearance of conflict while, in metropolitan areas, prestige and power go instead to those editors who are able to identify points of conflict in the community and bring them to the public consciousness.[31] The effectiveness of the mass media in handling intense social conflict is potentially a much more important one than the modest research literature on it to date would suggest. After all, when a social system is threatened from outside (for example, by disaster) or internally strained (as by a divisive political issue), the performance of its communication system is most critical.

This conflict-centered approach to the social effects of mass communication contrasts sharply with the earlier emphasis on attitude-management research in this field. The modification of one's feelings toward a class of objects has usually been studied in controlled situations where the target individual could be assumed to be invulnerable to outside influences. The Hovland group found what may be the optimal "field laboratory" in the Army's boot camp, where the soldier's daily life was extremely well controlled and practically identical from day to day and from one recruit to the next.[32] (Even so, some findings, such as the anomalous "sleeper effect," might be attributable to informal social organization within the barracks based on educational differences among the recruits.[33])

But even laying aside the methodological shift from controlled experimentation to the crisis- and conflict-management field studies that are proliferating today, an important conceptual change is apparent in the notion of "effective" communication. Hovland and his imitators began with an assumption that change of attitude (or behavior) in a certain direction was the desirable outcome. For instance, the Army needed to prepare its recruits psychoemotionally for combat; an effective orientation film would render them more enthusiastic about going to war alongside United States allies and against the Axis powers.[34] Similarly, in political research, an "effective" message persuades someone to vote for the candidate advocated. In marketing, the job of most advertisements is obviously to sell the advertised brand to consumers. Public relations speeches and releases are designed to build a favorable "image" or "climate of opinion" for the organization, agency, or firm that produces them. Messages that fail to accomplish these directional goals are deemed "ineffective."

This assumption is not made in crisis-management and conflict-resolution studies of media effects. Instead, "success" is inferred if the system survived the crisis without breaking apart. An effective resolution of a community conflict is indicated by a number of attibutes: the absence of bloodshed or the exercise of raw power; the speed and ease with which an outcome was reached; or the degree to which the various parties to the resolution are satisfied with it and with the process through which it was achieved. We might expect to see in communication-effects studies of the future more criteria of effectiveness with this nondirectional flavor.

Much of the day-to-day work of the news media does not deal with dramatic crises. "Slow news days" occur, and much routine coverage is made of the progress of bills through legislatures, of the campaigns of hopeful candidates for higher offices, and of distant events that have no clear connection to the immediate concerns of the bulk of the media audience. Are the media "ineffective" in their efforts to perform these humdrum tasks well, simply because they a) are not influencing attitudes in a particular direction and b) are not resolving any societal crises? One would like to be able to say, "No, of course these activities of the media are important, too." But present modes of research in effect define the nonpersuasive and noncrisis efforts of the mass media as ineffective by default.

Two current theoretical themes that involve content-specific psychological effects are interesting in that they do not presuppose any bias or directionality in media content. They find the "cause" in the simple variable of either mentioning or not mentioning a particular item in the media, even if it is mentioned in what seems to be a "neutral" fashion. The earlier of these themes in terms of research is the effect of "mere exposure" to a communicated item on one's attitudinal responses to it. The other is the concept of "agenda-setting" effects of the media, an idea that was around for many decades before its time for empirical test arrived.

The most thorough study of "mere exposure" is that of Zajonc.[35] He experimentally varied the frequency with which audience members saw particular photographs (of faces) during a series of presentations; a subsequent tendency arose to assign more favorable evaluations to those which had been seen most often. Becker and Doolittle applied this principle to the mass media, in an experiment using brief radio advertisements for political candidates.[36] Their finds were curvilinear; more frequent exposure to a candidate's name resulted in more favorable ratings up to a point—after which continued repetition produces a decline in evaluations. In a world where public figures vie for the spotlight and hire publicity agents to secure media exposure, that so little is known about the attitudinal impact of exposure per se is remarkable.

The agenda-setting hypothesis focuses on an effect that lies short of attitudinal persuasion, although the effect is essential to the persuasion. As the proposition has been put, the media may not be especially powerful in telling people what to think, but they can be quite successful in determining what people will think *about*.[37] McCombs and his colleagues have consistently found correlations between the rankings people make regarding the importance of various social "problems" and the frequency with which local mass media mention those problems.[38] McLeod and Becker have used a comparative design in which they examine the problem rankings of groups exposed to media that contain different content emphases; the rankings given by these different audiences resemble those of their respective media.[39] Despite these convergent results, however, the finding is apprently limited to certain groups of persons, such as those who are seeking guidance on political questions.[40] .

The current wave of interest in agenda-setting is centered in schools of journalism and is derived partly from ethical concerns within the news industry. The journalist's standard of objectivity has traditionally been considered satisfied where no directional bias could be demonstrated in content analysis of one's news. But direct persuasion is no longer deemed the only effect of importance. The issues a person considers important provide the cognitive background against which that person's specific opinions will be developed and tested. Agenda- setting has societal-level implications, too. The issues on which most problem-solving effort is likely to be expended are those that people consider most important; to the extent that the news industry controls which problems will be addressed, it also determines which will get ignored.

One final topic that has attracted considerable research attention in the past few years is the concept of a "knowledge gap" in society. The hypothesis is that the informational mass media are attended primarily by people who are already relatively well informed. Thus the gap is widened between the knowledgeable and the uninformed sectors of society, which in turn may make more difficult the functioning of the society as a total system.[41] While several studies, particularly in agrarian settings, have found a widening knowledge gap that can be attributed to media influence, some studies are also showing the reverse—that media inputs can bring the less-informed sector up to parity.[42] The conditions under which each of these patterns can be expected to occur pose an important research problem.

INTERVENING PROCESSES IN MEDIA EFFECTS

Many researchers, in writing their reports of studies in which some sort of effect of mas communication has been demonstrated, have betrayed a deep sense of unease about the inadequacy of their understanding of the phenomenon they have isolated. The two-variable model consists of a measure or manipulation of variation in exposure to media content (independent variable) and an observation of change in some aspect of thought or behavior (dependent variable) that is empirically linked in a systematic statistical fashion to the independent variable. Enough fairly impressive cause–effect research of this type has accumulated to assure us that the mass media do indeed have a variety of effects on individual behavior.

What has been lacking, although it too is beginning to accumulate, is three-variable research in which the psychological processes that intervene between media exposure and its effects are studied. If a boy is shown a filmed fight and subsequently acts more aggressively than before, we might conclude that the film has created an effect. But we may not understand what the intervening process has been and, lacking that knowledge, we may not have much idea how counselors or parents might themselves intervene to control the process after the media exposure has occurred. About as many different theories exist regarding these processes as there are theorists, and only slightly more active researchers.

In the example of the fight film, for instance, one interpretation might be that the boy is simply imitating the behavior he has been shown; perhaps that behavior was not included in his total repertoire of acts before, and now it is.[43] Or perhaps a process of "identification" is involved; he wants to behave like a grown, strong man, and what he has seen indicates to him that fighting is an appropriate mode of behavior for the type of person he is striving to become.[44] Still another account might be that the fight film aroused him to the point where he felt like doing *something* physically active; any form of activity would have sufficed, and his subsequent aggressive behavior was only one of many possible outlets for this generalized arousal.[45] All three of these hypothesized intervening processes have some empirical support, and perhaps all of the processes described occur in some viewers. The research problem is to determine the conditions under which one or another process becomes activated. The theoretical problem is more imposing, in a way, because it involves sorting out the relationships among the intervening processes which may interact with one another in various complicated combinations.[46]

Intervening processes have fascinated psychologists of media effects for years. Hovland and his associates set a model for careful experimental testing of alternative hypotheses based on different scenarios of intervening psychological events.[47] The new stimulus to better understand such processes is not simply an academic one. Some effects of mass media are considered undesirable outcomes (for example, aggression activated by media violence), and others are socially positive bits of socialization (for example, imitation of altruistic media models). Educators and social counselors would, as a rule, like to work from the presumed effects of media as a starting place; their programs would thus have to be tailored to minimize antisocial effects and to maximize desirable ones. This tailoring calls for a degree of fine tuning of social intervention programs that simply cannot be done with our present primitive state of knowledge about the processes at work in the production of media effects.

As an example, consider the concept of "perceived reality" of violent presentations. One set of experiments indicates that young people respond more aggressively to media violence when they are told it is real ("news clips"), and less so when they are told it is fictional ("just actors").[48] Correlational studies appeared to corroborate this finding.[49] But an attempt to teach grade school children how television shows make scenes look real, when they are not, failed to reduce the violence-aggression link.[50] A number of reasons might be advanced to explain this nonfinding. Perhaps the intervention program should have focussed on the unreality of plot lines rather than of dramatic production; perhaps a program of only a few weeks' duration is insufficient to counteract a lifetime of socialization; perhaps the experiments on perceived reality are not generalizable.[51] The point is that one is at a loss to pinpoint and pursue any one of these very different possible flaws; as things are, our understanding of the role of perceived reality as an intervening element in socialization through media is very limited. Even so, the role of perceived reality is one of the few intervening factors that has been investigated in any systematic or sustained way; we understand far less about most other suspected processes.

NEW METHODOLOGICAL PERSPECTIVES

As mentioned, recent media-effects research has made something of a shift toward the field study and, correlatively, away from laboratory experimentation. Hovland, to be sure, had the best of both worlds in his Army studies, where he took advantage of a highly controllable field situation in which his experimental manipulations would scarcely be noticed.[52] Upon returning to academe, though, he was forced to choose between the opportunities for control in the laboratory and the ring of generalizability that a field study lends to a finding.[53] In a well-known essay, he outlined the relative merits of the two methods and a number of reasons why one should expect media effects to be easier to demonstrate in the laboratory experiment than in the field survey.[54] Field studies have typically dealt with socially more momentous (and thus less modifiable) effects than have experiments; field studies are typically much more slipshod about such matters as precision of measurement or exact specification of either the causal variable(s) or the hypotheses at stake. Worse, they provide evidence that is at best more equivocal than that yielded by the controlled experiment. Each type of study is capable of showing a statistical correlation between media exposure and a suspected consequent behavior. The experiment is superior in its capacity to specify the time-order involved in this relationship; it guarantees that the cause precedes the effect, whereas in survey analysis, time-order must be inferred. Third variables that might influence (or account for) the observed correlation are handled differently in the two methods. In surveys, suspected third variables must be explicitly identified and measured; then they are partialed out statistically; those that escape the imagination of the investigator are not controlled at all. In the experiment, third variables (including those that fail to occur to the investigator) are controlled in two ways. Those variables that vary within individuals are controlled by random assignment of subjects to conditions; those that vary from one situation to another are controlled by force—that is, by standardizing the situation and not allowing it to vary. Thus one reviewer who has found a set of experiments at variance with his own findings has been prompted to complain that "they smell of the laboratory."[55]

A major shift in thinking about media-effects research in recent years has been the growing realization that *these methodological traditions are not necessarily in conflict.* They are different ways of bringing evidence to bear on the same questions. One should not feel obliged to choose one body of research to believe, and at the same time choose to ignore a second. If theoretical propositions are stated properly, both experimental and survey evidence should be relevant to them. Each camp has been fond of pointing to flaws in the other's methodology. Where the two approaches yield different conclusions, this criticism might make some sense, but the principal flaw lies in the fuzzy language in which hypotheses have been stated and generalizations drawn therefrom. Where the two methods yield similar conclusions, their respective shortcomings are of little consequence, because they do not share the same flaws. The prime case in point has been television violence research, where experimentalists and survey researchers found themselves quite in accord—and in both cases much more comfortable with their "tentative" conclusions once they saw the corroborating evidence derived from the alternative method.[56]

Still, the greatest boost for field-survey studies has come not from corroborating evidence from the laboratory nor from any theoretical innovations regarding media effects. Instead, advances in correlational methodology in general have in recent years provided an empirical rationale for inferring time-order relationships from nonexperimental data. Whereas experimenters employ *design* features such as random assignment and control groups to isolate relationships over time, survey researchers have had to turn to new modes of *data analysis* to accomplish this isolation. The approximation to an experiment's power to infer time-order is still distant; untested assumptions and equivocal interpretations remain in these developing forms of survey analysis. But one can no longer acceptably assert that "you can't say anything about causation from correlational data, because you have no evidence about time-order."

Two modes of analysis need to be distinguished. The more popular mode is path analysis.[57] Synchronous (single-wave) survey measures of a number of variables are organized according to a hypothesized sequence of causal events. The correlations among these variables are then analyzed as a single set; the result is an empirical model that indicates what the strength of each hypothesized "path" linking a set of variables would be if the total hypothesized causal model is valid. A complicated multivariate model with a number of time sequences can be tested; events that hypothetically occur near one another in time should be more strongly related than those the model assumes to be separated by greater time gaps and intervening events. Paths that turn out to be nonsignificant when partialed can be discarded and a simplified ("trimmed") version of the model accepted; or, if the data fit poorly with the model, the model can be discarded entirely and another hypothesized in its place. This method is hypothetico-deductive, not a theory-free inductive search for the single "best fit" model. To run an infinite series of such tests for all possible model linking a large set of variables is neither scientifically sound nor, often, feasible. Like experimentation, a path analysis begins with a set of integrated theoretical propositions about the relationships among some variables; these propositions are then tested as a set with empirical data. The fact that the investigator might accept a path model because it fits well with the data does not rule out the possibility that other theoretical models linking the same variables might also accord well with empirical findings. (The same is true of experimentation, with the major procedural difference being that the experimenter would have to devise an entirely different experiment to test a second hypothesis.) Examples of path-analytic hypothesis testing in communication effects research include those of McCrone and Cnudde, Bishop, and Jackson-Beeck and Chaffee.[58]

The second mode of analysis that has helped revive field-survey studies of media effects is cross-lagged panel correlation. Unlike path analysis, this method makes some special demands on design as well as on analysis, since it requires repeated measurement of both media exposure and the hypothesized effect at several points in time. This mode is also more limited in terms of the number of variables that may be involved in the hypothesis to be tested. Still, development of the Rozell-Campbell baseline[59] and other data-analytic models has helped to stimulate a surge of longitudinal panel studies in the communication-effects area. Nearly ten years elapsed between the suggestion by Schramm et al.[60] that this mode would be the optimal way to study the impact of media on developing children and the first reports of empirical findings in this area based on panel data; these early reports included the Lefkowitz et al. ten-year study of television violence and the acquisition of aggressive behavior,[61] and both short- and long-term contributions of media inputs to political socialization.[62] Unfortunately, the studies to date have involved only two time points; to have measures of both variables at three points in time is essential to assess reliability separately from the measurement of real change in either variable over time.[63]

A different kind of methodological formulation evident in recent media-effects research is based on the theoretical concept of contingent causation. That the mass media do not influence all persons in the same fashion has long been recognized; indeed, many persons are not affected in any perceptible way by many media inputs. This knowledge has led to a search for, and to some extent a discovery of, the contingent conditions that govern media effects. For instance, experimental exposure to filmed violence does not produce heightened aggression in all youngsters; this effect seems to be limited to those who are somewhat aggressive at the outset.[64] The agenda-setting power of the mass media does not extend to all citizens, only to those who for various reasons are seeking guidance in interpreting current events in their role as voters.[65] Nomothetic linear models such as path analysis and cross-lagged panel correlation, which assume that a hypothesized effect should hold for all persons, are inappropriate when one's hypothesis is instead that only under certain contingent conditions will any effect occur.

A procedure has been developed, and explicitly recognized as essential by a minority of investigators, in which a broad population sample is first separated into subgroups on the basis of the hypothesized contingent orientations that govern media effects; linear tests of the supposed effect are then run separately on each subgroup.[66] To the extent that this procedure is adopted, it can serve to render much more explicit the theories that are developed regarding media influence. A simple correlational analysis might conclude that a particular media campaign had a 10 percent effect; one's feeling about that result would be rather different if, instead of suggesting a change of 10 percent among all persons, the change could be shown to represent a 100 percent change specific to a group that comprised only 10 percent of the sample. Physically partitioning samples on the basis of contingent orientations that are necessary for a media effect to operate is likely to become more common in future research; this trend is a sign both that we understand quite a bit about the total influence process and that we are going to be able to learn more.

TWO MODEST PROPOSALS

Rather than try to summarize the ganglion of trends reviewed above, this chapter concludes with two suggestions for new directions in media-effects research that would build on several of these trends. Neither is limited to content-specific effects, nor to research with attitudinal persuasion, nor to individuals as such.

TELEVISION AND FAMILY CONFLICT

Schramm, Lyle, and Parker, in their seminal studies of television and children, found a great deal of evidence that those children who spent many hours with television were also the ones who reported considerable conflict with their parents over life goals and aspirations.[67] This correlation the researchers interpreted to mean that the family conflict led the child to seek escape into the ''fantasy-oriented'' world of television. But direction of causation is equivocal when one is working with purely correlational evidence; the thesis could be the reverse: the heavy use of television causes conflict to build within the home. Several reasons lead us to suspect that this latter proposition might be true. Television offers competing programs at the same time on different channels, and these programs are designed to appeal to different audiences. A significant amount of conflict might well arise between parents and children over which program to watch at a particular hour. We have evidence that children do not see the same kinds of programs when they are viewing television in the company of their parents as when only children are watching.[68] Specifically, youngsters are considerably more likely to watch violent programs with their parents than they are when viewing alone or with other children. This shift in viewing behavior may often involve some strain in the parent-child relationship. (The fact that the shift is followed immediately, in many cases, by exposure to television's stylized aggressive solutions to interpersonal conflicts is all the more disquieting.)

As Schramm has noted, time spent with television is considered by many to be a violation of the "work ethic" that permeates American society.[69] Whereas reading can be justified as "improving the mind," television is far less likely to be characterized that way. Since most children spend three to five hours a day with television, and since this viewing to some extent has cut into the time that might be devoted to more socially admired activities, we might hazard the guess that television viewing is a cause—rather than simply the effect—of parent-child conflict over the youngsters' long-range life ambitions.

A traditional topic of parent-child disagreement is that of bedtime. The general tendency is for children to attempt to stay up well after the time established by their parents as appropriate for them to go to their bedrooms. (In the age of television, it would not be totally facetious to define a "child" empirically as a person who goes to sleep when evening prime-time programming ends and the late-evening news comes on.) Daily viewing logs show that a majority of children in fact stay up until the news, a type of program that rather few of them care to watch.[70] In the United States, this news program typically occurs at 11 P.M. (10 P.M. Central Time); if the parents have set any earlier bedtime, battles will occur.

The standard sources of family conflict are thought to be sex and money, and one would be hard put to maintain that television might turn out to be a rival to either of these factors. But to some extent, television exacerbates problems in parent-child relations arising from both other factors.

Television has become increasingly permeated with broad sexual references, including both comedies and dramas built around prosti-

tution, homosexuality, rape, and such less weighty matters as pro-
miscuity, propositioning, and adultery. However clever or well done
these entertainments are, they raise problems within the family.
Parents differ enormously in the extent to which they care to discuss
sexual matters with their children and in their plans for the proper
timing of discussions of those topics they do intend to take up eventually. Television threatens to upset those plans, bringing into the
home intergenerational tensions that would not otherwise have existed
—or at least would not be so obvious. The traditional "birds and
bees" talk between parent and child may not easily be deferred until
the child reaches some point of passage in the life cycle such as the end
of grammar school or the onset of puberty; terms such as "gay" and
"hooker" occur commonly enough on United States television today
that a certain number of children are bound to inquire as to what they
mean. Some parents, themselves scarcely comfortable with street
language, surely find this usage a source of unease; at best, the situation seems unlikely to render parent–child communication any
smoother.

Money is the root of almost all commercial television, an industry
that thrives by delivering sponsors' products to the eyes of potential
consumers. One important target group is the children, who are exposed to many messages designed to instill a desire for various dolls,
toys, games, and so forth. Although research on "consumer socialization" has not yet proceeded very far, a valid distinction seems possible
between the orientations to the marketplace held by young children
and more mature viewers. While adults see advertisements as rival
claims in a competition for their limited financial resources, children
interpret them more in terms of a "want-get" situation. That is, they
have learned that to some extent they can get what they want; they do
not have much money—indeed, few families could afford to buy their
children all of the products that television advertisements induce them
to desire—so their method of getting is to pressure their parents into
buying things for them. The transaction becomes one of interpersonal
affection rather than a commercial one; the child whose demands are
indulged presumably is to feel more loved, while the deprived
youngster draws an opposite inference. Ward and Wackman have
opened up the study of the "family communication about consumption," to use their very neutral term, which is stimulated by television
ads.[71] We might hypothesize that a good deal of this communication
is rather tense and irascible.

The list above is based mainly on inferences from findings that previous researchers have not interpreted as indicators of family-conflict effects of television. Such a hypothesis is likely to arise only in a time when media effects on social units, rather than on isolated individuals, are coming to be considered.

DIVERSITY AND CONSTRAINT IN PUBLIC OPINION

A final suggested direction for new effects research is offered in the spirit of the Bicentennial of the American nation. The premise of our grand 1776–1976 pseudoevent was that we should reexamine the principles put forth by the Founding Fathers and consider how they can be renewed and extended today. In the area of mass communication, the most basic constitutional principle is that of freedom of the press. As Schramm has noted, Madison and Jefferson were concerned with "freedom from," while in the twentieth-century's preoccupation with social responsibilities of the media the stress is more upon "freedom for."[72] This attitude is more than an addition to the original intent; it is to a great extent a substitution. Freedom of the press *from* governmental constraints had, in principle, no particular goal other than to maximize the probability that a diversity of viewpoints would be able to vie in a "marketplace of ideas." A more content-specific view is taken today, in which the media are maintained as free institutions *for* the transmission of a variety of opinions; if some sides to a question lack access to the media, and thus to the public, current policy holds that access should be provided. In addition to obvious examples such as the "equal time" rule and the "fairness doctrine" in broadcast policy, many instances of efforts to maintain a competitive media system might be cited; competition, which is prized because it maximizes the chance for diversity, is thought to be thwarted by such phenomena as cross-media ownership, the one-newspaper city, media chains and networks, and other forms of consolidation and standardization.[73] The industry's plea in the face of complaints about these trends is generally that the news media's economic health, which is strengthened by business consolidations, is essential if they are to provide "common carrier" channels for diverse viewpoints—as they are expected to do under the "freedom for" approach.

The argument is an eternal one, resting in part upon untested assumptions about media effects. The criterion variable at stake is not any particular type of outcome but rather the total diversity of public opinion. The first premise, rather obscured in the financial and political debates in this age of Big Media, was that a wide range of viewpoints should find their way into public expression and thus be taken into account in the formulation of public opinion. This premise implies that the appropriate criterion for assessing the "effectiveness" of a media system would be the diversity—not the specific content—of viewpoints that are available to a wide audience via mass media and cognized and held by citizens. If the "fewness and bigness" which, Schramm notes, characterize today's news media exercise constraints over public opinion, these structural effects should manifest themselves in less diversity of media content and of public opinion.

Research on public opinion typically finds that a particular individual is rather consistent in political judgments across time, but considerable variation may be found from one individual to another on a topic at any given time. Given this finding, and the general value accorded to diversity of viewpoints in traditional democratic theory, to assess the "effectiveness" of the mass media solely by the extent to which they produce change within the same individual across time seems neither reasonable nor productive. Instead, we should expect to find assessments based on variation across individuals—that is, on diversity within the system as a whole.

A versatile measure of diversity has been available to communication researchers for several decades, in Shannon's definition of "entropy."[74] The uses of this tool for the study of human communication have been outlined by Weaver and have been considered explicitly for mass communication research by Schramm.[75] Shannon's measure of entropy *(H)* has several properties that make it potentially quite useful for assessment of system diversity. First, it is nondirectional; it can be applied to a set of nominal categories that are not themselves ordered in any evaluative way. Second, it yields a single summary estimate of diversity for each system at each point in time, and such estimates can be compared directly with one another. The computation of *H* for this purpose would require a set of mutually exclusive categories of public opinion that are as a group exhaustive of the total body of opinions possessed by the members of a system. While no such "perfect" opinion-content coding scheme has been devised, we have some reasonable approximations to it—close enough to permit some exploratory research at least.

The degree of entropy as measured by *H* is a function of two parameters of a set of categories: Entropy increases as the total number of categories increases; and entropy is greatest when as equal number of events falls into each of the several categories—decreasing to the extent that the number in one category exceeds that of another. These mathematical properties seem intuitively satisfying for an assessment of public opinion in terms of diversity. Greater diversity arises when the range of opinions is wider (more categories); less diversity is apparent when one or a few viewpoints dominate the scene (inequality of categories).

For example, in a highly popular war, little opposition is usually expressed, even via a "free" press. Only the one policy of fighting on to victory is to be found in people's opinions; diversity is zero. When the wisdom of a war policy is questioned, however, the range of alternatives may expand at least to two; one may approve the war or disapprove it. In the case of a limited war, such as the United States efforts in Korea and Vietnam, two "anti" positions are available: One may argue instead for all-out war or for complete withdrawal from hostilities. Opinion diversity, as measured by H, would be greater when three different positions are advocated by different citizens than if only two were advocated. And diversity would be greater the more nearly equable the numerical strengths of the different positions. If three positions were possible but one was accepted by no one, then from an empirical standpoint no more diversity would exist than if only two positions existed; use of the statistic H would reflect this empirical reality, since it takes no account of categories that are theoretically conceivable but that do not in fact occur with any frequency. A "far out" position held by only a very few people would not appreciably increase H as a measure of diversity.

The concept of a "community" need not be limited to the idea of a group of persons who reside in one locale. The mass media create their separate communities; for example, those who read newspapers (fewer than three of every four adult Americans) effectively constitute a separate community from those who rely mainly on television for their news. We might expect media subcommunities to differ from one another in terms of diversity of public opinion. For example, agenda-setting research has shown some differences between those who read one or another newspaper within the same city.[76] Use of H as a criterion variable shows some interesting effects of "media richness" on "agenda" measures in which the person is asked to identify the nation's (or state's) most important problem. A greater degree of entropy exists in communities that are served by *more than one* daily newspaper; in preliminary analysis of two large-scale surveys, this finding held up when the total population of the community was statistically controlled.[77] (Less difference in entropy occurs between one-newspaper towns and those with no daily, which suggests that this measure is indeed getting close to the issue of diversity itself.)

Questions about the nation's most important problem do not provide the optimal instrument for assessing diversity through the measurement of entropy, to be sure. Further, one cannot be certain that Shannon's H measure is sensitive enough to detect the subtle shadings of difference in the quality of public opinion that are at stake in the debate over the proper role of the press in a free society. The statistic has, however, proven itself capable of isolating differences in various kinds of media content, and its extension to the analysis of public opinion would enable researchers to address new hypotheses in the media-effects field.[78]

It would be possible to compare communities (or nations) that vary in their degree of control over media, or to examine much more thoroughly their media resources. Hypothetically, opinion entropy should be greater not only in media-rich locales but also where the press has greater freedom to present diverse viewpoints. Economic constraints could be assessed in the same fashion as legal and political constraints. The underlying "effects" proposition that some equivalence exists between media content and audience cognitions would also lead investigators to measure entropy in content, comparing locales with different politico-economic environments for their media. In all these cases, entropy should be stressed as an attribute of the community as a system; it need not extend to the level of the individual citizen, nor even to individual media, within that community. The collective diversity, across the many persons and media within a system, is at stake.

OVERVIEW

As is clear from both the review of recent trends and the speculation about future directions, this paper is grounded in the conviction that the mass media are indeed influential societal institutions. Historically, this original viewpoint was severely eroded in the 1940s and 1950s, when a belief that media effects are severely limited replaced the early fear of media domination.[79] Both conceptual broadening of the effects hypothesis and methodological advances that have refined our capacity for testing effects have contributed to a swing back. Noelle-Neumann has characterized this swing as a return to the image of "powerful media."[80] While no one should be so naive as to assume that whatever occurs in the mass media will immediately and thereafter color everyone's thinking, the limited-effects model provides an equally oversimplified image. Easy answers to the social questions raised by the growth of mass media cannot be arrived at from uncritical extensions of limited findings. They require the hard work of careful empirical analysis.[81]

NOTES

1. For a sociological analysis of the diffusion of mass media, see Melvin DeFleur, *Theories of Mass Communication*. New York: David McKay, 1966.

2. Consult Theodore Peterson, "The Social Responsibility Theory," in Fred S. Siebert, Theodore Peterson, and Wilbur Schramm, *Four Theories of the Press*. Urbana: University of Illinois Press, 1963.

3. Carl I. Hovland, Arthur A. Lumsdaine, and Fred D. Sheffield, *Experiments on Mass Communication*. Princeton, N.J.: Princeton University Press, 1949; Carl I. Hovland, Irving L. Janis, and Harold H. Kelley. *Communication and Persuasion*. New Haven: Yale University Press, 1953.

4. As examples: On credibility, Jack McLeod and Garrett O'Keefe, "The Socialization Perspective and Communication Behavior," in F. Gerald Kline and Phillip J. Tichenor, eds., *Current Perspectives in Mass Communication Research*. (Beverly Hills: Sage Publications, 1972; on persuasibility, Vernon A. Stone and James L. Hoyt, "The Emergence of Source-message Orientation as a Communication Variable," *Communication Research 1*: 89–109, 1974; on duration of effects, Steven H. Chaffee, "The Interpersonal Context of Mass Communication," in Kline and Tichenor, *op. cit.*

5. Fritz Machlup, *The Production and Distribution of Knowledge in the United States*. Princeton, N.J.: Princeton University Press, 1962.

6. Jon G. Udell, *The Growth of the American Daily Newspaper*. Madison, Wisc.: Bureau of Business Research and Service, University of Wisconsin, 1965. Newspaper production accounted for about 1.5 percent of manufactures, automobiles for 1.8 percent; meat products, drugs and medicines, lumber and many other industries ranked lower. Recent United States Department of Commerce figures show newspapers as the country's third largest source of employment, following the steel and auto industries (*U.S. Industrial Outlook,* January, 1976).

7. For a thoughtful discussion, see Wilbur Schramm, *Responsibility in Mass Communication*. New York: Harper & Bros., Ch. 9, 1957.

8. Wilbur Schramm, Jack Lyle, and Edwin B. Parker, *Television in the Lives of Our Children*. Stanford, Calif.: Stanford University Press, 1961.

9. Jack Lyle and Heidi Hoffman, "Children's Use of Television and Other Media." In Eli Rubinstein, George Comstock, and John Murray, *Televi-*

sion and Social Behavior, Volume IV. Television in Day-to-Day Life: Patterns of Use. Washington, D.C.: U.S. Government Printing Office, 1972.

10. For a comprehensive survey of current work in this area, see Jay G. Blumler and Elihu Katz, eds., *The Uses of Mass Communications.* Beverly Hills: Sage Publications, 1974.

11. Steven H. Chaffee and Fausto Izcaray, "Mass Communication Functions in a Media-rich Developing Society," *Communication Research, 2:* 367–395, 1975; Lee B. Becker, Jack M. McLeod, and Dean A. Ziemke. "Correlates of Media Gratifications," supplemental paper presented at roundtable discussion at American Association for Public Opinion Research convention, Asheville, N.C., 1976.

12. Paul K. Hatt and C. C. North, "Jobs and Occupations: A Popular Evaluation." In Reinhard Bendix and Seymour Martin Lipset, *Class Status and Power.* Glencoe: Free Press, 1953; Richard F. Carter and Bradley S. Greenberg. "Newspapers or Television: Which Do You Believe?", *Journalism Quarterly, 42:* 29–34, 1965; Schramm, Lyle, and Parker, *op. cit.*

13. An example is Bruce H. Westley and Werner Severin, "Some Correlates of Mass Media Credibility," *Journalism Quarterly, 41:* 325–335, 1964.

14. Hovland, Lumsdaine, and Sheffield, *op.cit.*

15. Heavy versus light exposure of children to televised violence, for example, was the basis for positive effects inferences in several studies reported in George Comstock and Eli Rubinstein, eds., *Television and Social Behavior, Volume III. Television and Adolescent Aggressiveness.* Washington, D.C.: U.S. Government Printing Office, 1972. Some success in predicting from heavy versus light viewing of television in general to stereotyped perceptions of society has been reported in George Gerbner and Larry P. Gross, "Living with Television: The Violence Profile," *Journal of Communication, 26:* 172–199, 1976.

16. Such nonexperimental methods as path analysis and cross-lagged panel correlation are discussed later in this paper. Consult Hubert M. Blalock, ed., *Causal Models in the Social Sciences,* Chicago: Aldine-Atherton, 1971, for a diverse set of perspectives.

17. A striking emphasis on informational uses of television is reported in Brenda Dervin and Bradley S. Greenberg, "The Communication Environment of the Urban Poor," in Kline and Tichenor, *op. cit.* See also Blumler and Katz, *op. cit.*

18. It has been pointed out that the study of media "uses and gratifications" through self-report and in a utilitarian framework probably biases both the results and their interpretation in the direction of overstating informational motivations. See James W. Carey and Albert L. Kreiling, "Popular Culture and Uses and Gratifications: Notes toward an Accommodation," in Blumler and Katz, *op. cit.*

19. An explicit learning model along these lines is presented as the conceptual basis for the studies reported in Hovland, Janis, and Kelley, *op. cit.*

20. Milton J. Rosenberg, "An Analysis of Affective-cognitive Consistency," in Rosenberg, Hovland, William J. McGuire, Robert P. Abelson, and

Jack W. Brehm, eds., *Attitude Organization and Change*, New Haven: Yale University Press, 1960. The appearance of this volume—based on models of cognitive inconsistency—in Hovland's Yale studies demonstrates that a sound research program can produce novel conceptual formulation.

21. Leon Festinger, *A Theory of Cognitive Dissonance*, Stanford, Calif.: Stanford University Press, 1957, especially chapters 4 and 5.

22. The discrepancy between these two types of effects is probably attributable to loose conceptualization of theoretical links between them and common causes in independent "variables" that are presented in the form of complex messages. See David R. Seibold, "Communication Research and the Attitude-verbal Report-overt Behavior Relationship: A Critique and Theoretic Reformulation," *Human Communication Research, 2:* 3–32, 1975; Steven J. Gross and C. Michael Niman, "Attitude-behavior Consistency: A review," *Public Opinion Quarterly, 39:* 358–368, 1975.

23. Herbert Hyman and Paul B. Sheatsley, "Some Reasons Why Information Campaigns Fail," *Public Opinion Quarterly, 11:* 412–423, 1947.

24. Harold Mendelsohn, "Some Reasons Why Information Campaigns Can Succeed," *Public Opinion Quarterly, 37:* 50–61, 1973; Dorothy F. Douglas, Bruce H. Westley, and Steven H. Chaffee, "An Information Campaign that Changed Community Attitudes," *Journalism Quarterly, 47:* 479–487, 492, 1970.

25. Hadley Cantril, Hazel Gaudet, and Herta Herzog, *The Invasion from Mars*, Princeton, N.J.: Princeton University Press, 1940.

26. The relationship between entertainment and other types of media content in preparing a society for organized social action is discussed in Charles R. Wright, "Functional Analysis and Mass Communications," *Public Opinion Quarterly, 24:* 605–620, 1960.

27. Donald J. McCrone and Charles F. Cnudde, "Toward a Communications Theory of Democratic Political Development: A Causal Model," *American Political Science Review, 61:* 72–79, 1967.

28. Wilbur Schramm, "Communications in Crisis," in Bradley S. Greenberg and Edwin B. Parker, eds., *The Kennedy Assassination and the American Public*, Stanford, Calif.: Stanford University Press, 1965.

29. James S. Coleman, *Community Conflict*, New York: Free Press, 1957.

30. George A. Donohue, Phillip J. Tichenor, and Clarice N. Olien, "Gatekeeping: Mass Media Systems and Information Control," in Kline and Tichenor, *op. cit.;* Tichenor, Jane M. Rodenkirchen, Olien, and Donohue, "Community Issues, Conflict, and Public Affairs Knowledge," in Peter Clarke, ed., *New Models for Mass Communication Research*, Beverly Hills: Sage Publications, 1973; Tichenor, Donohue, Olien, and J. K. Bowers, "Environment and Public Opinion," *Journal of Environmental Education, 2:* 38–42, 1971.

31. Olien, Donohue, and Tichenor, "The Community Editor's Power and the Reporting of Conflict," *Journalism Quarterly, 45,* 243–252, 1968. Conflict-avoidance in "shopper" newspapers that service local districts

within metropolitan areas is also stressed in Morris Janowitz, *The Community Press in an Urban Setting*, New York: Free Press, 1952.

32. Hovland, Lumsdaine, and Sheffield, *op. cit.*

33. This hypothesis is outlined in Chaffee, "Interpersonal Context," *op. cit.*

34. This global goal of the films was in fact not achieved, according to the findings of Hovland, Lumsdaine, and Sheffield; each film was rather successful in getting across its specific points and in modifying general attitudes toward the various peoples involved in the war, but the films had little or no effect on the individual soldier's eagerness to enter combat.

35. Robert B. Zajonc, "Attitudinal Effects of Mere Exposure," *Journal of Personality and Social Psychology, Monograph Supplement*, 9, 1–27, 1968. For similar findings using words as the objects of evaluation, see Steven H. Chaffee, "Salience and Pertinence as Sources of Value Change," *Journal of Communication*, 17, 25–38, 1967. The literature is reviewed in Michael L. Ray and Alan G. Sawyer, "Repetition in Media Models: a Laboratory Technique," *Journal of Marketing Research*, 8, 20–39, 1971.

36. Lee B. Becker and John C. Doolittle, "How Repetition Affects Evaluations of and Information Seeking about Candidates," *Journalism Quarterly*, 52, 611–617, 1975.

37. This statement is paraphrased from what is usually cited as the first appearance of the agenda-setting hypothesis, Bernard C. Cohen, *The Press and Foreign Policy*, Princeton, N.J.: Princeton University Press, 1963.

38. Maxwell E. McCombs and Donald L. Shaw, "The Agenda-setting Function of the Media," *Public Opinion Quarterly*, 36, 176–187, 1972; David Weaver, Maxwell E. McCombs, and Charles Spellman, "Watergate and the Media: A Case Study in Agenda-setting," *American Politics Quarterly*, 3, 458–472, 1975; Lee B. Becker, Maxwell E. McCombs, and Jack M. McLeod, "The Development of Political Cognitions," in Steven H. Chaffee, ed., *Political Communication*, Beverly Hills: Sage Publications, 1975.

39. Jack M. McLeod, Lee B. Becker, and James E. Byrnes, "Another Look at the Agenda-setting Function of the Press," *Communication Research, 1*, 131–166, 1974. For a comparison of the McCombs and McLeod approaches, see Becker, McCombs, and McLeod, *op. cit.*

40. Weaver, McCombs, and Spellman, *op. cit.*; McLeod and Becker, "Testing the Validity of Gratification Measures through Political Effects Analysis," in Blumler and Katz, *op. cit.*; Chaffee and Izcaray, *op. cit.*

41. Phillip J. Tichenor, George Donohue, and Clarice Olien, "Mass Media and Differential Growth in Knowledge," *Public Opinion Quarterly*, 34, 158–170; John T. McNelly and Julio Molina R., "Communication, Stratification and International Affairs Information in a Developing Urban Society," *Journalism Quarterly*, 49, 316–326, 339, 1972.

42. Examples include Tichenor, Rodenkirchen, Olien, and Donohue, *op. cit.*, and Douglas, Westley, and Chaffee, *op. cit.*

43. Albert Bandura, Dorothea Ross, and Sheila A. Ross, "Imitation of

Film-mediated Aggressive Models," *Journal of Abnormal and Social Psychology, 66,* 3–11, 1963.

44. Albert Bandura, "Social-learning Theory of Identificatory Processes," in D. A. Goslin, ed., *Handbook of Socialization Theory and Research,* Chicago: Rand McNally, 1969; Jack M. McLeod, Charles K. Atkin, and Steven H. Chaffee, "Adolescents, Parents and Television Use," in Comstock and Rubinstein, *op. cit.*

45. Percy H. Tannenbaum and Dolf Zillmann, "Emotional Arousal in the Facilitation of Aggression through Communication," in Leonard Berkowitz, ed., *Advances in Experimental Social Psychology, Vol. VIII,* New York: Academic Press, 1975; Zillmann, James L. Hoyt, and Kenneth D. Day, "Strength and Duration of the Effect of Aggressive, Violent, and Erotic Communications on Subsequent Aggressive Behavior," *Communication Research, 1,* 286–306, 1974.

46. An attempt to organize the major variables in social learning from television into a single theoretical scheme is presented in Chaffee and Albert Tims, "The Psychology behind the Effect," a chapter in George Comstock *et al., The Fifth Season: How Television Influences Human Behavior* (in preparation, Rand Corporation).

47. Perhaps the best example of the use of this model is Rosenberg *et al., op. cit.*

48. Seymour Feshbach, "Reality and Fantasy in Filmed Violence," in John Murray, Eli Rubinstein, and George Comstock, eds., *Television and Social Behavior, Vol. II. Television and Social Learning,* Washington, D.C.: U.S. Government Printing Office, 1972.

49. McLeod, Atkin, and Chaffee, *op. cit.;* John M. Neale and Robert M. Liebert, *Science and Behavior,* Englewood Cliffs, N.J.: Prentice-Hall, 1973, pp. 110–112.

50. John C. Doolittle, "Immunizing Children against the Possible Antisocial Effects of Viewing Television Violence: A School Intervention Curriculum," Ph.D. dissertation, Univerity of Wisconsin, 1975.

51. An attempt to manipulate perceived reality as a means of heightening sex-role learning has been reported by Suzanne Pinegree in "The Effects of Non-sexist Television Commercials and Perceptions of Reality on Children's Attitudes toward Women," a paper presented to International Communication Association convention, Portland, Oregon, 1976.

52. Hovland, Lumsdaine, and Sheffield, *op.cit.*

53. Hovland, Janis, and Kelley, *op. cit.;* Hovland, ed., *The Order of Presentation in Persuasion,* New Haven: Yale University Press, 1957; Hovland and Janis, eds., *Personality and Persuasibility,* New Haven: Yale University Press, 1959; Rosenberg *et al., op. cit.* The typical "laboratory" in these studies was a high school or (more often) college classroom, where different experimental conditions could easily be created in self-administered protocols.

54. Hovland, "Reconciling Conflicting Results Derived from Experimental and Survey Studies of Attitude Change," *American Psychologists, 14,* 8–17, 1959.

55. Jerome L. Singer, ed., *The Control of Aggression and Violence:*

Cognitive and Physiological Factors, New York: Academic Press, 1971, Chapter 2.

56. See, for example, Liebert, "Television and Social Learning: Some Relationships between Viewing Violence and Behaving Aggressively (Overview)," in Murray, Rubinstein, and Comstock, *op. cit.;* Chaffee, "Television and Adolescent Aggressiveness (Overview)," in Comstock and Rubinstein, *op. cit.*

57. This method can be traced back to Sewall Wright, "The method of Path Coefficients," *Annals of Mathematical Statistics, 5,* 161–215, 1934; its current ascendance in sociology began with Hubert M. Blalock, *Causal Inferences in Nonexperimental Research,* Chapel Hill: University of North Carolina Press, 1964.

58. McCrone and Cnudde, *op. cit.;* Michael E. Bishop, "Media Use and Democratic Political Orientation in Lima, Peru," *Journalism Quarterly, 50,* 60–67, 101, 1973; Marilyn Jackson-Beeck and Chaffee, "Family Communication, Mass Communication, and Differential Political Socialization," paper presented to International Communication Association convention, Chicago, 1975. The latter results are summarized in Chaffee *et al.,* "Mass Communication in Political Socialization," in Stanley Renshon, ed., *Handbook of Political Communication,* New York: Academic Press, forthcoming 1977.

59. R. M. Rozelle and Donald T. Campbell, "More Plausible Rival Hypotheses in the Cross-lagged Panel Correlation Technique," *Psychological Bulletin, 71,* 74–80, 1969. See also David R. Heise, "Causal Inference from Panel Data," in Edgar F. Borgatta and George W. Bohrnstedt, eds., *Sociological Methodology 1970,* San Francisco: Jossey-Bass, 1970.

60. Schramm, Lyle, and Parker, *op. cit.*

61. Monroe M. Lefkowitz, Leonard D. Eron, Leopold O. Walder, and L. Rowell Ruesmann, "Television Violence and Child Aggression: A Followup Study," in Comstock and Rubinstein, *op. cit.*

62. Chaffee, L. Scott Ward, and Leonard P. Tipton, "Mass Communication and Political Socialization," *Journalism Quarterly, 47,* 647–659, 666, 1970.

63. In path-analytic terms, a two-time cross-lagged model is "under-identified," because it lacks sufficient information to test the causal path represented by the coefficient between the Time 1 independent variable and the Time 2 dependent variable. See Otis Dudley Duncan, "Some Linear Models for Two-wave, Two-variable Panel Analysis, With One-way Causation and Measurement Error," in Blalock, *op. cit.,* 1971.

64. Leonard Berkowitz, *Aggression: A Social Psychological Analysis,* New York: McGraw-Hill, 1962.

65. Weaver, McCombs, and Spellman, *op. cit.;* McLeod and Becker, *op. cit.*

66. Peter Clarke and F. Gerald Kline, "Media Effects Reconsidered: Some New Strategies for Communication Research," *Communication Research, 1,* 224–240, 1974; Kline, Peter V. Miller, and Andrew J. Morrison, "Adolescents and Family Planning Information: An Exploration of Audience Needs and Media Effects," in Blumler and Katz, *op. cit.;*

Chaffee, "Contingent Orientations and the Effects of Political Communication," paper presented to Speech Communication Association convention, New York, 1973. A slightly different approach is to assess the person's degree of involvement with different topics and then to predict differential experimental effects for differing involvement orientations. For examples, see Michael L. Rothschild and Michael L. Ray, "Involvement and Political Advertising Effect: An Exploratory Experiment," *Communication Research, 1,* 264–285, 1974; Lawrence Bowen and Chaffee, "Product Involvement and Pertinent Advertising Appeals," *Journalism Quarterly, 51,* 613–621, 1974.

67. Schramm, Lyle, and Parker, *op. cit.*

68. Bradley S. Greenberg, Philip M. Ericson, and Mantha Vlahos, "Children's Television Behaviors as Perceived by Mother and Child," in Rubinstein, Comstock, and Murray, *op. cit.*

69. Schramm, Lyle, and Parker, *op. cit.*

70. Lyle and Hoffman, *op. cit.*

71. Scott Ward and Daniel Wackman, "Family and Media Influences on Adolescent Consumer Learning," *American Behavioral Scientist, 14,* 415–427, 1971.

72. Schramm, *Responsibility, op. cit.*

73. Since early in this century, the number of daily newspapers in the United States has declined steadily; a corresponding increase has occurred in the number of one-newspaper cities; in addition, historical trends point toward single business operations for competing papers, consolidation of independent newspapers into chains, and ownership of newspapers by businesses that also own other media outlets in the same markets. These trends have given rise to attempts to assess the impact of competitive factors on press content, but to date this effort has not been extended to effects analysis. For examples, see Raymond B. Nixon and Robert L. Jones, "The Content of Non-competitive vs. Competitive Newspapers," *Journalism Quarterly, 33,* 299–314, 1956; Guido Stempel III, "Effects on Performance of a Cross-Media Monopoly," *Journalism Monographs,* No. 21, 1973; David H. Weaver and L. E. Mullins, "Content and Format Characteristics of Competing Daily Newspapers," *Journalism Quarterly, 52,* 257–264, 1975.

74. Claude E. Shannon and Warren Weaver, *The Mathematical Theory of Communication,* Urbana: University of Illinois Press, 1949.

75. Shannon and Weaver, *op. cit.;* Schramm, "Information Theory and Mass Communication," *Journalism Quarterly, 32,* 131–146, 1955.

76. McLeod, Becker, and Byrnes, *op. cit.*

77. Steven H. Chaffee and Donna Wilson, "Media Rich, Media Poor: Two Studies of Diversity in Agenda-holding," paper presented to Association for Education in Journalism convention, College Park, Maryland, 1976.

78. A recent example is James H. Watt and Robert Krull, "An Information Theory Measure for Television Programming," *Communication Research, 1,* 44–68, 1974.

79. Joseph T. Klapper, *The Effects of Mass Communication,* New York: Free Press, 1960.

80. Elisabeth Noelle-Neumann, "Return to the Concept of the Powerful Mass Media," in H. Equchi and K. Sata, eds., *Studies of Broadcasting*, 9: 67–112 (1973). For a thorough rejection of the limited-effects position in the area of political communication, see Sidney Kraus and Dennis Davis, *The Effects of Mass Communication on Political Behavior*, State College, Pa.: Pennsylvania State University Press, 1976.

81. Preparation of this paper was partially supported by a grant from the Wisconsin Alumni Research Foundation, through the Graduate School of the University of Wisconsin. The author thanks John T. McNelly for his helpful comments on an earlier draft.

Denis McQuail describes the tensions among researchers, professional media people, and government in defining the role of a media science. The relationship he describes is remarkably similar to that of the journalist and public officials, one that ranges from cooperation to an adversarial stance. He clearly defines the field in terms similar to the article by Weaver and Gray, presented later in this book, but he stresses the need for the independence of media science. He argues forcefully that established principles of communication influence must be linked to a societal historical perspective that includes the key features of media institutions. This chapter is an edited version of Dr. McQuail's inaugural lecture as Professor of Mass Communication at the University of Amsterdam, given on November 6, 1978.

5

THE HISTORICITY
OF MASS MEDIA SCIENCE

Denis McQuail

The study of mass communication has grown in response to the real life activities of media institutions, which are themselves in a continuing relation of tension and cooperation with their society. This shapes the context in which scientific knowledge of the media is produced and disseminated. In turn, this knowledge may serve either the interests of media practitioners or the organized public power. In using the term *'historicity'*, I want to emphasize the dependence on circumstances of time and place of the object of study, the directions to be taken by enquiry, and the uses to which resulting knowledge may be put. The subject of mass communication is historicist in the even more important sense that the mass media are our main channel of connection with the events of history as they are happening now, and our response to these events is in significant ways dependent on the quality of mass communication.

There are other strands to my argument, which I will unravel later. It will be evident that my idea of history is a pragmatic one. I assume no determined direction in the longer term; I emphasize the particular, the descriptive, and the analytic rather than the predictive, at the same time appreciating the need to generalize from such evidence as we have about the probable in either past or future. The notion of a mass media science is quite novel to me, as it may be to my audience, but I do find it useful to distinguish the idea of an organized and assimilated body of knowledge from the aggregate of separate findings, or the techniques of research which any one may apply. In invoking the notion of a media science, I wish to suggest only that *if* we wish to make sense of the findings of media research in a holistic way, *if* we are to give fundamental thought to human communication, and *if* we are to establish the scope and boundaries of the subject, then

From Denis McQuail, "The Historicity of Mass Media Science," original manuscript.

we are obliged to refer in detail to the historical circumstances of our time and of our societies.

There are subsidiary reasons for the intrusion of the idea of history into my thoughts on this occasion. One is a real doubt about the future of mass communication in its present forms. The decline of mass communication, if and when it happens, will be not a cataclysm but the slow disappearance of those *mass* characteristics which have so clearly distinguished public communication systems in the twentieth century: the centralization of production and distribution, the separation of senders from receivers, the exceptional size and diversity of audiences.

Both technological developments and the preferred forms of social organization of the present time allow and favor a movement to what has been called a third stage in the development of communication (Maisel, 1973): a steady 'demassification' through specialization, and a consequent fading in importance of many of the questions which have been responsible for social scientific and public attention to mass communication, especially those questions which have to do with power and influence. This is certainly a possibility. Nevertheless, the present typical structures of mass communication still tend to maximize the benefits to producers and distributors: they have an attraction for major clients of the media, including governments and advertisers; and they also serve a limited but dominant set of audience interests. If there is a change, it will come about not through technology but through changes in the relative power of the different beneficiaries of mass communication. Whatever happens, it will be interesting to observe, and although I sense no danger of early obsolescence, it is not a bad thing to be prepared.

I began my explanation of my title by asserting that the actual media institutions as they work in society are the main continuing object of enquiry justifying a separate branch of study. In practice, this solves few problems of direction of boundary, since the media and what they do have quite diverse meanings. They constitute at one and the same time: an industry; an object of consumption; an instrument of individual, corporate, or collective purpose; a set of technologies; an embodiment of the principles, culture, and values of a people. In addition, since the phenomenon changes in response to human choice and technological possibility, there is bound to be a tension between the multiplicity of detail and the scientific urge to generalize. The changing diversity of the real world of mass communication makes it inappropriate to stake the claim of any one academic discipline to exclusive or dominant control, and my invocation of an historical sense is certainly not intended as such a claim.

My central concern is with the production of knowledge about the reality of mass communication, and it is a distinguishing, perhaps unique, feature of this activity that it occurs in some competiton with other vocal attempts to characterize and to generalize about the same reality, from somewhat different perspectives. The main protagonists in the debate are firstly the media scientist, whose position I take up, secondly the media practitioner or professional mass communicator, and thirdly, the politician or appointed guardian of the public interest. The second and third have their own message about the mass media, their own view of the actuality and purpose of these institutions. They are voices which compete with that of media science for attention, and it is likely that their message will diverge in its content.

Media practitioners are themselves often well informed and articulate and have general views about the purpose, character, and social effect of what they do. It is significant that a recent book by broadcasters about broadcasters could have been entitled 'The New Priesthood' (Bakewell and Garnham, 1970), without any too ironic intention. The mass media are a 'knowledge-making institution' in much the same sense as are education and research, and it is a small but significant part of their task to disseminate explicitly or implicitly information and ideas about themselves. The self-definition and self-image of the media, so promulgated, have the advantage of precedence in time over the message of media science, rather better access to the channels of communication, and perhaps greater audience appeal.

The second main competing voice, that of public guardian or politician, is less constant and less insistent, but present nonetheless in the formulated laws, regulations, codes of practice, communication policy statements, reports of commissions and enquiries and quasi-judicial bodies which in many countries have followed upon the expansion of mass communication and now appear at supranational levels. As a form of knowledge, the material takes on a different character from the self-view offered by the media, or the analysis and interpretation of media scientists. Its tendency is to prescribe and direct, by encouragement or restriction, and the overall purpose is to control in the general public interest or that of the state.

This does not exhaust the possibility of alternative sources of knowledge. There are interest groups which claim rights of access and of determination, and there is the common-sense knowledge of the media which we acquire and sometimes express as members of the general audience, based on experience and expectation. This, then, is the first feature of the context in which the study of mass communication has developed. It has come, effectively, last in a sequence. Its message has to be compared with other views which have independent sources and are supported variously by economic self-interest, claims to professional autonomy, the exercise of power, deeply held collective sentiments, and everyday experience.

It is not surprising that findings and generalizations of our subject receive close scrutiny on grounds of their validity and utility. The situation is one of reporting on an established, self-reflective, and authoritative institution which is itself in a position of potential tension with other, equally authoritative and well-organized, sources of political and economic power. Few other subjects are so exposed. There are few subjects in which the practitioner is so open to the possibility or risk of adopting the perspective appropriate to a different role, since we are also citizens and audience members and we might well be politicians or mass communicators in a small way.

Although we each have our own distinctive audience and reference groups, the likelihood of a mutual attention to one another on the part of my three named protagonists has seemed to increase over time, at least during the recent past, as issues of quality, control and access bring mass communications (along with much else) within the competence even of political systems in which a high value is placed on freedom of expression. If we consider only the modern period, then the first successful definition of the role of the press was made by the press itself, in the high tide of nineteenth-century liberalism, against a historical background of tension with established authority. A subsequent and quite successful reassertion of the claims of the state or society to the right of definition stems from two sources in the history of the media: the development of sections of the press into large-scale business enterprises and the rise of the newer media of film, radio, and television, which were open to regulation on grounds of morality, state security, and technological and economic management.

The official historian of the BBC, Lord Briggs (1961) tells us that it was born with no prior definition of purpose, and the same might well be said of these newer media in general. According to Raymond Williams (1974): "Unlike all previous communication technologies, radio and television were systems primarily designed for transmission and reception as abstract processes with little or no definition of preceding content. . . . It is only that the supply of broadcasting facilities preceded the demand; it is that the means of communication preceded their content" (Williams, 1974). The contrast with the press is a marked one, since newspapers had, generally, to struggle to achieve the right to print what they wished. In the circumstances, it cannot be surprising that organised social power has shown an interest in supplying, or adjudicating on, the missing components of purpose and content in the case of broadcasting. The incentive to control was reinforced by the increasing need of agents of government and the political interest to be involved directly as communicators as well as guardians of the public interest.

There is a good deal of evidence that government-media relations in a number of societies with liberal-democratic traditions have continued to be strained and acrimonious. At the heart of this tension is a fundamental question of the legitimacy and autonomy of the press and a series of recurring questions about whose and what version of a particular reality shall be disseminated. The history of mass media science has to be written differently according to national society; but there are signs of increasing convergence in its recent growth, and almost everywhere its concerns are related to the extending interface between the press (in general) and organized public authority.

It will now be clear why the independence of view which might be expected from a scientific enterprise with its own somewhat private academic world is far from assured. On the one hand, research and education as practical activities relevant to work in and for the mass media may draw us towards the application of knowledge in the industries of mass communication.

On the other hand, the growth of mass communication research partly reflects an element of societal response to a new and significant phenomenon. It is unacceptable that powerful media institutions should have control of the dissemination of knowledge of their own activities, and the emergence of mass communication as a branch of study may be interpreted as an increase of countervailing power, in the public interest.

My argument up to this point can now be summarized as follows: three separate sources of definition of public communication have emerged in sequence: the state, mass media themselves, media scientists. All seem to agree on the centrality of mass communication in society as a source of impressions of reality, an instrument of control or guidance, a forum where public happenings are enacted. This crucial assumption of centrality is based partly on evidence, partly on impression, partly on preference. It has been recently queried in a salutary way by Herbert Gans, who warns media researchers not to assign more importance to the media than does the audience itself, arguing that "for audiences, the media are near the margin of the society in which they live and which they construct" (Gans, 1978). He suspects that in forgetting this fact, media researchers are too inclined to look at social phenomena through the eyes of broadcasters and editors.

I have pictured a triangle of relationships, but I can offer a view from only one of the points. When I look along either axis I become aware of inconsistencies of image and expectation which reflect more than the occupational cultures of groups which are so different and so aware of their own identity. The strongest impression is that of a discrepancy between the 'practitioners'' view of themselves and the view disseminated by media science.

The media self-image is one of effective communication based on professional expertise rationally applied. The research-derived view is one of a process which is unpredictable in its outcome, barely accountable in its effects after the event, and more 'performance' than communication in any commonly accepted sense (Elliott, 1972).

Against the view of a profession closely sensitive and responsive to its audience as clients, research offers a view of the communicator as guided more by self-definition and an orientation to sources than by any urge to know the audience or to appreciate what can be learned of its capacities, interests, and needs (Burns, 1969). The autonomy, originality, and spontaneity which are the hallmarks of many professional communicators become, in the generalizations of recent research, a submission to tradition, routine, and the constraints of a system of mass production (Tuchman, 1978). Against the claim to be pragmatic, objective and nontheoretical, we find expositions of the implicit ideology of the products of communication activity (Glasgow Media Group, 1976). This contrast on critical main points is a fairly sharp one, and the picture drawn of mass communicators is not flattering.

The sharpness of contrast is partly to be accounted for by the divergence of the professional biases of the two groups. In general, journalists and other communicators lean towards the personal, the particular, the practical. They live in the present and impose a view of the moment on their work. Some capacity to define the needs of the audience, an insulation against self-doubt, an orientation to the present and future may all be in various ways essential to the work of journalists and entertainers.

By contrast, the craft of research has a long time-perspective and inclination to depersonalize and theorize, a fondness for the recurrent and the average, since these help to hold still a confusing universe of data. This tendency to overlook or discount deviations from the mean and to find unintended and unacknowledged regularity in the work of mass communicators is especially distressing to journalists, because they are professionally inclined to value the unique and the rare— the outstanding television program or personal performance, the reporting scoop, the significant moment captured on film, the eye-witness journalistic account of historic events. Such things are lost in the averaging and classifying of media content and of audience response undertaken by media research. It is understandable that the two groups feel some mutual antipathy.

There is the other axis of the triangle to consider; that which connects media science with agents of public authority. This is a relatively new relationship, growing in salience and probably increasing in sensitivity along with experience of contact. The situation is not unlike that which holds between research and mass communication practice, and it shows the same pattern of diverging aims and interest. Research was seen first as having a purely service function, defined as a set of useful techniques and concepts to be applied to specific problems chosen by those concerned with policy. The relationship then developed from both sides: public policymakers looked for occasional expert advice or adjudication, and the research community formulated requests for financial support, often justified on grounds of public interest. Put in this way, it seems to be a comfortable arrangement between two independent parties with a mutual interest in the activities of mass communication institutions. In reality, it is unlikely to be so comfortable.

In the first place the interest of organized public authority in the mass media is complex, with two most significant features: in one capacity it stands for public guardianship; in another it may represent the demands for access and advocacy of competing political agents. These two interests cannot easily be kept apart, since the possibilities of control for the public good inherent in one role are relevant to opportunities for intervention on political grounds. Social scientists can hardly be unaware of this, and no simple service-client relationship is possible, given the political uses of evidence and advice.

Secondly, public authority likes to receive objective evidence and technical advice that are uncontaminated by theory and ideas which cannot be adopted. This preference for the fact or the impartial adjudication is not easy to satisfy, tempting researchers to respond to expectations which they cannot properly meet.

The problem is again a complex one, deriving in part from divergent occupational and professional biases, in part from norms of impartiality which are imposed rather literally on public servants and commissioners. Some media research evidence is found to be too obscure to communicate to the uninitiated, or too 'soft' to be dependable, or simply too ideological.

The chairman of the recent British Committee of Enquiry into the future of television expressed a not uncommon view in writing after the event that "when tendentious arguments masquerade as research, it is important that some power should reside in the hands of men and women who are paid to be impartial" (Annan, 1978). That is an implicit advocacy of the need to have a voice of the public and the polity which is neither dependent on the media nor on media science.

In sum, the relationship, when it is activated, between media science and the world of politics and government is for the former a mixture of benefit and cost. There may be funding for research, some sense of satisfaction in what may seem to be serving the public good, some protected contact with the practicalities of the media world, perhaps some public esteem. At the same time, there is a risk of losing control of the application and interpretation of research, of being associated with conclusions and acts of policy which are not of one's choosing. It is hardly possible to have the rewards without the risks. It should not be assumed, however, that the link is without pain for the other partners. Some independence and authority may also be surrendered on their side, and advice once sought cannot easily be disowned.

The picture painted has been one of incipient conflict of relationship and fundamental divergence, yet there are some grounds for accommodation between the three main protagonists. One is an agreement about the importance of the media, for good or ill. This is flattering for mass communicators, reassuring for those who make a profession of the study of media, and often sincerely believed in by the guardians of the public interest. Another is a reference to majority interests or needs, a populism of one kind or another. This does, or should, present some problems for the media scientist, but it has its advocates amongst them. Thirdly, there can be an agreement about the importance of technology. Technicalism in various forms is relatively noncontroversial. Our protagonists can be brought together by considerations of the cost and organization of technology and its social implications. In some circumstances, a fourth solvent of difficulty could be an agreed conception of the national interest, expressed either in political or cultural terms. If these are grounds of accommodation, their effects may not always be beneficial. They are consistent with a continued neglect of minority interests, a failure to examine the real causes of problems, a misplaced belief in technological solutions, and a failure to consider alternative communication structures.

Having identified the competing sources of social knowledge of the media, I am concerned with the standing of media science and aware of its shortcomings. It is not necessary to claim either a monopoly of truth or an overriding dominance, given the multiplicity of the phenomena to be studied and of the stand-points from which they can be viewed. The only claim that has to be upheld is that the subject offers ways of systematically organizing knowledge about the media which are rational, consistent, self-correct, and ultimately useful. I would like to consider first some criticisms of the subject and, in a partial reply, some achievements.

Firstly, there is the view that the conclusions of the study of the media, where they are acceptable, are a laborious statement of what would be obvious to anyone of common sense. Secondly, it is pointed out that research is usually slow and too late for practical purposes, put to shame by those who work in the agencies connected with the "real world" of mass communication. Thirdly, the practitioners of media science are seen to depart from strict canons of objec-tivity. They promote views which may be partial (usually by being critical of mass media) or which are idealistic and impractical. Finally, it can be argued that the outpouring of work on the media is repetitive, contradictory, incon-clusive and noncumulative.

There is some substance to each of these charges, which are levelled from time to time at all the social sciences, and especially those which lie at the "soft" rather than the "hard" end of the scientific continuum. The questions taken on are large and complex, the object of enquiry very big and always changing, the methods too weak, and the common ground of approach too narrow.

Slowness and lateness are agreed. We work on a time scale which would not be accepted if day-to-day decisions were at stake; but resources are often limit-ed, and the required results are of a different order. Even so, I remember the chastening experience of reading in a press review of a long and laborious study of election television (Blumler and McQuail, 1968), on which I had collaborated, a quotation from the book claiming that the study had doubled our stock of tenable propositions about the political impact of British political television. The reviewer (now editor of the *Guardian*) found some amusement in pointing out that this had been achieved by adding one new finding to the previous stock of one.

The evidence of partiality seems to me quite strong, at the level of problem definition and interpretation of findings, although it is unusual that normal scientific procedures are disregarded in work which claims to be accepted as science. I admit a personal inclination to the view that knowledge bought at considerable public expense should ultimately be useful and I see no way to deny purposive social research under conditions of freedom and diversity of choice.

It is much harder, however, to accept the charge that we demonstrate the obvious. An illustrious predecessor in the field of mass communication re-search, P.F. Lazarsfeld, once answered a similar objection by producing, from the study he was reviewing, a short list of research findings which would be obvious to any person of common sense and asking his readers to reflect on their own reactions (Lazarsfeld, 1949). I could do the same, drawing on a series of studies of political communication which were made at the Centre for Television Research at the University of Leeds, over a period of more than ten years (Trenaman and McQuail, 1961; Blumler, et al., 1975). For example:

(1) The influence of political television is greatest where the motives and level of attention of the audience are highest. (Obvious, since we know television viewing is an unthinking habit for most people, and we cannot be affected by what we barely notice.)

(2) In the competition between parties for access to television, the effect of television is to increase the relative advantage of those parties which are already strongest. (Naturally people like to be on the winning side, and television emphasizes the success of larger parties.)

(3) Television has a large short-term impact on the attitudes of electors towards politicians and parties, but has no effect on information levels. (We can easily be stimulated emotionally by television, but learning takes some effort.)

(4) The more that young voters were exposed to political communication during their first election campaign, the less likely were they to want to vote. (We expect young people to be bored by politics or, if they have idealistic expectations, to be disappointed by the conventional reality.)

(5) The primary effect of newspapers in an election campaign is to inform, whereas that of television is to create loyalty to parties and their leaders. (Newspapers conduct rational arguments based on facts; television creates attractive images.)

Each statement is the direct opposite of the actual conclusion from research, but a little thought can soon produce a plausible explanation for each one which at least fits some tenets of popular belief. It is too easy a trick to bring a convincing answer to the charge, but it is no easier than discerning the obvious after it has been shown to be true by others.

The remaining charge—of repetitiveness, internal contradiction, and lack of cumulation— is the most serious, the hardest to reply to and, yet, the one by which the standing of the subject is likely to be judged. Without a reasonable increase in explanatory power over time, there is unlikely to be any science in the sense of an organized and growing body of relevant knowledge, but merely a collection of discrete items of information and miscellaneous ideas. The message derived from examination of the relationship between media science and its two potential clients—the practitioner and the policymaker—is that the subject has no secure future in the service of either, precisely because such clients are not interested solely in the application of research. They also have a strong and sometimes partisan interest in the total message, the overall interpretation of what research has to tell. In these circumstances, media science has to establish its own independent claims to utility and authority.

In seeking to support such a claim, some initial discouragement is felt, since there is much evidence of the weaknesses mentioned: an excess of trivial and repetitive studies and signs that fashion or convenience account for more work than any strategy for the progressive expansion of the frontiers of knowledge. However well it supports the claim to the circumstantiality of the subject, it is particularly distressing to notice that research attention has moved successively from press, to film, to radio, to television, often according to superficial judgments of social importance and popularity and with little attempt to learn from the recent past or even to establish what is distinctive about the medium being examined.

Among the omissions and imbalances of research, the subordination of the newspaper to television seems to be the most serious. The rather scarce studies that have been conducted into the effects of newspapers tend to support the view that the press is quite distinctive because of its capacity to be, in varying degrees, an object of long-term loyalty and identification for its readers; a full source of information for many and of specialised belief; a partisan influence on public opinion and a link to political parties; a medium relevant to specific local issues (McQuail, 1976). These points are additional to the fact that broadcast news still often relies rather heavily on the press for information and news judgment. Despite the scarcity of research, we are still being reminded by recent evidence that newspapers are, for the reasons given, an important influence on public opinion and political events (Clarke and Fredin, 1978).

Leaving aside faults of triviality and misplaced emphasis, there is academic conflict over these: whether portrayals of violence cause or reduce aggression; whether the media are necessarily subordinate to the economic or class system of their society; whether the audience tends to select actively according to interest and need or merely responds to what is offered; whether the media are a cause of change or a prop for the existing order of things.

In mentioning these disagreements, my first thought was that beneath the evident clash of ideology, the debats are normally conducted with close reference to details of evidence collected according to agreed criteria. My second thought was that a subject is only accepted as mature when it does exhibit unbridgeable internal differences on vital points.

Nevertheless, there is a limit to the number of matters that can be plausibly held to be in dispute and awaiting only the appropriate evidence. The general question of the power and influence of mass communication is one such issue by which the field of study is most publicly identified and where the charge of inclusiveness and contradiction is most likely to be raised. This is so despite the fact that if the media have no influence, then questions of their control, their content, and quality of performance have little interest and less practical relevance. Statements on the matter are always tentative and hedged by numerous conditions. Many enquiries into the effects of mass media find no such effects and sometimes positive evidence of their absence (Trenaman and McQuail, 1961).

One careful investigator has pointed out that communication effects are often likely to be smaller than the effects from questionnaires designed to measure them (Emmett, 1966). An influential review of empirical evidence compiled in the late 1950s reported that mass communication is not ordinarily a necessary and sufficient cause of audience effects, but is a contributory agent in a process of reinforcing what is there already (Klapper, 1960). The view that the main effect of mass communication is to reinforce what is already there is not, of course, without interest and not inconsistent with a notion of considerable media power. Equally, reinforcement and change are quite compatible processes, although the balance between the two is critical.

Assessments of media power have shown a cyclical pattern (McQuail, 1977), with early strong belief giving way to the more cautious assessments just referred to, whereas recent years have seen a strong renewal of interest in the thesis of media power, amounting to what Elihu Katz has described as a revival of "mass society theory" (Katz, 1978).

The range of views between theorists requires some explanation, as well, perhaps, as does the gap between the often cautious assessments of research and the strong claims of publicists or the beliefs which evidently underlie the political struggles for access and control. One response is to stress the complexity of the process in which the mass media play a part, only in interaction with other conditions. This is correct but also highly general, and may seem to evade the question. Another view is that the important social effects of the media occur in the long term, as by the slow dripping of water on stone, which can be worn away by increments too small to measure. Again, there is truth in this, but the common analogy of water on stone is misleading. Despite evidence of regularity, media content is not as costantly the same or as insipid as water. Unlike stone, media audiences both respond in some way to the flow of content and themselves change independently over time.

An alternative response which is consistent with the theme presented here and which helps to organize more of the successes of media research is suggested by the very fact of variation in media effects. I will introduce it by a quotation from James Carey (1978)

> The history of mass communication research must include, as a parallel, a history of the changing world of mass communication, of the purpose to which these institutions are put, the audiences that gather to them, the social structure they more or less shape. In terms of this latter history it can be argued that the basic reason behind the shift in the argument about effects from a powerful to a limited to a more powerful model is that the social world was being transformed over this period. . . . Powerful effects of communication were sensed in the thirties because the Depression and the political currents surrounding the war created a fertile seed for the production of certain kinds of effects. Similarly, the normalcy of the fifties and sixties led to a limited effects model. In the late sixties, a period of war, political discord and inflation combined to expose the social structure in fundamental ways and to make it permeable by the media of communication.

The point is made clearly enough that, in times of uncertainty and crisis, the mass media are more likely to be a source or channel of influence. This occurs in the sense that they originate, selectively concentrate, or amplify certain currents of opinion, interpretations of events, dominant images of society, a conclusion which would not have been accessible through most early research on effects conducted in the framework of social psychology. Such work sought actively to hold the world of external events constant in order to reveal more clearly the underlying principles of communication and attitude change. A subsequent, more sociological, tradition favored research which took account of the world outside the laboratory, especially in its attention to the institutional settings of production and reception of media messages. This work has had more chance of finding those conditions of effect which are related to the circumstances of society and a person's place in it. Susceptibility to influence from the media now has to be seen as dependent on: the strength or weakness of group affiliation; the degree and kind of motives for attending to the media; the extent to which the media are the principal source of information and ideas; the degree of trust, respect and attachment to, the media; the salience and interest of the message; the norms and structure of the media institution, especially in respect of such matters as diversity, balance, and objectivity.

At times of critical events, we can expect people to be more aware of needs for information and guidance, more directly reliant on mass media for knowledge and definitions of events. The more consistent the message of the media and the more trust and attachment the media attract, the more their definition will be accepted and reflected in opinion. The key variable condition is that of dependence. The mass media have, de facto, acquired for most people a position of being a legitimate and highly accessible source of knowledge on matters beyond direct and personal experience. A secular trend in modern societies has been the attenuation of social bonds and increased privatization. In exceptional times, the need for ties connecting people to each other and to their societies is more keenly felt and the substitution of media channels for personal ties more likely to occur. The name 'dependency theory' of effects has been given to a process close to that described (Ball-Rokeach and DeFleur, 1976). According to this theory, effects depend on the degree of reliance of audiences on mass media compared with other information resources, on the forms of social organization which define the role of the media, and on the conditions of change or novelty which give rise to information needs. The theory implies several things: an active audience; a limit to the accessible supply of information; constraining circumstances; some compelling or attracting force; a variability over time and between social groupings. It also largely rests on the assumption that mass communication in its present centralized forms continues to be of crucial importance as a source of public information for a majority.

More than a complicated way of saying that the effects of the media depend on the circumstances of time and place, this reminds us that, although the media are not often a primary *cause* of any significant phenomenon in society, they can be important in mediating and directing the course of events or reactions to events. Secondly, it underlines the importance of the detailed and laborious empirical investigations which are needed to support and test any higher-level generalization of this kind. Thirdly, if we accept this way of thinking, we have to pay attention, as far as we are able, to the 'climate of opinion,' the collective mood of the time. Fourthly, we should be more inclined to investigate significant moments and events and to find criteria for distinguishing them. Finally, it encourages the view that what the media choose to do may be important and that there may be significant moments in media content which count for more at a critical time than does the average over normal periods.

I associate this version of accumulating understanding with the label historicity, since the highest level of generalization about the effect of mass media is one which requires us to associate historical circumstances with key features of media institutions and with established principles of communication influence. The scope for error is large and the temptation to speculate is great, but we should look in this direction. As students of the media, we will at least be better insured against the historical calamity mentioned at the outset, the decline of the mass media, and better able to earn a living in accounting for it and its consequences.

There remain large areas where research mutually beneficial to public policy-makers, media scientists, and media professionals could take place on a cooperative basis, and I am unconvinced of the view that questions of policy must be intellectually uninteresting. Some concessions may be asked of media scientists, however, and we might begin by taking more seriously some features of the self-image of mass communicators. In particular, we might have more appreciation of what is unique, unpredictable, original, and timely about significant moments in mass communication. While the basis of power of the media does lie in structural conditions, the activation of that potential may depend on a person's doing something in a certain way at a critical moment. We might also be more open to the possibility that the language of the media, especially of news, is the only one which makes the current events of history assimilable. Further, we might be less impatient with journalism for not being a social science. It is forty years since Robert Park (1940) distinguished news from history as a "form of knowledge" in a most perceptive way, but we have not lost the tendency to assume that it must be an inferior form of knowledge.

There can be little doubt that questions of public policy and political decisions about the media will provide intellectual excitement, since ultimately they confront the ideal with reality, and the demand for useful contributions in this sphere will certainly increase. The utility of media science will often lie precisely in the independence which is so much disliked when it is manifested as partisan advocacy, criticism, internal disorderliness. But, if I were to name the most uniquely useful contribution of the subject, it would be in the description and formulation of social theories of communication, the exposition and analysis of the principles of operation of press and broadcasting in society. Policy cannot be made without a grasp of these things or without reference to alternative theory if policy asks for change.

Evaluative research on media performance cannot be carried out without appropriate concepts drawn from prescriptive theory. As the scope of mass media activity widens year by year, implicit theories legitimating what happens are slowly forged. Yet the nearest equivalent to a standard work on the subject of press theory in the world was written more than twenty years ago by an American historian, Frederick Siebert (Siebert et al., 1956). The book distinguished four theories of the press: the authoritarian, the libertarian, the social responsibility, the Soviet. The labels have some validity still, but the realities so labelled have inevitably changed. What is especially missing and missed is a discussion of theory which represents the interests and rights of the audience member. He or she appears as citizen, consumer, object of manipulation or protection, but rarely as a participant in a communication process with varied cultural and information needs which only mass communication may be able to meet. If this option for useful work is taken up by a development of theory which is more sensitive to the audience, then it will help to secure a firmer foundation for the independence of media science in its public dealings, from clients in the mass media or government.

As I conclude, I feel less apologetic about my choice of title, the more strands of argument it has helped draw together. My view of the study of mass communication is of an enterprise shaped by competing external forces and open to assimilation either by the institutional interests it should examine or by the political interests seeking control or change. The mass media themselves, despite their orientation to the present and cultivation of the ephemeral, are a product and indicator of long-term political and cultural developments of their society. They are also, for most people, the chief source of knowledge and understanding of the current course of history. The centrality or otherwise of the mediating role between ourselves and experience is the key to the problem at the core of the subject: the effects of mass media and mass message. In turn, an accout of these effects can only be given with the aid of an imaginative understanding of the time, the culture, and the society.

REFERENCES

Annan, L. (1978). "United Kingdom: Broadcasting and Politics." *Journal of Communication*, 28, 59-67.
Bakewell, J. and N. Garnham (1970). *The New Priesthood*. London: Allen Lane.
Ball-Rokeach, S.J. and M.L. DeFleur (1976). "A dependency model of mass media effects." *Communication Research*, 3, 3-22.
Blumler, J. and D. McQuail (1968). *Television in Politics: Its Uses and Influence*. London: Faber.
Blumler, J., D. McQuail, and T. Nossiter (1975). *Political Communication and the Young Voter*. Report to the SSRC. Leeds University. (mimeo)
Briggs, A. (1961). *The Birth of Broadcasting*. London: OUP.
Burns, T. (1969). "Public Service and Private World." In P. Halmos (ed.) *The Sociology of Mass Media Communicators*.
Carey, J. (1978). "The Ambiguity of Policy Research." *Journal of Communication*, 28, 114-9.

Clarke, P. and E. Fredin (1978). "Newspapers, Television and Political Reasoning." *Public Opinion Quarterly,* 42, 143-160.

Elliott, P. (1972). *The Making of a Television Series.* London: Constable.

Emmett, B.P. (1966). "The Design of Investigations into the Effects of Radio and Television Programmes and Other Mass Communications." *Journal of the Royal Statistical Society,* 129, 26-49.

Gans, H.J. (1978). "Social Research on Broadcasting: Some Additional Proposals." *Journal of Communication,* 28 100-105.

Glasgow Media Group (1976). *Bad News.* London: Routledge.

Katz, E. (1978). "Social Research on Broadcasting: Of Mutual Interest." *Journal of Communication,* 28, 133-141.

Klapper, J. T. (1960). *The Effects of Mass Communication.* New York: Free Press.

Lazarsfeld, P.F. (1949). "The American Soldier—An Expository Review." *Public Opinion Quarterly,* 13, 377-404. (I am indebted to Tom Burns for the idea of using this source.)

Maisel, R. (1973). "The Decline of Mass Media." *Public Opinion Quarterly,* 37, 159-170.

McQuail, D. (1977). "The Influence and Effects of Mass Media." In J. Curran et al. (eds.) *Mass Communication and Society.* London: Arnold. Pp. 70-94.

Communication and Society. London: Arnold. Pp. 70-94.

McQuail, D. (1976). *Review of Sociological Writing on the Press.* Royal Commission on the Press Working Paper no. 2. London: HMSO.

Park, R. (1940). "News as a Form of Knowledge." *American Journal of Sociology,* 45, 669-86.

Siebert, F.S. et al. (1956). *Four Theories of the Press.* Urbana: University of Illinois Press.

Trenaman, J. and D. McQuail (1961). *Television and the Political Image.* London: Methuen.

Tuchman, G. (1978). *Making News: A Study of the Construction of Reality.* New York: Free Press.

Williams, R. (1974). *Television: Technology and Cultural Form.* London: Fontana.

One of the liveliest debates in recent years is sparked by the Weaver-Gray paper on the history and future of research in the field. First presented at the 1979 annual convention of the Association for Education in Journalism at Houston, Texas, the paper documents for the first time the impact of funding on the focus of mass communication research. Further, Weaver and Gray argue that a major intellectual focus of research ought to be the institutional setting of the journalist. In his critique of the paper, James Carey, Dean of the University of Illinois College of Communications, stridently disagrees with the historical argument in the Weaver-Gray paper and objects to an intellectual linkage to professional journalism. Steven H. Chaffee, Vilas Research Professor of Journalism and Mass Communication at the University of Wisconsin—Madison, disagrees with the definition of the research field in the Weaver-Gray paper, but he is less critical of the suggested intellectual focus than is Carey. David H. Weaver is Director of the Bureau of Media Research at Indiana University; Richard G. Gray is Director of the School of Journalism at Indiana University—Bloomington.

6

JOURNALISM AND
MASS COMMUNICATION RESEARCH
IN THE UNITED STATES
Past, Present and Future

David H. Weaver and Richard G. Gray

MUCH AS THE PROVERBIAL FISH is unaware of the water in its world, so American scholarship has largely been unaware of journalism until recent times. Despite the fact that questions about the role of journalism in a democracy seriously concerned our Constitutional framers and despite the use journalists historically have made of empirical techniques of inquiry so central to much of modern scholarship, journalists essentially have been taken for granted by the traditional academic disciplines.

But pragmatic concerns about winning wars through journalistic propaganda, charting the great audiences for the big corporate media of the 20th Century, and worries about the short-term social effects of broadcasting have left an indelible stamp on the mass media research that has emerged in our time.

In the midst of the relative neglect by the established disciplines on the one hand, and the largely practical concerns of the government-funded and commercial research in the field on the other, schools of journalism have grown to maturity in many of the nation's great public universities. In these schools, a research tradition has slowly emerged that has the potential to combine the best of the applied concerns of professional journalists with the traditional strengths of the humanities and the social sciences.

This paper briefly reviews the major trends in journalism education and mass communication research in the United States, the major sources of funding for such research, and the relationships between sources of funding and research emphases. In addition, it suggests six areas which the authors feel should receive ongoing, programmatic research attention.

AUTHOR'S NOTE: We are indebted to Professors G. Cleveland Wilhoit (Indiana), Steven H. Chaffee (Wisconsin), James W. Carey (Illinois), and Richard R. Cole (North Carolina) for their contributions and suggestions. An earlier version of this article and the comments that follow were presented at the 1979 annual convention of the Association for Education in Journalism in Houston, Texas.

From David H. Weaver and Richard G. Gray, "Journalism and Mass Communication Research in the United States: Past, Present and Future," original manuscript.

Obviously, any paper of this length on such a wide-ranging subject must necessarily omit many details and give short shrift to many subjects. Our purpose here is not to provide an encyclopedic, detailed account of the development of journalism/mass communication education and research in the United States, but rather to step back and look at the relationships between what we perceive to be some major trends in journalism education, research and funding in this country during the past 200 years.

A COMPACT HISTORY OF JOURNALISM EDUCATION

One important influence on the kind of journalism and mass communication research conducted in this country was the way in which journalism education developed. This development can be organized roughly into four periods. The first, which is rather loosely defined, can be said to extend from the 1700s to the 1870s. During this time American journalism, as is still the case in Europe and much of the rest of the world today, was basically an apprenticeship system. Benjamin Franklin, for example, learned the trade as an apprentice in his brother's Boston print shop and later refined his skills in the House of Caslon in London. Subsequent early American journalists usually followed this apprenticeship path or perfected their writing skills through liberal arts education in the private universities of the Eastern seaboard.

The second period, which extends from the 1870s to the 1920s, saw the establishment of more formal programs of journalism instruction in institutions of higher education. For example, General Robert E. Lee, president of Washington College (now known as Washington and Lee University) started training in printing in the post Civil War period. Other universities followed suit. Kansas State College began instruction in printing in 1873, the University of Missouri In 1878, and the University of Pennsylvania in 1893. For the most part these classes were taught by former newspapermen. For example, Joseph French Johnson, a former financial editor of the Chicago *Tribune*, taught courses at Pennsylvania, and newspaperman Walter Williams headed the first separate school of journalism which was founded in 1908 at the University of Missouri. In this period, however, most programs were either adjuncts to English departments or got their start there. They primarily stressed technical courses and gained little respectability from academe or confidence from the profession.

The third period, which roughly extends from the 1920s to the 1950s, saw journalism programs established on a much firmer basis. A number followed the earlier pattern set by Missouri in 1908 and Columbia in 1912 of becoming an independent professional school within the larger university setting. Other programs gained momentum and respectability by becoming well established separate departments within colleges of liberal arts. This pattern was well-established at the

University of Wisconsin where Willard G. Bleyer had started teaching journalism classes in 1908 and the University of Minnesota where Ralph Casey, a Bleyer protégé, took over the journalism program in the 1930s.

In the early 1930s Bleyer created the Ph.D. minor in journalism in Wisconsin's doctoral programs in political science and sociology. Although his background was in English, Bleyer chose to locate journalism in the social sciences rather than in the humanities division of the university, and this decision had a significant impact on the kind of journalism research carried out and on the training of journalists at the university level.

Many of the founders of the major journalism programs around the country came out of the journalism-minor Ph.D. program at Wisconsin, including Chilton Bush, Ralph Nafziger, Kenneth Olson, Fred Siebert, Curtis MacDougall, and Ralph Casey. They carried the empirical social science assumptions with them to Stanford, Illinois, Michigan State, Northwestern and Minnesota.[1] The main thrust for programs at this time was to follow the Bleyer school of thought by integrating journalism education with the social sciences. As a result, journalism schools began hiring Ph.D.s on their faculties in this period and drew them primarily from such disciplines as political science, sociology and psychology. Some did come from the humanities, especially from history, and even they often took a social science point of view.

The final period, which extended from the 1950s to the present, might be said to have begun with the establishment of the Ph.D. in journalism and mass communications at the University of Minnesota in 1950. Other institutions—particularly in the Big 10—followed by establishing doctoral programs of their own. Stanford on the West Coast and North Carolina on the East Coast extended this tradition beyond the Midwest. Typically, these Ph.D. programs were run by scholars who had gained their terminal degrees in sociology, psychology, or political science. Their protégés, however, formed a discipline all their own, which often is referred to as journalism and mass communication. These recent scholars differ from other behavioral scientists such as psychologists and sociologists in that they often conceive research questions and approach scholarship from their own particular point of view. They tend, unlike the sociologists, to look at journalism research not as an outsider but from an inside point of view. Consequently the way they conceive research questions and interpret research data makes them more prone to conduct and write up studies that are more readily applicable and meaningful to the profession and to journalism education. While this pattern is not universal and while many leading scholars still slip back into the comfort of sociology and psychology, many are capable of striking out on their own to create a body of literature and a discipline that can truly be termed journalism and mass communication.

The research reviewed later in this paper closely parallels the major thrust of these historical patterns and reflects the composition of journalism faculties in the various periods discussed. For example, research for the first two periods (1700s-1920s) was conducted mainly by former newspapermen and consisted primarily of the history of printing, biographies of journalists, and descriptions of their journals.

Research in the third period (1920s-1950s) was conducted primarily by such behavioral scientists as Harold Lasswell, Leonard Doob, and Robert Park, Paul Lazarsfeld, and Carl Hovland, and often read as if it were a treatise in sociology, psychology or political science.

Research in the final period (1950s-present) tends to be conducted by scholars in media research centers who are the protégés of such pioneer journalism educators as Ralph Casey at Minnesota, Ralph Nafziger at Wisconsin, Chilton Bush at Stanford, and Wilbur Schramm of Illinois and Stanford. These more modern scholars may use behavioral science techniques, but they are capable and often do approach research questions from a journalistic or communication point of view.

PAST RESEARCH ON JOURNALISM AND MASS COMMUNICATIONS.

Prior to the 20th century, little systematic scholarly attention was paid to journalism or mass communication in this country. The studies that were done were mainly descriptive histories of newspapers and periodicals without much interpretation.[2] The focus of these histories was primarily on describing the lives of the most famous editors and publishers in very anecdotal terms, without much of an attempt to link what happened in journalism to larger forces and trends in society.

Examples of such histories include *The History of Printing in America* by Isaiah Thomas, which was published in 1810 and which is still relied upon as the definitive history of printing for the period up to the American Revolution.[3] Another early history was *Journalism in the United States* by Frederic Hudson, former managing editor of the New York *Herald*.[4] It contained detailed information on the growth, policies and newsgathering practices of New York penny newspapers, especially the *Herald*.

Between 1810 and 1927, five major histories of American journalism were written.[5] From 1927 on, beginning with Willard Bleyer's *Main Currents in the History of American Journalism*, four additional major histories of American journalism were produced, along with many other shorter historical studies.[6] But more importantly, 1927 marked the publication of Harold Lasswell's *Propaganda Technique in the World War*, one of the first studies of mass media content to employ systematic, scientific methods.[7] This study, prompted by the use of propaganda in

World War I by the British and Germans, marked the beginning of scientific research on the process and effects of mass communication. One of the primary assumptions made by Lasswell and other researchers was that mass media messages could not only provide information to the public, but also were powerful determinants of attitudes and opinions, a view that was challenged by later research in the 1940s and 1950s.

From the 1930s to the 1950s

Lasswell, a political scientist, was joined by other social scientists in the 1930s and 40s who were also interested in studying the uses and effects of mass media. Paul Lazarsfeld, a sociologist who emigrated from Europe to the United States in the 1930s, was interested in short-range effects of mass media on people's attitudes, opinions and decision-making behavior, especially during elections.[8] Kurt Lewin, a psychologist, was interested in personal influence and communication within small groups.[9] And Carl Hovland, also a psychologist, was interested in studying the effects of media message characteristics (such as credibility of source, one-sided arguments versus two-sided, etc.) on people's attitudes and opinions. During World War II, Hovland was employed by the U.S. Army to evaluate the effectiveness of its training films on the willingness of U.S. soldiers to go into combat and on their attitudes regarding the war.[10] (See Figure 1)

During the late 1930s and early 1940s, as British researchers Peter Golding and Graham Murdock have noted, "the need of the American commercial radio industry to chart its audience, and the demands of war-time propaganda research were important determinants of the directions studies took."[11] The interest in media effects during this time period was also spurred by a popular theory of "mass society," where social ties were presumably weakened in an urbanized, industrialized society and individuals were "atomized" and therefore more manipulable by the mass media.

Because of these and other influences, those scholars interested in studying journalism and mass communication turned their attention "to voting, an informed or uninformed electorate, (and) the process of persuasion and influence via the media."[12]

This view of mass media as influential social institutions—which was held initially by many of these early scholars—was eroded in the 1940s and 50s when the belief that media effects were severely limited replaced the early fears of media domination. This "limited effects" perspective grew out of research by these early scholars which focused on short-term changes in individual attitudes and opinions as a result of media exposure. Some changes were found in controlled experimental studies, but few such changes were found using survey research in more naturalistic settings.

During this 20-year period between the 1930s and the 1950s, other kinds of

Figure 1

Major Emphases of Journalism and Mass Communication Research

Time 1 (Early 1800s - 1930s)	Time 2 (1930s - 1950s)	Time 3 (1950s to Present)
1. Mostly descriptive histories of printing, newspapers and periodicals which focused on the lives and influence of major editors and publishers.	1. More interpretive histories of journalism which looked at the interaction between societal forces and journalistic institutions.	1. Studies of TV's effects on various kinds of behavior, especially aggressive actions.
	2. Studies of mass media content and propaganda messages by political scientist Harold Lasswell and others.	2. Studies of the impact of newspaper and TV coverage on riots and civil disorders.
	3. Studies of mass media effects on political attitudes and voting behavior by sociologist Paul Lazarsfeld and others.	3. Studies of the effects of pornography on antisocial and criminal behavior.
	4. Studies of personal influence and communication within small groups by psychologist Kurt Lewin and others.	4. Studies of the effects of TV advertising on children.
	5. Studies of the effects of message characteristics (e.g. source credibility, one-sided vs. two-sided arguments) on people's attitudes and opinions by psychologist Carl Hovland and others.	5. Studies of media uses and effects in political campaigns, especially TV and newspaper uses and effects.
	6. Studies of people's use of radio and newspapers.	6. A major nationwide study of working journalists.
	7. Scattered studies of press coverage of legal cases, newspaper management, working journalists, media and popular culture, newspaper content, TV's effect on magazine circulation, and press coverage of election campaigns.	7. Numerous studies of newspaper readership and use.
		8. Several nationwide studies of newspaper managers.

129

research were also being conducted on journalism in this country. (See Figure 1) There were studies examining press treatment of legal cases, a couple of studies on newspaper management, and several studies of working journalists, including U.S. correspondents stationed abroad, foreign correspondents covering the U.S., and telegraph editors.[13] In addition, studies of mass media and popular culture were beginning to find their way into *Journalism Quarterly*.

At the same time, more emphasis was placed on quantitative research methods from the social sciences, and on journalism and mass communication as a part of a larger society. As time went by, there were relatively fewer biographical historical articles and fewer articles by working newsmen (such as Arthur Krock and Virginius Dabney) in scholarly journals such as *Public Opinion Quarterly* and *Journalism Quarterly*. But even though social science methods began to be used by journalism scholars in the early 1930s, most of the research articles published in *Journalism Quarterly* through 1948 were "humanistic and non-quantitative," according to editor Raymond Nixon.[14]

By the mid-1950s, there were a few scattered studies of the content of competitive versus non-competitive newspapers, the circulation of magazines after the advent of television, and the amount of bias in press coverage of election campaigns. There were also a few studies of communicators during the 1930s to 1950s period, especially Leo Rosten's study of Washington correspondents in 1937, a study of the editorial staff of the *Milwaukee Journal*, of Oregon editorial writers, Kansas weekly publishers, American correspondents abroad, foreign correspondents in the United States, and David Manning White's "gatekeeper" study of a newspaper wire editor.[15]

But there was almost no attention paid to the workings of mass communication organizations, except for Warren Breed's study of the unwritten system of rewards and punishments in a newsroom and how these are learned by new staffers.[16]

Newspaper readership studies also became popular during this period, beginning with Iowa journalism professor George Gallup's 1930 *Journalism Quarterly* article.[17] The early studies were mostly descriptive, simply relating what percentage of persons in a sample read which items in the newspaper, but the later studies became more concerned with *why* and *how* people read, as well as *what* they read.

Wilbur Schramm, one of the most prolific and well-known researchers in journalism and mass communication, argues that there were three main currents of journalism/mass communication research running through the 20-year period from the mid-1930s to the mid-1950s: (1) Historical studies of the press and biographies of editors, with more of an emphasis on "social histories"—those that gave more recognition to the role of larger societal forces such as industrialization, urbanization and technology; (2) Studies of the press in society, including analyses of press philosophy, mass communication law, media ownership government-press relations, the role of the press in shaping public opinion, and press freedom and responsibility; and (3) Studies of the press as a communication institution and studies of the communication process.[18]

Schramm suggests several reasons to explain why these main currents of research developed during this time period:

1. Data on the communication industry became available from various sources, including the U.S. Census Bureau, the Audit Bureau of Circulation, the President's Committee on Social Trends in the 1930s, advertising research companies, and the United Nations Educational, Scientific and Cultural Organization (UNESCO).
2. More opportunities to do field research became available with the growth of university research centers such as the Bureau of Applied Social Research at Columbia University, the National Opinion Research Center originally at Denver and now at Chicago, and the Institute of Communications Research at the University of Illinois.
3. More quantitative research tools were developed by social scientists and statisticians to deal with the vast amounts of numerical data from readership studies, readability formulas, and systematic analyses of media content.
4. There was an increased willingness of foundations and other organizations to support research on journalism and mass communication. Such support came from various sources, including the Payne Fund, the U.S. Army, the Commission on Freedom of the Press (which received financial support from Henry Luce of Time, Inc. and Encyclopaedia Britannica, Inc.), the Department of Mass Communication of UNESCO, the International Press Institute, the Nieman Fellowship program at Harvard University, and various professional organizations in journalism, psychology, sociology and public opinion research—all of which now have sections on communication research. (See Figure 2)
5. Finally, during this 20-year period between the 1930s and the 1950s, schools of journalism in the United States moved away from being English-oriented schools of journalistic letters to becoming schools of applied social science. Such schools became more concerned with relationships between mass communication and society, and research became a major concern. As a result, research institutes and centers were begun, and they further encouraged systematic inquiry into journalism history, the study of mass media and society, and the study of communication institutions and processes.

Figure 2

Major Funding Sources for Journalism and Mass Communication Research

Time 1 (Early 1800s - 1930s)	Time 2 (1930s - 1950s)	Time 3 (1950s to Present)
1. Authors' own resources from publishing and printing businesses.	1. Authors' own resources from various sources.	1. Major funding from various government agencies, including the National Commission on the Causes and Prevention of Violence, the Surgeon General's Scientific Advisory Committee on Television and Social Behavior, the National Advisory Commission on Civil Disorders, the Commission on Obscenity and Pornography, the National Science Foundation, the National Institute of Mental Health, and the East-West Center in Hawaii.
2. University funding for sabbatical leaves, summer research support, etc.	2. University support for sabbatical leaves, summer research projects, etc.	
3. United States Census Bureau (for North's study of newspapers for the 1880 census).	3. United States government, including the U.S. Army, the U.S. Census Bureau, and the President's Committee on Social Trends in the 1930s.	
	4. The United Nations Educational, Scientific and Cultural Organization (UNESCO).	2. The American Newspaper Publishers Association (ANPA).
	5. Time, Inc. and Encyclopaedia Britannica (funded the Commission on Freedom of the Press in the 1940s).	3. The National Association of Broadcasters (NAB) and the Magazine Publishers Association (MPA).
	6. The International Press Institute (IPI).	4. The Frank E. Gannett Newspaper Foundation.
	7. The Nieman Fellowship program at Harvard University.	5. The Markle Foundation.
	8. The U.S. radio industry.	6. The Aspen Institute Program on Communications and Society (which is itself supported by numerous private and government foundations).
	9. Selected newspapers.	7. The Ford Foundation.
		8. The Twentieth Century Fund.
		9. Authors' own resources.
		10. Individual newspapers and television networks.
		11. University support.

Although much new research into journalism and mass communication was initiated between the 1930s and 1950s, many promising areas were somewhat neglected. In particular, the historical studies were still largely tied to a "Progressive" interpretation and a "great man" approach. And in the press and society area, very little research was done on media economics, especially the relationships between economics, freedom, responsibility and press performance. Also somewhat overlooked were the constraints placed on working journalists by different organizational structures, the role of individual values and professional attitudes in shaping the nature of news, and the training of individual journalists, their attitudes toward their jobs, and their financial and other rewards.

From the 1950s to the Present

With the advent of television in the early 1950s, journalism/mass communication research underwent a revolution of sorts. In the past 25 years or so, there have been literally hundreds of studies of the impact of television on American society. The majority of these studies have concentrated on short-term effects of television on children, many of them concerned with TV's role in stimulating subsequent violence and aggressive behavior.[19]

The introduction of television did not alter the interest of many researchers in the *effects* of mass media, but it did increase the level of funding—especially government funding—for journalism/mass communication effects research. (See Figure 2) Numerous field and laboratory studies on the effects of television were sponsored by such governmental agencies as the National Commission on the Causes and Prevention of Violence (appointed in 1968 by President Lyndon B. Johnson), the Surgeon General's Scientific Advisory Committee on Television and Social Behavior (appointed by the Secretary of Health, Education and Welfare in June 1969, with a budget of $1.8 million for 23 independent research projects and more than 40 technical papers), the East-West Center in Hawaii, and such government-funded agencies as the National Science Foundation and the National Institute of Mental Health.[20]

In addition to the widespread adoption and use of television, another stimulus for increased government funding for research on journalism and mass communication was the social and political upheaval of the 1960s.

Following riots in several American cities, President Johnson appointed a National Advisory Commission on Civil Disorders (the Kerner Commission) in 1967, which was charged to investigate the causes of—and means of preventing— these riots and also the impact of newspaper and television coverage on them. As a result of this concern, the Kerner Commission hired researchers to conduct quantitative content analyses of media coverage of the disorders in 15 different cities, to question ghetto residents about their attitudes toward newspaper and television coverage, and to discuss riot coverage with representatives of the news media.[21]

Another program of research which had implications for the study of journalism and mass communication was begun in the late 1960s with the forming of the Commission on Obscenity and Pornography by Public Law 90-100.[22] One of its tasks was to study the effect of obscenity and pornography on the public, and particularly minors, and its relationship to crime and other antisocial behavior.

Again, the concern was with media *effects,* but this time with more unconventional media than daily newspapers and television news programs. Both survey and experiments, as well as studies of the rates and incidences of pornography at community levels, were carried out with about $643,000 in funding provided by the Commission.

Concern over the role of advertising in the lives of children also led to government funding for studies on the potential harmful effects of television advertising on children, as part of the Surgeon General's program on Television and Social Behavior. A number of journalism/mass communication researchers with an interest in how children make buying decisions studied media content to see what kinds of commercials with what kinds of appeals were being directed toward children. Other researchers, who were more interested in the effects of commercials on children and their parents, used field experiments and surveys.[23]

Although many of these studies which received government funding in the 1960s and 70s dealt with the effects of television, a review of *Journalism Quarterly* from 1955 to 1974 reveals that of the 1,490 studies published there during that time, 835 or 56% concerned the print media, whereas about 5% concerned radio and television, about 21% dealt with both printed and electronic media, and about 18% were not specifically concerned with mass media.[24] This dominance of studies on the print media was due largely to numerous historical articles on newspapers, magazines and books.

In spite of the number of journalism research articles published in *Journalism Quarterly* during this period, an analysis of 122 randomly-selected articles from *Journalism Quarterly* and from the journalism/mass communication articles in *Public Opinion Quarterly* during the years 1954 through 1978 indicates that only about 26%, or one in four, of these studies were funded by some source, be it private, public or government. (See Table 1) A random sampling of 185 articles for the same years from the *American Political Science Review,* the *American Sociological Review,* and two psychology journals (the *Psychological Bulletin* from 1954 through 1963, and the *Journal of Personality and Social Psychology* from 1968 through 1978) suggests that about 50%, or one-half, of the studies published in these journals received funding from some outside source.[25] (See Table 1)

Table I
Percentage of Funded Studies in
Journalism/Mass Communication, Political Science, Sociology, and Psychology
From 1954 to 1978[1]

Field	1954	1958	1963	1968	1973	1978	TOTAL
1. Journalism/Mass Communication	35.7%	25.0%	27.8%	31.8%	14.3%	29.2%	26.2% (n = 122)
2. Political Science	27.3	36.4	33.3	69.2	54.5	46.2	45.6 (n = 68)
3. Sociology	54.5	50.0	72.7	62.5	60.0	75.0	63.0 (n = 54)
4. Psychology	50.0	50.0	62.5	55.6	47.4	80.0	57.1 (n = 63)
TOTAL	40	37	46	61	68	55	307

[1] These percentages are based on all the major articles in one randomly-selected issue of each of the following journals for the years indicated above: 1) *Journalism Quarterly* and only the journalism/mass communication articles in *Public Opinion Quarterly*; 2) *American Political Science Review*; 3) *American Sociological Review*; and 4) *Psychological Bulletin* (1954 – 1963) and *Journal of Personality and Social Psychology* (1968 – 1978). If the text or footnotes of an article acknowledged some funding source, be it a university fund, a private foundation, a government agency, etc., the article was coded as "funded."

Compared to the related fields of political science, sociology and psychology, then, published journalism/mass communication research appears to be substantially underfunded. Whereas one-half or so of the published studies in these other fields have been funded during the past 25 years, only about one-fourth of the journalism/mass communication published studies acknowledge a funding source of some kind.

Table 1 also suggests that political science was receiving funding roughly proportional to that of journalism/mass communication from 1954 through 1963, but that from 1968 through 1978 the proportion of published studies funded in political science nearly doubled while this proportion remained about the same in journalism/mass communication.

What funding there was for journalism/mass communication published studies was about evenly split among university, government and private sources from 1954 through 1963, and from 1968 through 1978. (See Table 2) This has not been the pattern, however, for the other social science studies included in our sample. Although the numbers of such studies are small, they suggest that published studies in both political science and sociology were funded primarily with university resources from 1954 through 1963, and psychological studies relied mainly on government funding. From 1968 through 1978, though, the primary source of funding for political science and sociology shifted from the university to the government, and psychology relied even more heavily on government funding. (See Table 2)

In short, while there has been more reliance in recent years on government funding by political science, sociology and psychology—at least according to our sample of published studies—those published journalism/mass communication studies which are funded continue to be supported about equally by the university, the government and private resources.

There is also evidence to suggest that what funding there has been for journalism/mass communication research has been provided for quantitative studies, primarily surveys, which are most likely to be concerned with the effects and uses of mass communication. (See Tables 3 and 4) Although a majority of the *unfunded* studies are also quantitative, the difference between the proportion of unfunded quantitative studies (66%) and funded quantitative studies (87%) is statistically significant.

Among the *unfunded* journalism/mass communication studies, historical-philosophical studies are the most common (39%), followed by surveys and content analyses. But among the *funded* studies, surveys are the most common (41%), followed by historical-philosophical studies and experiments. (See Table 3) In the fields of political science and sociology it is also true that a higher proportion of funded studies tend to be quantitative than do the unfunded studies, but a higher proportion of funded studies are also historical-philosophical in nature than is the

Table 2

Funding Sources for Published Studies in Journalism / Mass Communication, Political Science, Sociology, and Psychology from 1954 to 1978[1]

Funding Source

Field	University		Government		Private		Other[1]		TOTAL	
	(1954-1963)	(1968-1978)	(1954-1963)	(1968-1978)	(1954-1963)	(1968-1978)	(1954-1963)	(1968-1978)	(1954-1963)	(1968-1978)
1. Journalism/ Mass Communication	21.4%	27.8%	35.7%	27.8%	35.7%	33.3%	7.1%	11.1%	14	18
2. Political Science	50.0	23.8	20.0	52.4	10.0	4.8	20.0	19.0	10	21
3. Sociology	58.8	0.0	23.5	82.4	11.8	0.0	5.9	17.6	17	17
4. Psychology	22.2	14.8	55.6	81.5	22.2	3.7	0.0	0.0	9	27
Total									50	83

[1]See footnote "1" of Table 1 for a description of the sample of published studies and for the definition of a funded study.

[2]This category includes combinations of university, government and private sources of funding.

Table 3

The Relationship Between Funding and Use of Quantitative Research Methods
For All Journalism/Mass Communication Articles[1]

	Methodology[2]		
	Non-Quantitative	Quantitative	TOTAL
Funded	12.5%	87.5%	32
Not Funded	34.4	65.6	90
			122

Phi=.21, p=.03

[1] See footnote "1" of Table 1 for a description of the sample of published studies and for the definition of a funded study.

[2] A "quantitative" study is defined as one in which some quantitative data and/or data tables are presented. A "non-quantitative" study is defined as one in which no quantitative data tables are presented and in which the method used to arrive at the results did not involve counting or numerical procedures.

Table 4

The Relationship Between Funding and Type of Study For All Journalism/Mass Communication Articles[1]

Type of Study[2]

	One-time Survey	Trend Study	Panel Study	Lab Experiment	Field Experiment	Content Analysis	Historical-Philosophical	Other
Funded (n = 32)	40.6%	6.3%	0.0%	12.5%	6.3%	6.3%	28.1%	0.0%
Not Funded (n = 90)	26.7	4.4	1.1	5.7	0.0	18.9	38.9	3.3

TOTAL = 122

Cramer's V = .33, p = .12

[1]See footnote "1" of Table 1 for a description of the sample of published studies and for the definition of a funded study.

[2]A "trend study" refers to one which employs different samples from the same population over time; a "panel study" is one which uses the same sample of persons over time; a "lab experiment" is an experimental study done in a laboratory, classroom or other "artificial" situation; a "fieldexperiment" is an experimental study done in a more "natural" setting, such as an entire community; a "content analysis"is a systematic study of documents (usually media content) rather than people; a "historical-philosophical" study is one which does not employ the systematic gathering of primary data, but relies on a more mpressionistic synthesis of all kinds of evidence; and the "other" category refers to some combination of these types of studies.

case with journalism/mass communication studies.

These findings seem to be consistent with the argument that most of the public and private support for journalism/mass communication research in the United States from the 1950s to the present has been channeled into studies of the effects and uses of various media, with relatively little support available for other kinds of research, such as new historical studies of reporting and the changing nature of news, media economics, media organizations, and the training and socialization of journalists.

Another set of evidence which supports the argument that most funding for journalism/mass communication research has gone into audience uses and effects studies is a recent unpublished report by James Grunig on grant support for communication research. This report, based on the responses of 74 members of the Communication Theory and Methodology Division of the Association for Education in Journalism to a 1978 questionnaire, indicates that the most frequent grant proposals were for research on the uses and effects of television and other media. The most successful proposals (that is, those most likely to be funded) were in the areas of political, environmental and international communication. The least successful proposals were concerned with science communication, media management and policy, and studies of communicators.

As for a source of funding, Grunig's report suggests that the most frequent source of funding for communication research is universities, followed by the government-sponsored National Science Foundation and the private American Newspaper Publishers Association. Grunig's findings thus support the finding from our analysis of journal studies that journalism/mass communication research is funded about equally by the universities, the government and private sources. But Grunig does note that communication researchers tend to have the least success with major funding agencies such as the National Science Foundation and the Markle Foundation. That is, fewer proposals submitted to these agencies are actually funded than is the case for universities or other private sources.

One notable exception to the pattern of funding media effects and uses studies is the recent nationwide study of journalists by sociologist John W. G. Johnstone and others, which was funded by the Markle Foundation.[26] Another partial exception to the funding of media effects research is the Aspen Institute Program on Communications and Society, which has been supported by "numerous private and governmental foundations" since 1971 and which is concerned with identifying the main communication issues confronting society, such as public broadcasting, government and the media, television and social behavior, cable television and new technologies, and federal telecommunications policy-making.[27]

Still another recent exception to the media effects funding pattern has been The Twentieth Century Fund, which has commissioned studies of the economics of the daily press in the United States; how the wire services select, shape and distribute information; and the impact of government subpoenas on the free flow of news.

But throughout most of its history in the United States, journalism/mass communication research has received most of its quite modest funding support for the study of media *effects*. From the concern with wartime propaganda in World War I, a "mass society" in the 1930s and 40s, the effectiveness of advertising messages after the development of radio, the role of the news media in elections in the 1940s and after, the widespread adoption of television in the 1950s, and the role of the media in the political and social upheaval of the 1960s, both public and private funding has been provided primarily for the study of the short-term impact of media messages on individual persons, especially on their attitudes and opinions—and to some extent, their behavior.

There has also been some research funding for the study of people's *use* of mass media—especially newspapers and television—but this funding has generally not approached the level of support for the study of media effects. And much of the funding for studies of how people use media has come from media industries themselves. The American Newspaper Publishers Association, for example, began funding a series of studies in 1964 which concentrated on newspaper use and readership, characteristics of newspaper audiences, newspaper makeup and design, and news writing. Although the funding for such studies was initially quite limited, in the last two years or so it has been substantially increased and has focused more sharply on readership of newspapers.

Other research support from the communication industry has come from the National Association of Broadcasters and the Magazine Publishers Association, but this funding has been, for the most part, very limited. Indeed, as the data presented in Table 1 suggest, journalism/mass communication research has had only modest funding support from both public and private sources. During the 1960s, a time of considerable affluence for research generally, journalism researchers were not very aggressive in seeking outside support. And, as journalism professor Everette Dennis has noted, just as journalism/mass communication researchers began to receive substantial monies for their efforts—especially for studies of media effects—a new period of relative austerity in public and private research came about.[28]

This pattern of austerity has been somewhat reversed in the last few years by the support for journalism education from the Frank E. Gannett Newspaper Foundation, but most of this support has gone for equipment and training programs rather than for research. One exception to this trend has been the funding for research on newspaper managers which has resulted in the most thorough and wide-ranging research on this subject yet completed in this country.[29]

PRESENT RESEARCH ON JOURNALISM AND MASS COMMUNICATION

The history of journalism/mass communication research in the United States, which has been briefly sketched above, can also be viewed in terms of its relationship to schools and departments of journalism, and to journalistic institutions.

The early histories of printing and journalism, although very few and very descriptive, nevertheless were directly concerned with journalistic organizations and journalists. Beginning in the late 1920s, however, political scientists and other social scientists became interested in systematically studying the messages produced by journalists and, later, the effects of these messages on various audiences. This interest in effects was spawned and reinforced by several major factors mentioned earlier—concern over wartime propaganda, a mass society, effects of advertising, the role of the media in elections, the television explosion, and the role of news media in the political and social upheaval of the 1960s. As a result of their interests in messages and effects, however, many mass communication researchers began to be more concerned with audiences and the effect of journalistic messages upon them, than with journalists and the actual production of these messages.

Yet during this same time, schools and departments of journalism in this country were concentrating on developing courses of instruction in writing, reporting, editing, history, law and ethics, all with the aim of training students to be better observers and message producers. Although the programs of research on media uses and effects had some relevance to these courses, it was a limited relevance at best. And to the working journalist the research on media uses and effects often seemed to have no practical value whatever, in part because few effects researchers bothered to expound on the implications of their studies for journalists, and also because many such researchers wrote the results of their studies in barely comprehensible language.[30]

This is not to say that media uses and effects research has no value for journalism education or for working journalists, but it is to say that preoccupation with such research—largely because of the availability of funding for it—has led to little interest in journalists and journalism on the part of many journalism researchers, and to only sporadic research on journalistic training and values and the effect of such training and values on news production. Continued concern over media effects of society has also resulted in very little systematic research on the other side of the coin—the effects of society on the media—even though all journalists in this and every other country are greatly influenced by societal and organizational constraints each working day, and even though their training and values and news organizations are shaped to a large extent by political and economic forces.

Largely because of the availability of funding for media effects research, we argue, there are presently several fairly consistently-researched areas which fall under the broad heading of media effects. These include television and aggressive behavior, mass media and diffusion of information, the effects of televised advertising, and the fairly recent media "agenda-setting" studies.[31]

There are also numerous studies on the uses of mass media—especially newspapers and television—which build on each other and add up to ongoing programs of research, again because funding has been provided for such research. An example of such a program of research are the studies on newspaper readership which have been funded for the past 15 years by the American Newspaper Publishers Association. Other studies of media use have been funded by the radio industry, the television industry and various magazines in this country. And in this country and abroad, the "uses and gratifications" approach to mass communication research has enjoyed renewed popularity in the past decade or so.[32]

Another program of research which has been somewhat concerned with information-seeking from mass media is "coorientation," which has emphasized the influence of interpersonal perception upon communication behavior.[33]

But when one looks beyond these studies on the uses and effects of mass media, one generally finds widely scattered studies which usually don't build upon one another and which usually don't study the same subject over time. Most of the studies presently reported in *Journalism Quarterly* and elsewhere are one-shot experiments, content analyses or surveys which make only passing reference to related studies. In short, aside from the journalism/mass communication research concerned with audience effects and uses, there are few ongoing *programs* of research on journalism in this country, especially research on the sources of journalists' professional values and the role of these values in determining what is news and what is not.

Other areas which have received very uneven research attention include the relationships between media economics and professional freedom and responsibility, the relationships between journalistic job satisfactions and job performance, the entire general area of press performance, the impact of new technology on journalistic performance, and the relationships between universities and journalists.

CONCLUSIONS ABOUT U.S. RESEARCH ON JOURNALISM AND MASS COMMUNICATION

After briefly surveying the literature of journalism/mass communication research and quickly retracing the history of journalism education in the United States, we have reached the following conclusions:

1. Journalism—despite being one of the earliest social institutions in America and the only business specifically mentioned in the U.S. Constitution—for the most part has been ignored by traditional scholarship. The research literature on the press is sparse when compared to such other institutions as law, the church, business and government. But since the 1950s, there has been considerably more scholarly research on journalism.

2. What research there has been in large measure has been sporadic, disjointed and short-term, except for a few areas which deal mostly with media uses and effects.

3. Where there has been more systematic, long-range—and as a result more conclusive—research, there has been more significant, well-defined and directed funding.

4. Well-developed journalism/mass communication research in this country has followed the interests and concerns of funding agencies as much or more as it has followed the autonomous interests of individual scholars.

5. Research in the field generally has reflected the changing nature and make-up of journalism faculties. As the composition of journalism faculties has changed from ex-newspapermen in English departments, to behavioral scholars in schools of journalism, to communications scholars in colleges of journalism and mass communication, there has been a correlative move in scholarship. The field has moved from predominantly descriptive historical studies, to behavioral science studies, to present-day communication studies.

6. Journalism has borrowed heavily from other disciplines until recently. Now journalism scholars—educated under faculties who earned their doctorates in such fields as sociology, psychology, and political science—have at last produced a new scholarly generation of their own. These modern researchers, who can be called communication scholars, bring their own particular way of conceiving research questions, their own methods of interpreting and analyzing data, and their own point of view to bear on research questions and projects.

7. After assessing the research literature and finding some rather serious deficiencies and ignored areas of concern, it becomes apparent that certain streams of research need systematic study, prolonged attention, and long-range funding.

SUGGESTED PROGRAMS OF
JOURNALISM AND MASS COMMUNICATION RESEARCH

In light of the above observations, we recommend that ongoing programs of research be pursued in the following areas. This list is not meant to be exhaustive, but only suggestive. (See Figure 3)

1. *The impact of the social-intellectual climate on journalistic values, attitudes, and performance.*

Long-term research on the development and change of journalistic values—and the relationship of such values to journalistic performance—is sorely needed. Such research should include the role of both organizational and societal forces in molding these values, and the interaction of these forces and journalistic values in determining what comes to be defined as news. Such a research program could examine the impact of various factors—such as family background, personalities, journalism training, newsroom environment, size of news organization, kind of ownership of news organization, etc.—on the professional attitudes and values of journalists, their levels of job satisfaction, how they perceive their roles in society, and how they perform their jobs.

2. *The impact of new technology on journalism and on society at large.*

The field of journalism also needs, in our opinion, more long-term research on the way new technological innovations influence journalists' definitions of news and their methods of gathering information. Are new technological devices mainly cost-saving inventions for gathering and disseminating more information more quickly, or do they have an impact on what is considered newsworthy, how journalists perceive their roles in society, and how they perform their jobs? Do such technological devices also have an impact on the way in which people in the larger society use mass media, as well as an effect on what kinds of information are carried by the media?

3. *Trends, major issues, and directions of media criticism.*

Continuing research is needed, we think, on various kinds of media criticism, from media ombudsmen to press councils to journalism scholars, and on what effects this criticism has had on media coverage of various topics. Has the National News Council, for example, had an impact on journalists' conceptions of what is accurate and fair news reporting? Have the Council decisions had an effect on subsequent media reporting of the topics dealt with in the decisions? What effects, if any, have journalism educators had on news coverage through their research and analyses of media performance and effects?

Figure 3

Suggested Programs of Journalism and Mass Communication Research

1. Impact of social-intellectual climate on journalistic values, attitudes, and performance.
2. Impact of new technology on journalism and on society at large.
3. Trends, major issues, and directions of media criticism.
4. Media economics, role of the media in the capitalistic society, and implications for management and American society.
5. Possibilities, opportunities, and methods of developing new sources of information and new information outlets.
6. New historical approaches and fresh legal research on journalism.

4. *Media economics, role of the media in the industrial society, and implications for management and society.*

Relatively little ongoing, systematic research has been carried out on the impact of tax laws and other economic regulations on the concentration of ownership of various media, and on the effects of kind of ownership on journalistic attitudes, values, job satisfaction and actual performance. There is a need for continuing research, we feel, on these subjects, and also on the implications of economic trends and type of media ownership for media management and for the society at large. Do different forms of media ownership and management result in differing amounts and kinds of information being carried by the media? How well are citizens informed of the workings of their government and their economy under different systems of media ownership and management?

5. *Possibilities, opportunities, and methods of developing new sources of information and new information outlets.*

Research should be conducted into opportunities for the media to tap new sources of information, including computerized morgues and computerized records in city hall, the court house and other governmental agencies. Other new sources of information include the various computerized storage and retrieval systems such as the Educational Resources Information Center (ERIC), the Public Affairs Information Service (PAIS), the National Newspaper Index, and others. There is also a need for research, we feel, into the possibilities for news organizations to develop the information business far beyond the publication of a daily or weekly newspaper, or the preparation of a daily news broadcast. Such research could explore the possibilities of developing regional information centers that would provide business, scholars and other citizens with data.

6. *New historical approaches and fresh legal research on journalism.*

Although numerous histories of journalism have been published and several books on mass communication law have been written, we still lack a sound history of reporting which examines the nature of the news story and how it has changed over the years. We also lack an economic history of mass media which focuses on the impact of changing economic theories and practices on news values and news dissemination. The field also needs more long-term studies of mass communication law which consider in depth the relationships between the law and news reporting. Have various legal decisions regarding mass media helped to shape not only media organizations and their practices, but also the journalist's perception of his or her role in society and the journalist's definition of news?

Although these six areas don't begin to cover all the possibilities for programs of research in journalism/mass communication, they do suggest some alternatives to the audience-centered uses and effects studies which have dominated U.S. mass communication research for nearly half a century. And these six proposed areas of research shift the focus of attention more directly to journalism and journalists.

As we stated earlier, we have no doubt that media uses and effects research does have considerable value for journalists and journalism educators. But we hope that funding will be provided in the future for programs of research such as the ones we have briefly outlined above—research that is directly concerned with the institution of journalism and journalists, as well as with the larger society in which journalists work.

NOTES

[1] Personal communication from Professor Steven H. Chaffee, School of Journalism and Mass Communication, University of Wisconson, Madison, Wisconsin, April 2, 1979.

[2] For a description of the major historical studies of journalism in the United States prior to the 20th century, see Joseph McKerns, "The Limits of Progressive Journalism History," *Journalism History*, 4:88-92 (Autumn 1977). For a critique of the perspectives and methods used in these studies, see James Carey, "The Problem of Journalism History," *Journalism History*, 1:3-5 (Spring 1974) and David Weaver, "Frank Luther Mott and the Future of Journalism History," *Journalism History*, 2:44-47 (Summer 1975).

[3] Isaiah Thomas, *The History of Printing in America* (Worcester, Mass.: Isaiah Thomas, Jr., First edition, 1810). Also printed in Albany, New York by Joel Munsell in 1874. The 1874 edition was reprinted in New York by Burt Franklin in 1966.

[4] Frederic Hudson, *Journalism in the United States* (New York: Harper and Bros., 1873). ·

[5] These include Isaiah Thomas, *op. cit.;* Frederic Hudson, *op. cit.;* S.N.D. North, *History and Present Condition of the Newspaper and Periodical Press of the United States* (Washington, D.C.: Government Printing Office, 1884); James Melvin Lee, *A History of American Journalism* (Garden City, N.Y.: Garden City Publishing Co.; 1917, 1923); and George Henry Payne, *History of Journalism in the United States* (New York: D. Appleton and Co., 1920). See Joseph McKerns, *op. cit.,* for brief descriptions of these works.

[6] These include Willard G. Bleyer, *Main Currents in the History of American Journalism* (Boston: Houghton Mifflin, 1927); Alfred M. Lee, *The Daily Newspaper in America.* New York: Macmillan, 1941, 1960, 1962); and Edwin Emery and Henry Ladd Smith, *The Press and America* (New York: Prentice-Hall, 1954).

[7] Harold Lasswell, *Propaganda Technique in the World War* (New York: Knopf, 1927).

[8] One of Lazarsfeld's most well-known studies was *The People's Choice* by himself, Bernard Berelson and Hazel Gaudet (New York: Columbia University Press, 1948). This was a report of the 1940 election study conducted in Erie County, Ohio, which found that voters seemed to use the mass media to *reinforce* voting decisions, but that the media played an important role in stimulating interest in the campaign. See also Bernard Berelson, Paul Lazarsfeld, and W. McPhee, *Voting* (Chicago: University of Chicago Press, 1954).

[9] See Kurt Lewin, "Group Decision and Social Change," in Eleanor Maccoby, Theodore Newcomb, and Eugene Hartley, eds., *Readings in Social Psychology* (New York: Henry Holt & Co., 1958), and Kurt Lewin, *Resolving Social Conflicts* (New York: Harper & Brothers, 1948).

[10] See Carl Hovland, A. Lumsdaine, and Fred Sheffield, *Experiments on Mass Communication* (Princeton: Princeton University Press, 1949) for a summary of the Army-sponsored research on the effects of orientation films during World War II. Another important work summarizing the Yale communication studies through 1953 is *Communication and Persuasion* by Carl Hovland, Irving Janis and Harold Kelley (New Haven: Yale University Press, 1953).

[11] Peter Golding and Graham Murdock, "Theories of Communication and Theories of Society," *Communication Research*, 5: 339-56 (July 1978), p. 341.

[12] James Carey, "Social Theory and Communication Theory," *Communication Research*, 5:357-68 (July 1978), p. 365.

[13] Wilbur Schramm, "Twenty Years of Journalism Research," *Public Opinion Quarterly*, 21:91-107 (Spring 1957).

[14] Schramm, *op. cit.*, pp. 92, 94, and 95. See also Raymond B. Nixon, "Introduction," *Journalism Quarterly Cumulative Index*, Volumes 1-40, 1924-1963, p. 5.

[15] Schramm, *op. cit.*, pp. 95, 106; Leo C. Rosten, *The Washington Correspondents* (New York: Harcourt Brace, 1937); and David Manning White, "The 'Gate Keeper': A Case Study in the Selection of News," *Journalism Quarterly*, 27:383-90 (Fall 1950).

[16] Warren Breed, "Social Control in the News Room: A Functional Analysis" *Social Forces*, 33:323-35 (May 1955).

[17] George Gallup, "A Scientific Method for Determining Reader Interest," *Journalism Quarterly*, 7:1-13 (March 1930).

[18] Schramm, *op. cit.*, pp. 99-107.

[19] Major reviews of these studies include Charles K. Atkin, John P. Murray and Oguz B. Nayman, "The Surgeon General's Research Program on Television and Social Behavior: A Review of Empirical Findings," *Journal of Broadcasting*, 16:21-35 (Winter 1971-72); George Comstock and Marilyn Fisher, *Television and Human Behavior: A Guide to the Pertinent Scientific Literature.* (Santa Monica, Calif.: The Rand Corporation, 1975); George Comstock, "The Evidence So Far," *Journal of Communication*, 25:25-34 (Autumn 1975); and George Comstock, "The Impact of Television on American Institutions," *Journal of Communication*, 28:12-28 (Spring 1978).

[20] For a concise summary of these government funded studies, see Everette E. Dennis, *The Media Society: Evidence About Mass Communication in America.* (Dubuque, Iowa: Wm. C. Brown, 1978), pp. 21-33.

[21] Dennis, *op. cit.*, pp. 22-23. See also *Report of the National Advisory Commission on Civil Disorders*, New York Times Edition (New York: Dutton, 1968).

[22] See Dennis, *op. cit.*, pp. 25-27, and *The Report of the Commission on Obscenity and Pornography*, New York Times Edition (New York Bantam Books, 1970). The Commission had a budget of about $643,000 according to

United States Statutes at Large. 1968. Vol. 82 (Washington: U.S. Government Printing Office, 1969), p. 196.

[23] For a concise review of these studies, see Dennis, *op. cit.,* pp. 29-30, and also Scott Ward, Daniel B. Wackman and Ellen Wartella, *Children Learning to Buy: The Development of Consumer Information Processing Skills.*(Beverly Hills, Calif.: Sage Publications, 1977).

[24] Richard M. Perloff, "Journalism Research: A 20-Year Perspective," *Journalism Quarterly,* 53: 123-126 (Spring 1976).

[25] Although we realize that these journals do not cover the published research of journalism/mass communication, political science, sociology and psychology, time and money constraints prevented us from including more journals in this analysis. We do argue, though, that these journals are major sources of published research in their respective fields, and that much of the funded research in each field appears in these journals.

The *Journal of Personality and Social Psychology* was not analyzed for the entire 1954-1978 time period because it began publication in the 1960s. We chose it as one of the major journals in social psychology, because the research in social psychology is, we feel, more directly comparable to journalism/mass communication research than the research in other areas of psychology such as clinical and physiological. From 1954 through 1963, we analyzed the content of the *Psychological Bulletin* because several of our colleagues in the department of psychology at Indiana University described it as a more general journal, containing summaries and syntheses of research in various areas of psychology.

Rather than pick only three or four articles a year to represent each field for the 25-year period, we chose to analyze all the major articles in one randomly-chosen issue of each journal every fifth year, beginning with 1954 and ending with 1978. This sampling procedure produced a total of 122 articles in journalism/mass communication, 68 in political science, 54 in sociology, and 63 in psychology. Each article was coded as being funded or unfunded (see footnote a of Table 1), and quantitative or non-quantitative (see footnote b of Table 3). In addition, the source of funding for funded studies was noted (see Table 2), as well as the design of each study (see footnote b of Table 4). And the actual sample size was recorded for each study employing a sample.

[26] John W. C. Johnstone et al., *The News People: A Sociological Portrait of American Journalists and Their Work.*(Urbana, Ill.: University of Illinois Press, 1976).

[27] *Aspen Handbook on the Media: 1977-79 Edition* (New York: Praeger Publishers, 1977), pp. v and vi.

[28] Dennis, *op. cit.,* p. 31.

[29] See Christine L. Ogan and Gretchen M. Letterman, *Report and Evaluation: Conference on Women in Newspaper Management* (Bloomington, Ind.: School

of Journalism and Center for New Communications, Indiana University, 1977); David H. Weaver, Christine L. Ogan, Charlene J. Brown, and Mary I. Benedict, "Women in Newspaper Management: A Status Report," *Center for New Communications Research Report No. 2* (Bloomington, Ind.: School of Journalism and Center for New Communications, Indiana University, 1977); Susan Holly, "Women in Weekly Newspaper Management," *Center for New Communications Research Report No. 3*, 1978; and Christine L. Ogan and David H. Weaver, "Women in Newspaper Management: A Contradiction in Terms?" *Newspaper Research Journal*, 1:42-53 (April 1979).

[30] For a readable and concise explanation of the relevance of mass communication uses and effects research to working journalists, see Maxwell E. McCombs and Lee B. Becker, *Using Mass Communication Theory* (Englewood Cliffs, N.J.: Prentice-Hall, 1979).

[31] For major reviews of these programs of research, see George Comstock, Steven Chaffee, Natan Katzman, Maxwell McCombs, and Donald Roberts, *Television and Human Behavior* (New York: Columbia University Press, 1978); Steven H. Chaffee, Ed., *Political Communication* (Beverly Hills, California: Sage, 1975); Sidney Kraus and Dennis Davis, *The Effects of Mass Communication on Political Behavior* (University Park: Pennsylvania State University Press, 1976); Everett M. Rogers, "Communication and Development: Critical Perspectives," *Communication Research*, 3:99-240 (April 1976); John P. Robinson, "Mass Communication and Information Diffusion," in F. Gerald Kline and Phillip J. Tichenor, Eds., *Current Perspectives in Mass Communication Research* (Beverly Hills, California: Sage, 1972); and Donald L. Shaw and Maxwell E. McCombs, *The Emergence of American Political Issues: The Agenda-Setting Function of the Press* (St. Paul, Minn.: West, 1977).

[32] See ANPA News Research Reports and *News Research for Better Newspapers*, Volumes 1-7 (Washington, D.C.: American Newspaper Publishers Association, 1964-1979); and Jay G. Blumler and Elihu Katz, Eds., *The Uses of Mass Communications: Current Perspectives on Gratifications Research* (Beverly Hills, California: Sage, 1974).

[33] For a review of much of the coorientation research, see Steven H. Chaffee and Jack M. McLeod, Eds., "Interpersonal Perception and Communication," *American Behavioral Scientist*, 16:463-606 (March/April 1973).

7

COMMENTS ON
THE WEAVER-GRAY PAPER

James W. Carey

While I agree with many of the conclusions of the Weaver-Gray paper, I do have sharp and significant disagreements with the authors' argument. While the paper is a piece of historical analysis, it is part of a contemporary project. The implicit project it seems to me is to (a) wed journalism schools more closely to the profession and (b) enhance the likelihood of the funding of journalism research. In turn this project is embedded in a particular view of the history of journalism education and research. It sees the relevant history as the story of the growth of a professional class of journalists along with the apparatus of education and research which has supported the emergence of that class. In short, the view of history in the paper is the same as the end the paper wishes to foster. I do not wish to disagree with the project as such, though I have significant reservations about it, but I do not think the version of history offered in its name is a particularly usable or accurate one.

There is a partial truth to the argument that little research was done on journalism or mass communication research prior to modern times. The priorities of research rarely match the priorities of politics and society. For every article on the economics of the defense budget there are a thousand on the economics of the small firm, but which after all is the shaping force of the modern economy?

However, the truth in the argument which opens and organizes the Weaver-Gray paper is a misleading one. First, if you extend the word research to include scholarship it is not true that journalism and communication have been unstudied until recent times. Much of high intellectual quality has been written from the founding of the republic. Second, if one does a deeper analysis of the inherited tradition, one comes to quite a different view of the development of this scholarship.

It was a useful axiom of John Dewey that scholarship begins at the point that life becomes problematic. It is when something is unsettled, unclear, troubling that we turn our intellectual passions upon it. Journalism and communication were not troubling or problematic phenomena in the United States until after the Civil War except at one point—the problem of freedom. For most of our early history, ideas about the press, language, and communication were grounded in certain liberal and utilitarian assumptions that were relatively unquestioned. These were assumptions concerning the nature of human rationality, the ends of human action, the power of the marketplace of ideas, the nature of individual expression, the efficacy of a free market economy. The point of intellectual puzzlement and paradox in this tradition largely centered on the question of human freedom: what it was, how it was secured, what threatened it. Consequently, our earliest scholarly tradition and some of our most formidable argument surrounded the problem of freedom. Other aspects of the press and communication were not widely investigated because they were not primary nor did they raise troubling intellectual questions. In Germany, on the other hand, where as the old saw goes, the Enlightenment failed to cross the Rhine, liberal assumptions were persistently questioned and the press earlier became an object of systematic study and investigation. German scholarship whether descendent from a materialistic pole through Feuerbach and Marx or from an idealist pole from Kant and Hegel earlier took language, communication, the power of the press as central intellectual concerns.[1] In the period after the Civil War some of these same concerns began to surface in American literature because American scholars in the absence of a homegrown system of graduate education, were increasingly trained in Germany. But the press also came under investigation because developments in the late 19th century increasingly called liberal assumptions into question, increasingly turned the press from a settled institution into a problematic and troubling phenomenon. In one of the best known essays in our literature, Ralph Casey explicitly traced both the intellectual and social concern with the press to the late 19th century forces of industrialization, urbanization and the rise of mass literacy.[2] These movements undercut our received views concerning human rationality, the free marketplace of ideas, and the role of class conflict in the development and control of our institutions. Such movements made a concern with freedom an even more intense issue and also broadened the scope of thought about the press to include many previously unexamined aspects of this institution.

Consequently, cumulative traditions of scholarship on journalism and mass communication emerged in the last quarter of the 19th century. Those early traditions crested with the publication in 1922 of the first modern book exclusively devoted to the problem of what we learned to call "the media," Walter Lippmann's *Public Opinion*. Weaver and Gray's omission of this work is part of their serious underestimate of the amount of scholarly work on journalism and mass communication written prior to the contemporary era.

The early work on mass communication assumed two quite different intellectual and ideological postures, postures that are with us to this day. On the one hand, a tradition emerged in the Middle West late in the century—identified with John Dewey, George Herbert Mead, C. H. Cooley and later Robert Park and W. I. Thomas—that makes communication (not merely journalism or mass communication) the absolute center of scholarly analysis. Methodologically, this scholarship was critical and interpretive and had a normative end: the restoration of democracy, above all of small town democracy. In this tradition the central scholarly question became one of assessing the possibility that the new media, including the mass press, could restore or preserve democratic life. Not surprisingly, this tradition also examined the potential of the new media for destroying the basic conditions of democracy.

Almost simultaneously, a second tradition of research emerged and this one was more scientistic and positivistic. It attempted to examine the new media not in terms of an explicitly democratic ethos but in terms of the effects of the media on human behavior. This tradition itself is older than the Weaver-Gray paper estimates. In the 1890's as the mass press and the new illiterate medium of movies emerged, these forms were of great concern to one particular ideological group, social workers. As social workers assessed the influence of movies, particularly on children, they were explicitly attempting to shield people from what they took to be the baleful influences of modern life and from the social institutions associated with the immigrant class: pool halls, gambling parlors, taverns, street corners, the stage and movie theatres. For these influences they wished to substitute the home, the well-ordered park and playground and the school: places where middle class values and habits could be taught.[3] The concern with communication effects reflected then the desire both to shield people from some influences stemming from some sources and to open people up to alternative forms of social control, particularly to the new professional elites in commerce, politics and the helping professions.[4]

The major point is this: there has not been a cumulative and linear development of mass communication research. Rather there has been constant conflict and interaction of at least two different traditions and research programs; traditions which differ in theoretical assumptions, in method, in conclusions and in the implicit ideological positions they adopt.[5]

One final argument before a summary judgment. At the same time that a "new class" of social workers and other professionals was emerging late in the 19th century, journalists were also coming to constitute themselves as a class, developing professional organizations, creating codes of ethics, institutionalizing professional training in universities. This group, like the other nascent professions, pursued what can be called, not surprisingly, a professional model of knowledge and of history. Consequently, another stream of scholarship on journalism and mass communication was that which developed in interaction with and usually in support of the emergence of this new professional class. Much of the literature Gray and Weaver cite in the areas of history, law and ethics derives from this tradition. Included here are the histories of journalism, analyses of the conditions for the professionalization of the press, studies of the growth of the newspaper into an institution, treatises on the ethics of journalists, and legal treatments of the needs of the profession particularly in the area of First Amendment rights.

I think it is fair to say that the Weaver-Gray essay is a contribution to this professional literature. Its emphasis upon the funding of research (and the neglect of scholarship), its emphasis on the symbiotic relationship of the press and journalism education (and the neglect of the necessary conflict and distance between them), and its emphasis on the more or less single stream development of the literature (and the neglect of sharply differentiated intellectual traditions that make up that literature) reflects the telos of the paper as a whole: to contribute to the increased professionalization of the press, the university and the research tradition. Obviously, I have political differences with these views. However, the main emphasis in these remarks is to suggest that the paper does not contain a compelling and adequate interpretation of the history of this intellectual enterprise and, therefore, is likely to be misleading concerning the future directions scholarship and the funding of it ought to take.

NOTES

[1] For some documentation on this point see Hanno Hardt, *Social Theories of the Press: Early German and American Perspectives*, Beverly Hills: Sage Publications, Inc., 1979.

[2] Ralph Casey, "Communication Channels," in *Propaganda, Communication and Public Opinion*, Bruce Smith, Harold Lasswell and Ralph Casey, eds., Princeton : Princeton University Press, 1946, pp. 4-30.

[3] For a summary of much of the early literature and of the interest of social workers in the new media see Garth Jowett, *Film: The Democratic Art*, Boston: Little, Brown and Company, 1976.

[4] Some among these new elites merely wanted to "help"people; others merely wanted to relieve them of their votes and dollars. These were two wings of the same "new class." Both groups were concerned with the behavioral effects of the media, both advocated the growth of a scientific culture where science and the scientist replaced traditional forms of social control.

[5] Lippmann's classic work, *Public Opinion*, partook of both these traditions. On the one hand it was explicitly interested in preserving democracy in the face of the social changes that had led to and had been manifested in World War I. On the other hand the emphasis in his book on stereotypes gave the analysis an increasingly psychologistic and behavioral emphasis, and his solutions promoted the role of the new scientific elites in building an agency for the dissemination of objective data upon which to create social policy.

8

COMMENTS ON
THE WEAVER-GRAY PAPER

Steven H. Chaffee

Professors Weaver and Gray dealt with three major topics: how research on journalism and mass communicaton has developed historically, how it has been funded, and the paths it should pursue in the future. Their paper is a thoughtful contribution, and deserves comment on all three points.

1. What is the Field, and What Has It Done for Us Lately?

Their historical analysis, while it illuminates some important matters for the first time in print, is flawed in two respects. First, there is a decided lack of consistency in the conception of what the boundaries of the field are. Is it Journalism, or Mass Communication, or simply Communication Research? The scholarly domain starts small, consisting of traditional Journalism in their discussion of pre-1930s research; suddenly expands to include all of Communication in the 1930-50 era; then settles back to a Mass Communication definition in the 1950-present section. Finally, in their conclusions about where the field should go in the future, the authors return to a most narrow conception that centers on the world of the working journalist as the proposed hub of our intellectual concern.

I share with them this central focus on journalism, as a sphere of activity within larger concentric circles of Mass Communication and beyond to Communication in general. But, as I will argue at some length below, I believe they are a bit off-center in their identification of the heart of the target our research should aim at.

My other complaint about the historical presentation is the terribly short shrift given to the last 30 years. However one defines the field, it has grown enormously in this period, and the paper gives little hint of the qualitative innovation that has marked this growth. Instead it focuses on programmatic projects that were outgrowths of the media-effects trends that began in the 1940s. Even within the narrow scope of Journalism schools, a number of very healthy research traditions have built up since our doctoral programs were established in the 1950s. The three most impressive, to my eye, have been in historical, legal, and international research.

Mass communications history has rapidly taken up the procedures of empirical social science. It is not at all uncommon today to find a historian testing a hypothesis (Siebert's Proposition II is a popular one) by systematically gathering large quantities of relevant documentary evidence.[1] This movement toward quantification has led in turn to a vigorous counter-challenge on behalf of "qualitative" research.[2] The result has been a healthy continuing debate and a welcome growth in our comprehension of the societal and cultural role of the press that should not go unremarked.

Similarly, for some of the same scholars are involved, the fast-changing field of mass communication law has grown well beyond the old "Handbook on How to Avoid a Libel Suit" model. The authors of our leading legal textbooks conduct their own original scholarship, using the law library and the *Supreme Court Reporter* as capably as any professor of law.[3] Their research, and that of their doctoral students at schools like Minnesota and Wisconsin, has dug into such topics as privacy, courtroom procedure, regulation of the media, and the emerging concept of knowledge as property.[4] I concur with the call for "fresh legal research" but it needs to be recognized that we already have a number of diligent scholars working toward that end.

International communication studies are expanding in many directions. For some years this area consisted of little more than "airport research," i.e. the description by an itinerant journalism professor of the press system of a country where he happened to be spending a bit of time. But from the publication of *Four Theories of the Press* in 1956, there has developed a strong field of comparative analysis.[5] Two current offshoots of this effort are the empirical study of international news flow, and the massive volume of work on the role of mass communication in the development of Third World nations.[6] The latter can be traced back to studies of the dissemination of agricultural information by our land grant universities, most obviously the landmark work on the diffusion of hybrid seed corn.[7] These lines of research have also stimulated countervailing models, as Third World communication scholars have begun to assert their own position as a substitute for the western concepts that have traditionally been imposed upon their peoples.[8] A developmental concept of the press is emerging that corresponds to none of the "Four Theories" but instead borrows from all four to create a government-media model that is more suitable for struggling new nations.[9]

I mention these current research areas not to make the gratuitous point that Weaver and Gray have failed to include everything in their brief historical rundown; it could not be otherwise. My point is that their concentration on social-behavorial research traditions leads to a picture of much greater divergence between journalistic problems and research activities than is actually the case.

2. Funding: The Love-Hate Relationship

Weaver and Gray have done a thorough job of documenting the relationship between funding and research in mass communication and related social sciences. Their conclusion is that funding sources have led us astray, and I wholeheartedly concur.[10] Agencies seeking evaluation of their communication programs, and the government's preoccupation with television as the root of all manner of social behaviors, have drawn off scholarly energies that could have been more imaginatively and productively applied to the problems of our field as we see them.

I would warn, though, against the inference that what Journalism and Mass Communication needs is funding directed toward a narrow range of professional problems that have been studied less than they deserve. What is most needed is unspecified research support, and it need not be available in large amounts. Many of the most important studies in this field have been conducted at little expense, the scholar's psychic energy and the university's base-level support being the main outlays. Good research ideas grow out of the scholarly process itself; they are rarely developed in foundation offices or by action-oriented commissions, where "media effects" will indeed be the dominant conception to the detriment of all other research topics.

3. The Research Agenda: A Journalistic Paradigm

The underlying theme of Weaver and Gray's analysis is that our research should pursue the basic questions that evolve from our professional devotion to Journalism. Although many of my research colleagues would not agree with this, I do. But I would not concur with the identification of Journalism so directly with the performance of the professional journalist. The continuing concern within our Schools of Journalism is with the role of the press vis-a-vis government in a democratic society. This is what First Amendment research, and comparative "theories" of the press, and the recent revisionist movement in the study of political communication are all about.[11] Historians of Science tell us that only rarely does a field of inquiry undergo a shift in its dominant paradigm, the general framework of assumptions from which its research questions flow. I see reason to hope that we are on the brink of such a shift in mass communication research, which has long been controlled by a persuasional paradigm that inevitably generates questions about "media effects."

A journalistic paradigm would not direct attention to persuasional effects of mass communication at all. The purpose of a free press is not to channel people's attitudes and behaviors in a particular direction, but rather to provide people with information so that they will be able to make intelligent choices among alternative courses of personal and social action. Nowhere is the contrast between the persuasional and the journalistic paradigm so clearcut as in the political realm. Democratic theory assumes that the function of the press is to enlighten the electorate, so that voters can recognize those candidates and policies that most closely accord with their own needs and goals. To accomplish this, the press is left to its own devices on the assumption that various viewpoints will find their way to the public via many competing channels.

Now it is one thing to assume that an uncontrolled press system will serve a democratic society in this way, and quite another to examine empirically our institutions of press and government and their interaction with the populace. In the United States we have, for instance, developed a tradition of political campaigning that includes candidate speeches, press conferences, door-to-door canvassing, buttons and bumper stickers, expensive media advertising campaigns, direct mail solicitation, and reporters who trail candidates around the country, among other institutionalized practices. How well do these procedures work, and are they in need of reform? The kind of answer that is given will depend entirely upon the kind of question asked. The persuasional paradigm would evaluate campaign communication practices in terms of their effectiveness in winning votes, attracting contributions, or otherwise mobilizing political support to one side. But a journalistic paradigm would direct attention instead to "effects" of an informational sort, and to the bases upon which voters were enabled to construct their political decisions.[12]

Democracy is not a particularly popular concept nowadays. No more than one-fourth of the world's nations practice it, and in the United States it stands in some danger of atrophy. The age of television has witnessed a decline in such indicators of political participation as party affiliation, voting, and perceived efficacy.[13] This seems a propitious time to undertake an evaluation of our journalistic institutions in the context of democratic theory. With Weaver and Gray, I see the persuasional-effects paradigm as inappropriate to this purpose. But I also view their stress on the factors that shape the activities of professional journalists as overly narrow. A mobilization of audience-oriented, legal, historical, and comparative research efforts, structured around an explicitly journalistic paradigm such as I have alluded to here, seems very much in order.

NOTES

[1] Examples include Donald L. Shaw and Stephen W. Brauer,"Press Freedom and War Constraints: Case Testing Siebert's Proposition II, "*Journalism Quarterly*, 1969, 46: 243-54; John D. Stevens, "Press and Community Toleration: Wisconsin in World War I," *Journalism Quarterly*, 1969, 46: 255-59. Other hypothesis-testing historical studies are typified by Mary Ann Yodelis, "Who Paid the Piper? Publishing Economics in Boston, 1763-1775," *Journalism Monographs* No. 38, 1975; Maxwell E. McCombs, "Mass Media in the Marketplace," *Journalism Monographs* No. 24, 1972.

[2] One manifestation of this movement is the recent formation of the Qualitative Studies Division in AEJ. See James W. Carey, "The Problem of Journalism History," *Journalism History*, 1974, 1: 3-5 for a brief exposition of this intellectual viewpoint.

[3] Donald M. Gillmor and Jerome A. Barron, *Mass Communication Law: Cases and Comment*, St. Paul: West Publishing, 1974. Harold L. Nelson and Dwight L. Teeter, *Law of Mass Communication*, Mineola, N.Y.: Foundation Press, 1973.

[4] Examples: Don R. Pember, *Privacy and the Press*, Seattle: University of Washington Press, 1972; Everette E. Dennis,"Purloined Information as Property: A New First Amendment Challenge," *Journalism Quarterly*, 1973, 50: 456-62, 474; Chilton Bush, Walter Wilcox, Fred Siebert and George Hough. *Free Press and Fair Trial*, Athens; University of Georgia Press, 1970.

[5] Fred Siebert, Theodore Peterson and Wilbur Schramm, *Four Theories of the Press*, Urbana: University of Illinois Press, 1956.

[6] Wilbur Schramm, *Mass Media and National Development*, Paris: UNESCO, 1964; Daniel Lerner and Wilbur Schramm, *Communication and Change in the Developing Countries*, Honolulu: East-West Center Press, 1967; Herbert I.

Schiller,"Authentic National Development versus the Free Flow of Information and the New Communications Technology," in George Gerbner, Larry Gross and William Melody (eds.), *Communications Technology and Social Policy*, New York: John Wiley, 1973.

[7] Bryce Ryan and Neal Gross, "The Diffusion of Hybrid Seed Corn in Two Iowa Communities," *Rural Sociology*, 1943, 8: 15-24. A compendium of subsequent findings is Everett M. Rogers and Floyd Shoemaker, *Communication of Innovations*, New York: Free Press, 1971.

[8] Everett M. Rogers (ed.), "Communication and Development: Critical Perspectives," *Communication Research*, 1976, Vol. 3 No. 2.

[9] William A. Hachten, personal communication on work in progress.

[10]This was the main point of Chaffee, "Evaluation Research and Communication Theory," head's address to Communication Theory and Methodology Division, AEJ Convention, 1974.

[11] David Swanson, "Political Communication: A Revisionist View Emerges," *Quarterly Journal of Speech*, 1978, 64: 211-32.

[12] An example of application of a journalistic paradigm to "effects" research is Chaffee, "Presidential Debates—Are They Helpful to Voters?," *Communication Monographs*, 1978, 45: 330-45.

[13] Norman Nie, Sidney Verba and John Petrocik, *The Changing American Voter*, Cambridge: Harvard University Press, 1976.

Scholars in our field frequently are either apologetic, perplexed, or ambivalent about the term "mass" in mass communication research. Many, indeed, have charged that the term conveys an elitist bias. Others have seen the term as simply synonomous with "large." John Corner's essay points out the utility of the work in its designation of the kind of communication system our research deals with, as well as getting across the notion that (for the audience) the kind of communication experience mass communication provides is different. Dr. Corner is Lecturer in Mass Communication at the Centre for Communication Studies, University of Liverpool, England.

9

"MASS" IN
COMMUNICATION RESEARCH

John Corner

A defense of the suitability of "mass communication"
as a concept permitting research "capable of
reflecting critically on its own usages and concepts."

Social science has, in the last few years, become a good deal more theoretically anxious and self-critical than it was in the post-war phase of expansion and institutionalization. This increase in uncertainty has been accompanied by a shift in the focus of research from specific social phenomena to the methods and conceptual vocabulary through which the researcher both "knows" and systematically explores such phenomena. Although this change in emphasis can be observed throughout the social sciences, it is perhaps studies of communication, given the nature of the concerns, that are especially susceptible to a critical self-consciousness of discourse.

One concept which has been the subject of this questioning attitude has been the concept of "mass." At the recent setting up of a British Media Studies Association, for example, a strong objection was raised to the inclusion of the term in the constitution, a number of people being in favor of simply using "communication" wherever possible. There are a number of problems attending the discussion of this important concept, and these problems do not always seem to have been either adequately articulated or answered. I should like to consider a few of these "concealed" issues.

> *Dissatisfaction with the term "mass" has*
> *frequently been expressed by cultural historians,*
> *sociologists, and social psychologists.*

Raymond Williams, addressing a London conference called in 1973 to discuss the problems involved in establishing degree courses in communication studies, criticized the notion of "mass" as being misleading and pernicious (11):

> *And so it came about that the study of communications was deeply and almost disastrously deformed by being confidently named as the study of "mass communication". . . .*

Reprinted from "'Mass' in Communication Research" by John Corner in the JOURNAL OF COMMUNICATION 29 (Winter 1979) 26-32. Copyright 1979 by the Annenberg School of Communications.

Williams related the use of the term back to "mass society" theory and argued that the disabling characteristics of such a theory were inevitably transferred in applying the adjective to communication:[1]

> *The mass metaphor overtook us in its weakest meaning of the large ultimate audience, and then positively prevented the analysis of most specific modern communication situations and of most specific modern communication conventions and forms.*

The argument that the term "mass" involves an implicit idea of an undifferentiated, inert aggregate, and thus drastically ignores the varied and specific forms of social interaction is also developed by Robert Escarpit (6), who views the use of the term almost as an "error" in the social perception of the user:

> *The concept of mass thus stems from the inability to define or recognize a workable communication organization in a very large group.*

An almost identical position is held by Herbert Blumer (2) who asserts that "there exists little interaction or exchange of experience between members of the mass" and says of the "proletarian mass" that "they represent a large population with little organisation or effective communication."

Let us examine these positions in closer detail. The arguments which Williams brings to bear (11) against the use of the concept "mass" may be summarized as follows:

1. It unquestioningly inherits the notions concerning large-scale, homogeneous groupings from the mass society theorists.
2. In doing so it also and necessarily assumes that the masses "are inherently stupid, unstable, easily influenced."
3. It limits communication studies to "a few specialized areas like broadcasting and the cinema and what it miscalls popular literature."

[1] A very recent and useful survey by James Carey of some differences between British and American research traditions in communication gives something of a national dimension to the argument by reporting on the Williams lecture with the comment that "Americans have never been able to escape, despite their emphasis on small groups, the bias which the word 'mass' brings to their studies" (4, p. 411).

In subsequent publications, Williams has described mass communications as "a bourgeois concept" (13, p. 136) and, in a detailed commentary on the history of the notion of "masses" itself, sees "massification" as a mode of "disarming or incorporating the working class" (12, p. 163). Escarpit makes a similar point when he argues that the new techniques of diffusion

> are promoted by the dominant class with the hope that the massification of communication would be an excellent way of reinforcing the existing social structure and of counteracting the spread of class consciousness.

It is not my purpose to deal here with these theories of "massification" except to make the rather obvious point that a critique of a social process is not the same as a critique of the concept of it. If "mass communication" is a bourgeois concept, it must be for reasons other than that mass communication systems are, at the moment, largely bourgeois in their strategy—itself a questionable generalization.

> *I do not believe it either inevitable or even usual for*
> *researchers using the term "mass" to suffer*
> *distorted perspectives in the manner Williams describes.*

In short, I am not convinced that the "weakest meaning" of the concept has either overtaken us or prevented our attending to variation and complexity. Despite the shared use of the adjective, it does not follow that mass communication is necessarily a concept only "thinkable" within the social perspective of a mass society theory. Many researchers have employed the term while forwarding arguments grounded in positions ranging from liberal pluralism to the varieties of radical social theory. There is no evidence to suggest that the word exerts some special influence on its users, luring them ever closer to the pronouncements of Ortega y Gassett.

That "mass communications" has often been defined and researched in questionable ways is of course true, but to make this point is rather different from arguing some inherent flaw in the use of the concept itself. Nor has the notion led inevitably to a belief in the passivity and gullibility of audiences; indeed, the "uses and gratifications" approach (3) suggests quite the opposite, stressing audience activity while still retaining the word "mass" in its formulations. Such an example suggests it is simply not the case that, in the words of a British psychologist discussing the issue (1, p. 40),

> [T]he bottom is falling out of the "mass communication" concept as the study of media and their effects begins to take into account the audience's role in the communication process.

Williams' third point, that communication studies have been limited as a result of undue emphasis being placed on the large-scale networks of communication, seems equally overstated. Work on the social conventions and characteristics of speech, writing, nonverbal communication, and visual imagery has in the last decade gone on, unconstrained by mass media inquiry, in a variety of contexts, and has influenced research into mass communications processes where it has been found relevant to examining these specialized modes. There is naturally a vigorous debate among researchers about the nature and extent of the "relevance" in each case, but the huge increase in, for instance, linguistically informed research, bears witness to this influence. So does that work centering on symbolic experience in its analysis of the construction of sociocultural meaning through the media.

The principal arguments raised by media researchers in opposition to the notion of "mass communication" have been, then, (a) a general objection to what has been conceived of as a discredited social theory irredeemably linked to elitist anxieties, and (b) a belief that the specific conventions of meaning which make up a given TV program, newspaper feature or any media artifact cannot adequately be analyzed unless the very notion of "mass" is rejected for something more amenable to specificity and differentiation. Escarpit's formulation of this latter position is given at the end of his article:

> *The result is that the concept of mass is rapidly dissolving to be replaced by the puzzling yet far more workable image of an intricate network of communication channels in which new group-set identities are born year after year with corresponding behavioral patterns and balance of influences.*

It has been my argument that such "replacement" is unnecessary in communication studies except insofar as monolithic notions of "the masses"—an unacceptable shift from adjective to noun—are seen to be presumed by the researcher using the term. And there it is redefinition more than replacement that is required. I want now to discuss those characteristics of mass communication which, I feel, require us to retain the contentious concept while yet recognizing the important connections and parallels with other forms of communicative practice.

> *Many modern researchers have defined and used "mass communication" in such a way as to make it relatively independent of other "mass" concepts.*

One such account of working definitions is offered by George Gerbner (8). All of his considered formulations would appear to escape the censure of both Williams and Escarpit in that they demonstrate a conceptualization quite conscious of the cruder theories of "massification" and one able to handle the complex inter-relations at work in mass communicative practice. According to Gerbner,

> *mass communication is the technologically and institutionally based mass production and distribution of the most broadly shared continuous flow of public messages in industrial societies.*

He refers elsewhere to "mass produced message systems" and a process which goes "beyond the limits of face to face and any other personally mediated interaction." It is this stressing of the productive and distributive characteristics of the process which usefully forestalls the simple interpretation of mass communication as "communicating to *the masses*," a reifying slip from process to people which, once made, leads to the problems described above.[2]

The definition offered by Gerbner is one which rightly makes the adjective "mass" a description of the *communication system* rather than the *audience*. Such a usage importantly differentiates "mass communication" from "mass culture," a notion which is harder to defend in terms of a specifiable process.

A similar approach has been adopted by numerous other researchers, including Phillip Elliott, who concludes his study of production processes in British television (5) with the remark that *"the more mass the media* the more inhibitions are placed on a direct communication process"[3] (my italics).

> *Mass communication is often individually received*
> *by people who negotiate its meanings within*
> *a complex of social and interpersonal relationships.*

But to direct attention to this aspect of mass communication—its parasociality (9)—does not require us to change the name of our area of inquiry, and to admit the existence of widely differing readings of the same program or article does not entail regarding communication through broadcast and publication as just "another form of human communication." There are crucial and specific political and social determinants involved in this process, and also a general structure which makes any analysis a rather different matter from the investigation of primary group behavior or, for that matter, "group-set identities," though both these areas may well be relevant to the research.

One of the central characteristics of mass communication is the paradox between its usual individualized mode of reception and its vast productive and distributive networks, as referred to by Gerbner. It is this feature which seems to escape the notice of those commentators who use the example of the crowd, the congregation, and the public meeting in their search for an explanatory historical perspective for the idea of "mass communication." For the modern technological means of communication did not simply *extend* the possible size of a communicative network, adding ever more rapid distributive methods, but they also radically altered the *experience* of mass communication, linking it, through the personalized styles of television, radio, and newspaper address, to the registers and repertoires of general social discourse.

There is thus something of a disjunction between the social context of mass communication and the communicative register and style employed, since an

---

[2] An early and detailed reassessment of the concept, but one which is, significantly, phrased throughout in terms of "the mass," is provided by Eliot Freidson (7). Freidson interestingly concludes that the "concept of the mass is not accurately applicable to the audience" but that this "in no way questions the usefulness of the concept of the mass for other areas of research."

[3] In a monograph giving an overview of the field, Denis McQuail suggests a rather vulnerable compromise when he notes that "the means of mass communication are so called partly because they are designed for mass reproduction and partly because they are appropriate to communicating with a 'mass'—an internally undifferentiated aggregate of people. . ." (10, p. 165).

informality of address is sustained by a high degree of technical sophistication, professionally assumed roles, and the audience's habitual routines of attention in informal, frequently domestic, settings. The level of integrity of public performance which, say, a "live" speaker is forced to maintain towards a "live" audience," no matter what rhetorical devices may be permitted, breaks down in modern mass communication as the performance itself is assembled and subsequently attended to at discrete moments in the total communicative process. It is in the gap which thus opens up between these moments that the possibilities arise for social inauthenticity, intentional or otherwise.

The parasocial characteristic is the result both of the depth and range of social knowledge drawn upon variously by audiences to "realize" meanings from media output, and the variety of styles, formulae, and techniques which are employed by professional communicators to construct and inflect media texts, performances, and therefore to a greater or lesser extent the social meaning experienced (and "used") by the audience.

Here, the less obviously "voiced" modes of communication, ones offering to "reveal" rather than to "say," are even more important than direct forms of address. One might cite the television mode of dramatized, realist narrative, now widely used well beyond its conventionally fictive origins, both with and without additional commentary. Through a technologically developed repertoire which constructs an apparently ingenuous discourse, this mode strives to place the audience in the position of chance witnesses to "social events."

> *In mass communication the context, a prior social relationship, does not generate an appropriate communicative style; rather, a pre-fabricated communicative style generates and structures a "context."*

One sees Williams' point in stressing the need not to take these socially constitutive styles for granted, but to analyze them in their specific relationships to the primary behavior they affect to reproduce, and then to relate both to political and cultural formations and practices. The second of these tasks is essential, since mass communication systems often involve a vast number of people receiving simultaneously but independently the communications of a very few, with virtually no facility for contemporaneous effective response. The question is very much one of power, as Escarpit notes.

Since the analysis is concerned with the super-imposition and mutual modification of the varied modes of private and public discourse, achieved within the professional media practices of parasociality, mass communication is not amenable exclusively to functionalist or interactionist research. Yet finally the media researcher is primarily concerned with the structuring relationships and processes of mass communication agencies as they contribute to the generation of public meanings, thereby exerting an homogenizing influence both on the experiences and the definitions offered. The crucially totalizing aspect of this process is well indicated by the word "mass."

To conclude, it appears that the discussion of the notion of "mass" in communication research is still plagued by confusions which relate it directly to the theses of mass society theory, theses which are regarded as being far too culturally alarmist and sociologically unsound to support valid offspring. Other researchers, not directly anxious about general social theory, nevertheless feel that a notion of "mass communication" cannot do justice to the complex, highly differentiated nature of the phenomenon it labels.

I have tried to show, in response both to Escarpit's claims and to Williams' expressed fears, that a shift in the naming of the area of study is not required in order for theoretical development and argument to progress. A substantial body of communication research exists which is not crippled and crippling in the ways which, it has been suggested, must follow the use of "mass"; this body of research, moreover, is capable of reflecting critically on its own usages and concepts.

REFERENCES

1. Baggaley, J. "Communicators in Search of a Language." *The Media Reporter* 1(2), 1977.
2. Blumer, H. "The Mass, the Public and Public Opinion." In B. Berelson and M. Janowitz (Eds.) *Reader in Public Opinion and Communication* (second edition). New York: Free Press, 1966, pp. 43–50.
3. Blumler, J. and E. Katz (Eds.) *The Uses of Mass Communication.* Beverly Hills, Cal.: Sage, 1974.
4. Carey, J. "Mass Communication Research and Cultural Studies." In J. Curran (Ed.) *Mass Communication and Society.* London: Edward Arnold, 1977.
5. Elliott, P. "Mass Communication—A Contradiction in Terms." In D. McQuail (Ed.) *Sociology of Mass Communications.* London: Penguin, 1972, pp. 239–258.
6. Escarpit, R. "The Concept of Mass." *Journal of Communication* 27(2), Spring 1977, pp. 44–47.
7. Freidson, E. "Communications Research and the Concept of the Mass." *American Sociological Review* 18(3), 1953, pp. 313–317.
8. Gerbner, G. "Mass Media and Human Communication Theory." In F. E. X. Dance (Ed.) *Human Communication Theory.* New York: Holt, Rinehart and Winston, 1967, pp. 40–57.
9. Horton, D. and R. Wohl. "Mass Communication and Para-social Interaction." *Psychiatry* 19, 1956, pp. 215–229.
10. McQuail, D. *Communication.* London: Longman, 1975.
11. Williams, R. "The Hardening of an Infant's Arteries." Transcript of lecture given to C.N.A.A. Conference on Communication Studies 1973, in *Times Higher Education Supplement*, London, 7th December 1973. Reprinted as "Communications as Cultural Science" in *Journal of Communication* 24(3), Summer 1974, pp. 17–25.
12. Williams, R. *Keywords.* London: Fontana, 1976.
13. Williams, R. *Marxism and Literature.* Oxford: University Press, 1977.

Karl Erik Rosengren, a sociologist at the University of Lund, Sweden, and Director of the Swedish Cultural Indicators Project, reviews significant studies on the sociology of knowledge and mass communication in this chapter. Presented to the World Congress of the International Sociological Association at Uppsala, Sweden, in the summer of 1978, this chapter suggests how time series data from the Swedish Cultural Indicators Project will be used to remedy weaknesses Rosengren identifies in much contemporary research.

10

MASS MEDIA AND SOCIAL CHANGE
Some Current Approaches

Karl Erik Rosengren

I. INTRODUCTION

The theme "Mass Media and Social Change" borders on a fairly recent phenomenon in sociology: the social indicators movement. It also belongs to two older research traditions in sociology: the sociology of knowledge and the sociology of mass communications. The latter two traditions have many substantive problems in common, but in actual research they have been rather different. The sociology of knowledge has tended to produce a number of mostly theoretical, not to say speculative, treatises with possibly wide-ranging implications. The sociology of mass communications, on the other hand, has been characterized by a large number of fairly atheoretical, empirical studies of somewhat limited range. Partly identical problems, then, have been attacked in different ways by two research traditions without much mutual contact. Under such circumstances, a confluence of the two traditions may prove rewarding. It may well be that some recent developments within the tradition of social and cultural indicators research may be useful in such an attempt.

In this chapter some empirical studies within the tradition of mass communications research will be regarded in the light of theories and taxonomies drawn from the sociology of knowledge. An ongoing Swedish research program ("Culture Indicators: The Swedish Symbol System 1945-1975") will be presented and some tenative data from the program will be discussed, with a view to a possible confluence between the sociology of knowledge and the sociology of mass communications in terms of social and cultural indicators research.

From Karl Erik Rosengren, "Mass Media and Social Change: Some Current Approaches," original manuscript.

II. STUDIES OF SOCIOLOGY OF KNOWLEDGE

The question whether the mass media are agents of change or reinforcers of status quo cannot be answered in a general way. It could always be said, of course, that some mass media under some conditions may function as agents of some change, while other media under other conditions may function as reinforcers of some sort of status quo. But in order to answer the question in a more meaningful way, it must be broken down into more meaningful units, specified with respect to type of media and media content, type and sector of society, type and area of change and status quo, and so on.

Perhaps the first thing is to realize that the question about media as agents of social change or status quo is a special case of the old question of the relationship between culture and social structure. This, of course, is a question highly relevant to a Marxian view (base-superstructure, etc.). However, within the Marxian or marxisant tradition(s) few empirical investigations have actually been carried out in this area (see Williams, 1973; Murdock and Golding, 1977). On the other hand, wittingly or unwittingly, an almost Marxian way of looking at these matters is not alien to much research going on within what is usually considered a non-Marxian context (see sections III and IV below).

Peterson (1976) finds three types of relationships between culture and society, each with its proponents in the literature: cultural autonomy, culture creates social structure (idealism), and social structure creates culture (materialism). But there is at least one other obvious alternative to these three types: interdependence between culture and social structure (see Figure 1). Probably interdependence has more proponents today than has any of the three alternatives discussed by Peterson (1976). An eminent spokesman for an autonomy alternative is Bell (1976). It may well be that in coming years the discussion will concern the axis interdependence-autonomy rather than the axis materialism-idealism; and that it will be moving from a holistic, overall perspective to a more differentiated one. (For an excellent overview of related problems in the sociology of knowledge, see Eriksson, 1975.)

Central to culture is the notion of value. Meddin (1975) tries to create a typology of values, in terms of three "co-ordinates":

Level of abstraction (in descending order: value orientation, value, attitude, opinion)

Type of sub-component (cognitive: existential and evaluative beliefs; affective: sentiments; conative: action tendency)

Type of value (appetitive, normative).

The three coordinates are not completely independent. For instance, the higher the level of abstraction, the broader the extensions of the evaluative and existential beliefs. Appetitive values are hard to conceive at the highest level of abstraction. Thus, the level of abstraction seems to be more basic than the other two coordinates.

Social Structure Influences Culture

		Yes	No
	Yes	Interdependence	Idealism
Culture Influences Social Structure			
		Materialism	Autonomy

Figure 1: Four Types of Relationship Between Culture and Social Structure

Values change in different ways. Rescher (1969) created a preliminary typology—or rather, a list—of different types of value change (redistribution, deemphasis, rescaling, and so on). He has also discussed some ways in which value change can come about in a society (such as change of information, political change, and economic-technological change). Related to such substantive distinctions between types of value change and their causes are the familiar distinctions used by economists: short-term fluctuations, cycles, and trends— concepts which have also been used by anthropologists (for instance, Kroeber, 1952). The importance of time, however, has often been neglected when studying the relationship between culture and social structure and between mass media and social change. Depending on the level of abstraction (in Meddin's terms, from value orientations to opinions), values may change on a time scale ranging from millennia over centuries and decades to years or parts of years. "It would be strange indeed if the relations between culture and social structure would be the same under those very different circumstances" (Carlsson et al., 1979).

In studying value change it may also be fruitful to observe two other basic distinctions, namely: "Level of analysis (individuals, groups, institutions, society) [and] Area of change (social conditions; experiences of, and attitudes towards these conditions; standards, norms, goals and values)."

These distinctions, of course, are not original. They are often made, not least in social indicators studies (Zapf, 1975; Vickers, 1973).

Over the years a number o studies within the sociology of mass communication have touched on the question of values at the societal level, investigating the relationship between social structure and values mediated by the media. They have done this at different levels of abstraction (ranging from value orientations to values to attitudes and opinions), treating different types of change in terms of different scales of time (redistribution, deemphasis, rescaling; short-term fluctuations, intermediary cycles, long-term trends), and postulating or finding different types of relationship (cultural autonomy, interdependence, and so on) between culturally defined values and social structure. Let us turn to some examples of such studies.

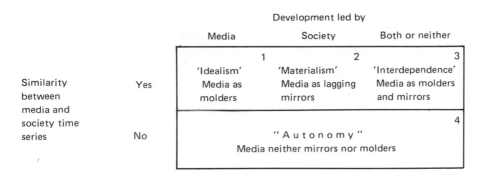

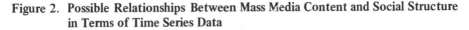

		Development led by		
		Media	Society	Both or neither
		1 'Idealism' Media as molders	**2** 'Materialism' Media as lagging mirrors	**3** 'Interdependence' Media as molders and mirrors
Similarity between media and society time series	Yes			
	No	**4** "A u t o n o m y" Media neither mirrors nor molders		

Figure 2. Possible Relationships Between Mass Media Content and Social Structure in Terms of Time Series Data

Inglis (1938). Comparing for the USA of periods 1900-1910, 1911-1920 and 1921-1930 the proportion of gainfuly employed women in fact and fiction, she found a tendency of fiction to reflect societal reality. However, fiction was also found to reflect the values rather than the facts of American life (although no independent measures of these values were given).

In a recent paper Lazer and Dier (1978) compared the occupational distribution of men and women in magazine short stories with U.S. Census Bureau figures for 1940, 1950, 1960, and 1970. Coupling their results with those of Inglis, the authors conclude that "the proportion of women working in fiction seem not to have changed very much since the turn of the century." Since the actual employment has risen substantially, "there must be an ever-widening discrepancy between the actual work experience of women and the portrayal of this experience" (1978: 180). (In terms of Figures 1 and 2: autonomy.) Yet, the final conclusion of the authors is that fiction influences society all the same: "The undesirability of work for women is the louder message" (1978: 181). As the authors themselves pointed out, however, in spite of that message the proportion of women actually gainfully employed *has* risen, but not so much, perhaps, as it would have done without the message of the media. A loud message, maybe, but is it effective or ineffective?

Middleton (1960) looked into American fertility during the years 1916, 1936, and 1956, finding a U-formed development in both fact and fiction, which points to cell 3 in Figure 2: interdependence.

In a study of crime, mass media reports of crime, and public perceptions of crime in Colorado during the period 1948-1950, Davis (1952) found indications that public perceptions reflected crime news rather than actual crime rates, while crime rates and crime news varied independently of each other (autonomy in terms of Figure 2). Funkhouser (1973) also found autonomy: no relationship between actual societal problems as rendered in official statistics, and the like

III. STUDIES OF THE SOCIOLOGY OF
MASS COMMUNICATION

In order to study the relationship between social structure and values mediated by the mass media, ideally one should have access to at least two, preferably three or four, sets of data. Data about the social structure and data about the value system mediated by the mass media represent the minimum demand. In order to get a better picture of the relationship under study, one should also have data about the values entertained by the population. Better still, one should also have data about the values of the producers and controllers of the media content. Finally, time series of these four types of data are to be preferred to cross-sectional data.

To the best of my knowledge, there is at present no study, completed or in process, based on time series of the four sets of data ideally needed to study the relationship between social structure and values mediated by the mass media. In fact, many value studies within the sociology of mass communication are limited to media data only, often cross-sectional or taken from two or three points or periods of time. In this section, only some typical examples will be given.

In an interesting cross-sectional study, Hubbard et al. (1975) studied not only about social problems presented in the media and public conceptions of these problems, but also official statistics about the same problems. Their results suggest that, especially in the emergence phase of a social problem, the news media may play a role in shaping conceptions of the *importance* of the problem. Public beliefs of the *prevalence* of the problem, on the other hand, parallel agency statistics, presumably because to some extent both are the products of the general culture of the society. (One wonders, though, why the news media should not be shaped by the same general culture of society.)

Hubbard et al. (1975) stress that the ideal test of hypotheses about the relationship between society and the mass media would entail a longitudinal design. Only such a design can really decide whether the media are mirrors or molders of society. A minimum design for such a longitudinal study of the relationship between the mass media and social structure would include time series data about media content and social structure. In case of some sort of similarity between the two time series (which, of course, can be measured in a number of more or less sophisticated ways), the question of the media as mirrors or molders could then be decided by relating the two time series to each other, in the simplest case just seeing which one leads the development. Figure 2 illustrates four theoretically possible outcomes of such a study (compare Figure 1 above).

Cell 4 implies that media are neither molders nor mirrors; cell 3, that media are both molders and mirrors; cell 1 represents the molder case. In cell 2, media mirror societal development, but with a lag.

Very few empirical studies of the interplay of mass media and society have been organized along the lines just discussed. An early example of such a study is and media coverage of the same problems (Vietnam, inflation, crime and so on) while the public's estimation of the general importance of issues was strongly related to the corresponding amount of coverage in the media during the time period under study (1964-1970). Jones (1976) also found no correspondence between crime rates and crime reports 1969-1973, while Antunes and Hurly (1977) even found negative correlations between types of actual crime and media reports about these types.

In a recent study of American crime in reality, in news media, in fantasy media content, and in public perceptions, Towers (1977), using a combination of time series data, analysis of variance, and factor analysis, found support for the hypothesis that public perceptions of crime as a social difficulty was related to real crime rates, and also that crime in news media reports was related to perceptions of crime as an issue, while fantasy crime showed no tendency to increase public perception of crime as a problem. He also found, however, a somewhat different relationship during different subperiods of the time period of his study (1964-1973).

Carlsson et al. (1979) studied the interplay between changes in economic conditions, media content, and political opinion in Sweden during the years 1967-1974. Their basic data were fetched from labor statistics, content analysis of editorials in a representative sample of the Swedish press, and political polls. The media did not stand out as mere mediators or reinforcers of influences stemming from other sources; they seem to have exercised an influence of their own on the political opinions of the population.

Shaw (1967) demonstrated that a specific change in the technical infrastructure of the mass media had reverberations on the content offered by the media. The introduction of the telegraph in the 1860s led to a marked decrease in value judgments in presidential campaign reporting of Wisconsin dailies from 1852 to 1916, since the dailies increasingly relied on the wired news of news agencies, sold to newspapers of different party affiliation. (In terms of Figures 1 and 2: a case of materialism.) Shaw's paper is interesting precisely because it relates data about the technical structure of society (introduction of telegraph) to data about media content (presidential reporting), and because it is so obvious that in this case changes in social structure must have caused changes in the media content, rather than the other way around. Often, as we have just seen, we do not have such clear-cut cases.

Half a dozen longitudinal studies, then, published during a period of no less than 40 years give only inconclusive, partly even contradictory evidence about the relationship between social structure; societal values as mediated by the mass media; and values, attitudes, and opinions among the public. There are many reasons for this, but three stand out as especially important:

(1) The piecemeal, ad hoc nature of the research in the area.
(2) The relatively short time series of mainly secondary data used.
(3) The lack of conceptual and empirical percision.

One way toward increased cumulativity in the field may be the establishment of common data bases of one sort or another, a solution advocated and exemplified, for instance, by Janowitz (1976) and Beniger (1978). In some research traditions important steps have been taken toward increased cumulativity by means of a common theoretical and/or methodological framework. For instance (in mainly cross-sectional studies), the "agenda setting" research tradition has been investigating the relationship between topics, attitudes, and opinions of the mass media and topics and attitudes of the public (see for instance, McCombs, 1976; Palmgreen and Clarke, 1977). Much the same relationship has been studied in an innovative way (including time series data) by Noelle-Neumann and her group (Noelle-Neumann, 1977), while O'Gorman and others attacked the area from the vantage point of pluralistic ignorance theory (O'Gorman and Garry, 1977, see Fields and Schuman, 1976). These approaches represent important steps in clarifying the societal role of the mass media, each in its way highlighting the intricate interplay between the media and their public, obviously a most important part of the total relationship between mass media and society.

If the example of these and similar research traditions could be emulated in sustained, possibly coordinated, theoretical and methodological efforts to create reasonably long time series of relevant social and cultural indicators, some weaknesses of prior research in the area could probably be overcome. Thus, we could hope gradually to arrive at a better understanding of the intricate relationship between social structure and culture as mediated by the mass media.

IV. SOCIAL AND CULTURAL
INDICATORS RESEARCH

Economic indicators have been around for centuries. The social indicators movement stems at least from the '30s, had a breakthrough around 1966, and is still very vital (see, for instance, the journal *Social Indicators Research*). Cultural indicators research has a less impressive record, but just as it has proved mandatory to establish indicators of a host of shifting social phenomena, it is also mandatory to create reliable and valid quantitative indicators of various cultural phenomena, such as values, opinions, and beliefs. Work along these and related lines is going on in several groups belonging to different research traditions.

The efforts of the groups around David McClelland and J. W. Atkinson represent an ambitious attempt at relating cultural, sociopsychological and politicoeconomic phenomena to each other (see, for instance, McClelland, 1975, and Atkinson, 1977). Changes in motivational factors within a nation—primarily the needs for achievement, power, and affiliation—are seen as somehow causing changes in the social structure of that nation, as well as changes in its relations to other nations, sometimes slowly (over centuries), sometimes dramatically (through wars). Two complexes of problems connected with the Mc-

Clelland and Atkinson approach seem to need further clarification: first, the relationship between individual needs of achievement, power, and affiliation and societal constellations of such motivational factors; and second, the relationship between such constellations and the overall value system of society. The size and complexity of these problem areas tell us something about the enormous difficulties connected with the whole complex relationship between cultural and societal change.

Based on the General Inquirer approach (Stone et al., 1966), the Lasswell value dictionary (Namenwirth and Lasswell, 1970) has been used in studies of changes in the American value system as manifested in American party platforms from 1844 to 1964 (Namenwirth, 1973; Namenwirth and Bibbee, 1976). Namenwirth finds long-term and short-term cycles in the value system. The long-term cycles (some 150 years) are supposed to result from sequential changes among four dominant clusters of Parsonian values (expressive, adaptive, instrumental, and integrative values), while the short-term cycles (some 50 years) presumably have to do with long waves of contraction and expansion in the economy. Regardless of the validity of these hypotheses, the Lasswell value dictionary, applied to mass media material and linked with relevant social indicators, would probably be highly relevant to the theme of mass media as agents of change or reinforcers of status quo. In its present form it cannot, however, be used directly to measure value constellations within the public.

Milton Rokeach has created an instrument especially for the standardized measurement of values and value change in the population, by means of which it is possible routinely to check the current value constellations, in a way similar to traditional polling procedures (Rokeach, 1973). Measurements for the period 1968-1971 are at hand (Rokeach, 1971). The measuring instrument is based on a typology of values encompassing 18 terminal and 18 instrumental values. Especially important among the former are the values of freedom and equality. A recent content analysis supported Rokeach's contention that these values can be used to characterize parsimoniously such ideologies as communism, socialism, liberalism, and facism (Rous and Lee, 1978). Content analyses of this type, of course, could be used to study mass media content from historical time periods, and such content analyses in combination with continued Rokeachian "value polls" could be used to throw further light on the interplay between the mass media and their public.

In his important research on cultural indicators, George Gerbner—the originator of the term "cultural indicators"—has been interested in mass media content as related both to social structure and to values and opinions of the public. He has also made the connection from the public's values back to social structure (Gerbner, 1970; Gerbner and Gross, 1976a, 1976b; Doob and Macdonald, 1979). Gerbner expresses the relationship between social structure and media content in almost Marxian terms:

> The cultural transformation of our time stems from the extension of the industrial-technological revolution into the sphere of message-production. The mass production and rapid distribution of messages create new symbolic environments

that reflect the structure and functions of the institutions that transmit them. [Gerbner, 1970: 69].

In the same context he also outlines the notion of cultural indicators and their usefulness:

> Informed policy-making and the valid interpretation of social behavior require systematic indicators of the prevailing climate of the changing symbolic environment. A central aspect of cultural indicators would be the periodic analysis of trends in the composition and structure of message systems cultivating conceptions of life relevant to socialization and public policy [Gerbner, 1970: 69].

Gerbner has applied this basic idea primarily to violence on TV, connecting measurements of the amount of TV violence with actual violence and with people's perceptions of actual violence. He thus shows that a high amount of TV violence consumed tends to lead to exaggerated beliefs about the actual amount of violence in society. Such distorted beliefs, Gerbner maintains, may ultimately prepare the way for a less democratic society than the present one.

It is obvious that this technique could have wide applications, and actually Gerbner's instrumentarium covers a broad field of sociocultural phenomena.

V. THE SWEDISH CULTURAL INDICATORS RESEARCH PROGRAM

With some important exceptions, the studies of mass communications referred to offer only scattered, inconclusive, and partly contradictory results. One way out of this melancholy state of affairs may be to apply distinctions, such as those presented in section II, to the empirical study of the relationship between the mass media and society. That would be the way of theoretical analysis. Along these lines it could fairly easily be shown, for instance, that at least part of the inconclusive and contradictory results referred to in section III may result from the simple fact that the changes of the value system have been approached at different levels of abstraction, with different time perspectives and different areas of change in mind. Another way may be to develop mutually relevant social and cultural indicators and apply them to reasonably long periods of time. That would be the way of methodology and empirical work. Such work could find a platform in the different research traditions mentioned in section IV, not least, perhaps, in Gerbner's cultural indicators research.

All this, of course, is rather easily said but not so easily done. However, somewhere a start must be made.

In Sweden, an interdisciplinary research program "Cultural Indicators: The Swedish Symbol System, 1945-1975," has been underway for about three years, and is to continue for at least another year. The aim is to develop cultural indicators for different areas of postwar Swedish society: to construct standardized instruments for measuring various aspects of the cultural climate as manifested in the symbol system of the mass media. The program is organized as a number of independent but coordinated subprojects, each led by a qualified specialist in the area. the initiator and coordinator of the program is the present writer. The program at present consists of the five following subprojects: domestic politics, foreign policy, religion, advertising, and literature. Each subproject is to deliver a number of cultural indicators time series to a common pool. The objective is ultimately to relate the various time series to each other and to other relevant time series (economic, social, and political), thus creating a coherent picture of the interplay between society and various sectors of culture mediated by the mass media of postwar Sweden. A series of reports from the subprojects will be published in 1979-1980 (the first of these reports is in press: Goldmann, 1979). A summarizing and synthesizing report will appear in 1980-1981.

While there are certainly many ways to tackle the problem of mass media and social change, the research program just outlined has at least one advantage compared with the research referred to in section III. It will be based on a number of fairly long time series of social and cultural indicators, relating to the same time period of the same society: postwar Sweden. Thus, there will be at least a possibility of escaping from the ad-hoc-ness of much of the research in the area. At the same time, the different time series from different sectors of society, relating to values at different levels of abstraction, will make it possible (and necessary) to study empirically some of the theoretical distinctions referred to in section II (level of abstraction, type and period of change, and so on).

As the data collection phase of the program is just now being finished, no definitive data can be offered as yet. However, Dr. Per Block, at the University of Lund, who is responsible for the subproject on religion in postwar Sweden, has some preliminary data relating to the phenomenon of secularization. They are presented here as an example of the many different time series that will be produced in the program. A short presentation of the background is necessary.

In Sweden, the deaths of most people are publicly announced by means of a paid advertisement in daily newspapers. These often contain a short poem or a religious sentence. Dr. Block content analyzed such announcements, regarding the presence or absence of a religious sentence in the advertisement as an indicator of religiosity or lack of religiosity. The data obtained from five leading Swedish newspapers from 1945-1975, suggest a fairly clear-cut trend of secularization, in that the proportion of religious sentences is more or less continually declining.

When more data are in, we will be able to relate this trend of secularization among the general public with parallel data on religion in more specific strata of society, visible in other parts of the newspapers. Preliminary data already at hand suggest that, at least among some critics and reviewers, there may have been something of a peak of religious interests in the 1950s. The later type of material, then, seems to vary in a way different from the decline in obituaries containing religious references. In order to understand such differential developments it seems necessary to apply some of the distinctions from section II. Because the different types of value change probably operate on quite different time scales (trends versus cycles), an ad hoc comparison between religious materials in the media and in other parts of society would have run a certain risk of drawing rather misleading conclusions, especially if it were limiting itself to a shorter period of time.

The ultimate aim of the program, however, is to relate value changes within different sectors of society (religion, advertising, literature and so on) to each other, to general and sector-specific changes in the social structure, and to impulses from outside Sweden. Especially interesting in this connection is the change in the cultural climate often being said to have taken place during the 1960s. Was there really an almost paradigmatic change, as many have contended, or was the change only taking place in more superficial layers of culture? If there was a change, where did it begin, in culture or social structure? In which sector of society? Which role did impulses from the outside play? The last question is not the least interesting one, for it suggests a radically different answer to the question of the relationship between society and the mass media.

Social structure and culture mediated through the mass media may change simultaneously, but the covariation may be due to common impulses from the outside. Reliable and valid measures of international tension, and of the international political structure, are available (Goldmann, 1974; Goldmann and Lagerkranz, 1977; Goldmann, 1979). In the foreign policy subproject, corresponding indicators from the Swedish debates on foreign policy are under construction. It seems reasonable to assume that this type of indicator may have relevance to other sectors of Swedish society as well. It may well be that at least some of the covariation between social structure and culture mediated by the mass media can be explained by such external impulses. If so, that would be an example of how the old problem of mass media and social change may be attacked from new angles by means of social and cultural indicators applied to both national and international phenomena.

REFERENCES

ANTUNES, G. E. and P. A. HURLY (1977) "The representation of criminal events in Houston's two daily newspapers." *Journalism Quarterly* 54:756-760.

ATKINSON, J. W. (1977) "Motivation for achievement," in T. Blass (ed.) Personality Variables in Social Behavior. New York: John Wiley.

BELL, D. (1976) The Cultural Contradiction of Capitalism. London: Heinemann.

BENIGER, J. R. (1978) "Media content as social indicators. The Greenfield Index of agenda-setting." *Communication Research* 5:437-453.

CARLSSON, G., A. DAHLBERG, and K. E. ROSENGREN (1979) "Mass media content, political opinions and social change. The case of Sweden, 1967-1974." Presented to the Nordic Symposium on Content Analysis, Rättvik, March 14-16, 1979. Stockholm and Lund: Depts. of Sociology. (mimeo)

DAVIS, F. J. (1952) "Crime news in Colorado newspapers." *American Journal of Sociology* 57: 325-330.

DOOB, A. N. and G. E. MacDONALD (1979) "Television viewing and fear of victimization: Is the relationship causal?" *Journal of Personality and Social Psychology* 37:170-179.

ERIKSSON, B. (1975) Problems of an Empirical Sociology of Knowledge. Uppsala: Almqvist & Wiksell.

FIELDS, J. M. and H. SCHUMAN (1976) "Public belief about the beliefs of the public." *The Public Opinion Quarterly* 40:427-448.

FUNKHOUSER, G. R. (1973) "The issues of the sixties: An exploratory study in the dynamics of public opinion." *The Public Opinion Quarterly* 37:62-75.

GERBNER, G. (1970) "Cultural indicators." *The Annals of the American Academy of Political and Social Science* 388:69-81.

GERBNER, G. and L. GROSS (1976a) "Living with television: The violence profile." *Journal of Communication* 26:173-199.

GERBNER, G. and L. GROSS (1976b) "The scary world of TV's heavy viewer." *Psychology Today* 9.

GOLDMANN, K. (1974) Tension and Détente in Bipolar Europe. Stockholm: Scandinavian University Books.

GOLDMANN, K. and J. LAGERKRANZ (1977) "Neither tension nor détente: East-west relations in Europe, 1971-1975." *Cooperation and Conflict* 12:251-264.

GOLDMANN, K. (1979) Is My Enemy's Enemy My Friend's Friend? Report No. 1 from the Research Program, "Cultural Indicators: The Symbol System of Sweden, 1945-1975." Lund: Studentlitteratur.

HUBBARD, J.C., M.L. DeFLEUR, and L.B. DeFLEUR (1975) "Mass media influences on public conceptions of social problems." *Social Problems* 23:22-34.

INGLIS, R. A. (1938) "An objective approach to the relationship between fiction and society." *American Sociological Review* 3:526-533.

JANOWITZ, M. (1976) "Content analysis and the study of sociopolitical change." *Journal of Communication* 26:10-21.

JONES, E. T. (1976) "The press as metropolitan monitor." *The Public Opinion Quarterly* 40: 239-244.

KROEBER, A. L. (1952) The Nature of Culture. Chicago: University of Chicago Press.

LAZER, C. and S. DIER (1978) "The labor force in fiction." *Journal of Communication* 28:174-182.

McCLELLAND, D. C. (1977) "Review of Inkeles and Smith, Becoming Modern." *Economic Development and Cultural Change* 25:159-166.

McCLELLAND, D. C. (1975) "Love and power: The psychological signals of war." *Psychology Today* January:45-48.

McCOMBS, M. E. (1976) "Agenda-setting research: A bibliographical essay." *Political Communication Review* 1:1-7.

MEDDIN, J. (1975) "Attitudes, values and related concepts: A system of classification." *Social Science Quarterly* 55:889-900.

MIDDLETON, R. (1960) "Fertility values in American magazine fiction." *The Public Opinion Quarterly* 24:139-142.

MURDOCK, G. and P. GOLDING (1977) "Capitalism, communication and class relations," in J. Curran, M. Gurevitch, and J. Woollacott (eds.) *Mass Communication and Society*. London: Edward Arnold.

NAMENWIRTH, J. Z. (1973) "Wheels of time and the interdependence of value change in America." *Journal of Interdisciplinary History* 3:649-683.

NAMENWIRTH, J. Z. and R. C. BIBBEE (1976) "Change within or of the system: An example from the history of American values." *Quality and Quantity* 10:145-164.

NAMENWIRTH, J. Z. and H. D. LASSWELL (1970) *The Changing Language of American Values*. Beverly Hills: Sage.

NOELLE-NEUMANN,E. (1977) "Turbulences in the climate of opinion: Methodological applications of the spiral of silence theory." *The Public Opinion Quarterly* 41:143-158.

O'GORMAN, H. J. and S. L. GARRY (1977) "Pluralistic ignorance—A replication and extension." *The Public Opinion Quarterly* 41:449-458.

PALMGREEN, P. and P. CLARKE (1977) "Agenda-setting with local and national issues." *Communication Research* 4:435-452.

PETERSON, R. A. (1976) "The production of culture." *American Behavioral Scientist* 19:669-684.

ROKEACH, M. (1973) The Nature of Human Values. New York: Free Press.

ROKEACH, M. (1974) "Change and stability in American values systems 1968-1971." *The Public Opinion Quarterly* 38:222-238.

RESCHER, N. (1969) "What is value change? A framework for research," in K. Baier and N. Rescher (eds.) Values and the Future. New York: Free Press.

ROUS, G. L. and D. E. LEE (1978) "Freedom and equality: Two values of political orientation." *Journal of Communication* 28:45-51.

SHAW, D. L. (1967) "News bias and the telegraph: A study of historical change." *Journalism Quarterly* 44:3-12, 31.

SMITH, E. V. (1978) "Four issues unique to socio-cultural indicators." *Social Indicators Research* 5:111-120.

STONE, P. J. et al. (1966) The General Inquirer. Cambridge, MA: MIT Press.

TOWERS, W. M. (1977) "Reality, pseudo-reality, and fantasy: The crystalization and reinforcement of crime as an issue 1964-1973." University of Oklahoma. (mimeo)

VICKERS, G. (1973) "Values, norms and policies." *Policy Sciences* 4:103-111.

WILLIAMS, R. (1973) "Base and superstructure in Marxist cultural theory." *New Left Review* 82:3-16..

ZAPF, W. (1975) "Systems of social indicators. Current approaches and problems." *International Social Science Journal* 27:479-498.

PART II

RESEARCH STRATEGIES AND
METHODOLOGY

Long-ignored issues of time as a variable in mass communication research are highlighted in several articles in the *Yearbook*. The lead chapter in this section summarizes the significance and application of time to research design.

The uses and gratifications research approach is thoroughly analyzed in two chapters. The utility of the approach and its pertinence to other research approaches are argued. An analysis of measurement questions and the reliability and validity of gratifications measures are considered.

A critical look at Scandinavian methods of content analysis of news bias is dealt with in the fourth chapter. A synthesis of various analytical approaches to news content is proposed.

The concluding chapter develops a new framework to combine various approaches to the study of mass communication in an institutional setting.

Several of the chapters in this book have pointed to the crucial importance of time in communication research. F. Gerald Kline's wide-ranging summary of how the concept of time has been used, misused, and neglected in our field is a very useful guide to sources and procedures for remedying a major weakness in communication research methodology. Dr. Kline is Director of the School of Journalism and Mass Communication at the University of Minnesota. His work refers to other articles (by Danowski and Cutler, and Krull and Paulson) that are available in the book from which this piece is taken: Paul M. Hirsch, Peter V. Miller, and F. Gerald Kline (eds.) Strategies for Communication Research (Beverly Hills: Sage Publications, 1977).

11

TIME IN COMMUNCATION RESEARCH

F. Gerald Kline

INTRODUCTION

TIME IN HISTORY

TIME HAS A LONG and honorable history. And a controversial one as well. Despite the noble and extended philosophical treatment the study of time has received, our operational assumptions about it remain surprisingly simple. Most of us take for granted the notion that there are different rates of change through time for different objects, topics or outcomes. Yet we only have to eavesdrop on the current discussions about the theory of relativity, quantum theory, and wave mechanics to sense what precarious ground we are on. While the physical scientists often place time at the core of their theoretical debates, among social scientists conceptualizing about time has lagged far behind. It is odd that this should be the case since time surely is as much—or perhaps more— at issue in continuous, dynamic social processes as in the more phlegmatic physical processes.

The inseparability of the consciousness of time from that of change was not readily agreed upon in early periods. As space was difficult to separate conceptually from its concrete state, so time was similarly difficult to separate conceptually from changes and events "taking place" in it. Greek, medieval, and modern philosophy center on the contrast between the timeless realm of Being and the temporal realm of change. Thus for Plato the basic reality belongs to the timeless essence while the temporal realm is that of change. In our contemporary work we find that the concern with "truth" or true knowledge as opposed to mere opinion is the epistemological parallel.

One of the most difficult problems to be faced is the notion of time, and consequently change, being continuous. For the reality of our conceptualization is always linked to the character of the mathematics we bring to bear on the concept. For example, both Berkeley and Leibniz held that time is the order of succession of perceptions and as such it is inseparable from concrete infinite events. Therefore the flow of "empty time" had no meaning. Thus for Berkeley that infinite indivisibility of time and change (in the sense of the calculus) is a fiction since durational instants are not perceptible and therefore not real. Leibniz, however, believed that time and change consisted of ever-perishing instants—divisible ad infinitum.[1]

Developments in philosophy and psychology as to the indivisibility of psychological time and physical time have raised issues that need to be examined. Questions of minimal intervals of time, either physical that coincide with elemental events of nature, or psychological that have to do with the activities or capabilities of a person, need to be raised for future scrutiny. A modest beginning is offered with our discussions of time sampling and choosing a particular model, i.e., a Markov chain model, with particular assumptions that match conceptualizations by the user.

RESEARCH DESIGN CONSIDERATIONS

In chapters that follow this, time will not be considered substantively. There is, however, much in our literature concerned with time as a resource in the sense of its allocation to different activities. Much reliance also has been placed on the amount of time spent (with a particular medium, or talking to another, etc.) as a fundamental measure in communication research. The relative simplicity of "time spent with" as a concept has also made it popular among those who are not specialists. The most obvious, and often inane, example is the repeated use of the statistic of the number of hours a child spends with television compared with the number of hours attending school. Heavy viewers as opposed to light viewers of television is another current example. Of course these statements assume a great deal about the homogeneity of the content in a medium across time as well as the cognitive capabilities of the user.

A more sophisticated use of time spent with the media is found in comparative time budget studies (Szalai, 1973). Here, within time spans or across sites, the effects of different cultures and social structures on time use and displacement are analyzed. However, the implicit notions of time spent with a medium, and homogeneous content in that medium, still remain.

It is seldom in any communication behavior study that the notion of time is explicitly set aside. In a survey design the ordering of variables in the analysis strategy has some kind of time ordering or, if the researcher wants to make statements about relationships between variables without the time ordering, there is usually the underlying notion that the parameter estimates being made are constant over time.

The experimental mode explicitly takes time into account with a before and after measure of the effect of a particular manipulation. Here we find little consideration given to the length of the period before a pre- and a post-test except as it affects the face validity of the design. When dealing with repeated measures experiments (Winer, 1962) time is essential to the designer. There is the occasional situation, however, when the experimenter uses such a design to be efficient (in the pooling of error variance for example) rather than out of concern for the time factor. In any experimental situation the choice of when to measure (see Arundale's chapter) assumes an effect has had time to take place. Or in situations with two or more independent variables the time it takes for each to have their independent, or jointly simultaneous, effect is critical. This is an area not usually dealt with explicitly in most designs.

In approaches that attempt to use nonexperimentally manipulated changes, such as surveys with respondents empaneled for repeated interviewing, we usually see causal interpretations of turnover tables or cross-lagged correlations. As Heise (1970) indicates, the lags between measurement periods must be sufficiently long for effects to take place, all of the lags must have approximately the same time frame, the period in which the measurement is taking place must be shorter than the lag that is assumed to be operating, and the choice of measurement times must be about the same as the lag period. These are stringent constraints that are usually assumed away or, as in most instances, overlooked entirely. Of course the experimental design can be combined with the panel design for a field experimental approach that attempts to take into account more of the threats to validity than either one can separately.

Another approach is to collect, or assemble, series of data over a period of time. Although not fraught with the same number and kinds of assumptions listed above they do need a great deal more data over longer time periods. Krull and Paulson's chapter will deal extensively with this approach.

A variant of the latter approach, in the sense that a number of time points are needed, is the cohort analysis outlined by Danowski and Cutler in the next chapter. Here the age of respondents, a time-related concept, is the focus for assembling the data from cross-section surveys over a number of years. Their approach attempts to simulate the correlation that exists between respondents repeatedly measured in panel surveys or repeated measures experimental design.

Finally, the level of measurement chosen for time-based research designs can be an important factor. If we consider the various measurement periods as a nominal rather than ordinal or interval level of measurement, we are making theoretical decisions that need explication. This will be discussed shortly in greater detail.

APPROACHES TO TIME IN THE STUDY OF SOCIAL CHANGE

Heirich (1964) offers a useful typology of time use in social research. He examines the use of time "as an explanatory factor, a causal link between other variables, a quantitative measure of them and a qualitative measure of their interplay" (p. 386). Let us examine each of these and provide some examples appropriate to communication research.

TIME AS A SOCIAL FACTOR

The first way in which we can conceive of time as a social factor is as a resource that is expendable. The allocation of time to a particular behavior means making some kind of judgment as to the relative worth of competing behaviors. Secondly, attitudes toward time create their own dynamic.

Time as a Resource

There is a finite quantity of time, often thought of as the twenty-four-hour day, that once used is not easily regained. This is one way of classifying the classic time budget study. Thus allocating more time to television and away from certain traditional activities can be conceived of as indexing a major cultural shift across cultures or over time in the same culture. It is such a shift, simply conceived in most instances, that apparently motivates much of the antagonism toward TV.

In the realm of media economics the obvious resource that concerns the analyst is the amount of money a person is willing to spend for a particular product. In many instances, though, the cost of the media product is less of a reason for not purchasing than the lack of time to devote to using it (Becker, 1977). As Heirich notes, however, one must distinguish between relative time allocated and the input-output relationship. Spending less time, as an input activity, with the evening newspaper may not have diminished its importance if the same output of information gain, from reading it, is maintained. If TV use was responsible for such a shift in time away from newspaper reading it will have gained in relative importance. Studies in the elasticity of demand for time spent in different communication behaviors are needed in this field and, if undertaken, would shed light on this general approach to the concept of time in social research.

Some thought also must be given to the way in which time as a social factor is accounted for in different cultures. In certain Asian societies, such as Indonesia, time is not treated as a linear concept but as a circular concept in which the beginning is the end and the end is the beginning. Does the arrival of a fast-paced television program in a culture which does not cherish change for the sake of change meet with the same perceptions as in the producing culture? The exportation of "Anglo-American media" (Tunstall, 1977) to developing nations with potentially varying evaluations of time would certainly warrant investigation for this reason, as well as by those concerned over the impact of "cultural imperialism."

Time as a Social Meaning

A second way in which we can conceive of time as a social factor is through its social meaning. Attitudes toward time can have a dynamic character all their own. Thus Carey and Sims (n.d.) write:

> Looking back over his life from 1907, Henry Adams fixed the precise moment when the United States entered the modern world, the instant of the shift from the old universe of genteel New England to that of industrial America, in 1844: "the opening of the Boston and Albany Railroad; the appearance of the first Cunard steamers in the bay; and the telegraphic message which carried from Baltimore to Washington the news that Henry Clay and James K. Polk were nominated for the Presidency." The points of departure Adams chose to mark the old from the new universe were, significantly, three changes in communications technology.

Of course, one can choose other examples: The period in time when the printing press began to affect those who previously had control over information; the development of the high speed rotary press; the lifting of the FCC's license freeze on TV spectrum allocation in the U.S.; or the launching of the first communication satellite. Here we are dealing with attitudes toward such periods of time, regardless of the truth or falsity of their causal nature, which affect how we view the past. They acquire a social meaning all of their own that has a dynamic in its own right.

The social meaning of time can also be examined in the context of interpersonal communication behavior. Who talked to whom first? This question, having to do with sequence of time in particular behavior, may symbolize social grade, class or authority. Whether the person indexing the behavior is the researcher making a measurement of such a behavior difference, or whether the participants themselves are making the judgment is irrelevant for our purposes. The social meaning can affect subsequent actions. Thus either as a resource, or by having a social meaning, time can be considered as a social factor.

TIME AS A CAUSAL LINK

Since concern with causality is of such importance in theorizing we most often think of time as a way to help establish causal inference. That B follows A in time is not sufficient for the inference that A causes B. It does, if it happens consistently, rule out the reverse situation that B causes A. When one can manipulate postulated causal factor A to determine whether B is absent, there is greater confidence in the inference. There are two main ways, Heirich argues, that theorists have used time as a causal link. The first is when time is used as a setting. The second uses time as a sequence.

Time as a Setting

Temporally bounded structural patterns are often used in causal models as a configuration, either through lack of specific knowledge or inability to specify some part of a sequence operating. Take for example, the patterns found in Table 1. The data, taken from a survey reported by Kline (1972) and Kline et al. (1970), indicate a pattern of relationships for two different age groups. One can see that the pattern of relationships for each age group is quite different. Tension between the family and peers was much higher for young adolescents than for the older ones. It appears that as one progresses through adolescence, independence of both family and TV as sources of information and opinion becomes stronger. For peers and television, the case is reversed. Reliance on the family and on TV portrayals conflict with activities in the peer environment. Treating the three variables together in this fashion allows us to construct a configuration pointing to differential interaction of these socialization sources among time settings.

Evaluating individual events or relationships in relation to their larger pattern is often more useful than viewing them as items independent of setting. Thus the use of time, in this instance age or stage of adolescence, to segregate patterns of interactions is an important function for analysis in social research.

A second example of the configurational approach is the way in which a number of variables go together in a particular pattern at a point in time using factor analysis. Although seldom conceived as a causal model, and even less as time-related, we can view the typical factor analysis equation as follows:

$$z_j = a_{j1}F_1 + a_{j2}F_2 + ... + a_{jm}F_m + d_jU_j \text{ (where } j=1, 2, ..., n)$$

The z's represent sets of intercorrelated variables while the a's and F's represent the loadings and factors extracted. As a causal diagram it would look like Figure 1. We can conceive of factor analysis in terms of causal analysis if we assume no causal links among our indicator variables (z's) and that they are caused by some underlying pattern or factor. This pattern is conceived of as what caused respondents to answer the questions, or undertake the behavior measured by the z's. In the instance of TV independence noted in Table 1, the measure was

TABLE 1

INTERCORRELATIONS OF FAMILY AUTONOMY, PEER AUTONOMY AND TELEVISION INDEPENDENCE FOR TWO AGE COHORTS[2]

	13-14 Year-olds	18-19 Year-olds
Family/Peer	−.45	−.05
Family/TV	+.21	+.38
Peer/TV	−.25	−.44

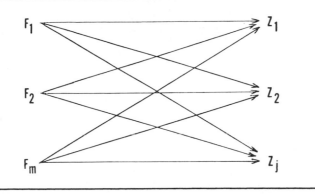

Figure 1.

derived from just such a causally conceived single factor model. Eight questions were administered to the adolescents, intercorrelated and factor analyzed. A one factor solution was derived with the factor loadings ranging from .11 to .57 while the items themselves intercorrelated over a range of −.36 to +.26 (see Kline, 1972, for further details and discussion).

Time as a Sequence

Another way to view time as a causal link is to examine relationships among variables where we can establish the sequence of events. If we have no knowledge about the time ordering of variables, or find that we cannot establish such an ordering, we cannot impute causality. Ordering on the other hand, can assist in this causal inference task.

Suppose we wish to determine whether the playing of a series of public service announcements on rock radio stations caused an awareness among adolescents that there was such a campaign going on. If we can establish the situation where in one location, or among one experimentally defined group, there is the potential to hear such a campaign, and if we can have a comparable group without such a campaign available, we should be able to make a reliable causal inference. Thus the playing of the material would cause those who heard it to discriminate messages while those that did not hear it, would not. Such a causal analysis—three field experiments that took account of the natural setting and the concomitant problems of audience interest, memory, or lack of hearing—was undertaken in Kline, Miller, and Morrison (1974) and Morrison, Kline and Miller (1976). Table 2 displays the data for experiments with messages concerning family planning, drug and alcohol use.

In each instance we had an appropriate design for making the time sequence operate on our behalf for the causal inference. We see the campaign was effective for family planning but had no impact for drugs and alcohol. Speculations

TABLE 2
MEAN CAMPAIGN MESSAGE DISCRIMINATION DIFFERENCES
AS A CONSEQUENCE OF RADIO ANNOUNCEMENT MANIPULATIONS

	Experimental City	Control City
Number of Messages Discriminated for:		
Family Planning	.72(N=90)	.18(N=95)
Drugs	.39(N=114)	.43(N=131)
Alcohol	.45(N=131)	.45(N=114)

concerning this lack of impact can range from the character of the stimulus presentation for each topic to the audience's interest in the topics at hand. For our present purposes this is a reasonable example of the classic causal analysis with a known time sequence. The next two examples will rest their interpretation on an assumed time sequence.

A configurational sequence is an elaboration of our last two examples. If we theorize that when we find A, B and C together we can expect to find D following from that pattern or configuration, we would expect a diagram such as that found in Figure 2. The coefficients shown in Table 3 are causal relationships estimated for young and old adolescents.

In this example it is clear that the family influence is predominant. The more autonomous adolescents are from their families, apparently the less they are socialized to give a positive evaluation of the institutions. The peers play a negligible role in the early period but, at a later age setting, the more one does rely on them, the more negative the institutional evaluation. And reliance on TV, although marginally important in the early teens, becomes negligible later on as a direct effect.[3]

Cycles are another aspect of time sequence that need to be considered. Here we are concerned with how A affects B which in turn affects A at a later time point. The most appropriate way to evaluate this kind of phenomenon is with measurement of the A's and B's at different time points. Krull and Paulson's chapter provides an insight into this issue for time series data.

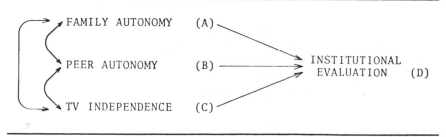

Figure 2.

TABLE 3
ESTIMATED CAUSAL RELATIONSHIPS FOR FAMILY
AUTONOMY, PEER AUTONOMY, AND TV INDEPENDENCE

Link	Age 13-14	Age 18-19
A ────▶ D	−.51 (−.57)	−.33 (−.36)
B ────▶ D	+.01 (−.01)	+.26 (+.21)
C ────▶ D	+.15 (+.15)	+.05 (+.04)
Variance Explained	34%	22%
A = Family Autonomy	C = TV Independence	
B = Peer Autonomy	D = Institutional Evaluation	

NOTE: Numbers in parentheses are understandardized path coefficients that allow comparisons across age groupings. The standardized coefficients with no parentheses should be compared only within age groupings.

Without time series or panel data, however, we are often forced to make certain conceptual assumptions that allow us to generate reciprocal causal parameter estimates using econometric techniques. In such a time-implicit analysis, we made the estimates shown in Figure 3 from data collected for a larger study in Minneapolis and St. Paul (Kline, 1969).

Here we see a mixture of uses of time for causal analysis. The demographics of income, age, education and occupation are all conceived as working together in a time setting, and as antecedent in time to the two dependent variables (in this instance time budget allocations). We postulated cyclical relationship between the use of time for TV viewing and newspaper reading. The finding that changes in TV time use dramatically affect newspaper reading time but not vice-versa needs close examination. And, the larger differences between income and age found in this analysis compared to Kline's earlier study (1969) reflect the greater number of influences controlled for in the latter paper. Although the relationship of the TV measure to that of newspaper time fits with perceptions by newspaper managements, it is only an example of how this kind of modeling can be done and should not be considered as definitive.

TIME AS A QUANTITATIVE RELATIONSHIP

Choosing the most appropriate time scale for the theoretical business at hand has been a neglected area in communication research. The length of time that a particular process operates will be importantly related to the consequences. Choice of time scale will also relate to the hypotheses being generated. If we use minutes, days, months, or years in our approach, such as the interval scale used in the Krull and Paulson chapter, there are quite different implications than if we choose to use a ordinal level of measurement as our time scale. And, as discussed earlier in our section on settings, we may be dealing at a nominal level.

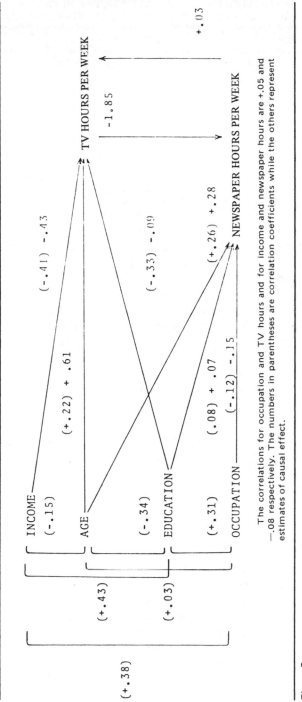

INCOME
(−.15)

AGE
(−.34)

EDUCATION
(+.31)

OCCUPATION

(+.43)

(+.03)

(+.38)

(−.41) −.43

(+.22) + .61

(−.33) −.09

(+.26) + .28

(.08) + .07

(−.12) −.15

TV HOURS PER WEEK

−1.85

+.03

NEWSPAPER HOURS PER WEEK

The correlations for occupation and TV hours and for income and newspaper hours are +.05 and −.08 respectively. The numbers in parentheses are correlation coefficients while the others represent estimates of causal effect.

Figure 3.

There are examples of the interval, ordinal, and nominal levels of time measurement to be found in our contemporary literature. Some obvious examples are diffusion rates across time, conceived of as an interval measure; stages of development such as those found in cognitive development and use of TV content, where time is treated as an ordinal scale; and the use of such time-related terms as stage of development found in comparisons of industrialized and nonindustrialized parts of the world. Let's look briefly at each.

Time as an Interval Level Measurement

Diffusion research (Rogers and Shoemaker, 1971; Deutschmann and Danielson, 1960; Greenberg, 1964) concentrates on the speed with which a practice has been adopted, or a news story has been heard, by a population of interest. For our purpose here we can rely on Figure 4, adapted from Chaffee (1975; 89). The abscissa is plotted in equal intervals of time and the major research concern is the speed with which the particular phenomenon of interest diffuses to the bulk of the population. Using notation found in Bartholomew (1973; 298-299) we can examine the source-stimulation, random, and receiver-constraints models found in Figure 4 as they relate to information diffusion.

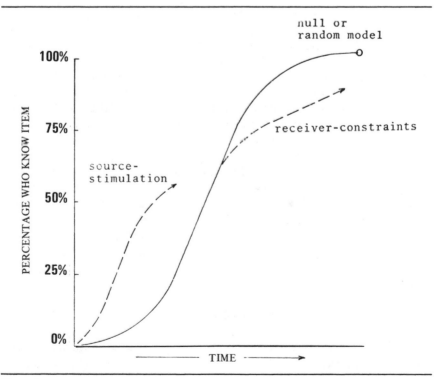

Figure 4.

Let E_s denote the transmission of the information from a source to any given member of the population. Assumed as a random event it would have the probability

$$Pr\ (E_s\ in\ (T,\ T + \Delta T\ )\ ) = \alpha\ \Delta T$$

This is the equivalent of saying the probability of transmission of information, E_s, to a random individual, from the news source, in the time period between T and some small increment of T, ΔT, is equal to the intensity of the source transmission, α, during that short period of time.

And, let us write the probability of the news, E_i, being communicated from one individual to another as

$$Pr\ (E_i\ in\ (T,\ T + \Delta T\ )\ ) = \beta\ \Delta T$$

Thus we can estimate α and β as the intensity of source and interpersonal transmission respectively. When exactly n people have received the information, the system is said to be in state n. We can write the probability of the system moving from state n to state n + 1 as follows:

$$Pr\ (n \rightarrow n + 1\ in\ (\ T,\ T + \Delta T\ )\ ) = \lambda \Delta T$$

For our purposes the system can only move from n to n + 1 so it will be possible to express n in terms of the parameters α and β when the process is complete. As there are N - n persons who have not heard, the contribution to n from the source is $(N - n)\ \alpha\ \Delta T$. The contribution from the interpersonal communication will be $n(N - n)\ \beta\ \Delta T$, for all possible pairs of one "knower" and one "ignorant," and our interpersonal intensity parameter. Combining these results gives us an estimate of λ in terms of α, β and N.

$$\lambda_n = (N - n)\ (\alpha + \beta\ n)$$

Although we have talked of the above as a diffusion process it is directly comparable to a pure stochastic birth process model for a population. And in diffusion, as in birth processes, we are particularly interested in the distribution of n(T), the number of hearers at time T, or in T_n, the time it takes to reach n people. A mathematical expression of n(T) is found in Bartholomew (1973; 300).

$$Pr\ (n(T) = 0\ ) = e^{-\lambda_0 T}$$

Since we can write λ in terms of α, β and N, as indicated above, the problem is solved in principle.

The practical problems of calculating the distribution, even for small N's, is formidable however. Bartholomew (1973; 302-306) shows how making assumptions about large N's can throw light on the process. Although further explication is beyond the scope of this chapter it is worth noting that we can obtain estimates of α, β, T_n, and n(T). T_n is a measure of the *duration* of the news diffusion process, while λ and β play a role in the *rate* process. From Figure 4 we would expect that there would be a different T_n to reach asymptote for each of the curves; α would be relatively larger for a source-stimulation curve, while β would be a more important parameter to examine for the receiver-constraint curve.

The advantage of treating time as an interval level concept as we have done in this example is in being able to pick up on the conceptually powerful notions of *rate* and *duration*. Additionally we can evaluate the *changes in rates* of change, such as those found at the inflections in our curves in Figure 4. To explore why such changes take place when they do, we can look for additional variables, or structural features (c.f. Chaffee, 1975) for a more complete explanation.

Time as an Ordinal Level Measurement

The widespread interest in cognitive development and comprehension of TV programming offers us an opportunity to examine the use of time as an ordinal level of measurement. Following work by Piaget (1954), Ward, Wackman, and Wartella (1977) examine the levels of comprehension of TV advertising by children at different age levels. The use of age in their research is a surrogate for the more ephemeral notions of stages of development in cognitive processing by children. Although age is used as an estimate of the isomorphism between chronological development and cognitive development, it is used as ordinal level measurement. The major premise is that the level of development of a four-year-old is less than, and prior to, the developmental level of a seven-year-old. And, in turn, the seven-year-old's level of development is less advanced than, and prior to, a nine-year-old's.[4] In effect, there is the equivalent of an ordinal scale (Schuessler and Strauss, 1950) underlying the conceptual notion of levels of cognitive development. A child must pass through stages of development that have an ordering and these stages are on a time dimension but are not necessarily equally spaced for all children. These stages have major implications for the cognitive differentiation, specification, and organization of media content.

Time as a Nominal Level Measurement

The debate over the last few decades as to the role of mass media in national development (Rogers, 1976) highlights certain mixed measurement perspectives on time. Some argue (Lerner and Schramm, 1967) for a stages of growth point of view in which stage one (whatever that might be) is a necessary condition for movement to stage two. Others argue (Bendix, 1967; Schramm and Lerner, 1976) that with the rapid development and dissemination of advanced communication technology there are opportunities for nation states to hurdle stages and move to advanced development without the painfully slow transitions from oral to print to electronic based societal information systems. Here we can see that some conceptual schemes would argue that if the stages can be hurdled then time is being treated nominally.

If we wish to argue that the widespread dissemination of advanced communication technology to less advanced parts of the world took place at different points in time than in the rest of the world, then we should be able to examine the mean incidence of media penetration among the population for major differences. Suppose for example we chose those countries that gained their political independence at different time periods. The argument that might support such a conceptual distinction would have to hinge on the cohesive political forces that provide for stable and sustained growth of the communication infrastructure along with the need for such communication to sustain continued stability. A second approach places these countries on a methodologically more attractive ordinal political modernization time scale. Let us examine Table 4a and b to see how the first nominal time measure contrasts with the latter ordinal approach.

The data in Table 4a, taken from Kline, Kent, and Davis (1970) indicate that choice of any of the nominal time periods prior to 1946 would not sustain the notion that the longer the period of political independence the more advanced the infrastructure and thus greater penetration. Rather, it appears that lumping the countries with political independence prior to 1946 and contrasting them with all others in the later time period would capture the relationship sought. The similarity among the first three time periods would seem to indicate that whatever penetration took place, did so independently of early political development. A reasonable guess would be that the countries that gained their independence subsequent to 1945 were former colonies of European nations and thus their lack of independence was correlated with lack of other elements that are necessary for media penetration.

The data in Table 4b show a strong relationship between development, media penetration measures and the ordinal time scale. With the possible exception of radio set use in the early and midtransitional stages it appears that the ordinal approach is quite appropriate. The data, however, are not complete, in the sense of newer communication technology such as TV and satellite developments. We would need that to determine whether the stages can be hurdled. If, for example, early transitional countries could obtain such developments, and support their effective use, whereas some or all of the midtransitional countries could not, we would have to question the ordinal level of our time measure.

This last section has outlined the interval, ordinal, and nominal use of time as

TABLE 4a

AVERAGE MEDIA PENETRATION AND DEVELOPMENT
SCORES BY DATE OF POLITICAL INDEPENDENCE

	Before 19th Century	1800-1913	1914-1945	After 1945
	(N=21)	(N=29)	(N=13)	(N=37)
Literacy	71%	63%	62%	32%
Newspapers	4.7	3.9	4.5	1.8
Radios	2.6	2.4	2.7	1.6
Cinema	3.8	3.5	4.1	2.1
Urbanization	11%	16%	15%	15%

TABLE 4b

AVERAGE MEDIA PENETRATION AND
DEVELOPMENT SCORES BY POLITICAL MODERNIZATION

	Modern	Mid-Transitional	Transitional
	(N=58)	(N=16)	(N=30)
Literacy	72%	46%	27%
Newspapers	4.6	2.8	1.8
Radios	2.6	1.9	1.7
Cinema	3.7	2.9	2.0
Urbanization	17%	12%	9%

a quantitative relationship. Other aspects must be kept in mind when using each of these approaches. Comparisons of rates of change in different cultures raise the question of whether intercultural or cross-polity comparisons will be valid if we do not have an understanding of how time and change are valued. In a society like the U.S., change is often valued for its own sake. Can we expect to find little impact of a particular rate of change in such a society, whereas in a more traditional situation the same rate of change would produce major dislocations? We are a long way from adequately handling such questions at present. To deal with such questions we will have to develop conceptual strategies for dealing with time as a quantitative measure.

TIME AS A QUALITATIVE MEASURE

We must distinguish between social processes and social change. In many instances social processes are part of an equilibrium phase of a stable situation. Tichenor and his colleagues (Donohue, Tichenor, and Olien, forthcoming) represent a school of thought that takes this viewpoint. And Kline (1972) has outlined the way in which this equilibrating process has played a major role in mass communication research theorizing. Social change, on the other hand, implies a qualitative difference as an outcome.

Suppose a person with a particular set of cognitions is confronted with a quite different social context; a situation in which the incoming persuasive messages are powerfully different from ones usually confronted. Heirich (1964: 389) argues that at least four outcomes are possible; suppression, routinization, adaptation or revolution. As the last term is not appropriate for our example a comparable term might be conversion. Let's examine them one at a time.

The literature on selective exposure and acceptance provides some rationale for the way in which incoming messages might be *suppressed*. *Routinization* might allow us to select those portions of the message that seem to fit with preexisting perspectives and thus treat the incoming messages, and perhaps even the producers of the messages, as if they were part of the previous situation. *Adaptation* is the more likely outcome. Here, those parts that could be exchanged for previous cognitions would be accepted with a new organizational outcome as a consequence. Finally, the recipient of the messages might be *converted*. Each of the four alternative outcomes represent a qualitative change of increasing effect.

With the realization that there are varieties of outcomes there must come the awareness of the role time plays. Time is relevant to the interplay of the dimensions already discussed. How long, for example, does the particular set of interacting measures of family and peer autonomy and TV independence remain in equilibrium in early adolescence before shifting to the new equilibrium found later? What set of political modernization characteristics go together during the early and mid-transitional periods and how does media penetration relate to such changes? What are the causal factors that produce qualitative shifts in the diffusion curve asymptote when we treat time as an interval measure? In short, the conjoint relationship between causal linkage and time as a quantitative measure can often be used to describe or explain qualitative outcomes of the process of change. Questions such as these need to be asked as we gain sophistication in handling time in our research conceptualizations and designs.

CONCLUSION

This has been a long and wide-ranging discussion of how the concept of time has been used, abused, and avoided in communication theory and research. Continued calls for process models of both mass and interpersonal communication alert us to inadequacies in our traditional research designs. But making the calls, hearing the calls, and acknowledging them are no excuses for inaction. Historians in our field claim time as their major stock in trade—but as Carey and Sims (n.d.) have pointed out we have a legacy of biographical studies which treat time even more casually than those whose research draws on the cross-sectional, descriptive survey. The experimental tradition inherited from the social psychologists of the 1940s and 1950s used time as a basis for causal imputation but seldom went further to explicate the conceptual question of when post measures are to be taken. Nor has this been addressed in more recent analyses.˙ In recent years there have been a number of attempts to use survey panel designs to examine shifts in communication behavior outcomes, but these suffer from the same kind of conceptual poverty that plagued the earlier laboratory experiments. Choosing the next time class meets, the next election, or when the money for experimental manipulation will run out, are not conceptually appropriate ways of defining when the T_1, T_2, or T_n measures are to be taken.

The following three chapters represent a healthy step in the direction of tackling some of these issues head-on. Each presents an original contribution to the topic of constructing time based designs in communication research.

NOTES

1. I am indebted to Milic Capek's essay on Time in *Dictionary of the History of Ideas.*
2. Family autonomy deals with the self-determination of the child living at home. Peer autonomy is conceived of as the independence an adolescent has vis-à-vis the peer group he or she is embedded in. Both of these concepts were operationalized by a number of items that related to each concept. A factor analysis procedure provided evidence of a simple structure for each concept. Factor scores were then generated for each respondent for each concept. Television independence was conceptualized as the manner in which content viewed on TV was considered real and useful. A similar factor analysis strategy was used to develop respondent scores from a battery of items. A person who is considered TV dependent is one who treats content on television as real and useful for everyday life and relies on it for information.
3. Not shown in this analysis, but reported earlier (Kline, 1972), independence does play a strong indirect role due to the configurational pattern found in late adolescence.
4. Misspecification is possible using this approach where one might find a child who has developed slowly yet placed in a stage category with other children of the same chronological age.

REFERENCES

BARTHOLOMEW, D.J. (1973). Stochastic models for social processes (2nd ed.). London: John Wiley.
BECKER, G. (1977). The economic approach to human behavior. Chicago: University of Chicago Press.
BENDIX, R. (1967). "Tradition and modernity reconsidered." Comparative Studies in Society and History, 9 (April): 292-346.
CAPEK, M. (1973). "Time." Pp. 389-398 in Dictionary of the history of ideas. New York: Charles Scribner.

CAREY, J.W., and SIMS, N. (n.d.). The telegraph and the news report. Unpublished manuscript from the Institute of Communications Research, University of Illinois.

CHAFFEE, S.H. (1975). "The diffusion of information." In S.H. Chaffee (ed.), Political communication: Issues and strategies for research. Beverly Hills, Calif.: Sage.

DEUTSCHMANN, P.J., and DANIELSON, W.A. (1960). "Diffusion of knowledge of the major news story." Journalism Quarterly, 37(summer):345-355.

DONOHUE, G.A., TICHENOR, P.J., and OLIEN, C.N. (forthcoming). Mass communication, policy, and community decisions. Beverly Hills, Calif.: Sage.

GREENBERG, B.S. (1964). "Person-to-person communication in the diffusion of news events." Journalism Quarterly, 41(autumn):489-494.

HEIRICH, M. (1964). "The use of time in the study of social change." American Sociological Review, 29(2):386-397.

HEISE, P.R. (1970). "Causal inference from panel data." In E.F. Borgatta (ed.), Sociological methodology. San Francisco: Jossey-Bass.

KLINE, F.G. (1969). Urban-suburban family structure and media use. Ph.D. dissertation, University of Minnesota.

——— (1971). "Media time budgeting as a function of demographics and life style." Journalism Quarterly, 48(summer):211-221.

——— (1972). "Theory in mass communication research." In F.G. Kline and P.J. Tichenor (eds.), Current perspectives in mass communication research. Beverly Hills, Calif.: Sage.

——— (1972a). Cross-sectional designs for communication research: path analysis. Invited paper for a symposium on advanced methodology at the meetings of the Association for Educational in Journalism.

KLINE, F.G., DAVIS, D.K., OSTMAN, R. VUORI, L., CHRISTIANSEN, N., GUNARATNE, S., and KIVENS, L. (1970). "Family and peer socialization and autonomy related to mass media use, mass institution evaluation and radical political activism: A descriptive analysis." Paper presented to the International Association for Mass Communication Research, Constance, Germany.

KLINE, F.G., KENT, D., and DAVIS, D.K. (1970). "Problems in causal analysis of aggregate data with applications to political instability," in J.V. Gillespie and B.A. Nesvold (eds.), Macro-quantitative cross-national analysis. Bevery Hills, Calif.: Sage.

KLINE, F.G., MILLER, P.V., and MORRISON, A.J. (1974). "Adolescents and family planning information: an exploration of audience needs and media effects," in J.G. Blumler and E. Katz (eds.), The uses of mass communications: current perspectives on gratification research. Beverly Hills, Calif.: Sage.

LERNER, D., and SCHRAMM, W. (1967). Communication and change in the developing countries. Honolulu: University of Hawaii–East-West Center Press.

MORRISON, A.J., KLINE, F.G., and MILLER, P.V. (1976). "Aspects of adolescent information acquisition about drugs and alcohol topics," in R.E. Ostman (ed.), Communication research and drug education. Beverly Hills, Calif.: Sage.

PIAGET, J. (1954). The construction of reality in the child. New York: Basic Books.

ROGERS, E.M. (1976). Communication and development: critical perspectives. Beverly Hills, Calif.: Sage.

ROGERS, E., and SHOEMAKER, F. (1971). Communication of innovations. New York: Free Press.

SCHRAMM, W., and LERNER, D. (1976). Communication and change: the last ten years— and the next. Honolulu: University of Hawaii–East-West Center Press.

SCHUESSLER, K., and STRAUSS, A. (1950). "A study of concept learning by scale analysis." American Sociological Review, 15:752-762.

SZALAI, A. (1973). The use of time: Daily activities of urban and suburban populations in twelve countries. The Hague: Mouton.

TUNSTALL, J. (1977). The media are American. London: Constable.

WARD, S., WACKMAN, D.B., and WARTELLA, E. (1977). How children learn to buy: the development of consumer information-processing skills. Beverly Hills, Calif.: Sage.

WINER, B.J. (1962). Statistical principles in experimental designs. New York: McGraw-Hill.

A typology of audience needs that helps focus uses and gratifications studies is developed in this article. Jay G. Blumler argues that cognitive, diversion, *and* personal identity *orientations make up a scheme that both generates hypotheses and guides uses and gratifications research strategy. Furthermore, he argues the merits of a gratifications approach and suggests that a "patch of common ground" may exist between gratifications and cultural perspectives. Dr. Blumler is Director of the Centre for Television Research at the University of Leeds, England.*

12

THE ROLE OF THEORY IN USES AND GRATIFICATIONS STUDIES

Jay G. Blumler

Although the uses and gratifications approach lacks a single general theory, it is not inherently atheoretical, and the author suggests how progress can be made in dealing with four conceptual issues facing this tradition: the nature of the "active" audience; the role of gratification orientations in mediating effects; the social origins of media needs and uses; and the interest shared with students of popular culture in perceptions of and cognitions about mass media content formed by audience members.

This paper will not discuss a series of recent "advances" in uses and gratifications theory. It aims instead to review the agenda of theoretical issues currently facing this tradition of mass communication research (a) in light of the major stock-taking that appeared three years ago (Blumler and Katz, 1974) and (b) in response to subsequent work and writings. Undeniably, a number of theoretical problems associated with this approach remain unsolved. Yet some critics' views about how they should be overcome seem misconceived.

A GRAND THEORY?

It has become fashionable to criticise practitioners of uses and gratifications research for a formidable array of *ultimate* theoretical shortcomings—for weaknesses, that is, that are supposedly lodged in the very underpinnings of their outlook. Sometimes virtually in the same breath (or rather in the same passage of type), they are taxed for being (a) crassly atheoretical (Elliott, 1974), (b) perversely eclectic (Swanson, 1976), (c) ensnared in the logical pitfalls of

From Jay G. Blumler, "The Role of Theory in Uses and Gratifications Studies," *Communication Research* 6, 1 (January 1979) 9-36. Copyright 1979 by Sage Publications, Inc.

functionalism (Carey and Kreiling, 1974), and (d) for flirting with positions at odds with their functionalist origins (Swanson, 1976). No wonder Swanson (1976) has concluded that, "The nature of *the* theory underlying uses and gratifications research is not totally clear" (the stress on the definite article is mine). Although uses and gratifications authors are at least partly responsible for this wealth of confusion, much of this line of criticism does seem to stem from a false expectation. To identify the fallacy, however, it is necessary to tread once again over familiar historical ground.

The uses and gratifications approach came most prominently to the fore in the late 1950s and early 1960s at a time of widespread disappointment with the fruits of attempts to measure the short-term effects on people of their exposure to mass media campaigns. It reflected a desire to understand audience involvement in mass communications in terms more faithful to the individual user's own experience and perspective than the effects tradition could attain. It sought to replace the image of the audience member as a passive victim, thought to be implicit in effects studies, with one of a person who could actively bend programmes, articles, films, and songs to his own purposes. It rested on the assumption that interesting and important differences of orientation to mass media fare obtained between different audience members. It was further supposed that variations in such orientations would covary with numerous other communication-relevant factors, such as (a) people's social circumstances and roles, (b) their personality dispositions and capacities, (c) their actual patterns of mass media consumption, and (d) ultimately, the process of effects itself.

Crucial to the argument is the equivalence of uses and gratifications research with effects research. The former is like, yet opposed to, the latter. Nobody would have dreamed of insisting that effects researchers should form a single school united around the same theoretical commitments. They were not castigated as eclectics because some aligned themselves, say, with Bandura, while others supported Berkowitz, and still others followed in the wake of Tannenbaum. Of course such scholars shared certain investigative points of departure, certain convictions about the phenomena that most merited research priority, and certain methodologies of attack. Yet it was not deemed a weakness that, under such a capacious umbrella, many different theories sheltered and engaged in mutual disputation. It was fair enough to expect each individual student of communication effects to explicate his own theoretical assumptions and hypotheses as clearly and coherently as possible. But a demand that each investigator of media effects should try to bring his theoretical framework into line with that of his colleagues would have seemed decidedly odd.

It is wrong to treat uses and gratifications scholarship any differently. Peruse Blumler and Katz (1974) in this spirit, and you will find that uses and gratifications theories abound in its pages. Wright defends a functionalist version. McQuail and Gurevitch outline two other theoretical approaches that could guide data-gathering about audience gratifications. McGuire, writing as a remarkably fertile card-carrying psychologist, seems able to conceive of 16 such theories? Rosengren puts forward a theoretical stance of his own—in which people's media requirements derive from deficiencies in their environmental and personality capacities to realise certain universal human needs (cf. especially Rosengren and Windahl, 1972). of Course, when each author enters the theoretical arena, he becomes a fair target for critiques of his logic, clarity, plausibility, and sensitivity to what really matters under the mass communication sun. The one complaint that should be ruled out of court is comment on their collective failure to evolve a fully corporate doctrine.

In short, there is no such thing as a 94 the) uses and gratifications theory, although there are plenty of theories about uses and gratifications phenomena, which may well differ with each other over many issues. Together, they will share a common field of concern, an elementary set of concepts indispensable for intelligibly carving up that terrain, and an identification of certain wider features of the mass communication process with which such core phenomena are presumed to be connected.[1] Rival theories may generate conflicting predictions about how those phenomena are empirically associated, but we should not be dismayed by or critical of their profusion and variety.

It is true that as functionalism lost its charm, uses and gratifications researchers could no longer situate their work within a comprehensive *weltanschauung,* fusing a model of man, a set of ultimate values, and a vision of how social structures, control systems, and cultural practices all bear down on the mass communication field. They certainly have no ideology/sociology/political philosophy/ethic all rolled into one to offer. Perhaps that explains why some academics, themselves armed with some such all-embracing creed, find them hopelessly atheoretical. But is the lack of this form of grand theory all that deplorable? After all, it is the distinctive mission of uses and gratifications research to get to grips with the nature of audience experience itself, which is ever in danger of being ignored or misread by (a) elitists who cannot partake of it and (b) grand theoreticians who believe they understand the significance of such experience better than do the poor benighted receivers themselves. Thus, uses and gratifications data supply the cautionary elements of our field, including antidotes against some of the more outlandish outcomes of extravagant theorising. The uses and gratifications position also reminds us that theoretical propositions in our field need to be tested for their plausibility against the realities of audience experience, which constitute an inescapable funnel through which all mass communication content must flow before it can effect whatever impact it is destined to exert.

None of the foregoing should be read as an excuse for avoiding theoretical issues or as a claim that fruitful theorising typically follows rather than precedes data collection. This author fully accepts one of Swanson's (1976) fundamental prescriptions—that "the importance of conceptual analysis must be recognised," and again that "conceptual analysis should be a priority for us all." The remaining four sections of this paper reflect a personal selection of conceptual problems that currently seem most urgent.

AN ACTIVE AUDIENCE?

In one respect, uses and gratifications writings have not been totally "ideology-free." In fact, their stress on the activity of the mass media audience stemmed from liberal-rationalist beliefs in human dignity and the potential of the individual for self-realisation. The issue to be considered here is whether what has hitherto been treated as an article of faith should now be converted into an empirical question.

This has not been seriously attempted so far for three main reasons. First, the notion of "the active audience" has conflated an extraordinary range of meanings, including those of *utility* (mass communication has uses for people), *intentionality* (media consumption is directed by prior motivation), *selectivity* (media behavior reflects prior interests and preferences), and *imperviousness to influence* (Bauer's, 1964, "obstinate audience"). Thus, little attention has been paid to the tasks of sorting out these distinct meanings, pondering their separate implications for other media phenomena, and finding ways of operationalising them as empirical tools. Second, the active audience has been treated as an either/or matter; either, in the company of uses and gratifications scholars, you regarded the audience as active, or, with other scholars, you relegated it to a more passive or reactive role. Consequently, the possibility of treating "audience activeness" as a variable was overlooked. Third, it was not appreciated that some media might invite more, or less, audience activity than others. Thus, its undifferentiated emphasis on the active audience left the uses and gratifications tradition vulnerable to statistical demonstrations—such as that recently offered by

Goodhardt et al. (1975)—that, when the television audience is examined behaviourally over time, few signs of a structuring of viewing by content preferences emerge.

If ideology is to be transcended in this sphere, then, a first step must be to distinguish and dimensionalise some of the different senses in which audience members could be active. One approach to this task might differentiate forms of "active-ness" likely to manifest themselves at different moments in a temporally ordered mass communication sequence: before exposure; during consumption; and after the media experience as such has been terminated. For example, a person might be regarded as more active in advance of exposure if he *consults information* about what is available; or *plans* when and what media fare will be consumed; or has a clear *prior expectation* of what he can get out of patronising some medium; or can specify the *criteria* of what counts as superior specimens of materials that interest him. During consumption, activity might be indexed by *degree of attention* paid to the output consumer or by ability to *recall* what it included. Subsequent activity would presumably depend on such after-exposure "uses" as a readiness to *reflect* on media materials, to *talk* about them with others, or to *absorb them into other activities* (e.g., in voting choices, purchasing behaviour, children's play, taking over styles of dress, singing, and so on).

Such an attempt to separate out the different possible meanings of audience activity would open up a number of interesting paths of empirical research exploration. How, for example, do the several indices of audience activity relate to each other? Are people more or less active across-the-board, as it were, or differentially so along the different dimensions of such activity? How do the several indices look when compared across different population sub-groups? Which sectors of the audience are more active in which respects? How do they look when compared across different media and media genres? Are some forms of media consumption more actively involving than others?

How does the unselective television audience depicted by Goodhardt et al. (1975) look when approached from these several angles? Finally, what are the implications of audience activity of various kinds for effects processes? This last question recalls an occasionally reported, yet still somewhat neglected, finding in television research—how the audience for a given programme form is divisible between a casually captive and a more committed element. By dimensionalising audience activity in the manner proposed, it might be possible to draw other significant distinctions within the mass audience, helping thereby to refine the detection of effects. In other words, there may well be many unnoticed analogues in people's uses of other forms of media content to the Blumler and McQuail (1968) discovery of profoundly differing reactions to election broadcasts on the part of those individuals who saw them because of their heavy customary viewing habits and those who followed them chiefly out of a keen political interest.

HOW DO GRATIFICATIONS MEDIATE EFFECTS?

The hope that the study of audience needs would revitalise the measurement of media effects has too often been voiced in a sort of theoretical vacuum. It is true that empirical research has yielded a scatter of indications that gratification orientations are indeed relevant to the effects process—sometimes by supplementing exposure influences (McLeod and Becker, 1974), sometimes by interacting with them (Blumler and McQuail, 1968; Kline et al., 1974). Yet one looks in vain for the theoretical advances that such findings should presumably have stimulated.

This lack has several sources. One is sheer neglect. A full list of published gratifications-by-effects studies would be exceedingly spare. Second, work on the involvement of gratifications in media effects has been far too reliant on retrospective speculation. It is not very far from the mark to characterise the prevailing strategy as one of feeding a number of audience orientations into the computer at the gratifications end and seeing what emerges at the effects end. Third, such audience orientations have often been represented by single-item measures rather than by scores compiled from endorsements of a number of items in a fairly homogeneous and reliable gratification factor. Fourth, the relationship between the focus of such gratification variables and the form of content assumed to exert some effect has sometimes been rather loose. Finally, little account has been taken of the multifunctionality of media content, which would presumably require a testing of hypotheses for effects based on combinations of gratifications sought.

At bottom we lack a well-formed prior perspective about which gratifications sought from which forms of content are likely to facilitate which effects. But before considering some elements that might belong to such a perspective, a confusion within the original uses and gratifications philosophy should be mentioned. Some pioneers of this approach perceived audience intentionality of any kind as serving to block message effects. Such is the line of thought which links the notion of an active audience to an obstinate one. And in at least one agenda-setting study, some evidence in support of this model has appeared (McLeod, Becker, and Byrnes, 1974). Yet this stance differs from the position of those uses and gratifications researchers who were sceptical about the limited effects model of media impact and who expected gratification variables to provide fine-tuned discriminators of diverse lines of media influence. The original design of the Blumler and McQuail (1968) study of the British General Election of 1964 illustrates this point of view:

> we expected a division of the members of a sample, according to their different motives for following election broadcasts, either to disclose previously undetected relationships between attitude change and campaign exposure, or to strengthen faint ones appreciably.

Yet Blumler and McQuail also neglected to specify in advance how particular motives might induce particular forms of attitude change.

This theoretical nettle can be grasped only by becoming specific and considering how certain impulses of audience motivation, which clearly underlie much mass media use, might plausibly be expected to facilitate certain influence processes. The numerous typologies of audience need that have emerged from recent work do provide empirical guidelines to the designation of such motives (Blumler, 1976; Dyckoff, forthcoming; Katz, Gurevitch, and Haas, 1973: Kippax and Murray, 1976). Despite many other differences, three orientations have surfaced from these studies with such regularity and distinctness that they clearly deserve focal attention from the standpoint of their likely effects repercussions. They include, first of all, a *cognitive* orientation, whereby the audience member looks primarily for information about some feature of society and the wider world around him—as in "surveillance" sought from the news, information about party policies and other issues of the day from election broadcasts, or perhaps "reality exploration" as a use of many fictional series and serials scheduled on television and radio. Second, people want *diversion* of many kinds, including, for example, the relief from boredom and constraints of daily routines derived from chat shows, music, comedy, and other forms of light entertainment, as well as the excitement generated by adventure serials, quizzes, sports and competitive games, and even the horse-race appeal of following an election campaign. Third, uses and gratifications studies have often highlighted a separate *personal identity* function, standing for ways of using media materials to give added salience to something important in the audience member's own life or situation. In a recent Leeds study, for example (Blumler, 1976), this orientation was represented by respondents' endorsements of the following statements:

It sometimes reminds me of past events in my life.

It shows what others are thinking about people like me.

It gives me support for my ideas.

I sometimes find examples of how to get on with others.

It makes me wish I were like some of the people I see or read about.

I can imagine myself in situations I see cr read about.

It makes me feel as if I really know the people I see or read about.

How might propositions about media effects be generated from this tripartite gratifications scheme? First, we may postulate that *cognitive motivation will facilitate information gain.* This hypothesis is not quite so obvious or trivial as its formulation initially suggests. Consider, for example, the viewing of TV news bulletins. In substance and presentation, they are not necessarily designed to reward only cognitive drives. The personalities of news-readers, the light-hearted sprinklings of humour and banter, and the highlighting of conflict and drama in many news areas may all cater powerfully to other than cognitive impulses. Moreover, gratification studies of news consumption have typically yielded diversionary/affective orientations that seem to match these content characteristics (Blumler, Brown, and McQuail, 1970; Levy, 1977). Thus, the proposed hypothesis postulates that in such a complex of multifunctional possibilities, the person who is more *strongly* and more *exclusively* moved to consume media materials for their informational content is more likely to acquire knowledge from them. And since such an orientation may well vary strongly and systematically across population subgroups (i.e., be more common among males, the middle-aged, the well-educated, and members of the professional and executive middle-class), exploration of this seemingly straightforward hypothesis might even help to shed light on the forces sustaining the so-called knowledge gap between different sectors of society.[2]

Second, *media consumption for purposes of diversion and escape will favour audience acceptance of perceptions of social situations in line with portrayals frequently found in entertainment materials.* This hypothesis stems from that school of thought which regards lack of involvement (Krugman, 1965) and distraction (Festinger and Maccoby, 1964) as facilitators of media impact under conditions in which people are exposed to content explicitly or implicitly projecting some consistent message. Central to this approach is the idea that when a person's perceptual guard has been lowered, he will be more open to influence by the frames of reference embedded in the materials he has been attending. And with repeated exposure to the same or similar materials, a drop-by-drop "over-learning" of its perspective (as Krugman has put it) may occur. What the uses and gratifications approach could offer this low involvement model of media effects is a missing motivational link. Media attendance for the purpose of diversion is likely to be literally diverting in another sense. By inhibiting conscious reflection on the frames of reference inherent in the materials he is enjoying, the individual may be encouraged to absorb them uncritically into the fabric of his own outlook. Thus, this particular gratifications-effects hypothesis might help researchers to study the processes whereby highly accessible and immediately appealing entertainment forms convey stereotypical impressions of real-life characters, roles, and conflict situations, which are widely absorbed in turn by audience members simply wanting to be relaxed, entertained, and thrilled.

Third, *involvement in media materials for personal identity reasons is likely to promote reinforcement effects.* In principle, of course, a preoccupation with the self during exposure could equally well stem from pressures on the individual to change his ways rather than entrench them. He might be hoping to resolve some personal dilemma or to find a rationale to justify some change in his outlook, way of life, or social and political allegiances. Individuals placed in situations demanding change and adaptation, however, are more likely to seek advice and support from personal acquaintances than from media materials, which can only rarely refer directly to the specific ingredients of people's problematic predicaments and choices. As McGuire (1974) has suggested in a series of acute observations on the psychological roots of media motivation, when people throw their identities into mass communication offerings, more often than not they will probably seek (and therefore presumably find) a reinforcement of what they personally appreciate, stand for, and value:

> Insofar as mass communication presents a culturally stereotyped and sanitized oversimplification of an untidy and unsatisfying reality, it offers the recipients an oportunity for the gratification of bolstering their implicit theories of the world.

> fictional material [in the media] . . . provides constant reaffirmation of the wisdom and ultimate vindication of one's choice of and persistence in a respectable life-style by showing that those who cling to it tend to be rewarded, while those who adopt unconventional life-styles that flaunt the rules of propriety or conventional morality tend to come to an evil end.

> The average person is presented with a range of materials by the newspaper, the television set, etc. that is far wider than one could possibly obtain in one's ordinary life which is typically spent with persons much like oneself. From this material one can extract information to construct one's self-concept, one's view of the world and of human nature and social relations as needed; and when one has already formulated such concepts, then mass communications allow one to bolster this image of oneself and one's world.

> the mass media, obviously in their fictional presentations and to an appreciable extent even in their factual ones, present people playing recognised and stylized roles. . . . . Even where the persons depicted are presented in pedestrian roles . . . the presentation is such as to emphasize and enhance the significance of these roles which in fact are shared by most members of the audience.

HOW DO MEDIA NEEDS
ORIGINATE IN SOCIAL CIRCUMSTANCES?

Uses and gratifications authors have always been strongly opposed to "mass audience" terminology as a way of
labelling the collectivities that watch TV shows, attend
movies, and read magazines and newspapers in their
millions. A diverse range of motives would impel different
members of the audience to tune in to the same events.
People's media requirements would also vary systematically according to their differing social roles and situations.
Nevertheless, when surveying the state of this art a few
years ago, Katz, Blumler, and Gurevitch (1974) confessed
that, "The social and environmental circumstances that
lead people to turn to the mass media for the satisfaction of
certain needs are . . . little understood as yet." Even though
they managed to extract, from previous writings, references
to five different routes along which "social factors may be
involved in the generation of media-related needs," they
still conceded how difficult it was "to conceive of a general
theory that might clarify the various processes that underlie
any such specific relationships." More recently, Levy (1977)
has noticed the same gap: "there is no general theoretical
framework which systematically links gratifications to their
social and psychological origins."

Attempts to supply one have been held back by several
factors. For one thing, the exercise required is dauntingly
vast. How could the derivation of media needs from, say,
restricted work experience, geographical mobility, high
education, social isolation, and sexual status all be brought
under one theoretical roof? Second, when the social origins
of audience gratifications have been empirically explored,
more often than not the task has been drastically reduced to
one of examining the role of a few standard demographic
variables—such as sex, age, and social class. Third, media
needs have rarely been visualised as springing from a
combination of multiple and interacting circumstances.

Fourth, speculation has largely focused on associations between certain social position variables and certain gratification tendencies. The processes in between, which might help to forge such links, have been virtually ignored. Finally, such overarching theory as has appeared in the literature has been one-sided. Compensatory thinking has largely dominated the field. The media have been regarded chiefly as substitute sources of satisfactions blocked for the individual by frustrating features of his environment. Audience gratifications, then, have been explained mainly in terms of environmental deprivation; the possibility that media use might occasionally feed on more positive interests and forces in the individual's life has been almost totally overlooked.

Fresh light has recently been thrown on some of these problems by the results of a project based for some years at the Leeds University Centre for Television Research.[3] Designed expressly to investigate the social sources of media satisfactions, this was based on a survey of approximately 1,000 British adults who (a) endorsed a set of 32 gratification statements as true or not true of their uses of newspapers, of television as a medium, and of four recently viewed TV programmes, and (b) answered many detailed questions about their social situations. Guided by factor analyses, the 32 gratification statements were reduced to four types of media satisfaction, scores for the attainment of each of which were assigned to each respondent: surveil-each of which were assigned to each respondent: Surveillance, Curiosity, Diversion, and Personal Identity.[4] Associations of social background features with these scores were examined not only variable-by-variable, but also in accordance with AID (automatic interaction detector) procedures. The latter analyses were not performed on the sample as a whole, however, since it was suspected that work status itself might determine which other background influences would be most operative for people in different situations. The AID analyses were therefore conducted separately on each of three major subsamples: full-time workers, nonworking housewives, and retired people.

A full summary of the results cannot be provided here, but two of their implications for further theory development do merit some comment. First, an attempt to look into the influence on peoples' media needs of social circumstances not often covered by conventional survey variables is apparently well worth the effort. In the Leeds study, measures of this kind were often involved in significant AID splits of the main media satisfaction scores. One example that can be mentioned is ownership or not of a telephone. Lack of such a facility was often associated with higher Diversion and Personal Identity scores. Moreover, having no telephone was more significant for individuals living at home all day—housewives and retired people—that in the case of full-time workers. Among such housebound groups, it mattered more for individuals of non-manual than of manual background, a class distinction that was particularly marked among the housewives. It was as if the deprivation arising from lack of a telephone, then, was felt more keenly by middle-class women, some of whose peers may use it as an instrument of more or less daily social contact. Other examples of hitherto little studied social background factors, which occasionally explained significant variation in media satisfaction scores, included geographical mobility, organisational affiliations, various indices of social contact opportunities, and various facets of people's work situations. When use of television for Diversion was examined among full-time workers, for example, the two highest-scoring groups turned out to be (a) women professing an instrumental rather than an expressive orientation to their work and (b) older people who felt dissatisfied with their jobs. The lowest-scoring group comprised individuals who were expressively oriented to work and highly satisfied with their jobs, range of social contacts, and opportunities to get out of the house.

Second, the Leeds survey findings prompted a quite comprehensive reconceptualisation of the relationship between people's social situations and their media-related needs. The evolution of this rethinking process can be traced through four tables. Table 1 lists all the study's social background variables, subdivided according to the categories under which they were originally grouped. It can be seen that they were at first classified along common-sense lines as: primary demographic particulars, social contact opportunities, variables of work experience, measures of leisure behaviour, and a miscellaneous set of "other variables."

Table 2 provides a summary overview of the AID results. This was arrived at by adding up the total amount of variance accounted for by each social position variable in each of the four main gratification areas (disregarding for this purpose subsample distinctions and differences between satisfactions gained from television and the press). Entries in the chart, then, list those variables which definitely appeared to account for relatively high proportions of variation in media satisfaction, falling roughly within the top three-eighths of the batting order for each gratification area.

The pattern displayed in Table 2 already sounds a strong warning against the previously mentioned tendency to think of audience involvement in the mass media as chiefly a compensatory affair. It is true that a mainly compensatory pattern shines through the variables listed in the chart under the Diversion heading (emphasising a lack of youth, education, organizational membership, social contacts, foreign travel opportunities, telephone, and car). It may also seem unsurprising that it is largely absent from the items listed under Surveillance (emphasising high education, middle-class social status, organisational affiliation, foreign travel, geographical mobility, and no felt need for more social contact). But the patterns for Curiosity and Personal Identity provide more interesting test cases of the validity of a compensatory perspective on the origins of media needs. Curiosity, for example, goes with, among other things, higher education, organisational affiliations, experience of travel abroad, frequent contact with friends, and an ability

TABLE 1
Initial Classification of Social Position Variables Examined for Associations with Media Satisfactions

Primary Demographic Particulars

Sex
Age
Education
Social grade
Marital status
Life-cycle position
Work status

Social Contact Opportunities

Household size
Frequency of seeing relations
Frequency of seeing friends
Frequency of seeing neighbours
Frequency of social interaction (above three items indexed)
Desire for more social contact

Work Experience

Work values (instrumental vs. expressive)
Job satisfaction*
Rating of social relationships at work*
Job perceived as dangerous
Job problems remain on mind after work*
Fear of loss of employment

* Equivalent items administered to women for views on housework

Leisure Behaviour

Frequency of going out in the evening
Desire to go out more
Satisfaction with leisure pattern
Weight of TV viewing
TV channel preference
Weight of newspaper reading
Individual morning papers read

Other Variables

Geographical mobility (frequency of recent housing moves)
Recent experience of foreign travel
Number of organisations joined
Frequency of church attendance
Possession of telephone
Availability of use of car
State of health and whether illness perceived as limiting/disabling

TABLE 2
Variables Accounting for Relatively High Proportions of Variance in AID Analyses of Social Position by Media Satisfaction Scores

	SURVEILLANCE	CURIOSITY	DIVERSION	PERSONAL IDENTITY
SEX	Male	Male	Female	
AGE	Older		Older	Older
EDUCATION	High	High	Low	Low
SOCIAL GRADE	Middle			
MARITAL STATUS	Married			
ORGANISATIONS	Yes	Yes	No	Yes
FOREIGN TRAVEL	Yes	Yes	No	No
GEOGRAPHICAL MOBILITY	High	Low	High	Both
HOUSEHOLD SIZE			Small	Large
FRIENDS' CONTACT		Often	Often	Often
RELATIONS' CONTACT		Rare		
OVERALL INTERACTION			Low	High
DESIRE FOR SOCIAL CONTACT	Less			More
GETTING OUT	Rare	Often		
TELEPHONE			None	None
CAR			None	None
ILLNESS				Ill
WORK VALUES			Instrumental	
JOB PROBLEMS ON MIND		Yes		Yes
FEAR JOB LOSS				Yes
JOB SATISFACTION		Low		
HOUSEWIFE'S SITUATION		Lonely		

to get out in the evening frequently. Personal Identity goes with organisational affiliation, being geographically mobile, living in large households, and relatively frequent interaction with other people. Intriguingly, it also goes and quite strongly, as it happens—with a desire for more social contact. Thus, it seems that in many cases the relationship between real-life situation and media satisfaction can be a more-the-more, not always a less-the-more one. And some gratifications, like Personal Identity, can be a hub of both compensatory and supplementary relationships to indicators of real-life opportunities and circumstances.

A further contemplation of these relationships resulted in Table 3, which outlines our attempt to reorder the background variables for their impact on media satisfaction. Three broad categories emerged from this attempt—with a further split for the middle category of the scheme. Thus, we postulated, there may be, first of all, *normative influences* on what individuals aim to get out of media fare. By virtue of a certain lifecycle position or a certain place in the social structure, certain expectations that people in those situations will go more for certain types of satisfaction and less for others are as if imposed on the individual. It may be socially expected, for example, that men will be more cognitively oriented to mass media provision than women. Notice, incidentally, how this category opens the study of media gratifications to a socialisation perspective: individuals may learn from forces in their social environment which satisfactions people like themselves are expected to derive from media use.[5] Second, the *socially distributed life-chances* an individual enjoys may have a bearing in two opposed ways. Some will be *factors which liberate* the individual, or are indicators of the possession of enabling experience that facilitate a more rich involvement with media contents. Organisational affiliation and frequency of social contact might operate in this way. Other factors, however, are sources of a *need to compensate* for the lack of such opportunities and capacities—as in, say, lack of a telephone, a car, or a satisfying job. Last, the *subjective reaction or adjustment* of the individual to his situation, whatever it may be, may be relevant to what he seeks to obtain from the media.

TABLE 3
Framework for Re-ordering Relationships Between Social
Background and Media Satisfaction

Differentially distributed opportunities and capacities: facilitators and enablers	Differentially distributed opportunities and capacities: compensatory mechanisms
Organisational affiliation	Ill health
Foreign travel	Instrumental work values
Geographical mobility	Desire for more social contact
Marital status	Desire to get out more
Household size	Lack of social interaction
Frequency of social contact	Job problems on mind
Frequency of getting out	Dangerous job
Telephone	Fear of loss of job
Car	
Church attendance	
Expressive work values	
Education	

Socially imposed norms and expectations	Subjective adjustment to situation
Sex	Work satisfaction
Age	Leisure satisfaction
Social class	Satisfaction with housewives' lot
Education	
Work status	

This typology not only reflected an attempt to order the linkages of social background factors with media satisfactions along other than merely ad hoc lines. Once attained, its utility was also put to a further empirical test. We had postulated that the satisfactions obtained from television viewing would tend more often to be of a compensatory kind, while those obtained from newspaper reading would tend more often to be of the facilitating, outer-world involving, more-the-more variety. This hypothesis was first suggested by the discovery that sample members' rates of actual mass media use seemed to show that the deprived, in some sense or other, individuals more often watched TV, while the more socially active individuals tended to read newspapers more often. Table 4 illustrates the outcome of a direct test of this intermedium difference hypothesis. It can be seen that it was confirmed for three of the four gratification score areas: Surveillance, Diversion, and Personal

TABLE 4
Comparison of Roles of AID Splitting Variables for
Newspapers and Television

	SURVEILLANCE		CURIOSITY		DIVERSION		PERSONAL IDENTITY	
	Press %	TV %	Press %	TV %	Press %	TV %	Press %	TV %
Social norms	29	24	18	2	30	26	0	36
Facilitators	55	19	16	42	27	13	53	17
Compensators	14	49	41	38	37	56	43	43
Other subjective	2	8	25	19	6	5	4	4
	100	100	100	101	100	100	100	100

Identity. That is, when for each gratification score on each medium we calculated the proportion of explained variance assignable to the variables we have classified as normative influences, facilitating factors, factors requiring compensation, and subjective reactions, respectively, the press scores were more often detemined by facilitating influences and the television scores by compensatory ones.

**TOWARDS A MEETING GROUND
WITH CULTURAL STUDIES?[6]**

Katz's (1959) hope that students of popular culture and investigators of audience gratifications would get together has proved stubbornly illusory. As a result, some items on the uses and gratifications agenda remain in a state of "unfinished business." As Carey and Kreiling (1974), writing from a cultural studies standpoint, have observed, "Uses and gratifications research fails to link the functions of mass media consumption with the symbolic content of the mass-communicated materials or with the actual experience of consuming them." And as Swanson (1976) has noted, such neglect contradicts the approach's own emphasis on the active audience. How else might such activity be more suitably manifested than in the process of arriving at perceptions and interpretations of the meanings of mass media contents?

But can a marriage be arranged between the cultural studies and uses and gratifications approaches, and, if so, on exactly what terms? Themselves deeply ambivalent in their attitude towards this question, Carey and Kreiling underline the difficulties involved in trying to answer it convincingly. They steer an erratic course between affirming the desirability of a merger and airing strongly-held suspicions that the fruits of any such union would only prove abortive. Sometimes they welcome uses and gratifications researchers as suitable partners to join forces with students of popular culture in the pursuit of common tasks. At other times they depict them as almost wholly disqualified to enter what is treated as a strictly bounded and near-sacrosanct cultural domain. Presumably that is why some of their stipulations and conditions read like terms not for a rapprochement, but for a takeover bid. Redemption awaits only those uses and gratifications researchers who are prepared to change all their spots.

It is true that several bridge-building suggestions are scattered throughout the essay. Even the complaint that uses and gratifications researchers have never seriously examined "mass communication as a system of interacting symbols and interlocked meanings that somehow must be linked to the motivations and emotions for which they provide a symbolic outlet" presupposes that such linkages exist and could profitably be explored. Unfortunately, this idea is not developed and is overwhelmed instead by a view of cultural studies as a self-contained and immaculate pursuit. Such uncompromising insistence on the unique properties of cultural studies recurs at many stages of the Carey-Kreiling analysis. For example, they will have no truck with behaviouralism in either its causal or its functional form. But such a wholesale rejection seems to rule out the investigation of linkages between meanings and motivations, an analysis of which would presumably necessitate the measurement of variation on both sides of the cognitive/conative divide. This sort of position is even more firmly asserted in Carey's other writings. In "Mass Communication Research and Cultural Studies: An American View" (Carey, 1977), for example, he categorically declares that cultural studies "does not seek to explain human behavior but to understand it . . . does not seek to reduce human action to underlying causes or structures but to interpret its significance . . . does not attempt to predict human behavior but to diagnose human meanings." Yet another example of the same outlook may be found in a passage in the 1974 essay with Kreiling, which obliges uses and gratifications researchers to accept—as a first precondition of moves toward accommodation—that "an effective theory of popular culture will require a conception of man not as psychological man or sociological man but as cultural man." Notice how these models are treated not as complementary but as opposed alternatives. It is from this standpoint, of course, that the essay criticises the reduction of cultural experience by uses and gratifications researchers to matters of tension reduction and role performance. The bald conclusion is inevitable: "The underlying uses and gratifications logic is inadequate for study of popular culture." Further doubts about merger prospects also arise from Carey and Kreiling's understanding of the essence of aesthetic experience. In contrast to the utilitarianism of uses and gratifications thinking, which is said to fit mass media use to a "means-ends model" of human activity, they proclaim the need to approach aesthetic values and interests as if essentially consummatory in character.

Such issues are too profound for resolution in the span of but a few paragraphs. But surely the heart of the matter, which such philosophical reflections may actually tend to obscure, is whether a patch of common ground does exist that students of audience gratifications and popular culture could till together without jeopardising their respective forms of integrity. Some sketch of its likely contours might begin to emerge by recalling how some of the earliest uses and gratifications studies showed how certain media materials *spoke to the condition* of their most loyal fans. The italicized phrase has been chosen advisedly. According to Herzog (1944) and Warner and Henry (1948), the appeals of radio soap opera, for example, stemmed in part from how they spoke to their listeners' (house-bound house-wives) conditions (presenting the housewifely role, then, in a certain light through the characters that symbolised it, the situations they inhabited, and the problems they coped with). Similarly, a British uses and gratifications study of *The Dales* (also a day-time radio serial) traced some of its appeals to the projection of meanings capable of being assimilated to listeners' own values and circumstances at a quite deep level (Blumler, Brown, and McQuail, 1970). For example, one cluster that emerged from fans' endorse-ments of a battery of reasons for liking to listen to *The Dales* reflected the program's "Reinforcement of Family Val-ues." Another stood for a "Reinforcement of the Social Role of Women." Overall, the programme was highly appreciated for its projection of a moral conservatism that older women associated with the standards of their own generation. Yet by injecting into the plots examples of such social problems as illegitimacy, homosexuality, infidelity, and so on, the series seemed to help some listeners to come to terms with potentially disturbing modern trends from within the shelter of a relatively secure normative perspective.

Implicit in such studies we may find the elements of a conceptual framework which might provide some of the terms of that elusive marriage contract between research-ers into popular culture and audience gratifications. Its point of departure would be the idea that audience mem-bers familiar with certain materials come to form percep-tions of what they have to offer. These in turn become their perceived *appeals,* which may include perceptions of the *meanings and values* conveyed by the materials concerned. Translated into *expectations,* these appeals become *motives* for attending to the same materials. And if confirmed in experience they become *satisfactions,* which will feed back into the complex of motives for continuing to consume them. Meanwhile, audience members' *social roles* help to shape their preceptions of such meanings and in this way also feature among the forces motivating attendance.

It is true that in order jointly to build on such elements as these, both parties would have to give a higher priority. than heretofore to the task of exploring the meanings that audience members ascribe to selected portions of media output. Theorists of popular culture would have to be prepared occasionally to shift their gaze from texts so as to focus it on reader, listeners, and viewers. Investigators of audience gratifications would have to put questions to people not only along the lines of "What are your reasons for viewing this programme?" but also of the kind "What about it do you find true-to-life? What does it seem to you to stand for? What picture of the world does it seem to convey?" But if such questions as these can be meaningfully raised with audience members, the prospects for jointly undertaking an exciting research venture are promising. The twofold aim of such an enterprise would be (a) to unravel how far, and in what ways, perceptions of content meanings contribute to media motivations, and (b) to ascertain lhow such perceptions, together with their motivational implications, vary across different audience subgroups, on the one hand, as well as across different content genres, on the other.

NOTES

1. It is such a body of shared elements that Katz, Blumler, and Gurevitch (1974) sought to identify in their definition of the uses and gratifications paradigm. Workers in this tradition, they said, "are concerned with (1) the social and psychological origins of (2) needs, which generate (3) expectations of (4) the mass media or other sources, which lead to (5) differential patterns of media exposure (or engagement in other activities), resulting in (6) need gratifications and (7) other consequences, perhaps mostly unintended ones."

2. The work of Nordlund (1976) strongly suggests the presence in less educated audience members of gratification orientations that may inhibit knowledge acquisition.

3. The research was conducted in collaboration with Dr. Michael Gurevitch and Professor Denis McQuail. Ms. Gayle Dyckoff and Ms. Peggy Newton also served the project in the early stages of its development. Computer analyses were organised by Mr. Alan Geekie.

4. The Personal Identity statements are itemised in the fourth paragraph of the third section of this paper. The statements representing the other forms of media satisfaction were as follows:

Surveillance:
—I use it to understand what is going on in the country and the world.
—I can use it to keep up with what the government is doing.
—It helps me to judge what political leaders are really like.

Curiosity:
—I can use it to find out about things I need to know about in my daily life.
—It helps me to satisfy my sense of curiosity.
—It shows me what society is like nowadays.
—It makes me want to learn more about things.

Diversion:
—It helps me to relax.
—It's a good way of passing the time when I don't feel like doing anything else.
—It sometimes gives me a good laugh or cry.
—It helps me to get away from everyday worries.
—It helps me when I want to be cheered up.
—It's a good thing to turn to when I'm alone.

5. Adoni (1976) has fruitfully applied a socialisation perspective to the study of media gratifications among Israeli adolescents.

6. The line of thought developed in this section profited from prior discussion with Professor Denis McQuail.

REFERENCES

ADONI, H. (1976) "The functions of mass media in the socialization of adolescents." Ph.D. dissertation, Hebrew University of Jerusalem.
BAUER, R. A. (1964) "The obstinate audience." Amer. Psychologist 19: 319-328.
BLUMLER, J. G. (1976) "The social sources of media satisfactions." Centre for Television Research, University of Leeds. (mimeo)
——— and E. KATZ [eds.] (1974) The Uses of Mass Communications: Current Perspectives on Gratifications Research. Beverly Hills, CA and London: Sage.
BLUMLER, J. G. and D. McQUAIL (1968) Television in Politics: Its Uses and Influence. London: Faber & Faber.

BLUMLER. J. G., J. R. BROWN, and D. McQUAIL (1970) "The social origins of the gratifications associated with television viewing." Report to the British Social Science Research Council. (mimeo)

CAREY, J. W. (1977) "Mass communication research and cultural studies: an American view," in J. Curran, M. Gurevitch, and J. Wollacott (eds.) Mass Communication and Society, London: Edward Arnold.

—— and A. L. KREILING (1974) "Popular culture and uses and gratifications: notes toward an accommodation," in J. G. Blumler and E. Katz (eds.) The Uses of Mass Communications: Current Perspectives on Gratifications Research. Beverly Hills, CA and London: Sage.

DYCKOFF, G. (forthcoming) "The role of the mass media in the socialization of immigrant community adolescents." Ph.D. dissertation, University of Leeds.

ELLIOTT, P. (1974) "Uses and gratifications research: a critique and a sociological alternative," in J. G. Blumler and E. Katz (eds.) The Uses of Mass Communications: Current Perspectives on Gratifications Research. Beverly Hills, CA and London: Sage.

FESTINGER, L. and MACCOBY (1964) "On resistance to persuasive communication." J. of Abnormal and Social Psych. 60: 359-366.

GOODHARDT, G. J., A.S.C. EHRENBERG, and M. A. COLLINS (1975) The Television Audience: Patterns of Viewing. Westmead, England: Saxon House.

HERZOG, H. (1944) "What do we really know about daytime serial listeners?" in P. E. Lazarsfeld and F. N. Stanton (eds.) Radio Research, 1942-1943. New York: Duell, Sloan & Pearce.

KATZ, E. (1959) "Mass Communications research and the study of popular culture: an editorial note on a possible future for this journal." Studies in Public Communication 2: 1-6.

———J. G. BLUMLER, and M. GUREVITCH (1974) "Uses of mass communication by the individual," in W. P. Davison and F.T.C. Yu (eds.) Mass Communication Research: Major Issues and Future Directions. New York: Praeger.

KATZ, E., M. GUREVITCH, and H. HAAS (1973) "On the use of mass media for important things." Amer. Soc. Rev. 38: 164-181.

KIPPAX, S. and J. P. MURRAY (1976) "Using the mass media: need gratification and perceived utility." Macquarie University, Australia. (mimeo)

KLINE, F. G., P. V. MILLER, and A. J. MORRISON (1974) "Adolescents and family planning information: an exploration of audience needs and media effects," in J. G. Blumler and E. Katz (eds.) The Uses of Mass Communications: Current Perspectives on Gratifications Research. Beverlyl Hills, CA and London: Sage.

KRUGMAN, H. E. (1965) "The impact of television advertising: Learning without involvement. Public Opinion Q. 29: 349-358.

LEVY, M. R. (1977) "The uses-and-gratifications of television news." Ph.D. dissertation, Columbia University.

McGUIRE, W. J. (1974) "Psychological motives and communication gratification," in J. G. Blumler and E. Katz (eds.) The Uses of Mass Communications: Current Perspectives on Gratifications Research. BEverly Hills, CA and London: Sage.

McLEOD, J. M. and L. B. BECKER (1974) "Testing the validity of gratification measures through political effects analysis," in J. G. Blumler and E. Katz (eds.) The Uses of Mass Communications: Current Perspectives on Gratifications Research. Beverly Hills, CA and London: Sage.

————, and J. E. BYRNES (1974) "Another look at the agenda-setting function of the press." Communication Research 1: 131-166.

McQUAIL, D. and M. GUREVITCH (1974) "Explaining audience behavior: three approaches considered," in J. G. Blumler and E. Katz (eds.) The Uses of Mass Communications: Current Perspectives on Gratifications Research. Beverly Hills, CA and London: Sage.

NORDLUND, J. E. (1976) "Mediaumgange: En explorativ studie." Ph.D. dissertation, University of Lund.

ROSENGREN, K. E. (1974) "Uses and gratifications: a paradigm outlined," in J. G. Blumler and E. Katz (eds.) The Uses of Mass Communications: Perspectives on Gratifications Research. Beverly Hills, CA and London: Sage.

————and S. WINDAHL (1972) "Mass media consumption as a functional alternative," in D. McQuail (ed.) Sociology of Mass Communications. Harmondsworth, England: Penguin.

SWANSON, D. L. (1976) "Some theoretic approaches to the emerging study of political communication: a critical assessment." Paper presented to the annual. meeting of the International Communication Association, Portland.

WARNER, W. L. and W. E. HENRY (1948) "The radio day time serial: a symbolic analysis." Genetic Psych. Monographs 37: 3-71.

WRIGHT, C. (1974) "Functional analysis and mass communication revisited," in J. G. Blumler and E. Katz (eds.) The Uses of Mass Communications: Current Perspectives on Gratifications Research. Beverly Hills, CA and London: Sage.

Jay G. Blumler is Research Director of the Centre for Television Research and Reader in Mass Communications at the University of Leeds, England.

One of the major problems of gratifications research has been a lack of attention to reality and validity of the measures. Lee B. Becker carefully performs secondary analysis and compares four major studies' measurement approaches. He shows that open-ended measures fail to elicit some gratifications that emerge from closed questions. Furthermore, the analysis suggests that gratifications measures applied to a limited subject matter—political content, for example—may have greater validity than those applied to media content in general. The clearest finding, however, is that gratifications are not media-specific in the studies reviewed here. Dr. Becker is Associate Professor of Journalism at Ohio State University.

13

MEASUREMENT OF GRATIFICATIONS

Lee B. Becker

Various operational problems confronting researchers working in the area of media gratifications are discussed. Strategies are delineated and difficulties inherent in each detailed. Data from four studies are presented to provide solutions to some of these problems.

One of the most difficult problems facing scholars conducting empirical research on the gratifications audience members seek from the media is measurement of the gratifications themselves (Katz, Blumler, and Gurevitch, 1974). Perhaps because of the very nature of the gratifications concept (it is audience- rather than researcher-oriented), operationalization is a particularly thorny issue.

At least three distinct strategies of operationalization exist. First, researchers can infer what gratifications audience members are seeking based on measurement of some separate, yet related, variable. The research of Kline, Miller, and Morrison (1974) is illustrative of this tactic. Inferences were made about the informational needs of audience members—and gratifications sought—based on locator variables such as age and sex.

A second, and certainly more common, strategy for measuring gratifications sought is to rely on reports from the audience members. This was the strategy employed by Blumler and McQuail (1969) in their seminal work on political gratifications. Respondents in the 1964 British

---

AUTHOR'S NOTE: *The author acknowledges the contribution of Jack M. McLeod at the University of Wisconsin, Madison, to this manuscript. Idowu A. Sobowale and Robin E. Cobbey, doctoral students at Syracuse University, assisted in data preparations.*

From Lee B. Becker, "Measurement of Gratifications," *Communication Research* 6, 1 (January 1979) 54-73. Copyright 1979 by Sage Publications, Inc.

study were provided a list of gratifications—developed from earlier research sessions—and asked to indicate which of the gratifications applied to them.

A third strategy open to gratifications researchers is to manipulate in field or laboratory settings the gratifications subjects have upon receipt of various communication messages. In a simple experiment, for example, subjects could be instructed to pay attention to a given message for a specific reason somehow related to the purpose of the experiment. These subjects then could be compared to others having been given different instructions—or gratifications—to learn of the implications of the gratifications on subsequent behavior. Other, more sophisticated settings could easily be created, though manipulation of gratifications to date has not been an explicit concern of researchers.

Each of these strategies of operationalization—by inference, by self-report, or by manipulation—has some strengths. But there are problems as well, some of which all three share. For example, each strategy assumes some knowledge on the part of the researcher of the population of gratifications from which audience members sample. Without that knowledge, it is impossible to designate surrogate measures, develop proper gratification lists or otherwise devise methods of soliciting relevant gratifications from audience members, or manipulate the important gratifications in an experimental setting.

Each of these tactics also assumes some understanding on the part of the researchers of the generalizability of any specific gratification. Gratifications may be media-specific, for example, or they may cut across media. Similarly, they may be content-specific or general in focus. Without knowing which of these possibilities is correct, however, the researcher is forced to devise measures—or manipulations—which may not adequately tap gratifications controlling specific media behavior.

The inferential, self-report, and manipulation strategies also are based on the assumption that the researcher adequately understands the relationship between positive gratifications which, presumably, lead audience members to certain media use behaviors, and negative forces, sometimes labeled avoidances, which result in nonuse of the media. While it is possible that the gratifications and avoidances share some common social antecedent, preliminary evidence presented by McLeod and Becker (1974) suggests they have some distinct implications in terms of eventual impact on audience member behavior. At present, however, relatively little is known about the role of these negative avoidance motivations.

In addition to the problems which the strategies share, each has some peculiar weakness. To employ the inferential approach, for example, researchers have to be able to identify some surrogate—either a cause, effect, or spurious covariate of the gratification. If the surrogate is a cause or effect, the researcher must be prepared to argue that the link is strong enough to rule out serious contamination due to problems of multiple causation. If the surrogate is spuriously related to the gratification, the researcher must be willing to argue that the relationship is stable enough to exist without serious variations across situations. In other words, the strategy assumes a rather high level of theorizing about the relationships between gratifications and other variables.

Special problems confront the researcher opting for the self-report strategy as well. It must be assumed that the respondent is *capable* of providing answers to the questions posed regarding relevant gratifications. Audience members, however, may not know which gratifications are important. Even if they do know, they may not be able to verbalize such answers.

While lists of gratifications may seem to get around the problems of recognition and verbalization, unless the items on the list are simply stated and in the vernacular of the respondents, the items may be rejected prematurely. Even when researchers may be able to circumvent difficulties resulting from the *capabilities* of the respondents, there remain difficulties stemming from the *willingness* of the respondents to report accurately controlling gratifications. Certain gratifications may well be more socially acceptable than others.

Manipulation of the gratifications in experimental settings also has limitations. If the manipulation is through intervention in the causal chain which produces the gratification, a detailed knowledge of the causal chain is necessary. If the manipulation is achieved through role-playing, experimental situations must be devised which avoid some of the problems inherent in the self-report tactic. The subjects, for example, must be able to understand the intricacies of the role-playing experiment, particularly as they relate to the gratification involved. Even if these difficulties can be overcome, the researcher opting for the experimental strategy still must deal with very real problems of external validity. Audience orientations would seem to be particularly difficult factors to isolate realistically in any laboratory setting.

VALIDITY CRITERIA

Each of these measurement problems presents a potential threat to the validity of gratification research. Yet relatively little empirical work has been done to establish guidelines for measurement or to offer suggestions as to the most viable strategy for studying a particular research problem involving gratifications.

Indirect empirical evidence of the validity of the gratifications measures can be derived from simple reliability estimates. To be valid, of course, gratification measures must be internally consistent and stable over relatively short periods of time. To date, however, there have been few reports of reliability coefficients for gratification measures.

Most often, validation of gratification measures has been of the content sort. Items are critically examined to determine if they logically measure the underlying gratification desired. For the most part, researchers have not used pragmatic validation processes, though several opportunities would seem to present themselves. Persons confronting an important decision on a public issue, for example, ought to be more likely to desire materials from the media to aid them in making that decision than persons not in the decision making mode.

The most powerful technique for validation, of course, results from the hypothesis testing procedure itself. Such construct validation has been slow to develop in the gratifications area, however, because the gratifications have not been well integrated into communications theory. As a result, relatively little strict hypothesis testing has been done. The strategy, however, was illustrated by McLeod and Becker (1974), who integrated the gratification measures into effects analysis.

To some extent, the relatively low level of knowledge about gratification measures exists because researchers have not reported data which bear on important measurement issues. In other words, some of the existent pieces of the empirical picture have not made it into the literature. Substantive speculation and findings, rather than discussions of methodological problems, have dominated.

What follows is a report on a series of studies conducted within the last several years. None of the studies was designed to deal exclusively with measurement problems in gratifications research, yet viewed together they speak to three of the general issues confronting researchers measuring gratifications by inference, self-report, or manipulation.

First, the studies address the question of relevant gratifications. Most deal with gratifications sought from the political content of the media and employ items derived from the work of Blumler and McQuail (1969). Together they provide information as to whether the battery of items in use is complete and what structure exists amongst the items.

Several of the studies also deal with the question of generalizability of the gratifications. This is done through examination of differences in gratifications sought from television and from newspapers as well as those sought from political and from nonpolitical materials in the media.

Finally, the studies present data regarding the relationships between positive gratifications and negative avoidances. This is accomplished through item analysis of separate measures of the two types of motivations.

1974 SYRACUSE VOTING STUDIES

The first of these studies was conducted in the fall of 1974 in Syracuse, New York. A list of ten items written to parallel some extent questions used in the original Blumler and McQuail (1969) research were presented to a sample of registered voters contacted in person. The voters were a probability sample of those registered in a district within the city chosen because of its diverse social makeup.

The items were asked separately for television and newspaper content and were designed to measure gratifications that audience members seek from the *political* content of the two media. Respondents indicated the extent to which the listed gratifications applied to them. The items are shown in Table 1 in the order they were presented to the respondents.

The items given the highest level of endorsement by the Syracuse sample measure what Blumler and McQuail have termed surveillance and vote guidance (items 1, 3, 6 and 8). The two items given the next highest endorsements (items 4 and 9) generally seem to measure reinforcement seeking. Excitement seeking (items 2 and 7) and the communicatory utility items (5 and 10) also were given significant endorse-

TABLE 1
Levels of Gratifications, 1974 Syracuse Voting Study

		Television	Newspapers
1.	To judge what political candidates are like (Surveillance)	2.23 (.70)	2.16 (.68)
2.	To judge which candidates are likely to win an election (Excitement)	1.83 (.76)	1.95 (.73)
3.	To help me make up my mind how to vote in an election (Vote guidance)	2.11 (.77)	2.14 (.79)
4.	To remind me of my candidates' strong points (Reinforcement)	2.00 (.74)	2.00 (.74)
5.	To give me something to talk about with other people (Communication)	1.64 (.71)	1.68 (.70)
6.	To see what the candidates would do if elected (Surveillance)	2.10 (.77)	2.08 (.79)
7.	To enjoy the excitement of an election race (Excitement)	1.73 (.79)	1.60 (.74)
8.	To see how the candidates stand on the issues (Vote guidance)	2.41 (.68)	2.50 (.63)
9.	To see (read) editorials and commentary about the elections which agree with my positions (Reinforcement)	1.90 (.78)	1.96 (.80)
10.	To use what I learn in political discussions (Communication)	1.85 (.77)	1.96 (.76)

NOTE: Entries are means and standard deviations. A high score indicates the reason for watching or reading political stories applies to the respondent. The scores are based on a three-point scale.

ments, though with less consistency than for the other dimensions.

The similarities between the two sets of gratifications shown in Table 1 is quite marked. There is only slight variation between the levels of the television items and those for newspapers. Little evidence seems to exist that the gratifications are media-specific.

Included in the 1974 Syracuse study was a series of items designed to measure negative gratifications—or avoidances. While the positive items had been presented to the respondents as "reasons some people have given for watching television programs [reading newspaper stories] which deal with political candidates and events," the avoid-

TABLE 2
Levels of Avoidances, 1974 Syracuse Voting Study

		Television	Newspapers
1.	Because I prefer to relax when watching television (reading a newspaper)	1.60 (.75)	1.42 (.67)
2.	Because usually my mind is already made up about whom to vote for	1.48 (.72)	1.49 (.71)
3.	Because the programs (stories) hardly ever tell me anything new	1.62 (.73)	1.71 (.74)
4.	Because I'd rather spend my time with (reading) other programs (stories in the paper)	1.74 (.76)	1.64 (.75)
5.	Because I'm not interested in watching (reading about) candidates I don't like	1.46 (.71)	1.42 (.66)
6.	Because it's hard to figure out what the programs (stories) are all about	1.41 (.68)	1.47 (.70)
	N=		(339)

NOTE: Entries are means and standard deviations.. A high score indicates the reason for watching or reading political stories applies to the respondent. The scores are based on a three-point scale.

ance items were presented as reasons for not watching or listening. Again, respondents were asked to indicate to what extent the items applied to them.

In general, the avoidance items shown in Table 2 were less well endorsed than the gratification items in Table 1. The most common reason for avoiding the political materials was to spend time with other stories. Again, there are few differences between the responses for the television and for the newspaper items.

This conclusion of little differentiation between media is reinforced by the actual correlations between responses to the items shown in Tables 1 and 2. The average correlation for the positive items is .61. For the negative items, the figure is .58. In other words, those respondents who reported watching political content for surveillance or vote guidance tended to report reading stories in newspapers for the same reasons.

In order to gain some understanding of the dimensionality of the items shown in Tables 1 and 2—and to determine whether the labels used above in describing the items have any empirical base—a factor analysis was performed. The analysis was designed to determine principal orthogonal components underlying the raw scores. The number of factors extracted was determined to insure that only components accounting for at least the amount of total variance of a single item were considered important. Varimax rotation was used.

The procedure produces the three-factor solution for the television items shown in Table 3. The first factor is clearly an avoidance cluster, picking up the primary loadings of each of the six avoidance items. Empirically, at least, the avoidance items are quite distinct from the positive gratifications. The second factor picks up the two surveillance items (1 and 6) as well as the vote guidance items (3 and 8). Also loading strongly on this factor is one of the two reinforcement items. The remaining items load primarily on the final factor. This is a pattern repeated almost perfectly for the newspaper items shown in Table 4.

The factor analyses in Tables 3 and 4 suggest the strong empirical tie which exists between the surveillance and vote guidance motivations as well as among the reinforcement, excitement seeking, and communicatory utility motivations. The avoidance items, as well, cluster together very strongly. This clustering together of various types of items serves to reinforce the finding from prior research that it is difficult to sort out the separate impact of various gratifications (Becker, 1976; McLeod and Becker, 1974).

1974 MADISON VOTING STUDY

The items used in the Syracuse study were incorporated into a study of voters in Madison, Wisconsin, that same year (McLeod, Brown, Becker, and Ziemke, 1977). The Madison study actually included two separate samples, one com-

TABLE 3

Factor Analysis of Television Gratifications and Avoidances,
1974 Syracuse Voting Study

Gratifications	Factor 1	Factor 2	Factor 3
1. To judge candidates	-.14	.71	.26
2. To judge who will win	.06	.42	.56
3. To help vote	-.15	.80	.17
4. To remind of strong points	-.06	.59	.43
5. To get something to talk about	-.05	.15	.78
6. To see what candidates would do	-.06	.77	.21
7. To enjoy excitement	-.09	.28	.62
8. To see stands on issues	-.13	.81	.21
9. To see editorials, commentary	.06	.20	.70
10. To use in discussions	-.08	.18	.82
Avoidances			
1. Prefer to relax	.74	.05	-.14
2. Mind made up	.72	-.13	.11
3. Nothing new	.68	-.24	-.01
4. Rather view other things	.76	-.05	-.15
5. Not interested	.76	-.09	.07
6. Hard to understand	.67	-.04	-.03

NOTE: Entries are correlations of the items with the rotated factors. N=339.

prised of voters under the age of 27 and the second of older voters. Only the latter group is examined here.

The levels of the gratification and avoidance items were almost identical with those shown for Syracuse voters. In fact, when comparably aged respondents are examined in the two communities, the average absolute deviation between the two samples is only .11.

Despite this similarity, a factor analysis of the 16 items used in the Madison study (presented in Tables 5 and 6) produces results somewhat different from those for Syracuse (Tables 3 and 4). The television items, shown in Table 5, factor into a reinforcement/excitement/communicatory

TABLE 4
Factor Analysis of Newspaper Gratifications and Avoidances,
1974 Syracuse Voting Study

Gratifications	Factor 1	Factor 2	Factor 3
1. To judge candidates	−.16	.62	.17
2. To judge who will win	−.08	.24	.55
3. To help vote	−.15	.79	.12
4. To remind of strong points	.03	.16	.37
5. To get something to talk about	.04	.14	.71
6. To see what candidates would do	.01	.75	.08
7. To enjoy excitement	.00	.09	.67
8. To see stands on issues	−.15	.73	.21
9. To see editorials, commentary	.02	.12	.57
10. To use in discussions	−.06	.13	.73
Avoidances			
1. Prefer to relax	.68	−.00	−.11
2. Mind made up	.63	−.13	.17
3. Nothing new	.64	−.25	.04
4. Rather view other things	.77	−.04	−.14
5. Not interested	.76	−.11	.01
6. Hard to understand	.69	.03	−.03

NOTE: Entries are correlations of the items with the rotated factors. N=339.

utility dimension somewhat similar to the one shown in Syracuse. One of the communicatory utility items, however, shows a somewhat weakened loading here. A clean surveillance/vote guidance factor also is produced. The avoidance items, however, are broken into two factors in Table 5.

In Table 6, however, which presents the factor analysis of the newspaper items, a clean avoidance factor emerges. Surveillance and vote guidance also load together. But here, the communicatory utility items break out separately, leaving the reinforcement and excitement seeking gratifications loading together.

TABLE 5
Factor Analysis of Television Gratifications and Avoidances,
1974 Madison Voting Study

Gratifications	Factor 1	Factor 2	Factor 3	Factor 4
1. To judge candidates	.20	.70	-.03	.07
2. To judge who will win	.71	.01	.14	-.13
3. To help vote	.07	.76	.03	-.11
4. To remind of strong points	.72	.23	.03	-.03
5. To get something to talk about	.54	.15	-.20	.46
6. To see what candidates would do	.21	.66	.05	-.19
7. To enjoy excitement	.61	.07	-.02	.26
8. To see stands on issues	.03	.80	-.02	-.02
9. To see editorials, commentary	.71	.16	.10	.01
10. To use in discussions	.33	.43	-.25	.52
Avoidances				
1. Prefer to relax	-.06	-.00	.75	.01
2. Mind made up	.02	-.26	.31	.67
3. Nothing new	-.11	-.37	.35	.58
4. Rather view other things	-.07	.09	.78	.08
5. Not interested	.15	-.12	.58	.13
6. Hard to understand	.14	.03	.61	-.02

NOTE: Entries are correlations of the items with the rotated factors. N=244.

In some respects, the factors in Table 6 are the cleanest shown so far. The minor discrepancies between the findings in Tables 3 through 6, however, indicate the fickle nature of such empirical solutions to the dimensionality problem.

1975 SYRACUSE VOTING STUDY

The analyses shown so far provide some indication of the levels and dimensionality of the gratifications and avoid-

TABLE 6
Factor Analysis of Newspaper Certifications and Avoidances,
1974 Madison Voting Study

Gratifications	Factor 1	Factor 2	Factor 3	Factor 4
1. To judge candidates	-.14	.68	.14	.19
2. To judge who will win	.03	.06	.73	.03
3. To help vote	-.06	.68	.10	.17
4. To remind of strong points	.10	.27	.64	.08
5. To get something to talk about	.01	.05	.21	.83
6. To see what candidates would do	.00	.59	.36	-.25
7. To enjoy excitement	.06	.06	.58	.31
8. To see stands on issues	-.13	.81	.08	.02
9. To see editorials, commentary	-.01	.16	.66	.22
10. To use in discussions	-.05	.17	.23	.77
Avoidances				
1. Prefer to relax	.71	-.17	.15	-.22
2. Mind made up	.66	-.01	.01	.05
3. Nothing new	.71	-.03	-.14	.10
4. Rather view other things	.70	.05	-.15	-.02
5. Not interested	.63	-.13	.20	-.01
6. Hard to understand	.62	-.17	.26	-.04

NOTE: Entries are correlations of the items with the rotated factors. N=244.

ances produced by the closed-ended procedure. They do not indicate how exhaustive the list of items is.

Data from a study conducted in the fall of 1975 provide some evidence on this point. Interviews were conducted with a sample of voters drawn from the same Syracuse voting district studied a year earlier. Included in the schedule were two open-ended questions designed to elicit from the sample members reasons why they sometimes "read newspaper stories or watch television or listen to radio news broadcasts dealing with local elections and politics" and reasons why they did not pay attention to such materials. Interviewers were instructed to probe for as many

TABLE 7

Open-Ended Responses to Gratification and Avoidance Probes
1975 Syracuse Voting Study

Gratification Dimensions	Responses	
Surveillance	46.8%	(153)
Vote guidance	39.4	(129)
Excitement	4.6	(15)
Reinforcement	2.1	(7)
Communication	1.2	(4)
Other	5.8	(19)
Total	99.9	(327)
Avoidance Dimensions		
Relaxation	36.9%	(106)
Alienation	34.8	(100)
Bias of Media	20.6	(59)
Partisanship	7.0	(20)
Other	.7	(2)
Total	100.0	(287)

NOTE: Each response to the gratification question was coded into one of the gratification dimensions. Avoidance responses were similarly coded. Respondents could give more than one answer. Several respondents gave no response to the avoidance question.

reasons as the respondent could give. The interviews were conducted in person.

The open-ended responses from the 299 respondents are shown in Table 7. Gratification responses were coded into five categories corresponding to the gratification dimensions shown in Table 1. The avoidance responses were coded into four categories: avoidance because of relaxation seeking, avoidance because of political alienation, avoidance because of perceived bias in the media, and avoidance because of partisan attitudes in conflict with the media content.

The dominance of surveillance/vote guidance types of comments is particularly strong in Table 7. The other gratifications, which were shown in Table 1 to be quite common, surface much less often when the respondents are asked to volunteer their gratifications. These other types of gratifications—reinforcement, excitement seeking, use because of anticipated utility of the information—are not readily verbalized or willingly volunteered by the respondents. While the focus of the question was on local politics for the 1975 study compared with politics in general for the 1974 Syracuse study, that difference hardly seems sufficient to account for the gross differences between Tables 1 and 7.

Many respondents were quite able and willing to give reasons why they sometimes avoided local political stories. Items dealing with perceived bias in the media were surprisingly common here. While this type of complaint may be exaggerated in Syracuse because of the poor quality of the media, similar complaints are likely to exist elsewhere in some form. Clearly, the item list shown in Table 2 is deficient in not including items of this sort.

1975 NORTHEASTERN NEWSPAPER AUDIENCE SURVEY

The data presented so far have dealt with gratifications that audience members report seeking from the political content of the media. Such content, of course, is only a fraction of what the media present. The relationship between gratifications sought from the political content of the media and gratifications sought from the media in general has not been explored.

Indirect inferences regarding this relationship can be made from data gathered as part of a readership study conducted in the fall of 1975 in a metropolitan newspaper market in the northeastern part of the United States. Included in the interview schedule was the list of gratifications shown in Table 8. Newspaper readers in the probability sample were asked in person to indicate to what extent the listed reasons applied to them.

The pattern of means shown in Table 8 is somewhat similar to those in Tables 1 and 2. Surveillance and guidance items (1-5, 7) received high endorsements comparable to those for similar items in Table 1. Reinforcement and com-

TABLE 8

**Levels of Nonpolitical Gratification,
1975 Northeastern Newspaper Audience Survey**

	Newspaper Readers
1. To keep up with the latest events	2.70 (.51)
2. To determine what is important	2.32 (.72)
3. To obtain useful information for daily life	2.34 (.70)
4. To help me form opinions about things going on around me	2.38 (.68)
5. To help me make decisions on issues	2.09 (.75)
6. Just to pass time	1.63 (.75)
7. To understand what's going on	2.53 (.59)
8. To be entertained	2.04 (.75)
9. To give me something to talk about with other people	2.09 (.76)
10. To use in discussions with my friends	2.08 (.76)
11. Because I agree with editorial stands	1.53 (.63)
12. To strengthen my arguments on issues	1.97 (.74)
13. To feel I am participating in current events	2.07 (.78)
14. For information in advertisements	1.71 (.77)
N=	(638)

NOTE: Entries are means and standard deviations. A high score indicates the reason for reading a newspaper applies to the respondent. The scores are based on a three-point scale.

municatory utility items were endorsed less often. The entertainment items, most similar of those listed to the excitement gratification in the political sphere, also were checked less often than the surveillance/vote guidance items.

TABLE 9
Factor Analysis of Nonpolitical Gratifications,
1975 Northeastern Newspaper Audience Survey

Gratifications	Factor 1	Factor 2	Factor 3
1. To keep up with events	.56	-.36	.08
2. To determine what is important	.65	-.24	.11
3. To obtain useful information	.62	-.26	.36
4. To help me form opinions	.70	-.27	.15
5. To help me make decisions	.65	-.29	.12
6. Just to pass time	-.02	.60	.52
7. To understand what's going on	.68	-.25	.11
8. To be entertained	.40	.45	.38
9. To get something to talk about	.69	.39	-.24
10. To use in discussions	.71	.30	-.34
11. Because I agree with stands	.41	-.33	-.13
12. To strengthen arguments	.67	.19	-.27
13. To feel I am participating	.66	.13	-.30
14. For advertisements	.26	.25	.41

NOTE: Entries are correlations of the items with the rotated factors. N=638.

A factor analysis of these gratifications, presented in Table 9, does *not* produce a structure closely matching those shown in earlier tables. The entertainment items, as would be expected, do factor out separately, and the single item on advertisements seems to be somewhat distinct. Every item but one, however, shows a fairly high loading on the primary factor, indicating a great deal of similarity in the way the respondents answered the whole battery of items. It remains somewhat unclear as to how similar the structure of the political and general gratifications may be. The preliminary evidence seems to be that the general gratifications are less well structured.

SUMMARY AND CONCLUSIONS

The data from the four studies allow for several conclusions regarding the exhaustiveness of existing gratifications measures. First, at least as far as political gratifications are concerned, the items developed by Blumler
and McQuail seem to cover adequately the range of relevant
motivations.

The list of political avoidances derived from the work of
Blumler and his colleagues and employed by McLeod and
Becker (1974), however, is deficient in at least one regard.
The list needs to be expanded to include avoidances be-
cause of perceived political bias in the media.

It also is clear that respondents will not necessarily
volunteer the same gratifications and avoidances to open-
ended questions as are tapped through the closed-ended
gratification and avoidance lists. In other words, respondents seem to be able to recognize an applicable gratification
when asked about it specifically, but not volunteer such
information without the specific probe.

Empirically, there are at least three distinct dimensions of
motivations. One cluster seems to be avoidance motivations
of various sorts. A second factor generally covers such
motives as vote guidance and surveillance. The final factor
consists of excitement seeking, reinforcement, and use of
the media for communicatory utility.

These empirical solutions, however, are rather divorced
from conceptual concerns. It is quite easy to distinguish
between a surveillance motivation, which would be expected to exist as a general state, and a guidance seeking
motivation linked to a specific decision confronting an individual. Empirically, that distinction does not seem to exist.
Clearly, efforts need to be made to differentiate via measurement between concepts as varied as some of those
appearing in the existing three clusters. Or more general
concepts need to be spelled out.

Those clusters, of course, are not totally consistent across studies. Where the nonpolitical materials are concerned, they cease to exist in any easily recognizable form. So while the data seem to suggest that the list of items being used is sufficient, they are quite inconclusive regarding conceptual questions of dimensionality.

The data are quite clear on one point: the gratifications do not seem to be media specific. The evidence suggests that people seeking a specific gratification from one medium seek that gratification from another as well.

It is not clear, however, that gratifications sought from the political materials in the media have some parallels in gratifications sought from other content or from the media in general. Again, this ambiguity results from the fact that the nonpolitical gratifications (in Tables 8 and 9) structure quite distinctly from those shown in earlier tables.

Finally, it is quite clear that the avoidance motivations are empirically quite distinct from the positive gratifications. In other words, the avoidances are not mirror-opposites of the gratifications—at least not those measured to date. While the gratifications seem to have a rather undifferentiated structure (there is little evidence of separate factors), their distinctiveness as a group calls for additional conceptual attention to them.

REFERENCES

BECKER, L. B. (1976) "Two tests of media gratifications: Watergate and the 1974 elections." Journalism Q. 53: 26-31.

BLUMLER, J. G. and D. McQUAIL (1969) Television in Politics. Chicago: Univ. of Chicago Press.

KATZ, E., J. G. BLUMLER, and M. GUREVITCH (1974) "Uses of mass communication by the individual," pp. 11-35 in W. P. Davison and F.T.C. Yu (eds.) Mass Communication Research. New York: Praeger.

KATZ, E., M. GUREVITCH, and H. HAAS (1973) "On the use of mass media for important things." Amer. Soc. Rev. 38: 164-181.

KLINE, F. G., P. V. MILLER, and A. J. MORRISON (1974) "Adolescents and family

planning information: an exploration of audience needs and media effects,"
pp. 113-136 in J. G. Blumler and E. Katz (eds.) The Uses of Mass Communications. Beverly Hills, CA: Sage.
McLEOD, J. M., and L. B. BECKER (1974) "Testing the validity of gratification
measures through political effects analysis," pp. 137-166 in J. G. Blumler and
E. Katz (eds.) The Uses of Mass Communications. Beverly Hills, CA: Sage.
McLEOD, J. M., J. D. BROWN, L. B. BECKER, and D. A. ZIEMKE (1977) "Decline
and fall at the White House: a longitudinal analysis of communication effects."
Communication Research 4: 3-22.

*Lee B. Becker is an Associate Professor in the School of Journalism at Ohio
State University. He received his Ph.D. from the School of Journalism and
Mass Communication at the University of Wisconsin, Madison.*

*Broadcast law in Sweden requires impartiality in news reporting by Swedish radio and television.
As a result of controversy about whether such regulation is successful, Swedish scholars have developed innovative ways to measure impartiality. Rosengren argues that maintenance of media credibility demands that news must always be* partial, *to some extent, to the basic values of the dominant
culture in which it is written and reported. As a result, he proposes a synthesis of the objectivity,
international news flow, and credibility news research "traditions." This chapter was first presented
as a paper at the ICA Convention in Berlin during the summer of 1977. Dr. Rosengren is a sociologist
at the University of Lund, Sweden.*

14

BIAS IN NEWS
Methods and Concepts

Karl Erik Rosengren

I.

The news presented in Swedish media has been investigated perhaps more than any other country's news. The results of the many investigations as a rule have been considered reassuring, especially for the Swedish Radio and Television(the SR). With few exceptions—such as the notorious Barsebäck Panic which was no panic (26)—the news of the SR has been found to be on the whole truthful, relevant, balanced and neutral. (These four characteristics have often been mentioned as corresponding to the general demands on the SR, raised by Swedish society and formulated in laws and agreements. They are explicated and discussed in, for instance, 10, 11, 29, 30.)

Most of these investigations have been carried out by professor Jörgen Westerståhl and his group at the Department of Political Science, University of Gothenburg (cf. 29, 30, 31). They represent a sustained, impressive and probably unique effort of "measuring objectivity" (29) in news reports. But they have one weak spot in common. The "objectivity" of the SR has been measured by means of comparisons with other media. If the SR has been found situated in the middle of the field, everything has been OK.

Over the years growing dissatisfaction with this method-

*Dr. Rosengren is a Research Fellow of the Swedish Research Council for the Humanities and the Social Sciences, currently active at the Department of Sociology, University of Lund, Sweden.

This paper, originally, was presented to the Mass Communication Division, ICA Convention, Berlin, May 29-June 4, 1977. It is published here by the permission of the author.

ology has been aired now and again. Comparisons between media is not enough, it has been maintained. Reality—as far as we know it—must be heeded, too. Possible "bias" in reality must somehow be controlled for. When in 1976 Westerståhl published his latest report, on the coverage of the Portuguese revolution in the SR (31), the debate kindled again. A foreign correspondent at the largest Swedish quality paper, Mr. Sven Öste at the *Dagens Nyheter*, expressed the criticism with journalistic verve:

> "What would have happened...if in 1965 the same technique should have been applied to the Vietnam reports in American radio and TV?...Safer...one of the few to see through the propaganda smoke screens...Safer would have been burnt at the stake." (17)

The criticism against the Westerståhl methodology, however, has been hampered by being unable to present any realistic alternative. Gradually, though, such an alternative has developed. The study of news reporting, it has been suggested, should to advantage be regarded as the study of a relation: the relation between reality (as far as it is known) and the picture of reality offered by the news media. Comparisons between the media, of course, will always be necessary. But reality, too, must be heeded.—Such a perspective is both necessary and fruitful, but it has some complications.

For example, it presupposes two sets of data—data about reality and data about the media picture of reality—which ideally should be independent of each other in the sense that they should not stem from the same source. Data about the media picture by definition come from the media; they are intra media data. Consequently, data about the known reality should as much as possible be fetched from sources outside the media; they should be extra media data (20, 22, 12).

The distinction intra/extra media data could certainly be discussed from several angles, philosophical as well as technical (23). One technical problem, though, is overriding: pure extra media data may be hard to come by. Over the years, several solutions to this basic problem have been suggested.

Extra media data of very diverse nature have been used, and may be used in the future.

For instance, one may use undisputable historical facts, as Walter Lippman did 57 years ago with respect to the Russian revolution, and as Lewis did 17 years ago with respect to the Cuban revolution (16, 14). One may check up with people appearing in the news (2,4,27). One may use planted observers (9, 13), photos (15), protocols (24), white books (28), surveys originally undertaken for other purposes (18), or carried out especially for the purpose (26). One may turn to official statistics (21).

But all the same there are cases where no ready-made extra media data are at hand. Then another solution must be resorted to. The researcher must himself establish a list of relevant events and conditions, and make this list the starting-point of his investigation. Often such lists may be compiled from calendars etc. such as, for instance, *Keesing's Contemporary Archives*. Then, of course, we are no longer dealing with pure extra media data, for very often the contents of such chronicles stem from the mass media. In these cases another distinction comes to the forefront: the distinction between event oriented studies and report oriented studies.

In event oriented studies events are studied with respect to the amount and type of reports it gets in the news media. ("Out of these 200 statements, how many were reported upon?") In report oriented studies, reports are studied with respect to what type of events they cover. ("Out of these 200 reports of statements, how many were made by social democrats?") Most news studies have been report oriented. In such studies it may be difficult to differentiate between bias inherent in reality and bias inherent in the reporting. One cannot "control for reality".

Now, if we combine the two distinctions intra/extra media data and event/report orientation, we arrive at the fourfold table of Figure 1. (The table is similar to, but does not coincide with the four types of tables discussed in 22.)

Fig. 1   Typology of News Studies

	Intra media data only	Intra and extra media data
Report oriented	1	2
Event oriented	3	4

Cell 1 contains most traditional news studies. Cell 2 represents cases where extra media data are used as some sort of a standard, in evaluative investigations of one sort or another. Cell 4 represents the most demanding, but also the most fruitful approach. It opens up the possibility of fairly sophisticated explanatory investigations. Often, however, one has to make do with studies of the type represented by cell 3. Such studies are based on intra media data only, but all the same event oriented.

With some simplification it may be maintained that, like cell 4, event oriented cell 3 controls for reality, something which cell 1 does not do. In some cases it is possible by means of secondary analysis to turn studies of type 1 into type 3. That is what I tried to do when the Swedish Radio Council asked me to evaluate professor Westerståhl's report on SR's news from the Portuguese revolution. In the next section, some results from this secondary analysis will be presented (cf. 31,23).

II.

Compare Tables 1 and 2. (Table 1 is taken more or less directly from Westerståhl's report (31), while Table 2 represents a secondary analysis of material collected by Westerståhl (23). Both tables treat the attention bestowed by various Swedish news media upon statements made by the several parties of the Portuguese revolution during the time period studied by Westerståhl (May-July 1975). But Table 1 is report oriented, while Table 2 is event oriented. Table 1 distributes media

Table 1   Reports of Statements from Parties in the Portuguese
Revolution in Six Swedish Media (per cent within media).*

	SR Straight News	SR Com- ments	DN (lib.)	SvD (cons.)	Arbt (soc. dem.)	Nfl (comm.)
MFA	24	20	21	20	15	35
Copcon	6	10	7	9	5	5
Governm.	5	5	6	7	5	5
Comm.	13	13	10	12	13	28
Left grps.	2	4	3	4	1	0
Socialists	37	40	41	36	49	23
Dem. P.P.	9	5	8	8	7	0
Others	4	2	4	3	4	5
Total	100	99	100	99	99	101
Number of mentions	141	340	220	245	202	40

*Adapted from (31).

Table 2   Percentage of Parties' Statements Reported
at Least Once by Swedish Media*

	SR Straight News	SR Com- ments	DN (lib.)	SvD (cons.)	Arbt (soc. dem.)	Nfl (comm.)	Statements registered
MFA	29	47	43	42	32	14	79
Copcon	25	57	50	54	32	7	28
Governm.	18	24	30	36	21	6	33
Comm.	20	31	27	29	31	11	75
Left grps.	4	46	25	38	8	0	24
Socialists	27	48	41	44	47	6	115
Dem.P.P.	44	39	61	50	50	0	18
Others	20	25	30	35	35	10	20
Per cent statements reported	24	41	38	40	35	8	392 (total)

*Recalculated from data in (31).   The table says, for instance, that the MFA
has been registered for 79 statements.   Of these, 29% were reported at
least once in the SR Straight News, which reported on 24% of the 392
statements registered in all.

reports about statements over the authors of the statements grouped into parties. The base of the percentages in this table is the total number of statement reports of each medium. Table 2 tells us what proportion of each party's statements was reported (at least once) by this and that medium. The base of the percentages is the total number of statements listed from each party.

In all, there were 392 such statements listed, found by Westerståhl in Le Monde, The Guardian, the SR and four Swedish newspapers covering the political spectre from communists to conservatives. They represent intra media data, of course, which makes Table 2 a type 3 table. But because of the wide range of sources used, it is not very likely that any important statement by any important actor has been missed. Therefore, the intra media data of the table may be used as a substitute for the extra media data demanded by strict methodology.

Table 2, then, may be said to "control for reality". (It takes care, for instance, of the fact that the Leftist groups produced only 24 statements, the Socialists no less than 115.) But on the other hand, Table 1 controls for the differential space of the various media, something which Table 2 does not do. In Table 1, then, comparisons must be made between media within parties; in Table 2, within media between parties. What is needed is a table which makes possible comparisons between media and parties at the same time. Table 3 is such a table. It has the combined advantages of event and report oriented tables.

Table 3 is built upon material from Tables 1 and 2. For instance, Table 1 tells us that SR straight news dedicated 24% of its statements mentioned to the MFA, while Table 2 tells us that the MFA produced 79 (=20%) out of the 392 statements listed. SR straight news, then, somewhat overrepresented MFA statements, compared to the statements actually listed (24 vs. 20%). This overrepresentation may be given the numerical expression $100 \times 24/20 = 120$. The corresponding values for all parties and media are given in Table 3, which has the combined advantages of event and report oriented tables.

Like Table 2 it "controls for reality", and like Table 1 it controls for differential space. It therefore admits comparisons between both parties and media. (Values over 100 denotes overrepresentation; values below 100, underrepresentation, compared to the number of statements actually listed from the different parties of the conflict.)

Table 3   Under- and Overrepresentation of Parties' Statements, Controlling for Number of Statements and Space*

	SR Straight News	SR Comments	DN (lib.)	SvD (cons.)	Arbt (soc. dem.)	Nfl (comm.)
MFA	120	100	105	100	75	175
Copcon	86	143	100	129	71	71
Governm.	63	63	75	88	63	63
Comm.	68	68	53	63	68	147
Left grps.	33	67	50	67	17	—
Socialists	128	138	141	124	169	79
Dem. P.P.	180	100	160	160	140	—
Others	80	40	80	60	80	100

*Recalculated from data in (31).   Values above 100 denote overrepresentation compared to the parties' proportion of statements registered in the material: under 100, underrepresentation

Several technical points could be discussed in connection with Table 3 (cf. 23).   Let me only point out that, just as Table 2, it must not be seen as an indirect proposal that all desks and media mechanically relay the same percentage of all statements from all parties in all conflicts.   Of course, there are a host of legitimate reasons why some or all media should under- or overrepresent the statements of some parties in some conflicts. But it should be an urgent task of research to ascertain the extent to which such over- or underrepresentation actually occurs, and then to discuss the facts against the background of common custom and consensual values.   Such a discussion may be based on tables like Table 3, but not on tables like Table 1.

And now, let us turn straight to the most important substantive content of Table 3. The leading Swedish news media (the SR and the three leading social democrat, liberal and conservative dailies) overrepresented the statements of the socialists, underrepresented those of the communists. For the communist daily, it was the other way round.

Since as a rule it is advantageous for the parties of a conflict to have its messages relayed by the media, it may be maintained that the leading Swedish news media were partial in favour of the socialists, to the disadvantage of the communists, while—quite naturally—the communist daily distributed its favours in the opposite direction. That the communist paper, "The Flame" is in favour of communists, is hardly any surprise. But that the SR—under law prescribed to be impartial—should be about as partial as the Flame—although in the opposite direction—may be news to some good citizens. It may seem surprising and even unpleasant, but it is indeed quite natural and understandable, only that there has been no hard figures to show it, since professor Westerståhl's tables have been type 1 tables.

III.

Journalistic work to a large extent consists in the evaluation of news, choosing between what to publish and what to throw away. The choices must be made very quickly, of necessity against a background of more basic values and evaluations. It is obvious that this background must make itself felt in the journalistic work. News therefore reflects the basic values of the journalists, and, ultimately, of their readers.

An overwhelming majority of the Swedish people—at least some 95%—does not share the basic values held by different communist parties. A very large minority—in some questions no doubt a large majority—does share the basic values held by Mario Soares' socialist party and their European sister parties, such as the Swedish social democrats. So it is quite natural that the greater part of the Swedish news system should be partial in favour of the Portuguese socialists, to the disadvantage of the communists. This holds true also for the SR, which in this case may be said to have been looking more to a paragraph prescribing it to "uphold democratic values" than to the paragraph about "impartiality". The case of the Portuguese revolution, then, rather nicely illustrates the thesis that the news disseminated in a country reflects the value system prevailing in that country. Another case in point is represented by Swedish news from the Middle East, which also has been shown to reflect Swedish sympathies for the Israeli side (25).

Knowing that partiality in news reporting often may be inevitable, it is all the more important from time to time to produce material such as Table 3 to show in concrete cases precisely how great the partiality may have been, against whom. It is also important to discuss how partial one should be allowed to be, roughly, against whom. And above all, it is important not to let the knowledge that partiality may be inevitable serve as a pretense for all sorts of conscious bias. On the contrary: the effort should be to curb as far as possible the seemingly inevitable partiality.

Accusations of unfairness, lack of impartiality etc. have been rather common in the Swedish debate about news reporting, just as in the corresponding debates in some other countries. If the arguments of this paper are correct, the combatants of such discussions may be more right than they think. All the same, the factual basis for these debates has been rather weak, one reason being that most studies of news reporting have been report oriented and based on intra media data only—an approach which makes correct evaluations of news reporting all but impossible. In this paper some alternatives to such an approach have been suggested. In the final section of the paper, the perspective will be broadened.

IV.

The study of news flow and news structure has taken place within several rather self-contained research traditions. One of these might be called the "objectivity tradition", in Sweden energetically represented by Jörgen Westerståhl (29, 30, 31). Another one is the "international flow tradition", represented by Galtung, Gerbner and others (6, 7, 22). A third related tradition is the credibility tradition, represented by Roper, Greenberg, Edelstein and others, in Sweden recently summarized and developed by Arvidson (1; cf. 3, 5, 8, 19). While the former two traditions deal with news reports and the process leading up to the news, the latter deals with the relationship between the news and the public. This paper represents an attempt to merge the "objectivity tradition" with the "international flow" tradition. However, a similar confluence with the "credibility tradition" might be worth trying, too.

It has been maintained in this paper that the news reporting in a country must be partial in a way reflecting the basic values and actual sympathies of the population. The reason for this is simply that otherwise the credibility of the media will disappear. Indeed, the whole Portugal debate in Sweden is a case in point here. It was triggered by a social democrat free lance journalist objecting to the allegedly communist perspective of a radio correspondent which seems to have deviated from the rest of the SR reporting. We have just seen, however, that in reality the SR reporting was as imbalanced or partial as that of a communist daily, only the other way round. But the SR was not criticized on this ground, it was criticized because one of its staff members may have been imbalanced or partial in the opposite direction. Thus, imbalance or partiality *per se* is not criticized. Only partiality which does not fit in with the basic values and sympathies embraced by a majority of the people is criticized. For such partiality does not produce reports perceived as trustworthy, credible, reliable. Imbalance and partiality—both key concepts in the objectivity tradition—are closely connected with trustworthiness and credibility—key concepts in the credibility tradition. Therefore, the two research traditions should be merged.

One possible starting-point for such a merger may be the simple conceptual scheme suggested by Arvidson (1) to bring

Fig. 2   Conceptual Scheme for Credibility Studies

		Perspective		
		Holistic Long-term Evaluative		Detailed Short-term Cognitive
	Medium	Trustworthiness	Credibility	Reliability
Characteristic of	Public in relation to medium	Trust	Credit	Reliance
	public at large		Credulity	

some order into the welter of more or less overlapping terms and concepts hampering the credibility tradition. The scheme is reproduced in Figure 2. Its details may be discussed, of course, but as a first step towards conceptual clarification it may be quite useful. Many credibility studies have moved about somewhat carelessly in the unknown property space outlined by the scheme.

Trying to relate the "objectivity tradition" and the "credibility tradition" to each other, it might be fruitful to try to create a similar conceptual scheme for the objectivity tradition. Starting from the Swedish radio law and from the agreement between the SR and the state, Westerståhl has made an attempt in this direction, much discussed in Scandinavia. It is rendered in Figure 3.

Fig. 3   Westerståhl's Classificatory Scheme (cf. *10, 29, 30*).

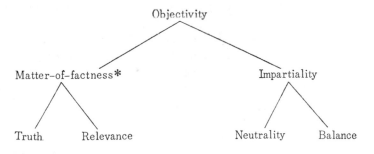

*Swedish "saklighet" is difficult to translate into English. (Cf. German "Sachlichkeit".) "Pertinence", perhaps?

Westerståhl's scheme has been criticized by many (cf. 10, 11, 23). All the same, Westerståhl is probably right in maintaining that truth and relevance go together in that both concepts are related to cognitions about the reported reality, while neutrality and balance have to do with evaluations, conflicts of interests etc. (30, p.12). But it is equally undeniable that truth and neutrality go together in that both are related to the contents of the news reports—the presentation part of the journalistic work, as it were—while relevance and balance have as much to do with what is not reported—i.e., with the selection part of the journalistic work. The dimensions mentioned so far are tentatively combined in Figure 4.

Fig. 4 Dimensions of News Assessment

		Criteria for assessment	
		Cognitive	Evaluative
To be assessed	Content, Presentation	Truth	Neutrality
	Selection	Relevance	Balance

It is, of course, necessary to add yet other distinctions, and that will complicate the outcome (cf. 23). Figure 4, therefore, must be regarded as a tentative sketch only. It has, however, the advantage of relating four important concepts to each other in a somewhat less rigid and hierarchical way than the original Westerståhl's scheme. It thus evades the contradiction between the hierarchical design of Westerståhl's scheme and the fact—pointed out by Westerståhl himself; (30, p.22)—that the four concepts may vary independently of each other (although truth is always the first demand).

Now, the logical next step should be to develop the two conceptual schemes of Figures 2 and 4 further, to relate them to each other, and to apply them in empirical research. It will be noted that one dimension is common to the two conceptual schemes: the cognitive-evaluative dimension. This gives us a hint about two possible conceptual chains. On the cognitive side: truth/relevance-reliability/reliance. And on the evaluative side: neutrality/ balance-trustworthiness/ trust (with credibility/ credit/credulity possibly falling somewhere in between). To be fruitfully applied in empirical research, of course, the two abstract conceptual chains have to be related to concrete beliefs about, and attitudes towards, the news events being studied.

Empirical and theoretical research along these tentative lines is about to start at the University of Lund, sponsored by the Swedish Board of Psychological Defense. Hopefully, it will tell us something about the cognitive and evaluative frames within which news must be kept in order not to lose drastically in credibility. Such knowledge should have some policy relevance, especially, perhaps, in a country like Sweden, which has a broadcast monopoly under law prescribed to disseminate in a neutral way truthful, relevant and balanced news.

References

1. Arvidson, P., "Trovärdigheten hos massmedierna"/Mass Media Credibility/, *Psykologiskt försvar* 81, 1977, Stockholm: Beredskapsnämnden för psykologiskt försvar.
2. Berry, F.C. Jr., "A Study of Accuracy in Local News Stories of Three Dailies", *Journalism Quarterly* 44, 1967, pp. 482–490.
3. Carter, R. and B.S. Greenberg, "Newspaper or Television: Which Do You Believe?", *Journalism Quarterly* 42, 1965, pp. 29–34.
4. Charnley, M.V., "Preliminary Notes on a Study of Newspaper Accuracy", *Journalism Quarterly* 13, 1936, pp. 394–401.
5. Edelstein, A.S. and D.P. Tefft, "Media Credibility and Respondent Credulity with Respect to Watergate", *Communication Research* 1, 1974, pp. 426–439.
6. Galtung, J. and M. Holmboe Ruge, "The Structure of Foreign News", *Journal of Peace Research*, 2, 1965, pp. 64–91.
7. Gerbner, G. and G. Marvanyi, "International News: The Many Worlds of the World's Press", *Journal of Communication* 27, 1977, pp. 52–66.
8. Greenberg, B.S. and M.E. Roloff, "Mass Media Credibility: Research Results and Critical Issues", *News Research Bulletin* No.6, 1974.
9. Halloran, J. *et al.*, *Demonstrations and Communication*, Harmondsworth: Penguin, 1970.

10. Hemánus, P., "What is News? Objectivity in News Transmission", *Journal of Communication* 26, 1976, pp. 102–107.

11. Hermerén, G., "Kvantitativ objektivitetsmätning"/Quantitative Measurement of Objectivity/,*Statsvetenskaplig tidskrift* 53, 1973, pp.151–163.

12. Hicks, R.G. and A. Gordon, "Foreign News Content in Israeli and US Newspapers", *Journalism Quarterly* 51, 1974, pp. 639–644.

13. Lang, K. and G.E. Lang, "The Unique Perspective of Television and Its Effects", *American Sociological Review* 18, 1953, pp. 3–12.

14. Lewis, H.L., "The Cuban Revolt Story: AP, UPI and 3 Papers", *Journalism Quarterly* 37, 1960, pp. 573–578.

15. Lindblom, B., ed., *Fallet Båstad*/The Case of Båstad/, Stockholm: Wahlström & Widstrand, 1968.

16. Lippman, W. and C. Merz, "A Test of the News", *The New Republic*, Aug. 4, 1920.

17. Öste, S., "Portugal i radion: Kan man mäta en reporters partiskhet?", *Degens Nyheter*, March 17, 1976.

18. Owen, J., "The Polls and Newspaper Appraisal of the Suez Crisis", *Public Opinion Quarterly* 21, 1957, pp. 350–354.

19. Roper B.W., *Trends in Public Attitudes Toward Television and Other Media 1959–1974*, New York: Telev. Inform. Off., 1975.

20. Rosengren, K.E., "International News: Intra and Extra Media Data", *Acta Sociologica* 13, 1970, pp. 96–109.

21. Rosengren, K.E., "International News: Methods, Data and Theory", *Journal of Peace Research* 11, 1974, pp. 145–156.

22. Rosengren, K.E., "International News: Four Types of Tables", *Journal of Communication* 27, 1977, pp. 67–75.

23. Rosengren, K.E., "Värderade nyheter"/Evaluated News/, *Statsvetenskaplig tidskrift* 57, 1977 (in press).

24. Rosengren, K.E. *et al.*, "Tidningsstruktur och politisk information"/ Press Structure and Political Information/, *Statsvetenskaplig tidskrift* 54, 1974, pp.78–90.

25. Rosengren, K.E. and G. Rikardsson, "Middle East News in Sweden", *Gazette* 20, 1974, pp. 99–116.

26. Rosengren, K.E. *et al.*, "The Barsebäck 'Panic': A Radio Programme as a Negative Summary Event", *Acta Sociologica* 18, 1975, pp. 303–321.

27. Scanlon, T.J., "A New Approach to the Study of Newspaper Accuracy", *Journalism Quarterly* 49, 1972, pp. 588–590.

28. Smith, R.F., "On the Structure of Foreign News: A Comparison with the New York Times and the Indian White Papers", *Journal of Peace Research* 6, 1969, pp. 23–36.

29. Westerståhl, J., "Objectivity Is Measurable", *EBU-Review* 121 B, 1970, pp. 13–17.

30. Westerståhl, J., *Objektiv nyhetsförmedling*/Objective News/, Stockholm:

Scandinavian University Books, 1972.
31. Westerståhl, J., "Ljudradions bevakning av händelserna i Portugal"/Radio Coverage of the Portugal Events/, Dept. of Pol. Science, Gothenburg 1972 (mimeo).

Contemporary controversies involving the performance of the mass media in the Watergate scandal and the Vietnam war have highlighted the importance of organizational studies of the media. This rediscovery of the organizational context has led to new work and to reanalysis of older research. Paul M. Hirsch summarizes and reinterprets much of this work, and, more importantly, he analyzes the strengths and theoretical interrelationships of the occupational, organizational, and institutional models of research. His work points macro-level studies across news and entertainment forms and and across media as well. Dr. Hirsch is a sociologist in the Graduate School of Business at the University of Chicago.

15

OCCUPATIONAL, ORGANIZATIONAL, AND INSTITUTIONAL MODELS IN MASS MEDIA RESEARCH
Toward an Integrated Framework

Paul M. Hirsch

PROLOGUE

THE STUDY OF MASS MEDIA is typically ordered around a principle of uniqueness which confuses the concepts of internal organization and institutional function. Institutionally, there are differences in the audience for (and prestige accorded) print versus broadcast journalists, and to all journalism versus (mere) entertainment. But in terms of how news and entertainment actually are produced and distributed, across media, the organizational similarities outweigh the differences. For example, both news and entertainment are forms of symbolic content created by employees to be utilized, modified, or discarded by employers whose organizations seek to earn profits or find subsidies. Under these (and other) common constraints, the creators and overseers of print and broadcast news and entertainment all share a preoccupation with organizational issues like budgets, salaries, deadlines, circulation, ratings, advertisers, and reputation. While the institutional functions served by each type differ significantly, both news and entertainment features are usually produced and distributed by the same organizations (newspapers, syndicates, broadcasting corporations) and supported by advertising (or other funding agencies). Their audiences also overlap, and both come from departments lodged in the same organizational entities. Each type of communication boasts high standards of craftsmanship, jealously guards its prerogatives against censorship, forms its own occupational community, and often complains about the same (bureaucratic)

AUTHOR'S NOTE: I wish to thank Michael Schudson for helpful comments, and the Rockefeller Foundation for supporting the research on which this chapter is based.

From Paul M. Hirsch, "Occupational, Organizational, and Institutional Models in Mass Media Research: Toward an Integrated Framework," *Strategies for Communication Research*, Paul M. Hirsch et al., eds. (1977) 13-42. Copyright 1977 by Sage Publications, Inc.

enemy. Interestingly, both occupational communities often accord higher honor to those members with audiences which are elite in status and small in size, such as columnists for the *New Yorker* or actors in theater rather than television. To point to these commonalities is not to suggest that either form is inherently corrupt because of its similarity to the other. Rather, it is to distinguish between the (similar) manner in which each is produced by organizations running rationally, on the one hand, and the social values placed on news versus entertainment on the other.

Against these similarities, the principle of uniqueness emphasizes distinctions between types of symbolic content. It assigns each to predesignated categories like "news" and "entertainment" and strongly asserts these are mutually exclusive, as well as internally differentiated according to which of the mass media they are created for. Generally, print is more serious; broadcasting more entertaining. These distinctions, however, derive from competing functions, interests, and professional rivalries more than from organizational differences in how each is created and distributed; and they are frequently exaggerated into ideologies and espoused by each specialty's practitioners and professional schools—of journalism versus radio and television versus theater arts, for example. Here, the categories "news," "entertainment," "print," and "broadcast" are effectively utilized to distinguish and segregate media and types of content that nevertheless remain strikingly similar in the manner that each is organized. In the university setting, analytical similarities have been downplayed, with each area more often concerned with substantive research and training students for their respective crafts and professions. In academic departments, particular slices of content or categories, across media, also are selected and predictably emphasized by researchers according to specialty—for example, election coverage by political scientists, drama and narrative form by English departments, sex role stereotypes and violence by sociologists. Studies of media audiences, economics and public policy (in marketing journals, policy institutes, and law and business schools, primarily) add useful ideas and information, though often these begin and end with very few words about the content of the particular media or industries on which they focus (see, for example, Aacker and Myers, 1975; Owen, 1975; and Noll, Peck, and McGowan, 1973).

This curious division of intellectual labor has fragmented the study of mass communication into an enormous number of fiefdoms and provinces, each with its own special interests or ideological stance. It has had the effect of inflating differences between the activities involved in producing different types of content, their meaning, and the significance of their appearance in different media. While the internal operation and institutional function of mass media organizations may be independent of each other, the ideologies of news producers and of their counterparts in entertainment have long and studiously resisted comparison, all claiming their activities are unique, in structure and mission. After a certain point, however, the respective ideologies appear short-sighted and often lead to unnecessary embarrassment, as when it is pointed out (and true but not shameful) that journalism reflects deadlines, or that much news is organizationally "manufactured," like spaghetti. Yet, perhaps because the ideology of each content group is lodged in such different settings, each continues to claim near-total uniqueness, based on those few dimensions on which it stands most apart from all the rest. What actually *is* unique about each area risks getting lost, for it is thereby merged with aspects which are not very unusual (as, for example, when the Associated Press once argued unsuccessfully for its immunity from the National Labor Relations Act, on the grounds that it had absolute and unrestricted freedom under the First Amendment to hire and fire its employees; cf. Gillmor and Barron, 1969). Such topics and issues, when improperly claimed as unique and defended as necessary for the maintenance of high standards, often become the stuff of "dirty laundry" as soon as outsiders discover and report them as such (e.g., Epstein, 1973; Altheide, 1976). The prospective loss of legitimacy, in turn, jeopardizes recognition of the important analytic distinction between the social functions served by particular symbolic content (e.g., news) and the manner in which it is produced.

This chapter is not intended to equate mass media information and entertainment content. As a field of study, however, mass communication must encompass both, and do a better job of treating the two comparatively in terms of a set of common dimensions, on some of which the two will vary. For example, utilizing recent work in industrial and organizational sociology and cutting across the different media and content categories, we can compare the administration of mass media organizations, social control of subordinates, organizational levels of authority, working conditions, organization size, uncertainty, boundary-spanning roles, and occupational communities. These and other dimensions for comparison will be incorporated in the occupational, organizational, and institutional approaches to be discussed shortly.

AN ORGANIZATIONAL PERSPECTIVE

My point of departure and basic conceptual framework is an organizational perspective on mass communication. This provides a useful counterweight to the insistence upon uniqueness asserted so often by spokesmen for particular media or types of symbolic content. It reverses the logic common to most professional schools by looking upon the people, crafts, and product as distinctive only after examining the bureaucracies in which they reside, and asking how these are similar to other organizations processing other types of tangible or intangible commodities, be they books, stock market prices, or automobiles. This perspective finds clear analytical similarities among the constraints on and organizational context in which reporters, writers, artists, actors, directors, editors, producers, publishers, executive vice presidents, and others learn and carry out activities characteristic of their respective roles, crafts and occupations. From an administrative standpoint, the symbolic content created or supervised by each is both vital to mass media organizations and produced and syndicated by many of the same entities. There also is substantial cross-ownership among the different media in which it appears. The organizational perspective thus emphasizes that since news and entertainment usually are produced and distributed through the same mass media bureaucracies, *each constitutes a mere department (or division) in large-scale organizations,* along with sales and advertising, audience and market research, printing, film processing, bookkeeping, and others. Its clear expectations are that (1) occupations and organizations engaged in the production of any symbolic content will share many characteristics in common (despite their own denials); (2) what is most distinctive about them is best understood by comparing them to occupations and organizations engaged in producing other types of products; and (3) we can learn more about how news and entertainment production differ by first inquiring into areas in which they are, in fact, similar.

As an example of the direction in which this approach leads, consider the economic concept of oligopoly. Firms in oligopolistic markets (regardless of the products or services they provide) are predicted by economists to act in similar ways regarding strategies in such areas as pricing policies, product differentiation, innovation, and wage rates. Today, the television industry, with three dominant firms (networks) acts remarkably like an oligopoly (Dominick and Pierce, 1976; Noll, Peck, and McGowan, 1973), as did the motion picture industry before it was divested of movie theaters by antitrust action and had to adapt to the advent of television (Hirsch, 1972). Like radio, it has since become more diverse in the subjects (or formats) treated, and more economically competitive. A similar relation between competition and innovation has been found in the recording industry (Peterson and Berger, 1975), and it is widely suggested that television content would become more diverse if the number of networks and channels available were to increase. Most newspapers, on the other hand, are best characterized as local monopolies, and tend to behave in the directions predicted by that economic model (Roose, 1967). As will be emphasized throughout, it is important for mass media researchers to keep in mind such nonmedia-based economic models, conditions, and contexts. The behavior of mass media organizations toward their product, mission, employees, regulatory agents, and audience cannot be explained solely by the type(s) of symbolic content (news, entertainment) which they provide, or by the personal desires of their owners and managers.

When taking the entire organization, rather than specific roles, units, or departments within it as a unit of analysis, this general perspective also offers a means of examining how professions and mass media organizations interact with audiences and agencies in their political and economic environments. It seeks to take account, for example, of the peculiar fact that significant portions of the mass media audience make few distinctions between informational, editorial, and entertainment content (Goodhardt, Ehrenberg and Collins, 1975). Nor, apparently do: political representatives conducting hearings about mass communication; mass media trade papers; many executives in media organizations; some citizens' groups in the United States; and many governments seeking to regulate print and broadcast content. When violence on television is deplored by respondents to surveys, it is violence on news broadcasts to which a majority objects (Robinson, 1972); and when American news programs seek to improve ratings, it is to more entertaining features, pacing, and attractive anchorpersons that television organizations have turned increasingly—as did many newspapers earlier, analogously, when there was greater competition in the cities where the survivors are located (Hirsch, forthcoming). Obviously, the distinction between news and entertainment content has become more complex during the last decade. As Tuchman points out (in this volume), such common distinctions as hard and soft news may derive more from internal organizational needs and bureaucratic convenience than from the nature or institutional functions of "news" itself. These types of questions, in turn, raise others about the general role of mass media in society, and the pros and cons of whatever degree of consensus is achieved by blanketing a nation with the same information and images. They call for the articulation of organizational and institutional models, in which mass media organizations *qua* organizations play a far larger role than they are usually accorded in case studies of single newsrooms, entertainment production units, or occupational communities. The intellectual roots of these questions trace back to a series of earlier, pioneering studies in precisely these latter areas, however. One of our major concerns is to explore ways to incorporate, draw on, and further develop their insights.

THREE MODELS OF MASS MEDIA ORGANIZATIONS

Three distinct models, or levels of analysis, characterize nearly all social science research on the operation of mass media. The *first* focuses on occupational roles, careers, and the interaction of mass media organizations with the individuals fulfilling them. The classic studies of gatekeeping, social control, and occupational socialization in journalism, or of conflicts between the ideals expressed by professional actors, directors, or reporters versus constraints found in the newsroom or other organizations exemplify this model. The *second* model takes the organization as a whole, and its administration, as the main object of analysis. Here, the task of coordinating the newsgathering activities of reporters and editors, or defining production requirements that affect filmmakers' decisions about scripts, casting, and the amount of running time for a finished work are more typical subjects for study. The *third* level, interorganizational and institutional analysis, examines relationships between organizations or professions and the larger societal environment in which they operate. Cross-ownership of media properties, postal rates' impact on magazine publishers' cost structures, and the derivation of news categories and journalistic traditions from the economic requirements of putting out a daily newspaper exemplify the types of issues taken up in interorganizational and institutional analyses. Like industrial sociology and social science more generally, mass communication research traditionally has focused on the individual creator/worker and his or her occupational experience. Studies taking the second or third approach have appeared more recently.

When these models are ranged on a continuum from "closed" to "open" systems, the earliest studies—of individuals and roles at the bottom of organizational hierarchies (actors, reporters)—come closest to utilizing the theoretical framework of a closed system. These take the organization in which people work as their surrounding environment. More recent examinations taking the organizations themselves, or sets of organizations as their units of analysis, encompass broader aspects of mass media environments—such as advertisers, government regulatory agencies, and audience demand factors. In so doing, they conform more to the theoretical tenets of open systems analysis by emphasizing larger units of analysis, activities on the boundaries of organizations, and external variables as primary agents of organizational change (Katz and Kahn, 1966; Hirsch, 1975a). These models, while analytically distinct, are not mutually exclusive. Rather, they work best when taken together, with each helping the others present alternative interpretations of findings or raise new questions for investigation. They are further interrelated in that the first examines how individuals work to create mass media content, while the second focuses on the organizational arrangements within which this occurs, and which corporately produce and distribute the finished product. The third is most useful for studying the cultural, economic, and political environments in which mass media and the professions comprising them act as a major social institution (albeit one among others).[1]

We will discuss and elaborate on each model in the order just presented. The attendant literature review is more illustrative than exhaustive in intent.

OCCUPATIONAL ROLES AND CAREERS

Occupational sociology, in theory, is concerned with the roles and careers of all organization members. In practice, surveys and field studies of people in occupational roles usually are confined to organizational participants of relatively low rank and status. Studies of professionals in the mass media, for example, cast light on the everyday routines and constraints felt by reporters or screenwriters far more frequently than on publishers or movie studio executives. For this reason, research about occupations, crafts, and professions—including those in journalism and entertainment—has come to be associated with the study of lower-level participants across many organizational hierarchies. This sample bias is due only in part to the personal tastes of scholarly investigators. For lower-level subordinates are typically more accessible to outsiders than their superiors (by rank). There are more of them, with fewer secrets to hide, less stake in their organizations, and possibly more interest in and time for an interviewer. In addition, however, university researchers often seem to prefer focusing studies on lower participants. For some, they are easier to control and pose fewer potential problems for the project; for others, they are simply more attractive and glamorous subjects.

Over time, an implicit difference between "occupational" and "organizational" sociology has thus developed. Each studies and "explains" its findings from the standpoint of different vertical levels in the same organization. What one subfield interprets as arbitrary or politically inspired interference and censorship, the other sees as perfectly reasonable in terms of the rationales and logic followed at the higher level of organization with which it is familiar. News media organizations' policies toward free-lance reporters provide an excellent example. News organizations are reluctant to accept controversial stories by nonstaff reporters (such as reports of the My Lai massacre in Vietnam, originally brought to the *New York Times* and other papers by Seymour Hersh, and rejected). Occupational analysts are likely to interpret this as unwarranted discrimination and editorial censorship, while the organizational analyst would more likely assert that where stories are particularly controversial, the reporters' reliability is a crucial element in the decision to print them. In such cases, staff members' credibility is generally higher than free-lancers', so the organization's policy of restricting investigative reporting to staff members and established wire or syndication services is seen as organizationally prudent, fair, and legitimate. (After his stories proved factually correct, Hersh was hired as a staff investigative reporter by the *New York Times.*). To a significant degree, occupational and organizational analyses have come to represent and argue for the contrasting standards and viewpoints embodied in their respective sets of respondents. Although there has been too little dialogue between them historically, research on mass media-based occupations and organizations has started to combine models, recently presenting a more integrated and sophisticated set of findings and interpretations.

THE GATEKEEPER TRADITION

With the publication of his classic study, "The Gatekeeper: A Case Study in the Selection of News," David Manning White (1950) began one of the most important traditions in communication research. The questions he posed include: By what criteria do editors select a small minority of stories from a far larger available universe for presentation to their publics? Are there hard and fast decision rules and, if so, are these universal? Or are individual decisions based more on subjective biases, idiosyncratic preferences, and questionable value judgments?

These questions have inspired studies in such disparate areas as journalism, entertainment, political elections, fine art, and popular culture—all of which are linked by an awareness of the surplus of potential items (news stories, screenplays, candidates for office, paintings, pop records, television series pilots) for adoption by mass media decision-makers. These share a common interest in learning what characteristics, if any, separate the losing candidates from those which make the front page, the best galleries, the academy awards, the top 40, or high Nielson ratings. As suggested in Table 1, the mass-media gatekeeper's mandate to filter out items for which there is not available space or air time occurs at several organizational levels, for virtually all types of content printed, filmed, or broadcast by the mass media. Occupational roles comparable to White's wire service editor include disc jockeys and radio station program directors, book publishers' readers and editors (discussed in Turow's article in this volume), and television network programming executives.[2] Analytically, the gatekeeping *process* is very similar across these media and occupations. Interpretations of its meaning, legitimacy, and inner workings vary substantially, however.

TABLE 1
GATEKEEPING ROLES IN THE FIELDS OF
MASS ENTERTAINMENT AND POLITICS

1. *The Artist*—provides the creative input. He is in constant demand because of the rapid turnover of product. The novelist, the politician, the playwright, and the clothing designer all exemplify the "artist."

2. *The Agent*—in service of a "producer." Agents operate in the field, linking the artist and producer. They serve as talent scouts for the book publisher. as political clubs in service of a party, as scouts for the Broadway producer, and for the clothing manufacturer.

3. *The Producer*—in the form of an entrepreneur or a corporation, supplies the capital and organization required to manufacture and/or promote the artist's product; e.g., the book publisher, political party influentials, the Broadway producer, the clothing manufacturer.

4. *The Promoters*—within the industry, are employed by the producer to create, plan for, and manage anticipated demand. Not all products at this level can be promoted with equal success. Promoters would: arrange for the book publisher's promotional parties, for the nomination of a candidate by party delegates, for the theater producer's "angels," and for fashion trade paper endorsements.

5. *The Gatekeepers*—linked by promoter to producer, they mediate between an industry and its consumers. Gatekeepers perform the crucial final filtering function of screening and selectively choosing from among the available products those which are to be publicized. The gatekeepers are mass media, e.g., book reviews, election editorials, theater reviews, coverage of new styles by fashion magazines.

6. *The Public*—votes upon and rank-orders those candidates who have successfully passed through all the previous stages of the filter, having thereby been pre-selected for the consumer to choose.

SOURCE: P. HIRSCH, "The structure of the popular music industry" (1969:7).
NOTES: 1. For authors and entertainers, the mass media often do not enter the picture until stage 5, when their performances, records or books receive (or are denied) publicity and reviews.
2. In this model, the "artist" is also the product to be processed. In terms of a comparison to journalism, the product would become the individual news story; the reporter would be the "agent" and the newspaper the "producer."

Gatekeeping by journalists has been researched more extensively and taken somewhat more seriously than gatekeeping by professionals with comparable tasks in other media fields. This reflects the larger role and institutional function of journalism in a democratic society more than it signals differences between constant categories at the production level, for a discovery that news editors' selection criteria are subject to personal bias and political pressure suggests more significant implications for public policy. Initial interpretations of editorial bias relied almost entirely on psychological explanations. As these have been supplemented by more sociological interpretations and hypotheses, the study of gatekeeping as a process has expanded to include organizational and institutional levels of analysis, in addition to the original emphases on individual traits and occupational roles. Taken together these provide complementary perspectives on the selection of mass media content.

One of the central issues raised by the gatekeeping tradition has been: How do decision-makers narrow down the glut of items competing for attention to a size manageable for the amount of space, time, or airplay available? A simple and attractive design for locating and interpreting variations in outcome and in the rationales employed is to search for individual differences among the decision-makers. Why does a news story run as a lead item in one newspaper but get buried in the back pages of a second? Or why have so many book publishers and record companies refused to sign artists whose works shortly became best-sellers for their competitors? If luck, intuition, probability theory, and, occasionally, politics leave too many unanswered questions, a search for personality differences between the individuals involved may yield additional information. Pool and Shulman (1959:156), for example, suggest that "accuracy of reporting is low on good and bad news alike when the news is incongruent with the tone of the reporter's [own] fantasies," predispositions, and stereotypes. By close analogy the same conclusion holds true for editors' selection and assignment of news stories, and comparable decisions by people in gatekeeping positions elsewhere.

Pool and Shulman also recognize, however, that professionals socialized into the norms of their occupation have learned to "distance" themselves from purely personal reactions and stereotypes. Personal tastes aside, they know how "this type" of story, or record, is supposed to read or sound. This is because mass media professionals do not work in isolation, but must meet the expectations of their organizations, occupation, and (to a less obvious extent) ultimate audience. The "subjective bias" of selection decisions can be individual, organizational, or both. Thus, the issue of accounting for decisions taken by lower-level and other gatekeepers becomes an analysis of variance—both statistical and conceptual. To what extent an employee gatekeeper can base decisions on personal rather than organizational criteria is a major question for additional research. What conditions are particularly conducive or detrimental to the exercise of personal discretion?

"Organizational logic," or the study of constraints imposed on an individual's selection decisions, enters the genre of gatekeeping studies through the work of Gieber (1956, 1964), Gans (1974), and Tuchman (in this volume), among others. The individual, occupational, and organizational components of gate-keeping are well illustrated by an analysis of White's original study of decisions by a wire service editor ("Mr. Gates"). White compared all stories from the major wire services which were rejected with those selected to appear in the newspaper, and also obtained a brief explanation for each decision from his respondent. One major result was a graphic demonstration of the extent to which gatekeeping occurs as an organizational necessity: White's "Mr. Gates" had to reject eight items for every one story there was space for in his paper's next edition.

White also coded all the items accepted or rejected into a set of common story types. Table 2 reproduces his comparison of the types and percentages of news stories received with those selected by the editor. We see that the types and proportions of news stories supplied by the wire services and the types and proportions chosen for the subscribing paper were *virtually identical*. In only three instances do the editor's choices, by category, differ more than two percentage points from the proportions sent by the wire services. From an

TABLE 2
AMOUNTS OF PRESS ASSOCIATION NEWS MR. GATES RECEIVED
AND USED DURING SEVEN-DAY PERIOD

| | Wire Copy Received | | Wire Copy Used | |
Category	Col. In.*	% of Total	Col. In.*	% of Total
Crime	527	4.4	41	3.2
Disaster	405	3.4	44	3.4
Political				
State	565	4.7	88	6.8
National	1,722	14.5	205	15.8
Human Interest	4,171	35.0	301	23.2
International				
Political	1,804	15.1	176	13.6
Economic	405	3.4	59	4.5
War	480	4.0	72	5.6
Labor	650	5.5	71	5.5
National				
Farm	301	2.5	78	6.0
Economic	294	2.5	43	3.3
Education	381	3.2	56	4.3
Science	205	1.7	63	4.9
Total	11,910	99.9	1,297	100.1

SOURCE: D.M. White, "The Gatekeeper: A Case Study in the Selection of News."
Journalism Quarterly, 27, 4(fall, 1950).
*Counting five lines of wire copy as one column inch.

organizational standpoint, this is the important finding and invites a reinterpretation of the more general conclusion that Mr. Gates's judgments (which later proved to be representative of most wire service editors) were strongly affected by his own personal and idiosyncratic biases. More likely, this editor was exercising discretion only within the latitude permitted for selecting particular stories to fit standard, widely agreed-upon categories, in the usual (expected) proportions that characterize a medium-sized, midwestern daily with a predominantly conservative readership.

The conclusion that editors are personally "subjective" in their decisions most often receives support when choices over individual news items are studied, rather than the aggregate totals of which types of stories consistently appear across papers over long time periods. White found, for example, that some individual stories were denied space because, as Pool and Shulman suggest, they violated the editor's own sense of reality. Reasons provided for rejection in these cases included: sheer "propaganda," "don't care for suicide stories," and "b.s." But even here, White's data show that out of 1,333 explanations for why a piece was rejected, almost 800 cited lack of space and about 300 cited overlap with stories already selected, or criticized the item for poor writing or absence of journalistic interest. Another 76 rejections dealt with events in areas too far from the paper's locale to expect reader interest. As a matter of interpretative emphasis, such craft-oriented norms and criteria statistically overwhelm personal bias in terms of the explanations provided by the editor and reported by White.

My reinterpretation of White's data—suggesting that occupational, craft, and organizational norms concerning news and story categories explain more of the variance in story selection than personal bias—represents a position forcefully argued in connection with other studies by Gieber (1964), Tuchman (1972), Wright (1975), Donahue et al. (1972), and Gans (1970), among others. An important intellectual bridge between these explanatory levels and interpretations was Warren Breed's (1955) classic analysis of the occupational socialization of newspaper reporters as a study in social control.

SOCIAL CONTROL IN THE NEWSROOM AND ON THE CUTTING ROOM FLOOR

For journalism more than for any other mass-media profession, charges of subjectivity and bias raise sensitive institutional and political issues. One can discount the importance of gatekeeping for pop records or pulp novels more easily by positing their functional or aesthetic equivalence. This is a less credible perspective in the area of news reporting, however. The issue becomes especially complex when we seek to take into account the phenomenological argument that all decisions by newspeople are *inherently* subjective and political, for "objectivity" is both a fictional construction and a defensive ploy (see Phillips's chapter in this volume, and Schudson, forthcoming). The model of mass media professionals and gatekeepers as socially controlled by the subtle reward systems and political preferences of their employers is closely associated with Warren Breed's (1955) early work, and receives more recent support from studies of news and entertainment organizations and producers by Cantor (1971), Sigal (1973), Sigalman (1973), Dreier (1977), and Metz (1975), among others. This model of social control also analyzes how the apprenticeships served by mass media professionals shape their later decisions. In so doing, it is closely related to the general study of occupational recruitment and socialization for all fields, and not restricted to research on the everyday actions of mass media organizations and personnel.

Breed's study yielded several interesting findings about journalists, which should also apply to professionals creating entertainment content. First was the observation that overt confrontations hardly ever occur. This is because most news stories do not raise issues of editorial policy. Rather, they fall into preset categories (see Tuchman in this volume) and follow established writing styles and routines. In addition to their statistical rarity, Breed pointed to the interpersonal dynamics of the newsroom as containing mechanisms to reduce the reporter's dissonance between the real and ideal: the neophyte's respect for his editor's superior news judgment, authority, and technical competence; a desire to advance as a constraint against dissent; sociability and the desire for friendly informal relations; a lack of intense feelings about the issue; and time pressures imposed by tomorrow's deadlines to seek "new" stories rather than agonize over those already located.

Breed's finding that both "policy" stories and disputes over them rarely arise has been replicated often enough to become an established proposition. In fact, his original formulation—which inquired into the reasons for their rarity—led to a reposing of the question to ask: Under what organizational conditions do such conflicts arise, and why *do* newspapers vary in the number of disputes which occur over policy stories, or concerning reporters' writing in general? These, in turn, encourage an examination of mass media organizations as a whole, leading away from the study of interpersonal relations between reporters and editors, and toward the study of administration and management of the larger corporate entities for which journalists work.

THE ORGANIZATION QUA ORGANIZATION

Historically, much of the best writing about the fields of journalism and entertainment has, in effect, discovered and addressed the occasional conflicts which follow from the necessary, if forced, subordination of individuals to the organizations they work for. As Breed (1955) also noted, this leaves unexamined the "normal," more harmonious, everyday routines which constitute the rule to which dissension over policy issues is the exception. The analytical perspective taking the entire organization as its object of analysis incorporates a broader interest in (1) the roles assigned and played by its managers and executives, and

(2) the importance of organization structure as the immediate context in which mass media content is produced and role relations are played out.

Within the broader framework of an entire organization, what may look like the "absolute" power of an editor or television producer over his reporters, writers, or directors loses some of its luster. Cantor (1971) points out, for example, that while television producers exercise full authority over writers, directors, and actors concerning story lines and their execution, their decisions are all subject to veto by the television networks for which the programs are being produced. (Network representatives, in turn, will explain their decisions in terms of having to meet sponsors' wishes and a need for high ratings.) In his own eyes, the producer becomes a mere "middle man," negotiating with both his staff and client for a product acceptable to all. Elite newspaper editors are described similarly by Sigal (1973). Whereas the reporter is aware mostly of what has been blue-penciled, desk editors must seek visibility for their staffs' reporting, argue its merits, and defend it against criticism from their colleagues and superiors. Their position is analogous to the factory foreman, who must frequently mediate between the demands of superiors and reactions of subordinates. Where the occupational analyst will focus on the reporter's potential frustrations at the hands of an editor, Sigal observes that changes in management or ownership affect reporters and content far more than a change in who occupies the desk of city editor. (For an interesting illustration of this point, see Whelton's [1977] personal description of "getting bought," as the *Village Voice* changed owners twice in a four-year period.) Knowledge of such varying perspectives by role occupants at different points in the hierarchy is best tapped through studies of the entire organization.

Sigal's study (1973:18) also illustrates how organization structure alone may affect the probability of reporters' copy being heavily edited or second-guessed:

> Geography complicates action channels at the *Times* by adding a bureaucratic layer between the national desk and the Washington bureau. . . . In the case of national news, the intervening layer . . . insulates the national desk in New York from the pressure of reporters covering Washington. This insulation probably gives rise to newsmen's perceptions of the *Times* as an "editor's paper," in contrast to the *Post,* which is seen as a "reporter's paper," When reporters work in the newsroom, as most Washington correspondents at the *Post* do, they can follow their story as it is edited. . . . New York is too remote to allow this feedback at the *Times*.

Here, the variable of physical proximity overrides individuals' predispositions or personalities as explanatory of differences between two otherwise similar media organizations. Organizational analysts also look to variations in technology, goals, and market opportunities and constraints in seeking to account for potential variations in how they operate and what is produced (Perrow, 1970; Roshco, 1975).

Lawrence and Lorsch (1967) report that where manufacturing firms face uncertain and changing markets, the most successful exhibit many competing departments (e.g., sales, promotion, quality control, research, manufacturing), each cherishing its autonomy and placing little value on the contribution of the others toward realizing organizational goals. At the same time, these departments require coordination, supervision and liaison staffs in order to function smoothly together. Successful organizations in simpler market environments exhibit simpler, more centralized structures. These guidelines might well apply to the mass media, where newspapers and television stations in major cities appear more complex in structure and subject to more rapid changes than their counterparts in smaller towns.[3]

Whereas the goal of business enterprises is usually profits, news media owners and publishers often are quoted and described as pursuing other values as well, e.g., personal prestige and influence. Searching for "norms of rationality" (Thompson, 1967), the organizational analyst refuses to rule out the balance sheet as a prime motive in frequent publishers' decisions to forego "quality" journalism and investigative reporting. Circulation studies repeatedly show these do not affect sales. As more local papers become absentee-owned, the owner's continued absence leads organizational researchers to propose the profit motive and a respect for the mass readership's actual preferences (sports, comics, advertisements, and human interest pieces) as significant and sufficient explanations of the most typical newspaper formats.[4] In this view, overt political bias on the part of publishers need not be presumed as the (only) cause of editors' discouraging expensive or investigative reporting. It is likely a frequently misplaced attribution in the current climate of chain ownership. A more realistic, of sadder reason, is a combination of cost accounting and disinterest.

These considerations are important in interpreting studies of mass media organizations from the standpoint of their lower participants. During the 1976-1977 television season, for example, the commercial networks responded to advertiser pressure and scheduled virtually no new series with on-screen violence for 1977-1978. The advertisers' main reason for vetoing this type of program content was, as usual, an unwillingness to associate their products with anything "controversial." An identical reluctance has long characterized the virtual absence of sponsors (with few exceptions, and then at discounted prices) for network-prepared documentaries. These advertisers' reasons are business-based: fear of boycotts, ill will, publicity from a subset of angered viewers (Metz, 1975). At the level of organization where program ideas and story lines are conceived, however, taboos are experienced as censorship and frequently seen as politically motivated. (This example is similar to the experience of free-lance journalists seeking to place controversial news stories with major newspapers, described earlier in this chapter.) From the standpoints of management and students of these broadcasters' and advertisers' behavior, the basis appears far more related to simple economics. In fact, government-sponsored public television has been more clearly responsive than commercial networks to direct political pressure. Organizational analysis reminds us that the issue here is not whether social control exists (for it is a constant), but rather who exercises power and for what reasons.

ORGANIZATIONAL PERSPECTIVES ON THE NEWSROOM

Newspapers' newsroom operations have been studied by Gieber (1964), Sigal (1973), and Bagdikian (1971) from the standpoints of the reporter and the organizations' management as a whole. Gieber both replicated White's study of gatekeeping by a wire service editor, and confirmed Breed's observation that disputes over policy issues seldom arise. He further noted that reporters are caught up in the machinery of newsgathering and writing to such a degree that it seldom if ever occurs to many that how individual stories are covered and "played" represents and carries out earlier policy decisions. Gieber presents the newsroom as an occupational culture, with standards of professionalism that derive from the organizational machinery of deadlines, beats, and accepted writing style. In his judgment, however, the resulting standards of reporting fail to qualify as truly professional, for they have confused means with ends by abandoning the goals of telling the reader what s/he really "needs" to know and of "critically evaluating" incoming (wire service) news stories.

Sigal (1973) and Phillips (1975 and in this volume) also have studied the organization structure of newspapers, and replicated Gieber's finding of little dissatisfaction among journalists with the demands it has placed on the craft. Sigal also conceives the newspaper as a set of structural arrangements consisting of hierarchy, goals, technology, roles, and individuals. Analytically, the resultant occupational constraints, opportunities, subculture, individual failures, and superstars are derived from the organizational context in which they function. Sigal (perhaps because his elite papers were what academic researchers consider the best) arrives at conclusions far less evaluative than Gieber's, however.[5] The idea that craft traditions and occupational norms interact with and follow from the organization's bureaucratic needs is a major contribution of Gieber, Bagdikian, Sigal, Tuchman and, more recently, Phillips and Dreier.

The organization *qua* organizational model focuses attention on the whole entity as the coordinator of, and environment surrounding, mass media occupations. It seeks to predict and explain variations in internal structure, administration, and individual roles, and lies midway between our first model of occupations (primarily of lower participants) in organizations and our final model inquiring into relations among mass media organizations and their larger role as a social institution.

THE INTERORGANIZATIONAL AND INSTITUTIONAL PERSPECTIVE ON MASS MEDIA

Interorganizational and institutional analysis both call attention to the single mass media organization as but one of many competitors, suppliers, distributors, and regulators which shape, and are shaped by, a broader and complex industry system. This larger system also constitutes an important social institution, that is, a large-scale organizational complex which collectively performs an important function for the surrounding society.[6] Mass media do this by collectively producing and disseminating the symbolic content of myths, fantasy, and hard information to entire populations.

All social institutions are influenced by the political and cultural values of their societies, and also play an important part in reinforcing and, less frequently, revising them. Institutional analyses of mass media focus on (a) the (reciprocal) influence of the content transmitted on the surrounding political and cultural environment, and vice versa; and (b) economic and organizational interrelationships among the elites of mass media corporations and those at the top in other institutional sectors. While interorganizational and institutional approaches often begin by studying the structure and operations of an entire industry, the former tends to focus on describing economic and managerial relationships, while the latter places more emphasis on interpreting their political ramifications.

INTERORGANIZATIONAL RELATIONS

When mass media are viewed as organizational complexes (tentatively holding aside differences in the types of content they produce), we find that all share a common set of needs and relationships. To reach its intended audience, for example, symbolic content must be not only created in (or for) production organizations; it also must obtain distribution and arrive at some form of retail outlet (Hirsch, 1972). Historically, the most successful organizations and media have combined each of these functions, but these also often become unbundled and embodied in entirely separate organizations. Today, as Table 3 suggests, virtually no mass media organization is entirely self-sufficient in all of these areas. While newspapers combine news-gathering, writing, and manufacturing facilities, for example, most are dependent on wire and syndication services for much of the copy in every edition. Magazines depend on autonomous distributors to get each issue onto the newsstand; television networks (as distributors) require station affiliates to "retail" their product to consumers; and movie production companies, distributors, and theaters share few common organizational boundaries or ties. Each medium thus contains an aggregation of organizations whose actions affect one another, and which have developed a variety of stable traditions, understandings, and pressure points. These customs and organizational interdependencies at different processing stages form the topic area researched by students of interorganizational relations.[7]

That mass media *content* is a product of interorganizational webs and relationships often seems clearer in retrospect than at a single point in time. Earlier models of mass culture and mass society, for example, equated the magazine medium with large circulation giants like *Life* and *Look,* and defined the radio and movie media as entertainment media dominated by a few major networks and production companies, respectively (see, for example, Rosenberg and White, 1957). While this was certainly the case in the 1940s, it hardly characterized the same media twenty years later. And as their market structures and forms of interorganizational relations radically changed, so did their content. The mass journalism or entertainment produced by these media was rooted in an environment comprised of a heterogeneous audience, few competitors, and close ties between organizations in the production and distribution sectors. As all of these attributes came to characterize commercial television, the others came to resemble "class" more than "mass" media, with more segmented and homogeneous audiences, more competition, and fewer ties between producer and distributor organizations. Their editorial and entertainment content was adapted accordingly, and the greater diversity they now offer, combined with more demographically homogeneous audiences, also accounts for the decline in political and cultural controversy surrounding these media. (It, too, has followed the mass audience to television.)[8]

Some organizational and content characteristics are less sensitive to changes in market structure than others, however. News organizations or departments remain more tightly integrated than their counterparts in entertainment. Here, as we have seen, source credibility and producers' reliability are weighed carefully due to the greater institutional importance of news in American society. At the major television networks, for example, all news must be developed in-house, whereas entertainment programs are generally purchased from outside production companies.[9] Where news stories and columns are taken by newspapers from wire services and syndicators, these "outside" sources are usually acknowledged in the text, and are not even subscribed to unless most journalists have reached a consensus about their general reliability.

In terms of combining separate production and distribution operations within one or a few organizations, newspapers and news are now the most tightly integrated content and media. In the U.S., power relations are more evenly distributed among wire services, syndicators, and subscribers than among television networks, program producers, and station affiliates. The latter two, while more formally autonomous, are less free in reality to expand their client roster (for programs) or locate alternative sources of popular program fare. Where many operations occur within the same formal organization, as with newspapers, the interorganizational conflicts experienced in other media appear in the guise of interdepartmental disputes.

The syndication of newspaper copy (opinion and advice columns, comics) and broadcasts (popular show reruns, movies, some documentaries) highlights a way in which interorganizational needs and relationships transform producers' categories into distributors' commodities, or "product." Here, form comes to take precedence over content, as "liberal" and "conservative" viewpoints (in separate columns) are distributed by the same syndicates, and often appear side by side in the same newspapers. The product (a "column") is the important currency exchanged by the organizations, irrespective of its particular orientation. In this way, newspaper syndication differs little from the independent distribution of broadcast talk programs, game shows, or series reruns. A major

TABLE 3

SCHEMATIC OUTLINE OF ROLES AND ORGANIZATIONS PROCESSING SYMBOLIC CONTENT

Medium	Supply Function (Input)	Processing Function (Throughput)	Distribution and Retailing (Output)	General Description (c. 1977)
Newspapers	Wire services Syndicators Correspondents	Newsroom reporters, editors, executives; manufacturing plant, printers; distribution facilities (truck drivers)	At retail: newsstands, coin boxes, subscriptions. Distribution handled directly by processing organization	Tightly coordinated; strong in-house control over content but responsibilities delegated to trusted supplier organizations; controls its own local distribution
Television	Entertainment production companies; Independent syndicators	TV Networks; Leased telephone lines (transmission)	At retail: local affiliates; independent stations	Dominated by the major networks. Suppliers and station affiliates vulnerable to nonrenewal of lucrative contracts. Where independent stations buy programs directly, there is no processing organization.
Movies	Production companies; Independent producers; directors; actors	Movie studios and distributors	Movie theaters, television, and cable television	Highly fragmented in re locus of control; many aspects negotiated on a case-by-case basis. Strong mutual distrust between sectors. (At earlier period, resembled television's current structure.)

Radio	Phonograph records; Syndicated features	Small staff, mainly for programming and local sales	None; local stations all received directly by consumers	Simplest organization system included here. Few national (network) interconnections; national formats tailored to local markets. Present organization of radio and newspapers makes them the most accessible and locally responsive mass media.
Magazines	Free-lance writers	Staff writers; editors; management	Mail subscriptions; distributors	National magazines highly dependent on distributor organizations; access to newsstands growing in importance as postal rates increase.
Book publishers	Authors	Editors; management	Distributors; retail stores; book clubs	Dependent on editors (for books), distributors (for placement at retail), and mass media for reviews and publicity. Promotion and distribution are key factors for trade book divisions.

reason for both is the reduction in costs permitted by the economies of scale involved. The resulting standardization of content—most localities receive the same programs and columns—is peculiarly democratic: the most "popular" columns or programs are featured, more so because to do so is economically rational than because they reflect the political or cultural preferences of media owners.

That this all occurs within legally sanctioned monopolistic (for newspapers) and oligopolistic (for television) market structures is also important to recall. It is in this economic context, for example, rather than because it broadcasts television programs, that the ABC network's introduction of new programming concepts like Monday-night sports, Olympics coverage, more youth-oriented and violent entertainment, and some tough investigative reporting, is best interpreted. In economic terms, it was as the poorest performer with the most to gain in a tight oligopoly that it undertook innovative documentaries and programming risks. That its product was communication and not widgets loses significance insofar as economic theory would expect firms in a comparable position in any industry to follow the same course (Scherer, 1970; Stigler, 1968).

One area in which interorganizational relations in mass media industries are distinctive is the extent to which formal vertical integration is considered unethical, or has been made formally illegal. Movie studios are barred from owning movie theaters; television networks forbidden to own cable television operations, program syndication services, or more than seven television stations; program producers are required to announce donations or payments from businessmen for using or naming their products on the air; and so forth. Much as newspaper editors filter the output of wire services, the legal separation of mass media production from distribution creates a large class of *organizational gatekeepers*. Radio station program directors, book review editors, talk show staffs, and other professionals who select the copy and programming for their organizations act as gatekeepers who filter the output of production organizations like record companies, book publishers, and filmmakers (Hirsch, 1969, 1972, 1975b). The latter seek to coopt them to feature their productions, for they cannot legally control which ones will be selected for coverage. Their inability to control this aspect of the distribution process provides mass media gatekeepers with substantial power over them, and sets up a situation in which periodic scandals over the latter's efforts to buy influence through forms of "payola" should be expected.[10] One reason for their persistence is the frequent inability of gatekeepers of both news and entertainment to pinpoint exactly which, if any, aspects of most individual news stories, popular records, or television shows account for their appeal to large audiences. And to the extent that "one is as good as another," there is added incentive for public relations departments and promoters to seek influence over decisions taken in gatekeeping organizations.

INSTITUTIONAL ANALYSIS

Interorganizational relations remain basically stable and avoid serious disruption so long as the external environment they share also cooperates. To maintain favorable conditions, or seek changes in those viewed as harmful, industry-wide trade associations lobby in Washington and keep a watchful eye on political developments relevant to their members' financial health or internal operation. The institutional role and relation of the mass media to other sectors of American society are well illustrated by the topics on which officials of the American Newspaper Publishers Association, National Association of Broadcasters, National Cable Television Association, and other groups testify before congressional committees, work to have legislation passed, or take to the courts on appeal.

Consider the issues of postal rates, mergers, copyright and tax law, television programming, and cable television. Each has the power to restructure the mass media industries it affects, even though it may seem (and is) far removed from the media organization's day-to-day operations. As a general rule, in fact, the farther away they are from the activities of its lower level participants, the more likely these issues are to be studied by lawyers and economists than by social scientists, for whose research they also have important implications. Mergers among newspapers, and their chain ownership, for example, often are attributed to American tax law, which makes it extraordinarily costly for families which own a newspaper to maintain outright control beyond two generations. Additionally, without the successful passage of the Failing Newspaper Act in the late 1960s, many recent newspaper mergers would probably be in violation of antitrust laws. For the magazine industry, the societal decision to trade off postal subsidies for a more balanced budget has meant sharp rises in costs for those with a small percentage of newsstand sales, and hastened the demise of several with the largest general circulation. An additional potential effect is a decline in the number of prospective small magazines of opinion, such as the *Nation* or *National Review,* and smaller circulations for those remaining, as subscription costs rise to meet postal rate increases.

Copyright law involves major stakes for authors and publishers, composers, television broadcasters, and cable TV operators. The transcript of speakers before congressional committees on this topic consistently reads like a *Who's Who* in the arts and mass media. It is on the topics of television violence and advertising that interest groups *outside* the industries affected directly are most likely to appear and be heard. (Earlier, when protesters were not awarded legal standing before the Federal Communications Commission, they were of far less political significance. It is not that protests of broadcast content are new, but rather the FCC's recent reaction which has made them a significant factor for the major networks to take into account.) Once the commerical networks agreed to institute a "family hour" featuring less sex and violence during the early evening hours, some television writers and producers litigated against the resultant restrictions on story lines and won a court ruling against their acceptability (as a matter of law rather than on the basis of the networks' own business or professional judgment).

Government policy towards mass media technologies—ranging from telecommunications satellites and cable TV networks, to allocating the broadcast spectrum for VHF and UHF television channels, citizens' band radio, and other uses—also impacts on the content produced for and distributed by these media channels and agencies. If all television stations had been assigned UHF frequencies during the early 1950s, for example, most major cities would have had more channels in operation earlier, sets could have been equipped to receive UHF signals better, and the amount and diversity of available programs might have been greater (Bagdikian, 1971; Kittross, 1960; Metz, 1975). Such "procedural" decisions by the Federal Communications Commission often exert indirect effects on content. A 1966 ruling forbidding AM and FM radio stations to broadcast the same programs throughout the day in cities of over 100,000 led to a search for successful new FM formats and audiences. One genre developed was the progressive rock music format, which featured recordings with music and lyrics previously passed over by AM radio "Top 40" stations (Hirsch, 1969; Denisoff, 1975). Within a short time, the FCC—apparently unaware of the correlation between its own ruling (to promote greater diversity) and the rise of a radical new format—issued a reminder to licensees to pay stricter attention to the content of records selected for air-play. Similarly, government regulatory policies toward cable television, regarding its legal status, access to programs, and public access to it, have long been affecting its growth rate and efforts to promote the new technology in urban and rural markets.[11]

Government agencies are not the only organizations whose policies have a substantial, albeit indirect, impact on mass media content. American movie scripts, for example, are commissioned and cast with an eye on financing and on distribution far beyond domestic movie theater box offices. Up to 50% of their gross receipts come from international sales; hence some producers seek to create films which will appeal to a worldwide audience, rather than "just" to the largest possible cross-section of Americans. Additionally, many films attain their largest audiences only after being rented or sold to television. Some movies are therefore produced in several versions: for distribution to American theaters, to television stations or networks, and to the world market. When producers seek financing, all of these are considered by both parties to any agreements signed.

Relations between advertisers and newspapers have affected not only editorial policies (this is studied quite often at the local level), but also the number of newspapers in a single city. Bagdikian (1971) notes that advertisters frown on the economic inefficiency entailed in having to place the same ad in several newspapers competing in the same city. A newspaper losing circulation may find advertising linage disappearing faster than the percentage drop in readers alone would warrant. If it ceases publication or merges, the advertisers' cost for reaching about the same number of readers decreases, even if the sole survivor raises (but does not double) its rates. Just as columns of opinion may be syndicated irrespective of the opinion contained, such advertising decisions, even though they determine the fate of newspapers, are usually based on circulation figures alone. This obviously has both direct and indirect effects on newspapers' availability and content.[12]

DIVERGENT INTERPRETATIONS

What are some of the other cultural and political consequences of these interorganizational relations, and their importance for our understanding of mass media as a social institution? On several points, there is a broad consensus among diverse sociologists (and others) employing functional analysis. For example, Breed (1958), Warner (1959), Phillips (1975), and Marcuse (1964) all conceive mass media as providing standardized, patterned rituals, with whose forms audiences are familiar and for which there are common expectations. Also, for mass newspapers and commercial television especially, mass media provide news, advertising, and entertainment content carefully designed so that every member of society can understand and participate in it. To the extent that certain media no longer fit this description, being "targeted" to segmented, homogeneous audiences (radio formats, special-interest magazines), then they no longer fulfill the functions classically attributed to mass media.

However, after agreeing that mass media function in this way in modern, capitalist, industrial societies, institutional analysts offer divergent interpretations of the social value of having these functions performed at all. Historically, the entertainment content of mass culture has been more widely debated than news or advertising, although the issues raised in connection with any one usually apply to the others as well. Debates over popular books, movies and broadcasting have been sparked by critics and advocates of catering to or manipulating mass taste, "engineering" a cultural consensus, or maintaining local diversity versus endorsing our technological capacity to create national markets for all types of products, including information and entertainment (Hirsch, 1977; Gans, 1974). More recently, the cultural politics surrounding mass entertainment have intensified, with large-scale exchanges and concern arising over the growth of pornography, violence in films and on television, and television's effects on children. (See McPhee's interesting model of mass entertainment producers in this volume.)

These have inspired more research on, and discussion of the very categories and aesthetic elements employed by entertainment producers but long taken for granted and, hence, seldom examined (see especially Gerbner, 1972; and Gerbner and Gross, 1976). Quantitative content analysis of slices of content (e.g., how many violent acts, or racial stereotypes) challenge and spotlight previously unarticulated assumptions about audiences, fantasy, and meaning held at the production level of entertainment-creating organizations. While many producers protest these analyses as misguided or out of context, they afford a rare opportunity for researchers to link occupational, organizational and institutional nexes and cross-pressures. Additional and related research opportunities abound for analysts of the prospective "deep" versus surface content of news and entertainment, and for considerations of whether popular culture is a meaningful cultural activity, merely a leisure time pursuit, or both.[13]

These developments in research on entertainment content and producers are closely paralleled in the fields of print and broadcast news. Much as Cantor's (1971) organizational analysis of television entertainment producers is related to the studies by Sigal (1973), Diamond (1975), and Breed (1955) of social control in the newsroom, Gerbner's strategy of interpreting television entertainment in terms of social science rather than producers' categories is paralleled by Tuchman's analysis (in this book) of newswriting and newsgathering. More than for producers of entertainment, the study of news categories touches on the legitimacy claims of the profession employing them. Modern journalism bases much of its claim to rewards and special privileges from society on the fairness and accuracy of its reporting. Earlier I noted that while news differs little from entertainment in how it is organized and coordinated at the production level, its institutional function and the attendant expectations differ markedly. Since news is defined by its practitioners and audience both as the more serious of the two, public awareness of the "tricks of the trade," and varying interpretations of their potential meaning by politicians or social scientists, pose a far greater potential threat to journalism's claims to legitimacy (cf. Phillip's chapter). As with the functions of mass media in general, sociological and cultural interpretations of objective journalism often agree as to its social role, but not on its social value. Phillips, Warner, and Breed contend it contributes by helping to set out and define a nation's common culture; Tuchman, Marcuse, Schiller, and others propose it (like all mass media) only distracts audiences from a truer reality; James W. Carey (1969) and Michael Robinson (1975) believe much of the institutional impact of objective journalism has been to disrupt and threaten widespread consensus.

These agreements and divergent interpretations of the very categories taken for granted by mass media professionals can promote increasing linkages between researchers employing the occupational model reviewed earlier and those engaged in institutional and content analysis. Research combining the levels of analysis each represents can better decompose the idea of biased reporting into the "professional bias" of the norms of journalism (cf. Gieber, 1964, on the use of denotive rather than evaluative symbols), and the personal bias of reporters or editors. The "personal bias" component of any analysis should now consist of the residual of what is left after accounting for the limits set by professional norms on how stories might best be covered. These norms, in turn, are seen by the organizational analyst as largely molded by the organizational constraints on, and bureaucratic convenience mandated by, mass media organizations (Molotch and Lester, 1974).

SUMMARY

In comparing occupational, organizational, and institutional models of mass media, I have suggested several commonalities among them, and proposed that they be linked more closely in empirical studies as well as in theories of mass communication. The organizational perspective underlying each analytical approach rejects the principle of uniqueness commonly held by practitioners. It sees clear similarities between news and entertainment forms, across media and in the manner they are organizationally produced.

We began by focusing attention on similarities in the roles and bureaucratic constraints found at the production level, across categories. This decreases the number of surface differences, and treats only the remaining "unexplained variance" as casting light on characteristics and attributes distinguishing the categories news, entertainment, print, and broadcast from each other. In presenting the three models side by side, I have noted places where each complements the others and thus increases our confidence in causal attributions when they appear in empirical studies. For example, before occupational analysts conclude that editors exercise near-absolute power over reporters' copy, the organization *qua* organization model insists they inquire to see how much discretion the editor is accorded by his or her *own* superiors in the organizational hierarchy. In relating studies of lower-level mass media participants to interorganizational and institutional research, and in linking the media content they produce and the corporations they work for to the surrounding societal environment, I have suggested these topics and levels of analysis are interdependent and will profit from further steps toward conceptual integration.

Occupational, organizational, and institutional models treat, in rough order, individuals in roles, occupational careers, organizational contexts, hierarchies, technologies and markets, interorganizational relations, and institutional roles and ramifications. In social science terms, these perspectives follow a continuum from closed to open systems analysis, and encompass substantive studies across specific topic areas and categories. Each model also was discussed (and sometimes evaluated) from the standpoint of the others. While each has an intellectual history of its own, all share a strong and common interest in linking the study of mass media occupations, organizations, and the societal conditions in which they operate. This chapter represents an effort to delineate their similarities and differences, dismantle unnecessary barriers between them, and point out frontier problems for organizational research.

NOTES

1. For an application of these categories to arts organizations, see DiMaggio and Hirsch, 1976.

2. In addition to the research on occupations in organizations discussed shortly, studies of importance also include: Alley (1977) and Miller and Rhodes (1964), on television

entertainment; Argyris (1974), Cater (1959), Cohen (1963), Donahue (1967), Eliot (1972), Johnstone et al. (1976), Rivers (1965), Rosten (1973), Tunstall (1974), and Warner (1971), on print or broadcast journalism; Peterson and Berger (1971) and Rosenblum (in press), on record producers and photographers, respectively; and Eliot (1977) and Riley and Riley (1959), on all mass media occupations at the production level.

3. American radio stations require few staff members and exhibit less variance by size of city. Newspapers and television stations in major cities may also be more complex organizationally simply because they are larger than the typical media organization in smaller cities. In addition to the organizational analyses discussed shortly, studies of importance also include: Johnstone (1976) and Talese (1969), on newspapers; and Brown (1971) and Lourenco and Glidewell (1975), on television.

4. A long-standing enmity between editorial and advertising or market research departments stems from the former's desire to give readers what they *need*, versus the latter's commitment to finding out what they actually *want*. Occupational studies' application of reference group theory to journalists and actors suggests that they see their "real" audiences as colleagues and peers rather than a mass audience of readers or viewers. However, these often stop short of also noting the limits to which creators may be permitted to actually "play" to these intended audiences. For small-town newspapers, Bowers (1967) reported direct interference by publishers in the decisions made by the editorial staff.

5. As a matter of logic, if all editors arrived at identical decisions—even the "right" ones—it is far from clear that this would be desirable from a public policy standpoint. As Pool and Shulman (1959) also suggest, such a prospect provides small likelihood of resolving the issue of biased reporting. Presently, where divergence is found, researchers infer distortion of the "true" account by one or more of the reports published; yet, if they were all the same, the resulting uniformity would very likely be experienced and described as oppressive. In the belief that divergence in opinion and reporting generally operates to the common good, American courts have chosen to permit high variance in editorial decisions and discretion, thus electing to take the good with the bad.

6. For example, business organizations collectively produce material goods and services, and educational organizations transmit knowledge, inculcate skills, and prepare young people for future jobs.

7. The division of activities into production, distribution, and retailing is further elaborated by Owen (1975). An excellent introduction to interorganizational relations is Evan (1976). Studies of the mass media which incorporate this perspective include: Brown (1968), DeFleur and Ball-Rokeach (1975), Hirsch (1969 and 1971), and Peterson and Berger (1972).

8. It is for this reason, for example, that the Nixon administration was so disturbed by CBS News' broadcasts about the Watergate scandal, which it was then trying to contain (Porter, 1976; Halberstam, 1976; Agnew, 1969). For until then, only the geographically and politically isolated *Washington Post* was according the story serious attention. CBS, however, was broadcasting it to a heterogeneous, nationwide audience. For further discussions of changes in magazines and radio, see Welles (1971) and Peterson (1964), on magazines; and Honan (1967) and Hirsch (1969), on radio.

9. Even for entertainment programs, however, a "track record" of earlier successes is sought. This provides networks more confidence that programs will be brought in on time, produced well, and appeal to their audiences.

10. This behavior would be subject to less scandal (and at one time was considered far more legitimate) if public opinion was not offended by practices like reporters' sources also buying them gifts and paying travel expenses, or record companies' artificially determining which songs were selected for radio station air-play.

11. These issues have been covered extensively by the press and in professional journals. See, for example, Schorr (1976), MacAvoy (1977), and Crandall (1974).

12. Such developments, in turn, affect the communities in whose geographical boundaries newspapers and broadcast media operate. On the relation between mass media and local communities, see Donahue, et al. (forthcoming), Tichenor, et al. (1976), and Janowitz (1967).

13. Several interesting volumes touching on this topic are Newcomb (1974), Cawelti (1976), Newcomb (1976), Sahlins (1976), and Arens and Montague (1976). See also Carey (1977).

REFERENCES

AACKER, D., and MYERS, J. (1975). Advertising management. Englewood Cliffs, N.J.: Prentice-Hall.

AGNEW, S. (1969). "Speech on television news bias." Pp. 195-204 in W. Hammel (ed.), The popular arts in America. New York: Harcourt Brace Jovanovich.

ALLEY, R. (1977). Television: Ethics for hire? Nashville: Abington.

ALTHEIDE, D. (1976). Creating Reality: How TV news distorts events. Beverly Hills, Calif. Sage.

ARENS, W., and MONTAGUE, S. (eds., 1976). The American dimension. Port Washington, N.Y.: Alfred Publishing.

ARGYRIS, C. (1974). Behind the front page. San Francisco: Jossey-Bass.

BAGDIKIAN, B. (1971). The information machines. New York: Harper and Row.

BLUMLER, J. (1969). "Producers' attitudes towards television coverage of an election campaign: A case study." Sociological Review, 13:85-116.

BOWERS, D.R. (1967). "A report on activity by publishers in directing newsroom decisions." Journalism Quarterly, 44(spring):43-52.

BREED, W. (1958). "Mass communication and social integration." Social Forces, 37:109-116.

――― (1955). "Social control in the newsroom." Social Forces, 33:326-335.

BROWN, L. (1971). Television: The Business behind the box. New York: Harcourt Brace Jovanovich.

BROWN, R. (1968). "The creative process in the popular arts." International Social Science Journal, 20(4):613-624.

CANTOR, M. (1971). The Hollywood television producer. New York: Basic Books.

CAREY, J.W. (1977). "Mass communication research and cultural studies." In J. Curran, M. Gurevitch, and H. Woollacott (eds.), Mass communication and society. London: Edward Arnold Ltd.

――― (1969). "The communications revolution and the professional communicator." Sociological Review, 13:23-38.

CATER, D. (1959). The fourth branch of government. Boston: Houghton Mifflin.

CAWELTI, J. (1976). Adventure, mystery, and romance. Chicago: University of Chicago Press.

COHEN, B. (1963). The press and foreign policy. Princeton, N.J.: Princeton University Press.

CRANDALL, R. (1974). "The profitability of cable television: An examiniation of acquisition prices." Journal of Business, 47, 4(October):543-563.

CROUSE, T. (1973). The boys on the bus. New York: Random House.

DeFLEUR, M., and BALL-ROKEACH, S. (1975). Theories of mass communication (3rd ed.). New York: David McKay.

DENISOFF, R.S. (1975). Solid gold: The popular record industry. New Brunswick, N.J.: Transaction Books.

DIAMOND, E. (1975). The tin kazoo. Cambridge, Mass.: MIT Press.

DIMAGGIO, P., and HIRSCH, P. (1976). "Production organizations in the arts." American Behavioral Scientist, 19, 6(August):735-752.

DOMINICK, J., and PIERCE, M. (1976). "Trends in network prime-time programming, 1953-1974." Journal of Communication, 26(winter): 70-80.

DONAHUE, G., TICHENOR, P., and OLIEN, C. (1972). "Gatekeeping: Mass Media systems and information control." Pp. 41-69 in F.G. Kline and P.J. Tichenor (eds.), Current perspectives in mass communication research. Beverly Hills, Calif.: Sage.

——— (forthcoming). Communication, policy and community decisions. Beverly Hills, Calif.: Sage.

DONAHUE, L. (1967). "Newspaper gatekeepers and forces in the news channel." Public Opinion Quarterly, 31(spring):61-68.

DREIER, P. (1977). The urban press in transition: The political economy of newswork. Unpublished doctoral dissertation. University of Chicago, Department of Sociology.

ELIOT, P. (1977). "Media organizations and occupations: An overview." In J. Curran, M. Gurevitch, and J. Woollacott (eds.), Mass communication and society. London: Edward Arnold Ltd.

——— (1972). "The making of a television series: A case study in the sociology of culture. London: Constable.

EPSTEIN, E.J. (1973). News from nowhere. New York: Random House.

EVAN, W. (ed., 1976). Interorganizational relations. Baltimore: Penguin.

GANS, H. (1974). Popular culture and high culture. New York: Basic Books.

——— (1970). "How well does television cover the news?" New York Times Magazine, January 11:30-45.

——— (1957). "The creator-audience relationship in movie-making." In B. Rosenberg and D.M. White (eds.), Mass culture. Glencoe, Ill.: Free Press.

GERBNER, G. (1972). "Violence in television drama: trends and symbolic functions. In E. Rubinstein, G. Comstock and J. Murray (eds.) Television and social behavior, vol. 1. Rockville, Md.: National Institute of Mental Health.

GERBNER, G., and GROSS, L. (1976). "Living with television: The violence profiles." Journal of Communication, 26: 172-199.

GIEBER, W. (1964). "News is what newspapermen make it." In L. Dexter and D.M. White (eds.), People, society, and mass communication. Glencoe, Ill.: Free Press.

——— (1956). "Across the desk: A Study of 16 telegraph editors." Journalism Quarterly, 43(fall): 423-432.

GILLMOR, D., and BARRON, J. (1969). Mass communication law: Cases and comment. St. Paul, Minn.: West.

GOODHARDT, G.J., EHRENBERG, A.S.C., and COLLINS, M.A. (1975). The television audience. Lexington, Mass.: Lexington Books.

HALBERSTAM, D. (1976). "CBS: The power and the profits" (parts 1 and 2). Atlantic, (January and February):33-71 and 52-91.

HIRSCH, P. (forthcoming). "Television as a national medium: Its cultural and political role in American society." In D. Street (ed.), Handbook of urban life. San Francisco: Jossey-Bass.

——— (1977). "Public policy toward television: Mass media and education in American society. School Review, 85, 4(August).

——— (1975a). "Organizational analysis and industrial sociology: An instance of cultural lag." American Sociologist, 10, 1(February): 1-10.

——— (1975b). "Organizational effectiveness and the institutional environment." Administrative Science Quarterly, 20, 4(September): 327-344.

——— (1972). "Processing fads and fashions: An organization-set analysis of cultural industry systems." American Journal of Sociology, 77, 4(January):639-659.

——— (1971). "Sociological approaches to the pop music phenomenon." American Behavioral Scientist, 14, 3(January): 371-388.

––– (1969). The structure of the popular music industry. Ann Arbor: University of Michigan Survey Research Center.

HONAN, W. (1967). "The new sound of radio." New York Times Magazine, December 3:56-76.

JANOWITZ, M. (1967). The community press in an urban setting (2nd ed.). Chicago: University of Chicago Press.

JOHNSTONE, J. (1976). "Organizational constraints on newswork." Journalism Quarterly, 53(1):5-13.

––– SLAWSKI, E., and BOWMAN, W. (1976). The news people: A sociological portrait of American journalists and their work. Urbana: University of Illinois Press.

KATZ, D., and KAHN, R. (1966). The social psychology of organizations. New York: John Wiley.

KITTROSS, J. (1960). Television frequency allocation policy in the United States. Unpublished doctoral dissertation. University of Illinois.

LAWRENCE, P., and LORSCH, J. (1967). Organization and environment. Cambridge, Mass.: Harvard University Graduate School of Business Administration.

LEUBSDORF, C. (1976). "Comment on campaign coverage." Columbia Journalism Review, (March-April):6-8.

LOURENCO, S., and GLIDEWELL, J. (1975). "A dialectical analysis of organizational conflict." Administrative Science Quarterly, 20:489-508.

MacAVOY, P. (ed., 1977). Deregulation of cable television. Washington, D.C.. American Enterprise Institute.

MARCUSE, H. (1964). One dimensional man. Boston: Beacon.

METZ, R. (1975). CBS: Reflections in a bloodshot eye. New York: Playboy Press.

MILLER, M., and RHODES, E. (1964). Only you Dick Darling. New York: William Sloane Associates.

MOLOTCH, H., and LESTER, M. (1974). "News as purposive behavior." American Sociological Review, 39:101-112.

NEWCOMB, H. (ed., 1976). Television: The critical view. New York: Oxford University Press.

––– (1974). TV: The most popular art. New York: Doubleday Anchor.

NOLL, R., PECK, M. and McGOWAN, J. (1973). Economic aspects of television regulation. Washington, D.C.: Brookings Institution.

OWEN, B. (1975). Economics and freedom of expression. Cambridge: Ballinger.

PERROW, C. (1970). Organizational analysis: A sociological view. Belmont, Calif.: Brooks/Cole.

PETERSON, R., and BERGER, D. (1975). "Cycles in symbol production: The case of popular music." American Sociological Review, 40:158-173.

––– (1972). "Three eras in the manufacture of popular music lyrics." In R. Peterson and R. Denisoff (eds.), The sounds of social change. Chicago: Rand-McNally.

––– (1971). "Entrepreneurship in organizations: Evidence from the popular music industry." Administrative Science Quarterly, 16:97-106.

PETERSON, T. (1964). Magazines in the 20th century. Urbana: University of Illinois Press.

PHILLIPS, E.B. (1975). The artists of everyday life: Journalists, their craft, and their consciousness. Unpublished doctoral dissertation. Syracuse University.

POOL, I., and SHULMAN, I. (1959). "Newsmen's fantasies, audiences, and newswriting." Public Opinion Quarterly, 23:145-158.

RILEY, J., and RILEY, M. (1959). "Mass communication and the social system." In R. Merton, L. Broom, and L. Cottrell, Jr. (eds.), Sociology today. New York: Harper and Row.

RIVERS, W. (1965). The opinion makers. Boston: Beacon.

ROBINSON, J. (1972). "Mass communication and information diffusion." In F.G. Kline and P. Tichenor (eds.), Current perspectives in mass communication research. Beverly Hills, Calif.: Sage.

ROBINSON, M. (1975). "American political legitimacy in an era of electronic journalism: Reflections on the evening news." In D. Cater and R. Alder (eds.), Television as a social force: new approaches to TV criticism. New York: Praeger.

ROOSE, J. (1967). "Daily newspapers, monopolistic competition, and economies of scale." American Economic Review, 57, 2(May):522-533.

ROSENBERG, B., and WHITE, D.M. (eds., 1957). Mass culture. Glencoe, Ill.: Free Press.

ROSENBLUM, B. (forthcoming). "Style as social process." American Sociological Review.

ROSHCO, B. (1975). Newsmaking. Chicago: University of Chicago Press.

ROSTEN, L. (1937). The Washington correspondents. New York: Harcourt Brace.

SAHLINS, M. (1976). Culture and practical reason. Chicago: University of Chicago Press.

SCHERER, F.M. (1970). Industrial market structure and economic performance. Chicago: Rand McNally.

SCHORR, B. (1976). "Television's scrambled signals." Wall Street Journal (June 29).

SCHUDSON, M. (forthcoming). A social history of American journalism. New York: Basic Books.

SIGAL, L. (1973). Reporters and officials. Lexington, Mass.: D.C. Heath.

SIGALMAN, L. (1973). "Reporting the news: An organizational analysis." American Journal of Sociology, 79(July):132-151.

STIGLER, G. (1968). The organization of industry. Homewood, Ill.: Irwin.

TALESE, G. (1969). The kingdom and the power. Cleveland: World.

THOMPSON, J. (1967). Organizations in action. New York: McGraw-Hill.

TICHENOR, P., NNAEMEKA, T., and DONAHUE, G. (1976). "Community pluralism and perceptions of television content." Paper presented at Association for Education in Journalism annual meetings.

TUCHMAN, G. (1972). "Objectivity as strategic ritual: An examination of newsmen's notions of objectivity." American Journal of Sociology, 77(January):660-679.

TUNSTALL, J. (1974). Journalists at work. Beverly Hills, Calif.: Sage.

WARNER, L. (1959). The living and the dead. New Haven: Yale University Press.

WARNER, M. (1971). "Organizational context and control of policy in the television newsroom: A participant observation study." British Journal of Sociology, 22, 3(September):283-294.

WELLES, C. (1977). "Can mass magazines survive?" Columbia Journalism Review, (July-August):7-14.

WHELTON, C. (1977). "Getting bought: Notes from the overground." Village Voice, (May 2):51.

WHITE, D.M. (1950). "The gatekeeper: A case study in the selection of news." Journalism Quarterly 27, 4(fall):383-390.

WRIGHT, C. (1975). Mass communication: A sociological perspective (2nd ed.). New York: Random House.

PART III

POLITICAL COMMUNICATION

Partly because it deals with such an enormously attractive and important human drama, political communication is the subject of many of the most important studies of mass communication. With the shift from attitude change to information-centered research, the role of mass communication in political reasoning has become a focal area. The studies presented in this section reflect this shift.

The first chapter analyzes a great volume of empirical work and draws valuable conclusions about the usefulness of televised debates by political candidates. The focus in the study is on usefulness as opposed to effects.

A comparison of the roles played by newspapers and television in the political reasoning of prospective voters emerges in the second chapter.

A Swedish study of the information value of various mass media is reported in the third chapter. Translated into English for this volume, the study presents a content analysis approach to both depth and breadth of news and its potential contribution to political reasoning.

The relationship of television news to political socialization of children is explored in the fourth selection. Cross-lagged correlation is used to draw interesting conclusions about this much-ignored problem.

The final chapter analyzes more than 100 articles to compare the uses and effects of newspapers and television.

Thirty empirical studies of the response of the electorate to the Carter-Ford presidential campaign debates of 1976 in the United States are analyzed in this article by Steven H. Chaffee. Evaluating the research from the perspective of the usefulness of the debates to the voter and the political system, Chaffee's careful analysis suggests the debates were clearly functional. The TV debates provided issue information, and a majority of voters saw the debates and learned from them. The voting intentions of persons who were regular viewers of the debate series changed most. The regular viewers were also least likely to be influenced by predispositional factors and more likely to vote according to their perceptions of policy differences between themselves and the presidential candidates. Dr. Chaffee is Vilas Research Professor of Journalism and Mass Communication at the University of Wisconsin—Madison.

16

PRESIDENTIAL DEBATES—
ARE THEY HELPFUL TO VOTERS?

Steven H. Chaffee

IN September of 1976 the nation had just eight weeks to decide whether to keep Gerald Ford as President or to replace him with Jimmy Carter, and half of the voters had not yet made up their minds.[1] The two major political parties had declined markedly in public attractiveness, and the Democrats were split into two wings that stood to the left and right, respectively, of the smaller Republican party on most policy questions.[2]

The position of the Democratic nominee on many of these issues was uncertain in the minds of a substantial minority of voters.[3] And in the wake of the Vietnam-Watergate era, there seemed to be as much concern about the characterological merits of the candidates as with the political interests they represented.[4] It was in this context of voter uncertainty, bred of deficiencies of party identification and of information about the policies and personal qualities of the candidates, that the Ford-Carter debates were held.

Voters interviewed prior to the debates expressed high hopes for them. In particular, they expected to learn where each candidate stood "on the

Mr. Chaffee is Vilas Research Professor of journalism and mass communication, University of Wisconsin-Madison.

[1] Estimates of the proportion of "undecided" voters are notoriously soft. In the week prior to the debates, a statewide probability sample of Wisconsin adults showed that 55% had a preference between Ford and Carter. In later interviewing waves, some of them became less certain of their voting intentions. On Election Day, a higher percentage of the "undecided" people did not vote. Of those who eventually did vote, only 31% had said they were "definitely" decided before the debates, and never expressed indecision in later waves. Whatever indicator is used, there appears to have been much more voter indecision on the eve of the 1976 debates than at comparable points in previous presidential election campaigns on which data are available. See S. H. Chaffee and J. Dennis, "Presidential Debates: An Empirical Assessment," paper presented at symposium on debates sponsored by the American Enterprise Institute for Public Research, Washington, D.C., October 1977; S. H. Chaffee and S. Y. Choe, "Time of Decision and Media Use During the Ford-Carter Campaign," paper presented to the Association for Education in Journalism meeting, Seattle, August 1978.

[2] On the decline of partisanship see N. H. Nie, S. Verba, and J. R. Petrocik, *The Changing American Voter* (Cambridge: Harvard University Press, 1976), pp. 47-73. The schism within the Democratic party is thoroughly documented in A. H. Miller et al., "A Majority Party in Disarray: Policy Polarization in the 1972 Election," *American Political Science Review*, 70 (1976), 753-78.

[3] There is no evidence of greater variation in people's perceptions of Carter's positions than of Ford's. But there was more inclination to respond "don't know" when asked Carter's position on a given issue (see Table 1 of the paper), and many voters had taken up the complaint of his various opponents (both those who were more liberal, and those more conservative) that Carter was "fuzzy on the issues."

[4] Of six personal "image" scales, the strongest correlate of vote changes during the fall 1976 campaign in Wisconsin was "honesty" and "integrity." J. Dennis, S. H. Chaffee, and S. Y. Choe, "Impact Upon Partisan, Image and Issue Voting," in S. Kraus, ed., *The Great Debates, 1976: Ford vs. Carter* (Bloomington: Indiana University Press, in press).

From Steven H. Chaffee, "Presidential Debates—Are They Helpful to Voters?" *Communication Monographs* 45 (November 1978) 330-353. Reprinted by permission of the Speech Communication Association.

issues" and they anticipated being able to make up their minds in great measure on the basis of what they learned in the comparative testing ground of the debates.[5] The candidates wanted the debates too, Ford because he saw debating as a possible means of overtaking Carter's lead in the polls, and Carter on the assumption that the net result of debating would be about 50-50, which would allow him to maintain his lead while time ran out.[6]

In the research community that had studied debates, notably those of 1960, there was less enthusiasm. Complaints were registered about the dual press conference format, in which some thought too much time was spent by reporters asking questions. There was little time for serious discussion of policy issues, many argued, and the 1960 debates had turned more on Nixon's celebrated five o'clock shadow and Kennedy's telegenic style than on political content.[7] Some questioned whether it

would be in the public interest for an incumbent President to place himself in the vulnerable debate setting where sensitive questions touching on national security might arise.[8] Political scientists saw the debates as part of a general process of erosion of political parties through personalization of the voting decision.[9] In all, there seemed to be as many reasons to be apprehensive about the Ford-Carter debates as there were grounds for optimism.

The purpose of this paper is to evaluate presidential debates as an emergent institution, with an eye to the question of whether they merit efforts to insure that debates are held in the future. The experience of 1976, as captured in some 30 studies of the debates and their audience, will form the main empirical basis for this evaluation.[10] The organizing point of view will be that of the *usefulness* of the debates, not necessarily that of their "effects." This means that the debates will be judged "effective" to the extent that the electorate gained from them, without regard to advantages won by either candidate over the other.[11] Putting it in somewhat

[5] Major sources of data on uses anticipated and gratifications received from the debates include J. M. McLeod et al., "Expanding the Context of Debate Effects," in Kraus, in press; G. J. O'Keefe and H. Mendelsohn, "Media Influences and Their Anticipation," in Kraus, in press; and L. B. Becker, R. E. Sobowale, and I. A. Cobbey, "Onondaga County and the 1976 Presidential Elections: A Report on Voter Reactions to the Debates," unpubl. paper, Syracuse University, 1977.

[6] A first-person account of the strategy underlying Ford's challenge to debate is provided by his former chief of staff and key campaign operative (R. Cheney, "The 1976 Presidential Debates: A Republican Perspective," unpubl. paper presented at symposium on debates). On Carter's side, the strategy outline is based on interviews of two central campaign planners, Patrick Caddell and Gerald Rafshoon, by a reporter who later joined Rafshoon's firm (S. Lesher, "Did the Debates Help Jimmy Carter?" unpubl. paper presented at symposium on debates).

[7] Post-hoc speculation as to what happened in the 1960 debates is ubiquitous throughout the literature on political mass communication. A good summary of this rather jaundiced view is E. M. Kirkpatrick, "Presidential Candidate 'Debates': What Can We Learn from 1960," unpubl. paper presented at symposium on debates. For supporting data, see S. Kraus, ed., *The Great Debates* (Bloomington: Indiana University Press, 1962).

[8] In the spring of 1963 the American Political Science Association appointed a Commission on Presidential Campaign Debates, which consisted of Carl J. Friedrich, Evron M. Kirkpatrick, Harold D. Lasswell, Richard E. Neustadt, Peter H. Odegard, Elmo Roper, Telford Taylor, Charles A. H. Thompson and Gerhart D. Wiebe. Their report, published in 1964, is now out of print. An updated summary of it has been written by Kirkpatrick. Many of the comments the commission received (from more than one-third of U.S. congressmen, governors, and state party chairmen) stressed the dangers of an incumbent President debating.

[9] Kirkpatrick summarizes this viewpoint extensively.

[10] This author has collaborated in a summary of 1978 debates studies (D.O. Sears and S. H. Chaffee, "Uses and Effects of the 1976 Debates: An Overview of Empirical Studies," in Kraus, in press) and an assessment of the value of debates (Chaffee and Dennis). The summative statements here are drawn largely from those collaborative papers, although the conclusions reached here are those of the present author.

[11] This viewpoint reflects the gradual shift in mass communication research from source-

broader perspective, this paper will focus upon the functions of the debates for the individual voter and for the total political system of which the voter is a part.

It is important to make clear what is meant here by "the debates." For purposes of this analysis, this term can be taken to refer collectively to all of those events that occurred in 1960 and 1976 because the candidates chose to hold debates. This would include voter decisions that were withheld in anticipation of the debates; the media hype that preceded them; other campaign events that did *not* occur because the debates did; the press's analyses of who won and why; and subsequent campaign efforts by the candidates that built upon (or attempted to erase) events that occurred during or as a result of the debates. For purposes of comparison, the alternative to debates in this collective sense is what would have occurred in 1976 and 1960 if the candidates had chosen not to debate. This requires some speculation; we should not assume that, say, the debateless landslide elections of 1964 or 1972 resemble what the much closer 1960 and 1976 contests would have been like without debates.

USES AND OPINIONS OF DEBATES

At the most superficial level of "use,"

that of mere exposure, presidential debates have been uniformly a great success. Estimates of the proportion of the electorate watching at least some of the debates ran as high as 90% in both 1960 and 1976.[12] The first Ford-Carter debate was turned on in 72% of all households according to the Nielsen ratings, and their final debate in 60%.[13] Gallup estimates for registered voters nationwide ran from 67% to 70% viewing the various Ford-Carter clashes.[14] High as these figures are, can they be explained by factors other than political interest? Viewers had little else to watch, since all three networks ran the debates in toto. But the same is true of other news events that do not attract nearly such large audiences: presidential addresses and press conferences, party conventions, congressional hearings. The debates were the subject of enormous advance publicity, and offered the spectacle of live broadcasting (a rarity nowadays) of a competitive event of high stakes and uncertain outcome. But those things are equally true of a number of major sporting events (Super Bowl, World Series, heavyweight title boxing matches) that draw huge audiences but still fall far short of a 72% Nielsen rating.[15]

If we assume that the political content of debates is at least partly responsible for attracting such large audiences, what is the nature of that attraction? Inferences from the 1960 studies suggest partisan motivations: to root for one's pre-

oriented concepts such as "persuasion" and "effects" to receiver-oriented concepts such as "uses and gratification" and "information." A fuller delineation of this trend is presented in S. H. Chaffee, "Mass Media Effects: New Research Perspectives," in D. Lerner and L. Nelson, eds., *Communication Research: A Half Century Appraisal* (Honolulu: University Press of Hawaii, 1977), pp. 210-241. The predominant model in the field today is probably the "transactional" one, which attempts to embrace both source and receiver orientations simultaneously (R. A. Bauer, "The Obstinate Audience: The Influence Process from the Point of View of Social Communication," *American Psychologist* 19 (1964), 319-328; S. Kraus and D. Davis, *The Effects of Mass Communication on Political Behavior* (University Park: Pennsylvania University Press, 1976).

12 Kraus, *The Great Debates*, pp 188-189; Sears and Chaffee; J. Robinson, "Poll Results on the Debates," in Kraus, in press.
13 Robinson summarizes the results of various polls, including Nielsen's.
14 The range for other polling organizations (Roper, Harris, Associated Press) was from 64% to 72% (Robinson).
15 There has been remarkably little academic study of the audiences for televised sporting events. Almost invariably a given contest is broadcast on only one network, whereas the presidential debates have had the advantage of blanketing all network prime time on the evenings they have been held.

ferred candidate and to find reasons for rejecting his opponent.[16] If, on the other hand, we are to believe the self-reported motivations of the voters of 1976, the main reasons (in descending order) were to learn the candidates' positions on issues, to compare them as personalities, and to help in deciding which way to vote.[17] For example, 90% of an Akron, Ohio sample said learning issue stands was "very important," and 75% said the same thing about learning what the candidates were like as people; 69% were looking for help in deciding between them, and 65% expected they would get that help from the debates.[18]

After the debates, and especially after the critiques of them in the press, people did not rate them so highly.[19] A Roper poll showed that only 14% considered the Ford-Carter debates #1 and #2 "very informative," and only 21% in Akron said they had learned something new and important about issues from debate #1.[20] The debates were also somewhat disappointing in terms of learning about the candidates as people, and in helping to decide how to vote. For example, 60% in one sample said it was at best "somewhat difficult" to get a true picture of the candidates, and only 16% of a national sample considered the debates "very revealing."[21] More undecided voters rated the first debate "poor" than "good" in one study, but in another considerably more said the debates had made their vote decisions easier (41%)

than harder (13%).[22] And the overall ratings, even if people's highest hopes were not totally realized, were favorable: 78% in Akron though the debates were a "good idea," 93% of a student sample rated the first debate "worth seeing," and 75% of those who watched the Dole-Mondale debate were "glad" they had.[23]

The tendency to downgrade the debates seems to have been partly a result of post-debate critiques by the press. Comparison of immediate and delayed (next day) reactions of college students to the first debate showed many more negative reactions after the interpolation of news media reactions.[24] These post-debate press accounts focused mainly on who had won and why, at the expense of coverage of what was said by the candidates.[25] Perhaps the content of the debates did not seem particularly newsworthy to journalists who had been covering the campaign for months. At any rate, voters found much more concentration on the issues they said interested them if they watched the debates rather than attending to subsequent press reports. One study found that 37% of the time in debate #1 was spent on economic issues. But this topic accounted for only 14% of newspaper reports and just 5% of television coverage of this debate.[26] A majority of the space in each medium was devoted to

[16] Kraus, The Great Debates, esp. Richard F. Carter, "Some Effects of the Debates," pp. 253-270; Kirkpatrick.
[17] See sources cited in footnote 5; also Sears and Chaffee.
[18] O'Keefe and Mendelsohn.
[19] Evidence that, despite favorable evaluations overall, the debates were not rated as favorably after they had taken place as they had been in anticipatory pre-debates ratings is reviewed in Sears and Chaffee.
[20] PBS/Roper polls press releases, WNET/13, New York City, 1976; O'Keefe and Mendelsohn.
[21] McLeod et al.; PBS Roper polls.

[22] McLeod et al.; R. P. Abelson, "Poll Analysis," unpubl. paper, Yale University, 1977.
[23] O'Keefe and Mendelsohn; G. E. Lang and K. Lang, "Immediate and Mediated Responses: Reaction to the First Debate," in Kraus, in press; D. R. Kinder, W. Denney and R. Wagner, "Media Impact on Candidate Image: Exploring the Generality of the Law of Minimal Consequences," paper presented to American Association for Public Opinion Research Convention, Buck Hill Falls, Pennsylvania, May 1977.
[24] Lang and Lang.
[25] A. H. Miller and M. MacKuen, "Informing the Electorate: Effects of the 1976 Presidential Debates," in Kraus, in press; M. Jackson-Beeck and R. Meadow, "The Triple Agenda of Presidential Debates," Public Opinion Quarterly, in press.
[26] Miller and MacKuen.

material about who had won, how the candidates had performed, the personal qualities they projected, and how the debate would affect their campaigns.[27] Paradoxically, then, the debates themselves brought out issue content but they also stimulated press activity that obscured that information by heavy emphasis on the outcomes rather than the content of the debates.

LEARNING FROM DEBATES

But our assessment of the debates should not rely upon manifest content, nor upon introspective ratings, either by voters or by the press. We should have evidence that people learned something from the debates, whether they thought so or not. In 1960, researchers were not especially concerned with informational functions. Most of their efforts were directed at "images," persuasive effects, and selective patterns of exposure and perception. One of the remarkable findings was that the debates, which effectively minimized selective exposure, were also not subject to selective perception insofar as informational content was concerned. That is, people learned a good deal of information and they were as likely to learn it from statements made by the candidate they supported as they were when it came from the opposition candidate. This was found in two different studies, although in one of them it was also shown that viewers tended to misattribute statements they agreed with to their own candidate and statements with which they disagreed to his opponent.[28]

Evidence consistent with the hypothesis that issue-position information came out of the 1976 debates is shown in Table 1. The data are from a panel of 164 Wisconsin residents, sampled statewide by the Wisconsin Survey Research Laboratory in 1976. Perceptions of Ford's and Carter's positions on four issues were tracked through the fall. In the week before the debates, uncertainty, as indicated by responding "don't know" when asked the candidates' positions,

[27] The result was not to distort the *relative* emphasis given to one issue over another, however. For example, economic issues were mentioned more than any other category, occupying 37% of the time of the debates. Economic issues were also the most prominent category in press reports, but occupied much less of total media time/space in percentage terms because of the overshadowing of issue content by other elements of "debate news." Miller and MacKuen.

[28] R. F. Carter, "Some Effects of the Debates," in Kraus, *The Great Debates*, pp. 253-270; Sebald cited in E. Katz and J. J. Feldman, "The Debates in the Light of Research: A Survey of Surveys," in Kraus, *The Great Debates*, p. 201.

TABLE 1

"DON'T KNOW" CANDIDATES' POSITIONS ON FOUR ISSUES,
WISCONSIN 1976

		Before debates	After 1st debate	After last debate
Government action to	Ford	14%	6%	4%
increase employment	Carter	21%	7%	5%
Change tax system				
so high income	Ford	12%	5%	3%
people pay more	Carter	17%	5%	4%
Government spending for	Ford	11%	9%	5%
defense and military	Carter	20%	13%	7%
Legalized abortions	Ford	20%	16%	12%
	Carter	21%	17%	13%

Entries indicate the percentage who said "don't know" when asked to locate each candidate on a five-position scale regarding the listed issue. Data are from Wisconsin statewide panel (see Dennis, Chaffee, and Choe, in press; Dennis and Chaffee, in press).

was about equally high for all four issues in Carter's case. There was somewhat more information about Ford's position on three of the four issues. When these same respondents were interviewed in the week after the first debate, there had been a decrease in "don't knows" on all four issues—but mainly on the two that were discussed in that debate (unemployment and tax reform); on these the Ford-Carter difference had all but disappeared. Then after all the debates were completed, the same people were interviewed a third time. There was a further decline in "don't knows" for all issues, but the drop from the previous interview was greatest for defense spending—a topic that had been prominent in the later debates. There remained after the debates considerable doubt about the candidates' positions on abortion, a topic that both of them steered away from in the debates. In other analyses of the same data set, Dennis, Chaffee, and Choe found little change over time in the mean positions attributed to Ford and Carter, but a steady decrease in variance around those means. While it is impossible to divine what the candidates' "true" positions were, it appears that there was a gradual clarification of the public's perception of where they stood.

Other studies found more evidence of clarification of issue positions, at least for the first Ford-Carter debate. For example, greater differences on employment policy, with Ford becoming more clearly understood as emphasizing private sector jobs, were found after (as compared to before) Debate #1 in three different studies.[29] A Syracuse survey

found a jump from 50% to 75% in the perception that Carter advocated reorganizing the federal government.[30] Four studies showed before-after increases in the perceptions that Carter favored and Ford opposed amnesty for Vietnam War draft evaders.[31]

Some clarification of issue positions would be expected over the course of a campaign in the absence of any debates on the topics, especially among people who are being repeatedly interviewed (e.g. abortion in Table 1). But in general, in the surveys that included waves just before and just after the first Ford-Carter debate, there is not much evidence of clarification on topics that were not discussed in that debate ("control" topics). After the debate, Ford and Carter were seen as neither closer nor farther apart on such policies as the B-1 bomber project, gun control, school bussing, abortion, or defense spending.[32] There was also no change reported in three studies on national health insurance (although some people saw this as a topic emphasized in the first debate).[33]

There were also in 1976 a number of studies in which standard predictors of issue-information (e.g. education, partisanship) were used in multivariate postelection statistical analyses. With these factors controlled, there remained a small but significant cumulative effect of debate exposure on several issues:

29 Becker, Cobbey, and Sobowale; Lang and Lang; A. J. Morrison, F. Steeper, and S. Greendale, "The First 1976 Presidential Debate: The Voters Win," paper presented to American Association for Public Opinion Research Convention, May 1977.

30 Becker, Cobbey, and Sobowale.
31 K. Baker and O. Walter, "The 1976 Presidential Debates and Political Behavior in Wyoming," paper presented to the Western Social Science Association, Denver, April 1977; W. R. Cantrall, "The Impact of the 1976 Presidential Debates on a Student Population," unpubl. paper, Illinois State University, 1977; Lang and Lang; Morrison, Steeper, and Greendale.
32 Becker, Cobbey, and Sobowale; Cantrall; Dennis, Chaffee, and Choe; M. B. Lupfer, "An Experimental Study of the First Carter-Ford Debate," unpubl. paper, Memphis State University, 1977; McLeod et al.
33 Cantrall; Lang and Lang; Lupfer.

federal job programs, governmental re-organization, B-1 bomber.[34] A national post-election survey found a significant contribution of debate exposure to a four-issue index of perceived differences between the two major parties when education, attention to politics, partisanship, and general media exposure were controlled.[35]

It seems safe to conclude that there was substantial political learning as a consequence of holding the debates in 1976. This was probably also true in 1960, although few studies attempted to document this kind of effect and many critics of those debates would agree with the judgment that "not even a trained observer could keep up with the cross-fire of fact and counter-fact."[36]

INFORMED VOTING

The next issue is whether it can be shown that this learning had anything to do with the quality of the electoral decision. Such a question, mixing as it does value judgments with knotty epistemological problems, can never be answered to the full satisfaction of every school of scholarly inquiry. But there is evidence from 1976 that an important contribution to rational issue-based voting can be traced to the debates.

Before considering this encouraging evidence, let it be clear that there were two classes of voters for whom the debates could make no impact in terms of policy voting: (a) voters who had already definitely made up their minds before the debates occurred, and (b) voters who did not watch the debates and who paid little or no attention to media reports of them. As already noted,

group (b) was relatively small, surely no more than 20% of the electorate and probably less than 10%.[37] Group (a) was smaller than in previous elections on which comparable data are available. In the Wisconsin statewide sample, only about 31% of those who voted were definitely decided in the week prior to the debates. Panel data from local samples produced estimates in this same range: 26% in Cedar Rapids, Ia., and 40% in Madison, Wisc.[38] The *possibility* that the policy issue content of the debates would guide voting decisions in 1976 probably remained, then, for something more than one-half of the voters.

The idea that the debates would influence the vote by providing people with information on the candidates' issue positions is in general contrast to the "limited effects" model, which stresses the tendency of mass political communication to strengthen commitments that have already been made.[39] The 1976 data will be approached with limited-effects hypotheses, bearing in

34 R. A. Joslyn, "Voter Belief and Attitude Change and the 1976 Debates," unpubl. paper, Temple University, 1977; McLeod et al.

35 Miller and MacKeun.

36 D. Cater, "Notes from Backstage," in Kraus, *The Great Debates*, p. 130.

37 This estimate is based on the facts that some 80% of the total adult population watched the debates, and that non-voters were drawn disproportionately from non-watchers.

38 Chaffee and Choe developed these estimates from secondary analysis of the panel data of McLeod et al.; S. L. Becker, R. Pepper, L. A. Wenner, and J. Kim, "Presidential Debates, Information Flow, and the Shaping of Meanings,' in Kraus, in press; and Dennis, Chaffee, and Choe.

39 The most comprehensive early exposition of the limited effects model is J. T. Klapper, *The Effects of Mass Communication* (Glencoe: Free Press, 1960). The interpretation of that model for this paper is the product of the present author, however, and is drawn from many sources including I. Pool, "The Effect of Communication on Voting Behavior," in W. Schramm, ed., *The Science of Human Communication* (New York: Basic Books, 1963), pp. 128-138; D. O. Sears and R. Whitney, "Political Persuasion," in I. Pool, W. Schramm, F. Frey, N. Maccoby and E. Parker (eds.), *Handbook of Communication* (Chicago: Rand McNally, 1973), pp. 253-289; B. B. Berelson and G. Steiner, *Human Behavior* (New York: Harcourt, Brace and World, 1964). Also included were the critiques of Kraus and Davis; and S. H. Chaffee ed., *Political Communication* (Beverly Hills: Sage Publications, 1975).

mind that an opposing theoretical view-point may be developed to the extent that the limited-effects model fails to hold up. Data from the Wisconsin state-wide panel study will be relied upon to arbitrate these theoretical issues (Table 2). The path model followed for the regression analysis in Table 2 is shown in Figure 1. Two factors that existed prior to the campaign—the person's party identification and socioeconomic status—are entered as the first predictors; it is assumed that these two will account not only for the vote but for reactions to the campaign itself. The next two predictors are specific to the campaign but occur prior to the debates: the perceived ideological differences (liberal-conservative) between the two candidates and the voter, and the person's stated voting intention just before the debates. The last two predictors, which in this model are also treated as results of the four prior predictors, are the differences the ·voter sees between Ford and Carter in terms of personal images, and their positions on issues as compared to his own position. The dependent variable is the vote the person actually cast on Election Day. In Table 2 this model is tested both for the entire Wisconsin sample, and then separately for three sub-samples that differed in the extent to which they watched the debates. In path-analytic terms, there are two exogenous variables (party identification, socio-economic status), two pre-debates endogenous variables (ideological difference, vote intention), and two post-debates endogenous variables (image difference, issue difference). While not exhaustive, this set of six predictors includes the major factors that previous research has shown account for voting decisions in presidential elections.[40]

40 Nie, Verba, and Petrocik.

Vote Stability

First, the limited effects model would predict that the more a person watches the debates, the more stable and predictable his vote will become. In the Wisconsin sample, respondents were classified into three groups according to the extent to which they had watched the four debates: Regular Viewers, who had seen all of some debates, and at least some of each debate; Occasional Viewers, who had seen some but not all of the debates; and Non-Viewers, who watched no more than part of one debate. The predictability of the vote from the person's vote intention prior to the debates was *highest among the Non-Viewers* and *lowest among the Regular Viewers* (Table 2). Thus, contrary to the limited effects model, the data indicate that those who watched the debates were less stable in their voting intentions than those who did not.

Party Affiliation

· A second set of predictions from the limited effects model are (1) that prior identification with a political party would be the strongest predictor of the vote, and (2) that party would have determined the vote before the debates began. Overall, party identification did have a strong total effect, and most of this was accounted for by its impact on the pre-debates vote intention (Table 2). There was also a significant direct effect of party, beyond that represented in early voting plans, but interestingly this latent effect of partisan ties was limited to the Occasional Viewers. Setting aside the terminology of a causal model, the behavior of the Occasional Viewers during the fall might be characterized as follows: they were the most party-oriented of voters, but they were somewhat unsure of the candidate nominated by their party; they tuned in to

TABLE 2

SUMMARY OF REGRESSION ANALYSES OF VOTE DECISION-MAKING MODEL, BY EXPOSURE TO DEBATES

Dependent Variable	Predetermined Variable	Total Sample (N = 164)		Low Exposure (N = 35)		Medium Exposure (N = 65)		High Exposure (N = 64)	
		Direct effect	Total effect	Direct effect	Total effect	Direct effect	Total effect	Direct effect	Total effect
Ideological difference	Party ID	.39***	.39	.14	.14	.35**	.35	.54***	.54
	SES	-.04	-.04	-.22	-.22	-.06	-.06	.06	.06
		$R^2 = .15$		$R^2 = .05$		$R^2 = .11$		$R^2 = .29$	
T_1 Vote intention	Party ID	.59***	.63	.49***	.51	.57***	.62	.67***	.72
	SES	.12	.11	.28	.25	.05	.04	.16	.17
	Ideology	.11	.11	.12	.12	.13	.13	.09	.09
		$R^2 = .43$		$R^2 = .42$		$R^2 = .41$		$R^2 = .52$	
Issue difference	Party ID	.10	.46	.43**	.58	-.07	.37	.08	.53
	SES	-.04	-.01	-.30	-.33	.19*	.18	-.02	.07
	Ideology	.35***	.39	.35*	.37	.47***	.52	.28*	.32
	T_1 Vote intention	.36***	.36	.19	.19	.45***	.45	.41**	.41
		$R^2 = .42$		$R^2 = .48$		$R^2 = .56$		$R^2 = .43$	
Candidate images	Party ID	.03	.46	-.05	.29	.16	.56	-.03	.49
	SES	-.09	-.03	-.25	-.12	-.08	-.07	-.03	.08
	Ideology	.20**	.26	.15	.23	.16	.23	.24*	.29
	T_1 Vote intention	.57***	.57	.63***	.63	.55***	.55	.55***	.55
		$R^2 = .45$		$R^2 = .36$		$R^2 = .53$		$R^2 = .44$	
Final vote	Party ID	.15*	.60	.12	.50	.27**	.67	.06	.61
	SES	.06	.09	-.08	.04	.09	.10	.01	.10
	Ideology	.04	.19	.16	.27	-.10	.04	.11	.30
	T_1 Vote intention	.41***	.61	.63***	.83	.41***	.59	.30*	.55
	Issue difference	.10	.10	-.12	-.12	.04	.04	.31**	.31
	Candidate images	.28***	.28	.35*	.35	.28**	.28	.22*	.22
		$R^2 = .69$		$R^2 = .79$		$R^2 = .73$		$R^2 = .69$	

Note: Direct effects entries are standardized regression coefficients (beta). Total effects include direct effects plus indirect effects (not shown in table) through intervening variables in the model.

*p < .05, **p < .01, ***p < .001

(Source: Dennis, Chaffee, and Choe)

305

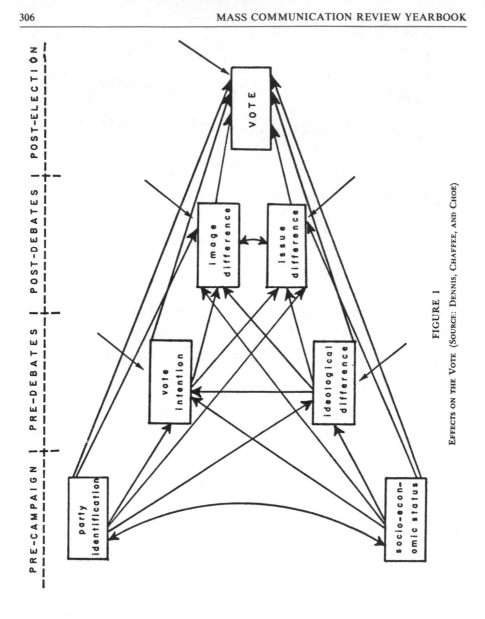

FIGURE 1

EFFECTS ON THE VOTE (SOURCE: DENNIS, CHAFFEE, AND CHOE)

the debates sufficiently to assure themselves that this candidate was indeed
worthy of their votes. The Non-Viewers,
although they changed the least in vote
intention, were the least party-oriented
in their voting. The Regular Viewers
were strongly guided by partisan considerations in their pre-debates vote intentions, but during the remainder of
the campaign they were the least influenced by party ties despite the fact
that they changed the most of any
group. It is the Occasional Viewers who
fit the limited effects model by finding
in the debates reinforcement of tentative
decisions to vote along party lines. Since

they comprise only about 40% of the sample, the evidence in support of that model in the aggregate is rather weak.

Image Voting

A variation on the limited effects theme has been to assert that presidential debates, rather than supplying voters with manifest issue information, serve simply to project appealing "images" of the candidates. This was the summary judgment from the 1960 debates studies.[41] The first hypothesis to be derived from this proposition is that those who watch the debates will be most likely to vote on the basis of the personality images they perceive of the candidates. The Wisconsin data are directly contrary to this prediction. In Table 2 favorable images (based on the sum of six scales) following the debates predict the vote most strongly among the Non-Viewers and most weakly among the Regular Viewers. These post-debates images are mainly determined by pre-debates events. There is practically no evidence in any study of changes in candidate images following the Ford-Carter debates. To be sure, this was not the case in 1960, when Kennedy's image was enhanced in several important respects as a consequence of his debate performance.[42]

In Table 2 the main predictors of post-debates image evaluations are pre-debates party identification and vote intention. Now, one might construe the difference in strength of these two predictors as an indicator of the impact of image alone. That is, the extent that one's vote intention is correlated with image perceptions, beyond the prediction based on the correlation of images with prior party identification, could be an implicit indicator of "image voting." If this reasoning is valid, image voting in 1976 was most common among Non-Viewers of the debates. Party identification was a weaker predictor of both pre-debates voting intention and post-debates candidate images for the Non-Viewers than for those who watched the debates. On the other hand, it was also Non-Viewers for whom post-debates images were most strongly predicted by pre-debates voting plans. Image voting, then, seems to have been a phenomenon that had already exercised most of its influence prior to the debates. There is no evidence that the debates enhanced this tendency in voters. It was if anything eroded by exposure to the debates.

Other Predisposition Factors

The limited effects model is built around the general concept of predispositions that determine one's interpretation of mass media content. We can examine in Table 2 two predispositional factors besides party identification. These are the measures of socioeconomic status and of ideological differences (liberal-conservative) between the candidates' and a voter's own position.

[41] Kraus, The Great Debates, see especially pp. 151-162, 201-205. This judgment may have passed irretrievably into the conventional wisdom with the unsubstantiated assertion by M. McLuhan, Understanding Media: The Extensions of Man (New York: McGraw Hill, 1964), that "TV would inevitably be a disaster for a sharp intense image like Nixon's, and a boon for the blurry, shaggy texture of Kennedy," p. 329.
[42] Katz and Feldman, pp. 203-205, after reviewing several studies in which this was found, suggest that it was due to the fact that "Kennedy had the 'advantage' of being all but unknown." If that were the reason, however, it should have applied as well to Carter, who made no comparable gain. A revised explanation might be that the less-known candidate does have the opportunity to enhance his image more, but that the first debate is the critical one for this pur-pose. Kennedy did rather well in his first debate, whereas Carter did not, and perhaps thereby lost his chance to pick up "image" points. Most studies show that the first debate is not only the one most people watch, it is also the one that makes much the greatest difference in perceptions of the candidates. Sears and Chaffee.

Neither of these proves to be a significant predictor of the vote when party identification and other, more immediate, factors are controlled. Overall, socioeconomic status is not significantly related to any of the other factors in the model. In the subgroup analyses, it is a significant predictor only of post-debates issue differences pereived by the Occasional Viewers. Ideology does predict issue differences, and to a lesser extent perceived images, and through these it makes some indirect contribution to the eventual vote.

Issue Voting

Although the limited effects model has not stood up very well to the empirical tests we have reviewed so far, its most important implications for evaluating debates are those having to do with issue voting. The limited-effects prediction would be that debates, even though they might contain considerable policy-related information, have little impact because the interpretation of that information is determined by prior political orientations. Put another way, people would not vote on the basis of their clarified issue perceptions, but rather would assimilate these perceptions into their earlier constructions of the situation. To examine the role of debate viewing in issue voting in 1976, an index of issue distances between each voter and the two candidates was calculated using the four issues listed in Table 1. The post-debates perceived issue difference was added to the model of vote decision-making in Table 2.

For the total sample, these issue differences did not significantly predict the vote, and were themselves strongly accounted for by predispositional factors. Among the Regular Viewers of the debates, however, this was not the case.

The votes of these citizens were more strongly predicted by issue differences than by any other factor in the model. Conversely, predispositions accounted less well for the post-debates issue perceptions of the Regular Viewers than of the other two groups.

SUMMARY

As a departure from expectations based on conventional theory, these are probably the most significant findings coming out of the 1976 debates studies: Prior to the debates, many voters reported that they were undecided, and they looked to the debates for information about the candidates' stands on policy issues. The debates provided issue information, and most voters watched and learned from them. Those who were the most regular viewers changed the most in their voting intentions, were the ones least influenced by predispositional factors, and were the most likely to vote in conformance with policy differences they perceived between themselves and the candidates.

DISCUSSION: INFORMED VOTING

Dennis et al. have used the term "bonding" and an analogy to chemistry to characterize what happened.[43] Just as various chemical elements can combine with one another to form stable molecules, so can the various perceptual and experiential elements of politics combine with one another. The end result is the vote, a molecular combination of various factors. The difficulty for researchers has been that, unlike elements in chemistry, such directional political factors as party, ideology, status, images, and issues tend to be positively inter-

---

[43] Dennis, Chaffee, and Choe. The bonding concept also appears in the study of adolescents by R. O. Hawkins, S. Pingree, K. Smith and W. Bechtolt, "Adolescents' Responses to the Issues and Images of the Debates," in Kraus, in press.

correlated so that all appear in aggregate analyses to be reinforcing one another. In individual cases, though, they may point in different directions, and only certain of them may be used in reaching a voting decision. The debates, controlled so that they are bi-directional, enter in the role of a *catalyst* rather than as an additional directional element. They modify the environment in which the directionally valenced elements are combining and help to determine which of these other elements has most to do with the final product, the vote.

It is a matter of which factors become most strongly reinforced. Given that most of them will tend to point in a similar direction for a particular voter, it is quite noteworthy that the "effect" of attention to debates seems to be a reinforcement of issue positions at the expense of images or global predispositions. More specifically, regular viewing of the debates in 1976 was associated with bonding of issues to the vote decision; occasional viewing with bonding of prior, partisan affiliations; and nonviewing with bonding of images and vote intentions.

The debates, then, were useful in different ways for different kinds of voters. Those who took most complete advantage of the information provided by the debates, as indicated by regular viewing, were enabled to vote on the basis of current issues. Those who only occasionally watched the debates seem to have gained reassurance that their parties had nominated candidates for whom they could vote. Those who did not watch the debates had little reason to modify their voting intentions during the fall campaign.

While this empirical analysis suggests an affirmative answer to the question posed in the title of this paper, some immediate caveats are in order. As already noted, the debates are helpful in providing policy-relevant information, but only for certain voters: those who have not already decided how to vote, and those who pay fairly close attention to what is said in the debates. In 1976 a majority of voters may have fit this description, but this would not necessarily be true in all, or even most, elections. It may well be that the kind of catalytic impact we found from the Ford-Carter debates is limited to campaigns in which (a) at least one of the candidates is not well known, (b) many voters are undecided, (c) the contest appears to be a close one, and (d) party allegiances are weak.

Having entered those qualifications, let it be further pointed out that those are precisely the conditions under which debates between presidential candidates are likely to recur. In 1960 there were many nominal Democrats who had voted recently for a popular Republican (Eisenhower) and who knew little about Kennedy. In 1976 party ties had weakened historically, and Ford was much the better-known candidate. Both elections were extremely close, and this closeness was probably more a cause than an effect of the debates of either year. Turning this proposition around, we can (in the absence of compelling legislation) expect both candidates to agree to debate only when they expect a close election and they have evidence that there are large numbers of votes yet to be won.

The general conclusion of this paper about the value of debates to individual voters can be expressed in two propositions that represent the lower- and upper-limit boundary conditions. As a lower-limit proposition, it appears that a considerable number of voters (perhaps half of the total electorate) can benefit from debates when conditions are such that candidates are likely to debate, i.e. in a very close and fluid election situation. The upper-limit situation is more hypothetical, since it would apply to conditions that have never been observed empirically: debates held despite a lopsided election situation in which almost all voters have decided and a large majority favor one candidate.

Let us suppose that the experiment of 1960 had led to an institutionalization of presidential debates, so that there would have been Johnson-Goldwater debates in 1964 and Nixon-McGovern debates in 1972. (It is most debatable what would have taken place in the three-cornered campaign of 1968.) What would the value of such debates have been to the voters in either of these landslide years? The closest to an empirical answer that can be provided is that the upper-limit value would have been a function of (a) the proportion of the electorate that was undecided and seeking information about the candidates and their positions, and (b) the degree of attention given to the debates by those voters. While it is impossible to reconstruct the actual conditions that existed in the Septembers of either 1964 or 1972, it is doubtless safe to surmise that this upper limit would have been a much smaller value than was the case in 1976, the year for which we have data in hand.

While we are in the realm of conjecture, let us assume that in 1964 or 1972 the upper-limit value of debates for the voters would have been quite low. Say, for purposes of argument, that only 10% of the voters were open to any information that could have been provided via presidential debates in the Octobers of those years. It could reasonably be argued that the question, "Are debates helpful to voters?" should still be answered affirmatively. It is unlikely that we will see in the imaginable future a U.S. election in which the upper-limit value of debates would shrink to zero.

The empirical problem is to evaluate the cost-benefit tradeoffs of various debates policies.

There is certainly ample reason, from the experience of 1976, to argue for maintaining the concept of presidential debates as a possibility for future elections. Conditions will doubtless arise again when each candidate sees a reason to debate. The potential benefits to voters will always be non-zero and in those cases where the candidates are likely to agree to debate, the possible gains for the electorate will be maximal. On the other hand, a policy under which a *requirement* to debate is written into the law, or one in which debating is made a condition for receiving federal campaign funds, would entail certain costs—not the least of which is severe strain on the principles of the Constitution. We should expect that an incumbent President will in most circumstances resist any compulsion to debate in a reelection campaign, so proponents of debates as a regular feature of all presidential campaigns will find themselves opposing the most powerful political institution in the country, the White House. Given barriers such as these, the marginal benefit to be realized on behalf of the electorate might well be outweighed by the inherent costs. Short of statutory institutionalization, but beyond the present system whereby debates are brokered by candidates the way prizefights are brokered by boxers, there are a number of intermediate steps that can be taken to increase the possibility that debates will be held in some—if not all—future national elections. The analysis of this paper can help to assess the potential benefits at stake in any such efforts.

LATENT SYSTEMIC FUNCTIONS

Beyond the direct usefulness of debates for voters, we are also beginning to get some idea of the functions debates can serve for the larger political system. There are at least two ways of looking at these latent functions: those which are of benefit to the enduring institutions of government and policy, and those which enable the administration that wins a particular election to govern effectively. There is beginning to accumulate some evidence that debates are functional at each of these levels of analysis.

In terms of enduring institutions, the Wisconsin data indicate that the 1976 campaign period was one of growing public confidence in the major components of the U.S. government. From before the debates to after the election, significant increases were found in measures of confidence in the presidency, the Congress, and the federal government.[44] There was also a slight (non-significant) gain in confidence in the Supreme Court. More important, these gains were positively correlated with various measures of exposure to the campaign, including the debates. With people's pre-debates level of confidence in the four institutions controlled in a hierarchical regression analysis, there was a significant positive relationship between total exposure to the debates and post-debates confidence (beta $= .14$).

The debates also can be credited with a role in political socialization, or the recruitment of new members into the body politic. In a panel study of 6th, 9th, and 12th graders in a small Wisconsin town, regression analyses showed debates exposure to be the strongest of eight predictors of post-debates interest in the election, with pre-debates interest controlled.[45] Among the older adolescents, discussion of the debates was also an important predictor of increases in

interest. Among the younger students, debate viewing and discussion also correlated with increases in perceived political efficacy and in partisanship. The socialization process as facilitated by the debates appears to be a smooth one. The older adolescents, in comparison with the younger respondents in the panel, reacted somewhat more like adults: they watched the debates more for issue information and less to be reminded of their candidates' strong points, and they determined their preferences more on the basis of party ties and less on image characteristics. Another study, designed to compare young voters with older voters, found similar reasons for watching, and reactions to, the debates for the two groups.[46] The younger voters were somewhat more affected by the debates, in terms of change in their perceptions of the candidates' issue positions.

The latent function of establishing a stronger basis for the successful candidate to govern once elected is not so well documented as are the general functions of the debates for the political system. Following the 1960 debates, Katz and Feldman speculated that "the debates might make for a greater acceptance of the winning candidate—even if one voted against him: one knew more about him, one felt that he was more human and more accessible."[47] This hypothesis was tested in the 1976 Wisconsin panel study, by separating the image evaluations of the candidates according to the respondent's eventual vote. There was a steady improvement from before until after the debates in the rating of the candidate the person was voting for, but the evaluation of the other candidate declined somewhat.[48] These changes were not significantly as-

44 J. Dennis and S .H. Chaffee, "Legitimation in the 1976 U.S. Presidential Election Campaign," *Communication Research*, in press.
45 Hawkins et al.

46 McLeod et al.
47 Katz and Feldman, p. 219.
48 Dennis and Chaffee.

sociated with the extent to which the person watched the debates, or paid attention to media follow-up reports and evaluations of them. But they were correlated with discussion of the debates. In hierarchical regression with the person's pre-debates evaluation controlled, debates discussion was a significant positive predictor of post-debates ratings of the candidate voted for (beta = .19), and a negative predictor of the equivalent ratings of the other candidate (beta = .12). No other campaign communication measure tested was as strong a predictor of these changes.[49] So if anything, we should consider that the evidence is against the hypothesis suggested by Katz and Feldman.

Also on shaky empirical ground is the possibility that the debates would enhance the international stature of a new administration. Although the 1976 debates were reportedly televised in 91 countries, we have data on reactions to them from only one nation, the Netherlands.[50] A survey conducted after the debates but before the election found that the Dutch respondents, even those who considered themselves liberals, overwhelmingly favored Ford in the U.S. election. This is probably attributable in large measure to the incumbent's much greater prominence in international news; a new government is probably always a bit suspect in the eyes of the rest of the world. The debates might have served to make Carter more acceptable abroad, and to make clearer that he was the more liberal candidate. The Netherlands data, while open to

alternative interpretations, are consistent with this hypothesis. Although only 31% of the Dutch respondents watched the debates, those who did were much more likely to have a preference between Ford and Carter; less likely to prefer the more familiar incumbent; and more likely to align their preferences with their general ideological positions.[51] We can at least tentatively infer that political learning from presidential debates is not confined to the American voters at whom the debates are directed.

The foregoing comprise the only latent functions of the debates on which evidence has been gathered. In general, they add to the overall accumulation of empirical arguments in favor of future debates. But there have been suggestions of latent dysfunctions as well. The personalization of politics that is associated with television may be exacerbated by candidate debates. This would implicate debates in the decline of U.S. political parties, which some attribute to television and many see as a serious loss for the political process.[52] Presidential debates also draw even greater attention to the presidency, which is only one institution in a multi-level, multi-branch system of government. This centralization of public attention may operate to the detriment of political rationality at less glamorous levels.[53] Another dysfunctional possibility is that debates may encourage the growing tendency to rely on television for one's information on public affairs.[54] Our better informed citizens are those who read newspapers

[49] The other communication measures tested in this analysis included attention to the campaign on television; attention to the campaign in newspapers and magazines; and discussion of the campaign. Separate measures of viewing of each of the four debates were also tested.

[50] H. de Bock, "The Influence of the Ford-Carter Debates on the Dutch Television Audience," unpubl. paper, Netherlands Broadcasting Foundation, 1977.

[51] This finding may be spurious, i.e. it may not indicate any "effect" of viewing the debates, but could simply be attributed to the high likelihood that people who watched the debates were in other respects more politically attuned and informed.

[52] Kraus and Davis; Kirkpatrick.

[53] Chaffee and Dennis; Kirkpatrick.

[54] Chaffee and Dennis.

and magazines to get their news.[55] The debates of 1976 had, at least in the short term, a tendency to lead to more attention to the campaign on television, although they also seem to have created a slight increase in attention to print and interpersonal channels.[56]

[55] The relationship between exposure to print and holding public affairs knowledge is probably a reciprocal one. Panel studies show both that reading the newspaper predicts gains in relative knowledge levels, and that high knowledge predicts gains in attention to newspapers. In adolescence, but apparently not in adulthood, the same reciprocal interplay exists between current events knowledge and exposure to television news. S. H. Chaffee, M. Jackson-Beeck, J. Durall, and D. Wilson, "Mass Communication in Political Socialization," in *Handbook of Political Socialization*, ed. S. Renshon (New York: Free Press, 1977), pp. 223-258.

[56] Analysis by Choe, described in Chaffee and Dennis, Appendix Table A.

CONCLUSION

We are far from having a full balance-sheet accounting of the functions and dysfunctions, manifest and latent, of presidential debates. Beyond the need for more evidence, there are many value judgments involved. Not everyone would agree, for example, that personalized rather than issue-oriented campaigns are undesirable, or that the maintenance of strong political parties and an electorate that gets its information from newspapers are desirable. But the burden of evidence to date, when intersected with traditional democratic values, should encourage us to attach a rather high net value to the debates as an emerging institution in the political process.

The reasonably positive assessment of the role of televised Carter-Ford presidential campaign debates on the political reasoning of voters (outlined in the preceding article by Chaffee) is somewhat overshadowed by the dismal picture of television's role in the 1974 senatorial elections in this study by Peter Clarke and Eric Fredin. The authors use data from a large national sample involving 67 news markets to show that newspaper use correlated positively with having reasons for senatorial candidate preference. Television use, on the other hand, was negatively related to political reasoning. In addition, intermarket comparisons suggest that newspaper competition and diversity may be related to public understanding of campaign issues. Dr. Clarke is Professor in and Chairman of the Department of Communication at the University of Michigan. Mr. Fredin is Assistant Professor of Journalism at Indiana University.

17

NEWSPAPERS, TELEVISION AND
POLITICAL REASONING

Peter Clarke and Eric Fredin

O NE OF THE most powerful hopes advanced by theories of representative government is that news media remain free so they may educate the public in making political choices. Ignorance condemns people to sway with the most available rhetoric. The uninformed person chooses randomly or out of habit to support candidates or policies.[1] Often he or she avoids the political arena altogether—perhaps because of hedonism or alienation.[2]

---

[1] An analogy to this point, drawn from laws of inertia, can be found in Converse (1962).

[2] The conventional image of the alienated and withdrawn citizen may be badly out of date, however. Recent studies have disclosed many people who are distrustful of government, but who combine this feeling with intensely held attitudes about political issues. Extreme conservatives and liberals can be expected to possess above average levels of information. See Miller (1974), and following comment by Jack Citrin and rejoinder.

Abstract Adults' use of newspapers is found to correlate positively with having reasons for preferring one U.S. senatorial candidate over another. Television exposure is negatively related to political "reasoning" to a nearly significant degree. Data were provided by a 1974 nationwide, postelection survey. Analysis was conducted at the aggregate level, examining media behavior and political knowledge in 67 news markets. News markets with competition among daily newspapers show greater levels of information than monopoly areas, controlling for education and interest in politics. Results suggest that a decline in newspaper penetration, lessened competition, or shift toward use of television for news would weaken peoples' understanding about partisan candidates.

Peter Clarke is Professor and Chairman, Department of Journalism, University of Michigan. Eric Fredin is a student in the Interdepartmental Doctoral Program in Mass Communication, University of Michigan. Data for this report were collected by the Center for Political Studies of the Institute for Social Research. Support was provided by grants from the National Science Foundation, the John and Mary R. Markle Foundation, and the Carnegie Corporation. Survey documentation and data are available from the Inter-University Consortium for Political Research, University of Michigan. Neither the original collectors of the data nor the Consortium bear any responsibility for the analyses or interpretations presented here.

From Peter Clarke and Eric Fredin, "Newspapers, Television and Political Reasoning." *Public Opinion Quarterly* 42 (Summer 1978) 143-160. Reprinted by permission of Elsevier North-Holland, Inc.

Researchers should take pains, therefore, to plot the educational role of journalism. The nature of this role, and how different media share in it, may yield hints about the future for rationality and order in American political life.[3] Studies have recently confirmed that this educational role exists, despite solemn, sociological pronouncements a few years back about "minimal effects." Agenda setting by media is widely recognized now.[4] Learning about public affairs from media has been documented, holding competing explanations constant.[5]

This article presents two amplifications to recent documentation. The first details the relative contributions of newspapers and television to the public informing process. These contributions may interest prophets of the American political future who note the steady slippage in per capita circulation of newspapers and the persistent rise in minutes spent viewing television news.[6] Although this shift may produce changes in levels of political understanding, it is also possible that informing functions traditionally served by newspapers are being assumed by electronic journalism.[7] The first findings reported below shed light on these alternative possibilities.

A second goal is to discern whether characteristics of media offered to citizens play a part in how informed people are. For reasons that will be made clear, amount of newspaper competition in markets is a key to understanding public information about political affairs. Since competition among newspapers is thought to be declining, any relationship between competition and levels of information would have implications for the future course of American political behavior.

Knowing about Public Affairs

What is the proper definition of being "informed"? The present analysis argues that possessing information about public affairs means

[3] Comparisons between print and broadcast media in political effects have been reported recently. See McClure and Patterson (1974 and 1976).

[4] Pertinent findings are reviewed in McCombs and Shaw (1976). See also Palmgreen and Clarke (1977).

[5] For a study comparing national and local public affairs issues, see Palmgreen (1975).

[6] Current criticism of both newspapers and local television news leads to the discouraging prediction that the public's grasp of "hard news" would be on the decline, whatever media they use. For pessimistic analyses, see Powers (1977), and Bordewich (1977). Trends in audience research are amply portrayed in minutes of meetings by the American Newspaper Publishers Association and in the pages of *Broadcasting Magazine*.

[7] Radio and word-of-mouth communication are omitted from this discussion because research has failed to show correlations with learning about public affairs. This analysis does not deal with persuasive effects of media on attitude formation and change. For contemporary studies of newspapers' editorial effects on voting decision see Erikson (1976), and Robinson (1972).

having reasons for favoring or rejecting political alternatives. Having reasons for perceiving or acting equips a person to explain choices—to self as well as others—lending order and pattern to political action. Reasons provide a cognitive framework for acquiring and processing additional information. Helping people develop reasons (to suit their own beliefs) is a goal to which schools and news media aspire.

This survey interviewed people at length about their reasons for supporting or rejecting political contenders in an important race—the election for United States senator in their state. (Other arenas of choice would also have been appropriate.) The senatorial contest can be used to compare the informing functions of two competing media systems, daily newspapers and television.

The analysis does not dwell on the specific reasons people offer. As one would expect, some citizens have no choice at all for U.S. senator or, having chosen, can present no explanation for their preference. Other people express reasons of a discouragingly conventional sort. A tiny minority fulfill the hopes of their civics teachers by enlarging on the candidates' policy positions or advantages that would accrue to certain groups if one were elected instead of the other. Expressing some reasons for senatorial choice, however primitive, is a precondition for having an elaborate point of view. The following analysis might be described as tracing the *minimum conditions* for an informed citizenry.[8]

Contrary to popular opinion, research demonstrates that the public relies on newspapers somewhat more than on television for political news.[9] Both vehicles are especially important in state and local affairs untouched by magazine journalism. This study considers extent of exposure to newspapers and television news as potentially informing vehicles and notes whether people discriminate political messages in these media. As the findings show, message discrimination represents a more direct and powerful contribution to learning than extent of exposure.

The concept of message discrimination (examined elsewhere[10]) is meant to replace the conventional idea of gross media use as evidence that communication events have transpired. Instead, the amount of communication people have experienced is reflected by their reports of having discriminated symbols about specified topics, not by minutes

[8] The authors avoid judgments about the completeness, sophistication, or even "accuracy" of reasons people give for their views of senatorial candidates. Possessing any reasons counts here—a blind acceptance that is justified by finding that the major point of variance is between persons who lack reasons altogether and persons with at least one criterion for choice between candidates.

[9] See, for example, Clarke and Ruggels (1970), and Edelstein (1974).

[10] See Clarke and Kline (1974), and Palmgreen et al. (1974).

spent exposed to media or frequency of reading or viewing. To measure message discrimination, the interview asked two kinds of questions that provided maximum opportunity to relate the political messages people found in media. One is whether they had read or seen anything having to do with an election campaign, recently concluded. The other is whether they had read or seen messages having to do with national political issues that they noted as important earlier in the interview. As with information holding, the concept of message discrimination provides latitude for people to report behavior they feel relevant to the political scene.

A variety of factors surely affect relationships between what the media convey about politics and growth in public awareness. Statistical controls might be imposed for many variables—race, income, sex of respondent, and more. A narrower path is followed here in order to concentrate attention on people's skills in making effective use of media and on their likely motivations for doing so. One step is to hold constant the level of formal education. This major stratification variable correlates powerfully with use of media and with knowing and participating in public affairs. Furthermore, media differ in the educational attainment of the audiences they reach. In the present analysis, education serves as a shorthand measure of ability.

People differ, also, in their willingness to follow public affairs. Some have been socialized by circumstances as well as institutions to concern themselves with political outcomes.

With education and interest controlled, there is some assurance that the remaining variance arises from the information environment to which people are exposed. This environment can fluctuate according to the demands of political events and the way in which events, like campaigns, are reported.

Research Methods

Data originate from detailed personal interviews with a weighted sample of 1,883 adults, a cross-section of the American public in states with Senate elections in 1974. The sample was selected by multistage, probability methods. Research design, field supervision of data collection, coding, and documentation were conducted according to high standards of the Center for Political Studies in the Institute for Social Research at Michigan. Details can be found elsewhere.[11]

[11] Persons interviewed here are eighteen years or older in households selected by probability sampling methods. Approximately two-thirds had been interviewed in 1972. Sampling, weighting, and other survey documentation can be found in Miller et al. (1975).

Interviewing took place following the off-year congressional election; this analysis is confined to 25 states in the continental region where the Center had designated sample points and where senatorial elections were underway. Sample clusters of households represent 67 media markets, ranging from metropolitan giants like New York and San Francisco to rural hamlets in Pitt County, North Carolina and Randolph County, Illinois. In the middle are such varied media locales as Louisville, Tulsa, Salt Lake City, Tulare, Bridgeport, and more.

One may examine these data in two ways: first, at the level of individual behavior, correlating variables across persons; or second, by aggregating data within media markets and correlating across them. The second strategy is followed in order to focus toward the end on a characteristic of media markets that may be associated with how informed people are. This characteristic is the level of media competition—the potential, at least, for a diversity of voices about public affairs, or a multitude of news presentations available to the public.[12]

MEASURES

The criterion variable is having reasons for liking or disliking the two major party candidates for Senate. The main questions read:"Was there anything in particular about the Democratic (Republican) candidate for Senator that made you want to vote for (against) him (her)?" Respondents were quizzed extensively about likes and dislikes, and as many as 12 responses were coded into an elaborate system of content categories.[13]

Admittedly, the measure favors people who consider themselves participants in the political process. Respondents who resolved not to vote after they studied the contenders and decided neither was worth support might have disclaimed having reasons to "vote for" or

---

[12] Individual analyses have not been overlooked. Patterns of results reported here are duplicated when we examine relationships between individuals' media use and information. We also recognize the imprecision of estimating mean levels of information, media use, and other market variables using data from a few interviews—even when based on probability samples. Imprecision attenuates any correlation with other factors like media competition. The substantial size of this relationship (see below) encourages some confidence that the data have attained reasonable accuracy across the 67 markets.

[13] When reasons people give are examined in detail, the majority cluster in four categories. Most frequent are references to the candidates' prior records of public service—general mentions of how well they have filled governmental or political offices. Mentions of being a good party man come second. References to integrity and honesty are third. The fourth most popular category is general expressions of having heard good things about the candidate. Respondents cite favorable characteristics much more often than criticisms. The respondent's party preference did not qualify as a reason.

"against." They would thus be misclassified in terms of the meaning we attach to this measure—a reflection of having reasons for political choice.[14]

Reading newspapers and viewing television news were measured with conventional items.[15] Message discrimination, as already explained, used one set of questions asking whether the respondent had read anything or seen any programs about the recent campaign, and another battery inquired into reading and viewing about an important national problem the respondent had noted and discussed earlier in the interview. Descriptions of these messages were also content analyzed according to a detailed coding scheme.[16]

Interest in public affairs was measured early in the interview with the following item: "Some people seem to follow what's going on in government and public affairs most of the time, whether there's an election going on or not. Others aren't that interested. Would you say you follow what's going on in government and public affairs most of the time, some of the time, only now and then, or hardly at all?"

Results

PREDICTING INFORMATION HOLDING

Correlations are first examined between having reasons for choice between senatorial candidates and use of news media. Table 1 shows zero-order coefficients between all predictors and information level. Correlations have been calculated between mean levels for each pair of variables across the 67 news markets in which there were elections for U.S. Senate in 1974.

The limited contribution of television coverage to public information is immediately apparent. Neither TV news viewing nor message discrimination in any television programing correlates significantly with knowing about senatorial contenders. Newspapers contrast by showing large correlations for both number of papers read and amount of message discrimination. Of course, levels of education and political interest in the 67 markets are associated with average information holding.

[14] All respondents, both voters and nonvoters, were asked these questions, however.

[15] Respondents named the daily newspapers they read. Television news viewing was measured for all parts of the daily cycle, since broadcasts at different times attract audiences of different ages. The basic question read: "How often do you watch (a kind of TV news)—frequently, sometimes, rarely or never?" Kinds included "national news in the early morning," "local news broadcasts in the early evening," "national news broadcasts in the early evening," and "local news broadcasts in the late evening." Responses were summed to yield an overall exposure estimate.

[16] See Miller et al. (1975).

Table 1. Zero-order Correlations between All
Predictors and Number of Reasons for Senate
Choice

	r
Exposure to TV news throughout day	.10
Number of newspapers read	.45
Discriminating problem and campaign messages on TV	.16
Discriminating problem and campaign messages in papers	.57
Interest in public affairs	.49
Education	.33

$r_{.05} = .24$.
$N = 67$ markets, less one market in the case
of TV news exposure for which there were insufficient data.

A more stringent test can be performed for the informing value of
television and newspapers, controlling for education and political
interest and distinguishing between types of communication variables
measured in this study. Only a minority in the audience is devoted to
television news or reads newspapers heavily for their political content.
To assess political informing functions one should hold media exposure
constant, along with education and interest in public affairs.

Multiple regression simultaneously invoking all predictors represents the appropriate analysis. Table 2 shows the fifth-order partials
and standardized betas for each predictor. Overall news viewing and
newspaper reading are eliminated as correlates of knowing about senatorial candidates. Discriminating messages in newspapers remains a

Table 2. Results of Multiple Regression between All Predictors and Number of Reasons for
Senate Choice

	Fifth-order Partials	Standardized Betas	t-value	Signi- ficance
Exposure to TV news throughout day	−.06	−.0164	n.s.	
Number of newspapers read	−.04	−.0490	n.s.	
Discriminating problem and campaign messages on TV	−.22	−.2431	1.77	.08
Discriminating problem and campaign messages in papers	.33	.5343	2.71	.01
Interest in public affairs	.28	.2969	2.25	.03
Education	.06	.0593	n.s.	

Multiple $R = .64$.

strong predictor; discriminating messages on television shows a *negative* relationship that approaches the .05 level of significance.

The partial correlations enclosed by a box in Table 2 (and their betas) supply persuasive evidence for a unique educational role by newspapers. Messages in newspapers confer information beyond what can be expected from general exposure levels. Television may actually exert an inhibiting effect on knowing about politics.[17]

Is this because people simply do not find messages about public affairs on television? Not according to this survey. Average scores are alike for measures of following the campaign and problems in newspapers and television (1.18, compared to 1.15—with nearly identical variances).

Are people who discriminate messages in newspapers fundamentally different from people who report this experience with television? Possibly. But that kind of explanation must confront the *positive* correlation between these two communication behaviors—a pearson coefficient of .49 at the market level, and a coefficient of .33 at the level of individual analysis.

Are there substantial differences in the kinds of messages people can read and those they can view and hear? Undoubtedly. But any differences do not extend to the *topics* those messages cover. We content-analyzed topics reported by newspapers (front pages only) and tape-recorded television news broadcasts before the election. Conclusion of this part of the research awaits coding of more of the news programs taped in the 67 markets. However, topic emphasis by a few stations that have been analyzed correlates highly with the same-city newspaper coverage, suggesting one would find more similarities than differences between media in their treatment of public affairs.[18] Like McClure and Patterson (1976:25), one is left for the moment with familiar speculations about why newspapers convey more

[17] The possibility of inhibition from television persists when the analysis is controlled for education, political interest, and message discrimination—leaving exposure levels unpartialed. The third-order partial for message discrimination in newspapers is .43 ($p <$ .01). For message discrimination in television the value is $-.24$ (beta $= -.2206, p = .06$). Our findings based on adults contrast with results from a longitudinal survey with adolescents. That study found equivalent television and newspaper correlations with scores from a paper-and-pencil test for students' current events knowledge. See Chaffee et al. (1970).

[18] Others have found impressive similarities between television and newspapers in quantity of coverage of *national* issues (McCombs and Shaw, 1972). Whether or not this finding is duplicated at the statewide political level depends on a number of influences— including, presumably, greater closeness between editors and events in their state, relative importance of state and national wire service priorities, and importance of local vs. national issues in each senatorial race.

information—their greater content and detail, audience control over the pace of exposure, and so forth.[19]

In any event, we turn to the second stage of analysis armed with a simplifying discovery. If reasoning about political choice (for U.S. senator) depends at all on the features of an area's media system, those characteristics will be found in the newspapers that circulate there, not in television coverage.

CAN DIFFERENCES AMONG NEWSPAPER MARKETS BE EXPLAINED?

Inferences based on this survey cannot lean on compilations of the "ten best" or "ten worst" newspapers or on normative views about journalistic excellence, because superior journalistic effort lies beyond detecting with the dependent variable as presently calibrated. The analysis distinguishes essentially between people who have no basis they can express for liking or disliking the senatorial candidates and those who have at least one reason.

In order to describe intermarket differences, each mean level of information holding was adjusted through regression analysis. Predicted market means were calculated through multiple regression against level of education and amount of interest in political affairs. The predicted value was subtracted from the observed value to yield a residual.

[19] Objections can be raised about permissiveness in accepting the ingredients of "reasoning" as reflecting a person's level of political information. (For an analysis using this kind of data to measure political ideology, see Converse [1964].) Since the reasons some persons express for liking or disliking candidates may be incorrect, according to a detached observer, or shallow, irrelevant, or otherwise unappealing, we conducted a parallel analysis using a more conventional test for knowledge—ability to name the senatorial candidates who competed in the election. Four major independent variables were introduced in simultaneous multiple regressions against both indices of information with the following results. Data are standardized beta weights with their statistical significance.

	Reasons		Candidate Names	
	beta	p	beta	b
Education	.0136	n.s.	.0465	n.s.
Interest	.3744	.004	.2814	.033
Newspaper mess. discr.	.3176	.009	.3629	.004
Television mess. discr.	−.0290	n.s.	−.0728	n.s.

Parallels between these results are striking. One can conclude that findings based on reasons for political preference, the less presumptuous measure of information, do not present a warped view of the weak educational role played by television.

Markets with positive residuals have greater levels of information than expected from their residents' ability and interest. Markets with negative residuals have lower levels of information than expected. The analysis concluded earlier implies that each market's residual should be related somehow to characteristics of newspapers that circulate within it. One could logically reason that circulation size would be a major factor; a study of completeness of coverage during the 1960 presidential race showed newspaper size to be important (Danielson and Adams, 1961). On other occasions the authors have examined regression analyses for cost data describing more than 400 daily newspapers. Both the size of editorial budgets and the average number of news pages produce large coefficients of determination (in the .90s) against raw circulation.

Volume of news output might make a dent in public information—as calibrated here. Accordingly, circulation of dominant papers was split to yield three groups of markets. The smallest markets are those with papers having 50,000 circulation or less. For these places the pattern is clear. Seventeen out of 22 showed large negative residuals ($-.26$ or greater, residuals expressed as standard scores), indicating that their citizens possess even less information than levels of education and political interest would predict. Three have near-zero residuals ($\pm .25$), and two show high positive residuals ($+.26$ or greater).

This neatness disappears among the two larger groups of markets— those dominated by papers in the 50,001 to 175,000 class, and greater than 175,000. These markets distribute nearly equally in terms of residual information holding; some are highly negative, some near zero, and some highly positive.

One insight into this apparent confusion is provided by shifting briefly from a market-by-market analysis to paper-by-paper comparisons. This eliminates the influence of nonreaders and can suggest whether newspaper characteristics other than size might affect the outcome.

Despite the limitation that many newspapers are represented by a handful of readers, interesting clues emerge from a look at each paper's residuals. Some multi-paper areas show marked differences in information holding between readership groups. Consider the following residuals, expressed in standard scores:

New York Daily News	$-.27$
New York Post	.31
New York Times	1.42
Baltimore News American	$-.34$
Baltimore Sun	.39

Chicago Sun-Times	−.49
Chicago Tribune	.38
Chicago Daily News	.72
Seattle Times	−.39
Seattle Post-Intelligencer	.21
Oakland Tribune	−1.33
San Francisco Chronicle	−.73
San Francisco Examiner	.27

In Chicago, to take one case, there is a world of difference between readers of the *Sun-Times* and the *Daily News*. Personal opinion governs whether this or any other comparison confirms the information level one would expect, controlling for education and interest. And, of course, some markets show only narrow differences. (Both Louisville papers have high positive residuals; Atlanta papers have large negative figures; Philadelphia is uniformly high positive.)

But differences among papers warn that public understanding in metropolitan zones depends not only on circulation penetration but on which newspapers penetrate. The variability of residuals in multi-paper markets suggests attention to media *competition* or diversity as a correlate of information.

Either of two expectations might be confirmed. The first is pessimistic. It holds that where newspapers compete on nearly equal footing for audience, they will battle for control of the "lowest common denominator." Given that politics interests only a few people, these competing papers would be expected to slight their public affairs obligations in favor of more popular fare. Through the years markets with more than one paper would come to have *lower levels* of information than predicted by other factors like citizens' ability and interest.

The more optimistic observer views diversity as producer of net social gain. Rival newspapers may not compete for the same readers; they may seek survival through differentiation. If at least one journal chooses to cover politics thoroughly, perhaps the audience for that kind of information will benefit, will develop levels of information beyond what could be expected from predisposing factors. The wide range of residuals in New York, Baltimore, Chicago, Seattle, the Bay Area and elsewhere is consistent with the more optimistic point of view.

From this brief and incomplete sketch it is clear that the causal imagery linking competition or diversity and knowing about politics is extremely complex. Its details cannot be laid bare here. But one can test whether the pessimists or the optimists have the greater support for their contrasting positions. The results, it will be seen, sustain the more encouraging point of view.

For each market, average differences were calculated in penetration by various dailies that circulate in the appropriate census unit containing the sample interview area (units might be a city, county, or SMSA). Actual circulation data were used (drawn from *Newspaper Circulation Analysis* by the Standard Rate and Data Service, Inc.), so that origins of the competition variable would be separate from the dependent variable under analysis. The index for competition represents environmental conditions surrounding citizens who were interviewed, not their individual use of that information environment. The competition variable signals, in part, the balance of newspapers' journalistic resources—even if under common ownership—and the availability of more than one report of political events—even if reports might differ only in the time of day they are delivered.

Some markets have little or no diversity, such as Toledo, where the *Blade* is the only Ohio paper circulating. Other markets have more competition, where papers differ from 70 to 30 percentage points in audience reach. The next category includes markets with 30 to 15 point gaps. The fourth group has gaps between 15 and 10 points. The most competitive markets have 10 to 0 point gaps in circulation reach by dailies. This category scheme divides markets into as nearly normal a distribution as can be accomplished—10 in the near-monopoly group, 18, 16, 12, and 11 in the most competitive environment.

Table 3 shows the results. The correlation between diversity and residual information holding is .50 ($p < .01$; Gamma coefficient). Whatever the words competition and diversity mean, and whatever philosophical passions they excite, closeness of market penetration is linked to a social condition of some value—the fact that citizens have reasons for making an important political choice.[20] A great variety of Senate contests and statewide political systems is represented by the 67 markets plotted in Table 3. It is reassuring that the relationship between newspaper competition and public understanding does not result from clustering of a state's media markets in a single area of the table. For example, three Ohio markets are found in the high positive row, two in the middle area, and two in the high negative row. New York has markets in all three rows of the table. So does California;

[20] The latter portion of this analysis can be misunderstood if read too literally. Individual towns and cities in Table 3 should not be labeled for all time as above or below expectations in level of information holding. Eugene, Ore., and Crawford County, Ia., are randomly drawn data points in the same sense that one views individual persons in the typical sample survey analysis. Markets studied here represent *classes* of markets; each is imperfectly described by the responses and behavior of a handful of adults in households chosen by probability methods. One can be confident of findings in the aggregate, especially when grouped into broad categories as here. We can be less certain that in a second survey Phoenix or Seattle would appear in the same cells of analysis.

Table 3. Markets by Newspaper Competition and Residual on Information Holding

Size of Residuals	Monopoly				High Competition
+.26 or more	Sioux Falls, S.D.	Bridgeport, Conn. Eugene, Ore. Knox, O. Oneida, N.Y.	New York Suburbs Philadelphia Suburbs Pittsburg Suburbs	Bronx, N.Y. Louisville, Ky. Philadelphia, Pa. St. Louis, Mo. St. Louis Suburbs Salt Lake City, Utah Tulare, Cal.	Cleveland, O. Cleveland Suburbs Indianapolis, Ind. San Francisco, Cal. Tulsa, Okla.
±.25	Logan, Colo. Manhattan, N.Y. Mississippi, Ark.		Chicago Suburbs Los Angeles, Cal. Los Angeles Suburbs Phoenix, Ariz. Plumas, Cal. Seattle, Wash.	Brooklyn, N.Y. Dayton, O. Hamilton, O. San Francisco Suburbs	Baltimore, Md. Chicago, Ill.
−.26 or less	Adair, Mo. Columbia, S.C. Currituck, N.C. E. Carroll, La. Lowndes, Ga. Miami, Fla. Orlando, Fla. Snyder, Pa. Toledo, O.	Acadia, La. Escondido, Cal. Hancock, O. Logan, Ill. Pitt, N.C. Sarasota, Fla. Sheboygan, Wisc. Stoddard, Mo. Waterloo, Ia. Whatcomb, Wash. Wilkes-Barre, Pa.	Clark, Ark. Crawford, Ia. Little Rock, Ark. Muhlenberg, Ky. New London, Conn. Ulster, N.Y. Vallejo, Cal.	Montgomery, Ala.	Atlanta, Ga. Baltimore Suburbs Randolph, Ill. Watauga, N.C.

Pennsylvania and other states are represented in two rows. In all these cases, media markets within individual states range widely in newspaper competition, as well.

A cluster of markets that contributes greatly to the correlation of .50 is found in the lower lefthand cells of Table 3. Most of these are small areas, some rural, with small circulation dailies that enjoy near-monopolies. Markets in the Midwest, the traditional South, Florida, the Middle-Atlantic, and even the West contribute to this group. If a single state or region of the country had dominated an area of Table 3, we would suspect that peculiarities of individual Senate campaigns or traditions of political competition intrude on the relationship between newspaper competition and the public's information holding. This does not seem likely.

Summary

Results are drawn from a nationwide sample including many media outlets. Findings underscore the superiority of newspapers as agents of information to help people identify assets and liabilities of important political contenders.

One cannot determine with these data why television should demonstrate a suppressing effect on information. Viewing and recalling political messages is strongly related to television news exposure, and is even related to message discrimination in newspapers. But when appropriate controls are made in analysis, areas where people use television for political news emerge as less informed than areas of equal education and political interest where people avoid the medium.

This conclusion coincides with findings by McClure and Patterson in their study of presidential campaigning in 1972. They measured the relationship between issue salience and gross media exposure. We charted the correlation between holding information and amount of message discrimination. Despite major differences in concepts and measurement, results coincide.

The more novel finding here is the association between public understanding and newspaper competition. The correlation, of course, does not resolve important causal issues at stake. Are competitive markets superior because of a qualitative richness in political news reporting about statewide races? Are they more informed because people have more than one opportunity each day to read about events? Or because aggregate newspaper readership is greater?

Demographic and cultural variables may contribute alternative explanations as well. It is conceivable that informed readers make for newspaper competition. This possibility might depend on an indirect process involving high levels of consumption among informed (and affluent) people. Consumption generates needs for advertising linage, so necessary for supporting more than one paper in a market.

Although all these factors need to be untangled, we have at least circumstantial evidence that competition and diversity are important social indicators of resources for political education in America. The meaning one can attach to words like competition and diversity remains equivocal, however. "Competition" usually refers to a condition of corporate or economic structure in a news market. "Diversity" refers to similarities or differences in the news products delivered by corporate structures.

One must recognize that closeness of circulation penetration is not a reliable indicator either of economic competition or of net diversity in news offerings. For example, morning and evening papers under the same ownership may publish quite different news accounts. Or competitive papers may rely on almost identical wire service reports.

Several kinds of competition may be available in different markets—other than the classic head-to-head battle between hometown dailies. Metropolitan papers may compete with suburban dailies within their commercial market sphere. Special editions of metropolitan papers may circulate to other cities within their state. Small towns that cannot support their own daily newspaper may lie in the zone of circulation overlap between nearby, larger cities. Or towns with dailies may be targets for market expansion by papers in larger towns nearby.

Examples of each kind of competition can be found in Table 3. It would be valuable to chart trends in penetration in these different types of markets as a barometer of opportunities for public education about political affairs. Researchers inquiring into media competition more deeply than this analysis may want to supplement data about audience reach with other information describing the structure of media markets. Structural factors like the distribution of education and wealth come readily to mind.

It is not obvious, however, that contextual variables accounting for media availability bear a conceptual correspondence to census data describing regions (cities, counties, or SMSAs). Media, whether print or broadcast, are consumed by household units. The physical location of a household governs whether or not it is within a zone to which a publication or broadcast signal will be delivered. But the physical location of a household says little about the size or character of the surrounding area which may help shape occupants' behavior, like learning about public affairs.

It is also troublesome and complicated to judge the size of census units whose structure may influence the capacity of media to cover political issues. For example, some large dailies enjoy support from prosperous core cities (Seattle). Others depend more on suburbs (Cleveland). What criteria should researchers use to decide the size of market context whose structure should be examined?

The analysis displayed in Table 3 also neglects to control for political structure, like amount of election competition that confronts citizens. Some anomalies in the relationship may result from lopsided senatorial contests that failed to excite political learning whatever level of media competition was available. In other cases lack of media competition may covary with one-party politics. At least one market off the diagonal in Table 3 is easy to explain. Adults in Sioux Falls, S.D., were not dependent on the resources of the *Argus-Leader* to inform them about one of the 1974 campaigners, Senator George McGovern.

Much remains to be learned about causal paths among richness of communication resources, public attention to these resources, skill and motivation to decipher messages, and retention of information. And one must distinguish between long-term developments in political understanding and the foreshortened learning that may take place between candidate nominations and election day, especially when new political figures emerge.

The present analysis has not been able to separate candidate attributes long familiar to the public (an incumbent's record in public office, for example) from attributes only recently communicated (e.g., a challenger's image of honesty or sincerity). Recent learning may correlate more than older learning with patterns of mass media use. Television portrayals may be especially important for learning during the closing days of a campaign—when apathetic citizens first pay attention to the passing political parade. All differences in time span and recency of learning have inevitably been mixed in the cross-sectional data analysis presented here.

Our results and those of Patterson and McClure do not dismiss television as a political force in America. The data simply call into question television's power to convey candidates' policy positions or personality in such a way that heavy viewers will retain more of this information than light viewers.

Results suggest we can legitimately feel unease over declining newspaper circulation and over any industry developments that limit the amount of newspaper competition within markets. Opportunity to reason about political events requires *having* reasons. If communication assets that are linked to public reasoning weaken, the quality of public judgments about partisan contenders may be in jeopardy.

References

Bordewich, Fergus M.
   1977   "Supermarketing the news." Columbia Journalism Review 16:23–30.
Chaffee, Steven H., L. Scott Ward, and Leonard P. Tipton
   1970   "Mass communication and political socialization." Journalism Quarterly 47:647–59.
Clarke, Peter, and F. Gerald Kline
   1974   "Media effects reconsidered: some new strategies for communication research." Communication Research 1:224–40.
Clarke, Peter, and Lee Ruggels
   1970   "Preferences among news media for coverage of public affairs." Journalism Quarterly 47:464–71.
Converse, Philip E.
   1962   "Information flow and the stability of partisan attitudes." Public Opinion Quarterly 26:578–99.
   1964   "The nature of belief systems in mass publics." Pp. 206–61 in David E. Apter (ed.), Ideology and Discontent. Glencoe, Ill.: Free Press.
Danielson, Wayne A., and John B. Adams
   1961   "Completeness of press coverage of the 1960 campaign." Journalism Quarterly 38:441–52.
Edelstein, Alex S.
   1974   The Uses of Communication in Decision-Making. New York: Praeger.
Erikson, Robert S.
   1976   "The influence of newspaper endorsements in presidential elections: the case of 1964." American Journal of Political Science 20:207–33.
McClure, Robert D., and Thomas E. Patterson
   1974   "Television news and political advertising: the impact of exposure on voter beliefs." Communication Research 1:3–31.
   1976   "Print vs. network news." Journal of Communication 26:23–28.
McCombs, Maxwell E., and Donald L. Shaw
   1972   "The agenda-setting function of mass media." Public Opinion Quarterly 35:176–87.
   1976   "Structuring the 'unseen environment'." Journal of Communication 26:18–22.
Miller, Arthur H.
   1974   "Political issues and trust in government: 1964–1970." American Political Science Review 68:951–72.
Miller, Warren E., Arthur H. Miller, and F. Gerald Kline
   1975   The CPS 1974 American National Election Study. Ann Arbor: Inter-University Consortium for Political Research.
Palmgreen, Philip C.
   1975   "Mass communication and political knowledge: the effects of political level and mass media coverage on political learning." Unpublished Ph.D. thesis, University of Michigan.
Palmgreen, Philip C., and Peter Clarke
   1977   "Agenda-setting with local and national issues." Communication Research 4:435–52.

Palmgreen, Philip C., F. Gerald Kline, and Peter Clarke
  1974 "Message discrimination and information-holding about political af-
        fairs." Paper presented to the International Communication Associa-
        tion, New Orleans, Louisiana.
Powers, Ron
  1977 The Newscasters. New York: St. Martins.
Robinson, John P.
  1972 "Perceived media bias and the 1968 vote: Can the media affect be-
        havior after all?" Journalism Quarterly 49:239–46.

Kent Asp of the Institute of Political Science at the University of Goteborg studies information depth and breadth in the mass media during a civic crisis about the contruction of an inner-city parking garage in Goteborg, Sweden. Asp develops a content analysis technique to study the information value of newspaper and broadcast news about the controversy. Morning newspapers had a higher information value than evening newspapers; newspapers contained greater information than broadcast news. Asp explores some of the reasons for these differences in this chapter, which is a translation from his book, Kungstorgsockupationen I Goteborg: Studier kring information och opinionsbildning *(Stockholm: Beredskapsnaemnden For Psykologiskt Forsvar, 1978).*

18

MASS MEDIA AS MOLDERS OF OPINION AND SUPPLIERS OF INFORMATION
A Study of an Extraparliamentary Action in Sweden

Kent Asp

EXTRAPARLIAMENTARY ACTION AND THE ROLE OF MASS MEDIA

Early one November morning in 1976, the Kungstorget market square was occupied in the center of Göteborg, the second largest city in Sweden. The occupation served as a protest against a decision by the city authorities to build a multistory garage under the square. After the occupation had lasted 11 days, a proposal was adopted which led to the abandonment of the parking scheme. The action had been successful.

The occupation of Kungstorget in Göteborg was by no means a unique event in Sweden. Occupations have earlier proved to be successful means for various groups in the community of giving vent to opinions when the normal parliamentary channels have been considered shut off or otherwise ineffectual. One such example of an extraparliamentary action which took the form of an occupation was the so-called "battle of the elms," which attracted attention abroad when it took place in the Kungsträdgärden Park in Stockholm in May 1971. Stockholm City Council had adopted a resolution to chop down the elms to make way for

From Kent Asp, "Mass Media as Molders of Opinion and Suppliers of Information: A Study of an Extraparliamentary Action in Sweden," original manuscript.

Both the elm tree issue and the occupation of Göteborg market square received a vast amount of attention in the Swedish mass media. Not only were the events as such covered but also the workings of representative democracy were laid bare. The issues raised by the protest action have come to be symbolic for the practical workings of democracy as well as a point of departure for discussions concerning the ability of private individuals to exert political influence.

Politicians have argued that the media coverage of extraparliamentary protest actions has, if not exactly encouraged, supported the cause of the demonstrators and thus obstructed the effecting of decisions which have been passed democratically. Journalists have retorted that democracy does not merely imply respect for decisions taken in accordance with proper democratic procedure but also respect for the rights of the private individual and the free press to handle and debate those decisions which have been arrived at in the course of democratic procedure.

The second main point of politicians' criticism of the media is their assumed failure to provide the public with factual information. The information, it is claimed, has been deficient, making it practically impossible for the man in the street to adopt an independent and rational position. This criticism has most frequently been voiced on occasions when the politicians responsible have been lamenting their own restricted opportunities to present the facts and motives underlying the planning measures adopted.

The content analysis presented here should be seen in light of this debate regarding the role of the media in the political decision process and their subsequent value as a basis for information when political attitudes are being molded. The main aim of our inquiry, therefore, is to study the part played by the mass media in contributing to the successful outcome of the occupation; and also in part to study the role played by the media in supplying information for the individual citizen on which to found an opinion of the case. The first task will be rather perfunctorally solved; the main results of the inquiry will be presented in descriptive form. The second task will be solved rather more thoroughly; it will be carried out primarily as a method study. The main purpose has been to develop a technique of analysis by which the value of the various media as bases of information can be quantitatively measured in a relatively simple manner. Before the results are presented, however, we shall first sketch a brief background to the Kungstorget occupation and the form the content analysis will take.

THE OCCUPATION OF KUNGSTORGET

A Brief Description

The proposal and decision to build the Kungstorget garage had been a hotly debated local political issue in Goteborg for almost 10 years. Project work on the scheme was begun as early as the 1960s, and it was the nonsocialist majority bloc in the city council which had driven the matter through in opposition to a socialist majority. The final formal decision was not, however, taken until May 1976.

The council elections held in September 1976 transferred majority power from the bourgeois parties to the socialist bloc comprising the Social Democrats and the Communist Party. Election results in Sweden at the local level, however, are not immediately operative and power does not change hands until the new year. Thus, the old nonsocialist coalition was still in power when it gave a construction firm license to commence work on the parking scheme on November 16. The principal reason for the start of construction, stated by the political parties concerned, was the fact that the matter had been reviewed and prepared for a considerable amount of time and a stoppage would constitute an irresponsible course of action. Attention was also called to the risk of high claims for damages being raised by the construction firm that had been engaged.

The main organization behind the occupation was the Göteborg Environmental Preservation Group. The group had been fighting the idea of an underground garage at Kungstorget for a number of years. The main point of argument was that the scheme would serve to boost the use of private cars in the city center and that the building of a multimillion dollar garage would tie the hands of the authorities and prevent the center from ever being free of private vehicles and impede progress toward an expansion of public transport. The occupants also maintained that if the garage materialized, it would threaten the service facilities of the suburbs by concentrating trade and business to the city center. The scheme would also result in a further increase in exhaust fumes and excessive noise in the central areas.

The Various Media Examined

The occupation of Kungstorget drew a lot of attention. During the 11 days and nights it lasted, over 25,000 column centimeters of copy and picture were used by 11 newspapers in the three biggest cities in Sweden to describe and comment on events at the market square. This included news reports, features, editorials, debate articles, as well as a prolific amount of illustrated material. Radio and television also showed a lot of interest in the incident. All in all, Swedish Broadcasting Corporation devoted about five hours of broadcasting time—radio and television—to the occupation in terms of news angle and, whenever content analysis of other types of material occur, these are accounted for separately. Figure 1 contains a brief outline of the newspapers and broadcasts surveyed. Abbreviations within parentheses will be used later on in the report.

Outline of Content Analysis

The content analysis takes its point of departure from the statements or actions of the people or groups of people who have appeared in the mass media. The person or group of persons featured in the mass media by virtue of his or their "statements and actions" is subsequently referred to as the "actor."

Newspapers

Göteborgs-Posten (GP): approx. 300,000 copies. Largest daily newspaper in Göteborg and the next largest in Sweden. About 80% of the local population read GP daily.

Göteborgs-Tidningen (GT): approx. 92,000 copies. Liberal. Local evening newspaper. Largest among evening newspapers in Göteborg.

Arbetet (Arb/west): approx. 103,000 copies. Social Democrat. Morning newspaper published in Malmö, with a special Göteborg edition of approx. 15,000 copies. This edition is the one covered by the present study.

Dagens Nyheter (DN): approx. 405,000 copies. Independent. Largest daily morning newspaper in the country. Published in Stockholm.

Svenska Dagbladet (SvD): approx. 180,000 copies. Independent conservative. Second largest daily morning newspaper in Stockholm.

Expressen (Expr and Expr/west): approx. 520,000 copies. Liberal. Published in Stockholm, it is the largest evening newspaper in the country. The study includes both the West Coast and Stockholm ed.

Aftonbladet (AB and AB/west): approx. 430,000 copies. Social Democrat. The second largest evening newspaper in the country and Expressen's keenest competitior. Two editions are covered by the study.

Sydsvenska Dagbladet (SDS): approx. 115,000 copies. Independent liberal. Morning newspaper published in Malmö, the third largest city in the country.

Skånska Dagbladet (SkD): approx. 30,000 copies. Principal mouthpiece of the Center Party. A Malmo morning newspaper.

Kvalls-Posten (KvP): approx. 110,000 copies. Independent liberal. Largest evening newspaper in Malmö.

Ny Dag (Ny D): approx. 18,000 copies. Principal mouthpiece of the Communist Party. Published in Stockholm twice a week. Quite a large distribution in Göteborg.

Television news programs

Rapport: 30 minute evening program broadcast in one of Swedish televisions's two national channels. The principal TV news program, watched daily by some 35% of the nation's viewers.

Aktuellt: Equivalent of Rapport on the other channel. Also broadcast later in the evening and watched by approx. 25%.

TV-nytt: Short news bulletin. Broadcast every evening one in each channel.

Radio news programs

Eko news desk (Eko-red): Sweden's main radio news program, consisting of more comprehensive news commentaries in radio channel one.

News summary 11 pm (23-nyh): Ten-minute news summary in radio channel 3.

West Coast news (West News): Local equivalent of the nation-wide Eko-red. broadcasts.

Figure 1: Description of the Swedish Daily Newspapers and Broadcast News Programs Studied

Four main groups of actors are involved in the Kungstorget occupation: the demonstrators, local Social Democratic and nonsocialist politicians, and the police. Other, less prominent actors were, for example, businessmen, the municipal parking corporations, as well as research scientists and traffic experts. In principle, these actors can appear in the mass media either by virtue of what they have done or what they have said. When only an *action* has occurred, this has been recorded merely as an appearance in the mass media.

The mass media coverage of the occupation consisted mainly of the various actors' *statements of opinion* and was concentrated around these. In principle the statements made are of three types:

(1) those of a slogan nature, a plain statement such as "No car park here"
(2) statements containing an argument for or against, that is, two assertions linked by a conjunctive *because*, such as "the garage must be stopped because it will lead to an increase in air pollution in the city center"
(3) statements making reference to other parties involved in the conflict, individual persons, or groups, such as "the occupants are left-wing extremists."

It should be remembered in this context that we are not only concerned with slogans, arguments, and private opinions expressed in the course of personal appearances (interviews, for example) but also reports from other sources of the views of the various actors.

About one-half of the statements made concerned other actors involved in the dispute. These statements, when recorded, have been divided into three categories: positive, neutral, or negative. The categorization of arguments for or against the scheme has been effected on the basis of news items, articles debating the issues, and other sources, including the minutes of the city council meetings and printed matter distributed by the Goteborg Environmental Preservation Group. There is a long list of arguments, and it has therefore been decided to group those of a similar nature into "type arguments." These are the arguments which have been recorded. They have been further subdivided into four categories: environmental and constructional, financial, traffic policy, and "democracy." In all, the various type arguments total 26: half in favor and half opposed.

A comparatively liberal assessment has been made of what constitutes an argument. If too high a demand is placed on *the wording* of the language, very few statements would qualify as pure arguments, and this would probably result in a misrepresentation of the actual issue at stake.

THE MASS MEDIA AS MOLDERS OF PUBLIC OPINION
—FOUR PATHS TO SUCCESS

The process of molding public opinion of the kind produced by the Kungstorget occupation is composed of an intricate combination of a number of different factors. The present study deals with only one of these factors—characteristics resident in the media content. What part, then, did the media content play in the process of molding public opinion? In retrospect, it would seem highly probable that the manner in which the media depicted the occupation was of major importance in enabling the activists to prevent the garage from being built. This much we know from declarations, for instance, made by responsible politicians subsequent to the occupation. They claimed after the event that with the help of the mass media, the demonstrators influenced public opinion enough to dissuade the authorities from going ahead with the scheme. In any case, the activists had evidently succeeded in creating climate of opinion which gave the political decision makers the *impression* that public opinion was against the scheme.

On the other hand, we do not know for certain whether the occupants *actually* managed to influence public opinion. Admittedly there is much to sustain the supposition, including more than 100,000 signatures gathered during the 11 days among a population figure for Göteborg of 440,000, in addition to a large number of declarations in support made by a variety of organizations. Notwithstanding this, the effect the action had on public opinion must solely be regarded as a reasonable working hypothesis.

That part of the inquiry which deals with the part played by the media content in enabling the demonstrators to halt the scheme will only be outlined in a descriptive summary. The findings of our inquiry into the role of the media in the opinion-molding process will be presented in the form of a number of hypotheses. These will suggest what factors are of importance if any action group relying on the reports of the mass media is to arouse public opinion or create a climate of opinion of sufficient impact to ensure success.

Roughly, the findings of the inquiry can be summarized as follows: Via the mass media, the occupants were able to influence a broad section of opinion in opposition to the scheme by achieving four prerequisites for success. These four paths to success may be characterized under the following headings:

(1) drawing attention
(2) drawing attention in a positive manner
(3) getting the message across
(4) gaining support.

Drawing Attention

The first and basic requirement for an action group is to draw sufficient attention in the mass media to reach a large section of the public. If this is not achieved, there will be little or no chance of influencing public attitudes. In this respect, the occupants of Kungstorget were highly successful. The first day of the occupations, the incident had appeared on the front pages of the big-city newspapers and was featured in the radio and television news programs. The news coverage was followed by letters from the general public, debate articles, review columns, and television panel discussion broadcast directly from the market square. The occupation of the square became the central news story in Swedish mass media during the period in question. This was particularly the case with the local press, whose coverage of the 11-day occupation took up about 10 times as much space on the news pages as the matter had received during 10 years as a controversial local political issue.

The first step toward success had thus been achieved. The success, however, was hardly an occasion for surprise. The means chosen by the demonstrators to ventilate their protest against the garage showed all the classical signs of becoming a big piece of news. The occupation of the square was, as such, both sensational and dramatic. In addition, the media were able to keep the interest and excitement alive each day by speculating on the possible police action and how the incident might end.

Drawing the mass media's attention to one's cause, however, is not enough. If the aim had merely been to attract media attention, perhaps even more sensational and dramatic methods should have been employed. An extraparlimentary action of this nature, however, requires a careful weighing of the chances of getting a good write-up as against the risk of incurring bad publicity. In other words, the action must be sensational and dramatic enough to interest the media but not to a degree that enables them to give the action negative publicity. The second requirement for success, then, is attracting positive attention—or at any rate attention which is not markedly negative in character.

Drawing Attention in a Positive Manner

There were two occasions when, from the demonstrators' point of view, a risk seemed imminent that the mass media would paint a negative picture of their action. The critical situations arose when the square was first occupied and then when the police forced the demonstrators to leave the square one week after the start of the action. (The police operation took 30 minutes, but the occupants were soon back again and the protest action was able to continue.) On both occasions, the activists were largely dependent upon the sort of picture the mass media gave to the course of events. Because of the large element of drama inherent in the incidents, a number of opportunities arose for the media to dramatize events and focus attention on scenes of violence and other features which far from enhanced the cause of the demonstrators.

In general, mass media reporting of the *activities* of the occupants on these two occasions avoided dramatic overtones. The initial stages, of vital importance to the occupants, during which they took possession of the square, were described in a concise manner informing readers, listeners, and viewers, in little more than one sentence, of what had happened without disparaging remarks about the occupants themselves. The latter also managed to avoid negative publicity at the time of the police action, and the event was actually referred to in later commentaries as evidence of the demonstrators' good sense and moderation. The police praised the demonstrators' conduct while they in their turn praised the sincere intentions of the police.

Besides the description of the occupants' activities, the depiction of the demonstrators as a *group* and as *individual persons* was of great significance. The mass media's picture of the occupants was a predominantly positive one. Attempts by sympathizers of the parking scheme, for instance, to brand the occupants as left-wing extremists failed. Instead, those responsible for initiating the action were depicted as belonging to an organization without political party affiliation.

In the portrayal of individual demonstrators, life around the market square during these 11 days and nights came to the forefront. This meant a series of news reports describing the songs, dancing, and musical activities of the demonstrators, their fighting spirit, and endurance of the cold November air. These reports together with detailed descriptions of the problems overcome in acquiring and preparing food served to present a picture of a predominantly good-humored popular festival. Thus the manner in which the general public experienced the occupation had a positive ring to it, eliminating any risk of alienation at an early stage. The second step toward success had now been achieved.

Getting the Message Across

Gaining access to the public's attention and avoiding a bad press at an early stage are not enough, however: The purpose of the action and the motives underlying it must also be properly put across, otherwise, very little opportunity will be available to swing public opinion in favor of the cause at stake.

The occupants' view of the dispute totally dominated the news columns of the press and the news broadcasts on radio and television. Between 80% and 90% of the views and arguments were either opposed to the scheme or to the nonsocialist parties' treatment of the issue; moreover, there were no significant differences from one paper to another or between the various newsrooms of the Swedish Broadcasting Corporation. As a result readers, listeners, and viewers were presented almost entirely with the views of the antiparking lobby. This majority viewpoint was backed by other important groups, chiefly via statements issued by Social Democrats, organizations, and experts of various kinds.

Gaining Support

The fourth factor required for an extraparliamentary action successfully to arouse public opinion via the mass media is the necessity to gain support from influential groups within the community and other acknowledged molders of opinion. The implication here for the action group is that the stronger and wider the support gained from groups with close reference to an individual, the better the chances of prevailing upon these attitudes and opinions.

Probably the most important reference group to influence public attitudes in the Kungstorget conflict was that of the *political parties*. Their approach to the occupation was first conveyed to the man in the street through the mass media.

The Kungstorget parking scheme was strongly party political. The non-socialist bloc had lent its support to the scheme during the course of many years while the Social Democrats had opposed it. Consequently, the occupants' demands for the abandonment of the scheme was widely supported by Social Democrat party officials in the mass media coverage of the occupation. The few expressions of censure of the action primarily concerned the use of extraparliamentary tactics as a democratic working method. Social Democrat support for the action was not, however, self-evident. This was due partly to the fact that the demonstrators also strongly criticized Social Democrat dealings in the Kungstorget dispute and partly to the fact that the adoption of an attitude favoring an extraparliamentary line of action represented a big political gamble even though the party's aims corresponded with those of the activists. The direct and indirect support received from the Social Democrats, however, quite probably made a significant contribution toward influencing the standpoint taken by Social Democrat sympathizers.

A less uniform picture presents itself if we examine statements made in the mass media by representatives of the bourgeois parties. The local politicians dissociated themselves completely from the demonstrators' case and action. This united standpoint was challenged, however, by views expressed by the nonsocialist parties on a national level. Here opinions were voiced mainly by the Youth Leagues. One statement, however, was issued by a member of the government: the Center Party Minister for Local Government criticized the nonsocialist majority in the Göteborg city council for not adopting a caretaker role in the few weeks remaining before the socialist coalition was due to assume the reins of government.

Returning again to our point of departure regarding the importance of references groups, it would seem that political supporters of the nonsocialist parties among the general public suddenly found that their closest points of reference were split. Admittedly the split was due in large measure to a number of statements by youth leaders belonging to the bourgeois parties, and this in itself probably had little effect on the run-of-the-mill liberal-conservative voter. The government minister's pronouncement, on the other hand, was undoubtedly far more influential. His criticism, however, was reported in much more detail by the mass media.

As a whole, then, the difference of opinion which existed within center-liberal-conservative circles made it considerably more difficult for voters of these political tendencies to dissociate themselves from the demonstrators' action than would have been the case had representatives of the bourgeois parties been united in their rejection of the occupant's cause. The support which a number of representatives of these parties gave must therefore be seen as a factor of quite some importance in enabling the demonstrators to persuade bourgeois voters of the validity of their action.

The second main type of reference group reported through the channels of the mass media and instrumental in steering public attitudes toward a definite position is the *professional molders of public opinion*. Here, too, the activists could count on overwhelming support. Among *newspaper editorials* only GP dissociated itself from the action, while *press columnists* were almost unanimously favorably inclined. In addition a large number of *debate articles* discussing the rights and wrongs of the issue pursued in depth the arguments of the opponents of the garage. A fourth group among these professional molders of opinion which probably played quite a significant role was made up of various *experts* within the fields of medicine and traffic research. Their remarks were to be found particularly on news pages and entirely centered around the unfavorable environmental consequences inherent in the building of an underground parking lot, including the risk of cancer.

The implication this support had for the demonstrators' ability to prevail upon public attitudes is difficult to assess precisely. What is clear, however, is that this support created a very *favorable climate of opinion* for the activists despite the alienation of Goteborg's leading press organ in its editorial columns. At the same time it should be observed that GP's portrayals of the demonstrators as individuals and as a group very seldom contained any assessments of a detailed nature.

The third type of reference group to probably have some effect on positions adopted by members of the public may be classified as "what other people thought." This was reflected in the mass media in three different ways. First, views expressed by ordinary people were reported in the normal way by the media; second, they appeared in letters written to the editor; and, third, public attitudes were revealed via press, radio, and television reports from the petition being signed in support of the demonstrators.

Views expressed by members of the general public occupied a prominent position in the press, on the radio, and on television: 8 out of 10 pronouncements by members of the public which appeared in the big-city newspapers supported the opponents of the parking scheme. Corresponding figures for radio and television were 7 out of 10. The media's news reports on what the general public thought about the Kungstorget dispute thus offered a picture of almost complete endorsement of the antigarage argument. Support for the demonstrators was somewhat cooler in the letter columns of the press.

The reporting of the work behind the petition of names was a very prominent feature of news coverage in the media. On average, just over every third article gave newspaper readers reports on the number of signatures collected, while every fourth news item dealt with the same subject on radio and television.

Once again, these reports in the media on "what other people thought" probably went a long way toward swinging public opinion in the activists' favor. Using the references group theory as a basis, we can group together the support gained via statements by the public appearing on news pages and the support expressed in the letter columns and conclude that the category we have called "what other people thought" in all probability exerted a very strong influence on the private individual's assessment of the situation.

The fourth and decisive step toward success had been reached. The action had received support from important groups in the community and other opinion-molding elements.

How can we account for the support given the action? Some of it was undoubtedly due to the positive treatment by the press, radio, and television. This suggested that supporting the occupants and their demands was not the same as supporting an extremist, violent action. This must have had a certain significance for Social Democrats backing the action . And yet the latter in reality had little alternative. They were able, it is true, to disclaim connection with the occupation as an extraparliamentary action, but they could hardly dissociate themselves from the criticism which the activists leveled against the scheme and the dealings of the nonsocial bloc. The building of a garage at Kungstorget had been one of the Social Democrats' election issues, and they could hardly now go back on their promises without sacrificing a certain amount of credibility.

THE MASS MEDIA AS SUPPLIERS OF INFORMATION

The previous sections have attempted to throw some light on the part played by media content in insuring the success of the demonstrators' action. My findings illustrated how media content in all probability was of major importance in determining public attitudes toward the parking scheme. In the present chapter I shall present a little more closely the type of information about the issue at stake which the mass media supplied, and which could provide a basis for a definite attitude in favor of or against the decision to build the underground garage.

The arrival at such a definite attitude may be seen as the result of a decision-making process in which the private person represents the decision maker basing his rational decision on the complete and correct information available. In the normal course of events, however, such an ideal situation would hardly exist and the public would not be able to adopt a position on these premises. This model, however, may serve as a suitable point of departure. The question, then, is what demands can be made on the mass media as suppliers of information to help the public arrive at a rational and independent position.

In order to be able to arrive at a rational decision, access must be had to *relevant information.* The Kungstorget issue concerned the acceptance or rejection of a decision to build an underground parking lot in the center of Göteborg. It could therefore be said that the information relevant to arriving at a decision consisted of all the reasons in support of and all the reasons opposed to the decision to build the garage.

The availability of information relevant to arriving at a decision is thus the first and basic requirement. This,however, is hardly a sufficient prerequisite from the point of view of readers, listeners, and viewers. The relevant information must appear with a certain frequency to avoid being swamped by irrelevant information. In other words, the relevant information must stand in reasonable proportion to the total flow of information issuing from the mass media. The second requirement may therefore be termed *density of information.*

A high degree of density of information does not, however, necessarily amount to a satisfactory field of material on which to base a decision. Density can be achieved, for instance, by the constant repetition of a small number of arguments tending toward a certain standpoint. Density of information must therefore be accompanied by a reasonable *breadth of information* in which, ideally, all the theoretically relevant arguments have been made available before a decision is made.

The fourth requirement concerns information about facts and motives as a basis for the various arguments. This means that with the help of the mass media, the individual is able to obtain a basis for a judgment of his own regarding the validity of the arguments. One instance affecting our study concerns information about the evidence put forward by the activists to support their claim that the scheme would lead to an increase in pollution from car exhaust in central Göteborg. Another concerns the facts the supporters of the scheme based their argument upon that the garage would be a profitable affair and not create financial difficulties for the city. Similar to our two earlier definitions, this requirement might be classified as *depth of information.*

Information Relevant to the Making of a Decision

My first requirement in assessing mass media output concerned the availability of information relevant to a decision. What exactly constitutes information of this kind in an issue such as the Kungstorget action can be subject for discussion. What is clear, however, is that any position adopted would not only take into account the building, environmental, and traffic policy aspects of the issue but it would also be a commentary on the democratic aspects of the decision to go ahead with the scheme and the form of extraparliamentary action the occupation involved. The issue confronting the general public thus concerned both fact and principle.

The point in question, then, is to what extent the general public was provided with arguments containing information relevant to the making of a decision.

The number of arguments varies considerably from one medium to another. Apart from the local press and the West Coast editions of two other papers, SvD alone records a figure of any significance. For calculation purposes the scarcity of arguments in some of the media creates a number of problems. There have, however, been no omissions as the findings are intended to present a complete picture, and the low number of arguments appearing in some of the media is relevant to the total result (see Table 1).

Some of these arguments presented in the media deal with concrete issues, such as environmental, building, financial, and traffic policy aspects, while others are concerned with democratic aspects.

TABLE 1:   Density of Information Index for 13 Swedish Daily Newspapers and
            6 Broadcast News Programs

Medium	No. of arguments	No. of col. cms.	Density of inf. index
Göteborgs-Posten	72	919	0.078
Göteborgs-Tidningen	22	813	0.027
Arbetet/West	43	773	0.056
Expressen/West	18	504	0.036
Aftonbladet/West	24	930	0.026
Svenska Dagbladet	31	399	0.078
Dagens Nyheter	13	377	0.034
Expressen	3	82	0.037
Aftonbladet	8	202	0.040
Sydsvenska Dagbladet	8	95	0.084
Skånska Dagbladet	9	100	0.090
Kvälls-Posten	5	324	0.015
Ny Dag	16	`179	0.089
All newspapers	272	5697	0.048
Aktuellt	5	96	0.052
Rapport	1	133	0.008
Eko news desk	3	96	0.031
TV-nytt	1	40	0.025
News summary 11 pm	1	28	0.036
West Coast news	9	272	0.033
All radio and TV news programs	20	665	0.030

The democratic aspects (46%) occupied almost as much space as the arguments concerning the heart of the matter: the effect of an underground garage on the environment and general traffic policy. This 46% primarily consisted of arguments in favor of stopping building plans because of the undemocratic conduct of the nonsocialist coalition in forcing a decision to be adopted and side-stepping an election result which amounted to a rejection of the garage. The coalition, so the argument ran, should be assuming a brief caretaker role. The opposing arguments stressed the democratic nature of the process by which the decision to build had been made, a democratic procedure which must be respected. Extraparliamentary actions such as the occupation of the market square, it was underlined, must not be allowed to govern local politics.

The factual arguments chiefly centered around traffic policy (32%). The most frequent argument here warned of the increase in automobile traffic. The scheme should be dropped and efforts channeled toward expanding the public transport network and establishing a car-free city center.

Factual arguments favoring and opposing the scheme for its environmental and building merits were given comparatively little space (14%) as were the financial arguments (8%). The latter arguments, which dominated for instance the election campaign, almost entirely disappeared during the days the occupation lasted.

The technical aspect which featured most was the question of exhaust pollution and noise level. Critics of the scheme claimed there would be an increase in car exhaust and noise as well as a larger concentration if the garage were built. Supporters of the scheme, on the other hand, spoke in terms of a decrease as traffic would be concentrated underground where it would also be possible to cope with pollution by means of a filtering plant installed on the roof of the garage.

Thus the factual arguments in the dispute were pushed somewhat into the background. This meant that the information from the media that the general public were able to base their opinion on was chiefly made up of *general political assessments*, while material to help form a judgment on the actual issue at stake was less in evidence.

Density of Information of the Media

The term density is intended as a measurement of the quality of media content necessary to be able to find the information upon which a position can be adopted. It means in practice that the longer time one must devote to a particular medium to obtain the relevant information, the lower the density of information of that medium. In the present context the density of information of a medium represents a measure of the relationship between the number of arguments and the total output dealing with the occupation of the market square.

In order to facilitate comparisons between the various types of media, it will be necessary to use the same basic measurements. The problem posed here is that newspaper volume is measured in written form while the broadcasting media are expressed orally. A number of tests have revealed, however, that a suitable common measurement is arrived at by making 1 column centimeter of newspaper copy equivalent to 5 seconds of broadcasting time. In Table 1 this common measurement has been expressed in column centimeters and a density of information index has been calculated. The index represents the number of arguments per column centimeter. This means that a medium containing 100 arguments per 1000 column centimeters obtains a frequency of information index of .100 while a medium containing 10 arguments in the same space would obtain .010.

As Table 1 shows, density of information varies considerably between the different media. Newspapers with high index values are SkD, Ny Dag, and SDS closely followed by GP and SvD. KvP has the lowest index figure. Low values are also recorded for GT and Aftonbladet's West Coast edition. Of the radio and television news desks, Aktuellt is highest and Rapport, lowest.

A clear distinction can be observed here between the daily morning press on the one hand and the evening newspapers and radio and television news broadcasts on the other. The difference between the broadcasters and the press is still there even when big-city newspapers are taken together, i.e., including the evening newspapers. The big-city press registers an index of .050 while radio and television news programs reach .030.

Breadth of Information of the Media

The requirement for density must also go hand in hand with a reasonable degree of breadth in the information supplied by the media, otherwise, readers, listeners, and viewers are restricted in their access to informative material on which to base and adopt a position. Ideally, then, every relevant argument in favor of or opposed to the building of the Kungstorget garage must be available before a decision can be arrived at.

We may therefore define the breadth of information provided by a medium as a measure of the proportion of different type arguments that medium provides to the total number of type arguments theoretically relevant. This means that a medium containing 13 different type arguments obtains an index of .50 (13/26) while another with 5 different type arguments shows a value of .19 (5/26) (see Table 2).

The index illustrated in Table 2 indicates the value the various media can claim for readers, listeners, and viewers in terms of breadth of information. The figures show that GP, SvD, and Arb had the greatest breadth of information. Next follow GT and the West Coast editions of AB and Expr. The Stockholm editions of these last two newspapers as well as KvP have a low count. Among the broadcasting media, Aktuellt and the regional news bulletins return high figures while Rapport, TV-nytt, and the 11 p.m. news report are low in the list.

Depth of Information of the Media

The Kungstorget parking scheme touched upon a number of aspects requiring information in depth for the individual to be able to adopt a position regarding the decision to build an underground garage. There was the question of car exhaust, for instance, with regard to which a number of research scientists warned of the danger of cancer being enhanced by poisonous substances in the exhaust fumes. There were also matters such as the financial side of the scheme, compensation claims, traffic plans for the downtown area, freehold agreements, and such and whether the taxpayers' money was to be made use of or whether the garage would pay its own way. But there was also the question of how the various political parties had arrived at their positions, how the political process toward a decision had been handled, what deliberations had taken place, and so on.

In this respect, the information output of the media in most cases is of such negligible proportions that it is unsuitable for estimates of the type I have made earlier in comparing the media. One half of the media examined contained no

TABLE 2:   Breadth of Information Index for 13 Swedish Daily Newspapers and
           6 Broadcast News Programs

Medium	No. of different types of argument	Theoretically possible no. of argument types	Breadth of information index
Göteborgs-Posten	20	26	0.77
Göteborgs-Tidningen	11	26	0.42
Arbetet/West	13	26	0.50
Expressen/West	10	26	0.38
Aftonbladet/West	10	26	0.38
Svenska Dagbladet	16	26	0.62
Dagens Nyheter	9	26	0.35
Expressen	3	26	0.12
Aftonbladet	3	26	0.12
Sydsvenska Dagbladet	5	26	0.19
Skånska Dagbladet	7	26	0.27
Kvälls-Posten	4	26	0.15
Ny Dag	6	26	0.23
Aktuellt	5	26	0.19
Rapport	1	26	0.04
Eko news desk	3	26	0.12
TV-nytt	1	26	0.04
News summary 11 pm	1	26	0.04
West Coast news	4	26	0.15

form of information in depth whatever, and in those instances in which it
did exist, background material amounted to between 2% and 7% of the total
news space devoted to the Kungstorget occupation. A note of interest is the
fact that the meager background material given appeared at quite a late stage.
The occupation had lasted one week before any newspaper had offered any background information as a comment on the incident.

The Informative Value of the Media

Density, breadth, and depth of information each have their intrinsic value
for reader, listener, and viewer alike. It is perhaps, however, a combination of
these three factors which determines the value a medium can claim as a basis
of information in forming public attitudes. Viewed in a rational perspective,
the ideal medium will clearly be one able to give proof of a high density of information, ample breadth, and detailed background material.

Diagram 1 illustrates a coordinate system in which the index values for density
of information and breadth of information have been recorded. This enables us
from two different angles to acquire a picture of the information value attributable to the various media. It is also theoretically possible to implant values
pertaining to information in depth to fit the pattern indicating the information

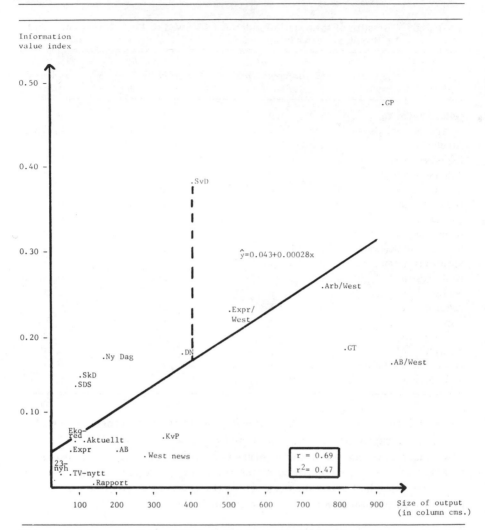

Diagram 1: Information Value of Media in Relation to Size of Output

value of the media output. For various reasons, chiefly the negligible scope of the material available, I have decided not to exploit this possibility here.

If initially we disregard the examples of Aktuellt and Arb/west, Diagram 1 would seem to suggest that there are four separate categories. The first group comprising SvD and GP reveals high values in respect of both density and breadth. A second group embraces SDS, SkD, and Ny Dag. As with GP and SvD, a high degree of density has been registered (somewhat higher, even, than these two), though considerably less breadth. These are newspapers, that is, in which the number of arguments is very large in relation to the amount of copy, while the material they provide on which a standpoint can be based is, on the whole, relatively incomplete.

The reverse is true of the third group which consists of DN, GT, and the West Coast editions of Aftonbladet and Expressen. These are newspapers with low frequency of information but which provide a somewhat broader basis of information. Although the difference in breadth is not particularly large, these four newspapers can still be classed in a separate group.

The fourth group is made up of the radio and television news programs and the evening newspapers Aftonbladet, Expressen, and Kvälls-Posten, all of which record low density and marginal breadth. Among these, Rapport occupies a special position. This program's six news items lasting a total of 12.5 minutes contained only *one* genuine argument which could be said to provide a basis for a position for or against the building of the garage.

The Informativity of the Media

In compiling the findings I have not paid any particular regard to the space the various media devoted to the incident. The comparisons that have been made between the media have concerned density, breadth, and depth of information in an absolute sense, the sum total of which I have termed "information value."

It is plain, however, that where more direct comparisons between various types of media are desired, account must be taken of the size of the media's output. A direct comparison of the television news rooms' coverage with that of the Göteborg press, for instance, is not strictly applicable. If greater resources are available for reporting on an event, it is reasonable to suppose that there are better opportunities for providing readers, listeners, and viewers with a fuller range of information. In other words, is GP's greater information value quite simply an indication of the fact that this newspaper has printed more material about the occupation than other newspapers?

Hitherto I have mainly dealt with two separate definitions, density of information and breadth of information, each of which in conjunction has served to clarify the information value of the media. My present task of analysis will be made the easier, however, if I devise a single unit of measurement which will embrace both frequency and breadth. One way of doing this is quite simply to multiply the density index by that of the breadth. The figure arrived at may then be termed the "media information value index."

A medium having a maximum information value is given an index value of 1: This figure derives from the fact that all statements, expressed or quoted, consist of relevant arguments, and all the theoretically relevant types of argument are present ($1.0 \times 1.0 = 1$). When, as in the case of GP, 60% of the statements consist of arguments and 77% of the type arguments are present, the medium is given an information value index of .46 ($.60 \times .77 = .46$; see Table 3).

Thus the information value index represents a combination of the density and the breadth of media information. It should be remembered, however, that the aim of this method of calculation is primarily to produce a simple measurement on which to base the correlation and regression analyses. The combined

TABLE 3:   Information Value Index for 13 Swedish Daily Newspapers and
            6 Broadcast News Programs

Medium	Density of information	Breadth of information	Information Value Index
Göteborgs-Posten	0.60	0.77	0.46
Göteborgs-Tidningen	0.43	0.42	0.18
Arbetet/West	0.47	0.50	0.24
Expressen/West	0.60	0.38	0.23
Aftonbladet/West	0.43	0.38	0.16
Svenska Dagbladet	0.62	0.62	0.38
Dagens Nyheter	0.52	0.35	0.18
Expressen	0.33	0.12	0.04
Aftonbladet	0.35	0.12	0.04
Sydsvenska Dagbladet	0.73	0.19	0.14
Skånska Dagbladet	0.56	0.27	0.15
Kvälls-Posten	0.38	0.15	0.06
Ny Dag	0.76	0.23	0.17
Aktuellt	0.28	0.19	0.05
Rapport	0.07	0.04	0.003
Eko news desk	0.43	0.12	0.05
TV-nytt	0.25	0.04	0.01
News summary 11 pm	0.14	0.04	0.01
West Coast news	0.29	0.15	0.04

measurement in itself does not say as much about the value of a medium as a basis of information as the two index values do separately.

Diagram 1 illustrates the relationship between the size of media output and the information value of the media. A standard system has been used, as previously, to facilitate direct comparisons between the various types of media. The dots indicate that there exists a quite definite and positive correlation between information value and output size. The correlation coefficient stands at .69 (using Pearson's r). The importance of the output for the information value can also be illustrated by the fact that r^2 equals .47, which is another way of saying that output size accounts for 47% of the variance in the media information value.

The line of regression which has been drawn in the diagram constitutes a guide to the significance of the various dots in the coordinate system. Deviations from this line thus attract interest, particularly those which are further away from the expected value which size of output would seem to suggest. The positive deviations—those occurring above the line of regression—can therefore be said to give proof of a higher informativity than those below the line. *Informativity* represents here a measure of the information value of a medium in relation to the value expected by the volume of material provided by that medium. Positive and negative deviations from the expected value correspond to positive and negative degrees of informativity.

As indicated by the diagram, the seven positive deviations comprise six morning newspapers plus the West Coast edition of Expressen. As the study embraces a total of seven morning newspapers, this means that the morning press evolves as the most informative of the media, with SvD as the most outstanding deviation in a positive sense. The conclusion here is that, according to this method of assessing the material, SvD was the most *informative* medium in news coverage of the Kungstorget occupation, while GP is credited with greatest *total information value.*

In assessing the informativity of each individual medium, I have been using all the media as a frame of reference. The following paragraphs will deal with the morning newspapers, the evening press, and radio and television separately. (Let it be repeated that the findings are based on a very small number of cases, and we should exercise a certain degree of caution in interpreting the correlation coefficients.)

Diagram 2 shows the line of regression for the morning press. Deviations from the line are insignificant and the correlation coefficient is as high as .76. The distance between the largest deviations (SvD and Arb) and the line of regression has been indicated by a broken line. Compared to the distance recorded for SvD when all the media were used as reference, the positive deviation in this case is smaller. Using the morning press exclusively as a frame of reference, SvD's role as the most informative of the media is less pronounced. The reverse applies to Arbetet, for which the negative deviation is somewhat larger compared with the earlier calculation.

The corresponding line of regression for the evening press is illustrated in Diagram 3. Again, deviations are minor and the ratio of output size and information value is high (r = .75). Only the West Coast edition of Expressen falls at any significant distance from the line. This medium was thus responsible for the most informative news coverage among evening newspapers, a fact which is corroborated by the earlier findings. Comparing the lines of regression of morning and evening papers, we find that the former travels along a higher level and is steeper. The steeper gradient suggests that an increase in a given volume of copy pushes up the information value in the morning press much more than in the evening press.

Very special care must be taken in interpreting the line of regression described in Diagram 4 for the radio and television news broadcasts. The reason is that no uniform pattern is evident in the relationship between information value and size of output. The correlation coefficient is low as a result (.36) as is the value for r^2 (.13). Even if we take into account the fact that we are dealing with very small quantities and that minor discrepancies can therefore be unduly magnified, the absence of a clear-cut relationship can be worthy of note, especially since both the morning and evening press show clear results. The findings here suggest that *factors other than* size of output are of considerably more significance in

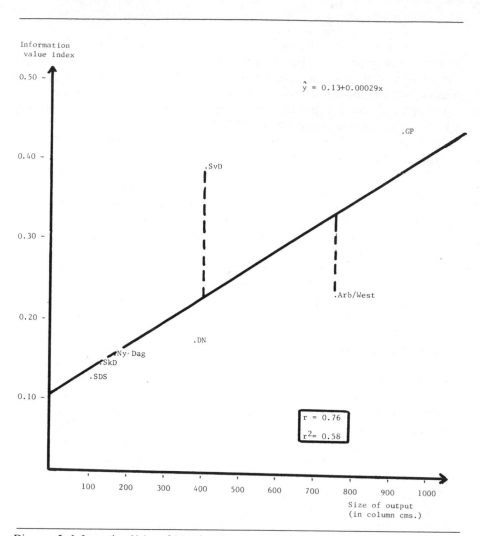

Diagram 2: Information Value of Morning Newspapers in Relation to Size of Output

radio and television, such as the personal contributions of individual members of the staff.

The main purpose of the analysis carried out here has been to test a certain analysis technique. The results should therefore be viewed chiefly in this light. But even if the scope of the material is small and we are only dealing with a case study, nevertheless the evidence should be plain that radio and television news broadcasts provided a weaker information base for the adoption of a position than did the newspapers. How do we then explain such a marked difference, unconnected as it is with the size of media output? One explanation naturally

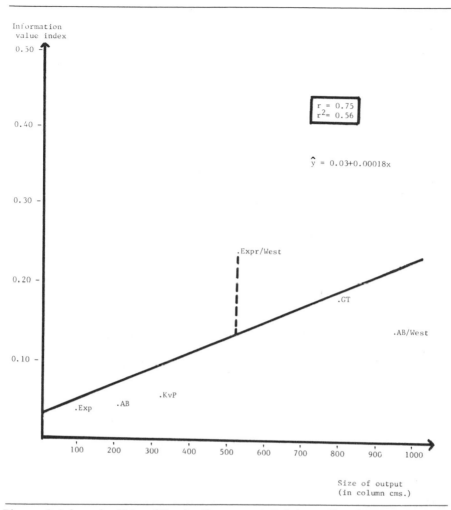

Diagram 3: Information Value of Evening Newspapers in Relation to Size of Output

can stem from differences in journalistic competence. Tempting though such an explanation may be for a number of commentators of the mass media world, the real reason probably lies in the different working methods employed. Radio and television journalists rely in an entirely different manner on the capacity for articulation of each actor. Broadcast news reporting is often concerned with direct interviews, whereas the newspaper journalist has an easier time editing a talkative interviewee, facilitating for example an intensification of the density of information.

In conclusion, this case study suggests that the information value of media content is dependent on two factors: qualities inherent in the actor (such as his knowledge of the issue, his desire to give information, his ability to express

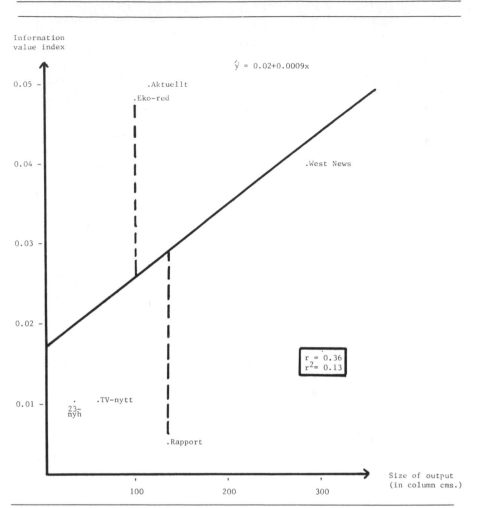

Information
value index

$\acute{y} = 0.02+0.0009x$

.Aktuellt

.Eko-red

.West News

r = 0.36
r^2= 0.13

.TV-nytt

23-
nyh

.Rapport

Size of output
(in column cms.)

Diagram 4: Information Value of Radio and Television News Programs in Relation to Size of Output

himself) and qualities pertaining to the medium (such as the journalist's knowledge of the situation, his ability to put relevant and intelligent questions, medium policy and resources).

The possible role of TV news in the political socialization of children has been a neglected area of published research. This work by Charles K. Atkin and Walter Gantz uses longitudinal questionnaire data from elementary students in kindergarten through fifth grade to look at the problem. Cross-lagged correlation analysis suggests a positive relationship between viewing TV news and political knowledge among older children (with news being the predominant causal factor). A random sub-sample of parents were interviewed by telephone, enabling the researchers to also conclude that parent-child discussion of news stimulated children's exposure to TV news. Dr. Atkin is Professor of Communication at Michigan State University. Dr. Gantz is Assistant Professor of Telecommunications at Indiana University—Bloomington.

19

TELEVISION NEWS AND POLITICAL SOCIALIZATION

Charles K. Atkin and Walter Gantz

WHILE MANY STUDIES have demonstrated that children learn a wide range of behavior from watching television, little research attention has focused on the role of TV in political socialization. Both entertainment and informational programing can have important consequences for the child's development of cognitive and affective orientations toward political actors, issues, and institutions.[1] Televised news presentations provide the most likely source of politically relevant stimuli, and this study examines the impact of national newscasts on child audiences.

The early evening adult-oriented news programs are shown at a time when most children are near the television set. Although the content is aimed well above the elementary school level of comprehension, young preadolescents might watch and learn from these newscasts. Furthermore, the CBS network has developed a new concept in news presentation: specially designed spot news broadcasts for child audiences. These innovative "In the News" programs are displayed for two

---

[1] Although most research has focused on news and public affairs content as the critical media stimuli in the political socialization process, some recent research indicates that television entertainment content may also affect orientations toward key elements of the political system, such as police. See Dominick (1974), and Rarick et al. (1973).

Abstract Elementary school children frequently watch child-oriented news segments on Saturday morning television, and occasionally view network newscasts. News viewing is mildly associated with both political knowledge and public affairs interest for older children, but younger viewers learn little. Parent-child discussion of news is also related to newscast exposure.

Charles K. Atkin is Associate Professor, Department of Communication, Michigan State University, and Walter Gantz is Assistant Professor, Department of Communication, State University of New York, Buffalo. This research was supported by grants from the DHEW Office of Child Development and the National Association of Broadcasters.

From Charles K. Atkin and Walter Gantz, "Television News and Political Socialization," *Public Opinion Quarterly* 42 (Summer 1978) 183-197. Reprinted by permission of Elsevier North Holland, Inc.

minutes every half-hour during Saturday and Sunday morning entertainment programing.

This investigation provides evidence regarding the effects of news viewing on four key variables that can be interpreted as political socialization criteria: political knowledge, discussion of news events, public affairs interest, and information seeking about events in the news.

Political Socialization

Political socialization is a developmental process by which children and adolescents acquire cognitions, attitudes, and behaviors relating to their political environment (Langton, 1969; Hess and Torney, 1967; Hyman, 1959). Several societal agents, particularly parents and schools, have been identified as transmitters of political orientations from generation to generation. Research shows that the socialization process typically begins with abstract emotional attachments and identification with political figures and institutions in the elementary school years. These vague affective allegiances are supplemented with specific knowledge during adolescence, when the child develops a more rational understanding of his political world (Greenstein, 1968).

Most political scientists have taken the individual as the primary unit of analysis. Greenstein (1965) has provided the most useful micro-level scheme in his rephrasing of Lasswell's basic question: Who learns what from whom under what circumstances with what effects? The current research literature has generally dealt with several agents influencing certain cognitive, affective and behavioral dependent variables for various subgroups of preadults.

Early political socialization research focused narrowly on the family as the major agent of political learning. The family environment appears to play an important role in the development of certain political variables such as party identification, knowledge, participation, and efficacy (Chaffee, McLeod, and Wackman, 1973; Dawson, 1966; Hyman, 1959; Greenstein, 1968). However, recent scholars have presented evidence which indicates that the potency of parental influence is overrated, particularly regarding the transmission of partisan attitudes and opinions across generations (Hess and Torney, 1967; Connell, 1972; Jennings and Neimi, 1968).

The second major agent of socialization examined in the research literature has been the school. According to Hess and Torney, the elementary school plays a crucial role in teaching conceptions, beliefs, and attitudes about the operation of the political system.[2] However,

---

[2] Hess and Torney (1967) say that "the school stands out as the central, salient and dominant force in the political socialization of the young child."

Langton (1969) reports compelling evidence that formal "civics" training in the secondary school has a minimal impact on most socialization indices.

Until the 1970s, most researchers did not consider the mass media as a potential agent of political socialization. Those few studies which included mass media variables actually treated exposure to political content as a dependent index of socialization rather than a causal agent contributing to the political learning process. Chaffee et al. (1970) speculate that the basis for ignoring the media role was the classic research evidence which showed that mass communication had limited effects on adult voting behavior. They argue that it is inappropriate to apply these principles to preadult socialization, when a young person is forming rather than defending political predispositions.

Recent investigations indicate that the mass media may be an important factor in political socialization. Studies of children's mass media usage patterns demonstrate a considerable amount of exposure to politically relevant information, especially in older age groups (Lyle and Hoffman, 1972; McLeod et al., 1972; Hawkins et al., 1975; Schramm et al., 1961).

To examine the consequences of mass media exposure, Chaffee et al. administered questionnaires to 1,300 adolescents in both May and November of the 1968 presidential campaign. They found that public affairs media exposure was correlated moderately with level of political knowledge and with campaigning activity at each point in time. Examining cross-lagged correlations across the six-month period, they discovered that public affairs media use in May correlated +.33 with November political knowledge and +.24 with November campaign activity. The knowledge correlation exceeded both the opposite time-order relationship and a "baseline" figure representing chance association, indicating a causal influence. However, the evidence for impact on campaign activity was somewhat less conclusive.[3]

Hawkins et al. (1975) reported that preadolescents who were heavy users of the mass media for political information in the 1972 campaign

---

[3] Chaffee, Ward, and Tipton (1970); these authors also asked students to rate the four primary socialization agents according to degree of importance in providing both information and personal opinion on two specific current topics. On the basis of self-reports on six-step rating scales, the mass media were clearly the most important information source (mean = 5.6), substantially above teachers (3.9), parents (3.3), and friends (2.6). As a source of opinion, the advantage still accrued to the media (4.5), followed by parents (3.3), teachers (3.2), and friends (2.5). Furthermore, students who relied primarily on the mass media scored substantially higher on the political knowledge index than those indicating that parents, teachers, or peers were primary sources of information and opinion. The degree of dependence on the mass media was correlated +.24 with knowledge, while level of dependence on each of the interpersonal agents was negatively associated with knowledge.

displayed substantially greater knowledge about Watergate the following spring, compared to less exposed respondents. In a study of upper elementary school students, Conway et al. (1975) showed that exposure to television news programing was moderately associated with perceptions of policy differences between political parties, awareness of the law-making process in government, and knowledge of governmental roles.

Several research investigations feature self-report perceptions of the role of the mass media versus other socialization agencies. Dominick (1972) administered questionnaires to junior high school students in New York City. The mass media were the primary sources of information about the president (83 percent), vice-president (85 percent), Congress (59 percent), and the Supreme Court (50 percent). In each case, television was cited most often. In three similar surveys, junior and senior high school students were asked to identify their sources of information about foreign affairs and war. Across a variety of specific topics, more than half of the respondents relied primarily on the mass media, particularly television.[4]

Exposure to television news may also stimulate the child to discuss news events with his peers and parents, or anticipated conversation about news topics may lead the child to seek out news shows in order to subsequently transmit or discuss the key stories. Schramm et al. (1961) discovered that sixth-graders in a town that was served by television tended to discuss the news twice as often as those in a town that had no television reception. Sixth- and tenth-graders highly exposed to media public affairs content were more likely to participate in family political discussion, according to a survey by Roberts et al. (1975). Atkin (1972) found that high school students in an experimental condition where they anticipated discussing national current events were more heavily exposed to television news than students who did not expect such discussions.

A study of high school students found a strong relationship between broadcast news exposure and political interest (Johnson, 1973). Research with adult voters further suggests that television news produces increased interest in political affairs (Atkin et al. 1976).

These studies provide a basis for predicting that television news exposure will contribute to political knowledge, discussion, and interest. In the present investigation, survey data were collected to examine the relationships between news viewing and political orientations among elementary school children.

---

[4] Hollander (1971), Coldevin (1972), and Tolley (1973). Other studies related to this topic are reviewed in Atkin (1975).

Method

Three data bases are used in this report: (a) questionnaires administered to 703 elementary school students in kindergarten through fifth grades during spring 1973; (b) telephone interviews with mothers of a randomly selected subsample of 235 students; and (c) second-wave questionnaires administered to a subsample of 200 of the original student sample during spring 1974.

In the main survey, questionnaire responses were gathered in schools indicated in inner city, suburban, and rural districts of central Michigan. Fourth- and fifth-graders filled out an instrument containing a number of open-ended knowledge questions, while younger children answered a slightly abbreviated version featuring multiple-choice items.[5] Following are the major sets of variables measured in the survey.

Political knowledge was measured by 10 questions reflecting concrete elements of the basic themes, personalities, and long-term news developments featured during the previous months in both national evening news programs and special Saturday morning news segments. Each item either asked a verbal question or posed a question about a picture printed on the page. Younger children could choose from among three alternatives; older children wrote answers in blanks for seven of the items.[6]

Three *interpersonal communication* items asked whether the child discussed news events with friends, mother, and father. Older children reported whether they had any *interest* in "the things the president does" and "things that happen in other countries," while the second wave students responded to an interest item dealing with "things that happen in Washington." To tap *information seeking*, all students were asked, "After you watch a story in the news, do you ever try to find out more about it—like looking in a book or asking someone questions?"

Television *news viewing* was measured with items asking about the frequency of exposure to (1) early evening network news ("How much do you watch the national news programs, like Walter Cronkite or John Chancellor—almost every day, sometimes, or almost never?") and to (2) the Saturday children's news segments ("How much do you watch the short In The News' programs that are shown between the cartoons

[5] Thirty-to-forty-minute questionnaires were administered in classrooms at each school. Children in the fourth and fifth grades filled out the questionnaires by themselves, with proctors assisting those having questions. In the first through third grades, proctors read each question and set of responses aloud to full classrooms or half-classes of students while other aides circulated through the room to help those with problems. The kindergaretn children filled out questionnaires in groups of three or four in a semi-interview setting.

[6] For a full description of the items in the questionnaire, see Atkin and Gantz (1975).

on Saturday mornings—a lot, sometimes, or almost never?" and diary reports of watching six specific newscasts the previous Saturday).

The data obtained from mothers supplemented the measures of news exposure and information seeking, but most items are not relevant to these analyses.[7]

One year after the initial survey, questionnaires were readministered to younger students at two of the schools.[8] A parallel set of political knowledge items was constructed to represent the events and personalities featured in the news in 1974. Identical items were repeated for the exposure, discussion, and information-seeking variables.

Results

The presentation of findings focuses on the relationship between television news exposure and the four political socialization variables. As a prelude, previously reported findings regarding the amount of news viewing are briefly described.[9] News watching begins early in elementary school and increases monotonically with age. Approximately one-half of the younger children and two-thirds of the older children report watching the adult-oriented early evening newscasts at least "sometimes"; somewhat higher proportions of each age group are exposed to the special Saturday morning news segments. Mother reports of child news viewing are somewhat more conservative, and most mothers indicate that their children do not pay close attention when watching adult newscasts. Furthermore, most youngsters are occasional rather than regular viewers of the news. Although some children actively seek out the news because they like it, much viewing is accounted for by sheer opportunity; inertial flow carries children from entertainment programs through dinner hour newscasts, while cartoons lead into Saturday news inserts.

What are the implications of this exposure to news on television? For several correlates of news viewing, it is difficult to clearly identify causal ordering; each variable in a bivariate relationship may produce

[7] In an attempt to contact a one-third sample of mothers, telephone numbers were randomly selected from the child questionnaire forms. In cases where two or more children from the same family attended the school, one child was randomly chosen as the focal point. Almost all mothers who were called cooperated in the 15-minute interview. Many of the questions paralleled those items in the child questionnaires, while others sought information from the mother's unique perspective.

[8] Among the 87 third-graders in the initial wave, 63 were resurveyed as fourth-graders; similarly 68 of 88 second-graders and 55 of 78 first-graders were questioned again one year later. Just 14 of the 37 kindergarteners were surveyed twice. The panel was restricted to the younger children because they all answered the same set of political knowledge items in the initial survey.

[9] For a complete description of these exposure findings, see Atkin (1978).

changes in the other in a reciprocal fashion. Nevertheless, these political socialization criteria can be considered as potential dependent variables at least partly affected by news exposure: knowledge, discussion, interest, and information seeking. In the first two cases, time-order analyses will attempt to determine the nature of causal flow.

POLITICAL KNOWLEDGE

The primary dependent variable in this investigation is political knowledge. The strongest predictor of 1973 knowledge is grade in school: fifth-graders score higher than fourth-graders on the advanced political knowledge items; within the younger group, there is correlation of +.44 between grade and the knowledge index.[10] Since knowledge was measured with different procedures for older and younger children, the results are considered separately.

Among the older children in fourth and fifth grades, national news exposure is moderately associated with political knowledge. The index

Table 1. Partial Correlations between News Viewing and Political Knowledge, Discussion, and Interest[a]

	News Exposure Variable	
Criterion Variable	Saturday News Viewing	National News Viewing
Older children (4th–5th grade, $N=291$)		
Political knowledge index	+.12*	+.23**
Interpersonal discussion index	+.19**	+.16**
Interest in presidential affairs	+.19**	+.13*
Interest in foreign affairs	+.05	+.09
Younger children (K–3rd grade, $N=412$)		
Political knowledge index	+.06	+.03
Political knowledge index[b]	+.19**	+.10*
Interpersonal discussion index	+.11*	+.25**
Interest in government affairs[b]	+.03	+.20**

[a] Partial correlations between the exposure variables and each criterion variable control for grade in school, sex, race, and school performace.
[b] This variable is based on second wave data gathered from $N=200$ younger children in 1974.
* $p < .05$.
** $p < .01$.

[10] Respondent characteristics such as race, sex, school performance, and social status are unrelated to knowledge in the younger age group, but moderate correlations emerge among the older children: blacks score lower than whites ($r = +.25$); higher status children are more knowledgeable than those from lower-class backgrounds (+.24); boys know more than girls (+.19), especially regarding political affairs; and those who do well in school display more knowledge than less able students (+.17). Thus, subgroup differences in current affairs information holding seem to develop as children move through middle elementary school.

combining the 10 knowledge items correlates +.27 with national news viewing. Since several of the child characteristics may be producing a slightly spurious relationship, partial correlations were computed controlling for grade, sex, race, and school performance. Table 1 shows that the zero-order correlation drops to a partial correlation of +.23 when these four factors are taken into account. Saturday children's news viewing correlates +.15 with the political knowledge index; the partial correlation is +.12. Although this Saturday news relationship is smaller, it is not significantly different from the national news relationship.

For illustrative purposes, Table 2 displays the proportion of children who correctly answered each knowledge item across three levels of self-reported national news exposure: heavy (almost every day), moderate (sometimes), and light (almost never). On the average, 48 percent of the light viewers have a correct answer, compared to 57 percent of the moderate viewers and 61 percent of the heavy viewers. The most dramatic difference occurs when children are asked to identify the picture of Henry Kissinger, a frequent television news personality. Just 8 percent of the light viewers knew his name, while 26 percent of the heavy viewers were aware of his identity.

For the younger children, national news exposure has a slight positive relationship with the political knowledge index. The 1973 raw correlation is +.08, with a partial of +.03. This relationship is significantly smaller than for older children ($p < .01$). Saturday news exposure

Table 2. Cross-Tabulations between National News Viewing and Political Knowledge, Discussion, and Interest in Fourth-Fifth Grade Sample

	National News Viewing		
	Light N = 83	Moderate N = 103	Heavy N = 105
Recognized Nixon in photo	90%	92%	98%
Identified Nixon's job as president	81	88	91
Knew Nixon taking oath in photo	17	36	35
Knew Watergate involved spies	30	36	47
Identified locale of Indian protest	64	71	78
Identified capital as Washington	55	67	59
Knew treaty signed with N. Vietnam	18	23	31
Knew captured soliders were POW's	71	84	87
Knew Mao's country was China	43	49	58
Recognized Kissinger in photo	8	22	26
Discussion of news with mother	62	67	71
Duscussion of news with father	50	55	58
Discussion of news with friends	55	63	72
Interest in presidential affairs	46	58	59
Interest in foreign affairs	66	73	74

correlates +.12, dropping to +.06 when demographics are controlled. The 1974 knowledge index computed with data from the panel subsample yields stronger associations (Table 1), which may be due to improved measurement or the children's more developed cognitive capacity one year later. Saturday news viewing is a nonsignificantly stronger predictor than evening news viewing.

These findings indicate a consistently positive relationship between viewing television news and knowing political information (although the strength of association is not impressive for younger children). The relationship also appears to be functional, since positive correlations remain when likely contaminating factors are controlled. One important issue is the direction of causality between these two variables: there is evidence from the information-seeking literature indicating that those who are more informed about political information environment will tend to seek additional messages because they are cognitively prepared to identify more content as relevant and to assimilate new developments into a context of existing understanding (Atkin, Galloway, and Nayman, 1976). Thus, previous political knowledge may produce news viewing, rather than news viewing causing political knowledge.

The direction of causality between news exposure and political knowledge can be tested with the cross-lagged correlation technique pioneered by Rozelle and Campbell (1969), since both variables were measured at both points in time. An application of this technique in other studies of the knowledge-exposure relationship is described in detail by Atkin et al. (1976) and by Chaffee et al. (1970).

The two lagged correlations between knowledge and exposure across time are of key importance. To determine causality, these cross-lagged correlations must be compared to a "no cause" baseline statistic that takes into account both the cross-sectional and time-lagged associations that may spuriously produce sizable diagonal relationships.

Conceptually, each cross-lagged correlation is compared to an average static correlation adjusted for unreliability due to temporal instability. It is inappropriate to compare a lagged correlation to a static correlation because the behavior measured changes over time, reducing the magnitude of the association; instability is particularly common among children studied over the period of a year. This genuine fluctuation can be taken into account by multiplying the average static correlation by the average stability coefficient that is obtained by dividing the time-lagged correlation by the internal consistency component of the reliability coefficient.

The cross-lagged correlational analyses indicate that news viewing is the predominant causal variable in the relationship with knowledge. For national news, the T_1 and T_2 static correlations average to $+.07$. The test-retest correlations across the one-year period indicate modest stability for each variable: T_1 national news viewing correlates $+.35$ with T_2 exposure, while the 1973 and 1974 political knowledge indices are correlated $+.37$. When these statistics are entered into the baseline formula, a chance cross-lagged correlation of $+.04$ is expected. The correlation between T_1 news viewing and T_2 knowledge is $+.11$, which exceeds the baseline and even the mean static correlation.[11] This provides solid evidence of causality, since time order is established and the association is functional (any set of antecedent or intervening factors that might have spuriously produced the correlation are taken into account with comparisons to the baseline).

A similar but stronger pattern of influence occurs for Saturday morning children's news. The mean static correlation is $+.19$ and the test-retest correlation for news viewing is $+.34$, yielding a baseline of $+.11$. The cross-lagged correlation from T_1 viewing to T_2 knowledge is $+.29$, which is considerably larger than the reverse knowledge-to-viewing correlation, the mean static correlation, and the baseline.[12] This demonstrates a strong causal effect from Saturday news exposure. There is also marginal evidence that knowledge leads to viewing, since the $+.13$ correlation across time is a bit higher than the chance baseline.

An alternative approach to testing-over-time relationships is multiple regression analysis. Knowledge in the second wave can be regressed on T_1 viewing and T_1 knowledge, and the first wave variables can also be used as predictors of T_2 viewing. Applying this technique, the beta weight for T_1 viewing and T_2 knowledge is $+.08$ for national news and $+.22$ for Saturday news. The reverse knowledge-to-viewing beta weights are $.00$ and $+.08$, respectively. These findings can be interpreted as further evidence that the contribution of viewing is more important than the role of knowledge in the relationship.

INTERPERSONAL NEWS DISCUSSION

It seems likely that news viewing will facilitate interpersonal communication about news events, and a reverse influence may also operate as conversations stimulate news exposure. Three items asking

[11] The reverse knowledge-to-exposure correlation is just $+.04$, the chance expectation. Although a difference is found between the exposure-to-knowledge correlation and the baseline, it is not statistically significant.

[12] The exposure-to-knowledge correlation significantly exceeds the baseline figure ($p < .05$).

whether the children talk about "things in the news" with peers, mother, and father were combined into an overall discussion index.

Grade in school is the strongest predictor variable, correlating +.30 with the discussion index. As children get older, they are particularly likely to increase discussions with peers (+.31), while mother (+.23) and father (+.14) conversations are less strongly related to grade. There are only weak associations with race, sex, academic performance, and social status. Again, these factors are controlled when examining the relationships between viewing and discussion of news.

For the overall sample, the partial correlation between national news viewing and the index of discussion is +.21, while Saturday news exposure correlates +.15. For national news, a stronger viewing-discussion correlation appears for younger than older children (Table 1). The opposite pattern emerges for Saturday news, as the relationship is stronger for older than for younger children. The item concerning talking with peers is slightly more strongly correlated with news viewing than the parental items, as illustrated in Table 2.

The mother-child subsample provides a broader measure of news discussion between mother and child, as both parties were asked whether such communication occurs. The combined index of mother-child news discussion correlates +.19 with national news viewing and +.15 with Saturday news viewing, when control variables are partialed out of the relationship.

The panel subsample yields evidence regarding the issue of causality between these two variables. Both variables were measured with identical items in 1973 and again in 1974. The cross-sectional national news relationships each year average to +.25. The no-cause baseline is +.12, since the average static correlation is diminished by the low test-retest correlation of +.25 for the discussion index. The T_1 viewing to T_2 discussion correlation is +.10, falling short of the baseline criterion for causality. On the other hand, the reverse correlation from earlier discussion to later viewing is +.15, which is lightly above the baseline.

The same basic pattern is found for Saturday news. The cross-lagged correlation from viewing to discussion of +.04 is smaller than the baseline, the reverse cross-lagged correlation, and the mean static correlation. On the other hand, the discussion-to-viewing correlation is +.11, indicating a modest causal influence.

Using regression analysis on these data, it is clear that the contribution of news exposure is minimal: the beta weights for T_1 viewing and T_2 discussion are +.05 for national news and +.03 for Saturday news. The regression of T_2 viewing on the first wave variables shows that discussion predicts viewing +.11 in the case of national news and +.10 for Saturday newscasts.

These panel findings can be interpreted as supporting the inference that interpersonal communication about the news stimulates exposure to television news. The data are not particularly conclusive, however, since these cross-lags barely exceed the baselines and are not larger than the static correlations. There is no evidence to show that the amount of news viewing serves to increase news discussion. Those who watch news do talk more about the news, but the act of exposure does not appear to be the causal influence in the relationship.

PUBLIC AFFAIRS INTEREST

The older subgroup was asked questions concerning their personal interests in foreign and national topics. It was anticipated that news exposure might produce more interest in the subject matter described in the newscasts, and that interest would lead to more viewing. Interest in "things the president does" is mildly related to news viewing in Table 1; the partial correlation is +.13 for national news and +.19 for Saturday news. The associations are smaller for interest in "things that happen in other countries." Table 2 shows that 46 percent of the light national news viewers are interested in presidential activities, compared to 59 percent of those heavily exposed; 66 percent of the light viewers and 74 percent of the heavy national news viewers are interested in foreign events.

During the second wave of the panel study, the younger students were asked about their interest in "things that happen in Washington." This measure has a partial correlation of +.20 with national news exposure and +.03 with Saturday news exposure (Table 1). Interest is expressed by 29 percent of the light national news viewers and 45 percent of the heavy viewers, taking into account grade in school as a control variable.

These data show that the children's interest in political affairs is modestly but definitely associated with news exposure. Since interest was not measured in the first wave of the panel study, it is difficult to infer causality in this relationship between news exposure and political interest.

INFORMATION SEEKING

Exposure to news programing may stimulate the child to seek further information from interpersonal or media sources. The children were asked, "After you watch a story in the news, do you ever try to find out more about it—like looking in a book or asking someone questions?" Overall, 40 percent replied in the affirmative, with a sharp increase from 25 percent at the kingergarten-first grade level to 51 percent for fourth-fifth graders. Mothers answered a parallel question: "We also want to find out whether or not these Saturday news programs stimulate children's curiosity. Does your son (daughter) ever try to get more information about something he (she) has seen on the news . . . either from you or someone else, or from books or magazines?" The 65 percent who said yes were asked how often this happens: 5 percent say "almost everyday," 15 percent "several times per week," 26 percent "once per week," and 19 "less than that."

Furthermore, there is a tendency for heavier viewers to seek more information. The self-report measure is modestly correlated with amount of news viewing, with partial correlations of $+.13$ for national news and $+.08$ for Saturday morning news. The mother-report measure, which is tied to Saturday morning news programing, has a partial correlation of $+.10$ with her report of the child's attention to Saturday morning news.

Thus, children who watch more news tend to seek more information afterwards, compared to those viewing less news programing. In addition, direct self-reported instances of seeking added information after viewing occur for about half of the children studied. To the extent that this information-seeking involves topics relating to politics, television news contributes to the political socialization of the child.

Discussion

This exploratory research represents the first comprehensive attempt to measure effects of television news programing among young people. Although it is difficult to obtain reliable data from elementary school students, some tentative conclusions can be drawn from the surveys.

The findings indicate that more than half of the children occasionally or frequently view news programing, and that exposure contributes to political knowledge, interest, and information seeking. Causal analyses with panel data indicate that influence flows primarily from news viewing to political knowledge; viewers become more informed about political matters, while previously knowledgeable children do not necessarily seek out news programing.

Children with different characteristics acquire varying amounts of knowledge from the news programing that they view. The findings clearly show that older children in fourth and fifth grade are more affected by the news than those in early elementary school, although this younger group does display limited learning from the simplified Saturday morning mini-newscasts. This developmental difference is due to their more sophisticated ability for processing, structuring, and storing incoming information; thus, they have a greater capacity for learning from news messages. The exposure-knowledge relationship is also stronger for middle-class than for working-class children, and among those children who like the news and are interested in news events. Thus, news programing has a much greater impact under certain conditions relating to the capacities and predispositions of the receivers. Future research should attempt to identify precisely these facilitating conditions rather than merely documenting that a relationship exists across the overall audience.

While discussion of news with parents and peers is moderately related to news viewing, this factor appears to be a cause of exposure rather than a consequence. The cross-lagged correlations from T_1 discussion to T_2 viewing are somewhat stronger than the T_1 viewing to T_2 discussion correlations for both national and Saturday news. Since the viewing-to-discussion correlates do not exceed the baseline, the evidence does not support the inference that news exposure exerts a causal influence. Thus, talking about the news with other people may mildly stimulate news viewing but is not directly stimulated by the viewing experience.

Interest in national political affairs is mildly associated with exposure to both early evening adult and children's news programing. The relationship is much weaker for interest in international affairs, although this measure probably reflected a broader attraction to foreign lands and peoples than specific interest in politically relevant events occurring abroad. Finally, the findings demonstrate that television news stimulates some child viewers to seek further information about topics covered.

In sum, television serves as more than a mere entertainment source for young children. TV news is a meaningful source of political knowledge acquisition and serves to arouse interest and curiosity about political affairs. Scholars examining the political development of the child should accord television a more significant role alongside the family and the school as a socializing influence.

References

Atkin, Charles
   1972   "Anticipated communication and mass media information-seeking."
           Public Opinion Quarterly 36:188–99.
   1975   "Communication and political socialization." Political Communication Review 1:2–7.
   1978   "Broadcast news programming and the child audience." Journal of Broadcasting 22:47–61.

Atkin, Charles, John Galloway, and Oguz Nayman
  1976 "News media exposure, political knowledge, and campaign interest."
        Journalism Quarterly 54:230–38.
Atkin Charles, and Walter Gantz
  1975 "The role of television news in the political socialization of children."
        Paper presented to the International Communication Association,
        Chicago.
Chaffee, Steven, Jack McLeod, and Daniel Wackman
  1973 "Family communication patterns and adolescent political participa-
        tion." Pp. 349–64 in Jack Dennis (ed.), Socialization to Politics: A
        Reader. New York: Wiley.
Chaffee, Steven, Scott Ward, and Leonard Tipton
  1971 "Mass communication and political socialization." Journalism Quar-
        terly 47:647–59.
Coldevin, Gary
  1972 "Internationalism and mass communications." Journalism Quarterly
        49:365–68.
Connell, R. W.
  1972 "Political sozialization in the American family: the evidence re-
        examined." Public Opinion Quarterly 36:323–33.
Conway, M. Margaret, A. Jay Stevens, and Robert Smith
  1975 "The relation between media use and children's civic awareness."
        Journalism Quarterly 52:531–38.
Dawson, Richard
  1966 "Political socialization." Pp. 214–28 in J. Robinson (ed.), Political
        Science Annual. New York: Bobbs-Merrill.
Dominick, Joseph
  1972 "Television and political socialization." Educational Broadcasting
        Review 6:48–56.
  1974 "Children's viewing of crime shows and attitudes on law enforce-
        ment." Journalism Quarterly 51:5–12.
Greenstein, Fred
  1965 Children and Politics. New Haven: Yale University Press.
  1968 "Political socialization." International Encyclopedia of the Social
        Sciences 14:551–55.
Hawkins, Robert, Suzanne Pingree, and Donald Roberts
  1975 "Watergate and political socialization." American Politics Quarterly
        3:406–22.
Hess, Robert, and Judith Torney
  1967 The Development of Political Attitudes in Children. Chicago: Aldine.
Hollander, Neil
  1971 "Adolescents and the war: the sources of socialization." Journalism
        Quarterly 48:472–79.
Hyman, Herbert
  1959 Political Socialization. New York: Free Press.
Jennings, M. Kent, and Richard Niemi
  1968 "Transmission of political values from parent to child." American
        Political Science Review 62:169–84.
Johnson, Norris
  1973 "Television and politicization: a test of competing models." Jour-
        nalism Quarterly 51:447–55.

Langton, Kenneth
1969 Political Socialization. New York: Oxford University Press.
Lyle, Jack, and Heidi Hoffman
1972 "Children's use of television and other media." Pp. 129–256 in E. Rubinstein, G. Comstock, and J. Murray (eds.), Television and Social Behavior: Television in Day-to-Day Life. Washington: U.S. Government Printing Office.
McLeod, Jack, Charles Atkin, and Steven Chaffee
1972 "Adolescents, parents and television use." Pp. 173–313 in G. Comstock and E. Rubinstein (eds.), Television land Social Behavior: Television and Adolescent Aggressiveness. Washington: U.S. Government Printing Office.
Rarick, D.L., J.E. Townsend, and D.A. Boyd
1973 "Adolescent perceptions of policy: actual and as depicted in TV drama." Journalism Quarterly 50:438–46.
Roberts, Donald, Suzanne Pingree, and Robert Hawkins
1975 "Do the mass media play a role in political socialization?" The Australian and New Zealand Journal of Sociology 11:37–43.
Rozelle, Richard, and Donald Campbell
1969 "More plausible rival hypotheses in the cross-lagged panel correlation technique." Psychological Bulletin 71:74–80.
Schramm, Wilbur, Jack Lyle, and Edwin Parker
1961 Television in the Lives of Our Children. Stanford: Stanford University Press.
Tolley, Herbert
1973 Children and War. New York: Columbia University Teachers College Press.

More than 100 uses and effects of television and newspapers are reviewed in this paper by David Weaver and Judith Buddenbaum. This work provides evidence that TV and newspapers are functional complements for knowledge and diversion, even though there is competition between them for the consumer's diversionary time. Newspaper use is more strongly associated with voting turnout and other political behavior than is television. Dr. Weaver is Director of the Bureau of Media Research at Indiana University; Buddenbaum is a doctoral student in the School of Journalism at Indiana. Their review was commissioned by the News Research Center of the American Newspaper Publishers Association and first published in the April 1979 ANPA News Research Report.

20

NEWSPAPERS AND TELEVISION
A Review of Research on
Uses and Effects

David H. Weaver and Judith M. Buddenbaum

The uses and effects of mass media have been systematically studied by hundreds of scholars in this country and others since the late 1920's.[47, 61, 62, 63] There are several reviews of such studies.[26, 41, 42, 48, 55, 57, 99, 112] But none have concentrated on the similarities and differences in the uses and effects of newspapers and television. In an effort to summarize what we know about these two important media, this review covers studies published since 1955 which look at the uses and/or effects of newspapers and television.

Findings in Brief

Review of the *uses* of television and newspapers finds that people value both television and newspapers and use both in a generally complementary manner for knowledge and diversion, and as an adjunct to interpersonal discussion. Although most people regularly use both television and newspapers, on any given day a person is more likely to read a newspaper than to watch televison *news*. Television typically is seen as fulfilling a more general-surveillance function while newspaper readership is associated with specific information seeking, in-depth knowledge about a subject and guidance at election time.

As a diversion, television and newspapers do compete with each other for the consumer's *time*, but people expect both to provide some entertainment. Only in the case of media use for escape does there seem to be a clear difference between television and newspapers. Persons who can be described as "alienated" are heavy viewers of fantasy-oriented television programming, but no correlation between alienation and newspaper use has been found.

The use of television as a substitute for other activities has been documented in several studies, but no studies were found on the use of newspapers as a substitute for interpersonal contacts. Use of both newspapers and television does seem to increase when people see the content as useful in conversations with others. Television seems to be favored by those who frequently *ask* others for information about a subject, while opinion *givers* seem to prefer newspapers.

In general, whites, males, persons with relatively high levels of education and high social and economic status say they prefer newspapers while blacks, females and persons of lower socioeconomic status say they are heavy television users.

As for the *effects* of newspapers and television, the studies reviewed here (mostly one-time surveys) suggest that exposure to newspapers is associated with reinforcement, rather than change, of pre-existing political attitudes. Exposure to television is somewhat more associated with the formation of new, short-term political attitudes and general political interest than is exposure to newspapers.

Newspapers seem to be more effective than television at increasing levels of political knowledge and at telling people what issues to be concerned about in a political campaign. And newspaper editorial endorsements of particular political candidates are associated with increased vote totals in elections, especially in non-partisan elections where there are few controversial issues.

A final conclusion suggested by studies of *political effects* of newspapers and television is that newspaper use is more strongly associated with voting turnout and other political activity than is television use.

Other conclusions suggested by the studies of *non-political effects* of newspapers and television are:

• Heavy television viewing—regardless of specific content—is associated with more distrust of other persons, more fear of the world in general, an exaggerated fear of being involved in violence and more dependence upon established authorities. Heavy newspaper exposure, on the other hand, is associated with less distrust of others, less fear of the world and less dependence upon established authorities. Heavy newspaper readers are also less likely to overestimate the number of persons involved in law enforcement than are heavy television viewers.

• Newspaper reading is associated with the formation of attitudes about topics which receive regular coverage in newspapers, but such coverage does not seem to have much systematic impact on the direction or the intensity of such attitudes.

• Newspaper exposure is associated with greater knowledge of topics covered in newspapers for both children and adults, and newspapers seem to be more effective at conveying detailed information than does television.

• Information loss seems to be greater from television than from newspapers, but there is a substantial loss of information (estimated at an average of 77 percent) from *both* newspaper and television news stories.

From David H. Weaver and Judith M. Buddenbaum, "Newspapers and Television: A Review on Uses and Effects," *ANPA News Research Report* 19 (April 20, 1979). Reprinted by permission of the American Newspaper Publishers Association.

• There seems to be a stronger association between the amount of space devoted to a topic in a newspaper and recall of information about that topic, than between the amount of time devoted to a subject by television and recall of information about that subject.

• Learning from newspapers seems to vary with a person's level of education. The more educated seem to learn more, thus perpetuating existing inequities in knowledge between better-educated and less-educated persons.

• Television plays a major role in making people aware of important breaking news (such as the assassination of a President or a disaster involving large numbers of persons), with newspapers tending primarily to supplement television and radio reports of such news. Those who rely on television for *important* breaking news seem to miss more details than substance.

• Children tend to develop a "high affection" for television before becoming involved with print media. And non-readers and light readers of daily newspapers tend to have negative attitudes about reading and regard it as "work."

• Readers of a weekly newspaper are more likely to be readers of a daily newspaper than not, and readers of a daily newspaper are more likely to watch televison *news* and to belong to a community organization than are non-readers of a daily newspaper.

Methodology

The conclusions in this review are based on more than 100 studies on the uses and effects of newspapers and television which were conducted between 1955 and 1977. Most of the studies reported here were published in one of four leading journals in the field of mass communications research: *Journalism Quarterly, Journal of Broadcasting, Public Opinion Quarterly* and *Journal of Communication.*

In addition to these journals, ANPA News Research Reports and Bulletins were scanned, as well as some of the newspaper readership study abstracts on file at the ANPA News Research Center, Syracuse University. A few recent books and unpublished papers dealing with newspaper and television uses and effects were also included in this review.

Uses of Newspapers and Television

Conventional wisdom tells us, on the one hand, that television is primarily an entertainment medium while newspapers are for information—and, on the other hand, that the two media are in competition with each other for the same audience. While there is some truth in both observations, the picture that emerges from a

review of mass communications research is of media audiences using both newspapers and television for knowledge, diversion and as an adjunct to interpersonal communication in a way that is more complementary than competitive.

For Knowledge

Of these three main uses, the use of television and newspapers for knowledge is the most thoroughly researched. However, to better understand both the complementary and competitive relationships between these media, we will subdivide this use for knowledge into surveillance, specific information seeking and guidance.

Diffusion studies by Budd, MacLean and Barnes[15] following significant news events indicate that, in general, one medium will be the source of awareness and the other will then be used for more specific information. However, which medium will fall into the surveillance category and which into the specific information-seeking category will be determined by a number of factors, including the time of occurrence of the event, the location of the audience at the time of the news break and the salience of the event.

For example, following a relatively *low-salience* event such as President Eisenhower's decision to run for re-election, Danielson[24] determined that although people who learned about the event from television heard about it much faster than those who learned about it from newspapers, more people learned about it from newspapers than from television. Following a *medium-salience* event such as George McGovern's decision to drop Thomas Eagleton from the 1972 Democratic ticket,[83] and a *high-salience* event like the John F. Kennedy assassination,[35] television is much more likely to be the first news source; but after hearing of the event, people generally turn to another medium for further information.

When the subject studied is routine daily news instead of a major news event, a similar pattern emerges. Studies by Stone[103] and Wade and Schramm[110] showed that most people consider television their most important news source—with newspapers their second choice—but this preference is not a case of "either/or." A study conducted by Ehrenberg, Goodhardt and Haldane[29] concerning duplication of viewing found that there is no special audience for television news and that viewing television news is not correlated with watching other public affairs programming. Other studies by Bogart[9] and Robinson[87] indicate that on any given day a person is much less likely to turn on television *news* than to read a newspaper.

Television news is used more for surveillance, and newspapers are used more for in-depth information. A study of television news recall by Neuman[81] showed that the audience consists primarily of casual viewers, while a study by Grotta, Larkin and DePlois[40] found that readers of small daily newspapers (circulation approximately 5,000) use them for local news and advertising and turn to television for national and international news. Metropolitan newspapers are seen by these readers as providing an additional source of news for those persons wanting more complete information.

For specific information, newspapers are generally the first choice. During an election campaign, Vinyard and Sigel[109] found that 98 percent of their respondents read at least one newspaper daily, and 87 percent watched television news and public affairs programs. Newspapers were rated the most important source for keeping informed.

For information about medicine and science, Wade and Schramm[110] found a similar complementary pattern, with newspapers being the primary source and television seen as a supplementary source. In a study of medical information, however, Wright[118] found that television and newspapers are used about equally, but respondents feel newspapers provide the most useful information. Most medical school faculty members surveyed by Shaw and Van Nevel[101] occasionally found new information about their specialties in the mass media, with 92 percent of that information contained in newspapers and in general magazines.

In a more general study of sources of science news, Swinehart and McLeod[105] found that before the launching of Sputnik, newspapers were the primary source of science news—but that following the launch, television increased in importance and replaced newspapers as the main news source for some groups.

Although many studies, particularly those of children, document some increase in knowledge following general non-news television use, studies documenting the deliberate use of general television content for knowledge purposes are practically nonexistent. Wright[118] found that people mention dramatic medical shows as a *not*-very-useful source of medical information, and Katzman[51] suggested that viewers of soap operas learn how to face life and handle certain kinds of interpersonal problems from their favorite shows; but this is not necessarily the same thing as watching such content in order to learn from it.

No studies included in the scope of this review dealt with the use of newspaper comic pages, filler material or other "non-news" items for knowledge purposes.

In addition, use of newspapers and television for guidance has not been well-researched. No studies concerning television were found in this review, and newspapers have been studied only in connection with elections. Vinyard and Sigel[109] found that 60 percent of Detroit registered voters surveyed depended greatly on newspaper endorsements for local candidate selection but relied less heavily on endorsements for state and national candidates. Surveying newspaper subscribers and voters in Oregon, Rarick[86] found that 42.2 percent would take newspaper advice on a local bond issue, but only 32.8 percent would take that advice in a presidential election. The same study indicated that women are more influenced than men by editorials on issues outside the home, while men are more influenced than women by editorials on domestic matters. But whether either sex turns to editorials for specific guidance in matters beyond elections is not clear.

For Diversion

According to Robinson,[90] the average person devotes 28 percent (or 92 minutes daily) of all leisure time exclusively to television, 7 percent to newspapers and an additional 36 minutes daily to other leisure activities while also watching television as a secondary activity. Although all of this is "diversion" in the sense that it is time spent outside the confines of the normal working day, these totals include media use for knowledge and as an adjunct to interpersonal communication, as well as for the strictly diversionary purposes of entertainment, escapism and time passing.

As diversionary activities, television and newspapers clearly compete with each other for audience *time* even though their contents are not strictly competitive.

Studies from the early years of television conducted by Hamilton and Lawless[43] indicate that the chief reason for wanting television, and one of the chief values to those having it, was as a cheap form of entertainment. In a somewhat later study, Mehling[74] asked respondents which mass medium they would keep if they could have only one. Of the 52 percent who selected television, 53 percent mentioned "entertainment" and 40 percent "variety" as their reason. By comparison, 26 percent selected newspapers—but of those, only 25 percent mentioned either "entertainment" or "variety" as the reason for their choice.

Although television, particularly during daytime hours and prime time, offers many programs that are usually classified as entertainment and newspapers carry such entertainment features as comics, crossword puzzles and certain columns, the question of exactly what content people use when they want to be entertained has not received much study.

Working with a convenience sample of children aged 6 to 12, Streicher and Bonney[104] found that most made a distinction between their regular viewing and programs from which they could "learn something." For entertainment, boys preferred cartoons, drama and fantasy, while the top choices for girls were situation comedies, drama and cartoons.

Schramm, Lyle and Parker[96] found that soon after children learn to read, they begin turning to newspapers to read the comics. This use continues even after they develop an interest in other content.

That adults expect to be entertained by mass media is documented by a number of studies dealing with political content. Cranston[23] notes that soon after telecasts of political conventions began, entertainment became a part of the format as a way of holding audience attention; Kelley[52] points out that a proportion of the audience for campaign debates comes from those who are interested in the "game" aspect of elections; and Atkin and others[6] found that people's attitudes toward candidates at least partially depend on the entertainment value of the candidates' commercials.

In a study of television viewing across the Canadian-American border, Sparkes[102] found that Canadian viewers turn to U.S. television primarily for entertainment, and United States viewers turn to Canadian stations to supplement local offerings, particularly of sports.

Katz and Foulkes[50] state that mass media may serve for individual retreat or for keeping "close" to desired others, but that no particular medium is associated with escapism. They further caution that "escape" content does not function as "escape" for everyone using it and suggest that, therefore, the term "escape" should apply to consequences rather than to a pattern of use.

However, Pearlin[84] found a relationship between stressful experiences and escape viewing, while studies of alienation by McLeod, Ward and Tancill[73] and Sargent and Stempel[95] found that those who can be described as "alienated" spend more time with television, especially its fantasy content, and apparently use television as an escape medium. No correlation was found between alienation and newspaper readership.

Television and newspapers can both serve as a mechanism for passing time. Mehling[74] found that 2 percent of those who selected television as the one medium they would keep and 2 percent of those who selected newspapers gave "time killing" as their reason. Neuman[81] in his study of television news recall found that 12 percent of television news viewers surveyed watch in order to relax, and Davis[25] determined that one function of television for older adults is to divide the day into meaningful segments.

For Communication

As an adjunct to interpersonal communication, television and newspapers may be used in three ways: to keep people close together, to substitute for personal relations and to provide something to talk about.

Hamilton and Lawless[43] found that "keeping the family at home" was the most important reason for having a television set and the second-most important reason for wanting one, and Merrill[76] determined that children under five watch televison most frequently after 7 p.m. when they can be with other family members.

In a study of leisure activities, Meyersohn[77] found that most heavy viewers also participate in other forms of recreation including people-oriented activities, such as visiting, but that higher income people who are heavy viewers do not engage in many other leisure activities. Like the elderly persons surveyed by Davis,[25] they apparently turn to television for companionship.

Several studies document an increase in television and newspaper use when people see the social utility of this activity. For college students, Atkin[4] determined that the number of newspapers read and the time spent reading newspapers and magazines is positively correlated with the number of groups in which news is discussed. Troldahl and Van Dam[106] found that persons who frequently give opinions or ask for information are more likely to use several media than are those who seldom talk about the news. Givers and askers differ from each other in their media selection, with more opinion *givers* reading newspapers and more *askers* watching television. Radio and magazine use is very similar for both groups. Among senior citizens, Graney and Graney[33] found that television use is positively correlated with telephone use and attendance at meetings.

Who Uses Newspapers and Television

Clearly, both newspapers and television can be used for knowledge, diversion and as an adjunct to interpersonal communication. The total time and attention devoted to either medium, as well as the amount of that time and attention that will be devoted to any one of the uses, depend on the individual. But these differences frequently can be predicted from demographic and attitudinal characteristics.

In general, persons with higher incomes and more education are more likely to read newspapers than are those with lower levels of education and income, who generally devote more time to television.

Williams and Lindsay[113] found that time spent with newspapers and television is more closely correlated with social stratification than with age, sex or race. Although this study showed little difference in source of "important news" for persons classified as "influential," "social workers" and "clients," major differences were found in the amount of time devoted to newspapers and television.

Among the "influentials," 90 percent read a newspaper every day, but only 6 percent watched more than three hours of television. Among the "clients," the figures were 53 percent and 39 percent, respectively. "Social workers" were intermediate in their media habits.

A similar study by Greenberg and Dervin[37] found that low-income persons are much more likely to rely on television as a source of world and local news, and they are much less likely to use newspapers for that information. Wade and Schramm[110] reported that television is the source of news for most people during a national election campaign, but newspapers are preferred by highly educated, professional and white collar workers, and by high-income groups.

Considering education as a predictor separate from socioeconomic status, Vinyard and Sigel[109] found that reliance on multiple media increases as education increases; but Kline[56] and Samuelson, Carter and Ruggels[94] reported that as education levels increase, the total amount of time spent with media decreases. Much of this decrease comes at the expense of the diversionary content of television.

Considering race as a predictor of media use, Allen[1] and McCombs[68] found that television is more important for blacks than for whites; but studies by Sharon[100] and by Williams and Lindsay[113] suggest that most media differences between the races are more closely correlated with socioeconomic status than with race itself. Furthermore, work by Williams, Dordick and Horstmann[114] suggests that ethnic subgroup and community standards, as well as economic conditions, may be responsible for differences that are usually reported as racial.

In the area of newspaper readership, racial differences persist even when controls are applied for socioeconomic status. Bogart[11] found that newspaper readership for blacks and whites follows generally the same pattern by sex, age and income—with the exception that it falls off more sharply among blacks with very low income and those with less than a college educaton. Sharon[100] determined that whites read more of all kinds of printed matter than do blacks, regardless of economic status, and that this difference is particularly apparent in newspaper readership. Among those of both races who do read newspapers, blacks read less of the editorials, society pages and regular advertisements and more sports and television-radio listings than do whites.

Sex is usually one of the demographic characteristics used to predict newspaper and television use; however, like race, it is unsatisfactory when considered apart from education and economic status. Greenberg[36] found that women prefer television to newspapers as a news source, but work by Wade and Schramm[110] and Kraus, Mehling and El-Assal[58] suggests that this pattern is reversed for women with high education levels. Furthermore, results obtained by Rarick[85] indicating that

women tend to be home- and family-oriented in their newspaper reading—while men are more oriented toward matters outside the home—may be more a function of time spent at home than of innate sexual differences. By way of comparison, Katzman[51] determined that women make up 71 percent of the audience for daytime soap operas, but the other 29 percent of the audience comes from the children and unemployed and retired men—who also happen to spend much of their time at home.

As a general model, Greenberg and Kumata[38] found that television use peaks during high school, then decreases through age 50, but increases again thereafter.

Children begin their media use with television. According to Merrill[76] the initial appeal is the medium itself rather than any particular content. The heaviest viewing occurs between the ages of 4 and 12. By age 13, most have begun to use other media. Schramm, Lyle and Parker[96] found that while newspaper readership begins after television use, by the end of high school two-thirds of children read a newspaper daily. Comics are generally the first thing children read.

Clarke[19] found that, in general, children's newspaper reading is associated with parental values—but that family status alone is predictive of children's attention to newspapers. In a later study,[18] he concluded that for teen-age boys, readership of science and sports news is more predictive of lasting interest in newspapers than is readership of teen supplements.

Effects of Newspapers and Television

To enhance comparison, each of the studies on newspaper and television *effects* was assigned to one of six categories—political, violence and aggression, general world views, general learning, media use and interpersonal communication, and consumer affairs. Within each of these six groupings, the effects on attitudes, knowledge and behavior were analyzed where possible.*

Political Attitudes

The three panel studies by Bogart,[10] Rollings and Blascovitch[92] and McCombs and Weaver,[71] and most of the surveys on political attitudes, suggest that newspapers mainly reinforce pre-existing political attitudes and contribute somewhat to the formation of new attitudes. The single experiment by Atkin[5] suggests that

---

*This is a review of newspaper and television news content on these attitudes, knowledge and behavior. For example, the extensive specialized literature on the effects of advertising (e.g., [30,34] and [117]) is not included here.

newspaper reporting of public opinion polls can influence attitudes toward a specific political candidate, especially if the polls tap the opinions of highly valued reference groups.

In spite of Atkin's contradictory experimental evidence, some other studies of political attitudes[16, 21, 49] suggest that exposure to newspapers is not enough to cause more long-term change in political attitude, at least not by itself. Some of the studies which examine correlates of both newspapers and television exposure[7, 49, 71, 92] further suggest that television may be more effective at stimulating the formation of new, short-term political attitudes and general political interest, whereas newspapers may be more effective at reinforcing already-formed political attitudes.

Political Knowledge.

Both panel studies and surveys found that exposure to newspapers is associated wtih increased political knowledge (variously defined).[7, 10, 17, 21, 49, 53, 72, 98] All of these studies, except one by Bogart,[10] also included measures of television use (usually television news viewing), and all but one concluded that exposure to newspapers is more strongly correlated with increased political knowledge than is exposure to television news. The exception is a survey of elementary school children in Maryland; it found that television news viewing was more strongly correlated with knowledge of which roles were governmental than was reading newspaper current events material.[22] There are no experimental studies dealing with political knowledge.

A number of fairly recent studies,[70, 78, 115] several of them done over time with the same persons,[66, 71, 107] also suggest that newspaper emphasis on specific political issues is more strongly correlated with overall audience concern about the same issues than is television emphasis on such issues, leading to the inference that newspapers are more effective at telling people what issues to think about in a political campaign than is television, especially earlier in a campaign.[60]
As a whole, the findings from these studies are surprisingly consistent: exposure to newspapers seems to lead to more concern over political issues and to more political knowledge than does exposure to television.

Political Behavior

A number of studies, mostly analyses of newspaper editorials and voting records, suggest that newspaper endorsements of particular political candidates are associated with the winning of elections, especially nonpartisan races where there are few salient or controversial issues.[39, 44, 65, 67, 98] Two studies by Robinson also found aggregate correlations of editorial endorsements with winning the 1968 and 1972 presidential elections in this country.[85, 89]
Most of the studies on political behavior which include measures of both newspaper and television exposure suggest that newspaper use tends to be more strongly associated with voting turnout and various other kinds of political activity than does televison use, even when only television *public affairs* viewing is measured.[17, 32] This conclusion seems to hold for both adults and children.

Likewise, the studies of political behavior which include only measures of newspaper exposure also conclude that such exposure is positively correlated with political participation in Japan,[60] with voting turnout in Ohio,[64] with general political activity in North Carolina[8] and with voting choice in Wisconsin and North Carolina.[5, 8]

Violence and Aggression

Only three studies of violence and aggression were found which considered newspaper exposure as a factor.[31, 119, 120] The first, a survey of U.S. adults, found that heavy TV viewing—regardless of specific content—is associated with more distrust of other persons, more fear of the world in general, an exaggerated fear of being involved in some kind of violence and more dependence upon (positive attitudes toward) established authorities. Heavy newspaper readers, however, showed just the opposite trends—less distrust of others, less fear of the world and less dependence upon established authority.

With regard to knowledge, one of these studies also found that heavy newspaper readers were less likely to overestimate the number of persons involved in law enforcement than were heavy TV viewers, and heavy newspaper readers seemed to have a more trusting picture of the world than did heavy TV viewers. These patterns held for all persons except less-educated, lower-income blacks.

With regard to behavior, the second and third studies[119, 120] examined crime statistics for Detroit, Cleveland, Minneapolis and Vancouver, British Columbia, during and before newspaper strikes in these cities. These studies found that the rates of some crimes (burglary, robbery, larceny and auto theft) declined significantly during newspaper strikes in Detroit, but there was no evidence of any general relationship between newspaper strikes and crime rates in the other cities, leading the author to conclude that the relationship found in Detroit was probably due to chance and that "there appears to be no general relationship between newspaper publication and crime rates." (p. 612)[120]

General Views of the World

Four surveys (including one panel study) which dealt with newspaper use and general attitudes toward real-world phenomena found that newspaper use is associated with the formation of attitudes about topics receiving coverage in newspapers, such as fluoridation[14] and world pollution.[80] Newspaper exposure is also associated with innovativeness, empathy and cosmopolitanism among farmers in Colombia.[91]

The fourth study, involving Indiana University students, found that newspaper editorials and editorial cartoons advocating the same point of view result in more opinion change than either would by itself. Editorials alone seem to produce more opinion change than do cartoons alone.[13]

In the late 1950's, some seven or eight years after the introduction of television throughout the United States, most people perceived that they obtained most of their general news from newspapers rather than television.[59] But by the early 1970's, most people said they obtained most of their general news, especially impressions of international affairs, from television rather than newspapers.[20, 80]

Yet during the 1962-63 New York newspaper strike, Kimball,[54] in a panel study of 200 newspaper readers, found complaints about "lack of detail" and lack of opportunity to "absorb the news" from other media, especially television. Those questioned also said they wanted to know more about general news, sports, advertisements and financial news, suggesting that this kind of information normally was obtained from newspapers.

Newspaper exposure seems to be correlated not only with various kinds of real-world knowledge for adults. There also is evidence from surveys conducted by Schramm, Lyle and Parker[97] that as children grow older, they increasingly use newspapers (and other print media) for learning about the real world, whereas television is used primarily for entertainment and escape.

General Learning

An experiment with 160 university students by Dommermuth[28] found that a printed version of a message produced significantly more change in opinion than a televised version of the same message. Seven other studies which examined the relationships between newspaper exposure and general learning suggested that both newspaper stories and television news shows can convey information and increase the salience of various topics, but information *loss* seems to be greater from television than from newspapers. Printed messages seem to result in more information retention than do televised messages,[28, 116] but there is still a substantial amount of information loss (estimated at an average of 77 percent for radio, television and newspapers combined in an experiment by Wilson). In an earlier experiment, Hazard[45] also found that less exposure to newspapers was associated with less information gain from television newscasts.

A combined content analysis and survey by Booth[12] found that the association between *space* devoted to a topic in a newspaper and recall of information about that topic is stronger than the association between the amount of *time* devoted to a subject by television and recall of information about the subject. In both newspapers and television, accompanying pictures seemed to increase recall of information about the subjects.

Although most of the evidence on information loss and retention from different media is experimental, several surveys by Tichenor, Donohue and Olien[106] find that learning occurs from newspapers but varies with one's initial level of education. These researchers found that knowledge levels differ more in a community with a regularly published newspaper than in a community with a newspaper strike. They also found that the association between level of education and understanding of "more publicized" topics is greater than the association between level of education and understanding of "less publicized" topics. These findings led Tichenor, Donohue and Olien to conclude that newspapers may serve to reinforce existing inequities in knowledge between better-educated and less-educated persons.

Other studies suggest that television plays a major role in delivering important "breaking" news (such as the assassination of a President or a disaster involving many persons), with newspapers tending primarily to supplement television and radio reports of such news.[27] And even though evening television news broadcasts report fewer key events than do the front pages of newspapers, those who rely on television news rather than newspapers don't miss much substance but rather the *details* of major stories.[44]

The single experimental study which dealt with the relationship of general problem-solving behavior to print-media use found that for seventh-grade children, printed messages resulted in more creative problem-solving behavior than did televised solutions, but the differences were not statistically significant.[75]

Media Use and Interpersonal Communication

The single study which considered the relationship between newspaper use and attitudes toward other media involved focus-group discussions with non-readers and light readers of newspapers in Canada.[2] This study found that non-readers and light readers tended to have negative attitudes about reading in general (they regarded it as "work"), and they tended to like radio and television more than newspapers because they perceived radio and TV to be better at presenting what is happening in the world "right now."

Two studies suggest that regular daily newspaper readers tend to be more aware of other print and broadcast media offerings in their communities than do non-readers of daily newspapers.[2, 3] A related study by Deutschmann and Danielson[27] also found that information about important news seems to go directly from television, radio, and—to a lesser extent—from newspapers to their audiences without much interpersonal relaying. These studies also indicate that persons generally do talk with others about major news learned from both newspapers and television.

Further, readers of a weekly newspaper are more likely than not to be readers of a daily newspaper,[2] and readers of a daily newspaper are more likely to watch television *news* on a regular basis than are non-readers.[3] In addition, daily newspaper readers are more likely to belong to community organizations than are non-readers, and thus are more likely to engage in interpersonal communication about community issues and problems.

Summing Up

These studies of the uses and effects of newspapers and television provide many insights into the similarities and differences between these two media, but they also leave many questions unanswered.

With regard to *uses* of newspapers and television, we need more studies which concentrate on people's *motives* for use as well as on various *situational factors* (such as jobs, families, living areas, etc.). While use of newspapers and television for *knowledge* has been fairly well-researched, we know less about use of these and other mass media for *diversion* and as an adjunct to *interpersonal communication.* That is, there are not many studies which look at mass media in relation to other communication activities, either in terms of motives or in terms of the effects those media have on individuals.

With regard to the *effects* of newspapers and television, we *do* have quite a few studies on *political* effects, but not many on the impact of these media on people's *emotions, values* and *propensity to act aggressively* toward others.

But the studies to date do establish one point very clearly: in speaking about competition or differences between newspapers and television, it is necessary to specify precisely what *kind* of competition or difference is under discussion.   ■

References:

[1] Allen, Thomas A. (1968), "Mass Media Use Patterns in a Negro Ghetto." *Journalism Quarterly,* 45:525-7.

[2] American Newspaper Publishers Association News Research Center (1975-76), "Canadian Newspaper Readership Study." ID Number 0218.

[3] American Newspaper Publishers Association News Research Center (1976), "Newspaper Readership Study." ID Number 0193.

[4] Atkin, Charles K. (1972), "Anticipated Communication and Mass Media Information Seeking." *Public Opinion Quarterly,* 36:188-99.

[5] Atkin, Charles K. (1964), "The Ipact of Political Poll Reports on Candidate and Issue Preferences." *Journalism Quarterly,* 46:515-21.

[6] Atkin, Charles K., Lawrence Bowen, Oguz B. Nayman and Kenneth C. Sheinkopf (1973), "Quality vs. Quantity in Televised Political Ads." *Public Opinion Quarterly,* 37:209-224.

[7] Atkin, Charles and Gary Heald (1976), "Effects of Political Advertising." *Public Opinion Quarterly,* 40:216-228.

[8] Becker, Lee B. (1977), "The Impact of Issue Saliences." In Donald L. Shaw and Maxwell E. McCombs, *The Emergence of American Political Issues: The Agenda-Setting Function of the Press.* St. Paul, Minn.: West, Chapter 8:121-31.

[9] Bogart, Leo (1968-69), "Changing News Interests and the News Media." *Public Opinion Quarterly,* 32:560-74.

[10] Bogart, Leo (1957-58), "Measuring the Effectiveness of an Overseas Information Campaign: A Case History." *Public Opinion Quarterly,* 21:475-98.

[11] Bogart, Leo (1972), "Negro and White Media Exposure: New Evidence." *Journalism Quarterly,* 49:15-21.

[12] Booth, Alan (1970-71), "The Recall of News Items." *Public Opinion Quarterly,* 34:604-610.

[13] Brinkman, Del (1968), "Do Editorial Cartoons and Editorials Change Opinions?" *Journalism Quarterly,* 45:724-26.

[14] Brinton, James E. and L. Norman McKown (1961), "Effects of Newspaper Reading on Knowledge and Attitude." *Journalism Quarterly,* 38:187-95.

[15] Budd, Richard W., Malcolm S. MacLean Jr. and Arthur M. Barnes (1966), "Regularities in the Diffusion of Two Major News Events." *Journalism Quarterly,* 43:221-30.

[16] Byrne, Gary C. (1969), "Mass Media and Political Socialization of Children and Pre-Adults." *Journalism Quarterly,* 46:140-42.

[17] Chaffee, Steven H., L. Scott Ward and Leonard P. Tipton (1970), "Mass Communication and Political Socialization." *Journalism Quarterly,* 47:647-59.

[18] Clarke, Peter (1968), "Does Teen News Attract Boys to Newspapers?" *Journalism Quarterly,* 45:7-13.

[19] Clarke, Peter (1965), "Parental Socialization Values and Children's Newspaper Reading." *Journalism Quarterly,* 42:539-46.

[20] Coldevin, Gary O. (1972), "Internationalism and Mass Communication." *Journalism Quarterly,* 49:365-68.

[21] Converse, Philip E. (1962), "Information Flow and the Stability of Partisan Attitudes." *Public Opinion Quarterly,* 26:578-99.

[22] Conway, M. Margaret, A. Jay Stevens and Robert G. Smith (1975), "The Relation between Media Use and Children's Civic Awareness." *Journalism Quarterly,* 52:531-38.

[23] Cranston, Pat (1960), "Political Convention Broadcasts: Their History and Influence." *Journalism Quarterly,* 37:186-94.

[24] Danielson, Wayne A. (1956), "Eisenhower's February Decision: A Study of News Impact." *Journalism Quarterly,* 33:433-41.

[25] Davis, Richard H. (1971), "Television and the Older Adult." *Journal of Broadcasting,* 15:2:153-59.

[26] Dennis, Everette E. (1978), *The Media Society: Evidence About Mass Communication in America.* Dubuque, Iowa: Wm. C. Brown.

[27] Deutschmann, Paul and Wayne A. Danielson (1960), "Diffusion of Knowledge of the Major News Story." *Journalism Quarterly,* 37:345-55.

[28] Dommermuth, William P. (1974), "How Does the Medium Affect the Message?" *Journalism Quarterly,* 52:441-7.

[29] Ehrenberg, A. S. C., G. C. Goodhardt and I. R. Haldane (1969-70), "The News in May." *Public Opinion Quarterly,* 33:545-55.

[30] Fisk, George (1959), "Media Influence Reconsidered." *Public Opinion Quarterly,* 23:83-91.

[31] Gerbner, George and Larry P. Gross (1976), "Living with Television: The Violence Profile." *Journal of Communication,* 26:2:172-197.

[32] Glaser, William A. (1965), "Television and Voting Turnout." *Public Opinion Quarterly,* 29:71-86.

[33] Graney, Marshall J. and Edith E. Graney (1974), "Communications Activity Substitutions in Aging." *Journal of Communication,* 24:4: 86-96.

[34] Grass, Robert C. (1977), "Measuring the Effects of Corporate Advertising." *Public Relations Review,* 3:39-50.

[35]Greenberg, Bradley S. (1964), "Diffusion of News of the Kennedy Assassination." *Public Opinion Quarterly*, 28:225-32.

[36]Greenberg, Bradley S. (1966), "Media Use and Believability: Some Multiple Correlates." *Journalism Quarterly*, 43:665-70, 732.

[37]Greenberg, Bradley and Brenda Dervin (1970), "Mass Communication among the Urban Poor." *Public Opinion Quarterly*, 34:224-35.

[38]Greenberg, Bradley S. and Hideya Kumata (1968), "National Sample Predictors of Mass Media Use." *Journalism Quarterly*, 45:641-46.

[39]Gregg, James E. (1965), "Newspaper Editorial Endorsements and California Election, 1948-62." *Journalism Quarterly*, 42:532-38.

[40]Grotta, Gerald L., Ernest F. Larkin and Barbara DePlois (1975), "How Readers Perceive and Use a Small Daily Newspaper." *Journalism Quarterly*, 52:711-15.

[41]Halloran, James D. (1965), *The Effects of Mass Communication.* Leicester, England: Leicester University Press.

[42]Halloran, James D. (1970), *The Effects of Television.* London: Panther.

[43]Hamilton, Robert V. and Richard H. Lawless (1956), "Television within the Social Matrix." *Public Opinion Quarterly*, 20:393-403.

[44]Harney, Russell F. and Vernon A. Stone (1969), "Television and Newspaper Front Page Coverage of a Major News Story." *Journal of Broadcasting*, 13:2:181-88.

[45]Hazard, William R. (1962), "Some Personal and Social Influences on Telecast Viewing." *Public Opinion Quarterly*, 26:429-434.

[46]Hooper, Michael (1969), "Party and Newspaper Endorsements as Predictors of Voter Choice." *Journalism Quarterly*, 46:302-5.

[47]Hovland, Carl I., I. L. Janis and H. H. Kelley (1953), *Communication and Persuasion.* New Haven, Conn.: Yale University Press.

[48]Hovland, Carl I. (1954), "Effects of the Mass Media of Communication." In Gardner Lindzey, ed., *The Handbook of Social Psychology,* Volume 2. Cambridge, Mass.: Addison-Wesley, pp. 1062-1103.

[49]Katz, Elihu (1971), "Platforms and Windows: Broadcasting's Role in Election Campaigns." *Journalism Quarterly*, 48:304-14.

[50]Katz, Elihu and David Foulkes (1962), "On the Use of Mass Media as 'Escape': Clarification of a Concept." *Public Opinion Quarterly*, 26:377-88.

[51]Katzman, Nathan (1972), "Television Soap Operas—What's Been Going on Anyway?" *Public Opinion Quarterly*, 36:200-12.

[52]Kelley, Stanley Jr. (1962), "Campaign Debates: Some Facts and Issues." *Public Opinion Quarterly*, 26:351-66.

[53]Kent, K. E. and Ramona R. Rush (1976), "How Communication Behavior of Older Persons Affects Their Public Affairs Knowledge." *Journalism Quarterly*, 53:40-46.

[54]Kimball, Penn T. (1963), "New York Readers in a Newspaper Shutdown." *Columbia Journalism Review*, 2:3:47-56.

[55]Klapper, Joseph T. (1960), *The Effects of Mass Communication.* New York: The Free Press.

[56]Kline, F. Gerald (1971), "Media Time Budgeting as a Function of Demographics and Life Style." *Journalism Quarterly*, 48:211-21.

[57]Kraus, Sidney and Dennis Davis (1976), *The Effects of Mass Communication on Political Behavior.* University Park. Pa.: Pennsylvania State University Press.

[58]Kraus, Sidney, Reuben Mehling and Elaine El-Assal (1963), "Mass Media and the Fallout Controversy." *Public Opinion Quarterly*, 27:191-205.

[59]Krieghbaum, Hillier (1968), "Newspaper is Main Channel for News for Most People." *Editor & Publisher*, 91:35:11.

[60]Kuroda, Jasumasa (1965), "Newspaper Readership and Political Behavior in a Japanese Community." *Journal of Communication*, 15:171-181.

[61]Lasswell, Harold D. (1927), *Propaganda Technique in the World War.* London: Kegan Paul.

[62]Lasswell, Harold D. and D. Blumenstock (1939), *World Revolutionary Propaganda.* New York: Knopf.

[63]Lazarsfeld, Paul F. (1940), *Radio and the Printed Page.* New York: Duell, Sloan and Pearce.

[64]MacDonald, James (1972), "Turned off Readers." *Bulletin of the American Society of Newspaper Editors*, 563:3-5.

[65]McClenghan, Jack Sean (1973), "Effect of Endorsements in Texas Local Elections." *Journalism Quarterly*, 50:363-66.

[66]McClure, Robert D. and Thomas E. Patterson (1976), "Print vs. Network News." *Journal of Communication*, 26:2:23-28.

[67]McCombs, Maxwell E. (1967), "Editorial Endorsements: A Study of Influence." *Journalism Quarterly*, 44:545-48.

[68]McCombs, Maxwell E. (1968), "Negro Use of Television and Newspapers for Political Information." *Journal of Broadcasting*, 12:3:261-66.

[69]McCombs, Maxwell E. (1977), "Newspapers Versus Television: Mass Communication Effects Across Time." In Donald L. Shaw and Maxwell E. McCombs, *The Emergence of American Political Issues: The Agenda-Setting Function of the Press.* St. Paul, Minn.: West, Chapter 6:89-105.

[70]McCombs, Maxwell E. and Donald L. Shaw (1972), "The Agenda-Setting Function of Mass Media." *Public Opinion Quarterly*, 36:176-87.

[71]McCombs, Maxwell E. and David Weaver (1977), "Voters and the Mass Média: Information-Seeking, Political Interest, and Issue Agendas." Paper presented to the American Association for Public Opinion Research, Buck Hill Farms, Pa.

[72]McLeod, Jack M., Ramona R. Rush and Karl H. Friederich (1968-69), "The Mass Media and Political Information in Quito, Ecuador." *Public Opinion Quarterly*, 32:575-87.

[73]McLeod, Jack, Scott Ward and Karen Tancill (1965-66), "Alienation and Uses of the Mass Media." *Public Opinion Quarterly*, 29:583-94.

[74]Mehling, Reuben (1960), "Television's Value to the American Family Member." *Journal of Broadcasting*, 4:4:307-13.

[75]Meline, Caroline W. (1976), "Does the Medium Matter?" *Journal of Communication*, 26:3:81-89.

[76]Merrill, Irving R. (1961), "Broadcast Viewing and Listening by Children." *Public Opinion Quarterly*, 25:263-76.

[77]Meyersohn, Rolf (1968), "Television and the Rest of Leisure." *Public Opinion Quarterly*, 32:102-12.

[78]Mullins, L. E. (1973), "Agenda-setting on the Campus: The Mass Media and Learning of Issue Importance in the 1972 Election." Paper presented to the Association for Education in Journalism, Fort Collins, Colo.

[79]Mullins, L. E. and Maxwell E. McCombs (1975), "Young Voters and the Mass Media." *News Research for Better Newspapers*, 7:222-230.

[80]Murch, Arvin W. (1971), "Public Concern for Environmental Pollution." *Public Opinion Quarterly*, 35:102-106.

[81]Neuman, W. Russell (1976), "Patterns of Recall among Television News Viewers." *Public Opinion Quarterly*, 40:115-123.

[82]Newspaper Advertising Bureau (1975), "Print Competition for Newspaper Readership."

[83]Ostlund, Lyman E. (1973-74), "Interpersonal Communication Following McGovern's Eagleton Decision." *Public Opinion Quarterly*, 37:601-10.

[84]Pearlin, Leonard I. (1959), "Social and Personal Stress and Escape Television Viewing." *Public Opinion Quarterly*, 23:255-59.

[85]Quarles, Rebecca C. (1977), "Mass Communication and Political Accuracy: A Comparison of First-time and Older Voters." Paper presented to the Communication Theory and Methodology Division, Association for Education in Journalism, Madison, Wis.

[86]Rarick, Galen R. (1970), "Political Persuasion: The Newspaper and the Sexes." *Journalism Quarterly*, 47:360-64.

[87]Robinson, John P. (1971), "The Audience for National TV News Programs." *Public Opinion Quarterly*, 35:403-5.

[88]Robinson, John P. (1972), "Perceived Media Bias in the 1968 Vote: Can the Media Affect Behavior After All?" *Journalism Quarterly*, 49:239-46.

[89]Robinson, John P. (1974), "The Press as King-Maker: What Surveys From the Last Five Campaigns Show." *Journalism Quarterly*, 51:587-94, 606.

[90]Robinson, John P. (1969), "Television and Leisure Time: Yesterday, Today and (Maybe) Tomorrow." *Public Opinion Quarterly*, 33:210-22.

[91]Rogers, Everett M. (1965-66), "Mass Media Exposure and Modernization Among Colombian Peasants." *Public Opinion Quarterly*, 29:614-625.

[92]Rollings, Harry E. and Jim Blascovich (1977), "The Case of Patricia Hearst: Pretrial Publicity and Opinion Change." *Journal of Communication*, 27:2:58-65.

[93]Roshwall, Irving and Leonard Resnicoff (1971), "The Impact of Endorsements and Published Polls in the 1970 New York Senatorial Election." *Public Opinion Quarterly*, 35:410-14.

[94]Samuelson, Merrill, Richard F. Carter and Lee Ruggels (1963), "Education, Available Time, and Use of Mass Media." *Journalism Quarterly*, 40:491-96.

[95]Sargent, Leslie W. and Guido H. Stempel III (1968), "Poverty, Alienation and Mass Media Use." *Journalism Quarterly*, 45:324-26.

[96]Schramm, Wilbur, Jack Lyle and Edwin B. Parker (1960), "Patterns in Children's Reading of Newspapers." *Journalism Quarterly*, 37:35-40.

[97]Schramm, Wilbur, Jack Lyle and Edwin B. Parker (1961), *Television in the Lives of Our Children*. Stanford, Calif.: Stanford University Press.

[98]Schweitzer, John C. (1975), "Daily Newspaper Readership Among 18 to 29 Year Olds." *News Research for Better Newspapers*, 7:213-222.

[99]Seymour-Ure, Colin (1974), *The Political Impact of Mass Media*. Beverly Hill, Calif.: Sage.

[100]Sharon, Amiel T. (1973-74), "Racial Differences in Newspaper Readership." *Public Opinion Quarterly*, 37:611-17.

[101]Shaw, Donald L. and Paul Van Nevel (1967), "The Information Value of Medical Science News." *Journalism Quarterly*, 44:548.

[102]Sparkes, Vernone (1977), "TV Across the Canadian Border: Does It Matter?" *Journal of Communication*, 27:40-47.

[103]Stone, Vernon A. (1969-70), "Sources of Most News: Evidence and Inference." *Journal of Broadcasting*, 14:1:1-4.

[104]Streicher, Lawrence H. and Norman L. Bonney (1974), "Children Talk About Television." *Journal of Communication*, 24:3:54-61.

[105]Swinehart, James W. and Jack M. McLeod (1960), "News about Science: Channels, Audiences, and Effects." *Public Opinion Quarterly*, 24:583-89.

[106]Tichenor, Phillip J., George A. Donohue and C. N. Olien (1970), "Mass Media Flow and Differential Growth in Knowledge." *Public Opinion Quarterly*, 34:159-70.

[107]Tipton, Leonard, Roger D. Haney and John R. Baseheart (1975), "Media Agenda Setting in City and State Election Campaigns." *Journalism Quarterly*, 52:15-22.

[108]Troldahl, Verling C. and Robert Van Dam (1965-66), "Face-to-face Communication About Major Topics in the News." *Public Opinion Quarterly*, 29:626-34.

[109]Vinyard, Dale and Roberta S. Siegel (1971), "Newspapers and Urban Voters." *Journalism Quarterly*, 48:486-93.

[110]Wade, Serena and Wilbur Schramm (1969), "The Mass Media as Sources of Public Affairs, Science, and Health Knowledge." *Public Opinion Quarterly*, 33:197-209.

[111]Weiss, Carol H. (1974), "What America's Leaders Read." *Public Opinion Quarterly*, 38:1-22.

[112]Weiss, Walter (1969), "The Effects of the Mass Media of Communication." In Gardner Lindzey and Elliot Aronson, eds., *The Handbook of Social Psychology*, Second Edition, Volume 5. Reading, Mass.: Addison-Wesley, pp. 77-195.

[113]Williams, Frederick and Howard Lindsay (1971), "Ethnic and Social Class Differences in Communication Habits and Attitudes." *Journalism Quarterly*, 48:672-78.

[114]Williams, Frederick, Herbert S. Dordick and Frederick Horstmann (1977), "Where Citizens Go for Information." *Journal of Communication*, 27:1:95-99.

[115]Williams, Wenmouth Jr. and David C. Larsen (1977), "Agenda-Setting in an Off-Election Year." *Journalism Quarterly*, 54:744-49.

[116]Wilson, C. Edward (1974), "The Effect of Medium on Loss of Information." *Journalism Quarterly*, 51:111-115.

[117]Wright, Peter L. (1974), "Analyzing Media Effects on Advertising Responses." *Public Opinion Quarterly*, 38:192-205.

[118]Wright, W. Russell (1975), "Mass Media as Sources of Medical Information." *Journal of Communication*, 25:3:171-73.

[119]Payne, David E. and Kay Price Payne (1970), "Newspapers and Crime in Detroit." *Journalism Quarterly*, 47:233-38, 308.

[120]Payne, David E. (1974), "Newspapers and Crime: What Happens During Strike Periods." *Journalism Quarterly*, 51:607-612.

PART IV

INFORMATION-SEEKING

Two quite different studies are included in this section, one dealing with information-seeking at the level of the individual and the other looking at information choices and information diffusion at the community level. Both represent valuable work.

The first study looks at individual styles of information-seeking and suggests a model that thoroughly charts the decision points in information decision-making. The second study is representative of an extemely important research program that assumes a macro-level approach to information diffusion and control.

A model of information-seeking is developed in this work. Experimental data suggest four distinct styles of information-seeking behavior: loners, formal seekers, risky seekers, and informal seekers. Although the different styles appear unrelated to success as defined in the experiment, the possibility of differential quality of information gain and decision-making exists for the four styles. Dr. Donohew is Professor of Communication at the University of Kentucky. Dr. Tipton is Associate Professor of Journalism at the University of Kentucky. Mr. Haney is Assistant Professor of Journalism at Murray State University.

21

ANALYSIS OF
INFORMATION-SEEKING STRATEGIES

Lewis Donohew, Leonard Tipton, and Roger Haney

Distinct "styles" of information seeking have different moods and communication behaviors.

► Rational decision-making, whether it involves weighty matters like careers or marriage or more routine activities such as shopping or home repairs, requires answers to certain basic questions involving information choices. Do we need more facts, or can we decide on the basis of what we know now? Should we consult other people or go to more formal sources, such as books?

¹ Lewis Donohew, "Decoder Behavior on Incongruent Political Material: A Pilot Study," *Journal of Communication,* 16: 133-42 (1966); Steven H. Chaffee, Keith R. Stamm, J.L. Guerrero and Leonard Tipton, "Experiments on Cognitive Discrepancies and Communication," *Journalism Monographs,* 14 (1969); Leonard Tipton, "Effects of Writing Tasks on Utility of Information and Order of Seeking," JOURNALISM QUARTERLY, 47:309-17 (1970); Donohew and Philip Palmgreen, "A Reappraisal of Dissonance and the Selective Exposure Hypothesis," JOURNALISM QUARTERLY, 48:412-20 (1971); Donohew and Palmgreen, "An Investigation of 'Mechanisms' of Information Selection," JOURNALISM QUARTERLY, 48:627-39, 666 (1971); Donohew, Joanne M. Parker and Virginia McDermott, "Psychophysiological Measurement of Information Selection: Two Studies," *Journal of Communication,* 22:54-63 (1972); Donohew and John R. Baseheart, "Information Selection and Galvanic Skin Response," JOURNALISM QUARTERLY, 51:33-39 (1974).

² Peter Clarke, "Some Correlates of Selectivity in Information Seeking," paper presented to Association for Education in Journalism convention, Syracuse, 1965; Edwin Parker and William Paisley, *Patterns of Adult Information-Seeking* (Stanford: Institute for Communication Research, 1966); Peter Clarke and Jim James, "The Effects of Situation, Attitude Intensity and Personality on Information Seeking," *Sociometry,* 30:235-45 (1967); Charles K. Atkin, "Communicatory Utility and News Information Seeking," paper presented to Association for Education in Journalism Convention, Washington, D.C., 1970; Steven F. Chaffee and Jack M. McLeod, "Individual vs. Social Predictors of Information Seeking," JOURNALISM QUARTERLY, 50:237-45 (1973); Other more-recently published studies along similar lines include Charles K. Atkin, "Instrumental Utilities and Information Seeking," in Peter Clarke, ed., *New Models for Mass Communication Research* (Beverly Hills: Sage, 1973); Alexis S. Tan, "Exposure to Discrepant Information and Effect of Three Coping Modes," JOURNALISM QUARTERLY, 53:678-84 (1975).

We often go through this process without pausing to articulate a particular information-gathering strategy. But we do, nonetheless, tend to favor particular strategies—some of us methodically gather and weigh all sides of questions while others pick out what they think is the heart of the matter and decide based on that information. In coping with problems in our environment, some persons plunge in with apparent confidence, defining the questions they want answered, then going quickly to key sources and building an information base for decision-making. Others approach this process with considerable hesitation, tentatively defining what they think they need, gingerly checking out some sources, then perhaps redefining their needs several times before finally arriving at a decision.

Are such strategies related to how much persons already know, or to their personality—such as open-mindedness, self-esteem, or need for variety? Are they related to their moods—how they feel at the moment? Does one kind of strategy lead to success and another to failure? These are some of the questions the study reported in this article seeks to answer.

Background

Over the past several years, the authors have been engaged in a number of studies involving approaches to information seeking and processing.¹ On the basis of these and others done by colleagues in our field,² we proposed a con-

►Lewis Donohew is professor of communication and Leonard Tipton is associate professor of journalism at the University of Kentucky. Roger Haney is assistant professor of journalism at Murray State University.

From Lewis Donohew et al., "Analysis of Information-Seeking Strategies," *Journalism Quarterly* 55 (Spring 1978) 25-31. Reprinted by permission.

FIGURE 1

A Flow Model of Information Seeking, Avoiding, and Processing

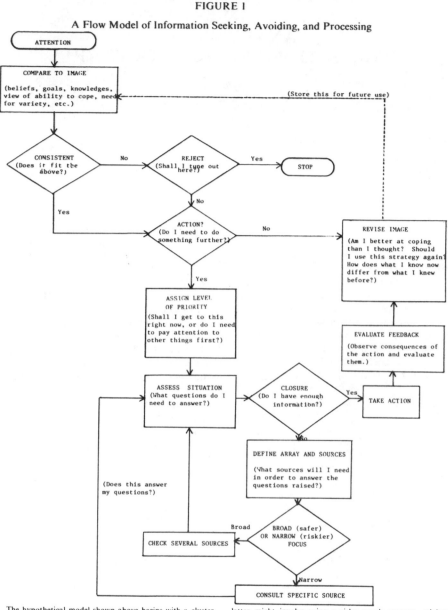

The hypothetical model shown above begins with a cluster of stimuli which define a situation or problem that could require further information-seeking. These stimuli reach the attention of individuals and are compared to elements in their "images of reality"—their hierarchies of values, knowledges, views of their ability to cope with situations, level of need for stimulation, (see Footnote 7) and information-handling "set," or style of coping with information.

Other components include situational elements affecting information search, such as time pressures and availability of information, and type of information search conducted. The latter might involve using a risky search strategy—relying on one or a few key sources—or taking the safer course of gathering everything one can find, then sorting out the pieces. It also includes the type of sources (formal, such as books and "experts"; informal, such as peers), and the point at which one decides on closure ("I have enough information to make a decision."). Following closure, the individual takes some action, evaluates its consequences and possibly revises the image of reality as a result. This may include changing (or reinforcing) beliefs about information strategies to be used another time.

ceptual model of information seeking, avoiding, and processing whose central component is the kind of information search conducted.[3] A hypothetical flow version of the model is shown in Figure 1. At this stage, the authors are studying broad patterns of regularities—what goes with what—before proceeding to further experimentation and attempts to offer causal explanations. The study reported here is a further effort in this direction.

In an earlier examination of strategies of information-seeking, a group of students had been asked to keep diaries for a semester on their thoughts and steps in writing a term paper. The data, reported in the article describing the model, were unsatisfactory from several points of view—among them that they took too long to gather and were too subjective. The authors sought an information-seeking situation that would last hours rather than months and which would permit

more control over such variables as availability of information, content and time pressure.

Procedure

The authors set up a race-horse game, using videotapes and information on horses, odds and payoffs from a day's actual races. Students in freshman communication classes (N = 85) played the role of bettors. The students were issued play money and instructions on how to play the game. Before each race, they were given the opportunity to buy various kinds of information from sellers at a table. They could buy information comparing several horses on such attributes as best racing times, odds or handicapper's picks. They also could buy information on individual horses—such as racing records (these roughly correspond to the pertinence/salience distinction of an early Carter paradigm).[4] The primary objective of the exercise, as described to participants, was to increase the amount of money held. Subjects could bet or pass, buy all information available or buy none of it, as they chose. They were instructed not to exchange purchased information with other participants, but they could reveal their betting decisions in advance of placing bets. Records were kept of what information subjects bought, the bets they placed and the winnings they collected.

After each race, students were asked to indicate whom they had advised and who had given them advice. The investigators also sought to assess, through use of a mood scale, how they felt at the moment: anxious, pleasant, relaxed, etc.

Variables. In this particular study, the variables can be catergorized as "personality" measures, "information-strategy" variables and "mood" variables. The first and last might also be viewed as "antecedent" and "consequent" variables.

The personality measures used were *self-esteem,*[5] *dogmatism* (which was treated conceptually as a style of information-processing),[6] and *sensation-seeking,*[7] which was used as a measure of

[3] Lewis Donohew and Leonard Tipton, "A Conceptual Model of Information Seeking, Avoiding, and Processing," in Peter Clarke, ed., *op. cit.*, pp. 243-68. In a recent review of information processing literature, the model was described as one using a "gratifications" approach (See Michael L. Ray and Scott Ward, "The Relevance of Consumer Information Processing Studies to Communication Research," *Communication Research*, 2:195-202, 1975).

[4] Richard F. Carter, "Communication and Affective Relations," JOURNALISM QUARTERLY, 42:203-12 (1965).

[5] See Morris Rosenberg, *Society and the Adolescent Self-Image* (Princeton: Princeton University Press, 1965). The scale used here also appears in John P. Robinson and Philip Shaver, *Measures of Social Psychological Attitudes.* (Ann Arbor: Institute for Social Research, 1969).

[6] An elaboration on the rationale for this interpretation is contained in Donohew and Palmgreen, "An Investigation . . .," pp. 627-39, 666, and in Donohew and Baseheart, *loc. cit.* The measuring instrument was one developed by Troldahl and Powell, "A Short-Form Dogmatism Scale for Use in Field Studies," *Social Forces*, 44:211-15 (1965).

[7] This is based on activation level or variety theories, which hold that human beings attempt to maintain a level of activation to which they are accustomed. See D.W. Fiske and S.R. Maddi, *Functions of Varied Experience* (Homewood, Ill.: Dorsey, 1961); S.R. Maddi, "The Pursuit of Consistency and Variety," R.P. Abelson, *et al.*, eds., *Theories of Cognitive Consistency: A Sourcebook.* (Chicago: Rand McNally, 1968); Elizabeth Duffy, *Activation and Behavior* (New York: John Wiley, 1962). In our chapter presenting the model, we have suggested that when persons go beyond preferred limits of variety in information-seeking (i.e., they become too aroused), they will tend to reduce the input of variety and seek consistent or even redundant information. When they exceed preferred levels on the consistency end of the continuum (i.e., their arousal is too low), they will seek more novel content. This response tendency is measured here through a scale developed by Zuckerman, *et al.* See M.E. Zuckerman, A. Kolin, L. Price and I. Zoob, "Development of a Sensation-Seeking Scale," *Journal of Consulting Psychology*, 28:477-82 (1964).

one's need to seek variety. A fourth "antecedent" variable measured before subjects played the game was *prior knowledge*, measured with a set of questions about horse-racing.

The information-strategy variables included two interpersonal measures. *Information given* was the number of people to whom the subjects reported giving information or tips before a race started. *Information received*, the other side of the coin, was the number of people each subject reported receiving information *from* before each race.

Amount of information bought was the number of different items (tips, track records, etc.) a subject purchased.

Broad-focus or narrow-focus strategy[8] was defined in terms of both the type of information bought and the sequence in which it was purchased. Subjects were placed on a 1-5 scale. The broadest focus was assigned to subjects who first bought the information comparing all entries on shared attributes, then proceeded to acquire information on specific horses. The narrowest focus was assigned to persons taking the riskier path of buying only a single piece of information. Other positions on the index were assigned to combinations between these two ends of the continuum.

Risk-taking was computed by multiplying the odds on the horse chosen (subjects were allowed only one bet per race) by the percentage of the subject's stake being bet (including the original stake plus any payoff from previous races). This number was divided by 2 if Ss bet to place, and 3 if Ss bet to show.

Closure was the amount of time lapsed —as recorded by stopwatch—between the time information tables opened after each race and the time Ss placed their bets; i.e., the time between attention and closure in the model. Closure times were divided into quartiles.

Success and *perceived availability of information* are actually consequent variables. The former is the amount of money won on a race. The latter is the

students' estimates (on a 1-5 scale) of the adequacy of their information choices.

The mood scale was one adapted by Greenberg[9] and further modified by Donohew and Palmgreen.[10] It measured eight moods: *aggression, concentration, deactivation, social affection, anxiety, depression, egotism* and *pleasantness*.

In all, there were 76 separate measures taken: the four personality or antecedent variables, a "pre-experiment" and four post-race assessments of the eight moods, measures of risk-taking and success for each race and four post-race assessments of the six information-strategy variables.

Analysis Procedure. Data were analyzed through Q-technique factor analysis. This procedure identifies clusters of *people* who, considering all the characteristics studied, tend to resemble each other—that is, it identifies "people types." A companion procedure then was applied to determine which characteristics were unique to particular types and which were common to all types.[11] The factor-analytic portion of the analysis, using a principal-axis solution with varimax rotation, accounted for 60% of the total variance.

Findings

Results of this analysis indicated that

[8] The strategies referred to here originally were conceptualized by Jerome Bruner, J.J. Goodnow and G.A. Austin in *A Study of Thinking* (New York: John Wiley, 1956) and modified slightly for use in this study. As presented in our original article (Donohew and Tipton, *op. cit.*), a broad-focus strategy is one that initially involves identifying potential sources of information and inputting them on a relatively non-selective basis—i.e., mapping a number of possible sources. Then the broad-focuser would review the information, select the best of it, and organize other information around it. A narrow-focus strategy, on the other hand, is one in which the individual at first focuses on one source of information and adds sources and ideas as he or she comes across them.

[9] Bradley S. Greenberg, "Performance and message consequences of encoding behavior under cognitive stress," unpublished Ph.D. dissertation, University of Wisconsin, 1961.

[10] *Ibid.*, 627-39.

[11] Under the procedure used here (see G. Norman Van Tubergen, *Quanal User's Guide*, Lexington, 1975), weightings for the factor matrix were computed according to the formula:

$$weight = \frac{r}{1-r^2}$$

where r = factor loading

Each row of the weighted factor matrix is examined and the highest positive loading for the person is located in order to compute factor arrays. All other loadings for the person are *(Continued)* there *were* distinct "styles" of information-seeking behavior consistently employed in coping with the situation involved here. Our analysis produced four types of persons, with information-seeking variables emerging as important attributes of three of the types. The characteristics described below discriminated among types by a z-score of absolute 1.0 or greater.

Type 1: Loners. This type, which had less prior knowledge than any of the others going into the game, seemed to be more affected by mood than by anything else. Persons falling into this type consistently indicated fewer feelings of pleasantness and egotism and more feelings of depression and deactivation than any of the others. They also interacted less with other people in giving and receiving information.

Type 2: Formal Seekers. A second type consistently scored higher than all other types in seeking information before making decisions. Persons belonging to this type perceived more information as being available to them and bought more of it. They also pursued the more comprehensive broad-focus strategy of seeking described in our model, choosing the safer course of buying comparative information about several horses rather than taking chances on one or two early choices. Their caution also extended through the point of decision-making. They extended their information search and brought about closure later than any other type. In contrast with the "loners," members of this type felt less depres-

set in zero. Here: N = number of people. n = number of items. P = number of types of F^{ik} is the weighted factor value of the jth variable on the kth type and D^{if} is the response of the Jth variable to the ith observation. Then:

$$A_{ik}^n = \Sigma$$

$j = 1$ D_{ij} F_{jk}, where $i = 1$. n and $k = 1$.

Since $F_{jk} = 0$ or F_{jk} = the highest positive loading for the jth variable, it is possible for a particular k that all F_{ij} are zero. The resulting array A_{ik} then also would be zero. If such a condition occurs, the zero array is eliminated at this point.

Following the check for zero arrays and completion of any necessary eliminations, the arrays A_{ik} are standardized to yield the arrays Z_{ik}. These present a standard (z) score for every item, i, on each type, k. Thus, the higher a given z score is for an item on a type, the stronger the response to that item by the people falling into that type.

sion, deactivation and aggression than anyone else. They also felt more pleasantness and less anxiety than any of the others.

Type 3: Risky Seekers. This type had more prior knowledge of the subject than any others. Perhaps as a consequence, its members took the riskier, though more parsimonious, path of information-seeking which we called a narrow-focus strategy. They tended to select quickly one or two horses from the list of entries, then to seek additional information about those horses. Possibly also as a result of their sophistication, they were more discriminating and perceived less information as being available to them. They also consistently reported feeling more egotistical, aggressive and depressed, and were lower in their reported need for variety. As might be expected, this type placed bets sooner than any of the others.

Type 4: Informal Seekers. This fourth type was distinguished from the others on two variables. First, the members reported the highest need for variety. They also were higher than all others on interpersonal communication. Members of this type reported giving information to and receiving it from more persons than those of any other type. These same persons also were lower than any of the others on the amount of information bought for three of the four races.

Discussion

The variables comprising the four types identified by the Q analysis fit together in logical and consistent ways and suggest some interesting questions for further research.

One fact that is obvious is the way our "antecedent" variables fell into the different types. Prior knowledge seems to be the most important, since it most clearly discriminates the "loners" and "risky seekers" from the other types. It makes intuitive sense that high prior knowledge would lead to the narrow-focus strategy and early closure adopted

FIGURE 2

Characteristics Describing The Four Types

Type I Loners	Type II Formal Seekers	Type III Risky Seekers	Type IV Informal Seekers
Higher than all other types on:	Higher than all other types on:	Higher than all other types on:	Higher than all other types on:
Feelings of deactivation p, 1, 2, 3, 4	Perceived avail. of Information 1, 2, 3, 4	Prior knowledge of topic	Variety seeking information given 1, 2, 3, 4
Feelings of depression p, 2*	Late closure 1, 3, 4	Feelings of egotism 1, 2, 3, 4	
Feelings of aggression 3	Feelings of pleasantness 2*	Feelings of anxiety 1, 4	Information received 1, 2, 3, 4
Early closure 1	Amt. of inf. bought (on races 2, 3, 4)	Feelings of depression 2*, 3, 4	Late closure 2
	Broad-focus strategy (on races, 1, 2, 3, 4)	Feelings of aggression 2, 4	Feelings of pleasantness 2*
		Narrow-focus strategy 2, 3, 4*	Narrow-focus strategy 4*
		Early closure, 2, 3, 4	
Lower than all other types on:	Lower than all other types on:	Lower than all other types on:	Lower than all other types on:
Prior knowledge of topic 2, 3, 4	Information rec'd, 1	Variety seeking	Amt. of inf. bought 2*, 3, 4
Info. given others 2, 3, 4	Feelings of deactivation p, 1, 2, 3, 4	Perceived avail. of info. 1, 2, 3, 4	Perceived avail. of info. 4
Info. received from others 3*, 4	Feelings of depression p, 2, 3, 4	Info. given others 1	Feelings of aggression 2*
Feelings of egotism 1, 2, 3*, 4	Feelings of aggression 2*, 3, 4	Info. received from others 2, 3*	Feelings of pleasantness 4
Feelings of pleasantness 2, 3	Feelings of anxiety 4	Amt. of info brought 2*	

p = pre-measure, before races stated
1, 2, 3, 4 = measured during or after race 1, 2, 3, 4
*tie with one other type

by the risky seekers. Along these same lines, we might also interpret the consistently higher feelings of egotism as "antecedent" rather than "consequent" variables. The relationship between low prior knowledge and the behavior of the "loners" is not so intuitively apparent. Perhaps these people simply did not get into the spirit of the game. Their consistently higher "deactivation" scores—indicating they were tired, sluggish and drowsy—support this suggestion.

Sensation (variety) seeking was the personality variable associated with the "informal seekers." After the first race, they used few formal sources. Instead they consistently went to interpersonal channels, both giving and receiving information. Whether or not their need for variety caused them to seek out other people, however, is not yet known.

One thing that is apparent in this situation is that people *didn't* change mood or seeking strategy from race to race, even though their winnings went up and down. In other words, observing the consequences of their actions from a prior race didn't seem to change their "images of reality" for later races. Some of the results were slightly different following the first race, but, as Figure 2 indicates, what they did or how they felt early on is how they continued to feel and do throughout, with few exceptions.

In this study, no single type had greater success than the others. In this instance, even those who didn't do much of anything in the way of information search before making decisions did as well as those who diligently tried to get good information before betting. In designing this study, we did not manipulate this success variable.

Winnings were awarded wherever they fell. It probably is fortunate that the winnings did not turn out to be concentrated in any one group. Otherwise they might have affected strategies that people used in later races and confused the patterns of "what goes with what."

Whether the same types of people—as defined largely by what they felt, thought and did—would be found in other situations is, of course, unknown. Would these same variables fit together in situations involving extremely serious issues? In trivial ones? Would there be considerably more information search by all types on the grave issues, for example? On this latter question, it would be difficult to predict at this point, because one can think of many examples in which persons have made far-reaching decisions basically affecting their lives almost on a whim.

On the basis of what is known up to now, there is not much to guide us in answering those questions. There have been numerous studies of decision-making and of information processing, but, beyond the studies that have been cited here, not much attention has been paid to the strategies that people use in *gathering* information—or to their reasons for not gathering it. Yet it seems that information-seeking must be one of our most fundamental methods for coping with our environment.[12] The strategies we learn to use in gathering information may turn out to be far more important in the long run than any specific pieces of knowledge we may pick up in our formal education and then soon forget as we go about wrestling with our day-to-day problems.

[12] See Harold M. Schroder, Michael J. Driver and Siegfried Streufert, *Human Information Processing* (New York: Holt, Rinehart and Winston, 1967).

Despite its importance, very few researchers have taken a macro-level, community perspective on mass communication. An exception is a research program that has been in progress for some time at the University of Minnesota. In this article, C. N. Olien, G. A. Donohue, and P. J. Tichenor describe data from nineteen Minnesota communities that illustrate the thesis that community size and structure tend to shape both the type of mass media and their coverage and the uses made of those media by the citizens of those communities. They conclude from their data that community structure is a principal element of media environment and information control. Dr. Olien is Associate Professor of Sociology; Dr. Donohue is Professor of Sociology; Dr. Tichenor is Professor of Journalism and Mass Communication, with a joint appointment in sociology; all are at the University of Minnesota.

22

COMMUNITY STRUCTURE AND MEDIA USE

C. N. Olien, G. A. Donohue, and P. J. Tichenor

*Media use and preferences
in 19 Minnesota communities
are related to community
size and structure.*

► Citizen choice among different media as sources of news is vital to the maintenance of a well-informed public. Several studies conclude that media choices are related to levels of understanding of public issues.[1] Usually, the higher the use of and preference for print media, the higher the level of knowledge about public affairs topics.

Given the relationships between media choice and understanding, it is important for both theory and social policy to understand better the circumstances that tend to determine or limit media choices. The purpose of this article is to analyze data on the extent to which community type and structure may affect media choice, both in terms of *use* of media, and in terms of *preference* for different media as sources of information. A closely related question is whether structural differences are more important than community educational level in explaining such differences.

The central thesis is that community size and structure, as determinants

of the type of newspaper that covers that community, tend to shape uses that citizens make of newspapers and television and their relative preferences as well. Daily newspaper reading is expected to be higher and television use lower in communities in which the principal local newspaper is a daily rather than a weekly. Correspondingly, preference for newspapers as a source of news is expected to be lower, and preference for television higher, in weekly newspaper communities than in larger and more pluralistic communities served by daily papers. These differences are expected to hold regardless of differences in level of education, according to the principle that structural factors tend to operate over and above individual differences in directing and limiting human behavior.

Communities with semi-weekly papers would be expected to be intermediate on these measures. The emphasis is on television rather than radio, since television is generally found to be a major and growing source of news among citizens.[2]

Community Structure and Type of Newspaper. The hypothesis under test assumes that community structure determines the type of local newspaper. In Minnesota, among 293 communities with populations of 10,000 or less,

[1] John P. Robinson, "Mass Communication and Information Diffusion," Chapter 3 in F. Gerald Kline and P. J. Tichenor, editors, *Current Perspectives in Mass Communication Research*, Vol. I, Sage Annual Reviews of Communication Research, 1972. Also, see Wilbur Schramm and Serena Wade, *Knowledge and the Public Mind*, Stanford University Institute for Communication Research, Stanford, California, 1967.

[2] *An Extended View of Public Attitudes toward Television and Other Mass Media, 1959-1971*, Television Information Office, N.Y., 1971. Also, see Leo Bogart, "Changing News Interests and the News Media," *Public Opinion Quarterly*, 32: 560-574 (Winter 1968-69).

► The authors are associate professor, professor of sociology and professor of journalism and mass communication, respectively, at the University of Minnesota. Data are from studies supported by projects 27-18 and 27-19, Minnesota Agricultural Experiment Station, and by the Minnesota School of Journalism & Mass Communication Research Division. The study is also partially supported by the University of Minnesota computer center.

From C. N. Olien et al., "Community Structure and Media Use," *Journalism Quarterly* 55 (Autumn 1978) 445-455. Reprinted by permission.

all except four (1.4%) have weekly or twice weekly papers. Above that population level, 54.7% have dailies, and above 50,000, all except one (a suburb) have daily newspapers.[3]

Size is important, not in itself, but because it produces greater structural heterogeneity leading to different media functions and choices. Weekly papers tend to cover communities which are relatively homogeneous and which place a high value on news about the community. Newspapers in such communities are both maintained and limited by existing institutions—economic, political, educational, ethnic and voluntaristic. Weekly papers in small communities tend to concentrate on the consensus aspect of local affairs in the interest of maintaining a state of tranquility and avoiding social disruption which small community structures, based upon personal contact and communication patterns, do not tolerate well.[4]

If a community is more pluralistic, in the sense of containing more diverse centers of potential social power, it is more likely to be served by a daily newspaper since both diversity and daily publication are products of increased size. A daily in a more complex urban setting is more likely to report a broad range of local as well as state and national news, emphasizing the controversial aspect of public issues in the interest of maintaining communication among the multiple interest groups in the community and in society at large. Such emphasis on conflict is not necessarily disruptive, but is part of the process of resolving conflicts and managing them at tolerable levels. In this sense, conflict reporting may be functional for maintaining the stability of the system as a whole.

Semi-weeklies, usually in communities intermediate in size between those of weeklies and dailies, also tend to be intermediate in coverage of state topics and of external matters generally.

Theoretically, newspapers depend upon their link to community identity in fulfilling their functions.[5] But if none of the available daily newspapers serves that link, citizens are not likely to have the same attachment for newspapers as a whole. Weekly newspapers are faced with a perpetual paradox. They may be highly valued for maintenance of the local community and its institutions, but they deal little or not at all with the larger social system. State, national and international issues are increasingly relevant to communities of all types as society becomes increasingly complex. *Inter*dependence among regions and communities, and *de*pendence of the community on external forces both grow in proportion to the increases in diversity and in control by centralized decision-making structures which have occurred in recent years. With its nearly exclusive concentration on the local scene, the weekly community paper leaves a functional void in the reporting of the larger social system.

One might ask whether this "missing function" in a weekly newspaper town is filled largely by out-of-town daily newspapers, or by television. There are several reasons why the tendency might be toward television rather than dailies. One is the very fact that, being oriented toward a specific but *different* community, the out-of-town daily is less functional even if it is relatively easy to receive. In spite of its regional coverage, a daily from a more or less distant and larger city does not address local concerns the way the hometown weekly does, or the way the daily itself does for its own urban locality. Regional dailies

[3] Minnesota Newspaper Association annual directory. Minneapolis, Minnesota, 1976. In an Iowa study, the correlation between community population and newspaper circulation was .84. See L.R. Whiting, Mass Media Gatekeepers and Community Development: Aspects of role, perceptions and performance, unpublished M.S. Thesis, Iowa State University, 1976.

[4] G. A. Donohue, P. J. Tichenor and C. N. Olien, "Mass Media Functions, Knowledge and Social Control," JOURNALISM QUARTERLY, 50: 652-659 (Winter 1973).

[5] Leo Bogart and Frank E. Orenstein, "Mass Media and Community Identity in an Interurban Setting," JOURNALISM QUARTERLY, 42:179-188 (Spring 1965).

do not cover the local routine in outlying towns, but highlight only the more universal occurrences in those places, which are also likely to be covered by television.

It is not merely a case of "reader demand" working against an out-of-town daily newspaper, although individual reader preferences may be involved. The out-of-town daily, as a result of its identification with the group, economic and political life of another place does not have the same institutional support locally as does the hometown weekly. Support of local institutions is expressed in several ways, through such acts as bringing news to the paper, developing relationships with editors and reporters, and providing advertising. As Larkin and Grotta learned in an Oklahoma study, a small daily may be highly valued in its hometown for its advertising, which may be seen as a major part of the paper's community role.[6] Such advertising in the newspaper concentrates on retail establishments within the home city and, therefore, is of little relevance to populations outside that community's trade area.

Television, on the other hand, may derive much of its popularity as a source of external news from the very fact that it has minimal community identification. The entertainment content of television is largely national and advertising is mostly for individual products not tied to specific local stores. Television has no classified ads. Yet, television is easily available, with its news programs covering much of the same state, national and international events that appear on front pages of daily newspapers. Its dramatic oral and visual character add to its news appeal. Such appeal, coupled with television's detachment from any specific community and its more or less equivalent treatment of different communities may add to the relatively greater dependence upon television compared with dis-

tant newspapers, as a source of regional, state, national and international news. Whereas distant newspapers may be rejected because of their other-town character, television may be acceptable partly because it lacks that negative feature.

The reasoning thus far applies to larger cities and smaller separated towns. But what about suburban areas served by weeklies? Would the easy availability of metropolitan dailies lead to as high a dependence on newspapers as in the urban center itself? According to the perspective here, the expected answer would be no, acknowledging the likelihood that suburbanite reading of the big city daily varies directly with the strength of surburbanites' ties to that city. Within that setting, suburban communities have a degree of independence which is born of interdependence. Functioning as politically separate bedroom communities, they make it possible for residents to establish a relatively autonomous home life among neighbors with a relatively narrow range of ethnic and socioeconomic background, in school districts totally separate from the inner city. Suburban independence depends heavily on carefully maintained political separation, whereas small town independence results from physical distance as well as political boundaries. Just as reading about one's home town in a regional daily is not the same as reading about it in the local weekly, reading about one's suburb in the "neighborhood" section of a metro daily may be far different from seeing it in the suburban community press.

The 19 Communities Analyzed. Data for analysis are from survey studies conducted in 19 different community areas in Minnesota since 1969. Each community was represented by an area probability sample of adults interviewed in their homes by local interviewers trained specifically for the respective study. Sample sizes varied from 88 to 183. The communities were selected to reflect variation in size and structure, type of newspaper and occurrence of pub-

---

[6] Ernest F. Larkin and Gerald L. Grotta. "Consumer attitudes toward and use of advertising content in a small daily newspaper." *Journal of Advertising,* 5: pp 28-31 (Winter 1976).

TABLE 1

Characteristics of Communities and Their Newspaper Content

Community Characteristics	Weekly Newspaper Towns (N:10)	Semi-Weekly Newspaper Towns (N:3)	Daily Newspaper Towns (N:6)
Average population	5,770.00	8,533.00	39,733.00
Average number of businesses	288.00	460.00	1,650.00
Average number of voluntary groups	8.20	52.67	9.00
Average number of churches	14.40	15.67	54.50
Average number of schools	7.80	9.00	35.00
Newspaper Content Characteristics*			
Newshole, average size in column inches per edition	1,058.00	959.00	1,349.00
Average percent newshole devoted to *all* local news and public affairs	90.8	90.0	40.5
Average percent newshole devoted to *local public affairs only*	21.0	19.3	17.8
Average percent of newshole devoted to state and national public affairs	7.3	8.7	55.8

*Content measures are based on per-edition averages for all editions published the month before the survey study was conducted.

lic affairs issues. Ten of the communities are served by weekly papers, three by semi-weekly papers and six by dailies.

Daily newspaper use in each community is the average number of daily papers which respondents reported reading twice per week or more. Television use is average hours reported spent viewing each day. Preference measures for each medium are based upon answers to the following question: Between television, radio and the newspapers, which *one* do you prefer most as a source of news these days?

While this question emphasizes the *one* medium most preferred, there were frequently small percentages, usually less than 7%, who nevertheless mentioned two media or more, even following a restatement of the question. Since the overlap is negligible, it was not separated out in this analysis, and preference scores are the *total* percentages in each community mentioning each medium.

Differences in Communities and Newspapers. The assumption that community structure is related to type of local newspaper is also supported by data from these 19 communities (Table 1). The weekly communities average 5,770 in population, with an average of 288 businesses per community. By contrast, the six daily communities average nearly 40,000 in population, with 1,650 businesses each. The three semi-weekly newspaper communities are intermediate on all pluralism measures, although they are clearly more like the weekly than the daily communities.

Similarly, differences in newspaper content are sharpest between the weeklies and semi-weeklies on the one hand, compared with dailies on the other. About 90% of the weekly and semi-weekly news space is devoted to local news, compared with just over 40% for the dailies. However, proportion of space devoted to local *public affairs* news differs little across

FIGURE 1

Type of Newspaper and Mean Daily Reading
in 19 Communities

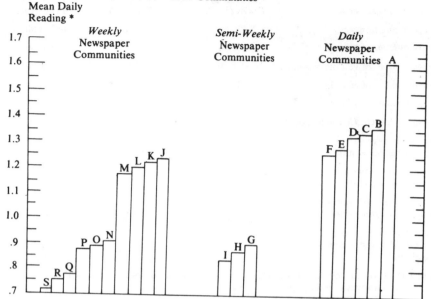

* "Mean Daily Reading" refers to the average number of daily newspapers reported as read twice per week or more by respondents in each community.

Difference between communities p <.025 by Mann-Whitney U Test, weeklies compared with others.

papers. The bulk of the news in the smaller papers is social events and athletics, quite apart from political news or reports of public agencies and institutions. Also, the larger diet of state and national news in the dailies is apparent; over half (55.8%) of the daily paper news is state and national public affairs, compared with well under a tenth for weeklies and semi-weeklies.

Results

Use of Daily Newspapers and Television. The first part of the proposition under test is that daily newspaper reading will be lower, and television viewing higher, in communities in which the local paper is a weekly rather than a daily. The data in Figure 1 generally provide strong support for this. Average daily reading is higher

in each of the six daily communities than in any one of the non-daily communities. Two specific findings here are especially noteworthy. One is that weekly communities S (lowest daily reading of all) M and N are metropolitan suburbs, contiguous with each other, in a county in which morning and evening daily papers with circulation in excess of 200,000 are published. A second point is that daily newspaper reading is extremely low in the three communities served by semi-weekly newspapers, a finding which is not consistent with the expectation that semi-weeklies would be intermediate on all measures. All three are similar in size and are predominantly rural areas that are well outside the fringes of urban centers where dailies are published.

In the non-daily communities, television viewing tends to be higher as expected (Figure 2). Again, the three semi-weekly

FIGURE 2

Type of Newspaper and Median TV Viewing
in 19 Communities

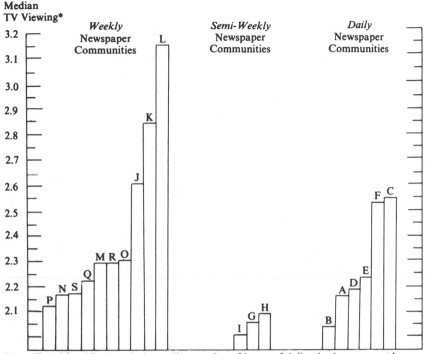

* "Mean Television Viewing" is the median number of hours of daily viewing reported by respondents in each community.

Difference between communities, p <.05 by Mann-Whitney U Test weeklies against others.

communities stand apart, this time having lower levels of television viewing than either of the other two groups of communities.

The relationship between weekly availability and use of other media is also illustrated by a comparison of level of weekly reading with levels of other media use, across the 19 communities. The rank correlation coefficient for weekly and daily reading is -.52, significant at the .05 level; for weekly reading and television viewing it is positive as expected (.35) although not significant.

In general, then, data support the conclusion that community structure, through determining types of newspapers available, tends to determine uses which citizens make of different media.

Type of Community and Media Preference. Data also tend to support the second part of the hypothesis that type of medium covering a community is related to preferences for media as sources of news. Findings for percent mentioning newspapers as a "preferred source of news" are in Figure 3, for the 16 communities where the question was asked.[7] Four of the five daily communities are at or near the top of the distribution. The one daily community

[7] Communities D, N and P are not included in the preference tables, since the preference question was not asked in those places in the same way and results are therefore not comparable.

FIGURE 3

Type of Newspaper and Percent Preferring Newspapers
as Source of News in 16 Communities

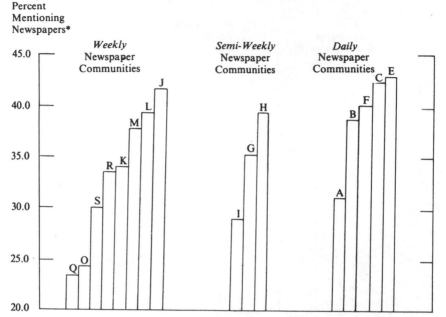

*The question asked in each community was "Between television, radio and the newspapers, which one do you prefer most as a source of news these days?" The three first communities studied—Osseo, St. Cloud and Wright County—are not included, since the item was worded differently in those cases.

with under 35% mentioning newspapers, community A, has one of the smallest dailies in circulation in the Midwest. Weeklies tend to be lower on preference with semi-weeklies intermediate on this measure. So while the differences are not as sharp as with measures of use, they are clearly in the predicted direction.

Similarly, television preference as a source of news is higher in the weekly communities, again as predicted (Figure 4), with daily communities lower. As with newspaper preference, semi-weekly communities tend also to be intermediate on television preference.

Level of weekly reading is inversely related to newspaper preference and positively related to television preference, again in line with the test proposition. The

rank correlation coefficient across these 16 communities for level of weekly reading and newspaper preference is -.52; for weekly reading and television preference it is .50. With daily reading, the relationships are opposite in sign, .59 for newspaper preference and -.36 for television preference. The first three of these coefficients are significant at the .05 level.

Level of Education and Media Use and Preference. Among different aspects of community structure, level of education is often related to media use and preference. Westley and Severin found education not related to time spent reading newspapers but

FIGURE 4

Type of Newspaper and Percent Preferring TV
as Source of News in 16 Communities

Percent
Mentioning
Television

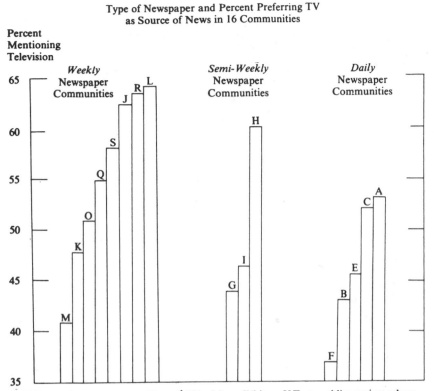

Difference between communities p < .05 by Mann-Whitney U Test weeklies against others.

closely related to preferences.[8] As education went up, preferences for newspapers increased and preferences for television declined, a finding reported in other studies.[9] Within the communities in this study, correlations tended to be low and positive between respondent education and daily newspaper reading, and low and negative between education and television viewing time.

Shifting to the community level of analysis, one might ask whether education level of the community is a key variable underlying the observed differences in media uses and preferences among communities. The larger and more pluralistic communities served by dailies in the study also have higher average levels of education. But given the fact that a community has a particular kind of

newspaper, does the overall level of education make a further difference?

The data support the structural hypothesis that community differences are more important than educational level. The rank correlations between community education level and use and preference measures are consistently weaker than between community pluralism ranking (based on a summary index of items in Table 1) and media scores. The rank correlation between pluralism and daily newspaper reading across the 19 com-

[8] Bruce H. Westley and Werner Severin. "How Wisconsinites use and appraise their daily newspapers and other media," School of Journalism mimeo report, University of Wisconsin, Madison, 1963.

[9] See, for example, Bradley S. Greenberg and Brenda Dervin, "Communications and related behaviors of a sample of low-income urban adults compared with a general population sample," Project CUP report sl, Department of Communication. Michigan State University, East Lansing, 1967.

FIGURE 5

Mean Daily Newspaper Reading
According to Type of Newspaper and Level of Education
in 19 Minnesota Communities

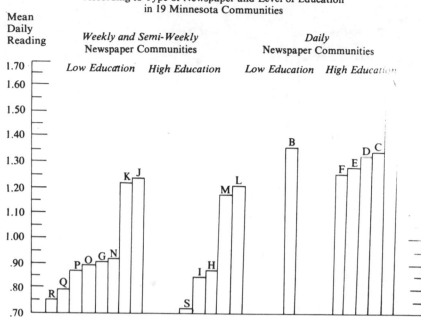

High Education includes communities with a median level of education of 12 years or higher.

munities is .64 (p<.05) whereas the correlation between educational level and daily newspaper reading level is only .22 and nonsignificant.

As a further check, communities are separated according to whether their median level of education is under or over 12 years (Figure 5). The only daily community with education below the median level is B, which is second highest on the daily reading score. Among weeklies and semi-weeklies combined, there is little difference in reading, with both high and low education communities spread across the range.

Community level of education may, however, be somewhat of a factor in newspaper *preference* when community type is controlled. The one daily community with low education (B) is second lowest of the five daily communities on the preference measure. Among high-education communities with non-daily papers, H, L and M are next to the top of the distribution on preference, but S and I are well below the middle of the range for smaller papers.

It is clear that the principal differences are by type of community and type of medium, which go together. Level of education is secondary, with its effects conditioned by community structure. The findings as a whole are consistent with the conclusion that community structural factors tend to determine the media available in a community, and that this media environment both produces and limits, to a considerable degree, the uses that the community population as a whole makes of media and their preferences among media as sources of information. This finding would probably not be apparent using high and low educated respondents as the units of analyses, as the data indicate.

Uses and Preferences in Suburban Areas. Importance of the media structure may be illustrated in another way in three cases where weekly papers cover communities which are suburban, rather than rural. These are suburban communities M, N and S, with S having the lowest daily reading of all. All three are contiguous, in the same area of a metropolitan county, and the results should be viewed as tentative and with considerable caution.[10] Nevertheless, the fact that daily newspaper use and newspaper preference are relatively low and television preference is high in these communities seems illustrative of the difficulty metropolitan newspapers often have in maintaining circulation in their nearby suburbs.[11] The question clearly merits further and more extensive research, but these findings raise a question about whether suburban weeklies do or do not compete directly with metropolitan daily newspapers for customers. Suburban citizens have a high level of choice may not produce a high community-wide orientation toward newspapers, but may instead lead to high media *specialization* in a suburb. Such specialization arising from multiple sources of information may have far-reaching implications for distribution of social power that thrives on imbalances in information.

Discussion

Community structure, then, is a principal element of information control. Through determining the type of media environment, structure tends to shape the use that citizens make of different media, and their relative preferences for these media as sources of news. As a consequence, the configuration of information available to the average citizen tends to differ sharply from one community to another.

Quantitative differences in newspaper information can be estimated by comparing a typical community having a weekly, such as 0, with a typical community having a daily, such as C. By weighting the content data in Table 1 by the average number of dailies read in these two communities, one can conclude that in a week the average adult in community C is potentially exposed to about 2000 column inches of local public affairs, or 133% as much as in community O. In state and national affairs news, the estimated potential exposure each week is to about 6,300 column inches in community C, which in this case is about 154% as much as in O. So the typical citizen in the community served by a weekly gets less newspaper news in both catetories and has a lower preference for the papers that report it, compared with his or her urban cousin.

Such differences in the newspaper information environment in the two communities may have a number of outcomes for level of citizen understanding and participation in public issues, one being a lower level of familiarity with state, national and international affairs. For understanding of local issues, however, the outcomes are not entirely clear and require additional study.

A quite different set of consequences might be expected if one takes into account the greater homogeneity of interests in the community with a weekly and also assumes, as Chaffee and Wilson found, that there is less diversity in information held in areas that are "media poor" as well as less diverse in other structural characteristics.[12] If the information in the system is confined to a smaller num-

[10] These data do not necessarily conflict with Bogart and Orenstein's finding that readership of newspapers from a given city among "interurban" residents is related to strength of ties to that city by individuals. See Bogart and Orenstein, op. cit.

[11] Leo Bogart, "The future of the metropolitan daily," *Journal of Communication,* 25: 30-43 (Spring 1975).

[12] Steven H. Chaffee and Donna Wilson, "Media rich, media poor: Two studies of diversity in agenda-holding," paper presented to Association for Education in Journalism, College Park, Md., August, 1976.

ber of issues and points of view, there is less competion for attention and concern if one of those issues is heavily publicized. An important proposition for testing is that less diversity in both information and total structure of the community will lead to more total involvement of the population in those cases, perhaps relatively rare, when community newspapers concentrate on a crisis situation. This proposition is consistent with Coleman's conclusion that "self-contained" communities (economically homogeneous) may, although infrequently, produce highly intense con-

[13] James S. Coleman, *Community Conflict*, (New York: Free Press, 1957), p. 6.

troversies.[13] In cities having dailies, conflict is a way of life; there are different controversies in the more pluralistic city environment and citizens are more likely to develop a more balanced perspective as a result. Urban citizens have more information about more conflict issues but may be less intensely aroused by any one of them, compared with their small-town counterparts. This proposition, about diversity in community structure and information as they relate to citizen involvement, could have far-reaching consequences for information control and therefore social control if it is borne out by further evidence.

PART V

CRIME AND VIOLENCE
IN MASS COMMUNICATION

This section is a symposium of studies and essays organized around the cultural indicators of George Gerbner and Larry Gross. Both European and American analyses of the cultural indicators work are included.

In general, the attempt by Gerbner and Gross to theorize about the cultural-ideological role of television is applauded. But researchers from both sides of the Atlantic question the validity of the cultural indicators methodology. Other research raises questions about the survey methodology of the cultivation analysis.

23

THE DEMONSTRATION OF POWER
Violence Profile No. 10

*George Gerbner, Larry Gross, Nancy Signorielli,
Michael Morgan, and Marilyn Jackson-Beeck*

*Annual progress report sums up findings suggesting that
fear and inequity may be television's most pervasive
lessons; 1978 Index shows violence up in children's hours.*

"Then," asked Socrates in Plato's *Republic*, "shall we simply allow our children to listen to any stories that anyone happens to make up, and so receive into their minds ideas often the very opposite of those we shall think they ought to have when they grow up?"

Plato was probably not the first to articulate a concern over the effects of story-telling on young minds; he certainly was not the last. Parents have always been understandably wary of those who wish to entertain or educate their children.

Traditionally, the only acceptable extra-familial storytellers were those certified by religious institutions. With the growth of educational institutions, also originally religious, a new group of storytellers interceded between children and the world.

The emergence of mass media fundamentally altered the picture. Children were increasingly open to influences which parents, priests, and teachers could not monitor or control. Beginning with the widespread availability of printed materials for the literate, enlarged by the availability of movies and radio, and culminating with the omnipresence of television, the opportunities for children

George Gerbner, Larry Gross, Nancy Signorielli, and Michael Morgan are members of the Cultural Indicators research team at The Annenberg School of Communications, University of Pennsylvania. Marilyn Jackson-Beeck is Assistant Professor at the Department of Communication, Cleveland State University. This research is conducted under grants from the National Institute of Mental Health and the American Medical Association. A Technical Report is available for $17.50 from the first author (checks to be made payable to the Trustees of the University of Pennsylvania). Portions of this article will also appear in (6).

to directly consume mass-produced stories have rivaled traditional methods of instruction about the world. Plato's ancient question reverberates vividly for parents as they confront today's storyteller.

The televised stories that generate the most concern seem to be those that contain scenes of violence. Why should this be? Even when committed in the name of law and order, acts of physical aggression are suspected of inciting impressionable viewers to commit similar acts. This is, as we shall see later, an invariable reaction of "established classes"—adults in this case—when members of "subservient classes"—children, here—are exposed to mass-mediated stories.

Another reason for concern about TV violence is the frequency of aggressive acts depicted in television drama, particularly in programs aimed specifically at children. It has often been noted that by the time the average American child graduates from high school, he or she will have seen more than 13,000 violent deaths on television. Given the sheer amount of children's potential exposure to televised violence, we worry that children will become jaded, desensitized, and inured to violence not only on television but in real life as well.

In the thirty years that we have lived with television, public concern with the medium's predilection for violence has been reflected in at least eight separate congressional hearings, a special report to the National Commission on the Causes and Prevention of Violence in 1969, and a massive study of television and social behavior commissioned by the Surgeon General. These hearings and reports have focused largely on the prevalence and effects of televised violence and culminated in a five-volume report issued in 1972 (2). In the years since 1972, the flow of research and debate has continued. While scientific caution requires us to proceed carefully, some conclusions can be drawn from the wealth of data and evidence that has been accumulated.

First, violence is a frequent and consistent feature of television drama. In our research violence is defined as the overt expression of physical force, with or without a weapon, against self or other, compelling action against one's will on pain of being hurt or killed, or actually hurting or killing. Using this definition we have been analyzing a sample of prime-time and weekend morning network dramatic television programs annually since 1967-68 and have found that, on the average, 8 out of every 10 programs and 6 out of every 10 major characters are involved in violence. The average rate of episodes of violence has been 7½ per hour, and in weekend daytime children's programs, violent episodes average almost 18 per hour.

Second, there appears to be a justifiable fear that viewing televised violence will make people, children in particular, somewhat more likely to commit acts of violence themselves. At the time of the Surgeon General's report in 1972, about 50 experimental studies indicated that viewing violence increases the likelihood of children engaging in violent behavior, at least in the short-term context of the laboratory. Although the experimental findings are not always generalizable to real-life situations in which many other behavioral factors, e.g., reprisal, are included, the impact of these experimental studies was strengthened by survey research which found positive correlations between everyday vi-

"Of course it makes a big difference whether they learned that from some heroic John Wayne movie or a cheap crime program."

olence viewing and aggression among adolescents in real life (1). Moreover, these relationships were not accounted for by other factors—socioeconomic status, sex, school achievement—which often prove quite helpful in explaining adolescent behavior. Our own research (4) also has found that young viewers who watch a lot of television are more likely to agree that it is "almost always all right" to hit someone "if you are mad at them for a good reason."

Yet, if the most consistent effect of viewing television violence were that it incited real acts of violence, we would not need elaborate research studies; the average sibling, parent, and teacher would be reeling from the blows of television-stimulated aggression. Clearly this is not the case. Imitative aggression among children may be frequent but it is relatively low-level. Widely publicized cases of serious violence which seem to be influenced by television programs or movies are rare. At any rate, spectacular cases of individual violence threatening the social order (unlike those enforcing it) have always been "blamed" on some corrupter of youth, from Socrates through pulps, comics, and movies, to television. Are there no other grounds for concern?

> *In order to answer this question, we must begin with a fuller understanding of the total phenomenon of television.*

All societies have ways of explaining the world to themselves and to their children. Socially constructed "reality" gives a coherent picture of what exists, what is important, how things are related, and what is right. The constant cultivation of such "realities" is the task of rituals and mythologies. They legitimize actions along lines which are conventionally acceptable and functional.

Television is the mainstream of that cultural process (see 3,4). It is an agency of the established order and as such serves primarily to maintain, stabilize, and reinforce—not subvert—conventional values, beliefs, and behaviors. The goal of the greatest audience appeal at the least cost demands that these messages follow conventional social morality.

Two further assumptions underlie our research, called Cultural Indicators. One is that commercial television, unlike other media, presents an organically composed total world of interrelated stories (both drama and news) produced to the same set of market specifications. Second, television audiences (unlike those for other media) view largely non-selectively and by the clock rather than by the program. Television viewing is a ritual, almost like religion, except that it is attended to more regularly.

Most regular viewers are immersed in a vivid and illuminating world of television (mostly drama) which has certain repetitive and pervasive patterns. One feature is that men outnumber women three to one. Thus much of the action revolves around questions of social order and of power, on the streets, in the professions, and in the home.

Violence plays a key role in television's portrayal of the social order. It is the simplest and cheapest dramatic means to demonstrate who wins in the game of life and the rules by which the game is played. It tells us who are the aggressors and who are the victims. It demonstrates who has the power and who must acquiesce to that power. It tells us who should be feared—and by that achieves the goal of real-life violence. The few incidents of real-life violence it incites only serve to reinforce this fear. In the portrayal of violence there is a relationship between the roles of the violent and the victim. Both roles are there to be learned by the viewers. In generating among the many a fear of the power of the few, television violence may achieve its greatest effect.

We have addressed this hypothesis in the Cultural Indicators project by analyzing the world of television drama, including measures of violence, and by determining the extent to which exposure to this *symbolic* world cultivates conceptions about the *real* world among viewers. Our Violence Profile No. 10 focusing on the 1978-79 season continues to report what we have found.

> *Violence in weekend children's and late evening*
> *programming on all three networks rose to near*
> *record levels in the fall of 1978.*

The 1978 sample was composed of one week of prime-time dramatic programming and one weekend of daytime (children's) dramatic programming (8 a.m. to 2 p.m.) for all three networks. This yielded 111 programs and 298 major characters for analysis. The levels of violence were measured by determining the prevalence and rate of violent actions and characterizations. To compute the Violence Index we sum five measures: percent of programs containing any violence, twice the rate of violent incidents per program, twice the rate of violent incidents per hour, the percent of characters involved in any violence, and the percent of characters involved in killing. A summary of the components of the annual Violence Index for the years 1967-1978 is presented in Table 1.

The 1978 Violence Index (see Table 2) shows an increase over the 1977 Index for weekend children's and late evening (9-11 p.m. EST) programming, although a decrease was shown in the prevalence and rate of violence in the former "family hour" (8-9 p.m. EST) programs (see Figure 1). This overall in-

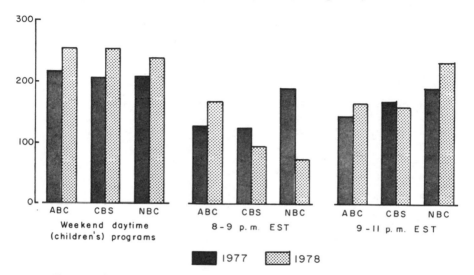

Figure 1: Changes in Violence Index by network and program time, 1977-1978

crease comes after declines in the level of violence registered for the 1977-78 season and network declarations and assurances of further reductions, especially during children's programming hours.[1]

The overall level of weekend (children's) programming containing violence climbed to 97.9 percent. The rate of violent incidents in children's programs zoomed from 15.6 per hour in 1977 to a near record level of 25.0 per hour in 1978 (more than five times the prime-time rate). The index for new children's programs jumped 52 points over last year's index for new children's shows, the largest increase in any category. Continuing children's programs became more violent by 31 points. By contrast, continuing prime-time programs increased in violence by only 3 points.

---

[1] For example, Frederick S. Pierce, President of ABC Television, told the National Education Association convention in the spring of 1978 that "we have set some specific goals and standards for children's programming. A critical one has been the elimination of interpersonal violence." In the fall of 1978, all measures of violence in ABC children's programming were significantly higher than the year before. The ABC weekend daytime rate of violent incidents per hour, for example, jumped from 16.0 in 1977 to 26.3 in 1978. The ABC Violence Index for weekend daytime programming in 1978 was its highest since our study started in 1967-68 (see Tables 2 and 3).

Table 1: Violence Index components (1967-1978)

	67-68[1]	69-70[1]	71-72[1]	1973	74-75[2]	75-76[2]	1976	1977[3]	1978[4]	Total 67-78
All Programs N =	183	232	203	99	192	226	110	192	111	1548
% Programs w/violence	81.4	80.6	79.8	72.7	80.7	77.4	89.1	75.5	84.7	79.9
Rate per program	4.8	4.9	5.0	5.3	5.4	5.2	6.2	5.0	5.8	5.2
Rate per hour	7.2	8.1	7.2	7.0	6.9	7.7	9.5	6.7	8.3	7.5
% Characters involved in violence	69.5	65.1	58.8	55.7	64.6	64.2	74.8	60.9	64.8	64.0
Violence Index	190	178	174	160	183	177	204	166	183	178
Weekend-Daytime N =	62	107	81	37	77	92	49	53	48	606
% Programs w/violence	93.5	97.2	88.9	94.6	93.5	90.2	100.0	90.6	97.9	93.7
Rate per program	5.2	6.5	6.0	6.7	5.1	5.1	6.9	4.9	7.5	5.9
Rate per hour	22.3	25.5	16.0	13.2	12.2	14.2	22.4	15.6	25.0	17.7
% Characters involved in violence	84.3	89.7	73.5	77.2	71.7	81.1	85.6	77.2	86.0	80.3
Violence Index	242	253	208	212	201	211	247	209	249	223
Prime-Time N =	121	125	122	62	115	134	61	139	63	942
% Programs w/violence	75.2	66.4	73.8	59.7	72.2	68.7	80.3	69.8	74.6	71.0
Rate per program	4.5	3.5	4.4	4.5	5.6	5.3	5.6	5.0	4.5	4.8
Rate per hour	5.2	3.9	4.8	4.9	5.4	6.0	6.1	5.5	4.5	5.1
% Characters involved in violence	64.4	49.4	53.9	41.1	60.5	55.0	67.4	55.5	52.9	55.7
Violence Index	176	140	159	132	174	160	183	154	153	159
8-9 P.M. EST N =	74	73	55	32	54	61	25	65	27	466
% Programs w/violence	77.0	60.3	74.5	56.3	63.0	52.5	72.0	66.2	59.3	65.0
Rate per program	4.9	2.8	4.2	4.6	3.6	2.7	3.8	4.2	3.0	3.8
Rate per hour	6.4	3.9	4.8	5.1	3.9	4.1	4.7	5.3	4.0	4.7
% Characters involved in violence	66.3	46.1	50.0	40.9	46.2	37.0	55.1	53.2	39.2	49.0
Violence Index	186	127	150	126	138	104	145	140	116	139
9-11 P.M. EST N =	47	52	67	30	61	73	36	74	36	476
% Programs w/violence	72.3	75.0	73.1	63.3	80.3	82.2	86.1	73.0	86.1	76.9
Rate per program	4.0	4.3	4.5	4.3	7.4	7.6	6.9	5.8	5.6	5.7
Rate per hour	3.8	3.9	4.8	4.7	6.6	6.9	6.8	5.7	4.8	5.4
% Characters involved in violence	61.5	54.2	57.1	41.3	72.8	68.4	75.7	57.1	62.5	61.8
Violence Index	162	158	167	137	205	203	209	165	180	178

[1] These figures are based upon two samples collected in the fall of each of these years.

[2] These figures are based upon two samples -- one from the fall and one from the spring.

[3] The Fall 1977 sample consists of two weeks of prime-time and one weekend of daytime network dramatic programs. A total of 192 programs and 585 major characters were analyzed.

[4] The Fall 1978 sample consists of one week of prime-time and one weekend of daytime network dramatic programming. A total of 111 programs and 298 major characters were analyzed.

Table 2: Violence Index components for 1977 and 1978 by network

	All Networks		ABC		CBS		NBC	
	1977[1]	1978[2]	1977[1]	1978[2]	1977[1]	1978[2]	1977[1]	1978[2]
All Programs N =	192	111	59	35	80	48	53	28
% Programs w/violence	75.5	84.7	74.6	88.6	70.0	85.4	84.9	78.6
Rate per program	5.0	5.8	4.3	5.7	5.0	5.5	5.7	6.5
Rate per hour	6.7	8.3	6.0	8.1	7.4	9.8	6.4	6.9
% Characters involved in violence	60.9	64.8	55.8	66.3	58.0	63.9	70.7	64.3
Violence Index	166	183	154	186	159	183	190	179
Weekend-Daytime N =	53	48	16	11	21	26	16	11
% Programs w/violence	90.6	97.9	93.8	100.0	85.7	100.0	93.8	90.9
Rate per program	4.9	7.5	5.4	9.5	4.5	6.7	4.8	7.2
Rate per hour	15.6	25.0	16.0	26.3	15.2	26.8	15.7	20.6
% Characters involved in violence	77.2	86.0	79.2	81.5	80.8	86.0	71.1	91.3
Violence Index	209	249	216	253	206	253	206	238
Prime-Time N =	139	63	43	24	59	22	37	17
% Programs w/violence	69.8	74.6	67.4	83.3	64.4	68.2	81.1	70.6
Rate per program	5.0	4.5	3.9	3.9	5.2	4.0	6.1	6.0
Rate per hour	5.5	4.5	4.5	4.6	6.4	4.4	5.3	4.6
% Characters involved in violence	55.5	52.9	48.3	60.0	51.2	44.6	70.6	54.1
Violence Index	154	153	136	165	146	136	188	159
8-9 P.M. EST N =	65	27	21	12	27	8	17	7
% Programs w/violence	66.2	59.3	66.7	83.3	55.6	50.0	82.4	28.6
Rate per program	4.2	3.0	3.1	2.3	4.0	2.0	5.8	5.6
Rate per hour	5.3	4.0	4.5	3.4	5.9	2.9	5.4	5.6
% Characters involved in violence	53.2	39.2	44.3	62.1	46.2	33.3	76.6	20.7
Violence Index	140	116	126	167	123	93	188	72
9-11 P.M. EST N =	74	36	22	12	32	14	20	10
% Programs w/violence	73.0	86.1	68.2	83.3	71.9	78.6	80.0	100.0
Rate per program	5.8	5.6	4.6	5.6	6.2	5.2	6.3	6.3
Rate per hour	5.7	4.8	4.6	5.4	6.8	4.9	5.3	4.1
% Characters involved in violence	57.1	62.5	51.1	58.3	55.3	50.0	66.7	84.4
Violence Index	165	180	143	164	166	158	188	230

[1] The Fall 1977 sample consists of two weeks of prime-time and one weekend of daytime network dramatic programs. A total of 192 programs and 585 major characters were analyzed.

[2] The Fall 1978 sample consists of one week of prime-time and one weekend of daytime network dramatic programs. A total of 111 programs and 298 major characters were analyzed.

Breaking down the figures by networks, both ABC and CBS boosted the violence saturation of children's programs to 26.3 and 26.8 incidents per hour, respectively—a record high for both networks. NBC's rate went up to 20.6, its fourth highest level. Major characters involved in violence in children's programs climbed from nearly eight to almost nine out of ten. Figure 2 compares the components of the Violence Index for 1977 and 1978.

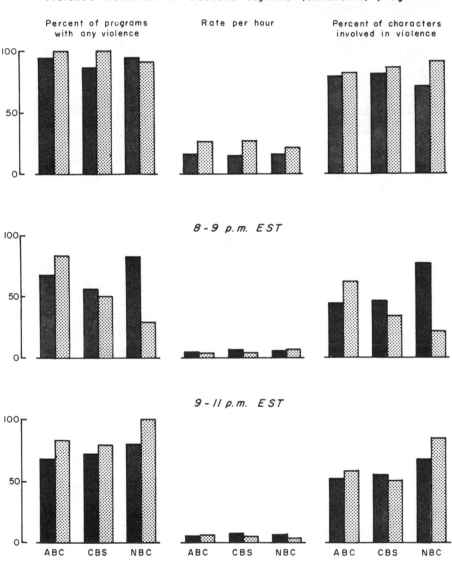

Figure 2: Changes in Violence Index components by network and program time, 1977-1978

A summary of long-term trends can be seen in Table 3. The late evening increase in violence was due primarily to NBC's increase in violent programming, followed by ABC, but not CBS. However, NBC also led in reducing early evening prime-time violence to its lowest level on record. Unlike the other networks, ABC increased its violent programming in the former "family hour," as well as the late evening and weekend daytime hours. Figures 3 and 4 present long-term trends for children's and prime-time programming overall and by network.

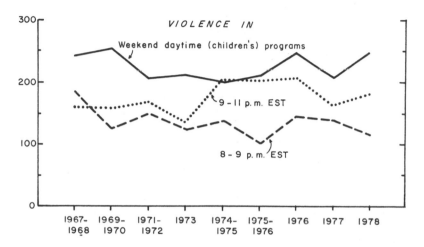

Figure 3: Violence Index in children's and prime-time programming, 1967-1978

The portrayal of violence on television drama also continues to demonstrate a pattern of unequal relative risks among characters of different age, sex, and social groups. Over the past ten years our research has shown that certain groups of dramatic characters consistently were victimized more often than they committed a violent act. As can be seen in Table 4, these include women of all ages, but especially young adult and elderly women, as well as young boys, nonwhites, foreigners, and both members of the lower and upper (but not middle) classes. In 1978, the relative risks of female victimization further increased. In 1977 there were 1.05 male and 1.13 female victims for every male or female violent. In 1978, the male ratio of risk rose to 1.21 but the female ratio rose to 2.14. Female victimization increased the most for weekend children's programming, rising from 1.09 in 1977 to 2.80 in 1978.

Having established that violence has continued to be an integral part of dramatic programming, what can we say about the viewers' perceptions of social reality? Our findings continue to show stable associations between patterns of TV content and conceptions of social reality held by heavy viewers. The current analyses are based on data collected from two samples of adolescents, one from a public school in suburban/rural New Jersey (N = 447) and one from a New York City school (N = 140). Students filled out questionnaires which offered two

Table 3: Summary of Violence Index (1967-1978)

	67-68[1]	69-70[1]	71-72[1]	1973	74-75[2]	75-76[2]	1976	1977[3]	1978[4]	Change 1977 to 1978
All Programs	190	178	174	160	183	177	204	166	183	+17
Prime-Time	176	140	159	132	174	160	183	154	153	- 1
Weekend-Morning	242	253	208	212	202	211	247	209	249	+40
8-9 P.M. EST Programs	186	127	150	126	138	104	145	140	116	-24
9-11 P.M. EST Programs	162	158	167	137	205	203	209	165	180	+15
Cartoons	246	254	224	218	207	228	273	228	252	+24
TV Plays	173	137	140	122	157	149	185	137	137	0
Movies	211	198	226	186	258	252	220	265	248	-17
Comic Tone Programs	144	183	144	149	171	162	227	151	203	+52
Prime-Time	108	72	76	43	54	70	133	99	119	+20
Weekend-Daytime	222	265	202	225	226	229	270	241	274	+33
Serious Tone Programs	-	187	208	197	211	206	216	203	192	-11
Prime-Time	-	187	210	200	217	211	214	209	183	-26
Weekend-Daytime	-	207	167	178	168	183	228	181	230	+49
Continued Programs	182	173	175	159	183	181	197	174	190	+16
Prime-Time	171	149	155	135	170	168	180	166	169	+ 3
Weekend-Daytime	231	251	217	222	209	207	244	215	246	+31
New Programs	201	188	172	163	181	168	216	154	165	+11
Prime-Time	184	119	166	124	188	145	192	134	112	-22
Weekend-Daytime	253	256	192	202	169	221	250	203	255	+52
Action Programs	236	226	220	212	224	213	231	214	207	- 7
Prime-Time	237	221	223	213	237	220	234	219	185	-34
Weekend-Daytime	256	254	225	218	201	206	230	209	239	+30
ABC Programs	210	162	159	138	188	186	207	154	186	+32
CBS Programs	159	173	170	174	173	153	182	159	183	+24
NBC Programs	204	204	195	172	189	194	224	190	179	-11
Prime-Time Programs										
ABC	203	119	146	101	196	180	196	136	165	+29
CBS	128	129	150	152	152	122	150	146	136	-10
NBC	201	176	187	147	178	182	212	188	159	-29
8-9 P.M. EST Programs										
ABC	200	105	140	120	181	129	197	126	167	+41
CBS	157	123	132	127	112	46	102	123	93	-30
NBC	201	161	175	136	119	133	139	188	72	-116
9-11 P.M. EST Programs										
ABC	209	146	150	79	210	222	196	143	164	+21
CBS	92	137	161	174	187	171	175	166	158	- 8
NBC	201	196	200	161	224	222	282	188	230	+42
Action Programs										
ABC	241	223	225	196	232	211	251	208	230	+22
CBS	234	238	230	238	235	224	206	231	192	-39
NBC	235	221	209	211	209	207	234	204	202	- 2
Weekend-Daytime Programs										
ABC	242	239	192	208	178	200	237	216	253	+37
CBS	257	250	210	238	213	210	239	206	253	+47
NBC	229	278	220	202	213	227	264	206	238	+32
Cartoon Programs										
ABC	242	239	226	208	178	202	239	217	253	+36
CBS	257	252	219	238	219	240	263	243	260	+17
NBC	237	280	231	215	233	258	333	219	238	+19

[1] These figures are based upon two samples collected in the fall of each of these years.

[2] These figures are based upon two samples -- one from the fall and one from the spring.

[3] The Fall 1977 sample consists of two weeks of prime-time and one weekend-morning of network dramatic programs.

[4] The Fall 1978 sample consists of one week of prime-time and one weekend of daytime network dramatic programming. A total of 111 programs and 298 major characters were analyzed.

Table 4: Risk ratios[a] for major characters in all programs (1969-1978)

	All characters				Male characters				Female characters			
	N	Involved in violence	Violent-victim ratio	Killer-killed ratio	N	Involved in violence	Violent-victim ratio	Killer-killed ratio	N	Involved in violence	Violent-victim ratio	Killer-killed ratio
All characters	3949	63.3	−1.20	+1.90	2938	68.4	−1.18	+2.02	956	46.1	−1.34	+1.20
Social age												
Children-adolescents	415	60.5	−1.60	+3.00	297	65.0	−1.69	+3.00	116	49.1	−1.33	0.00
Young adults	813	64.5	−1.36	+2.00	539	69.6	−1.23	+2.17	270	53.7	−1.82	+1.33
Settled adults	2212	59.8	−1.12	+2.07	1698	65.7	−1.12	+2.13	513	40.0	−1.12	+1.60
Elderly	106	47.2	−1.15	−1.75	80	50.0	+1.07	1.00	26	38.5	−3.33	−0.00
Marital status												
Not married	1873	65.6	−1.23	+1.90	1374	69.7	−1.18	+2.02	491	53.8	−1.44	+1.30
Married	987	45.5	−1.27	+1.67	626	52.9	−1.27	+1.82	361	32.7	−1.25	+1.11
Class												
Clearly upper	269	59.5	−1.38	+1.50	182	67.6	−1.26	+1.57	87	42.5	−2.00	+1.25
Mixed	3549	63.4	−1.19	+2.07	2650	68.3	−1.17	+2.20	844	46.3	−1.29	+1.20
Clearly lower	131	69.5	−1.25	−1.11	106	73.6	−1.20	−1.13	25	52.0	−1.71	1.00
Race												
White	3087	60.1	−1.19	+1.97	2235	65.1	−1.16	+2.11	852	46.9	−1.31	+1.26
Other	360	55.0	−1.33	+1.69	280	61.1	−1.27	+1.69	77	31.2	−1.83	0.00
Character type												
"Good"	2304	58.4	−1.29	+2.93	1659	63.7	−1.24	+3.85	622	43.2	−1.51	−1.60
Mixed	1093	61.4	−1.22	+1.33	807	65.8	−1.21	+1.27	262	44.7	−1.31	+1.50
"Bad"	550	88.0	1.00	+1.84	471	89.4	−1.01	+1.86	71	77.5	+1.15	+1.67
Nationality												
U.S.	3100	58.1	−1.20	+2.06	2263	63.2	−1.16	+2.23	827	43.9	−1.38	+1.18
Other	264	73.5	−1.31	+1.31	203	80.8	−1.29	+1.27	61	49.2	−1.47	+2.00

[a] Risk ratios are obtained by dividing the more numerous by the less numerous within each group. A plus sign indicates that there are more violents or killers than victims or killed and a minus sign indicates that there are more victims or killed than violents or killers. A ratio of 0.00 means that there were no victims or killers or violents or killed. A +0.00 ratio means that there were some violents or killers but no victims or killed; a −0.00 ‑tio means that there were victims or killed but no violents or killers.

413

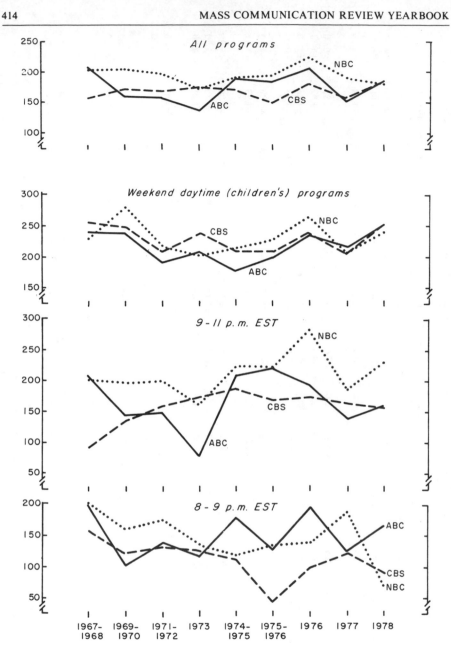

Figure 4: Violence Index by network and program time, 1967-1978

answers to each question, one answer based on facts or statistics (or some other view of reality), and one "television answer," which expresses the "facts" as depicted on TV. Information on viewing habits and demographic variables was also requested and is summarized in Figure 5.

Tables 5-8 summarize the results[2] in four areas of investigation—chances of involvement in violence, fear of walking alone at night, perceived activities of

---

[2] The full analysis, including all tables summarized in this article, is presented in (5).

	New Jersey school children		New York school children	
Date	Dec. 76; May 77		June 77	
Location	Rural/suburban New Jersey		New York City	
Sampling	Student population of a public middle school		Population of 10 to 17 year olds at a New York private school	
Number of respondents	447		140	
Collecting organization	Cultural Indicators		Cultural Indicators	
Method of collection	Self-administered questionnaire		Self-administered questionnaire	
Demographic characteristics		%		%
Sex	boys	45.9	boys	51.4
	girls	54.1	girls	48.6
Grade in school	seventh	47.7	5–8	51.4
	eighth	52.3	9–12	49.6
Age	$\bar{X} = 13.09$		$\bar{X} = 14.1$	
Perceived ethnicity	American	76.4	American	69.1
	Italian	7.2	Italian	0.7
	Black, Afro	0.8	Black, Afro	8.8
	Jewish	4.1	Jewish	6.6
	German	1.3	German	1.5
	Irish	1.5	Irish	0.7
	Other	8.7	Other	12.6
Parents' education	Neither went to college	42.0	Neither went to college	10.8
	Father or both went to college	58.0	Father or both went to college	89.2
TV viewing light	up to 4 hrs/day	43.6	2 hrs/day or less	51.5
heavy	4 hrs & up/day	56.4	Over 2 hrs/day	49.5
Newspaper reading light	almost never	15.0	almost never	14.3
medium	once in a while	46.1	once in a while	46.4
heavy	almost daily	38.9	almost daily	39.3

Figure 5: Adolescent data bases used in cultivation analysis

the police, and mistrust. Three measures are provided for each question—the percent of light viewers who give the answer that reflects the television world (the "television answer"), the Cultivation Differential or CD (percent of heavy viewers minus the percent of light viewers giving the "television answer" within a comparison group), and the gamma coefficient (with the statistical significance indicated by asterisks).[3]

The percent of heavy viewers who responded in terms of the television world can be determined by adding the Cultivation Differential to the percent of light viewers. For example, in Table 5 we see that 62 percent of the light viewers in the New Jersey school sample overestimated the proportion of people involved in violence. Since the CD is +11, the percent of heavy viewers responding in this way would be 73 percent. Finally, two numbers of respondents (Ns) are reported—the overall number of children responding to the question and the total number of light viewers who gave the "television answer."

These analyses reveal that adolescent heavy viewers see the world as more violent and express more fear than do light viewers in a variety of ways, ranging from estimates of the number of people involved in violence, to perceived danger, to assumptions about the use of violence by the police.

Heavy viewers in both the New York and New Jersey schools are more likely than light viewers to overestimate the number of people involved in violence and the proportion of people who commit serious crimes (see Table 5). In the New York sample, the finding is especially strong for boys, those of lower socioeconomic status, those who have not had a personal or family experience as a victim, and those with middle or low achievement scores. In the New Jersey sample, the relationship is stronger among girls, frequent newspaper readers, and heavy TV news viewers, as well as among those whose fathers did not attend college. Despite these variations, the association remains consistently positive for each comparison group: heavy viewers in every case are more likely than are light viewers to believe that a greater number of people are regularly involved in violence. Similarly, heavy viewers in the New Jersey sample are generally more likely to overestimate how many people commit serious crimes. The relationship is the strongest among females and occasional newspaper readers.

Most of the New Jersey students (about 80 percent) feel that it is dangerous to walk alone in a city at night (see Table 6). Yet within every comparison group, heavy viewers are more likely than light viewers to express this opinion. This pattern is most evident among girls, occasional newspaper readers, and infrequent viewers of network news. Although most consider it dangerous, there is a fair degree of variation in who is afraid to walk alone in a city at night. The New Jersey students are more afraid than the New York students; in both samples and again, especially in New Jersey, the females are considerably more afraid. Within every group, however, heavy viewers are more likely than are light viewers to express this fear. This pattern is not as consistent in the New York sample, although it persists notably for females, those of lower SES, low achievers, and those who have not been victims of crime.

---

[3] In the New Jersey sample light viewers are those who watch less than four hours of television a day; in the New York sample light viewers watch less than two hours of television a day. The levels of viewing are determined by a median split of the samples.

Table 5: Summary of cultivation analysis focusing upon involvement in violence

	Percent overestimating the percent of people involved in violence[a] New York City (N = 123)[f]				Percent overestimating the percent of people involved in violence[b] New Jersey (N = 425)[f]			Percent overestimating the number of criminals[c] New Jersey (N = 406)[f]		
	% Light viewers[d] (N = 39)	CD[e]	gamma		% Light viewers[d] (N = 114)	CD[e]	gamma	% Light viewers[d] (N = 136)	CD[e]	gamma
Overall controlling for:	62	+21	.51**	Overall controlling for:	62	+11	.26**	77	+ 8	.26*
Sex				Sex						
Male	58	+29	.67**	Male	64	+ 4	.10	76	+ 2	.05
Female	67	+12	.31	Female	60	+17	.38**	79	+12	.46**
Grade in school				Grade in school						
Grades 5–8	71	+17	.48*	7th	68	+12	.29*	81	+ 2	.08
Grades 9–12	56	+19	.40	8th	57	+10	.20	74	+13	.39**
Socio-economic status				Ethnic group						
Low	71	+22	.70*	Ethnic	58	+14	.30	72	+17	.53**
High	47	+15	.30	Non-ethnic	60	+14	.30**	80	+ 3	.11
Achievement				Newspaper reading						
Low	67	+27	.79*	Every day	57	+16	.33*	79	+ 2	.07
Medium	50	+26	.52*	Sometimes	66	+ 8	.19	75	+12	.39**
High	61	+15	.35	Network news watching						
Experience as victim				Almost daily	53	+26	.54**	78	+12	.42
Yes	70	+18	.50*	Once in a while	67	+ 4	.09	77	+ 4	.14
No	29	+46	.76**	Hardly ever	61	+13	.28	76	+10	.31
				Father's education						
				No college	65	+12	.28*	84	– 1	–.04
				Some college	58	+ 8	.16	75	+ 9	.27

* p ≤ .05 (tau)   ** p ≤ .01 (tau)

[a] "Think about the number of people who are involved in some kind of violence each year. Do you think that 3 percent of all people are involved in some kind of violence in any given year, or is it closer to 10 percent?"

[b] "Think about the number of people who are involved in violence each week. Do you think one person out of every 100 is involved in some kind of violence in any given week, or is it closer to 10 people out of every 100?"

[c] "About what percent of all people commit serious crimes—is it closer to 3 percent or 12 percent?"

[d] Percent of light viewers giving the television answer

[e] CD (Cultivation Differential) is the percent of heavy viewers minus the percent of light viewers giving the "television answer."

[f] Total number of respondents

Table 6: Summary of cultivation analyses focusing upon the danger of walking alone at night

New York City

	Percent afraid to walk alone in a city at night[a] — New York City (N = 122)[f]			Percent afraid to walk alone in own neighborhood at night[b] — New York City (N = 130)[f]		
	% Light viewers[d] (N = 27)	CD[e]	gamma	% Light viewers[d] (N = 9)	CD[e]	gamma
Overall	46	+ 6	.13	13	+19	.50**
controlling for:						
Sex						
Male	41	−13	−.27	6	+ 6	.36
Female	52	+25	.52*	21	+32	.63**
Grade in school						
Grades 5–8	59	+ 2	.05	16	+20	.49*
Grades 9–12	38	− 6	−.14	12	+10	.36
Socio-economic status						
Low	29	+24	−.47	11	+18	.52
High	62	−38	−.69**	20	−14	−.62
Achievement						
Low	32	+31	.57*	4	+28	.82**
Medium	65	−29	−.52*	16	+ 7	.22
High	47	+ 6	.12	14	+27	.62*
Experience as victim						
Yes	51	− 3	−.07	14	+17	.47*
No	23	+38	.68*	7	+26	.73*

New Jersey

	Percent who think it's dangerous to walk alone in a city at night[c] — New Jersey (N = 407)[f]			Percent afraid to walk alone in a city at night[a] — New Jersey (N = 414)[f]		
	% Light viewers[d] (N = 139)	CD[e]	gamma	% Light viewers[d] (N = 116)	CD[e]	gamma
Overall	79	+ 7	.24*	64	+10	.24**
controlling for:						
Sex						
Male	76	+ 4	.14	45	+15	.31*
Female	83	+ 7	.32*	81	+ 3	.09
Grade in school						
7th	75	+10	.31*	59	+17	.38**
8th	83	+ 5	.20	68	+ 5	.11
Ethnic group						
Ethnic	82	+ 4	.12	65	+ 9	.21
Non-ethnic	79	+ 7	.25*	62	+12	.28*
Newspaper reading						
Every day	80	+ 2	.05	61	+ 7	.16
Sometimes	78	+10	.36*	66	+12	.29*
Network news watching						
Almost daily	83	+ 7	.28	65	+11	.26
Once in a while	81	+ 4	.13	60	+10	.22
Hardly ever	76	+12	.38*	68	+12	.30
Father's education						
No college	77	+ 9	.28	60	+11	.25
Some college	79	+ 8	.30	64	+13	.30*

* p ≤ .05 (tau)   ** p ≤ .01 (tau)

[a] "Would you be afraid to walk alone in a city at night?"
[b] "Are you afraid to walk alone in your own neighborhood at night?"
[c] "Is it dangerous to walk alone in a city at night?"
[d] Percent of light viewers giving the television answer
[e] CD (Cultivation Differential) is the percent of heavy viewers minus the percent of light viewers giving the "television answer."
[f] Total number of respondents

Responses to a question about one's willingness to walk alone at night in one's *own* neighborhood show a strong and consistent relationship between the amount of viewing and being afraid. Females and young students are more afraid overall; these two groups also show the strongest relationship between amount of television viewing and expressing the fear of walking alone at night in one's own neighborhood.

Television viewing also seems to contribute to adolescents' images and assumptions about law enforcement procedures and activities. Among the New Jersey students, more heavy than light viewers in every subgroup believe that police must often use force and violence at a scene of violence (see Table 7). Among the New York students, there is a consistent positive relationship between amount of viewing and the perception of how many times a day a policeman pulls out his gun. Adolescents in New Jersey show a positive relationship across the board between amount of viewing and the tendency to believe that policemen who shoot at running persons actually hit them.

Finally, adolescent heavy viewers also tend to express mistrust in people and to express the belief that people are selfish (see Table 8). Although the differences are not as pronounced as they are for violence- and fear-related questions, the patterns are stable across most groups. Those who watch more television remain more likely to say that people "are mostly just looking out for themselves" (rather than trying to be helpful) and that one "can't be too careful in dealing with people" (rather than that they can be trusted).

These findings provide considerable support for the conclusion that heavy television viewers perceive social reality differently from light television viewers, even when other factors are held constant. There is considerable variation between groups in the scope and magnitude of these patterns: the extent of television's contribution is mediated, enhanced, or diminished by powerful personal, social, and cultural variables, as well as by other information sources. Yet the relationships remain positive in almost every case. The amount of viewing makes a consistent difference in the responses of these adolescents, even the "more sophisticated," "less impressionable" New Yorkers.

Parallel results were also found for a slightly younger age group. In a survey of 2200 seven- to eleven-year-old children and their parents conducted by the Foundation for Child Development, a significant relationship was found between amount of television viewing and violence-related fears even with controls for age, sex, ethnic background, vocabulary, and the child's own reports of victimization (7). We may conclude, then, that heavy viewers' expressions of fear and interpersonal mistrust, assumptions about the chances of encountering violence, and images of police activities can be traced in part to television portrayals.

Given these findings that heavy TV viewing cultivates fear of violence, why is the most vocal concern about TV-incited violence? The privileges of power most jealously guarded are those of violence and sex. In the public realm it is government that claims the legal prerogative to commit violence (in defense of law, order, and national security), and to regulate the commission and depiction of sexual acts (in defense of "decency"). In the private realm parents assert the same prerogatives over their children—the power to determine the range of

Table 7: Summary of cultivation analyses focusing upon activities of the police

Controlling for (NYC)	Percent overestimating number of times police draws guns on average day[a] — New York City (N = 121)[f]			Controlling for (NJ)	Percent overestimating how often police find it necessary to use force[b] — New Jersey (N = 419)[f]			Percent overestimating how often police shoot fleeing suspects[c] — New Jersey (N = 423)[f]		
	% Light viewers[d] (N = 4)	CD[e]	gamma		% Light viewers[d] (N = 82)	CD[e]	gamma	% Light viewers[d] (N = 97)	CD[e]	gamma
Overall	6	+12	.52*	Overall	45	+11	.21*	53	+11	.22**
controlling for:				controlling for:						
Sex				Sex						
Male	0	+10	1.00*	Male	44	+ 5	.11	59	+ 5	.10
Female	13	+13	.39	Female	46	+15	.28*	47	+17	.33**
Grade in school				Grade in school						
Grades 5-8	9	+13	.51	7th	45	+15	.31*	50	+14	.27*
Grades 9-12	5	+ 1	.10	8th	45	+ 6	.11	55	+ 9	.18
Socio-economic status				Ethnic group						
Low	8	+15	.55	Ethnic	52	+ 8	.16	56	+10	.19
High	0	+ 6	1.00	Non-ethnic	42	+12	.24*	50	+12	.24*
Achievement				Newspaper reading						
Low	8	+11	.43	Every day	42	+ 9	.17	56	+10	.20
Medium	0	+19	1.00*	Sometimes	47	+11	.22*	51	+11	.23*
High	6	+14	.62	Network news watching						
Experience as victim				Almost daily	47	+16	.32	55	+ 6	.11
Yes	6	+10	.49	Once in a while	43	+ 5	.10	51	+14	.29*
No	7	+13	.56	Hardly ever	43	+17	.31*	55	+ 8	.17
				Father's education						
				No college	47	+17	.32*	65	+ 2	.05
				Some college	41	+ 5	.09	43	+13	.26*

* p ≤ .05 (tau)   ** p ≤ .01 (tau)

[a] "On an average day, how many times does a policeman usually pull out his gun—less than once a day or more than five times a day?"

[b] "When police arrive at a scene of violence, how much of the time do they have to use force and violence—most of the time or some of the time?"

[c] "How often do you think policemen who shoot at running persons actually hit them?"

[d] Percent of light viewers giving the television answer

[e] CD (Cultivation Differential) is the percent of heavy viewers minus the percent of light viewers giving the "television answer."

[f] Total number of respondents

Table 8: Summary of cultivation analyses focusing upon mistrust and alienation

| | Percent saying that you must be careful in dealing with people[a] | | | Percent saying that people are selfish rather than helpful[b] | | |
| | New Jersey (N = 420)[e] | | | New Jersey (N = 413)[e] | | |
	% Light viewers[c] (N = 97)	CD[d]	gamma	% Light viewers[c] (N = 101)	CD[d]	gamma
Overall	52	+10	.21*	56	+ 8	.17*
controlling for:						
Sex						
Male	56	+10	.21	62	+ 2	.05
Female	48	+12	.22*	50	+13	.27*
Grade in school						
7th	49	+16	.32**	56	+ 3	.06
8th	54	+ 5	.10	56	+13	.28*
Ethnic group						
Ethnic	62	− 2	−.03	60	+ 7	.16
Non-ethnic	48	+14	.28**	53	+ 9	.19
Newspaper reading						
Every day	49	+16	.31*	59	+ 4	.10
Sometimes	55	+ 6	.12	54	+10	.20
Network news watching						
Almost daily	53	+13	.26	57	0	−.00
Once in a while	53	+ 8	.16	57	+ 5	.12
Hardly ever	48	+13	.26	52	+18	.36*
Father's education						
No college	56	+12	.23	60	+ 5	.10
Some college	48	+ 8	.17	54	+ 3	.06

* p ≤ .05 (tau)

** p ≤ .01 (tau)

[a] "Can most people be trusted, or do you think that you can't be too careful in dealing with people?"

[b] "Would you say that most of the time people try to be helpful, or that they are mostly just looking out for themselves?"

[c] Percent of light viewers giving the television answer

[d] CD (Cultivation Differential) is the percent of heavy viewers minus the percent of light viewers giving the "television answer."

[e] Total number of respondents

permissible and forbidden behavior. It would stand to reason, therefore, that the representatives of established order would be more worried about television violence as a threat to their monopoly over physical coercion, however limited that threat might be, than about insecurities that drive people to seek protection and to accept control.

In 1776 John Adams wrote that fear is the foundation of most governments. By demonstrating the workings of a social power hierarchy, television drama may contribute to the cultivation of assumptions that tend to maintain this hierarchy. The durable message of unequal power and victimization in television vi-

olence is clear. Any real-life violence that television incites may serve to reinforce the fear created by symbolic violence.[4]

The meaning of violence is in the kinds of social relationships it presents and
the lessons of power—and fear of power—that may be derived from them. Conventional wisdom and fearful people, themselves victimized by images of violence around them, might stress the one or two in a thousand who imitate violence and threaten society. But it is just as important to look at the large
majority of people who become more fearful, insecure, and dependent on authority, and who may grow up demanding protection and even welcoming repression in the name of security. The most significant and recurring conclusion
of our long-range study is that one correlate of television viewing is a heightened and unequal sense of danger and risk in a mean and selfish world.

REFERENCES

1. Chaffee, S. "Television and Adolescent Aggressiveness (An Overview)." In G. A. Comstock and
   E. A. Rubinstein (Eds.) *Television and Social Behavior,* Volume 3: *Television and Adolescent
   Aggressiveness.* Washington, D.C.: U.S. Government Printing Office, 1972.
2. Comstock, G. A., E. A. Rubinstein, and J. P. Murray (Eds.) *Television and Social Behavior* (five
   volumes). Washington, D. C.: U.S. Government Printing Office, 1972.
3. Gerbner, G. and L. Gross. "Living with Television: The Violence Profile." *Journal of Communication* 26(2), Spring 1976, pp. 173-199.
4. Gerbner, G., L. Gross, M. Jackson-Beeck, S. Jeffries-Fox, and N. Signorielli. "Cultural Indicators:
   Violence Profile No. 9." *Journal of Communication* 28(3), Summer 1978, pp. 176-207.
5. Gerbner, George, Larry Gross, Nancy Signorielli, Michael Morgan, and Marilyn Jackson-Beeck.
   "Violence Profile No. 10: Trends in Network Dramatic Programming and Viewer Conceptions of Social Reality, 1967-1978." Annenberg School of Communications, University of
   Pennsylvania, April 1979.
6. Gross, Larry. "Television and Violence." In Kate Moody and Ben Logan (Eds.) *Television Awareness Training* (second edition). Nashville, Tenn.: Parthenon, 1979.
7. Zill, Nicholas. Personal communication, Foundation for Child Development, New York, April
   1979.

---

[4] A striking example of what we mean can be found in *Tales of a Fourth-Grade Nothing,* a story
book in its fourteenth printing by Dell Publishing Company, sold coast-to-coast. Chapter 4 begins
this way:

> *We live near Central Park. . . . Jimmy Fargo has been mugged three times—twice for his bicycle
> and once for his money. . . . I've never been mugged. But sooner or later I probably will be. My
> father told me what to do. Give the muggers whatever they want and try not to get hit on the
> head. Sometimes after you're mugged, you get to go to police headquarters. You look at a bunch
> of pictures of crooks to see if you can recognize the guys that mugged you.*

Luc Van Poecke, Mass Communication Researcher at Catholic University in Leuven, Belgium, reviews the work of George Gerbner and Larry Gross on cultural indicators. Dr. Van Poecke is excited about the theoretical implications of the cultural indicators approach, but he argues that classical content analysis is not equal to the theoretical task of studying mass communication as the production of ideology.

24

GERBNER'S CULTURAL INDICATORS
The System Is the Message

Luc Van Poecke

INTRODUCTION

The notion of cultural indicators results from George Gerbner's discontent with classical methods. In analyzing media effects, the secondary facts have, according to Gerbner (see Gerbner, 1969a, 1972b, 1973a, 1973b; Gerbner and Gross, 1976), been falsely treated as the most important facts. For Gerbner, those things which are an immediate reality to the consciousness of both communicator and receiver are of secondary importance; most researchers remain at this level in their analysis. Typical of this traditional approach is the amount of attention paid to direct and intentional changes in specific patterns of behavior, opinions, and attitudes caused by an isolated message or campaign.

Gerbner argues that this archaic research strategy is totally inadequate for researching the effects of television. Television, as no other medium, fulfills a function which entirely escapes the traditional methods: "These earlier modes of study were based on selectively used media and focused on attitude or behavior change. Both assumptions are largely inadequate to the task of conceptualizing and investigation of the effects of television" (Gerbner and Gross, 1976: 175).

For Gerbner, the primary function of the mass media in general, and of television in particular, is to produce an *ideological effect*.[1]

IDEOLOGY AND MASS MEDIA

The symbolic functions

All societies, according to Gerbner (see Gerbner and Gross 1976: 176), produce explanations of reality for themselves and for their posterity. This socially

From Luc Van Poecke, "Gerbner's Cultural Indicators: The System Is the Message," original manuscript.

constructed reality produces a coherent, homogeneous picture of what exists, what is important, what relates to what, and what is right. In other words, each society cultivates—through dominant rites and myths—a kind of grammar which rule the conduct of its members, which decides what is compulsory, forbidden, and allowed and what is seen as right, reasonable, and wholesome. Gerbner calls these sociocultural processes the "symbolic functions." They create an indispensable environment of symbols (see also Gerbner 1972b: 153). This system of established values and "truths," this logic of relationships and structures, makes the members of a society feel at home. In other words, the symbolic functions legitimize the social organization and rationalize, motivate, or naturalize it. They serve the established powers:

> Common rituals and mythologies are agencies of symbolic socialization and control. They demonstrate how society works by dramatizing its norms and values. They are essential parts of the general system of messages that cultivates prevailing outlooks (which is why we call it culture) and regulates social relationships. This system of messages, with its story-telling functions, makes people perceive as real and normal and right that which fits the established social order [Gerbner and Gross, 1976: 173].

Gerbner seldom uses the concept, but it is clear that we are confronted here with what in Marxist tradition is called an ideology, a praxis which transforms concrete individuals into members, subjects of a certain society. This definition comes from the French Marxist, Althusser (as elaborated, for instance, in 1970). Gerbner is more lucid than Althusser when it comes to understanding modern mass culture. They both agree that this function used to be fulfilled mainly by religion. However, Althusser thinks that school has now taken over this function in our capitalistic society. Gerbner argues the mass media, and television in particular, have assumed the function.

The primary role of the mass media

For Gerbner—as for Althusser—an ideology does not consist of "wandering ideas." Ideology has a concrete, material status; it develops itself in texts, *messages*, that are produced by *institutions*; and this is how a (collective) *consciousness is cultivated*. The ideology unfolds itself in concrete communication processes which can thus be defined as social interaction through messages (see Gerbner, 1970: 72; 1972b: 153), whereby a symbolic environment is created. As such, Gerbner sees ideology as a humanizing process.

It is clear, according to Gerbner (compare 1970: 69; Gerbner and Gross, 1976), that the industrial-technological revolution reveals itself in the domain of the production of messages. The mass production and the ultrafast distribution of messages have created a new symbolic environment which reflects the structures and function of the institutions that produce them. Gerbner believes that by this means the mass media produce a short-circuit in the other fields of social communication: The collective consciousness they create and the public they form take the place of the former social relationships. Ideology develops mainly, and with all its consequences, through the mass media and through television in particular.

According to Gerbner and Gross (1976) television is the ideal ideological machinery. No other medium can reach everyone. It can wipe out the heterogeneity within the public and shape all subjects according to standard patterns. As no other medium, television possesses the flexibility, directness, and interpolative force to exercise the ideological function optimally. The medium accompanies the human being from early childhood to the grave. Television is the big mythteller, the flagship of the industrial mass culture, the all-embracing socialization machine. Gerbner says:

> TV penetrates every home in the land. Its seasonal, cyclical, and perpetual patterns of organically related fact and fiction (all woven into an entertainment fabric producing publics of consumers for sale to advertisers) again encompass essential elements of art, science, technology, statecraft and public (as well as most family) storytelling. The information-poor (children and less educated adults) are again the entertainment-rich held in thrall by the myths and legends of a new electronic priesthood. [Gerbner and Gross, 1976: 175-176].

One could say (see Gerbner and Gross, 1976: 181) that what was already present in other mass media is realized in all its consequences by television, namely the production of an all-embracing mass ideology for a mass public (created by the media themselves). This could be described as the specificity of the medium.[2] Also, it becomes clear now that for Gerbner the search for changes caused by certain messages is irrelevant. One should rather talk about the creating, reinforcing, and consolidating of a certain ideology, whereby every insisting change will be resisted (see 1973a: 267).

As Katz (1979) remarked, Gerbner's vision belongs to the trend in media research that rejects what earlier researchers considered as relevant, and vice versa. Before, the term *media effect* was only used to point out a change in behavior or attitude. Gerbner and Gross argue that

> stability may be *the* significant outcome of the sum total of the play of many variables. . . . We cannot look for change as the most significant accomplishment of the chief arm of established culture if its main social function is to maintain, reinforce and exploit rather than to undermine or alter conventional conceptions, beliefs and behaviors [Gerbner and Gross, 1976: 180-181].

One has to admit also that the first and only aim of media research ought to be the study of this process (Gerbner, 1972). A further examination of the ways Gerbner describes the mechanism of the ideology/socialization will give us a better insight of Gerbner's motives for calling the mass media the dominant ideological institutions.

The hidden curriculum

Mass communication is a form of "subjection," not so much violent as instructive.[3] In short, throughout communication one can discern a global curriculum, "a lesson plan that no one teaches but everyone learns. It consists of the symbolic contours of the social order" (Gerbner, 1973a: 269).

Central to all this are, of course, the messages by which this culturalization process takes place. In this connection we can discern three main theses in Gerbner's work.

First, Gerbner argues that mass mediated messages form a structure, a system ("message systems"). The primary function of communication is the production of a global ideological world. The individual messages are parts of a bigger structure in which the parts obtain their significance and value. The whole must be the starting point of analysis (see, for example, Gerbner, 1969a: 128). The starting point should, for instance, be the television drama as a whole: Which symbolic world is created by this configuration, which axiology is developed here, which causal relationships are here shown as natural, obvious, and probable?

In this connection Gerbner is a structuralist. Paraphrasing McLuhan, he states that "the system is the message" and that, if one wants to analyze the effects of individual messages, one should start from the sociocultural structure. Any other strategy puts the cart before the horse (see Gerbner, 1973a: 269).

Secondly, Gerbner argues that message systems function primarily in an implicit way. Beneath the explicit and fragmentary nature of the individual messages, one must look (see Gerbner, 1973a: 270) for the symbolic patterns and functions which sustain the collective moral and the dominant sensibility of the social order. Beneath those things which are given as direct data to the consciousness (more important than the intention of the communicator, more relevant than the superficial opinions and functions), is the symbolic order at work, an order that could at least be called nonconscious. For example, television drama has a hierarchy of values, a "natural" succession of actions, "obvious" roles, (in short: a public agenda) whereby one sees "basic assumptions about the facts of life and standards of judgments" (Gerbner and Gross, 1976: 175). Therefore Gerbner calls the curriculum that unfolds itself here *hidden* (1973a).

Gerbner's third thesis concerning the ideological effect of the media, is that the message systems are text-immanent. This means that the effectiveness of the media cannot be judged from an intention, function, or want that precedes the system or is external to it. One can, according to Gerbner (1973b: 570; 1972b: 158) never speak of a failure in communication, but only of failures of private intentions or campaigns. These "failures" are not relevant for the primary working of the medium. One could even say that failures on the superficial level (the conscious intentions, functions) can be interpreted as successes on the deeper level (the ideological). The receiver "understands" the message better than the communicator. Furthermore, message systems can exercise their primary function in a way that escapes the consciousness of both communicator and receiver.

The primary function of the media lies not in representing but in producing a coherent mythology.

A FORM OF CONTENT ANALYSIS

The cultural indicators

The "symbolic environment" is analyzed by what Gerbner calls "cultural indicators." This analysis starts from questions such as: What are the relationships between the media institutions and the other social institutions? How and on which level are message decisions made? How is the production of the message systems organized? In short, "the analysis must consider all major powers, roles and relationships that have a systematic and generalized influence on how messages will be selected, formulated and transmitted" (Gerbner, 1973b: 559). Instead of the traditional concern for the intention, the want, and the function of messages, Gerbner emphasizes the anonymous, not immediately conscious and systematic order of the hidden curriculum: "Nothing happens in it independently of man's will, although much that happens may escape individual awareness or scrutiny" (Gerbner, 1973a: 267).

Gerbner's model for content analysis (see 1970; 1973b) examines, within a chosen message system and in an empirically quantifying way, these dimensions: namely, the *existence* of *priorities*, of *values* and of *relationships*. The obtained measurings are combined into cultural indicators such as the violence index of television drama (see Gerbner, 1969b, 1972a; Gerbner et al., 1976, 1977, 1978).

Gerbner (1972a: 29; 1973b: 570) insists on the structural and systematic character of the fields studied. One does not study (count) violence on television as such, but units that are related. When the structure changes, the meaning of these units changes also: "When the symbolic context changes, the significance of acts changes. . . . Such observations enable us to ask questions about what *that* message might cultivate in public conceptions and behaviour" (Gerbner, 1973b: 570).

Also important is the "cultivating differential" (Gerbner and Gross, 1976: 181). If one wants to examine what is cultivated by the symbolic system that unfolds itself through television, then one has to take into account that there are still other factors that help to create the public's view of the world. By comparing the ideas about the world of a group of "heavy viewers" with that of a comparable group of "light" viewers; the "cultivation differential" is approached.

Let us consider Gerbner's favorite domain: violence on television. From the preceding, it is clear that one should not look for the "inciting" theory. Gerbner and Gross say: "It is clear, at least to us, that deeply rooted sociocultural forces, rather than just obstinacy of profit-seeking, are at work" (1976: 189). Heavy viewers have internalized a certain view of society and a sense of values and norms coupled with it: a logic of winning and losing, a system of victims and aggressors, a certain role-partition, an idea about the risks in life and the price that should be paid for breaking the law (see Gerbner and Gross, 1976: 178; Gerbner et al., 1978: 184). Gerbner and Gross (1976: 191) have found in their research that for intensive TV viewers the world appears more threatening than it is in reality and that this concept of the world awakens the demand for more order and authority and also legitimizes the latter. In this way, television produces myths that have a social function: The medium acts here as the most important instrument for socializing and for social control; the repressive powers are strengthened and justified. This concrete example shows what Gerbner sees as the character of the media: They act as the established religion of the industrial society; they have, in other words, exactly the same relation to governance that the church used to have to the state (Gerbner and Gross, 1976: 194).

EVALUATION

Gerbner's global vision of the relation of media, culture, and society is more persuasive than his content analysis model. The latter is influenced too greatly by the trademark of all content analysis models: an obsession for measures and numbers as reassuring guarantees of the truthfulness of the scientific discourse. It is not that one regards culture as a sacred cow that might choke on a computer program, or that one considers the idea that culture can be measured economically as an infamous attack on the human richness and complexity of our culture. It is striking, though, that Gerbner's research strategy shows once more that the idea that the concrete analysis should be quantifying results in the simplification of the theoretical problem. In other words, the fact that the starting point of the model is quantitative influences the whole theoretical base; the latter is weakened in its explaining capacity in order to provide the "hard" figures for the concrete analysis. In concrete terms, this means that Gerbner leaves a couple of problems unsolved.

SOME GAPS

Gerbner poses that culture unfolds itself in communication (that communication is culture). Further, culture can be defined as ideology, and ideology consists of symbolic systems. It is striking here that Gerbner leaves the specificity of the symbolic, as such, nearly unconceptualized (nor will this specificity, as a consequence, be found in the concrete analysis model). It is true that Gross is interested in the problem (Gross, 1973; Worth and Gross, 1974), and Gerbner is sometimes a bit more explicit about it (see Gerbner, 1972). But it is clear that a serious elaboration of the symbolic character of the object of analysis— and this elaboration is also necessary for a further definition of ideology— demands some kind of *semiotics*. A theory of signs can answer the questions: What is a symbol? What is the relation between the symbolic and the real?

Although a bit more explicitly elaborated, the *system character* of the symbolic also remains unclear in Gerbner's work. It is true there is a hasty reference to Rapoport's system theory (Gerbner, 1969a), but here also many things remain unsaid. Hence, a valid structural analysis model does not yet emerge from Gerbner's work.

Gerbner's approach demands a theory of the process of making things probable, a *rhetoric* of what makes the world seem real to a media consumer. One can thus readily see that, within the theoretical problem, a project of *semiotics* is necessary. The semiotics should be supported by an elaborated *system* or structure theory, and should include a *rhetoric*. Classical content and analysis is not equal to the task at hand.

For Gerbner, the symbolic is active on a nonconscious level. It is clear, though, that further theorizing of the fact that the conscious seems to be the product of the subconscious would lead Gerbner further than he (or his analysis model) would like. Such a theory is nevertheless necessary to get a better insight into the process Gerbner calls "cultivation," the process that transforms the individual into a member of a certain society. Gerbner's theoretical vision loses some of its explanatory value because it lacks a theory of the subconscious and a culture theory that is linked to it.

Gerbner emphasizes that the message systems are immanent. The thesis, though, that the force and the meaning of symbolic functions lie in their difference from reality (Gerbner, 1973: 571), makes it at least necessary to start the content analysis model from a *narrativity theory* and a *genre theory*. For how much value has an analysis of the television drama when one does not have an insight into the specific logic that rules the story and the laws that characterize each genre? Here, also, we can see a discrepancy between the potential richness of Gerbner's viewpoint and the impoverishment that is caused by the necessary quantification.

Finally, one can also say that, in spite of the careful analysis of the institutional processes, the relation between the symbolic/ideological processes and their social context is insufficiently conceptualized. A more extensive ideology-theory is needed to explicate the instances that determine an ideology and the way shifts in symbolic systems take place. Because, although cultural indicators can be used to indicate these changes, Gerbner reveals few elements to explain and describe the mechanism of change as it relates to a theory of history (at least, a history of ideas).

CONCLUSION

Gerbner is a structuralist when he stresses the contextual differential in message systems. But the question is whether this structural intention can be realized in the concrete analysis carried out by Gerbner and his team. The structuralism, in the definition of his categories, always tends toward differentiation, to a nonreducible specificity. Gerbner's vision of the media as producers of ideology contains a potential richness on the theoretical level, but this richness cannot be elaborated through a quantitative content analysis model. It is argued here that to study mass communication as the production of an ideology, one must proceed from a semiotic point of view. This demands not only a rhetoric and a narrativity and a genre theory, but also a more elaborate system or structure theory.

It appears the crucial objection of Cicourel (1964: 28) is applicable here: "It is the language of measurement (in its generic sense) which imposes the necessary equivalence classes, not the theoretical concepts." This objection can only be eliminated if one sets up research from a radically different point of view. If not, the cart is before the horse once again.

NOTES

1. In this context see also E. Katz's paper (1979; given at the Eighth Flemish Congress of Communication Sciences in Brussels), where the different points of view for conceptualizing media effects are brought together. Katz opposes here the traditional research models (concentrated on limited and direct effects and on the selectivity and the interpersonal relationships of the receivers) with some new approaches that are characterized as "theories of powerful mass media." The theory of the "ideological effect," which Gerbner supports, is one of these new approaches.

2. In this context we would like to point out, if not an incoherence, then certainly a kind of ambiguity. In their attempt to define the specificity of the television as sharply as possible, Gerbner and Gross manage to create the impression that television caused a fundamental break in the history of the mass media. Not only is the "ideological" effect presented as the privilege of television, but it is also suggested that the traditional approach is still relevant for the other mass media. This opinion, which is already weakened in the above-mentioned article (see Gerbner and Gross, 1976: 181), cannot be found so profiled in Gerbner's other articles. There he usually demonstrates that the primary function of mass communication (and of communication in general) is ideological, so that notions like selectivity and change can be regarded as secondary. Here television plays a specific but not a unique role.

3. According to Althusser (1970), the state apparatus (the "superstructure") can be divided into the juridical-political and the ideological. The first group has a dominant (but not exclusively) repressive function; the second group has a dominant (but not exclusively) ideological function.

REFERENCES

ALTHUSSER, L. (1976) "Idéologie et appareils idéologiques d'état," pp. 67-125 in Althusser, Positions. Paris: Ed. Sociales.
BAKER, R. K. and S. J. BALL [eds.] (1969) Violence in the Media. Washington, DC: Government Printing Office.
CICOUREL, A. V. (1964) Method and Measurement in Sociology. New York: Free Press.
COMSTOCK, G. A. and E. A. RUBINSTEIN [eds.] (1972) Television and Social Behavior. Volume 1, Media Content and Control. Washington, DC: Government Printing Office.
FAUCONNIER, G. et al. (1979) 25 Jaar Televisie in Vlaanderen: Aanpassing of Transformatie van een Cultuur? Leuven: Centrum voor Communicatiewetenschappen, K. U. Leuven.
GERBNER, G. (1977) "Comparative cultural indicators," in Gerbner, 1977.
——— (1973a) "Teacher image in mass culture: symbolic functions of the 'hidden curriculum,'" pp. 265-286 in Gerbner et al., 1973.

—— (1973b) "Cultural indicators: the third voice," pp. 555-573 in Gerbner et al., 1973.

—— (1972a) "Violence in television drama: trends and symbolic function," pp. 28-187 in Comstock and Rubinstein, 1972.

—— (1972b) "Communication and social environment." Scientific American 227, 3: 153-160.

—— (1970) "Cultural indicators: the case of violence in television drama." Annals of Amer. Academy of Pol. and Social Sciences 388: 69-81.

—— (1969a) "Toward 'cultural indicators': the analysis of mass mediated public message systems," in Gerbner et al., 1969.

—— (1969b) "Dimensions of violence in television drama," in Baker and Ball, 1969.

GERBNER, G. and L. GROSS (1976) "Living with television: the violence profile." J. of Communication 26, 2: 173-199.

GERBNER, G. et al. (1978) "TV violence profile 9: cultural indicators." J. of Communication 28, 3: 176-207.

—— (1977) "TV violence profile 8: the highlights." J. of Communication 27: 171-180.

—— (1976) TV Violence Profile 7: Trends in Network Television Drama and Viewer Conceptions of Social Reality. Philadelphia: Annenberg School of Communications.

GERBNER, G. [ed.] (1977) Mass Media Policies in Changing Cultures. New York: John Wiley.

GERBNER, G. et al. [eds.] (1973) Communication Technology and Social Policy: Understanding the New "Cultural Revolution." New York: John Wiley.

—— (1969) The Analysis of Communication Content. New York: John Wiley.

GROSS, L. (1973) "Modes of communication and the acquisition of symbolic competence," pp. 189-208 in Gerbner et al., 1973.

KATZ, E. (1979) "On conceptualizing media effects," pp. 27-51 in Fauconnier et al., 1979.

WORTH, S. and L. GROSS (1974) "Symbolic strategies." J. of Communication 24, 4: 27-39.

Divergent conceptions of violence that relate to both culture and time, and problems of validity and causality in laboratory and field experiments are used by James D. Halloran to question our knowledge of the effects of media violence. Professor Halloran sees promise in George Gerbner's cultural indicators approach because it is sensitive to the possibility that televised violence is actually used to legitimize and maintain power and authority of established elites, a far more realistic and serious effect than the individual modeling behavior so often researched in experiments. Professor Halloran is Director of the Centre for Mass Communication Research, University of Leicester, and is President of the International Association of Mass Communication Researchers.

25

MASS COMMUNICATION
Symptom or Cause of Violence?

James D. Halloran

In recent years there has been abundant evidence, ranging from government-sponsored inquiries and research to expressions of concern in the media and elsewhere, and the formation of pressure groups, that the alleged, although ill-defined, relationship between the mass media and violence is considered by many people to be important and problematic. The problem as popularly perceived is not a new one. Much of what is now being said about television has been said before about the other media, and throughout history innovations in communication technology have frequently been blamed for producing social disruption. Nevertheless, the portrayal of violence by the media, particularly by television, is increasingly seen as a major social problem, particularly in Western Europe and North America.

The concern is expressed in a variety of ways. People complain, they group together, they attend meetings, they exert pressure and plan collective action in the hope that this will lead to a solution, usually a censorious one, to the problem as they see it. Whether or not the concern is justified is a different matter. The evidence suggests that the process of influence, the role of the media and the nature of violence are not understood and that consequently the problem is inadequately defined. In view of this, the solutions put forward are not likely to be appropriate, and in fact the whole debate is characterized by inconsistencies and internal contradictions.

The approach to the problem outlined here is essentially a social scientific one. A social scientist must never take the definitions of problems and expressions of concern at face value. He should not ignore them, but he has to distinguish the latent from the overt, probe beneath the surface and seek to establish, amongst other things, why people are concerned, why and how they express the concern and define the problems in the way they do, and how their definitions square with

James D. Halloran is professor and director of the Centre for Mass Communication Research, University of Leicester, 104 Regent Road, Leicester LE1 7LT, United Kingdom. He has been a consultant to Unesco and the Council of Europe, for which he has written various reports, and had published numerous books and articles on communication, including Mass Media and Society: The Challenge of Research *(1974).*

rticle from the INTERNATIONAL SOCIAL SCIENCE JOURNAL, Vol. XXX, No. 4. © Unesco
'8. Reproduced by permission of Unesco.

reality. He must also emphasize that we live in highly differentiated, pluralistic societies, where issues are viewed and problems defined from different standpoints, where one man's media meat may be another man's media poison, and where neither social science nor the available social philosophies provide us with clear, unambiguous guidelines for social policy and action.

Our societies are complex, interlocking structures, and this means that we should not attempt to study any single institution or social process in isolation. The problem of media violence should be studied in relation to other institutions and to violence in society as a whole, and it should be set within the appropriate social, political and economic frameworks. This problem may be seen, as may other social problems, as the price we have to pay for the nature and organization of the institutions that characterize our societies. In a sense we get the problems we deserve.

As far as the media/violence issue is concerned the general tendency—and this applies to much of the research as well as to the media and the public debate—is to grossly oversimplify the problem. People often talk about media violence and violent behaviour almost as though there were no other sources of violence in society. They seek neat, convenient, uncomplicated answers that illustrate simple causal relationships. Once having identified a fixed point of evil, external to self, they use this as a scapegoat, and this helps them to maintain their own particular view of self and society.

Assuming that the media/violence relationship is worth examining, then the first thing to do is to remove the media from the centre of the stage. We should accept from the outset that the main focus of our examination is violence or violent behaviour in society, and that our interest in the media—at least as far as this problem is concerned—is what, if any, is the relationship between the media on the one hand and violent behaviour on the other.

Violence may be categorized in several ways; for example, we may make a distinction between collective or political violence and personal or individual violence. If we accept this distinction and look at collective violence from an historical perspective, we shall see that it is much more normal, central and historically rooted than many would have us believe. Tilly has written:

Historically, collective violence has flowed regularly out of the central political processes of western countries. Men seeking to seize, hold or realign the levers of power have continually engaged in collective violence as part of their struggles. The oppressed have struck in the name of justice, the privileged in the name of order, and those in between in the name of fear.

Much of what we now accept, take for granted and enjoy, is the outcome of violent action in the past, although this will now have been fully legitimated, and the media, together with educational and other institutions, will have played a part in the legitimation process. Certain important aspects of our history offer a tempting model of violence for those with a sense of grievance who might seek to solve their problems and achieve their goals by emulating their illustrious forebears.

Most people think of violence, both in the collective and individual sense, in terms of assassinations, murders, riots, demonstrations, assaults, robberies, rapes, acts of vandalism, and so on. In fact, for many, this sort of 'illegitimate' behaviour represents the totality of violence. But there are others who adopt a different and wider approach and include in their definition war, capital punishment, corporal punishment and certain aspects of penal practice, police behaviour and school discipline. A still broader definition might include poverty, deprivation, economic exploitation and discrimination—and it has been argued that the behaviours in these categories are interrelated and feed off each other. In fact, society may contribute to violence by the seal of approval it gives to certain forms of violence, particularly those that have been legitimated in the name of social control.

There is no need here to favour any one of these definitions, and it is accepted that valid distinctions can and must be made between different kinds of violence. Nevertheless, it is important to stress that research and discussion on media violence should not be confined to 'illegitimate violence' as this is defined by most of those who express concern about media violence. Many of these people, feeling that they have a firm stake in the established system, loudly condemn 'illegitimate violence' but urge the use of what they regard as legal or 'legitimate violence' to protect the existing order, and thereby their own position or vested interest. There is, of course, a difference between legitimate violence and legal violence. The former depends on consensus. Legal violence is not necessarily legitimate.

When violence is examined within the appropriate historical and cultural contexts, we can see many examples of how it has been culturally, and even subculturally, defined. Fortunately, there is much more to life than violence, but it is always with us, and throughout history man has had to deal with it and use it in a variety of ways. Some forms of violence are acceptable and approved, others are not, and the acceptance and approval usually depend more on the objective, the perpetrator and the victim than on the nature and form of the violent behaviour. There never has been, nor is there ever likely to be, any agreed definition of violence by which all the forms of behaviour covered by the various approaches would be universally condemned.

Like the definition of the concept, neither can the sources or roots of violent behaviour be adequately studied outside the appropriate national, historical, cultural and economic contexts. The roots obviously differ from country to country. For example, in the United States it has been suggested that the 'frontier factor', the patterns and extent of immigration, the War of Independence, the industrial revolution, urbanization, rapid social change and mobility, unprecedented prosperity and affluence, the class system and relative deprivation—some of these unique to the United States, some common to several countries—have all played a part in contributing to the present situation in that country.

The media are not mentioned in the above list, and it is worth noting that, in the United States and elsewhere, few of those who have systematically and scientifically studied violent behaviour have cited the media as a major cause. They find the roots of such behaviour elsewhere, as we shall see. However, we shall also see that quite a few researchers, particularly in the United States, whose approach to the problem has been via media and communication studies, have been more inclined to indict the media. The reasons for these differences make an interesting study in themselves. It all depends on how the problem is defined and on what questions are asked.

Even allowing for the aforementioned national and cultural differences, it is still possible, albeit in general terms, to make suggestions about some of the main sources of violent behaviour—and this will be done here without referring to peculiarities in biological makeup. In a report (*The History of Violence in America*) to the National Commission on the Causes and Prevention of Violence in the United States—claimed to be 'the most comprehensive, authoritative study of violence ever published'—we may read that although many factors impinge on what is a complex process, there is considerable evidence that supports the assumption 'that men's frustration over some of the material and social circumstances of their lives is a necessary precondition of group protest and collective violence', and that 'Probably the most important cause of major increases in group violence is the widespread frustration of socially deprived expectations about the goods and conditions of life men believe theirs by right. These frustratable expectations relate not only to material well-being but to more intangible conditions such as security, status, freedom to manage one's own affairs, and satisfying personal relations with others'.

Rapid social change can inflame the situation, particularly in the case of the 'rising expectations among people so situated that lack of opportunity or the obdurate resistance of others precludes their attainment of such expectations'. This is especially true where the country concerned has proudly lived under the flag of material prosperity for all. The role of the media in this connection will be examined later.

It has also been suggested that the situation could be exacerbated where a country (e.g. the United Kingdom) experiences a period of 'sharp relative decline in socio-economic or political conditions after a prolonged period of improving conditions'. The repercussions could be widespread and take several forms, for 'people whose dignity, career expectations, or political ambitions are so frustrated are as likely to rebel as those whose pocket-books are being emptied'. A further problem occurs when people in such situations 'believe that they cannot make their demands felt effectively through normal, approved channels and that "the system" for whatever reasons has become unresponsive to them'.

The above passages from the report to the National Commission are couched mainly in terms of group or collective protest or political behaviour, but they are applicable *mutatis mutandis* to individual behaviour as well. Studies of the violent behaviour of delinquents and criminals show that in many cases there is a lack of appropriate or legitimate ways of problem-solving at a variety of levels. In addition to the economic level, these include the search for identity and satisfactory interpersonal relationships. Those whose opportunities to respond to the demands of life are severely limited and who can visualize no other solution may resort to violence. Violence may come to be regarded as an alternative—perhaps the only—road to success, achievement and status which they have been led to believe society values so highly.

The above comments are not meant to provide a comprehensive explanation of violent behaviour—there are several other approaches, each with its own emphasis. The main intention is to place the media/violence problem in perspective, to draw attention to the complexity of the situation and to the many factors involved, and—above all—to provide a wider, more relevant framework than is normally used, within which the problem may be examined and discussed.

In view of what has been said, it is important to emphasize that it is not being suggested here that the media have no influence. The main points are that violence tends to be inadequately conceptualized, that the role of the media and the process of influence are not properly understood, that the nature and direction of influence are not what they are commonly supposed to be, and that both in research and the public debate the right questions about media influence and about violence in society are rarely asked.

It should be noted that the report of the United States National Commission quite rightly does not absolve media institutions and practitioners from their responsibilities. Although television is not regarded by the commission as a principal cause of violence in society, both the nature and amount of violence on the small screen are roundly condemned. However, in the way they address the problem, the members of the commission—like so many before and after them—do not always ask the right questions. But this is not surprising in view of the fact that they appeared to rely so heavily on the research results from those who oversimplify the problem and think of causal relationships in terms of imitation, increased aggressive drives, attitude change, and so on. Unfortunately, the commission did not really face up to the media implications of its own conclusions about relative deprivation and frustration, which were referred to earlier, although there was a reference in the report to 'additional complications (which might) arise from the high visibility of both violence and social inequalities'.

Clearly violence is not unrelated to frustration, even though the relationship is not as direct and simple as some psychologists seem to have indicated. Consequently, it is certainly worthwhile asking the question: What, if anything, do the media contribute to frustration in our society, and—through this—to aggression and violence?

As we have seen, the situation will vary from country to country, and will clearly be influenced by a variety of factors, media and non-media, including advertising, degree of urbanization, and so on. But let us assume that we are dealing with a commercially oriented, industrialized, urban society where advertising plays an important part in media operations and in the economy generally. The main goals, aims and objectives of this kind of society will be closely related to the achievement of material prosperity, and a great deal of effort, time and money (not just through advertising) will be expended on the promotion of these goals. We know that one of the tasks of advertising is to make people dissatisfied with what they have and to stimulate them to want more, irrespective of their economic circumstances. Society places far greater stress on materialistic goals than on the legitimate ways of achieving these, and the media reflect this imbalance. For the poorer, deprived sections of the community, all this could exacerbate feelings of frustration and discontent.

In these circumstances, deprived groups in society are reminded, by a daily bombardment, of what is available to others, what is said to be theirs for the asking, yet what they certainly do not possess and, moreover, are not likely ever to achieve. There are, of course, other powerful agents of frustration operating at a variety of levels, from the interpersonal to the environmental, but it would be foolish to ignore the possibility that the media, in their normal day-to-day operations, by the presentation of these norms and values, may increase expectations unrealistically, aggravate existing problems, contribute to frustration and consequently to the aggression and violence that may stem from this.

This, however, is not the sort of relationship people normally have in mind when they speculate or pontificate about the link between the media and violence. This type of relationship is certainly not central to those who vociferously condemn media violence.

As might be expected from what has already been said, the condemnation of media content is highly selective. Not all forms of media violence are condemned, any more than are all forms of violent behaviour. In passing, it is interesting to note that quite a number of those who regard media violence as a serious problem not only tend to be aggressive in the way they express this but also adopt a somewhat negative and punitive approach to several other social issues. They favour the death penalty, corporal punishment and tougher discipline generally. They also exhibit racist tendencies, and oppose penal and other social reforms. Overall, they tend to be conservative, conformist and authoritarian. This does not apply by any means to all those who, at some time or other, have expressed concern about the media portrayal of violence.

Just as violence is defined selectively, so research results are used selectively. This is particularly true in the case of some of those just mentioned, that is, in so far as they find it necessary to refer to research at all in support of their claims.

Earlier it was stated that, although those researchers whose work centred on violent behaviour and violence in society had not found the media to be a major source of violent behaviour, others—those whose main focus had been the media and violence—had been more inclined to indict the media. On the whole, most of these researchers are psychologists who have addressed themselves directly to some form of hypothesized relationship between the media's portrayal of violence, on the one hand, and violent or aggressive behaviour on the other. In many cases, their work has been commissioned, and is financially supported, for this specific purpose.

The United States Surgeon General's $1 million twenty-three-project research programme on television violence represents the biggest and most expensive, if not the most sophisticated and co-ordinated, exercise in this area. Since the findings and interpretations of this research programme are frequently quoted by those who claim that a causal link (media violence = violent behaviour) has been established, we must obviously, despite the many criticisms levelled against the individual projects, look at what the report has to say.

In view of the way it has been used to prove a case against television, it is surprising to find that the Surgeon General's report is really quite cautious in its conclusions. It refers to a preliminary and tentative indication of a causal relation between viewing violence on television and aggressive behaviour, operating only on some children who are predisposed to be aggressive and only in some circumstances. It is also recognized that both the heavy viewing of violence and violent or aggressive behaviour could be the joint products of some other common source. They could both be symptoms of a wider condition.

This last point confirms our own research on television and delinquency, carried out in England some years before the Surgeon General's work. In this research, it was also found that the television viewing patterns of the delinquents did not differ significantly from those of their non-delinquent peers from the same socio-economic background. Neither were any significant differences in television viewing and preferences discovered when the media behaviour of aggressive and non-aggressive teenagers in the north-east of England were compared.

These and other studies led us to state, some years ago, that no case had been made where television (or the other media) could be legitimately regarded as a causal, or even as a major contributory, factor of any form of violent behaviour. A more recent conclusion, following a survey of work in this country and elsewhere (including research from the United States) is that it has still not been established that the mass media have any significant effect on the level of violence in society. In fact, the whole weight of research and theory in this field would suggest that the mass media, except just possibly in the case of a small number of pathological individuals, are never the sole cause of such behaviour. At most they play a contributory role and, at that, a minor one.

We should not be surprised at this; rather we should be surprised at the persistence with which researchers still look for simple cause-and-effect relation-ships. In the strict sense we shouldn't really be asking questions about the effect of television. We rarely ask such questions about other institutions such as the family, religion or education.

Two points need to be made with regard to the above comments. First, they refer for the most part to studies that conceptualize the problem in terms of imitation, increased aggression, attitude change, and so on. These represent what may be termed the conventional approach, which, so it is argued here, is based on an inadequate understanding of the media, of violence, of the communication process, and of the nature of society. As we shall see later, the media do have influence, but not primarily in this way. Second, most of the conventional research—the results of which are often used to support the causal argument—has been carried out in the United States. The United States is different from the United Kingdom and other countries in a variety of ways, particularly with regard to the nature and amount of violence both on the screen and in society at large. What obtains in one country need not obtain in another.

More to the point, however, is the possibility that this work, or at least certain interpretations of it, does not even hold in the United States. It has been criticized on several grounds (theoretically, conceptually and methodologically), particularly for the lack of clarity and consistency in the use of such concepts as violence and aggression. In many cases the operationalization of the concepts is also very questionable. There is likely to be a substantial gap between behavioural, verbal and attitudinal responses in a laboratory and anti-social aggression or violence in the home or street. The major weaknesses in the experimental laboratory work are the artificiality in the setting, the type and time of the measurements, and the nature of the 'victim' (e.g. dolls, balloons, recipients of electric shocks, etc.). Moreover, it is by no means always clear what is really being measured. Validity is low. Generalization to antisocial behaviour in real-life situations must be very suspect indeed. Survey work—the results of which, so it is claimed, point in the same direction as those from the laboratory work—is more realistic but is not susceptible to causal explanation.

Perhaps the last word on this highly controversial topic should be given to George Comstock, who is thoroughly familiar with the work, and who has been closely and supportively associated with the Surgeon General's research and its follow-up over the last few years. Writing in late 1976, Comstock, fully aware of the convergence of the different research approaches, reports as follows:

It is tempting to conclude that television violence makes viewers more anti-socially aggressive, somewhat callous, and generally more fearful of the society in which they live. It may, but the social and behavioral science evidence does not support such a broad indictment.

The evidence on desensitization and fearfulness is too limited for such broad conclusions at this time. The evidence on aggressiveness is much more extensive, but it does not support a conclusion of increased antisocial aggression. Such a conclusion rests on the willingness of the person who chooses to sit in judgement to extrapolate from the findings on interpersonal aggression to more serious, non-legal acts.

Most important, the evidence does not tell us anything about the degree of social harm or criminal antisocial violence that may be attributable to television. It may be great, negligible, or nil.

However, in making these comments and criticisms let me also confirm what was said earlier, namely, that there is no intention here to absolve those who work in the media from their responsibilities—the gratuitous insertion of violence for kicks or profits is to be deplored. But deploring the portrayal of violence is one thing; linking it with violent behaviour is another entirely different matter.

Neither is there any attempt to play down the role of the media. The media are certainly not without influence; it is the process of influence that is more complex and probably more far-reaching than is commonly realized. For example, the way the media report violence and deviant behaviour plays a part in defining problems and gives focus to public concern. Violence and deviant behaviour, particularly in their extreme forms, are extensively covered by the media in most Western societies. There is nothing new about this practice, nor about the style or manner of presentation, unless it is that it is not quite as sensational as it once was. Yet it could be that, because of the nature of our fragmented, plural, industrial society, where many believe mediated culture plays an increasingly prominent part in shaping our values and behaviour, media portrayals of violence and deviance have more important social repercussions today than they had in the past.

Some years ago an American sociologist, Marshall Clinard, writing on 'The Newspaper and Crime', argued:

The press has been charged with generally promoting and glorifying crime because of the volume of its news items . . . The amount and prominence of space devoted to crime in the newspapers and the amount of conservation based on these stories present a bewildering picture of immorality in our society. By continually playing up crime, it is likely that newspapers are important in making us a crime-centred culture. As a result crime often seems more frequent than it is.

Although this claim and others like it are rarely accompanied by hard supporting evidence, it is not unreasonable to hypothesize that what people read in the papers, hear on the radio and see on television might influence their views about the nature and extent of violence in our society. Some years ago studies carried out in the United States indicated that public estimates of the amount and type of crime in the community were more closely related to newspaper reports than to the actual amounts of crime as recorded by the police. Although other studies have been more ambiguous, there is no need here to argue the pros and cons of conflicting research results. The main point is to draw attention to one of the ways in which the media may be related to public perceptions of violent behaviour.

The media help to set the social/political agenda. They select, organize, emphasize, define and amplify. They convey meanings and perspectives, offer solutions, associate certain groups with certain types of values and behaviour, create anxiety, and legitimate or justify the status quo and the prevailing systems of social control. They structure 'the pictures of the world' that are available to us and, in turn, these pictures may structure our beliefs and possible modes of action. It is in these complex and difficult ways that we must examine the influence of the media.

The media, of course, do not work in isolation. What we should really study is the mix, the interaction or interrelationship between media experiences on the one hand, and non-media or situational experiences on the other. These will differ from issue to issue, from person to person, from country to country, and so on. For example, we know from our research on race relations and racial conflict that the media may have a disproportionate influence in conveying meanings and perspectives where personal experience is lacking. Our work on the media and race showed that, over a seven-year period, the media portrayed non-white people essentially as a threat and a problem, and that this was reflected in public attitudes. Here we have a clear example of the media exacerbating conflict, and reinforcing, if not actually creating, social problems. Our research also shows that the coverage by the British media of the hostilities in Northern Ireland is another example of conflict exacerbation.

There are, then, several questions we might ask. For example, what kind of pictures are being presented to us? Are they false pictures in which the extent of violence and deviance is exaggerated and its nature distorted? Is it true that by designating violence as news (the more violent, the more newsworthy), a climate of alarm is created, and fears, anticipations and expectations about violent behaviour built up?

These questions bring us to even more fundamental ones. What is news? Do the mass media create new 'facts' by making non-news news? Must the negative, deviant, violent or sensational always predominate? There are other questions, too, that need not be detailed here, but one of the things we can say at this stage is that, on the whole, the way the news about violence and related issues is presented by the media makes it unlikely that the facts will be placed in a meaningful context, or that the issues behind the story with regard to offence, offender, victim or official agency will be adequately covered.

It is often argued by those working in the media that, when events are reported, it is natural to focus on the immediate case. That is where the drama lies, where the action is, and what the public wants to know about. This may be true, but it provides a poor base from which an adequate understanding of the problem can be developed.

The formation of sound social policy typically depends on knowledge of changes in the development rate and distribution of the relevant events, but policies more frequently are formed in reaction to certain extreme cases. The media deal in extreme cases, and we know they are widely used as the main source of information and are regarded by many as highly credible.

One of the reasons why the media portray situations as they do is because they operate within a socio-economic system where readers and viewers have to be won and kept. The presentation of violence and related phenomena have become vital in this connection.

For the daily news media, persons, events and happenings (particularly negative ones), are the basic units of news. One reason for the concentration on events is the 'publication frequency' of the media themselves. Events are more likely to be picked up by the media working to a daily publication cycle if they occur within the space of one day. For example, a demonstration is a possible news event, while the development of a political movement over several years does not have the correct 'frequency'.

The concentration on events itself makes some aspects of a story more likely to be regarded as newsworthy than others. The issue of violence, for example, is directly related to the visible forms of events in the streets. But this preoccupation with events and incidents tends to exclude consideration of background development and of the issues involved.

One of our research projects, which focused on the media coverage of a large political demonstration, provides a good illustration of some of the foregoing points. It also raises several important questions about the influence of this form of presentation on the general public's assessment of the events going on in the world, and its consequences for social action.

In this research, differences between the various media in the treatment of the demonstration were obviously detected, but we were also able to show a more important and fundamental similarity between practically all branches of the media. In all but one case, the story was interpreted in terms of the same basic issue which had originally made it news. Viewers and readers were not presented with various interpretations focusing on different aspects of the same event, but with basically the same interpretation that focused on the same limited aspect, namely, the issue of violence. Yet violence need not have been central—in fact, in reality it was not central. The 'set' of violence was used because, together with the other implications of news values, it was the logical outcome of the existing organization of the news process, and of the assumptions on which it rested.

As indicated earlier, these news values are an integral part of professional news selection and presentation as this has developed within our particular socio-economic system. No matter what lofty ideals are claimed, numbers of readers, listeners and viewers, and the economics of advertising, play an important part in shaping these values and the news which they underlie.

It is also important to note that the images created in this way may endure, and may be capable of being extended to related areas. The coverage of student demonstrations and, in the United Kingdom, the reporting of the anti-apartheid demonstrations against the visiting South African rugby team, are but two of many examples of the apparent pervasiveness and durability of the image of violent confrontation and other related negative stereotypes.

But, argues the media man, we know what the public wants and we provide this. The public likes what it is familiar with, what it has been given over the years, what it has come to accept and expect. Supply influences demand. It is of course clear that many people like their news to be action-packed and incident-oriented, lively, entertaining, even sensational and violent. This sort of material may meet different needs for different people, but the emphasis on action, visual attractiveness and immediacy (rather than on what is socially significant), doesn't stem solely from some basic human need. It receives plenty of help and reinforcement from the media.

What, then, are the results of this form of news presentation? One interpretation is that the way the media deal with these situations may lead to labelling, to the association—perhaps unjustifiable—of certain groups with violent behaviour, and possibly to the acceptance of violence as a legitimate way of dealing with problems or as a necessary form of retaliation.

In the case of the demonstration project, given the climate of public opinion at the time of the research, the largely negative presentation was almost bound to devalue the case of the protesters. Moreover, in the long run this might increase rather than reduce the risk of violent behaviour. Because of the way the media operate, a minority group may have to be violent before there is any chance of its case being presented to the general public.

It would also appear from this and related research that, whether we are dealing with student demands for reform in the universities, anti-apartheid marches, anti-war demonstrations, drug-taking, alcoholics, homosexuals, prisoners' unions, racial questions, or strikes, there is a very good chance that the news story will centre on violence and confrontation. The account will be largely isolated from antecedent conditions and convey little understanding of either root causes or aims. In fact, the whole presentation is likely to be fragmented and out of context.

Research has shown that, in reporting violence and deviance, the media exaggerate, sensationalize and stereotype, and that public perceptions derived from these presentations may modify or even create the behaviour in question. For example, the images of drug use obtained from the media, so it is claimed, have influenced court and police behaviour and, in turn, this has influenced the behaviour in such a way as to make it conform with the stereotypes. The stereotypes were fulfilled, the behaviour—previously marginal—became more central and more frequent, and this was followed by further (reinforcing) social reaction. The problem was confirmed at a redefined level, and all sides behaved as they were 'expected' to behave.

At a different level, the overall effect of this type of presentation of deviance and social problems could be to eliminate or play down alternative conceptions of social order. The news-selection process, therefore, may have an ideological significance for the maintenance of the status quo of power and interest by managing conflict and dissent in the interest of the establishment.

This represents a more complex and indirect approach to media influence than is normally postulated, but surely the study of the media in this way is much more valid and rewarding than the relatively simple-minded causal stimulus-response approaches that have been frequently if unproductively utilized in the past.

But these newer approaches do not provide all the answers. For example, the labelling-amplification approach mentioned earlier, although useful and interesting, does not account for deviant behaviour—still less for the initial deviation. It also has a limited application, for it does not apply equally to all forms of deviant behaviour, some of which are clearly visible.

The importance of public definitions and expectations about violence, as contributory factors to the processes by which the behaviour is publicly defined, labelled or stereotyped, and even on occasions amplified, should always be borne in mind, without exaggerating the possibilities. People do have experiences other than media experiences and, although the agenda may be set by the media, the ability of the public selectively to use and interpret what the media make available should not be underestimated. The media may inform public perceptions and beliefs about violence, but there are other sources of information, even though, in many societies, most of the population have little or no personal experience of violence.

Generally, media violence is viewed negatively, and is criticized or condemned because of its alleged disruptive effects. But we have already referred to the possibility that the media, in their portrayal of violence and deviance, may serve a 'positive' function by acting as an instrument of social control and by maintaining the status quo. The function may be regarded as positive from the standpoint of the establishment, although not necessarily from the standpoint of other groups in society who are seeking change.

The media may reinforce the status quo by maintaining a 'cultural consensus'. It is possible that the media coverage of violence could enhance normative consensus and community integration. Where people have little firsthand knowledge of violent crime they are likely to depend on the media for most of their information. The media inform, bring to light, create awareness, redefine the boundaries of what is acceptable and what is not, and structure perceptions of the nature and extent of violence. In doing this they bring people together in opposition to disorder, reinforce a belief in common values, facilitate the imposition of sanctions, and strengthen social control. But in order to do this the violence must be made visible throughout society—hence the importance of the media.

Although many of the hypotheses that stem from this approach have still to be put to the test, there is nothing new in the view that regards violence as a catalyst. Marx, Durkheim and Mead all stressed the unanticipated functions of crime in creating a sense of solidarity within the community by arousing the moral and aesthetic sentiments of the public. More recently, Lewis Coser developed a related idea when he argued that not only criminals but law-enforcing agents also may call forth a sense of solidarity against their behaviour. In certain circumstances the use of extra-legal violence, particularly when exhibited under the glare of television cameras, and made highly visible to the public at large, could lead to awareness, indignation and revulsion that might result in the rejection of a hitherto accepted practice. Many questionable things that we don't know about—or at least that do not intrude too much into our everyday lives—are done in our name and in the name of social order and justice. But passivity and acquiescence become more difficult with an increase in visibility. It has been suggested that the media coverage of racial disturbances in the southern states in the United States in the early 1960s is a case in point.

The media coverage of racial disturbances in the United States, as well as drawing attention once more to the different definitions of violence and to its functional or dysfunctional consequences, also shows the complexity of this whole problem in a heterogeneous, pluralistic, stratified society. After seeing racial disturbances in the streets on their television sets, some people may reach for their guns in the name of law and order, others may learn a lesson or two that they will put into practical use when their time comes, and still others—as the hitherto invisible or partly visible becomes clearly visible—may be jolted out of their apathy and stirred into social action directed at the roots of the problem. Here, as in other situations, different people take different things from the same message. There are no easy decisions for the responsible broadcaster in deciding what to present and how to present it in situations like this. In reminding broadcasters of their responsibilities, we must also recognize their difficulties, and try to understand their problems.

In the last few pages we have been dealing with non-fictional media material, but George Gerbner, one of the most prominent mass-communication researchers in the United States, is much more concerned with fictional material. He would agree with some of the criticisms made earlier in this article about the inadequacies of the conventional research approaches, particularly those that focus on attitude and behavioural change and the stimulation of aggression. He is also critical of studies that are based on selectively used media, and this in part stems from his firm conviction that television is essentially different from the other media, and that research on television requires an entirely new approach: 'The essential differences between television and the other media are more crucial than the similarities . . . the reach, scope, ritualization, organic connectedness and non-selective use of mainstream television makes it different from other media of mass communications.'

Gerbner argues that television should not be isolated from the mainstream of modern culture because 'it *is* the mainstream'. It is 'the central cultural aim of

American society', a 'major force for enculturation [that permeates] both the initial and final years of life as well as the years between'. His interest is not so much in individual programmes or specific messages as in 'whole systems of messages' and their consequences for 'common consciousness'.

He sees little point in making the conventional distinction between information and entertainment. He regards entertainment, particularly television drama, as highly informative—'the most broadly effective educational fare in any culture'—and maintains that all of us, whatever our status or educational background, obtain much of our knowledge of the real world from fictional representations. Television entertainment provides common ground for all sections of the population as it offers a continuous stream of 'facts' and impressions about the many aspects of life and society: 'Never before have all classes and groups (as well as ages) shared so much of the same culture and the same perspectives.'

This is not just a speculative exercise on Gerbner's part, for he supports at least part of his case with some of the most impressive systematic analysis of television content ever carried out. Naturally, he recognizes and accepts that content analysis by itself tells us nothing definitive about the viewing public's reactions to the content. He claims, however, that his studies of the public, although as yet in their early stages, demonstrate quite clearly the ability of television to cultivate its own 'reality'. In all the cases studied, heavier viewers had versions of social reality that squared more with 'the television world' than did the versions of the lighter viewers.

Gerbner's work, then, provides some support for the main themes of this article, namely, that television is not without influence (Gerbner would put it much more strongly than this), but that the nature and directions of the influence are not as commonly supposed, or of the kind that conventional researchers seem anxious to trace and identify. He also supports the view that the concern about media violence, based on the possibilities of disruption that threaten the established norms of belief, behaviour and morality, is ill-conceived and badly directed.

Gerbner, then, is certainly worried about television's portrayal of violence, but this is not because of its potential for disruption or even change, but because it might function to legitimate and maintain the power and authority of the establishment. Change is more likely to be impeded than facilitated as television demonstrates the values of society and the rules of the game 'by dramatic stories of their symbolic violations'. In this way, it serves the social order of the industrial system. 'The system is the message' and the system works well—perhaps 'too well in cultivating uniform assumptions, exploitable fears, acquiescence to power and resistance to meaningful change'.

Gerbner sees television violence as the simplest and cheapest dramatic means available to demonstrate the rules of the game of power, to reinforce social control, and to maintain the existing social order. He supports this view with data from his research, suggesting that the maintenance mechanism seems to work through cultivating a sense of danger, risk and insecurity. This leads, especially for the less powerful groups in the community, to acquiescence to and dependence upon established authority. It also facilitates the legitimation of the use of force by the authorities in order to keep their position.

As far as the influence of television is concerned, this reinforcement or maintenance function is considered to be far more important than any threat to the social order that might stem from television-induced imitation, attitude change, or increased aggressive drives. In fact, Gerbner states that 'media-incited criminal violence may be a price industrial cultures extract from some citizens for the general pacification of most others. . . . Television—the established religion of the industrial order—appears to cultivate assumptions that fit its socially functional myths'.

Violence and its portrayal by the media clearly serve specific social functions, although these will differ from country to country, as will the nature and extent of media violence. Veikko Pietilä, the Finnish scholar, in comparing television violence in the United States and the Soviet Union, shows that in the two countries, it is presented in different contexts and serves different functions.

In the Soviet Union, televised violence tends to be presented in historical, societal and collective contexts, whilst in the United States, the emphasis is on individually oriented aggression that is frequently linked to personal success, achievement and private property. In the United States, one of the main aims is to create excitement and attract and keep an audience in a fiercely competitive system where profits have to be made. In the Soviet Union, according to Pietilä, the purposes are more often propagandistic and educational.

Pietilä comments on both the commodity (box office) and ideological functions of televised violence in the United States, and asks a question not unlike some of those already posed in this article. He asks if television violence represents a vital aspect of the essential nature of this society, because a core element in its history and development has been individual success by means of violence or aggression. This form of violence is deeply rooted in the society, and the media portrayal of violence is a manifestation of this state of affairs that ought not to surprise us. It is also suggested that the constant emphasis on this theme by reinforcement, diversion, or some other process, helps to preserve the existing order.

Pietilä confines this type of speculative analysis to capitalist societies and refers to television content contributing 'to the directing and regulating of social process in such a way that the existing order and form of these societies is protected'. We saw that Pietilä's research indicated that televised violence in socialist societies is different in content and context from that in capitalist societies. Not surprisingly, he argues that media violence functions in different ways in the two countries. However, at another level, it serves both systems by reinforcing the existing order. At this level the system is the message in both countries.

This and similar topics could be pursued much further and at greater depth, but enough has been written to illustrate one of the main aims of this article, which is to suggest some of the social and political consequences that may possibly stem from the ways in which the media deal with violence and related phenomena—ways that do not figure prominently either in the general debate or in the research programmes of most mass-communication researchers.

It must be emphasized, however, that at this stage we are mainly theorizing and talking in terms of possibilities and hypotheses. We are not in a position to make clear, definitive statements, supported by evidence, on the precise role of the media in the areas and directions outlined in this article. The necessary research has not been carried out. Moreover, even if the recommended research were carried out the neat, simple, packaged, convenient, unequivocal answers sought by so many are still not likely to be forthcoming. The nature of the problem is not susceptible to this type of answer. The process is too complex.

Of course, new research is required—it always will be if we are to have informed policies. To accept that research by itself is unable to provide an answer to all our questions, like a catechism, is not to reject its usefulness. We must not be unrealistic in our expectations, but there is no doubt that research has a substantial contribution to make to our understanding of social institutions and social processes. I am writing, of course, about a particular type of research.

I am convinced that it will be more profitable to explore the avenues of inquiry outlined in this paper, difficult though it may be—even just to speculate on these approaches—than to persist in the much simpler conventional search that attempts to establish causal links between media violence and real-life violence.

One final point needs to be made. As far as research is concerned, although a great deal remains to be done we are not entirely ignorant, as I hope the references to the results from quite a number of projects will have established. We have enough information now to know where to start if we wish to reduce violent behaviour in our societies. The final report of the United States National Commission on the Causes and Prevention of Violence called in 1969 for 'a reordering of national priorities and for a greater investment of resources—to establish justice and to ensure domestic tranquillity'. The emphasis was on social reform and increased expenditure to facilitate the achievement of essential social goals. The needs and the priorities are still the same, and are likely to remain that way for some time.

Bibliography

COMSTOCK, G. *The Evidence of Television Violence*. Santa Monica, Calif., Rand Corporation, 1976.

CROLL, P. The Nature of Public Concern with Television, with Particular Reference to Violence. Unpublished paper. Leicester, United Kingdom. Centre for Mass Communication Research.

DEMBO, R. Critical Factors in Understanding Adolescent Aggression. *Social Psychiatry 8*, 1973.

Final Report of the National Commission on the Causes and Prevention of Violence. Washing-

Bibliography (*continued*)

ton, D.C., United States Government Printing Office, 1969.

GERBNER, G.; GROSS, L. Living with Television: A Violence Profile. *Journal of Communication*, spring 1976.

GRAHAM, H. D.; GURR, T. R. (eds.). *The History of Violence in America*. A report to the National Commission on the Causes and Prevention of Violence. New York, N.Y., Bantam Books, 1969.

HALLORAN, J. D. Probleme der Berichterstattung in den Massenmedien über Kriminelles Verhalten. *Universitas*, August 1976.

HALLORAN, J. D.; BROWN, R. L.; CHANEY, D. C. *Television and Delinquency*. Leicester, United Kingdom, Leicester University Press, 1970.

HARTMANN, P.; HUSBAND, C. *Racism and the Mass Media*. Davis-Poynter, 1974.

HARTMANN, P.; HUSBAND, C.; CLARK, J. Race as News: a Study in the Handling of Race in the British National Press from 1963 to 1970. In: *Race as News*. Paris, Unesco, 1974.

HOWITT, D.; CUMBERBATCH, G. *Mass Media, Violence and Society*. Elek, 1975.

HOWITT, D.; DEMBO, R. A Subcultural Account of Media Effects. *Human Relations*, Vol. 27, No. 1.

Patterns of Violence. *The Annals of the American Academy of Political and Social Science*, March 1966.

PIETILÄ, Veikko. Notes on Violence in the Mass Media. *Instant Research on Peace and Violence*, No. 4. Tampere Peace Research Institute, Finland, 1976.

Television and Growing Up: The Impact of Televised Violence. Report to the Surgeon General, United States Public Health Service, from the Surgeon General's Scientific Advisory Committee on Television and Social Behavior. Washington, D.C., United States Department of Health, Education and Welfare, 1972.

Although applauding George Gerbner and Larry Gross for their innovative research and for high-lighting television as the dominant cultural system of the modern world, Horace Newcomb questions the basic validity of their violence profile research. Newcomb argues that the cultural indicators approach is couched in terms of a ritual model of culture studies, but that lurking in the actual con-duct of the research is the old, outmoded transportation model of communication. In a rebuttal, Gerbner and Gross argue that survey data provide evidence of the validity of their work, particularly when comparing heavy and light viewers on their perceptions of crime. Furthermore, they see their analysis as doing far more than a simple transportation model suggests because they see the social sources of television content as rooted deeply in our societal structure. Dr. Newcomb is Associate Professor of English at the University of Texas at Austin. Dr. Gerbner is Professor of Communica-tions and Dean of the Annenberg School of Communications at the University of Pennsylvania. Dr. Gross is Associate Professor of Communications at the Annenberg School.

26

ASSESSING THE VIOLENCE PROFILE STUDIES OF GERBNER AND GROSS
A Humanistic Critique and Suggestion

Horace Newcomb

By defining television as an "environment of symbols," Gerbner and Gross raise questions that are congenial to and problematic for humanistic study. A difficulty arises when the "environment of symbols" must be interpreted. In their interpretation TV becomes a world "ruled" by violence. Other content factors must be interpreted in terms of this dominant symbol. More serious problems emerge when audience responses are interpreted in terms of these prior interpretations. The difficulties are caused in part by the use of a "transportation" model of communication in spite of a rhetoric that reflects a "ritual" model. Application of a ritual model to the world of TV content would require the location of television's symbols in a culture's history of symbolic construct, definition of the reorganization of these symbols in TV content, and careful analysis of how meanings are appropriated by audiences.

Every nomenclature has its implications, leading us to such-and-such observations rather than such-and-such others. And in that sense even the most empirical of term-guided studies (and there can be no other kind) has a built-in deductive aspect, by turning our observations in one direction rather than some other. Hence, instead of telling ourselves that we can dodge this inevitable terministic limitation, shouldn't we begin by asking ourselves what kind of terms might best reveal the complexity of the problem? There is a sense in which all key terms are reductionist, being related to a subject in much the way that the title of a book is related to its contents. But there is a vast difference between nomenclature that over-simplifies and one that is, rather, like the glimpse into the possible details of a panorama.

—*Kenneth Burke*, Dramatism and Development

From Horace Newcomb, "Assessing the Violence Profile Studies of Gerbner and Gross: A Humanistic Critique and Suggestion," *Communication Research* 5, 3 (July 1978) 264-282. Copyright 1978 by Sage Publications, Inc.

More than any other research effort in the area of television studies the work of Gerbner and Gross and their associates sits squarely at the juncture of the social sciences and the humanities.[1] Nowhere is this better illustrated than in their article, "Living With Television: The Violence Profile" (1976),[2] and it is primarily to that discussion that this essay is addressed, though I will also take into account Gerbner's (1971) contribution in the collection of papers prepared for the U.S. Surgeon-General's report. There it is clear that the broad concern with violence might be defined in social scientific terms as a "social problem." But the definitions of what television is, how it works in American culture, and how culture itself works, are humanistic in nature. One might wish to quarrel with the inclusion of a view that is essentially anthropological in the domain of the humanities, but the particular approach to culture outlined by Gerbner and Gross places them in the humanistic camp among various anthropological positions.

In their analysis questions about *what* to study are framed in humanistic terms. Methods of quantitative measurement and analysis are applied to the fictional world of television. Interpretations of the data supplied by this description raise problems that are, again, essentially humanistic in nature. The television audience is approached with questions framed on the basis of these interpretations and, once again, statistical profiles are established about the relationship between the audience and the medium. Broad conclusions are drawn from these profiles and these conclusions have often been referred to in the complex process of policy formulation. This application of information gathered in such intricate procedures of definition, interpretation, and measurement makes the close examination of the studies all the more necessary. Some attention has been given to the methods and results of the quantitative portions of the studies and the definitions of categories of measurement. When that attention has resulted in negative commentary responses have been offered by Gerbner and Gross.[3]

The intention of this essay is to analyze from a humanistic point of view some of the basic assumptions, definitions, assertions, and arguments in the Violence Profile studies. I should say here that I focus on the Gerbner-Gross studies not only because of their prominence, but because they have been open and forthright in their use of mixed methods of analysis and in their call for the development of new techniques of study appropriate for a new medium. Almost all social scientific studies are at times involved in complex interpretive issues, and many are far more veiled in these steps, or are unwilling to admit to the complexities involved. But the question, "What does it all *mean*?" is, essentially, a humanistic question. Gerbner and Gross have taught us that we shall have to be open to many methodologies in answering that question for television. Indeed, what their work often demonstrates is that rigid distinctions between humanistic and social scientific questions may be useless in this area. Though many of my own comments here are negative criticisms of their research, they are offered on the assumption, shared I think by Gerbner and Gross, that television shatters many of our disciplinary boundaries. The usual dismissal of the Annenberg projects as "body counts" or "numbers studies" are thoroughly insufficient whether offered by humanists or magazine journalists. There is no easy "us" or "them" approach. My goal here is to enrich the dialogue around television.

That Gerbner and Gross have a strong basis on which to converse with the humanistic disciplines is clear from their definition of television as an object of study.

> The environment that sustains the most distinctive aspects of human existence is the environment of symbols. We learn, share, and act upon meanings derived from that environment. The first and longest lasting organization of the symbolic world was what we now call religion. Within its sacred scope, in earlier times, were the most essential processes of culture: art, science, technology, statecraft, and public story-telling.
>
> Common rituals and mythologies are agencies of symbolic socialization and control. They demonstrate how society works by dramatizing its norms and values. They are essential parts of the general system of messages that cultivates prevailing outlooks (which is why we call it culture) and regulates social relationships. This system of messages, with its story-telling functions, makes people perceive as real and normal and right that which fits the established social order.
>
> The institutional processes producing these message systems have become increasingly professionalized, industrialized, centralized, and specialized. Their principle locus shifted from handicraft

to mass production and from traditional religion to formal education,
to the mass media of communication—particularly television
[p. 173].

While there may be parts of this definition that are problematic,
while in some cases there is a need for clarification, the general
approach, the willingness to identify and discuss an "environment of symbols," is thoroughly congenial to the humanistic
perspective.

From that perspective, from that part of it that has been involved with the study of television formulas rather than with the
significance of individual programs, the most significant contribution of the Gerbner-Gross projects has been the careful
mapping of television's social world. It is crucial to know the
details of, rather than intuit patterns in, that world. For instance,
our "sense" that there is a television "type" is made far more
definite when we can point to the fact that "while only one in
three male leads is shown as intending to or ever having been
married, two of every three females are married or expect to
marry in the story," or that "nearly half of all females are concentrated in the most sexually eligible young adult population, to
which only one-fifth of males are assigned." We feel familiar
with, and much more sure of generalizations based upon the observation that "children, adolescents, and old people together
account for less than 15 percent of the total fictional populations"
(p. 183). Similar statistical definition regarding employment patterns, types of activity, racial demography, and social class add up
to a fictional world that is not in any sense a reflection of the statistical patterns of American society as television viewers experience it. Because of this work the specific content of that
"environment of symbols" is made far more precise. Such careful
work is rarely offered by humanists. Too often we have assumed
that significant patterns observed and subjectively marked by
trained analysts are equally obvious to viewers. We have asserted
our own responses as generalizations. The Annenberg studies
offer far more precise indications of the relationship of the
"world" of TV fictions to the world of experience.

A strain on this synthesis of the humanities and the social
sciences begins to develop, however, when it becomes necessary

to interpret this environment of symbols. That strain can be illustrated by focusing on a series of assumptions and assertions about how television works, how viewers perceive it, and what, finally, the symbols mean. Ultimately the strain is sufficient to cause us to return to the initial definition of "symbol" and "environment of symbols" and demand clarification in the use of these terms.

An early difficulty arises when we are told that "The substance of the consciousness cultivated by TV is not so much specific attitudes and opinions as more basic assumptions about the 'facts' of life and standards of judgment on which conclusions are based" (p. 175). I take this to mean that distinctions among programs are far less significant than similarities. On one level this could refer to the plots of individual television dramas in which we notice varying motivation for actions, individual responses to events, speeches or lines or small bits of reaction on the part of actors. On a different level the same judgment could be held against formulaic structures rather than pieces of content. Put concretely this distinction would suggest that it is far more significant that violent actions in westerns and detective formulas are seen as (for example) the actions of certain social types—white, middle-aged, males—than that one is a cowboy and the other a detective, or that one shoots a man in a ritualistic gun duel and the other in a dodging street battle. The implications are that all viewers are "getting" similar messages and that they get certain messages rather than others.

No evidence is offered for this most basic assumption, other than the observation that television viewing is nonselective. That is to say, "Individual tastes and program preferences are less important in determining viewing patterns than is the time a program is on. The nearly universal, nonselective, and habitual use of television fits the ritualistic pattern of its programming. You watch television as you might attend a church service, except that most people watch television more religiously" (p. 177). Without commenting on the possibility that this view of television and religion reflect an essentially Catholic as opposed to Protestant view, I would suggest that the leap from nonselective to nonperceptive is unwarranted. There is, so far as I know, no evidence to support the assumption that "specific attitudes and opinions" are less strongly cultivated by television than " 'facts' of life."

A similar problem emerges in a discussion of the aesthetic composition of television drama. Gerbner and Gross assert that

> The realism of TV fiction hides its synthetic and functionally selective nature. The dominant stylistic convention of Western narrative art—novels, plays, films, TV dramas—is that of representational realism. However contrived television plots are, viewers assume that they take place against a backdrop of the world of television drama. It is also highly informative. That is, it offers to the unsuspecting viewer a continuous stream of "facts" and impressions about the way of the world, about the constancies and vagaries of human nature, and about the consequences of actions. The premise of realism is a Trojan horse which carries within it a highly selective, synthetic, and purposeful image of the facts of life [p. 178].

Many of the terms of this definition are exceptionally congenial to humanistic discussion. But the question again is, on what grounds do the authors assert that "Nothing impeaches the basic 'reality' of television drama." The very quoted nature of "reality" and "facts" indicates that in the totality of the television world the *authors* do not consider these things as factual or real. They are significant, symbolic distortions whose meanings must be interpreted. Much hinges here on the assertion that the viewer is "unsuspecting." The Trojan horse metaphor implies deceit and subversion. The additional suggestion is made that there may be in television "subtle patterns against whose influence we may all be somewhat defenseless" (p. 179) and that there are other "seductively persuasive" sorts of imagery there. These negative definitions, so crucial to the argument, rest on the unsupported assumptions that viewers are unsuspecting and do not perceive TV constructs as essentially fictional, that nothing impeaches the realistic base of television, and that perception is selective in this, rather than other, directions. Consequently, it is broad facts rather than specific meanings that are assumed to be getting through to the viewer.

Questions of televised violence must now enter our analysis for it is not merely any or all "basic assumptions about the 'facts' of life" that are most often raised about TV. The effects of violence have been the primary concern. Measurement of content has focused on violence portrayed on TV. In part, perhaps, that choice is historical, reflecting our society's generalized concern with the topic and its willingness to fund studies in this area. The Annenberg projects have, of course, been expanded, and it may be that some of the findings with regard to sex role stereotyping and other, broader social areas, will modify findings in this initial area of study. But procedures for discussing violence on television are beset with certain basic problems that go beyond the assumptions I have discussed so far. If the same or similar procedures are applied in other areas it is important that these problems be clearly identified.

The first, from the perspective of the humanist, is that of definition. In measuring violence on television Gerbner and Gross use "a clear cut and commonly understood definition,"

> the overt expression of physical force against self or other, compelling action against one's will on pain of being hurt or killed, or actually hurting or killing [p. 184].

While this definition may be commonly understood by researchers and other citizens in the world of experience, the application of any stipulated, a priori, definition to a world of fiction is highly questionable. From the humanistic perspective it would be both more cautious and useful to try to determine a meaning of violence as it is understood by the characters themselves in the fictional world of television. One could then compare that definition with others, "commonly understood," in order to take the first interpretive step toward understanding the *meaning* of the symbolic distortion. Instead, Gerbner and Gross measure the incidence of violence as they have defined it, impute aesthetic and behavioral effects to the incidence so measured, and then interpret the world of television in light of that effect.

Let me be more specific by using figures averaged over the years 1967-1975. Nine hundred twenty-four programs, 630.2 hours, and 2649 leading characters were analyzed. 79.8% of the programs and 83.6% of the hours contained some violence as defined for the study. Measuring all hours there was an average of 7.4 violent episodes per hour. Of all leading characters 62.9% were involved in some violence, 10.2% were involved in some killing. Presumably it is on this basis, for I can determine no other that does not rest purely on interpretation (and if that is the case the substance of the interpretive process should be presented rather than merely the conclusion), that Gerbner and Gross assert that television provides a "symbolic world *ruled largely by violence*" (p. 178; my emphasis). This is the effect of the incidence of violence as found in fictional television. Yet, it is a long and clearly unwarranted leap from the measured incidence of violence (or any other dramatic element for that matter) to the assertion that that dramatic world is "ruled" by the single, particular dramatic factor in which the researcher is most interested. What Gerbner and Gross seem to be saying, and I emphasize seem because it is not clear, is that we all see violence as more prominent than other aspects of television. The incidence of violence, it is implied, is the most important dramatically in that it governs all sorts of other fictional interactions. It is suggested that violence is more easily understood than attitudes toward it or the context in which it occurs. Such conclusions are obviously dependent upon the earlier assertion that we perceive facts rather than attitudes and opinions. As a consequence of this chain of reasoning, the implication goes, much of what we learn from television is learned in terms of this dominant symbol.

It is crucial that we understood here that violence, for Gerbner and Gross, is a symbol. Perhaps it would be better to say that violence is a metaphor that must be interpreted, for having demonstrated that violence is widely present in television fiction, the authors go on to tell us that fictional violence does not mean violence, in the sense that its primary effect is the stimulation of similar actions. Rather, "TV violence is a dramatic demonstration of power which communicates much about social norms and relationships, about goals and means, about winners and losers, about the risks of life and the price for transgressions of society's rules" (p. 178). Violence structures a world that places, types, and directs viewers.

> Representation in the fictional world signifies social existence; absence means symbolic annihilation. Being buffeted by events and victimized by people denotes social impotence; ability to wrest events about, to act freely, boldly, and effectively is a mark of dramatic importance and social power. Values and forces come into play through characterization; good is a certain type of attractiveness, evil is a personality defect, and right is the might that wins. Plots weave a threat of causality into the fabric of dramatic ritual, as stock characters act out familiar parts and confirm preferred

notions of what's what, who's who, and who counts for what. The
issue is rarely in doubt; the action is typically a game of social
typing, group identification, skill, and power [p. 182].

It is at this point in their analysis that Gerbner and Gross offer
their specific demographic outline of the television world and then
go on to say that "Violence plays a key role in such a world. It is
the simplest and cheapest dramatic means available to demonstrate the rules of the game of power" (p. 183). *That violence, on
a statistical basis, plays a key role in the world of television fiction
is self-evident. But the meaning of that world as presented by
Gerbner and Gross in the interpretation offered above is highly
debatable.* The generalization that violence is the "simplest and
cheapest dramatic means available to demonstrate the rules of
the game of power," is, equally, an interpretation and would hold
only in terms of the prior interpretation of the meaning of the
television world. Other interpretations of that world have been
offered, and in those interpretations the meaning of violence,
even in its documented incidence, is very different.[4] In those
interpretations it is often impossible to assert that the world of
fictional television is "ruled" by violence. This prior interpretation
of the meaning of fictional structures in television seriously
weakens the interpretation put forward by Gerbner and Gross
with regard to the meaning of television content.

My suspicion, however, based in part on comments by Gerbner,[5] is that these interpretations of the fictional content of the
world of television drama are less crucial for the validity of their
studies than are their assumptions about and interpretation of
the TV audiences' response to fictional content. To obtain this
Gerbner and Gross have developed their techniques of "message
system analysis" and "cultivation analysis."

We have begun that [message system] analysis with the most
ubiquitous, translucent, and instructive part of television (or any
cultural) fare, the dramatic programs (series, cartoons, movies on
television) that populate and animate for most viewers the heart-
land of the symbolic world. Instead of guessing or assuming the
contours and dynamics of that world, message system analysis
maps its geography, demography, thematic and action structure,
time and space dimensions, personality profiles, occupations and
fates. Message system analysis yields the gross but clear terms of

location, action, and characterization discharged into the mainstream of community consciousness [182].

The complementary "cultivation analysis" is designed to determine "what, if anything, viewers absorb from living in the world
of television." Here television messages are turned "into questions of social reality. To each of these questions there is a
'television answer,' which is like the way things appear in the
world of television, and another and different answer which is
biased in the opposite direction, closer to the way things are in
the observable world" (p. 182). The results of these studies are
well known. They indicate a difference in response by heavy and
light television viewers even when other factors are held constant. The responses indicate that heavy viewers are more likely
to select the "television answer" than the "observable world"
answer. This information has been widely circulated as an indication of television's ability to distort perception and, by implication,
behavior or choice of behaviors. My concern here is that these
studies are skewed not in terms of their measuring procedures,
but precisely in terms of interpretive and definitional assertions
that I have cited above. *If* we cannot assume that certain parts
of the television message are more directly perceived and absorbed than others, or *if* the world of television is not interpreted
as being "ruled by violence" then, very simply, one would ask
different questions of the audience. *In the Gerbner and Gross
procedures the research model assumes and is based on the
validity of the very interpretations and hypotheses that should be
tested.*
Directly related to this problem of the type of question to be
asked is the problem of the specific questions put to the audience.
Certain of these questions contain prior interpretations of the
meaning of their answers. Let me illustrate. The cultivation
analysis shows that heavy viewers select the television answer to
the question regarding the proportion of people employed in law
enforcement. From this finding Gerbner and Gross report a next
step in their analysis.

An exaggerated impression of the actual number of law enforcement workers seems to be a consequence of viewing television.
Of greater concern, however, would be the cultivation of a con-

comitantly exaggerated demand for their services. The world of
television drama is, above all, a violent one in which more than
half of all characters are involved in some violence, at least one-
tenth in some killing and in which over three-fourths of prime-time
hours contain some violence. As we have suggested, the cultivation of fear and a sense of danger may well be a prime residue of
the show of violence [pp. 192-193].

To test this assumption viewers were asked, "Can most people be
trusted?" The television answer. on the questionnaire, to which
heavy viewers responded more frequently, was "Can't be too
careful." I would suggest that for many respondents, whether
heavy or light viewers, this last phrase does not *mean* that people
cannot be trusted, nor that television produces an exaggerated
demand for the services of law enforcement employees, nor that a
residue of fear or sense of danger pervades their lives. The conclusion drawn from the data is once again a restatement of the
premise designed to be tested.

Even more problematic are the responses to another question,
"During any given week, what are your chances of being involved
in some type of violence?" Again, heavy viewers selected the
television answer. We know how the figure in the television
answer is arrived at. But how many viewers in responding to the
question are framing their responses in terms of violence defined
as "the overt expression of physical force against self or other,
compelling action against one's will on pain of being hurt or
killed, or actually hurting or killing." The question for researchers
is not how much violence might be available for personal involvement, but rather, what does violence *mean* to the respondent? What does "involvement" mean? if the respondent is
thinking in terms of automobile accidents, how different is the
measure? if the viewer counts as involvement the witnessing of
an automobile accident on the expressway is the result affected?
What if the respondent is counting as involvement the visiting of
a hospitalized friend who has been injured in an industrial accident?

My point is that any attempt to determine "the way things are
in the observable world" is equally, if not far more, problematic
as determining meanings in fictional constructs. That determination requires just as much interpretation. The cultivation analysis,
then, yields findings, often referred to in working toward policy

decisions, which are equally clear but of necessity *equally as gross* as the findings in the message system analysis. In summary, the conclusions hold only if the incidence of violence means what they say it means and is perceived as they say it is perceived. A deep and basic flaw in the Gerbner-Gross analysis is that they operate, at least in the definitions and reports of their findings, with a monosemic and univocal theory of symbols.

Many of these problems arise, I think, because implicit in this sort of analysis is a particular model of communication. It is a model that frequently leads to difficulties for humanistic approaches or for social scientific approaches heavily dependent on the hermeneutic exercise. The Gerbner and Gross studies appear at the first glance to adopt a different model of communication, one that is less problematic for these orientations. In their discussion of symbol, ritual, myth, and story they evoke what James Carey has referred to as a "ritual theory of communication." With such a perspective we observe

> a process through which a shared culture is created, modified and transformed. The archetypal case of communication is ritual and mythology, for those who come at the problem from anthropology; art and literature, for those who come at the problem from literary criticism and history. A ritual view of communication is not directed toward the extension of messages in space, but the maintenance of society in time (even if Marxists are less than sanguine about this); not the act of imparting information or influence, but the creation, representation, and celebration of shared beliefs [1975: 177].

As I have said, much of the definition bears an apparent relationship to the stated assumptions of Gerbner and Gross. What is often unstated, however, relates far more directly to Carey's opposing category, a "transportation theory" in which communication is seen as "a process of transmitting messages at a distance for the purpose of control. The archetypal case of communication then is persuasion, attitude change, behavior modification, socialization through the transmission of information, influence, or conditioning" (p. 177).

In their own survey of television research paradigms Gerbner and Gross seem to reject models which focus on the transportation aspects of television. They reject the view that consequences can be presumed "without the prior investigation of content, as the conventional research paradigms tend to do," and point out that the content studied "cannot be limited to isolated elements (e.g., news, commercials, specific programs)" (p. 180). They point to the weaknesses in the experimental method, weaknesses that cluster around the search for change as the only important indicator of influence. Their own view is that stability may be more important than change. They also rule out methodologies that focus on "exposure to one particular type of television programming," and point to errors in previous violence related research caused by ignoring the complex and systemic nature of the medium.

The definitions, procedures, and reports of results, however, place the Violence Profile work firmly in the "transportation theory" realm. The location of messages in a system is little different from locating them in specific programs or bits of programs if one is seeking and defining message effects. It leads to broader generalizations based on more heroic assumptions. Analytically, however, the difference is merely one of magnitude. Similarly, the cultivation of consciousness fits the transportation model as well as does the cultivation of specific behaviors, so long as it is cultivation and its effects that one is attempting to measure.

Among the most direct indications of this transportation view of television communication is the choice of metaphors for television and its processes in the culture. TV is "the central *arm* of American society. It is an *agency* of the established order." Aspects of the television world are *discharged* into the mainstream of community consciousness" (my emphasis).

This brings us to a central problem with transportation theories of communication. In using them one must eventually identify sender and receiver, and the criticisms, ultimately, are ideological ones. The critic does not agree with the message content or does not approve of its use. The attacks, explicit or implicit, are on groups or societies that propagate the flawed messages rather than on the medium. Alternatives are limited. One can change the sender or perhaps correct the social ill that is the "cause" of the message, e.g., eliminate racism so that racist messages will no longer be a "normal" aspect of the communication content. But there is no firm assurance that such a change will produce a "better" content even though it might be more agreeable to certain critics.

Gerbner and Gross are cautiously ambivalent in identifying the sources of television's problematic content. When TV is described as "the central arm of American society . . . an agency of the established order," it is unclear whether or not American society and the established order are to be seen as synonymous. Again, they suggest that "Once the industrial order has legitimized its rule, the primary function of its cultural arm becomes the re-iteration of that legitimacy and the maintenance of established power and authority." Is the "industrial order" definable? Are they setting forth an "establishment theory?"

On the one hand that, or something like it, would seem to be the case, though it is a far more complex process than often depicted.

> It is clear, at least to us, that deeply rooted sociocultural forces, rather than just obstinancy or profit-seeking, are at work. We have suggested earlier in this article, and have also developed else-where, that symbolic violence is a demonstration of power and an instrument of social control serving, on the whole, to reinforce and preserve the existing social order, even if at an ever increasing price in terms of pervasive fear and mistrust and of selective aggres-siveness. That maintenance mechanism seems to work through cultivating a sense of danger, a differential calculus of the risks of life in different groups in the population [p. 189].

"Selective aggression" and "risks of life in different groups" clearly indicate that certain individuals and groups are more interested in maintaining the "existing social order" than others. But other comments indicate that such complicity is not always predictable in conventional terms of power or social status.

> The world of television drama is a mixture of truth and falsehood, of accuracy and distortion. It is not the true world but an extension of the standardized images which we have been taught since child-hood. The audience for which the message of television is primarily intended . . . is the great majority of middle-class citizens for whom America is a democracy (our leaders act in accordance with the desires of the people), for whom our economy is free, and for whom God is alive, white, and male [pp. 179-180].

Presumably, if this great majority already believes in the meanings expressed through television they too are interested in the maintenance of those meanings. Simple versions of this model of communication argue that television merely "mirrors" what is already there. The version here is more complex than that.

Gerbner and Gross are careful to point out that all societies have created such systems of socially constructed reality for similar purposes. To the degree that television is different (that is, to the degree that their research represents an analysis of the *medium*), it is in terms of uniformity and pervasiveness. "The institutional processes producing these message systems have become increasingly professionalized, industrialized, centralized, and specialized. Their principal locus shifted from handicraft to mass production and from traditional religion and formal education to the mass media of communication—particularly television" (p. 173). And again, "We assume, therefore, that TV's standarizing and legitimizing influence comes largely from its ability to streamline, amplify, ritualize and spread into hitherto isolated or protected subcultures, homes, nooks, and crannies of the land the conventional capsules of mass produced information and entertainment" (p. 181). I suggest here that such technological distinctions and innovations do not necessarily lead to an increase in the manipulative or exploitative power of the symbolic environment, though that interpretation is the most common one. Equally as plausible is that they merely increase the pervasiveness of the symbols. In either case, mass dissemination makes it all the more important to establish the meanings of the symbols as fully as possible.

The observation that much of the message content of television (or any other dominant symbol system) reflects what is established, what is already believed, and the observation that this new medium conveys those shared meanings to larger populations, are precisely the sorts of observation that indicate the weakness of transportation models as explanatory theories. They simply do not tell us very much about how such meanings operate. If, on the other hand, we accept the full significance of a ritual theory of communication rather than merely invoke the key terms—myth, ritual, story—we will study the communication process in very different terms, and, I believe, learn more. In concluding, then, I will suggest some alternative hypotheses and methods of study that emerge from the application of the ritual model to the study of television.

As I have tried to indicate, much of what Gerbner and Gross say about television supports the idea that such a ritual model is more appropriate. I believe that they are absolutely correct in arguing that television is the central symbol system in American culture. I also agree that television content confirms our received views and extends "standardized images which we have been taught since childhood." As they say, "The world of television drama is a mixture of truth and falsehood, of accuracy and distortion." A full understanding of the medium, then, must find ways of accounting for these mixtures of symbol and the resultant mixtures of meaning and experience. Such an understanding cannot afford to reduce such multiplicity of meaning to simple messages.

Anthropologist Marshall Sahlins sheds important light on the analytical processes necessary here in his discussion of the cultural role of advertisers, market researchers, and fashion designers. All, in his view, are "hucksters of the symbol." I think it quite possible to include television producers and sponsors in this list. The role of these professions, Sahlins argues, is not to create their products and symbols "de novo." Rather,

> In the nervous system of the American economy, theirs is the synaptic function. It is their role to be sensitive to the latent correspondences in the cultural order whose conjunction in a product-symbol may spell mercantile success. Or perhaps more frequently theirs is to respond to the ceaseless reformulation of symbolic relations within the national social life. Such change proceeds, on one side, from constant revision of the economic grid, changes in the structure of production which impose new coordinates on other social relations. . . . On the other hand, reformulation of the symbolic correspondence may be initiated from the opposite direction: from events unfolding in the superstructural sphere—wars, a new radical movement, an increase in the divorce rate, a return to religion—such as alter the context of production. We think of these as a kind of cultural climate, just as we think of designers as plucking their ideas out of thin air. But the fashion expert does not make his collection out of whole cloth; like Levi-Strauss's famous bricoleur, he uses bits and pieces with an embedded significance, from a previous existence to create an object that works, which is to say that objectively synthesizes a relation between cultural categories, for in that lies its salability [1976: 217].

This description suggests at least a three step process in coming to a thorough, satisfactory understanding of television as

America's central symbol system. First we must recognize that the ideas and the symbols that express them on television are not "created" there. They have a history in American culture. They are "used" ideas and symbols, or, as Sahlins suggests, they have an "embedded significance." Research of the meaning of the symbols, then, must begin with the complex of previous meanings associated with such symbols. In concrete terms we will have to recognize the fact that for Americans "violence" has had many meanings and uses. It is not a concept that is easily defined. Symbolic analysis that takes this into account will begin with conventional "history of idea" work, though the focus on the symbolic nature of the ideas may add a dimension for some analysts that approaches a sort of "archeology of ideas."

The second step of the process is to examine the organization and expression of these ideas in the world of television. At this stage close analysis of program formulas, and even of individual programs may prove to be helpful. On one level this simply leads to the careful description of what violence means for the characters who populate the television fictions. On another level we will have to recognize the potential for different meanings of similar symbols when those symbols are combined in different forms and patterns, for possible changes in television forms and meanings over time, and for the modifying influence of the styles of individual producers and companies. The more complex understandings can then be related to the ideas as they exist outside of and before television.

The final, and most crucial, step in examining television from the vantage point of a ritual model of communication is the analysis of the audience. Here, of course, humanists have most to learn from social scientists. But we should all be open to the possibility that different members of the mass audience will attach different meanings to the same messages. Those meanings will emerge from individual and group systems of belief and meanings. They will change. We must recognize the possibility that violence will mean one thing to a viewer on one evening, something else on another evening. I do not believe that simple surveys can adequately gather such complex information. We will need to develop techniques for audience ethnography, for the collection of data on long-term bases, for understanding the variations of human response to art and entertainment. These or similar methods can lead us to a fuller understanding of the complexities of our subject.

It should be clear from this sort of proposal that the Annenberg projects have been innovative ones. Their foresight to collect data on a systematic, long-term basis, to move out of the laboratory and away from the closed experimental model, will enable other researchers to avoid costly mistakes. Their material holds a wealth of information. The violence topic provides only one of many symbol clusters to be examined. As they move into new areas, and hopefully retrieve more, and more complex information from audiences, we should see whole new sets of questions and answers emerging to aid us in explaining television's role in our culture.

I do not wish to be misunderstood here. I am not attacking the "negative" findings of Gerbner and Gross. I am not asserting that by applying techniques built on a ritual model we will discover television to be the pure and gleaming center of a wholesome mass American culture. Societies can formulate rituals celebrating evil symbols and ideas; their fictional worlds can be constituted around both negative and positive meanings; they can maintain themselves around repression as well as liberation. But I think it more likely that most societies are radical mixtures of both. Symbol systems speak of both. Indeed, they speak of both simultaneously. Surely, in religious systems the fear of hell and the joy of salvation can operate together, perhaps in creative tension. Television is no less complex. I believe it more than likely that some members of the TV audience fear and resist change, and at the same time work to insure the equal rights of all people. My common sense tells me that it is possible to be afraid in city streets, and, at the same time, abhor the idea of a police state. I believe, finally, that television is fully as complex as the American "mind," the cultural force out of which it is created. It may be that all the messages of television speak with a single intent and are ruled by a single dominant symbol whose meaning is clear to a mass audience, or to that part of the audience heavily involved with those messages. But I have yet to see evidence sufficient to warrant such a reductive view of human experience in America.

NOTES

1. I recognize the involvement of many individuals in the research supporting the published material I will be examining here. For purposes of convenience I will refer to the work as that of the principal authors.

2. All references are to this article and are indicated in the text by page number. Some of my analysis as presented here might be modified in light of the content of unpublished research reports. If that is the case I would welcome the publication of all pertinent material.

3. See the *Journal of Broadcasting* (Summer 1977) for an exchange of views on this topic.

4. Newcomb (1974, 1976); Cater and Adler (1975, 1976); Alley (1977); Real (1977).

5. Colloquium at the National Humanities Institute at the University of Chicago, May 1977.

REFERENCES

ALLEY, R. (1977) Television: Ethics for Hire? Nashville: Abingdon.

CAREY, J. W. (1975) "Communication and culture." Communication Research 2: 173-191.

CATER, D. and R. ADLER [eds.] (1976) Television as a Cultural Force. New York: Praeger.

————— [eds.] (1975) Television as a Social Force. New York: Praeger.

GERBNER, G. (1971) "Violence in television drama: trends and symbolic functions," in G. Comstock and E. Rubinstein (eds.) Television and Social Behavior, Vol. 1. Washington, DC: Government Printing Office.

————— and L. GROSS (1976) "Living with television: the violence profile." J. of Communication 26: 173-199.

NEWCOMB, H. [ed.] (1976) Television: The Critical View. New York: Oxford Univ. Press.

————— (1974) TV: The Most Popular Art. Garden City, NY: Doubleday/Anchor.

REAL, M. (1977) Mass Mediated Culture. New York: Prentice-Hall.

SAHLINS, M. (1976) Culture and Practical Reason. Chicago: Univ. of Chicago Press.

Horace Newcomb is Associate Professor of English at the University of Texas, Austin. He is the author of TV: The Most Popular Art *(1974) and editor of* Television: The Critical View *(1976). His articles on television in American culture have appeared in* Prospects, Christian Century, *the* Wall Street Journal, *and the* Journal of Popular Culture. *He is Associate Editor of the* Journal of Popular Film and Television.

27

EDITORIAL RESPONSE
A Reply to
Newcomb's "Humanistic Critique"

George Gerbner and Larry Gross

Newcomb's essay on "Assessing the Violence Profile Studies of Gerbner and Gross: A Humanistic Critique and Suggestion" (1978) is a welcome contribution to the dialogue of the "two cultures," although perhaps the contrast is a bit overdrawn.

After noting that our social scientific approach to the study of television as an "environment of symbols" is "thoroughly congenial to the humanistic perspective" (p. 267), Newcomb questions our emphasis on the similarities among television plays in preference to the differences in style, format, and nuances of plot, and so on. Our reason for this emphasis is that we consider most television plays assembly-line drama rather than works of unique craftsmanship. The patterns that the corporate assembly-line imparts to its products become the aggregate and repetitive terms of common exposure and usage. Our main interest is in the commonalities of exposure and association that cultivate public conceptions, rather than in the variety of individual differences. When a certain type of dramatic action (such as violence) is presented an average of seven, eight, or nine times an hour, and viewed nonselectively by most viewers, we are dealing with a standardized and cumulative pattern which is not traceable to single programs. It is like looking down from a plane as it flies over a familiar neighborhood: the view is different but it is still the same territory. As Hirsch (1977) noted recently, "it is well to remember that many more people are hooked on television itself than specific programs."

Newcomb questions our assertion of television's realism. He claims we do not consider the world of television "real," but assume that viewers do. However, our assumptions are not that simple. Viewers may suspect or even dismiss contrived plots (although accept them as explanations for motivations, actions, and outcomes, thus for much of how things may actually *work,* rather than what they *are*), but they may still absorb much of the authentic-looking background detail. For example, viewers seem to "know" what courtrooms, police stations, or surgical operating rooms look like, how people work and act in them, what social types are likely to succeed or fail. This type of "knowledge" relates to the informational qualities of the realistic style of presentation of background "facts" and acts, and not necessarily to whether viewers believe the foreground plots (although many do).

In addition to our analyses of survey questions addressed by ourselves or others to samples of viewers, we have encouraged auxiliary studies which investigate viewers' perceptions in greater depth. In her recent doctoral dissertation, Schwartz-McDonald (1977) describes the conceptions of crime and law enforcement of a sample of Philadelphia residents who respond to extended individual interviews. These respondents typically reported the sort of incidental, background learning from television which we believe characterizes the way most of us have formed our images of many social institutions and processes. These television-related images can range from technical details—

Q: What makes you think that lawyers are not supposed to lead witnesses?

A: Television. "I object, your Honor, Counsel is leading the witness."

Q: Seriously.

A: I'm dead serious. I've never been in a courtroom in my life (99).

to more general assessments of credibility—

Q: Do you have any idea whether the plots are realistic? (On "The Streets of San Francisco")

A: They seem to be. They seem to be things that could happen to anybody. I don't think they're particularly exaggerated.

Q: What sorts of crimes do they have on there?

A: All kinds. Rapes, robberies, murders. The run of the mill (p. 138).

to extreme faith in the realism of television—

A: Most of the shows are realistic because if they weren't, they wouldn't be able to produce them on TV (p. 110).

Our most recent report (Gerbner et al., 1978) provides further evidence that viewers do absorb "broad facts" from their experience of many hours in the world of television. Whether they believe any specific plot is irrelevant to our argument.

Next, Newcomb tackles our definition of violence and, in the process, misinterprets some fundamentals of the analysis of communications content. Our definition is minimal, commonly understood, and unambiguous: it essentially entails hurting and/or killing, or forcing some action on pain of being hurt or killed. Newcomb asks why we don't "determine a meaning of violence as it is understood by the *characters* themselves in the fictional world of television," and then compare that with other definitions. That suggestion is much more puzzling and problematic than anything we are doing.

Of course, we recognize that not all violence is alike. Striking out against brutality and injustice is not the same as perpetrating them. But, as noted, we deal with violence as an industrial ingredient injected wholesale into formula plays. The overall patterns of violence as demonstrations of social power are little affected by exceptions to the rule and by subtle differences in "meaning." Victimization denotes vulnerability whether deserved or not. Plots may add "meanings" to standard fates assigned to different social types, but do not change the calculus of risks implicit in those fates.

Newcomb also objects to our observation that television provides a "symbolic world ruled largely by violence," even though he notes that it occurs an average of 7.4 times per hour. But rule does not rest entirely on numbers. Perhaps we can be charged for rhetorical excess, but we mean "ruled" literally. We attempt to explain (and in the latest report, to elaborate) the finding that the ratio of victims to violents within any group sets up a hierarchy of social powers, a "pecking order." That order is, of course, the regulatory component in a social structure.

We do not mean (or say) that violence is more prominent than other actions, as Newcomb suggests (although it may be); we only find that it tends to exemplify power relations in the symbolic social order. Newcomb calls that "highly debatable." Perhaps. But some of the findings in our latest report provide additional evidence of the connection between television violence and symbolic demonstrations of power.

Newcomb questions our procedure designed to assess the contribution of television to viewers' conceptions of social reality. The objection goes like this: we define what is presented on television, then turn around and question viewers to determine whether the patterns implicit in those presentations are acually confirmed by heavy viewers more than by light viewers. The validity and reliability of our definitions determines the soundness of the test.

That indeed is what we do. We spend much time and effort assuring (and measuring) the validity of our definitions. We find that heavy viewers *do* tend to answer our questions in line with the television presentations, even when we control for demographic and other characteristics. Therefore, it seems that they do learn at least some of the lessons brought out in our analysis, and learn them independently of other media exposure and real-life differences. Newcomb does not offer an alternative explanation for these findings, nor another way to assess TV's contributions to what people think and do.

The fact is that heavy viewers overestimate their chances of involvement in violence and their general vulnerability (compared to light viewers in the same social groups) *however defined*. Newcomb's big question, "what does violence mean to the respondents" is not only irrelevant but distracting. We study what exposure to violence-laden television contributes to their conceptions of the realities of their own lives.

Newcomb's "point that any attempt to determine 'the way things are in the observable world' is equally, if not far more, problematic as determining meanings in fictional constructs" (p. 274) is puzzling. The fictional meanings our type of analysis attempts to determine are simple and unambiguous events reliably coded and commonly recognized. The real world conceptions we study are those our respondents reveal in their answers. The two sets of data can be related in fairly straightforward ways. The procedure may be painstaking, but not particularly problematic.

Newcomb thinks that these "problems" arise from an implicit model of communication. He notes correctly that we reject simple "opinion change" theories in favor of "cultivation" or "ritual" theory. But then he suggests we implicitly follow the "transportation theory" designed to study influence and control, not just ritual. Newcomb's reasoning ignores the fact that ritual *must be learned*. We are not born with rituals and stable images; nor are they "transported" into us. We are born into and grow up in a symbolic environment of which television is now the mainstream that *cultivates* stable images after some of its own patterns.

The "transportation theory" claim transports Newcomb into an interesting discussion of the social sources of television content. He correctly elaborates our view that those sources are deeply rooted in the structure of our society, and that television mainly standardizes, ritualizes, streamlines, and spreads assembly-line symbol mass production into the life-space of an otherwise heterogeneous public. But then Newcomb suggests that "such technological distinctions" may "merely increase the pervasiveness of the symbols" (p. 278). That is like saying the coming of the automobile merely increased the pervasiveness of movement. It did, and in the process it transformed and standardized significant aspects of living. In any case, Newcomb adds, "mass dissemination makes it all the more important to establish the meanings of symbols as fully as possible" (p. 278). We can only respond that we study the relationships between patterns of messages and images regularly presented on television and what viewers think and do, especially as these relate to issues of public policy. That is enough "meaning" for us and, we submit, for most practical research purposes.

Toward the end of his essay, Newcomb develops some useful suggestions for studying the history of ideas and symbols. We hope the rest of us will not be required to await their conclusion before we are permitted to investigate the relationships between television, ideas, and action.

Unfortunately, puzzling nonsequiturs mar Newcomb's concluding comments. He asserts that symbol systems can have both negative and positive meanings, that "the fear of hell and the joy of salvation can operate together, perhaps in creative tension" (p. 281). And he goes on:

> Television is no less complex. I believe it more than likely
> that some members of the TV audience fear and resist
> change, and at the same time work to insure the equal
> rights of all people. My common sense tells me that it is
> possible to be afraid in city streets, and, at the same time,
> abhor the idea of a police state [p. 281].

One can believe anything one wishes about "some members" of the TV audience. One can listen to the voice of "common sense" to justify anything, however historically improbable.

The cultivation of fear, insecurity, and social rigidity does not contribute to the tendency to accept the massive changes that would be necessary for the realization of equal rights of all people. Fear of city streets tends to strengthen the demand for police protection and even repression, no matter how "abhorrent" that might seem to some people in the abstract. To obscure these overriding general relationships in the name of some particularistic observation of presumably greater sophistication or complexity violates not only the lessons of social science, but also the principles of humanism.

Newcomb is incorrect when, in his last sentence, he dubs our research on TV's contribution to viewer conceptions as "a reductive view of human experience." But as we move further into the investigation of different dimensions, such as television's contributions to occupational choice, assumptions about politics, aging, health, law, minorities, and so on, we welcome the serious attention and critique of scholars like Newcomb and accept the charge of the need to be more precise, cautious, and clear.

REFERENCES

GERBNER, G., L. GROSS, M. JACKSON-BEECK, S. JEFFRIES-FOX, and N. SIG-
    NORIELLI (1978) "Cultural indicators: violence profile no. 9." J. of Communi-
    cation 28, 3: 176-207.
HIRSCH, P. (1977) "The medium of the motive." *The Wall Street Journal* January
    17.
NEWCOMB, H. (1978) "Assessing the violence profile of Gerbner and Gross:
    a humanistic critique and suggestions." Communication Research 5: 264-282.
SCHWARTZ-McDONALD, S. (1977) "Learning about crime: concept of crime and
    law enforcement as they relate to use of television and other information
    sources." Doctoral dissertation, University of Pennsylvania. (unpublished)

*George Gerbner is Professor of Communications and Dean of the Annen-
berg School of Communications at the University of Pennsylvania. He is
editor of the* Journal of Communication *and editor of* Mass Media Policies
in Changing Cultures *(Wiley-Interscience, 1978). His research is on the
social aspects of mass communications.*

*Larry Gross is Associate Professor of Communications at the Annenberg
School of Communications at the University of Pennsylvania. He is co-
editor of* Studies in the Anthropology of Visual Communication. *His research is in the cultural determinants of symbolic behavior.*

One of the most widely discussed findings in research in recent years—in both the popular and the scholarly press—is the dramatic difference in situational perceptions found by George Gerbner and Larry Gross in their studies of "heavy" and "light" TV consumers. In survey data from four major U.S. cities (Philadelphia, Chicago, Los Angeles, and Dallas), Gerbner and Gross have found heavy TV watchers exaggerate the likelihood of their becoming crime victims. Anthony N. Doob and Glenn E. Macdonald use survey data from both high- and low-crime areas of Toronto to challenge the Gerbner-Gross conclusion that TV is the causal agent. Drs. Doob and Macdonald are psychologists at the University of Toronto, Ontario, Canada.

28

TELEVISION VIEWING AND FEAR OF VICTIMIZATION
Is the Relationship Causal?

Anthony N. Doob and Glenn E. Macdonald

Previous findings have suggested that people who watch a lot of television are more likely to fear their environment than are those who report being less frequent viewers of television. From this simple correlation, previous authors have suggested that television causes people to overestimate the amount of danger that exists in their own neighborhoods. The present study attempted to replicate this finding and to determine if the apparent effect was due to a previously uncontrolled factor: the actual incidence of crime in the neighborhood. Respondents to a door-to-door survey indicated their media usage and estimated the likelihood of their being a victim of violence. Neighborhoods were chosen so as to include a high- and a low-crime area in downtown Toronto and a high- and a low-crime area in Toronto's suburbs. Pooling across the four areas sampled, the previous findings were replicated. However, the average within-area correlation was insignificant, suggesting that when actual incidence of crime is controlled for, there is no overall relationship between television viewing and fear of being a victim of crime. A multiple regression analysis and a canonical correlation analysis confirmed these findings.

A variety of social problems have been attributed to television viewing. It is said that television makes people more violent, that it lowers the level of literacy in the population, and that it distorts the viewer's perception of the world. There is little denying that the picture of reality that comes into people's homes is not an accurate reflection of their own society. That we learn from television, as we learn from every other medium, seems intuitively plausible independent of research results. Gerbner and Gross (1974, 1976a, 1976b; Gerbner et al., 1976), however, have suggested something even more serious than simple learning effects: that people not only learn factual information, such as the proportion of people involved in law enforcement, but that they generalize from the information that they get from television. In particular, Gerbner and his associates show that those who watch a lot of television are more likely to feel that they might be involved in some kind of violence during a given week than do those who watch relatively little television. This same pattern of results shows up in a variety of questions having to do with the viewers' perceptions of various aspects of the society in which they live. As Gerbner et al. (1976) point out, "Their heightened sense of fear and mistrust is manifested in their typically more apprehensive responses

We wish to thank Julian Roberts for his help and useful suggestions at all phases of this work and Bob Gebotys for his help in analyzing the data. The Metropolitan Toronto Police were very open and helpful to us in providing the data necessary for choosing our experimental neighborhoods. The research was supported by the (Ontario) Royal Commission on Violence in the Communications Industry, and a version of this study is published in Volume V of that commission's report. We wish to thank Mr. C. K. Marchant, the Director of Research of that commission, for his help and encouragement throughout all phases of the work. The data analysis was supported, in part, by funds provided to the Centre of Criminology, University of Toronto, by the Ministry of the Solicitor General, Canada.

Requests for reprints should be sent to Anthony N. Doob, Department of Psychology, University of Toronto, Toronto, Ontario, Canada M5S 1A1.

From Anthony N. Doob and Glenn E. Macdonald, "Television Viewing and Fear of Victimization: Is the Relationship Causal?" *Journal of Personality and Social Psychology* 37, 2 (February 1979) 170-179. Copyright 1979 by the American Psychological Association. Reprinted by permission.

to questions about their own personal safety, about crime and law enforcement, and about trust in people" (p. 9).

Obviously, heavy television viewing is not independent of other social factors. Gerbner and Gross (1976a) have found that "heavy viewing is part and parcel of a complex syndrome which also includes lower education, lower mobility, lower aspirations, higher anxieties, and other class, age, and sex-related characteristics" (p. 191).

Because of the problem of confounding variables, Gerbner has been careful to break down his data on various other characteristics of television viewers such as age, sex, educational level, news reading, news magazine reading, prime-time viewing, and viewing or nonviewing of TV news. The notable finding in all of these comparisons is that although there may be main effects of some of these other characteristics, in all cases, heavy viewers are more likely than light viewers to feel that they might be involved in some violence.

No list of possible confounding variables can be complete. The worry of any researcher doing correlational research and wishing to make a causal statement is that some other variable would, in fact, account for the effect apparently demonstrated. We felt that there is one quite plausible factor that might account for the correlation between viewing and fear of violence: People who watch a lot of television may have a greater fear of being victims of violent crimes because, in fact, they live in more violent neighborhoods.

The study that this explanation suggests, then, is quite obvious: A survey of the television viewing habits of people and their perception of being involved in violence should be performed in both high- and low-crime neighborhoods. Pooling across neighborhoods, we should be able to replicate Gerbner's and his associates' findings; within neighborhoods, however, the effect should be substantially reduced or eliminated.

Method

For purposes of efficient distribution of resources, the Metropolitan Toronto Police have divided Toronto into approximately 210 patrol areas. The size of these patrol areas varies not only as a function of the resident population but also as a function of the number of calls of all types that the police receive in the area: Busy areas thus tend to be smaller in terms of the size of the population served and in terms of geographic area. The police identified for us the 10 patrol areas with the highest number of reported assaults and woundings and the 14 areas with the lowest number of reported assaults and woundings for the 7-month period ending 2 months before the beginning of the survey. From these data, four geographic areas, approximately equal in size, were chosen. Two (one within the city of Toronto, the other suburban) were high in reported crime; two (one city, one suburban) were low in reported crime. It is difficult to estimate the exact rates of crime for the four areas. However, very rough estimates would suggest that the rates of assaults and woundings per 100,000 resident population for the 7-month period for the four designated areas would be the following: high-crime city, 614; low-crime city, 8; high-crime suburb, 195; low-crime suburb, 6. It must be emphasized that these are very rough figures: The low-crime areas each had only two reported assaults (and no woundings) for the entire 7-month period; hence the estimates are bound to be unstable. There were eight patrol areas constituting the high-crime city area; one patrol area was sampled for the high-crime suburban area and two each for the low-crime areas.

Obviously, the four areas differ considerably on a large number of social variables other than reported crime rates. The high-crime city area contains a portion of the downtown commercial/entertainment district of the city, the largest block of public housing in the metropolitan area, and much of the poorest portion of the population. The low-crime city area is largely expensive, single, detached houses and is one of the more exclusive residential areas. The high-crime suburban area contains a high concentration of low-rise public housing and is generally fairly poor. The low-crime suburban area is mostly single, detached, middle-class housing.

Random households were chosen within each of these areas. Interviewers, employed by a commercial survey company, did a door-to-door survey. The person who answered the door was asked to list all of the people over 18 years of age living in the household. One of these people was then chosen at random by the interviewer. If this person could not be interviewed at that time or at some mutually acceptable time, the interviewer went on to the next randomly chosen household, and the procedure was repeated. The effect of this selection procedure was an oversampling of women (70.5%) and, presumably, a general oversampling of those who spend much of the time at home. Although this effect would be unfortunate if one were interested in estimating population values for the measures that were taken, it was less relevant in our study, where we were interested in the relationship between television viewing and fear of criminal victimization.

Table 1
Mean Fear-of-Crime Factor Scores for Each
of the Sampled Areas

	City		Suburb	
Area	M	n	M	n
High crime	.28	83	.15	69
Low crime	−.34	71	−.13	77

Note. The higher the number, the more fear.

Respondents were first asked to indicate those programs that they had watched during the previous week. According to our interviewers, very few people had any difficulty in doing this. They were then asked to complete a 37-item fixed-alternatives questionnaire. This questionnaire consisted of six questions dealing directly with the person's estimate of his or her own likelihood of being a victim of a crime; four questions dealing with estimates of the likelihood of particular groups of people being victims; four questions dealing with the perception of crime in general being a problem and there being a need for more police personnel; two questions dealing with the necessity to arm oneself; eight questions of a factual nature dealing with crime; three questions dealing with society's response to crime; four questions dealing with the respondents' view of Toronto with respect to crime; three questions dealing with the respondents' prediction of their response to a request for help; and three questions dealing with media usage. The whole interview took approximately 45 minutes on the average.

For purposes of analyzing the types of television, we decided to use the number of programs watched as an index of total viewing. In addition, programs were coded by a research associate into violent and nonviolent types before the tabulation of the other data. It should be pointed out that this last measure is, necessarily, somewhat subjective. However, as will be seen, this turns out not to be a serious problem in understanding the results.

Results

In order to reduce the number of measures to a somewhat workable number, a factor analysis was performed [1] on the 34 opinion questions. Using a varimax rotation, only one factor accounted for a substantial amount of the common variance. The percentages of the common variance accounted for by the first 4 of the 11 factors were 35.9%, 12.5%, 10.8%, and 8.4%. The questions that loaded highest on the first factor are shown in Table 4; they were the six questions related to the

respondents' estimates of their own chances of victimization, two of the questions dealing with the chances of victimization of particular groups, and one of the questions dealing with crime as a general problem. Generally speaking, it seems fair to label this factor "fear of crime." Each of the next three factors had substantial loadings from only one or two questions.

As one would expect, the residents of the four areas differed significantly on their overall fear of crime. The average factor scores for the four areas are shown in Table 1. Analysis of variance on the factor scores revealed a main effect for high-/low-crime area that was highly significant, $F(1, 296) = 17.79$, $p < .01$. Neither the city/suburb effect nor the interaction was significant. It is clear, then, that people who live in high-crime areas are, in fact, more afraid.

The four areas sampled also differed on their exposure to the various media. Table 2 presents these data. Overall, people in high-crime areas watched more television and, generally speaking, tended to watch more violent television. Although there were interactions between the two factors on these two measures, for the purposes of this article, these interactions are not very important. As one might expect, since the areas differed on so many dimensions, there were also effects on self-report of exposure to radio news: People living in low-crime areas tended to report listening to radio news more frequently. Furthermore, the reported frequency of newspaper reading was higher in low-crime areas and in the city.

Gerbner and his associates (Gerbner & Gross, 1974, 1976a, 1976b; Gerbner et al., 1976) do not directly present measures of association between the total amount of tele-

---

[1] The input for the factor analysis consisted only of those 300 respondents (of the total of 408) who answered every question. Most of the other 108 respondents failed to answer only a few of the questions. The proportion of complete questionnaires varied somewhat from area to area. The numbers of complete/total questionnaires are as follows: high-crime city, 83/119, or 70%; low-crime city, 71/118, or 60%; high-crime suburb, 69/85, or 81%; low-crime suburb, 77/86, or 90%.

Table 2
Media Usage for the Four Areas

| | High-crime area | | Low-crime area | | F value | | |
| | | | | | High/low crime | City/ suburb | Inter-action |
Medium	City(119)	Suburbs(85)	City(118)	Suburbs(86)			
Total TV	36.25	31.71	18.89	25.03	25.21**	<1	4.98*
TV violence	6.97	3.73	2.11	3.33	23.25**	2.72	18.11**
TV news	3.07	2.99	3.72	3.74	2.83	<1	<1
Radio news	5.07	4.96	5.44	5.37	9.79**	<1	<1
Newspaper reading	4.78	4.58	5.26	4.80	6.89**	6.01*	<1

Note. For TV viewing, numbers refer to mean number of programs watched during the previous week. The other measures are mean values on a scale where 1 equals never and 6 equals daily. *n*s are in parentheses.
* $p < .05$.
** $p < .01$.

vision viewed by their respondents (in response to the question "How many hours a day do you usually watch television? Please include morning, afternoon, and evening") and their fear of being a victim of a violent crime (in response to the question "During any given week, what are your chances of being involved in some type of violence—about a 50–50 chance, about a 1-in-10 chance, or about a 1-in-100 chance?"). However, estimating from the data that are presented in the various reports, we calculated a phi coefficient of .13 and a contingency coefficient of the same value.

Looking at our data, then, we calculated the (Pearson) correlation between our fear-of-crime factor scores and our various measures of media usage. These correlations are presented in the first column of Table 3. It

is quite clear that the basic effect is much the same as that found by Gerbner and his associates: Across the four areas, those who watched the most television (or violent television) tended to be those who were the most afraid. However, the effect *within* area is not quite so simple: Although the effect would appear to hold in the high-crime area of the city, it tended to disappear for the other areas. Indeed, the average correlations (last column of Table 3) indicate that there is essentially no relationship between media usage and fear of crime when the effect of neighborhood is removed. We have suggested that the artifact that created the first two correlations in the first column might be labeled "actual incidence of crime." However, in terms of the focus of this article (the relationship of media usage to fear of crime), the

Table 3
Correlations Between Media Usage and Fear-of-Crime Factor Scores for all Subjects (Pooled), for Each of the Four Areas, and for the Average of the Four Areas

| | Pooled across all areas | High crime | | Low crime | | Average correlation |
Medium		City(83)	Suburb(69)	City(71)	Suburb(77)	
Total TV	.18**	.24*	.16	.06	−.09	.09
TV violence	.18**	.22*	−.03	.14	−.04	.07
TV news	.05	.14	−.04	.05	.06	.05
Radio news	.05	.18	−.09	−.02	.21	.07
Newspaper reading	−.07	−.20*	−.14	.09	.15	−.03

Note. Positive correlations indicate more fear associated with higher media usage. *n*s are in parentheses.
* $p < .05$.
** $p < .001$.

Table 4

Fear-of-Crime Questions and the Correlations Between Responses to Each Question and Total TV Viewing and TV Violence for the Four Areas Pooled and the Average of the Four Areas Calculated Individually

	Total TV		TV violence		
Question	Pooled	Average within area	Pooled	Average within area	High TV viewing associated with
1. To what extent are crimes of violence a serious problem in your neighborhood? (399)	.07	−.02	.16*	0	Serious problem
2. What do you think the chances are that if you were to walk alone at night on the residential streets of your neighborhood each night for a month that you would be the victim of a serious crime? (391)	.18*	.10*	.19*	.05	High probability (1 in 10)
3. If a child were to play alone in a park each day for a month, what do you think the chances are that he would be the victim of a violent crime? (382)	.12*	.02	.22*	.12*	High probability (1 in 10)
4. If you were to walk by yourself in a park close to your home each night for a month, what do you think the chances are that you would be the victim of a serious crime? (391)	.10*	.02	.14*	.04	High probability (1 in 10)
5. What do you think the chances are that an unaccompanied woman would be the victim of a violent crime late at night in a Toronto subway station? (389)	.10*	.04	.09	.04	High probability (1 in 10)
6. What do you think the chances are that you, one of your family, or one of your close friends might be the victim of an assault during the next year? (385)	.13*	.02	.12*	−.02	High probability (1 in 10)
7. How likely do you think it is that you or one of your close friends would have their house broken into during the next year? (405)	−.04	−.07	.01	−.01	Extremely unlikely
8. Do you ever decide not to walk alone at night because you are afraid of being the victim of a violent crime? (402)	.05	.06	−.04	−.04	Very often
9. Is there any area around your home (i.e., within a mile) where you would be afraid to walk alone at night? (403)	.12*	.05	.02	−.06	Yes

Note. ns of respondents for each question are in parentheses.
* $p < .05$.

name given to this variable is unimportant: When the effect of neighborhood is removed, the "effect" of television is reduced to almost nothing.

Clearly, however, the artifact (whatever it is called) measures in only the crudest way the amount of crime that a person is exposed to. For example, a person living in one part of what we have labeled as a high-crime section of the city might, in fact, be quite safe: The crimes might well be in a different section of that patrol area. However crude the measure might be, the size of the correlations does drop dramatically.

It should be pointed out that correlations are responsive to effects other than the strength of the relationship between two variables. In particular, as McNemar (1962) points out, "the magnitude of the correlation coefficient varies with the degree of heterogeneity (with respect to the traits being correlated) of the sample" (p. 144). Given that we have divided our overall sample (into the four areas) in a manner that clearly relates to both of the variables (see Tables 1 and 2), this curtailment of the variance could be a problem. It turns out, however, not to be a serious problem in this case. The ratios of the standard deviations of the "curtailed" distribution (average of the four areas' standard deviations) to the uncurtailed distribution (standard deviation for the four areas pooled) are .965, .917, and .844 for the factor scores, total TV viewing scores, and TV violence scores, respectively. McNemar (1962) indicates that "formulas for 'correcting' for double curtailment are not too satisfactory" (p. 145). However, correcting for the curtailment of the range for the most curtailed distribution (TV violence) would only raise the average correlation between fear and amount of violent TV watched (averaged across the four areas) from .07 to .09.

The data look very much the same when analyzed question by question. The nine questions with the highest weight on the first factor of the factor analysis are shown in Table 4. In addition, the overall correlations for all subjects pooled across areas are shown in the first column (for each question with total TV viewing) and the third column (for

Table 5
Stepwise Multiple Regression Summary[a]

Variable	R when entered[b]	F when entered[c]	F in final equation[d]
High/low crime	.234	17.234**	16.704**
City/suburb	.235	.186	.051
Interaction: Crime × City/Suburb	.251	2.335	2.322
Sex	.350	19.858**	21.176**
Age	.376	6.605*	5.206*
Total TV	.385	2.363	.058
TV violence	.391	1.703	1.537
Radio news	.401	2.637	3.002
Newspaper reading	.403	.389	.389

[a] Variables entered in the order indicated.
[b] R achieved with this and all variables above it included.
[c] Equivalent to a test of the significance of the partial correlation between this variable and fear of crime with all variables listed above it partialed out.
[d] Equivalent to a test of the null hypothesis that the beta for this measure in the final equation involving all nine variables is zero.
* $p < .05$ ($df = 1$ and ≥ 290 for all Fs).
** $p < .01$.

the responses to each question and violent TV). All of the significant correlations are in the direction consistent with the Gerbner (Gerbner & Gross, 1974, 1976a, 1976b; Gerbner et al., 1976) findings (i.e., more TV associated with higher likelihood of victimization, etc.). Generally speaking, it is clear that the correlations tend to decrease substantially in size when they are run within the four areas and then pooled.

An alternative method of analyzing these data is in a stepwise multiple regression analysis using the fear-of-crime factor scores as the criterion and various other social and media exposure data as predictors. In order to control for neighborhood, this was entered first into the regression equation (coded as three variables: high/low crime, city/suburb, and their interaction). Next, two subject characteristics, sex and age, were entered, since both of them related to the fear-of-crime measure. (Not surprisingly, women and older people reported higher levels of fear than did men and younger people.) After these more "basic" variables had been entered, total TV viewing and TV violence were entered. Finally, the frequency of listen-

Table 6
Standardized Canonical Variate Coefficients

Variable	High score indicates	Variate 1	Variate 2	Variate 3
Outcome set				
Question 1	No problem	.536	−.102	.339
Question 2	Low chance	.064	−.108	.266
Question 3	Low chance	.365	−.012	−.773
Question 4	Low chance	.107	−.175	.283
Question 5	Low chance	−.159	−.059	−.806
Question 6	Low chance	.394	.216	.541
Question 7	Unlikely	−.420	.131	.131
Question 8	Never	−.501	−.451	.417
Question 9	No	.028	−.577	−.281
Predictor set				
Total TV	Much	.079	.088	−.063
TV violence	Much	−.136	−.017	.335
Radio news	Little	−.177	−.194	.430
Newspaper reading	Little	−.014	−.168	.032
High/low crime area	High	−.609	.472	−.178
City/surburb	City	−.279	−.145	−.845
Interaction: Crime × Location	High suburb/ low city	.465	−.283	−.236
Age	Older	.010	.163	.096
Sex	Female	.229	.889	−.110
Canonical correlation		.608	.468	.305
p value[a]		<.001	<.001	<.002

[a] Using Wilks' lambda. Using the method of the greatest characteristic root, the third pair of canonical variates is not significant. For a discussion of this problem, see Harris (1976).

ing to radio news and newspaper reading were entered into the equation.

The results are shown in Table 5. It is clear that after the subject characteristics had been entered, the media questions had no significant predictive value. Most relevant to the Gerbner results is of course the lack of importance of total TV viewing when it first entered the equation.

Finally, a canonical correlation analysis was done, using the nine fear-of-crime questions (see Table 4) as the criterion set and the same nine variables as in the multiple regression analysis (see Table 5) as the predictor set. Three significant canonical correlations were found. The variates associated with these correlations are shown in Table 6.

The first pair of canonical variates suggests that those who do not see crimes of violence as a problem in their neighborhood (Question 1), who do not think that a child playing alone in a park is in danger (Question 3), and who do not think that they themselves are likely to be victims of an assault (Question 6), but who are afraid that their houses will be broken into (Question 7) and who do not walk alone at night (Question 8), tend to be females living in low-crime (city) areas.

The second pair of canonical variates appears to indicate that people who have areas near them that they will not walk in at night (Question 9) and who fear walking alone at night (Question 8), but who do not think that they will be victims of a violent crime (Question 6), tend to be females living in high-crime (city) areas who listen to a lot of radio news.

The third set of variates suggests that those who think that unaccompanied female subway riders (Question 5) and children playing alone in parks (Question 3) are vulnerable to attacks, but who themselves do not feel vulnerable (Question 6) and do not worry about walking alone at night (Question 8), since their neighborhoods are safe (Question 1), tend to be suburban (low-crime area) residents who watch a lot of violent TV and do not listen to radio news.

The total amount of television watched did not seem to be important, and the amount of violent television watched entered into the interpretation only in the third canonical variate. Even in this case, it appears that the amount of violent TV watched related positively to the perceived vulnerability of particular groups (female subway riders and children playing alone in parks) but negatively to the perceived likelihood of the respondents themselves being victims of violent crime.

In summary, then, looking at these data from three somewhat different points of view, it appears that the amount of television watched did not relate to the amount of fear a person felt about being a victim of crime when other, more basic variables were taken into account.

Other Findings

As indicated earlier, we asked 25 other questions. Most of these questions related, directly or indirectly, to the respondents' views of the nature and frequency of crime or violence around them. In 14 of the questions, there was a significant relationship (pooled or calculated individually and then averaged) between TV viewing and the response to the question. The questions and the relationship of each question to TV viewing are shown in Table 7. What is noteworthy about these correlations is that there is generally not a substantial drop when the correlations are computed within area and then averaged (column 2 of Table 7). Thus, it appears that the relationship between total TV viewing and responses to these questions is not mediated by the area in which the respondent resides. These were the only other questions that correlated with TV viewing, and, at least from our point of view, they are qualitatively different from those that were large contributors to the "fear index" (see Table 4). Because it is not of central interest

to this study, we did not look at other possible factors that might account for the correlations that we have presented.

Discussion

A number of things are reasonably clear from these data. First of all, the basic findings of Gerbner and his associates (Gerbner & Gross, 1974, 1976a, 1976b; Gerbner et al., 1976) are replicable: People who watch a lot of television are more likely to indicate fear of their environment. It is equally clear, however, that this relationship disappears when attempts are made to control for other variables, including the actual incidence of crime in the neighborhood. Thus, it would appear that television itself is not likely to be a direct cause of people's fear of being victims of crime.

Although clearly at the level of speculation, it is interesting to note that Gerbner's (Gerbner & Gross, 1974) own data on this issue were collected by telephone interview in four cities: Philadelphia, Chicago, Los Angeles, and Dallas. One can assume that there exists in these cities some variability in the dangerousness of different neighborhoods. Since households for that survey were selected randomly from telephone books, it seems reasonable to expect that neighborhoods differing in actual dangerousness would be included from each city. This variation could be sufficient to produce the apparently small correlation that Gerbner found. More interesting, however, is the possibility that for some unspecifiable reason, the relationship only holds in high-crime areas, or in high-crime cities in particular. As shown in Table 3, we, too, got significant correlations within the high-crime area of the city of Toronto. One possible admittedly post hoc explanation for this result is that television violence in the form of police shows and so forth deals mostly with high-crime city neighborhoods. It is possible that people outside of such areas do not feel that the violence on television has any relevance for them; hence, there is no relationship between the amount of television watched and the perception of the likelihood of being a victim.

Table 7
Questions Associated Significantly With TV Viewing: Correlations Between Responses to Each Question and Total TV and TV Violence for the Four Areas Pooled and the Average of the Four Areas Calculated Individually

Question	Total TV		TV violence		High TV viewing associated with
	Pooled	Average within area	Pooled	Average within area	
10. Would you imagine that you would be more likely to be seriously harmed by someone you knew previously or by a complete stranger? (400)	.12*	.09*	.04	.06	Previously known
12. How dangerous do you think it is for a female driver of a car to pick up a male hitchhiker who is a stranger? (404)	.09*	.06	.06	.06	Dangerous
13. Do you think that it would be a good idea to spend more money on police patrols of your area of the city? (403)	.11*	.06	.12*	.08	Definitely yes
17. Do you think that it is useful for people to keep firearms in their homes to protect themselves? (405)	.31*	.20*	.25*	.11*	Definitely yes
20. Should women carry a weapon such as a knife to protect themselves against sexual assault? (405)	.18*	.17*	.19*	.18*	Definitely yes
21. Some people have suggested that one way to reduce the incidence of violent crime is to encourage people to stay away from areas thought to be high in crime. Do you think that this is a good way of dealing with the problem of crime? (403)	.09*	.07*	.09*	.06	Definitely yes
22. What proportion of murders in Toronto do you think are committed by people who could be classified as mentally ill? (381)	.11*	.10*	.08*	.09*	High proportion
23. Approximately what proportion of assaults in Toronto are directed against members of racial minorities (i.e., nonwhites) by whites? (359)	.10*	.12*	.09*	.11*	High proportion
24. What proportion of serious assaults in Toronto do you think are carried out by nonwhites? (364)	.08	.11*	.08	.12*	High proportion
25. How many murders do you think took place in metropolitan Toronto during 1975? (372)	.17*	.16*	.16*	.13*	Large number

Table 7   (continued)

| Question | Total TV | | TV violence | | High TV viewing associated with |
	Pooled	Average within area	Pooled	Average within area	
26. During the last 5 years, how many people do you think were murdered in the TTC subway? (384)	.15*	.12*	.09*	.08*	Large number
31. If you were walking alone on a residential street at night and someone asked you for directions, would you stop and give him the directions? (404)	.10*	.11*	0	0	Definitely not
32. If a person were to have an epileptic seizure on the street in front of you, how likely do you think most people would be to help? (405)	.10*	.07	.08	0	Very likely
33. If, in the middle of the night, a stranger knocked on your door and asked to use your telephone to call someone to help him start his car that had apparently stalled on your street, which of the following would you be most likely to do? (404)	.11*	.12*	.05	.03	Not help

Note. ns of respondents for each question are in parentheses.
* $p < .05$.

The second general point that should be made about our data is that although the correlation between TV viewing and fear dropped off when neighborhood was used as a controlling factor, this same factor did not eliminate the relationship between TV viewing and other factors (see Table 7). It is possible that the questions listed in Table 7 are, in fact, related to television viewing because they deal with matters of a more factual nature than the questions having to do with the person's own level of fear. Thus, television may well act as a source of information with regard to questions of fact, whereas it does not change people's views of how afraid they should be.

References

Gerbner, G., & Gross, L. *Trends in network television drama and viewer conceptions of social reality, 1967–1973. Violence profile number 6.* Washington, D.C.: Educational Resources Information Center, 1974.

Gerbner, G., & Gross, L. Living with television: The violence profile. *Journal of Communication,* 1976, *26,* 172–199. (a)

Gerbner, G., & Gross, L. The scary world of TV's heavy viewer. *Psychology Today,* April 1976, pp. 41–45; 89. (b)

Gerbner, G., Gross, L., Eleey, M. F., Fox, S., Jackson-Beeck, M., & Signorielli, N. *Trends in network television drama and viewer conceptions of social reality, 1967–1975. Violence profile number 7.* Philadelphia, Pa.: The Annenberg School of Communications, University of Pennsylvania, 1976.

Harris, R. J. The invalidity of partitioned-U tests in canonical correlation and multivariate analysis of variance. *Multivariate Behavioral Research,* 1976, *11,* 353–366.

McNemar, Q. *Psychological statistics* (3rd ed.). New York: Wiley, 1962.

Received February 24, 1978 ■

PART VI

IMPACT OF MASS COMMUNICATION: TELEVISION

Ambitious syntheses of voluminous research on the social effects of television are presented in this section. Several of the articles portray television's effects in a different conception from the tradition of "limited effect."

The first chapter summarizes several thousand studies on television and argues that the social impact of television is much greater than many have assumed.

The impact of the celebrated TV series *Roots* is analyzed in the second chapter, with selectivity processes shown to limit the program's effects.

A synthesis of research dealing with television and children is contained in the third selection, which argues that children are active in their uses of television, and that they are not passive sponges of TV content. Age-specific programming for children is called for in this piece.

An analysis of major experimental research since 1956 is presented in the fourth chapter. The role of improved methodology and the possible impact of increased television-watching on experimental results are suggested.

A provocative analysis of a possible sexist bias in the execution and interpretation of research results on violence and pornography concludes this section.

The 1978 publication by Columbia University Press of Television and Human Behavior, *a synthesis of thousands of studies, has been widely noted in the popular and the scholarly press. Here, the senior author of that work, George Comstock, distills much of the larger Rand Corporation report. He points out that the conclusion of minimal effects has been inadvertently applied to television largely because of the failure to document a large, independent impact on viewers. The perspective has now changed. Even though the independent effects of television appear small—because they are interrelated with a host of other factors—their social importance may be great. Dr. Comstock is Samuel I. Newhouse Professor of Public Communications at Syracuse University. The original version of this chapter was first presented as a paper at the annual meeting of the International Industrial Television Association in Anaheim, California, in 1976.*

29

TELEVISION AND ITS VIEWERS
What Social Science Sees

George Comstock

Television and human behavior is a topic about which there will always be question marks. There are many reasons. The procedures of social science are too imperfect. The questions are too many and too difficult. Both the medium and the society are too subject to change. Nevertheless, in the 25 years since television began its conquest of the environment, there has accumulated a sizable scientific literature about the relationships between the medium and people.

It is sometimes said that very little is known about television and people beyond the popularity of the former and the fickleness of taste of the latter. This is not really true, if one is willing to accept a scientific definition of "knowing." That is, there is a great deal "known" if one is willing to define the concept of knowing as a state in which there is verifiable evidence that disposes an observer toward one or another set of possible facts or explanations without establishing that such is the case with absolute certainty.

The relevant literature amount to over 2500 items. The variety is so great than no simple or concise statement is possible. For example, the studies include:

- A psychologist who modified the thumb-sucking of a young child by shutting off the set whenever the act was performed (Baer, 1962).

From George Comstock, "Television and Its Viewers: What Social Science Sees," original manuscript.

- A team of epidemiologists who videotaped the living room behavior of Kansas City, Missouri, families from mobile units parked in their yards while they watched television (Bechtel et al., 1972).

- The international battery of sociologists who recorded the time spent on television and other activities, including work and sleep, in major industrial cities throughout Western Europe, the United States, and Latin America (Szalai, 1972).

- The psychologists who filmed children's expressions as they watched one man attack another in a violent television portrayal. They related the degree to which those expressions revealed positive or negative emotional reactions to the children's later inclination to help or hinder another child in playing a game (Ekman et al., 1972).

- The many social psychologists who have compared the subsequent aggressiveness of children and adolescents who viewed violent television with the aggressiveness of those who saw no television or less violent television. The aggressiveness was measured in such varied ways as the voicing of insults (Wells, 1973; Feshbach and Singer, 1971), the punching of a Bobo doll (Bandura et al., 1936a, 1963b), the playing with guns or knives (Liebert and Baron, 1972), the infliction of electric shocks (Berkowitz and Alioto, 1973; Berkowitz and Geen, 1966), and actual physical interpersonal aggression (Steuber et al., 1971; Parke et al., forthcoming), in such varied settings as university psychology laboratories, classrooms, homes, and residential schools.

- The many social scientists who have investigated television's role in politics, including the effect on West Coast voters of early predictions of the presidential winner based on East Coast returns (Fuchs, 1965, 1966; Mendelsohn, 1966; Tuchman and Coffin, 1971; Lang and Lang, 1968b); the effects of televised debates between presidential candidates (Kraus, 1962); the degree to which television sets the agenda of issues and personalities to which the public gives attention (McCombs and Shaw, 1972, 1974); the role of television in reshaping the events of which it is supposedly a neutral reporter (Lang and Lang, 1953, 1968a); the effects on voters of exposure to television news and televised political advertising (McClure and Patterson, 1974a, 1974b; Dreyer, 1971; Rothschild, 1975; Atkin et al., 1973; Chaffee et al., 1970); and, of course, the effects of television on the conduct and outcome of political campaigns (Mendelsohn and Crespi, 1970; Robinson, 1972; Blumer and McQuail, 1969; DeVries and Tarrance, 1972).

- The analysts of content, who have measured such varied attributes of the medium as the quantity and character of violence in entertainment (Gerbner and Gross, 1973, 1974; Gerbner, 1972); the content and bias of television news (Frank, 1973; Russo, 1971; Singer, 1970; Stevenson et al., 1973; Efron, 1971); sex stereotyping in cartoons (Levinson, 1973), in family programs (Long and Simon, 1974), in commercials (McArthur and Resko, forthcoming), and in drama (Seggar and Wheeler, 1973); trends in regard to portrayals of blacks in entertainment and cartoons (Dominick and Greenberg, 1970); the behavior of the characters in soap operas (Katzman, 1972); the way various occupations are portrayed (DeFleur, 1964); and the methods employed by characters in dramatic entertainment to outwit antagonists, overcome barriers, and achieve goals (Larsen et al., 1963).

Clearly, we can only draw some meaning from this diverse array if we focus on specific themes. Let us take four major ones:

First, the role of television in behavior modification.

Second, the influence of television on the way people spend their time.

Third, the contribution of television to politics.

Fourth, what the American public thinks of television.

Before we begin, certain caveats are necessary. Science by its very nature is always tentative. Social science is particularly so, because of the clumsiness of its tools. The findings we will review have the status of hypotheses for which there is some support. We should not mistake that status for "proof" or "incontrovertibility," two criteria largely beyond the social sciences.

TELEVISION AND BEHAVIOR MODIFICATION

There are two kinds of behavior modification that follow communicatory experiences—voluntary and involuntary. In the first instance, the individual enters into an implicit contract regarding the outcome. Examples are education and smoking control. In the second, there is no such contact. An example would be a change in the probability of engaging in some behavior as the consequence of being entertained. There is evidence that television can contribute to both voluntary and involuntary behavior modification.

Voluntary Modification

As you know, television can be an effective teacher (Chu and Schramm, 1968). However, its instructional capacities are not limited to the conveying of facts, manual skills, or presentations that substitute for the ordinary instructor-student relationship. It appears that television can also modify behavior that is annoying or pathological.

Such modification is in its infancy. Nevertheless, the work done so far suggests that the medium is far from limited to instruction, entertainment, and news.

The key is apparently that the observation of the behavior can alter the viewer's inclination to behave in the same way. Television, in this instance, "teaches" that the world is a little different than the viewer thought or provides a model which the viewer can emulate.

Let us look at some examples:

- The subjects are children between the ages of four and seven whose parents report they are afraid of the dentist. They are divided into two groups. One group sees no film. The other group sees a film about an eight-year-old boy. The cast includes a four-year-old girl and a dentist's chair. The boy climbs without fear into the chair, while the girl, who is visibly frightened, watches. As the film progresses, the girl loses her fear. At the end of the film, the girl climbs voluntarily into the chair. Subjects in the group that saw the film increased in their willingness to visit the dentist, while those in the group that saw no film did not (Poulos and Davidson, 1971).

- The subjects are preschool children afraid of dogs. The design is similar. One group sees films of Disneyland and Marineland. The group sees a series of films in which young children interact to a progressively increasing degree with a dog. Subjects in the group that saw the dog-and-children films increased in their willingness to approach and play with a dog. Those that saw the Disneyland and Marineland films did not. Moreover, the decrease in fear proved to be maintained a month later (Bandura and Menlove, 1968).

- The subjects are preschool children who are considered to be socially withdrawn. The design is similar. The experimental film portrays a child of the same age as the subjects engaging in successively more demanding social activities, and at each stage being rewarded for participation. Those who saw this film increased markedly in social interaction within the setting of the nursery school (O'Connor, 1969).

Television has also been used with reported success in various adult therapeutic situations. The usual procedure has been to employ television to provide feedback to the patient that would otherwise not be possible.

Here are some examples:

- Group psychotherapy sessions are videotaped. The patient then views the proceedings in the company of the therapist and sees his behavior removed from the emotion-laden circumstances in which it occurred. As a result, several therapeutic forces are set at work. There is added feedback to that already provided by the group. The patient's "direct confrontation" with himself gives him the perspective of those with whom he interacted (Danet, 1969). There is also an attack on the psychological defense of denial. This is the maneuver in which the individual restructures the past so that what is agreed upon by observers is believed not to be true by the individual. The video provides a not-easily refutable correction (Melnick, 1973). Furthermore, the opportunity to reexperience the events in a reflective state is said to encourage the acceptance by the viewer of things about himself which he would reject in the more argumentative interaction with therapist and fellow patients (Berger, 1971).

- Marriage and family counseling sessions are videotaped (Alger and Hogan, 1969; Hogan and Alger, 1966). It is claimed that a more democratic exchange results, because therapist and client have access to the same record; that communicatory patterns are better revealed; and that family members are able to become more objective about themselves. These are presumably all steps toward a successful resolution of whatever the problem(s) may be.

In both these cases, one key would seem to be the accuracy and faithfulness to events which television can achieve. There is no other means of transcribing events that combines television's audio-visual veracity with portability and convenience.

Involuntary Modification

Involuntary behavior modification occurs when there is a change in behavior as the result of exposure to some communication, and when the change was not consciously sought by the individual or someone legitimately responsible for him. "Brainwashing" is an example. It has received much popular attention as a major part of F. Lee Bailey's defense of Patty Hearst. The concept is inherited from the experience of American prisoners in the Korean war who were subjected to a calculated program of physical discomfort, isolation, and information manipulation to alter their attitudes and subsequent behavior (Schein, 1956). We are inclined to think of involuntary modification as rather sinister, involving such exotica as radio-activated brain implants, mood-altering drugs, hypnotism, and conditioning of the sort dramatized in Richard Condon's *The Manchurian Candidate*. However, it also has an everyday face. We are surrounded by the media from birth to death, and we encounter many messages that we do not seek. We sometimes respond in ways that we would not have expected or are not conscious of as a response traceable to exposure to the media. This is an unavoidable part of modern life, but it is also involuntary modification of behavior.

The fact that television is supported by the sale to advertisers of access to audiences is implicit evidence that television can be persuasive when its messages are designed to be. Moreover, there is evidence that at least under some circumstances its entertainment programs can maintain or alter behavior.

The majority of research has been devoted to the modification of the behavior of children and adolescents, and in particular to the question of the influence of violent television entertainment on their subsequent aggressiveness. There are many issues unexplored, but the accumulated evidence does permit the tentative acceptance of certain propositions.

It was once widely argued that television violence has a cathartic effect on young viewers. The viewer presumably would act out his hostile impulses vicariously as he watched the violence on the screen. As a result, exposure to television violence would reduce subsequent aggressiveness. Although it seems obvious that such an effect must occur for certain individuals, there is no evidence that it is a typical occurrence (Goranson, 1969). When exposure to television violence does reduce subsequent aggressiveness, and it has been demonstrated that it can do so, it appears to be the result of the violence heightening anxiety about aggressive impulses, thereby leading to increased self-control (Berkowitz and Rawlings, 1963).

On the contrary, the most justifiable interpretation of the total array of findings is that the viewing of television violence increases the likelihood of subsequent aggressiveness on the part of children and adolescents (Bandura, 1973; Berkowitz, 1962; Bogart, 1972; Chaffee, 1972; Comstock, 1972; Goranson, 1970; Krull and Watt; 1973; Liebert et al., 1973; Shirley, 1973; Singer, 1971; Surgeon General's Scientific Advisory Committee on Television and Social Behavior, 1972). However, there are some very important caveats. The first caveat is that this conclusion does not rest on a single irrefutable demonstration that the effect is an everyday event of real life, but on the convergence of findings from a variety of studies, each of which has its own weaknesses for inferring real-life impact. The result is that subsequent studies could overturn the conclusion. The second caveat is that the research tells us very little about other functions or purposes for the young served by violent television drama. It has been suggested that it may teach empathy and other socially desirable reactions (Hyman, 1973). Third, we know very little about the degree of social harm, if any, attributable to this relationship. The impact may be negligible, or it may be great.

The evidence comes from three major sources:

- experiments which demonstrate that the observation by children of a television portrayal may lead to imitation of that portrayal

- experiments which demonstrate that the observation by adolescents of a television portrayal of interpersonal violence may increase their level of aggressiveness toward others

- various surveys which find a positive correlation among young persons between aggressiveness and the amount of violent television viewed.

Let us look at a typical imitation experiment. The subjects are nursery school children. They are divided into four groups. The first group sees a live adult attack a Bobo doll in a number of specific ways—with fists, by kicking, with a mallet, by throwing rubber balls, and by verbal abuse. The second group sees the same attack by a human being occur in a televised portrayal. The third group sees the same attack occur in a televised portrayal, but this time the attacker is a costumed "cat lady" such as might appear in a cartoon. The fourth group sees no attacks of any kind. Afterwards, each child is taken to a playroom where there is a Bobo doll and the other paraphernalia available to the attacker. The child's behavior is surreptitiously observed. The children who saw the attacks—live human, televised human, or cartoon-like—performed many more acts resembling those of the attacker than not exposed to the attacks. In addition, the children who saw the cartoon-like portrayal performed more behavior like that in the portrayal than those who saw no attacks, although the degree of imitation was less than in the case of the live human (Bandura et al., 1963a).

Three hypotheses are supported. First, the observation of a televised portrayal can result in the imitative display by young children of what has been portrayed. Presumably, the children who saw the televised attacks acquired responses previously novel to them. Second, the effects of televised and real-life experience can be similar. This is indicated by the fact that both the attacks by the live human and by the televised human resulted in increased imitative aggression. Third, cartoon-like portrayals can have an influence similar to that of portrayals involving humans. This suggests that whatever we may infer about the influence of television on children, Saturday morning programming cannot be considered exempt simply because it largely consists of cartoons.

Let us look at another imitation experiment. The subjects again are nursery school children. They are divided into three groups. One group sees a televised sequence in which an adult attacks a Bobo doll in the same specific ways as before—with fists, by kicking, with a mallet, by throwing rubber balls, and by verbal abuse. At the end, another adult rewards the attacker by serving candy and soda. The second group sees an identical televised sequence except that instead of rewarding the second adult punishes the attacker by tripping and spanking him. The third group sees the same sequence, except that there is neither reward nor punishment. Again, after seeing one of the film portrayals, each child is taken to a playroom with a Bobo doll and the other paraphernalia, and his behavior is surreptitiously observed. The group that saw the attacker punished engaged in fewer aggressive acts like those of the attacker in the film than the groups that saw the very same aggressive behavior but also saw the attacker either rewarded or not punished. However, when the children were offered a small reward for performing the acts they had seen, the differences disappeared (Bandura, 1965).

Two hypotheses are supported. First, the way that an aggressive act is portrayed on television can affect its influence on children's subsequent imitation. In this instance, reward for portrayed aggression was shown to increase the likelihood of imitation. Second, even when there is no performance of portrayed behavior, such behavior may have been added to the repertoire of the young viewer. The implication is that such acquired behavior may be stored for use at a later time.

Let us look at a typical experiment concerned with the effects of television violence on adolescents. The subjects are college males and females. They are first angered by receiving electric shocks administered by a confederate of the experimenter as feedback in an experimental puzzle-solving task. Then they see a film portrayal of a very violent boxing match from the film *Champion* under a variety of circumstances. Or they see a nonviolent film.

Later, the puzzle-solving task is repeated, but this time the subjects have the opportunity to deliver electric shocks to the confederate. In one of the circumstances for viewing the violent film, the subjects are told the name of the experimenter's confederate is "Kirk," the same as the victim in the fight film. In the other circumstances for viewing the violent film, the events behind the portrayed fight are depicted as making the beating administered to the victim either justified or unjustified. The adolescents who saw the fight film delivered a higher level of shocks than those who saw the nonviolent film. The adolescents who believed the confederate had the same name as the film victim delivered a higher level of shocks than those who believed the names were not the same. The adolescents for whom the film beating was depicted as justified delivered a higher level of shocks than those for whom it was depicted as unjustified (Berkowitz and Geen, 1967).

Three hypotheses are supported. First, the televised portrayal of aggression can result in increased aggression by adolescents against another person, and aggression so affected can be different in kind from what was observed. Second, similarity between the elements of the portrayal and the real-life situation can stimulate such effects. In this case, it was the overlap of names. Third, the likelihood of such effects is enhanced by the portrayal of violence as justified.

Of course, as a method, the experiment is limited because it measures behavior in a restricted, artificial context. However, it has the strength of permitting causal inference, and in the experiments cited and about 75 other experiments published in reputable scientific journals, there is a clear demonstration within the context of the experiment of the modification of behavior by exposure to television.

There are also experiments with similar results where the circumstances are relatively if not wholly nonartificial. Let us look at one. The subjects are the teenage residents of three schools for delinquent boys in the United States and Europe. In each school, the boys are divided into two groups. One group sees a series of violent films during a week, including *Death Rides a Pale Horse, Champion,* and *The Chase.* The other group sees a series of nonviolent films. Everyday interaction is recorded for three weeks before the film week, during the film week, and for two weeks after the film week. During and subsequent to the viewing of the films, the sum of verbal and physical aggressiveness is greater for the boys who saw the violent films (Parke et al., forthcoming).

When we turn to evidence from everyday life, we find a number of instances in which there is a positive correlation between measures of aggressiveness and the viewing of violent television entertainment (McLeod et al., 1972a, 1972b; Lefkowitz et al., 1972; Chaffee, 1972). Furthermore, the data indicate that the relationship is not explained by more aggressive youths preferring more violent television (Chaffee, 1972).

These are the threads of research which converge on the conclusion that television violence can modify behavior in the direction of increased aggressiveness. It must be emphasized that our knowledge is largely limited to the direction of the effect. We have no index of the actual degree to which real-life aggressive behavior, whether against person or property, whether relatively acceptable or open to police intervention, is influenced by television.

The television industry, under pressure from the Federal Communications Commission and the Congress to which the social science evidence contributed to at least some small degree, adopted in 1975 the "family viewing hour" during which violence is restrained in primetime. The effects—on families, on children, and on television during the "family" hour and later in the evening—are yet to be evaluated. However, we can readily recognize that if television does not contribute to actual social harm, the remedy may not be so easily found.

We do not have an index of the quantitative impact, but we do know that in certain rare circumstances, especially provocative portrayals can result in dangerous antisocial behavior on the part of very few, presumably emotionally unstable individuals. The clearest example was the tendency for airliner bomb threats to follow upon the broadcasts of the Rod Serling play, *Doomsday Flight* (Bandura, 1973). If it turns out that the major threat is such singular productions, rather than the general level of television violence, we may be unable to protect ourselves before the fact, because of uncertainty over the eventual impact of a given portrayal and because of our concern not to censor the arts or the media.

There is also some evidence that one factor contributing to increased aggressiveness subsequent to the viewing of violent television may be its capacity to arouse the viewer physiologically (Tannenbaum and Zillmann, 1975). The corollary is that arousing but nonviolent content may also increase the level of subsequent aggressiveness, and there is some evidence to support this proposition (Zillmann, 1971; Tannenbaum, 1972). If arousal is a major factor, and if it often follows upon exposure to nonviolent content, violence reduction may be a remedy high in appeal but low in curative effect.

TELEVISION AND OUR TIME

Television also influences human behavior by the attention given to it by the audience. The television industry is primarily interested is how this attention varies among programs and networks, and how it can be maximized. There are, however, a number of other questions to be asked, and on which there is some scientific evidence. They include the kind of behavior accompanying viewing, the place of television in total leisure time, and the influence of television on other activities.

Viewing Behavior

What do people do when they view? Often, something else. In one study, families were videotaped while they watched television in their own homes (Bechtel et al., 1972). It documented what we know—"television viewing" is an activity *interruptus*, a discontinuous experience with spurts and disconnections, and often accompanied by some other activity, which in these particular video records most often was eating. In addition, attention to the screen while "viewing" rises and falls depending on what is being shown, with commercials getting the lowest attention (about two-thirds of the rating for the content getting the greatest attention, movies).

Television and Leisure

In 1965, a team of UNESCO social scientists engaged in an extraordinary investigation of the way modern humans spend their time. Diaries of 24 hours of activity were obtained from large samples in each of 15 industrialized cities located in the United States, Western Europe, and Latin America (Szalai, 1972; Robinson, 1972; Robinson and Converse, 1972). Because spending time with the mass media was one of the activities recorded, these data tell us how television fits in with the rest of daily life.

Americans spend about 40% of their total leisure time with television. The time spent with television is three-fourths of the total time spent with the mass media. Among 37 primary activities recorded, television ranked third behind sleep and work as a consumer of time. When the United States was compared with other countries, the U.S. consumption of television per capita was highest; but surprisingly; when only persons with access to a set were examined, the amount of viewing per day was surprisingly similar despite the great differences in cultures and programming.

Influence on Other Activities

The same UNESCO data tell us something about the impact of television on other activities, because they permit the comparison of owners and nonowners of sets in sites where ownership is not universal. The two most striking effects seem to be an increase in time devoted to the mass media and a decrease in time devoted to sleep, although the fastidious might argue that the apparent decrease in attention to household tasks is equally noteworthy. When set owners and nonowners are compared across the twelve countries, set owners spend about an hour a day *more* in mass media consumption as the result of the time devoted to television, and about 13% *less* time sleeping. Set owners also spend less time attending social gatherings away from home, listening to the radio, reading books, engaging in miscellaneous leisure activities, attending the movies, conversing, watching television away from home, and doing household tasks.

The impact of television is best evaluated against the effects of other major innovations. In temporal terms, the effect of the automobile on time spent on housework has been slight compared to the full hour's increase in mass media consumption and the necessary readjustments in other activities apparently attributable to television (Robinson, 1972). Television has done no less than reshape daily life.

TELEVISION AND POLITICS

This year, each network will send crews of between 500 and 800 to cover the presidential nominating conventions, and coverage of the primaries has been extensive and competitive. The list of television's major political events is long; it includes the Nixon "Checkers" speech, the "great debates" between Nixon and Kennedy in 1960, the Kennedy assassinations, the long count in 1968 before Nixon clearly became the winner, and the Watergate hearings. There are many instances in which television campaigns appear to have won congressional or gubernatorial elections.

Television has clearly transformed American politics, yet it would be an error to attribute too much to television exposure *per se* in the way of voter turnout or choice. Television has more clearly affected politicians. It has encouraged the manipulation of the nominating convention so that the performance carried by television makes a favorable impression, altered the organization of campaigns so that television access through the news or paid advertising is a major thrust, and redirected the expenditure of campaign funds toward the media (Mendelsohn and Crespi, 1970).

Despite noteworthy exceptions, effects on voter turnout and choice are less certain. The reasons include the tendency for many voters to make up their minds early in the campaign, before there is much exposure to campaign-related television; the typical presence of long-standing predispositions toward one or the other of the major parties; the inclination for people to "filter out" information contrary to their own viewpoint; and the conflicting and self-canceling nature of the various political news items and paid advertisements carried by television. They also include the fact that political situations vary widely and there are often some unique elements, which makes the absence of any general or typical effect of exposure to television not so surprising.

The most widely accepted view of television's influence is that it has the very limited effect of strengthening or maintaining predispositions (Klapper, 1960). This is an important effect, but not one that appears in the form of changed votes.

However, we should not ignore the very many conditions under which strong effects may occur. For example, four studies of the effect on Western voter choice and turnout of the broadcasting of early East Coast returns and computer projections in 1964—returns and projections making it clear that Johnson would be the winner over Goldwater—found that the broadcasts had little influence (Fuchs, 1965, 1966; Mendelsohn, 1966; Tuchman and Coffin, 1971; Lang and Lang, 1968a). We should not forget that this was a race in which feeling was strong and Johnson's lead was established so well before the election that most voters had taken it into account in reaching their decision. Such notice about trends might well alter voter decisions and electoral outcomes when it disconfirms expectations.

Television has a greater opportunity to affect voters the later in the campaign they make decisions. There is some evidence that the number of "undecideds" is growing, and that television is especially favored by them for political information. Television also has a greater opportunity to affect voters who do not identify with a political party. There is evidence that such party identification has been declining since 1952 (Dreyer, 1971). In both cases, there is a historical trend which may lead to an increase in the political influence of television.

There are other factors which suggest that television's influence may be increasing. Between 1952 and 1974, expenditures for paid political broadcasts increased 600%, six times the rate of inflation (Rothschild, 1975). Television advertising is usually thought of as primarily having a persuasive impact, but with television news devoting so much attention to visual coverage rather than issues, political advertising may become a major source of information about the positions of candidates. Furthermore, because the broadcast of paid advertising cannot be predicted by the viewer, people cannot avoid messages as easily as they can with convention coverage or news commentary.

Because degree of exposure to television does not seem to dramatically influence voter turnout or choice during campaigns, this should not lead us into the error of dismissing television as a political factor. Television is the stage on which personalities and issues play out their political roles. Politics has fitted itself to television, and television in turn has increased the public's vicarious participation in politics. Politics has been altered, and in the future it may be altered still further by television if, as some observers believe, long-time political loyalties are lessening, established voting patterns are falling apart, and politics is becoming less stable (Blumler and McLeod, 1974).

TELEVISION AND THE PUBLIC

What do the American people think of television? We know that they think it is better to have the set on than off. The most recent Nielsen figures indicate that in the average household, television is on between six and a half and six and three-quarters hours per day. During the preceding decade, television use per household increased steadily.

There have also been many criticisms of television. When we turn to public opinion surveys designed to discover the general public's evaluation of television (Steiner, 1963; Bower, 1973; Roper, 1975), we find:

- The public's overall evaluation of television is largely favorable.

- Between 1960 and 1970, the public became somewhat less satisfied with television. Although viewing increased, so did complaints, while praise declined.

- The most criticized aspect of television is the commercial. About 70% of Americans believe there are too many commercials. However, 70% also believe commercials are a "fair price" to pay for the medium.

- When compared with other media, television has become increasingly favored by the public. In 1960, the public was about equally divided as to whether television, magazines, or newspapers presented things most intelligently and which was most educational, and newspapers led television by ten percentage points as "doing most" for the public. By 1970, television led on all these points by a clear margin.

No aspect of television has drawn more controversy than network news. During the Nixon years, it was generally portrayed by administration officials as unfair, too liberal, biased, and the product of an elite out of touch with the average American.

The fact is that the public as a whole evaluates television news very, very favorably. The public not only believes it to be their major source of news, but thinks it to be the medium to believe if there are conflicting or different reports of the same news item (Roper, 1975). There is no evidence that either liberals or conservatives are more dissatisfied or disturbed over the balance of television news (Bower, 1973). About half of Americans believe television reporting to be "more objective than it is biased," while only about a third believe it is "more biased than it is objective" (Hickey, 1972). Furthermore, the degree to which there is criticism tends to be self-canceling. For example, in 1971, about 25% believed there was bias *for* the administration, and about 25% believed there was bias *against* the administration (Hickey, 1972).

About 65% of the American people say that they usually get most of their news "about what's going on in the world today" from television (Roper, 1975). It must be emphasized that this is a perception or public declaration in regard to television's symbolic status. It does not "prove" that this is indeed the case. In fact, the evidence is that the public's declarations overestimate the true role of network news, because far fewer watch it than most would guess. For example, in a national sample of 7000 adults, more than half did not watch a single national evening news program over a two-week period.

In sum, the relationship between the American public and television is a love-hate one. The public dallies endlessly with television, carps but accepts the faults as a fair price for the pleasures, acclaims it the major source of news yet does not fully pay attention to its reports.

THE SOCIAL IMPORTANCE OF TELEVISION

In the past, social scientists inadvertently have probably contributed to an impression that television's noteworthy effects are minimal. This has occurred because they have tended to reserve the conclusion that television has an important effect for instances in which there has been some large, independent impact on the average viewer, and typically they have not found one. We are becoming more sophisticated in our thinking. It has always been recognized that television has its influence in conjunction with a multitude of other variables; that it may only have it influence when some particular set of circumstances is present; that it may only have a particular effect on viewers with special characteristics; and that its independent contribution to any outcome may be small. What has changed is that it is now widely acknowledged that such impact, although quantitatively small, may be large in terms of social importance. The shift of a percentage point in an election seems trivial until it is remembered that Kennedy defeated Nixon by a smaller margin. Shifts of small magnitude in other areas also often represent important social effects. There is no general statement that summarizes the scientific literature on television and human behavior, but if it is necessary to make one, perhaps it should be that television's effects are many, typically minimal in magnitude, but sometimes major in social importance.

REFERENCES

Alger, I. and P. Hogan. (1969) Effects of videotape playback experience on family and marital relationships. *American Journal of Orthopsychiatry, 39,* 86-94.

Atkin, C. K., L. Bowen, O. B. Nayman, and K. G. Sheinkoph. (1973) Quality versus quantity in televised political ads. *Public Opinion Quarterly, 37,* 209-224.

Baer, D. M. (1962) Laboratory control of thumbsucking by withdrawal and representation of reinforcement. *Journal of the Experimental Analysis of Behavior, 5,* 525-528.

Bandura, A. (1965) Influence of models' reinforcement contingencies on the acquisition of imitative responses. *Journal of Personality and Social Psychology, 1,* 589-595.

Bandura, A. (1973) *Aggression: A Social Learning Analysis,* Englewood Cliffs, New Jersey: Prentice-Hall.

Bandura, A. and F. Menlove. (1968) Factors determining vicarious extinction of avoidance behavior through symbolic modeling. *Journal of Personality and Social Psychology, 8,* 99-108.

Bandura, A., D. Ross, and S. A. Ross. (1963a) Imitation of film-mediated aggressive models. *Journal of Abnormal and Social Psychology, 66,* 3-11.

Bandura, A., D. Ross, and S. A. Ross. (1963b) Vicarious reinforcement and imitative learning, *Journal of Abnormal and Social Psychology, 67,* 601-607.

Bechtel, R. B., C. Achelpohl, and R. Akers. (1972) Correlates between observed behavior and questionnaire responses on television viewing. Pp. 274-344 in E. A. Rubinstein, G. A. Comstock, and J. P. Murray (eds.) *Television and Social Behavior.* Volume 4. *Television in Day-To-Day Life: Patterns of Use.* Washington, D.C.: Government Printing Office.

Berger, M. (1971) *Videotape Techniques in Psychiatric Training and Treatment.* New York: Bruner and Mazel.

Berkowitz, L. (1962) *Aggression: A Social Psychological Analysis.* New York: McGraw-Hill.

Berkowitz, L. and J. T. Alioto. (1973) The meaning of an observed event as a determinant of its aggressive consequences. *Journal of Personality and Social Psychology, 28,* 206-217.

Berkowitz, L. and R. G. Geen. (1966) Film violence and the cue properties of available targets. *Journal of Personality and Social Psychology, 3,* 52-530.

Berkowitz, L. and R. G. Geen. (1967) Stimulus qualities of the target of aggression: a further study. *Journal of Personality and Social Psychology, 5,* 364-368.

Berkowitz, L. and E. Rawlings. (1963) Effects of film violence on inhibitions against subsequent aggression. *Journal of Abnormal and Social Psychology, 66,* 405-412.

Blumler, J. G. and J. M. McLeod. (1974) Communication and voter turnout in Britain. Pp. 265-312 in T. Leggatt (ed.) *Sociological Theory and Survey Research.* London: Sage Publications.

Blumler, J. G. and D. McQuail. (1969) *Television in Politics: Its Uses and Influences.* Chicago: University of Chicago Press.

Bogart, L. (1972) Warning, the Surgeon General has determined that TV violence is moderately dangerous to your child's mental health. *Public Opinion Quarterly, 36,* 491-521.

Bower, R. T. (1973) *Television and the Public.* New York: Holt, Rinehart and Winston.

Chaffee, S. H. (1972) Television and adolescent aggressiveness. Pp. 1-34 in G. A. Comstock and E. A. Rubinstein (eds.) *Television and Social Behavior.* Vol. 3. *Television and Adolescent Aggressiveness.* Washington, D.C.: Government Printing Office.

Chaffee, S. H., L. S. Ward, and L. P. Tipton. (1970) Mass communication and political socialization. *Journalism Quarterly, 47,* 647-659, 666.

Chu, G. C. and W. Schramm. (1968) *Learning from Television: What the Research Says.* Washington, D.C.: National Association of Educational Broadcasters.

Comstock, G. A. (1972) *Television Violence: Where the Surgeon General's Study Leads.* P-4831. Santa Monica, California: The Rand Corporation.

Comstock, G. (1975) *Television and Human Behavior: The Key Studies.* R-1747-CF. Santa Monica, California: The Rand Corporation.

Comstock, G. and M. Fisher. (1975) *Television and Human Behavior: A Guide to the Pertinent Scientific Literature.* R-1746-CF. Santa Monica, California: The Rand Corporation.

Comstock, G. and G. Lindsey. (1975) *Television and Human Behavior: The Research Horizon, Future and Present.* R-1748-CF. Santa Monica, California: The Rand Corporation.

Danet, B. N. (1969) Videotape playback as a therapeutic device in group psychotherapy. *International Journal of Group Psychotherapy, 19*, 433-440.

DeFleur, M. L. (1964) Occupational roles as portrayed on television. *Public Opinion Quarterly, 28*, 57-74.

DeVries, W. and L. Tarrance, Jr. (1972) *The Ticket-Splitter: A New Force in American Politics.* Grand Rapids, Michigan: Eerdmans Publishing.

Dominick, J. R. and B. S. Greenberg. (1970) Three seasons of blacks on television. *Journal of Advertising Research, 10*(2), 21-27.

Dreyer, E. C. (1971) Media use and electoral choices: some political consequences of information exposure. *Public Opinion Quarterly, 35*, 544-553.

Efron, E. (1971) *The News Twisters.* Los Angeles: Nash Publishing.

Ekman, P., R. M. Liebert, W. V. Friesen, R. Harrison, C. Zlatchin, E. J. Malmstrom, and R. A. Baron. (1972) Facial expressions of emotion while watching televised violence as predictors of subsequent aggression. Pp. 22-58 in G. A. Comstock, E. A. Rubinstein, and J. P. Murray (eds.) *Television and Social Behavior. Vol 5. Television's Effects: Further Explorations.* Washington, D.C.: Government Printing Office.

Feshbach, S. and R. D. Singer. (1971) *Television and Aggression: An Experimental Field Study.* San Francisco: Jossey-Bass.

Frank, R. S. (1973) *Message Dimensions of Television News.* Lexington, Massachusetts.

Fuchs, D. A. (1965) Election day newscasts and their effects on Western voter turnout. *Journalism Quarterly, 42*, 22-28.

Fuchs, D. A. (1966) Election-day radio-television and Western voting. *Public Opinion Quarterly, 30*, 226-236.

Gerbner, G. (1972) Violence in television drama: trends and symbolic functions. Pp. 28-187 in G. A. Comstock and E. A. Rubinstein (eds.) *Television and Social Behavior. Vol. 1. Media Content and Control.* Washington, D.C.: Government Printing Office.

Gerbner, G. and L. P. Gross. (1973) The violence profile no. 5: trends in network television drama and viewer conceptions of social reality. Annenberg School of Communications, University of Pennsylvania. (unpublished)

Gerbner, G. and L. P. Gross. (1974) Violence profile no. 6: trends in network television drama and viewer conceptions of social reality: 1967-1973. Annenberg School of Communications, University of Pennsylvania. (unpublished)

Goranson, R. E. (1969) The catharsis effect: two opposing views. Pp. 453-459 in R. K. Baker and S. J. Ball (eds.) *Violence and the Media. A Staff Report to the National Commission on the Causes and Prevention of Violence.* Washington, D.C.: Government Printing Office.

Goranson, R. E. (1970) Media violence and aggressive behavior: a review of experimental research. Pp. 1-31 in L. Berkowitz (ed.) *Advances in Experimental Social Psychology.* Vol. 5. New York: Academic Press.

Hickey, N. (1972) What America thinks of TV's political coverage. *TV Guide*, April 8, 6-11.

Hogan, P. and I. Alger. (1966) Use of videotape recording in family therapy. Paper presented at the meeting of the American Ortho-Psychiatric Association.

Hyman, H. H. (1973) Mass communication and socialization. *Public Opinion Quarterly, 37*, 524-540.

Katzman, N. I. (1972) Television soap operas: what's been going on anyway? *Public Opinion Quarterly, 36,* 200-212.

Klapper, J. T. (1960) *The Effects of Mass Communication.* New York: Free Press.

Kraus, S. (ed.) (1962) *The Great Debates.* Bloomington, Indiana: Indiana University Press.

Krull, R. and J. H. Watt, Jr. (1973) Television viewing and agression: an examination of three models. Paper presented at the meeting of the International Communication Association, Montreal, April.

Lang, K. and G. E. Lang. (1953) The unique perspective of television and its effects: a pilot study. *American Sociological Review, 18,* 3-12.

Lang, K. and G. E. Lang. (1968a) *Politics and Television.* Chicago. Quadrangle Books.

Lang, K. and G. E. Lang. (1968b) *Voting and Nonvoting.* Waltham, Massachusetts: Blaisdell.

Larsen, O. N., L. N. Gray, and J. G. Fortis. (1963) Goals and goal-achievement in television content: models for anomie? *Sociological Inquiry, 33,* 180-196.

Lefkowitz, M. M., L. D. Eron, L. O. Walter, and L. R. Huesmann. (1972) Television violence and child aggression: a followup study. Pp. 35-135 in G. A. Comstock and E. A. Rubinstein (eds.) *Television and Social Behavior.* Vol. 3. *Television and Adolescent Aggressiveness.* Washington, D.C.: Government Printing Office.

Levinson, R. M. (1973) From Olive Oyl to Sweet Polly Purebread: sex role stereotypes and televised cartoons. Paper presented at the meeting of the Georgia Sociological Society, Atlanta, November.

Liebert, R. M. and R. A. Baron. (1972) Some immediate effects of televised violence on children's behavior. *Developmental Psychology, 6,* 469-475.

Liebert, R. M., J. M. Neale, and E. S. Davidson. (1973) *The Early Windowd: Effects of Television on Children and Youth.* Elmsford, New York: Pergamon Press.

Long, M. L. and R. J. Simon. (1974) The roles and statuses of women on children and family TV programs. *Journalism Quarterly, 51,* 107-110.

McArthur, L. Z. and B. G. Resko. (forthcoming) The portrayal of men and women in American television commercials. *Journal of Social Psychology.*

McClure, R. D. and T. E. Patterson. (1974a) The people's choice revisited in the age of television: comparing the voter impact of the mass media during a presidential election campaign. Paper presented at the meeting of the American Association for Public Opinion Research, Lake George, New York, May.

McClure, R. D. and T. E. Patterson. (1974b) Television news and political advertising: the impact of exposure on voter beliefs. *Communication Research, 1,* 3-31.

McCombs, M. E. and D. L. Shaw. (1972) The agenda-setting function of mass media. *Public Opinion Quarterly, 36,* 176-187.

McCombs, M. E. and D. L. Shaw. (1974) A progress report on agenda-setting research. Paper presented at the meeting of the Association for Education in Journalism, San Diego, August.

McLeod, J. M., C. K. Atkin, and S. H. Chaffee. (1972b) Adolescents, parents and television use: adolescent self-support measures from Maryland and Wisconsin samples. Pp. 173-238 in G. A. Comstock and E. A. Rubinstein (eds.) *Television and Social Behavior.* Vol. 3. *Television and Adolescent Aggressiveness.* Washington, D.C.: Government Printing Office.

McLeod, J. M., C. K. Atkin, and S. H. Chaffee. (1972b) Adolescents, parents and televised use: self-report and other-report measures from the Wisconsin sample. Pp. 239-313 in G. A. Comstock and E. A. Rubinstein (eds.) *Television and Social Behavior.* Vol. 3. *Television and Adolescent Aggressiveness.* Washington, D.C.: Government Printing Office.

Melnick, J. (1973) A comparison of replication techniques in the modification of minimal dating behavior. *Journal of Abnormal Psychology, 81,* 51-59.

Mendelsohn, H. A. (1966) Election-day broadcasts and terminal voting decisions. *Public Opinion Quarterly, 30,* 212-225.

Mendelsohn, H. A. and I. Crespi. (1970) *Polls, Television, and the New Politics.* San Francisco: Chandler.

O'Conner, R. D. (1969) Modification of social withdrawal through symbolic modeling. *Journal of Applied Behavior Analysis, 2*, 15-22.

Parke, R. D., L. Berkowitz, J. P. Leyens, S. West, and R. J. Sebastian. (forthcoming) Film violence and aggression: a field experimental analysis. *Journal of Social Issues.*

Poulos, R. W. and E. S. Davidson. (1971) Effects of a short modeling film on fearful children's attitudes toward the dental situation. State University of New York, Stony Brook. (unpublished)

Robinson, J. P. (1972) Television's impact on everyday life: some cross-national evidence. Pp. 410-431 in E. A. Rubinstein, G. A. Comstock, and J. P. Murray (eds.) *Television and Social Behavior.* Vol. 4. *Television in Day-To-Day Life: Patterns of Use.* Washington, D.C.: Government Printing Office.

Robinson, J. P. and P. E. Converse. (1972) The impact of television on mass media usages: a cross-national comparison. Pp. 197-212 in A. Szalai (ed.) *The Use of Time: Daily Activities of Urban and Suburban Populations in Twelve Countries.* The Hague: Mouton and Company.

Roper Organization, Inc. (1975) *Trends in Public Attitudes Toward Television and Other Mass Media, 1959-1974.* New York: Television Information Office.

Rothschild, M. L. (1975) The effects of political advertising on the voting behavior of a low involvement electorate. Doctoral dissertation, Stanford University.

Russo, F. D. (1971) A study of bias in TV coverage of the Vietnam War: 1969 and 1970. *Public Opinion Quarterly, 35*, 539-543.

Schein, E. H. (1956) The Chinese indoctrination program for prisoners of war. *Psychiatry, 19*, 149-172.

Seggar, J. F. and P. Wheeler. (1973) World of work on TV: ethnic and sex representation in TV drama. *Journal of Broadcasting, 17*, 201-214.

Shirley, K. W. (1973) Television and children: a modeling analysis review essay. Doctoral dissertation, University of Kansas.

Singer, B. D. (1970) Violence, protest and war in television news: the U.S. and Canada compared. *Public Opinion Quarterly, 34*, 611-616.

Singer, J. L. (1971) The influence of violence portrayed in television or motion pictures upon overt aggressive behavior. Pp. 19-60 in J. L. Singer (ed.) *The Control of Aggression and Violence: Cognitive and Physiological Factors.* New York: Academic Press.

Steiner, G. A. (1963) *The People Look at Television.* New York: Knopf.

Steuer, F. B., J. M. Applefield, and R. Smith. (1971) Televised aggression and the interpersonal aggression of preschool children. *Journal of Experimental Child Psychology, 11*, 442-447.

Stevenson, R. L., R. A. Eisinger, B. M. Feinberg, and A. B. Kotok. (1973) Untwisting *The News Twisters:* a replication of Efron's study. *Journalism Quarterly, 50*, 211-219.

Surgeon General's Scientific Advisory Committee on Television and Social Behavior. (1972) *Television and Growing Up: The Impact of Televised Violence.* Report to the Surgeon General, United States Public Health Service. Washington, D.C.: Government Printing Office.

Szalai, A. (ed.) (1972) *The Use of Time: Daily Activities of Urban and Suburban Populations in Twelve Countries.* The Hague: Mouton and Company.

Tannenbaum, P. H. (1972) Studies in film- and television-mediated arousal and aggression: a progress report. Pp. 309-350 in G. A. Comstock, E. A. Rubinstein, and J. P. Murray (eds.) *Television and Social Behavior.* Vol. 5. *Television's Effects: Further Explorations.* Washington, D.C.: Government Printing Office.

Tannenbaum, P. H. and D. Zillmann. (1975) Emotional arousal in the facilitation of aggression through communication. Pp. 149-152 in L. Berkowitz (ed.) *Advances in Experimental Social Psychology.* Vol. 8. New York: Academic Press.

Tuchman, S. and T. E. Coffin. (1971) The influence of election night television broadcasts in a close election. *Public Opinion Quarterly, 35*, 315-326.

Wells, W. D. (1973) Television and aggression: replication of an experimental field study. Graduate School of Business, University of Chicago. (unpublished)

Zillmann, D. (1971) Excitation transfer in communication-mediated aggressive behavior. *Journal of Experimental Social Psychology, 7*, 419-434.

Widespread popular speculation about the possible effects of Roots, *an eight-episode TV series about the origins and history of slavery in America, accompanied the broadcasts in January 1977. Kenneth K. Hur and John P. Robinson study some of the effects of the program in this survey of Cleveland, Ohio, viewers. They conclude that selective exposure and selective perception limited the program's influence on white racial attitudes. Dr. Robinson is Director of the Communication Research Center at Cleveland State University. Dr. Hur is Assistant Professor of Communication at Cleveland State University.*

30

THE SOCIAL IMPACT OF "ROOTS"

Kenneth K. Hur and John P. Robinson

Blacks were more likely to watch, to consider program accurate and to discuss it with others. Influence on racial attitudes of whites less than suggested by various media observers.

► "Roots," a television drama on slavery, was a national television phenomenon. ABC-TV's unprecedented 12-hour dramatization of Alex Haley's book was not only one of the most watched programs in television history but also stimulated unprecedented reaction and discussion in the print media. Both the Associated Press and *Time* magazine reported that "Roots" was a "nightly Super Bowl" for most Americans.[1] The eight-episode series attracted the largest audience in the history of television; seven of the eight episodes ranked among the "top 10" in all-time television ratings, with between 62% and 68% audience share. The last episode drew an estimated audience of some 80 million, a 71% audience share. In all, 130 million Americans were reported as having watched at least part of the series.[2]

Perhaps more important that "Roots'" sheer audience size was the public's reactions to the program. Despite the criticisms made by some historians and media reviewers,[3] the series received overwhelming praise both from critics and public. A Harris survey indicated that Americans nationwide gave it a positive rating (by an 83-15% majority), and 50% of those who saw the program thought it was "one of the best" television programs they had ever seen.[4] Some observers compared "Roots" to the aftermath of the John F. Kennedy assassination, or Orson Welles' Martian invasion radio broadcast as a major broadcasting event, as the series appeared to produce some immediate effects on many viewers. Many white viewers of "Roots" expressed feelings of guilt, anger and sympathy in response to the series and joined the many blacks who suddenly expressed an intense interest in their own genealogies.[5] "Roots" was also blamed for racial disturbances at schools in Pennsylvania, Michigan and Mississippi and for a siege in Cincinnati in which a man took hostages and demanded the return of his son he had abandoned 19 years previously.[6]

This raises a number of interesting questions about the relation between mass media and mass behavior: How

[1] Jerry Buck, "'Roots' is TV's Topper," Associated Press wire, Jan. 29, 1977, and "Why 'Roots' Hit Home," *Time*, Feb. 14, 1977, pp. 69-71.

[2] *Ibid.*

[3] Many television critics and historians criticized "Roots" for its historical inaccuracies, omissions or distortion of facts on slavery history, and stereotyping of characters on the show. Most observers of "Roots" also objected to nudity, violence and a strongly emotional theme presented on the show. John J. O'Connor, "TV Weekend," New York *Times*, Jan. 28, 1977, and Richard Schickel, "Viewpoint: Middlebrow Mandingo," *Time*, Jan. 24, 1977.

[4] Louis Harris, "'Roots' has Little Impact on Opinions," news release, April 1977.

[5] "Why 'Roots' Hit Home," *Time, op. cit.* The article reported that following exposure to "Roots," letters to the National Archives in Washington requesting information about genealogy tripled in a week and applications for permits to use the research facilities jumped by 40%.

[6] "Hostage-takers are 'Loners'," Washington *Post*, Feb. 20, 1977, and "Race Trouble Laid to 'Roots'," Associated Press wire, Jan. 27, 1977.

► Kenneth K. Hur is assistant professor of communication at Cleveland State University and John P. Robinson is professor and director of the Communication Research Center at the same university.

From Kenneth K. Hur and John P. Robinson, "The Social Impact of 'Roots,'" *Journalism Quarterly* 55 (Spring 1978) 19-24. Reprinted by permission.

did the mass TV audience react to the specific content in the "Roots" series? What differences are found between whites and blacks in their exposure to the program and their perceptions of the program content, particularly its depiction of American black history and portrayal of whites and blacks? Did "Roots" viewers perceive the show's presentation of black history as accurate or consider the hardships of slavery as horrible as the series intended to portray? What demographic and attitudinal factors influenced or were related to exposure to "Roots" and viewers' perceptions of the hardships of slavery? The present investigation was undertaken to provide empirical answers to these questions.

The social effects of particular programs and kinds of programming on television, such as commercials, television violence and public-affairs and news programs, have been examined by many researchers. There has been increased social science attention given to television entertainment, recognizing the various entertainment functions that television viewing performs.[7] A recent series of studies of "All in the Family" provides one such example. Vidmar and Rokeach, Surlin and Tate, and Tate and Surlin, among others, have examined the relationships between audience racial attitudes and viewing and perceptions of the series.[8] Although findings vary by studies, most of the research indicates that both selective exposure and selective perception hypotheses hold for the audiences of "All in the Family," such that the dominant effect of the series appears to have been the reinforcement of existing attitudes. Such findings are not unfamiliar in communication research,[9] but they have come at a time when increasing research evidence points to a return to the notion of "powerful mass media."[10] Although "All in the Family" and "Roots" differ in form (comedy vs. epic drama), their themes overlap in that one deals with whites' racial bigotry against blacks and the other deals with whites' brutal treatment of blacks.

Thus, our analysis proceeded along two main avenues. First, differences between whites and blacks were tested in terms of exposure to "Roots" and reactions to the series. It was expected that a higher percentage of blacks than whites would watch "Roots," and among "Roots" viewers, blacks would also watch more episodes and perceive the series more favorably than whites did. Secondly, among white viewers did existing racial attitudes influence or relate to exposure to "Roots" and to perceptions of black people and the hardships of slavery as presented in the series? To accomplish this latter goal, viewers and non-viewers were compared on their racial attitudes, both attitudes closely related to the material shown on "Roots" (e.g., the hardships of slavery) and attitudes not related to the program (e.g., open housing.)

[7] Raymond A. Bauer. "The Audience." Ithiel de Sola Pool. Wilbur Schramm, et. al., eds., Handbook of Communication (Chicago: Rand McNally, 1973), pp. 141-52; Robert T. Bower. Television and the Public (New York: Holt, Rinehart and Winston, 1973); George Gerbner and Larry P. Gross, "Living with Television: The Violence Profile," Journal of Communication, 26: 173-199 (1976); William J. McGuire, "Psychological Motives and Communication Gratification," Jay G. Blumler and Elihu Katz, eds., The Uses of Mass Communications (Beverly Hills: Sage Publications, 1974), pp. 167-96. Gary A. Steiner. The People Look at Television (New York: Knopf, 1963); William Stephenson. The Play Theory of Mass Communication (Chicago: University of Chicago Press, 1967).

[8] Neil Vidmar and Milton Rokeach, "Archie Bunker's Bigotry: A Study in Selective Perception and Exposure." Journal of Communication, 24: 36-47 (1974); Stuart H. Surlin and Eugene D. Tate. "All in the Family: Is Archie Funny?" Journal of Communication, 26: 61-68 (1976); Eugene D. Tate and Stuart H. Surlin. "Agreement with Opinionated TV Characters Across Cultures," JOURNALISM QUARTERLY, 53: 199-203 (1976); Stuart H. Surlin, "Bigotry on Air and in Life," Public Telecommunications Review, 2: 34-41 (1974); John C. Brigham and Linda W. Giesbrecht, "All in the Family: Racial Attitudes," Journal of Communication, 26: 69-74 (1976); John D. Leckenby and Stuart H. Surlin, "Incidental Social Learning: 'All in the Family' and 'Sanford and Son'." Journal of Broadcasting, 20: 481-94 (1976).

[9] Raymond A. Bauer, op. cit.; Joseph T. Klapper, The Effects of Mass Communication (New York: The Free Press, 1960); Wilbur Schramm, "Channels and Audiences," Ithiel de Sola Pool, Wilbur Schramm, et. al., eds., Handbook of Communication, op. cit., pp. 116-40; Walter Weiss, "Effects of the Mass Media of Communication," Gardner Lindzey and Elliot Aronson, eds., Handbook of Social Psychology, Vol. 5 (Boston: Addison-Wesley, 1969), pp. 77-195; Eunice Cooper and Marie Jahoda, "The Evasion of Propaganda," Journal of Psychology, 23: 15-25 (1947).

[10] E.g. Elizabeth Noelle-Neumann. "Return to the Concept of Powerful Mass Media." Studies of Broadcasting. pp. 66-112 (1973); John P. Robinson, "The Press as Kingmaker," JOURNALISM QUARTERLY, 51:589-94 (1974).

Method

A cross-section sample was drawn from Cleveland and its vicinity using the random-digit sampling method of telephone numbers. Telephone numbers drawn at random from the city's telephone directory were used to establish a base number to generate a random sample (including unlisted numbers). To each base number, the numbers 100, 200, 300, 400 and 500 were both added and subtracted, generating 10 random numbers. The resulting list of about 1,200 numbers was assigned to trained student interviewers who were instructed to make at least three call-backs to that number. Males and females were randomly selected by contacting males at odd phone numbers and females at even numbers. This survey was conducted during the week of Jan. 31 thru Feb. 6, shortly following the broadcast of "Roots'" last episode in order to capture short-term effects of the show. A total of 529 telephone interviews was completed, with an adjusted completion rate of 64% after non-working and business telephone numbers were taken into account, and almost 80% if no answers (7%) and refusals (14%) are excluded.

Persons interviewed were asked questions concerning their viewing of "Roots," their perceived accuracy of the program's presentation of American black history and of the picture of blacks and whites portrayed in the program, and the extent of post-viewing discussion about the program. Following the questions on "Roots" viewing, respondents were asked about their general racial attitudes. The questions of racial attitudes consisted of four items, an opinion on open housing and endorsements of basic racial stereotypes about intelligence, trustworthiness and general behavior. The item that was most directly related to "Roots" asked whether re-

spondents felt what blacks went through in slavery was equivalent, worse or much worse than what white immigrants to America had to endure. At the close of the interview, respondents were asked about background and control factors, such as television viewing hours, age, education, race and sex.

The 529 respondents were 82% white and 18% black, and 42% male and 58% female. Fairly heavy exposure to "Roots" was reported, with 75% of respondents reporting watching at least part of the series, a figure slightly higher than the national data reported by both Harris and Nielsen surveys.[11] More than 30% of the respondents reported watching all eight episodes, 18% between 5 and 7 episodes and 26% between 1 and 4 episodes. Across the sample, the mean number of "Roots" episodes seen was just more than 4.

Results

Table 1 shows comparisons between the white and black portions of the sample on different measures. The two portions of the audience varied widely in their responses with significant t-ratios at the .05 level being found for all 11 measures.[12] Not surprisingly, the two samples differed most on racial attitudes, with white respondents believing that whites are more intelligent, trustworthy and behave better than blacks, and being less in favor of open housing than blacks.

As expected, the white and black samples also differed significantly in their viewing of "Roots." A higher percentage of blacks than whites watched "Roots," and among "Roots" viewers, black viewers also watched more episodes on the average than did white viewers. Almost 90% of black respondents reported watching part of the series, compared to 71% of the white respondents, and about 44% of black viewers, compared to 27% of white viewers, reported watching all eight episodes.

In line with the hypotheses of selective interpretation, black viewers also considered the series to be more historically accurate than white viewers. When

[11] The National Nielsen Ratings indicated "Roots" drew an average 46.7% of the total Nielsen sample and the Harris survey showed that "Roots" was seen by 69% of the 1,549 adults sampled nationwide.

[12] The white sample and black sample did not differ significantly on sex and education, but did on age with blacks being younger.

TABLE 1

Mean Comparisons for White and Black Samples[1]
on Responses to "Roots" and Racial Attitudes

	Whites (N)	Blacks (N)	t	P
1. Exposure to "Roots" (0-1)	.71 (430)	.89 (88)	3.56	.001
2. "Roots" Episodes Seen (0-8)	5.47 (300)	6.33 (78)	2.69	.01
3. Accuracy of Black History[2] (1-5)	2.30 (276)	1.90 (71)	2.54	.01
4. Accuracy of Picture of Blacks (1-5)	2.12 (261)	1.84 (74)	1.89	.05
5. Accuracy of Picture of Whites	2.29 (272)	1.96 (73)	1.96	.05
6. Discussion About "Roots"[3] (1-5)	2.15 (299)	2.55 (77)	3.32	.001
7. Open Housing[4] (1-5)	4.43 (384)	4.88 (85)	2.88	.01
8. Intelligence[5] (1-5)	2.63 (360)	3.08 (77)	3.88	.001
9. Behavior[5] (1-5)	2.41 (353)	3.27 (73)	7.09	.001
10. Trustworthiness[5] (1-5)	2.50 (345)	3.37 (71)	7.02	.001
11. Slavery Condition[6] (1-5)	2.87 (381)	3.93 (81)	5.71	.001

Notes: [1] Means were calculated for only those who answered questions. Thus, Ns vary by questions.

[2] The 1-5 scale ranges from "very accurate" to "not very accurate."

[3] The score represents the number of people respondents talked to about the program; the number 3 represents more than 5 people with whom the respondent discussed the program.

[4] The scale represents 1 being favorable and 5 being unfavorable.

[5] The scale represents 1 in favor of whites, 5 in favor of blacks and 3 for in-between.

[6] The scale represents 1 perceiving the hardships of black slavery as "roughly similar" to white-immigrant conditions, 3 perceiving black slavery as "worse" and 5 as "much worse."

asked to gauge the accuracy not only of the program's presentation of black history, but of its portrayal of blacks and whites in that history, black viewers' responses were consistently closer to the "very accurate" side of the question than were white viewers' responses. Also, there was a significant difference between black and white viewers in their perceptions of the hardships of black slavery. When asked how the conditions of black slavery compared to those of white immigrants, black viewers were significantly more likely to say it was "much worse" than were white respondents.

Black and white viewers also differed significantly in "selective behavioral response" to the program, i.e., the amount of post-viewing discussion of the program. Blacks reported talking with more people about the program than did white viewers.

Did "Roots" influence and relate to racial attitudes? Most observers of "Roots" thought that it would improve race relations in the long term, mainly because of its impact on whites. Thus, *Time* magazine suggested that "Roots" would leave whites with "a more sympathetic view of blacks by giving them a greater appreciation of black history."[13] The assumption was that once whites had witnessed the vivid first-hand portrayal of slavery in "Roots," their appreciation of how much blacks had endured and how far blacks had come would be enhanced. Presumably, this in turn might lead to more pro-black or sympathetic feelings in other attitude areas as well.

Relation between viewing "Roots" and racial attitudes within the white audience

[13] "Why 'Roots' Hit Home," *op. cit.*

TABLE 2

Mean Comparisons for White Viewers
and Non-Viewers on Racial Attitudes

	Viewers (N)	Non-Viewers (N)		t	P
Open Housing*	4.58 (281)	4.01	(115)	3.53	.001
Intelligence	2.70 (262)	2.45	(98)	2.31	.05
Behavior	2.47 (253)	2.24	(100)	2.01	.05
Trustworthiness	2.58 (249)	2.27	(96)	2.73	.05
Slavery Condition	2.96 (273)	2.65	(108)	1.79	.07

* For scale ranges of the racial attitude measures, see Notes 4-6 under Table 1.

is shown in Table 2. White viewers and non-viewers differed as expected on the five general racial-attitude questions included in the survey. White respondents who watched the series consistently expressed more liberal racial attitudes than whites who did not watch the show. "Roots" viewers were more in favor of open housing and more likely to perceive blacks as similar to whites in intelligence, trustworthiness and general behavior. White non-viewers, then, were more likely than white viewers to oppose open housing and to perceive blacks as inferior to whites in intelligence, trustworthiness and behavior. For the most part, however, these attitudes relate only tangentially or implicitly to the content and messages in "Roots" and probably existed prior to exposure to "Roots." Thus it is how viewers and non-viewers differ in their perceptions of slavery that becomes a central test of the impact of the program. According to Table 2, "Roots" viewers were in fact more likely than non-viewers to see what blacks went through in slavery as "worse" than what happened to white immigrants, but the level of significance (as gauged by the value of t) is lower

than the traditional 5% level. To the extent that the program was successful in affecting attitudes, one might have expected the differences in slavery attitudes to be at least as great as those found on basic racial attitudes. The differences in basic racial attitudes noted earlier also suggest that many non-viewers avoided "Roots" because they were already less sympathetic to its content— a factor mentioned by several non-viewers when asked why they did not watch the program.

Nonetheless, these are not complete tests of the impact of the program, and we now turn to some multivariate analyses that provide a more controlled test than is possible in Table 2.

Multivariate Analyses. In order to determine further what factors influenced and were related to whites' exposure to "Roots" and their perceptions of the series, we performed two multiple classification analyses (MCA),[14] one for exposure to "Roots" and one for the items dealing with perceptions of the hardships of slavery. As seen in the analysis in Table 3, whites' exposure to "Roots" was strongly related to attitudes on open housing as well as age and amount of television viewing. All three variables remained strong predictors after other factors were introduced and controlled in the regression equation (the multiple R was .39, indicating that all five factors predict to just over 15% of the variance in viewing the program). Although sex was related to viewing, its significance was attenuated in the multi-

[14] Norman H. Nie, et al., eds., *SPSS: Statistical Package for the Social Sciences* (New York: McGraw-Hill, 1975), pp. 409-418. Multiple Classification Analysis (MCA), available in the SPSS computer program, enables the researcher to know the net effect of each dependent variable when the differences in the other factors are controlled. It is particularly useful when the dependent variable is measured on an interval scale and the independent variables are of both metric and non-metric variables, such as our variable measurements. One disadvantage of MCA in the SPSS program is that a maximum of only five independent variables can enter into a single analysis.

TABLE 3

MCA Regression Weights Predicting
Exposure to "Roots" of Whites

Exposure to "Roots"

	Eta[1]	Beta[2]
Sex	.13*	.12
Education	.06	.10
Age	.21*	.20*
Open Housing	.16*	.16*
TV Hours	.24*	.25*
(N = 361)		

Notes: 1. Eta values are straightforward, un-
corrected correlation ratios.

2. Beta values are partial-correlation
ratios and can be viewed as standardized partial regression coefficients.
*Values are significant at the .05 level.

variate context of MCA. The white viewers of "Roots" were more liberal on
the topic of open housing, even after
other significant predictors of viewing
were taken into account. In conjunction
with the racial viewing differences in
Table 1, this is consistent with the presence of selective exposure in decisions
to watch the program both within the
white audience and between whites and
blacks.

The matter of selective perception or
selective interpretation within the white
audience was also examined via MCA.
In Table 4, perceptions of the hardships
of slavery was the dependent variable,
and viewing "Roots" was introduced as
an independent or predictor variable,
Here, perceptions of slavery were related to viewing, but were much more
strongly predicted by attitudes on open
housing, age and education. All three
variables survived as significant predictors when the other independent factors
are controlled, but viewing "Roots" was
reduced even further once these three
predictors were taken into account. The
relationship between exposure to "Roots"
and perceptions of the hardships of
slavery proved insignificant in five additional MCA analyses, which included
other racial-attitude predictors as independent variables.[15]

TABLE 4

MCA Regression Weights Predicting Whites'
Perceptions of the Hardships of Slavery

Perceptions of Slavery Hardships

	Eta[1]	Beta
Sex	.00	.00
Age	.20*	.17*
Education	.21*	.18*
Open Housing	.21*	.18*
Exposure to "Roots"	.08	.04
(N = 365)		

Notes: 1. See Table 1 for explanation of values.
*Values are significant at the .05 level.

Conclusions

These data hardly suggest that
"Roots" had the influence on the racial
attitudes of whites that was widely attributed to it by media critics and observers. While differences were found
between viewers and non-viewers on
the hardships of slavery, differences on
other racial attitude predictors as in-
the program were more significant and
these racial attitudes were significantly
related to perceptions of slavery.

Inspection of our data shows that
about a third of white viewers of "Roots"
remained unconvinced after the program
that what blacks went through during
slavery was any worse than what white
immigrants to this country endured and
that less than 40% of non-viewers shared
this view. This suggests that the possible
effects of "Roots" on the perceptions of
the hardships of slavery were mainly
felt by those whites already sympathetic
to the program's content.

We interpret our data as consistent
with both selective -exposure and perception hypotheses being at work among
our white sample. In contrast to the assumptions of most media analysis and
commentary, while a majority of our
white sample did watch "Roots" and

[15] Separate analyses indicated that amount of viewing of the
series, in terms of episodes seen, was unrelated to perceptions
of slavery. That is, people who saw all eight episodes were not
much different than those who missed a few or several episodes, in terms of their perceptions of slavery.

most thought it historically informative and accurate, there is little evidence of it producing conversions in racial attitudes.

Our data do seem rather inconsistent with certain characterizations of the black audience, however. Navita and McCain have hypothesized that blacks prefer serious and realistic black-oriented programs to non-serious, non-realistic black-oriented programs.[16] Yet almost 90% of the black respondents in our sam-

[16] James C. Navita and Thomas A. McCain, "Predicting Black Viewer Preferences in Black-Oriented Television Programming," paper presented to the Mass Communication Division at the annual meeting of the International Communication Association, Portland, Oregon, April 1976.

ple watched the program, leaving too few non-viewing respondents to gauge the impact of the program as we have done with our white sample.

Considering the fact that there have been few serious black-oriented programs on television, with its realistic and serious treatment of black identity, "Roots" might have produced more revolutionary effects on the black audience. Given the greater media reports of black behavior in response to the program, particularly among adolescents, the impact of "Roots" on blacks may have been the more significant phenomenon.

No subject of public media policy draws more controversy than television and children. The debate ranges from TV as a "plug-in drug" to the fantastic potential of television as a learning tool. Ellen Wartella's careful review of a wealth of research and thought on the subject questions the view of children as passive sponges of TV and suggests that children are active in cognizing their television worlds. She concludes there is a need for age-specific programming that is geared to stages of children's development. In addition, she argues that television, with appropriate parent-teacher intervention and supplementation, may be used to advance the age at which children become sophisticated about advertising and media persuasion. Dr. Wartella is a mass communication researcher at the Institute of Communications Research, University of Illinois. This review was first published as a staff document for the Federal Communications Commission.

31

CHILDREN AND TELEVISION
The Development of the
Child's Understanding of the Medium

Ellen Wartella

Children have long been recognized as a special audience for media presentations, particularly television (Schramm et al., 1961). From an adult's perspective, children have different cognitive or thinking abilities and more limited experience to help them make sense of television. The work of Jean Piaget (1928, 1950, 1954) and American cognitive developmental researchers (Flavell, 1977) has provided the general orientation to research examining children's understanding of television. What is it about how children think about television, how they construe meaning from television messages, and how they understand the televised world that makes them a "special audience"? This chapter will attempt to answer these questions by reviewing the current state of research regarding how children make sense of television and its contents. In sections two and three, a review will be offered of age-related differences in children's interpretations of television entertainment content in general and advertising content in particular.

The thrust of the most recent research regarding children's understanding of television messages is that children of different ages bring different information-processing skills to the television-viewing situation. That is, during childhood, children are growing and changing both in the available cognitive abilities

From Ellen Wartella, "Children and Television: The Development of the Child's Understanding of the Medium," original manuscript.

and in their understanding of their social world. These developing abilities are then reflected in the ways in which children of different ages understand television messages. Thus, the nature of the age differences is how children "think" about and understand television and its content is the focus of this review.

The organization of the chapter is as follows: First, a brief analysis and description of the fundamental principles of cognitive development theory will be offered in section I. Since previous reviews of research on children and television have offered fuller descriptions of cognitive development theory (see, for example, Roberts, 1979; Ward et al., 1977; and Wartella, 1979), a brief review of the crucial terms, assumptions, and characterization of the changing cognitive skills available to children will be presented. Furthermore, critiques of cognitive development theory, especially Piaget's theory, will be offered. Second, the growing literature on children's information-processing of television dramatic programs content will be reviewed in section II. Third, the discussion in section III will focus on several specific pragmatic questions regarding children's understanding of the purpose of television advertising and their information-processing of advertising content. In the last section, a postscript, I will examine some of the possible policy options which seem unwarranted by the preceding review.

I. FUNDAMENTAL PRINCIPLES OF COGNITIVE DEVELOPMENT THEORY

This section will present a theory of child development which is widely used in research in developmental psychology, cognitive development theory. Some of the basic concepts, assumptions, and broad outlines of cognitive development theory are discussed. Furthermore, a brief review of major criticisms of cognitive development theory is offered. This section concludes with a recommendation that research on children's understanding of television messages be examined for age-related differences, since children's abilities to make sense of television change greatly as they grow older.

The truthfulness of the statement that children think differently than adults is fairly self-evident. Any adult who has spent even passing time with a preschooler or elementary school child recognizes that young children are not miniature adults. The young child (those below middle childhood or about age seven) in particular has a qualitatively limited manner of perceiving, thinking, and interacting with other people, when measured by adult-standards. Attempts to describe how children grow and develop in the way they think about and interact with their physical and social world has led to the emergence of cognitive development theories. The most famous cognitive development theory, and thus the one which has received the most research attention, is that of the Swiss psychologist Jean Piaget (Gruber and Voneche, 1977; Flavell, 1963, 1977).

Cognitive development theory is a "theory of knowing" (Gruber and Voneche, 1977: ix): It attempts to describe how children think or process information. Piaget's nearly 60 years of work (Piaget, 1923) has been devoted to the articulation of a theory of how humans come to know their physical and social world. Certain aspects of his theory are crucial for understanding the thrust and meaning of cognitive developmental notions: First, Piaget's theory is a stage theory of development. That is, he posits that children undergo qualitative changes in the way they organize and use information. Second, he posits a set of cognitive structures to characterize children's thought processes at distinct, age-related stages of intellectual development. The development of cognitive structures is universal and proceeds through the process of an active child both accommodating to and assimilating new cognitive events into his or her level or cognitive abilities.

A particular stage of development is a description of the cognitive abilities children possess at that level of development. Each stage roughly approximates certain age levels—roughly, that is, since current research is being devoted to examining how closely particular cognitive abilities follow the expected age guidelines suggested by Piaget's theory (see, for example, Case, 1974). The different periods of development in Piaget's theory—his stages—then are correlated with age, but are not synonymous with the age of the child. Moreover, the range of abilities available to children at any given stage of development is said to form a structured whole (Kohlberg, 1969); that is, one stage is different and discontinuous from the next stage, and at a given stage of development a child will respond to a *variety* of tasks according to this underlying thought organization or stage of cognitive abilities. Thus, the different cognitive abilities available to a child at a given level or stage of development are organized into a whole pattern of responses across a variety of tasks which may not seem similar on the surface.

While the age ranges typically associated with Piaget's theory are not hard and fast, the crucial concept of stage serves as a convenient term for summarizing and describing children's cognitive abilities through the course of childhood development. Piaget posits four major stages in the course of cognitive development: the sensorimotor stage (birth to about age two); the preoperational stage (ages two-seven); the concrete operational stage (ages seven-12); to the formal operational stage (12+). Descriptions of the four stages of development Piaget identifies are a useful way of elaborating the differences in children's thinking.

The *sensorimotor* stage is characterized by behavioral patterns of thought—what Piaget calls schema. It is through touching, grasping, sucking, and operating on objects that the child is "thinking." There is no symbolic representation of objects, since the importance of this stage is that the child develops a sense of separateness between self and the world around him. It is during this stage that the child is learning to react to objects and people immediately present.

It is during the next stage, *preoperational* (ages two to about seven years), that the child begins to develop cognitive reasoning ability, symbolic ability, and mental imagery. Piaget characterizes the mental process of this stage as a "mental experiment" in which the child duplicates in mental imagery the various objects he or she is "thinking" about. Children's thoughts are very closely linked to perception—they rely on the immediate perceptible qualities of objects as the basis of logical reasoning, what has been referred to as perceptual boundedness (Wohlwill, 1962; Ward and Wackman, 1973; Wartella and Ettema, 1974). For example, Ward and Wackman (1973) illustrate the concept of perceptual boundedness by noting that the five- and six-year-olds they studied focused on the visual aspects of TV messages rather than the content of functional distinctions among different kinds of messages. That is, the younger children were "bound" to the "perceptual" or surface characteristics of the television stimuli. Furthermore during this stage children tend to be egocentric in their dealings with the world—they tend to see the world from their own perspective.

With the development of *concrete operations* (ages seven-12) the child acquires the ability to separate perceptions from other forms of thought and knowledge—in other words, appearances from reality. This stage of cognitive development is characterized by the growth of certain basic logical operations: elaborated cognitive abilities. For instance, during the stage of concrete operations, while the child has available all of the necessary cognitive abilities, he or she is limited to applying these abilities to images of concrete objects and events; abstract thought does not develop until the next stage of cognitive development.

Formal operations (which develops by about age 12) is characterized as the beginning of true adult-like thought patterns, in that the child develops abstract thought, hypothetical reasoning, and propositional thinking.

This brief description of Piagetian stages of development points out how children become increasingly more "thoughtful" in their behavior as they grow older. A major dimension of development is increasingly less reliance on the apparent perceptual characteristics of objects and events. Two major dimensions of this thoughtfulness operate in tandem. First, children become less perceptually bound; they become less tied to the immediate surface or perceptual characteristics of objects and events and are able to take into consideration other dimensions, such as the functional differences among objects. A second dimension of "thoughtfulness" is that as children grow older they become better able to coordinate multiple dimensions of phenomena, what has been called the dimension of decentration. Decentration again can be illustrated with reference to Ward and Wackman's (1973) research. They found that their older (nine- to 12-year-old) children were able to discuss visual, message content, and functional distinctions between TV advertisements and programs—the older children examined multiple dimensions of television messages.

These Piagetian stages of cognitive development are based on research on how children think about the physical world, such as their conceptions of time (Piaget, 1946), space (Piaget and Inhelder, 1948), and physical causality (Piaget, 1927). Piaget and other developmental psychologists argue, however, that the same logical, thinking abilities are reflected in children's thoughts about the social world (Flavell, 1977; Shantz, 1975).

The major thrust of development in social cognition for children is the decline of egocentrism and the development of role-taking skills. Egocentrism is the lack of ability to take another person's perspective into account. According to Selman (1971), children move through distinct stages of role-taking abilities. The lower boundary of these stages is egocentric perspective-taking, when children confuse their perspective on objects and events with others' perspectives. This is characteristic of children below age six. Children gradually become aware that other people may have motivations different from their own point that the child is able to assume a third-person point of view, such as when the child can say "Mother wants me to clean my room because it's dirty, but I want to play." For Selman, mutual perspective-taking (age ten through adult) is developed when children understand that just as they can look at others' perspectives, so can others mutually examine their perspective.

Thus, role-taking skills involve the child gradually learning that other people have feelings, thoughts, motivations, and inner states different from the child's own and from what may be apparent on the surface.

In short, as children grow older they learn to put themselves in the other's shoes to look at the world. They become less "gullible," self-centered, and naive in social interactions. They become more flexible and capable of making inferences about how and why people behave as they do and about what others see, feel, think, intend, and are like (Shantz, 1975).

What brings about development of cognitive and social inference-making abilities? According to Piaget, development occurs through children interacting with their environment and involves both maturation of physical abilities and experiences with the world. Children, in a sense, are constantly structuring and restructuring their ways of thinking about the world. Piaget uses the term equilibration to refer to this self-regulatory process that propels development. Children try to cope with their environment by constantly accommodating to new events and assimilating these new events into their current level of cognitive abilities.

Here we come to one of the basic criticisms of Piagetian cognitive development theory: whether development in terms of the stages Piaget describes unfolds universally in the same manner at the same rate. Can developmental growth be accelerated? Can children acquire a cognitive ability earlier than cognitive developmental theory would predict? Do children have to be "ready" before they can develop new cognitive abilities?

There are some preliminary answers to these questions. First, there is evidence from cross-cultural research that suggests there is a "time lag" in the development of cognitive abilities as Piaget describes them among children in nonwestern cultures. Dasen (1977), in a collection of cross-cultural studies, argues that there may be a pro-western culture and high social class bias in Piaget's work. There is cross-cultural evidence, however, that children do show competence for cognitive structures as Piaget defines them. Moreover, the appearance of these cognitive abilities in a given situation is culturally determined. In short, while there is some evidence that Piaget's stages of cognitive ability are universal, the rate of development and the appearance of these stages may vary culturally.

A second problem with cognitive development research is that children may not always perform up to their highest level of ability on any given task used to assess cognitive development. For instance, one potential confounding ability is language use. Siegal and Brainerd (1978) in particular argue that the typical Piagetian tasks used to assess cognitive ability are suspect because they rely on language abilities beyond the level of the children. Therefore, these authors argue that children may be cognitively able to perform a given task but aren't able to use language well enough to explain the concepts they understand. The competence (or the possession of a given cognitive ability) versus performance (demonstration of that ability in a given situation) distinction raises issues regarding cognitive development research. Seigal and Brainerd (1978) in particular argues that nonverbal testing methods must be used to assure that we are not confusing language difficulties with the lack of a given cognitive ability. Even aside from language use abilities, children may not always perform at their highest level of competence.

Third, there is evidence from a variety of studies that children may be able to "learn" a cognitive operation earlier than Piaget's theory suggests can occur. Research by Case (1974), Pascual-Leone (1970), and Field (1977) indicate that when the learning environment appropriately respects the child's existing cognitive abilities and elicits the child's own activity in the learning situation, acceleration of development can occur. In short, by matching the learning environment to the child's ability, there is evidence that one can "teach" the child new cognitive skills earlier than Piaget's theory of development suggests they would occur. This is not to say that research uniformly supports the notion of accelerating development. Research is mixed. Similarly, it is difficult to offer a typical rate of acceleration. In one study, Case (1974) reports a successful training procedure which increased eight-year-olds' ability to solve a complicated logical procedure which, according to Piaget, could not be learned until a child is 14 or 15. On the other hand, Flavell (1977) in discussing research on children's abilities to communicate a listener's perspective on stories, notes the general lack of success in training children who have an egocentric perspective to adopt an other-directed perspective in communicating stories verbally.

The implications of these critiques of Piagetian cognitive development theory are multiple. First, they suggest that one should be wary of making inferences from more theoretical literature on children's general cognitive development to children's responses to television. Second, they suggest that attention should be given to the particular tasks and measures utilized in research to assess children's ability levels. Third, the critiques argue that one should be wary of arguments which maintain that children of given ages "can't do" certain things. To argue on the basis of Piagetian theory that five- or six-year-olds are incapable of some, even if modest, accelerated cognitive growth in the absence of specific training programs may be premature. The recent neo-Piagetian research seems to suggest that where optimal learning environments can be developed, modest cognitive growth may be encouraged for children. Finally, these critiques would suggest that any review of the status of research on children's understanding of television should not be too closely tied to a discussion of "stage-related" differences in comprehension of television. The stage concept may be less meaningful than simple descriptions of how children of various ages make sense of television.

On the other hand, there are positive contributions of cognitive development theory and research to our understanding of children and television. First, the literature that has been discussed above argues rather strongly for the notion that children's thinking and interpreting abilities change radically as they grow older. The ways children attend to, interpret, and comprehend the world around them seem to follow general dimensions of change. As I noted above, children become less bound to their immediate perception for cues to assess objects, and they become better able to use mutiple dimensions of objects when trying to make sense of them. These processes have been referred to as the decrease in perceptual boundedness and the development of decentration as children grow older. Similarly, research on the development of social cognition presents evidence that children only gradually develop an understanding of other people and the motivations and consequences of human actions. Thus, this literature offers *strong* evidence for the importance of age as a variable of interest in research on children.

Second, the theory of cognitive development and related research from this perspective offers some guidelines for research and policy. In particular, it suggests at what ages we might expect children's interpretations of television messages to change and the likely directions these changes might take. For instance, as I noted previously, major changes in cognitive abilities occur around middle childhood—what Piaget refers to as the shift from preoperational to concrete operational thought. Between the ages of seven and nine, children acquire a host of new thinking skills and reasoning abilities, such as the ability to reverse thought processes and discover inconsistencies in logic. Similarly, we might expect there to be changes in children's interpretations of television occurring around middle childhood. Research findings addressing this point will be discussed in the next two sections.

Thus, with this brief overview of cognitive development theory and this introduction to developmental changes in children's thinking and interpreting abilities, this review will now turn attention to children's interpretations of television content.

II. CHILDREN'S INFORMATION-PROCESSING OF TELEVISION CONTENT

In this section, research on age-related differences in how children attend to (look at and listen to) and comprehend (construe meaning from) television content will be presented. While most research on television and children has been concerned with whether or not children "learn" aggressive behaviors from watching television, there has been particular stress played on *what children do to and with television*. The focus here will be on how children's developing cognitive abilities and social experiences lead to increasingly better understanding of television messages. In order to examine how children process television content, the discussion will focus on two aspects of information-processing: children's attention to television messages and their comprehension of these messages. Third, a general discussion of children's understanding of television as a phenomenon will be presented.

A few brief comments about the concept of age differences might be in order before the review begins. Several recent reviews of children's responses to television (Comstock et al., 1978; Dorr, forthcoming; Wartella, 1979) have argued for the adoption of a developmental perspective in examining children's reactions to television. Typically, what is meant here are age-related descriptions of how children make sense of or process television messages. Age serves as a good marker or locator of both the child's level of cognitive development and degree of experience with the social world useful for judging television reality. Thus, while age, in and of itself, is not a "cause" of differences in how children make sense of television, it merely serves to locate where differences will occur. Unfortunately, the adoption of this sort of age-related description of how children make sense of television is a relatively recent phenomenon. As Comstock et al. (1978) note, there are few studies which adopt a developmental perspective on children's social learning from television. Furthermore, most of this research has occurred within the last ten years. Therefore, many gaps in our ability to identify precisely age-related changes in children's processing abilities will be found. However, the review of the status of research in the remainder of this chapter will try to describe developmental changes in how children make sense of television messages.

Attention to Television

Marie Winn, author of *The Plug-In Drug* (1977), is only one of the popular commentators who have referred to children's "passive, zombie-like" attention to the television screen. The analogy to drugs (television as a narcotic) is conjured up by images of five- and six-year-old children sitting quietly with eyes fixed on a television set. How accurate are these descriptions? In general, what do we know about how children of different ages attend to television? What visual and auditory factors capture children's attention?

The view of children passively watching the television screen is counter to the current psychological view of the child as an active cognizer of his or her world. Cognitive development theory, as I pointed out in the preceding section, views children as active participants in their environment, actively striving to make sense of the world about them. The literature on children's development of attention processes tends to support the active nature of attention development.[1]

Children's attention processes have been found to undergo decided developmental changes during the first seven or eight years of life: As children grow older they acquire greater control in allocating their attention to tasks and their attention becomes more selective. They are better able to ignore the irrelevant information and to focus on the relevant. In short, attention becomes more flexible and adaptable (Pick et al., 1975; Flavell, 1977). These same developmental principles of attention have been demonstrated in the few studies which have been conducted on children's attention to television.

First, the evidence regarding the passive or active nature of television viewing may be considered. It would appear that much of the criticism of "zombie-like" viewing of television comes from casual observation of children watching television. Observational studies of children's visual attention to the television set indicate that viewers pay varying levels of attention to television programs and commercials. In one study Levin and Anderson (1976) report that, on the average, preschoolers they observed looked at and away from the television about 150 times per hour. These studies have utilized various age groups from children as young as one year of age (Levin and Anderson, 1976) through adolescence. Furthermore, observations have been made in homes (Bechtel et al., 1972; Ward and Wackman, 1973), in schools (Wartella and Ettema, 1974), and in special laboratory viewing rooms (Anderson and Levin, 1976; Anderson et al., 1979; Krull and Husson, 1979).

The studies on television attention discussed here rely primarily on measures of visual attention; for example, observers' records of visual eye contact. Since children may still be listening to the television set although not watching the screen, visual attention measures may underestimate total attention to the program.

Anderson and his colleagues (1979) have conducted a series of laboratory studies of children's attention to "Sesame Street" segments. Anderson's program of research highlights the active nature of children's attention to television: Up until about age two and a half, children tend to orient themselves away from the television—they seldom look at the screen. Starting at age two, however, children have been observed in engaging in what adults would consider television viewing: Their bodies are oriented to the television set, and even when not watching the set intently they are monitoring it frequently to see if they should attend further. In Anderson et al.'s (1979) observational studies among preschoolers, age is a good predictor of the amount of attention children will show to the television set: The older children more frequently gazed at the set, and, past age three, the duration of any one glance at the set is longer. They report that by age five or six, children's viewing of television is selective. However, while age appears to predict amount of attention to television among young children, Anderson et al. (1979) and others (Wartella and Ettema, 1974; Poulos et al., 1975) report that there is individual variation in attention at any age. It is therefore important to look at the factors other than age which affect attention.

Several factors have been found to influence children's attention to the television: distractions in the viewing environment, the content and form of the television message, cycles or patterns of attention, and the comprehensibility of the message.

One of the few observational studies of children's attention to television in the home was conducted by Bechtel et al. (1972), who used in-home videotape cameras to survey family viewing patterns. Although they observed relatively few children in their study, they did note that children's television viewing was interrupted by time for reading, playing with pets and siblings, and talking to other people. It would seem that, in the normal course of watching television, other distractions in the room take children's as well as adults' attention away from the television set.

Anderson et al. (1979) report a recent laboratory experiment which demonstrates that even five-year-old children's attention is affected by distractors in the viewing condition—in this case, toys in the room. Two groups of five-year-olds were shown a "Sesame Street" program in two viewing conditions: one in a room which contained toys the other in a toyless viewing room. Visual attention to the screen was monitored continuously by an observer, who depressed a recording button when the child looked away. Attention to the screen by the group of children who watched TV without toys in the viewing room was nearly double the attention of the children who watched with toys available.

However, the presence of other children in a viewing situation in one controlled laboratory study was not found to distract four-year-old attention to a segment of "Sesame Street" (Sproull, 1973). Several researchers have attempted to examine the relationship between the content of television and children's attention behavior.

Two studies have examined the kinds of content on television which tends to elicit young children's attention. There are some consistencies and inconsistencies in these two studies. Anderson and Levin (1976), as noted earlier, recorded preschoolers' attention to an hour-long "Sesame Street" program. Poulos et al. (1975) similarly recorded six- to eight-year-old children's visual attention to an episode of "Sesame Street." In both studies the researchers examined the relationship between the children's attention and the presence or absence of particular visual and auditory elements on the television program. Across the two studies, attention was found to increase in the presence of activity or movement on the screen, child actors, animation, puppets and eye contact. Poulos et al. (1975) also report that animals on the screen, panned camera shots, and camera cuts also increased attention. Anderson and Levin (1976), however, found camera activity to have little effect on visual attention . Another discrepancy between the two studies is that while the presence of an adult female on "Lassie" was found to decrease six- to eight-year-olds' attention, adult females on "Sesame Street" were found to increase preschoolers' attention. Static images in both studies tended to decrease attention.

In both studies, auditory elements such as background music, auditory changes, rhyming, repetition, alliterations, and peculiar voices tend to increase the young children's attention to the set. Anderson et al. (1979), after further investigation, argue that auditory factors are most important in bringing children back to attention after they have "tuned out" for some reason. Comparable findings have been made in other work by Wartella and Ettema (1974) and Huston-Stein (1977).

Anderson et al. (1979) further explored the effects of these "bit changes" or changes in visual and auditory elements on the screen on eliciting, maintaining, and terminating children's attention. They find that all bit changes—that is, whenever there is a change in the visual or auditory elements on the screen— strongly influence a look at the screen for children who are not looking and tend to terminate a look when children already have their eyes on the set. Furthermore, it seems plausible that bit changes in the audio portion of the program would elicit the most impact on inducing visual attention, as Anderson and his colleagues have found. On logical grounds, if the children are not watching television, only the auditory message *could* bring them back to visual attention— by cueing them that something new is on the screen.

Research on the range of formal features of television—the kinds of bit changes and content which do elicit movement in attention among young children—is still very preliminary. It seems likely that although preschool children may be highly susceptible to the perceptual changes on the screen (as indicated by Wartella and Ettema [1974] and Levin and Anderson's [1976] work), older children's and adults' attention to television may also be influenced by such characteristics of the television message.

Moreover, there is some evidence that across all age levels attention to television is also influenced by patterns or cycles of attention which may not be related to cognitive developmental growth. For instance, Anderson et al. (1979) and Krull and Husson (1979) refer to a pattern of attention they call "attentional inertia," a term which refers to the notion that viewers can become engrossed in a program with almost continual attention and without looks away from the set for at least short periods of time. By "patterning," Anderson et al. (1979) refer to regularities in viewing, not viewing the television set. For instance, Anderson et al. (1979) found that preschool children typically look at the TV for short periods: these authors report that 54 percent of all "looks" are for less than three seconds. They noted, however, that when a look at the set lasted longer than about 10 seconds, the probability increased that the viewer would continue watching initially for several minutes in a state of attention inertia. Krull and Husson (1979) similarly found that a major factor influencing their four- and five-year-old subjects' attention to differing segments of a "Sesame Street" program was attention to the previous segment. In other words, there was high attention interdependence. Krull and Husson noted that these young four- to five-year-olds seemed slower to react and change their attention level across bit changes than were seven- to nine-year-old children they observed watching an "Electric Company" program.

These cycles in attention, and the notion of attentional inertia, may describe a general process of attention. Anderson et al. (1979) report that such attentional inertia patterns have been demonstrated to characterize college students' television-watching behavior in their laboratory tests. The question not yet answered is whether young preschool children are more susceptible to such attention inertia, and what conditions might increase the likelihood of such a pattern of viewing. If young children are found to be "more susceptible" to such attentional inertia, such a pattern of viewing might be what Marie Winn and other critics are referring to when they talk about the "zombie-like" television viewing patterns of young children.

A final factor which may influence young children's attention behavior is that of the comprehensibility of the message. Anderson et al. (1979) report a recent experiment examining two-, three-, and five-year-old children's attention to a specially produced version of a "Sesame Street" program which was made unintelligible through various editing techniques and running the soundtrack backwards. At each age of two, three, and five, children attended less to the bits of the program that were rendered less intelligible.

It seems likely, then, that during the preschool years children begin to orient to the television set. By about age five, children's patterns of attending to television fairly much approximates adult styles of looking and not looking at the television. While at times children may appear glued to the television set (zombie-like viewing), these periods—at least in laboratory studies—appear to be of relatively short duration. Moreover, this attentional inertia is found not just among young children (although there is some evidence it may be more pronounced among children under age five than over age seven), but among older children, including college students. Further, there is increasing evidence that, rather than the passive television viewing critics contend children engage in, children are very active in attending to television. Between about two and three years of age children acquire televiewing behavior; they begin to orient themselves to the television set, tuning in and out during the programs and commercials. Monitoring of television is elicited and maintained by various kinds of visual and auditory elements on television, and some of these elements are more successful in capturing young children's attention than are others. Moreover, it appears that changes in the audio have the greatest impact in drawing children's attention back to the set if they are not attending. Finally, there is some initial evidence that the comprehensibility of the television message is important in maintaining the child's attention: When the message is relatively unintelligible for children of a certain age level, then continued attention is unlikely. In short, the picture emerging regarding how children attend to television is very much in keeping with the active nature of cognition: Children do appear to be *actively* and selectively attending to the television screen.

Although the literature surveyed regarding children's patterns of attention to television appears in contrast to much of the conventional discussions of television's narcotic effects and the passive nature of television-watching, this may not be the case. An argument can be advanced that watching television is inherently less active than "doing" some other activity, such as playing games or engaging in sports. Actively "watching" television should not be equated with actively "doing" some other sport or activity which engages the child's body and mind.

Comprehension of Television Messages

The literature surveyed so far regarding children's attention to television has relied on observation of visual attention by the child viewers. Measures of visual attention alone do not provide an indication of what aspects of the message children are extracting from the television screen. In order to acquire indications of this, researchers have relied on postviewing measures of children's recognition and recall of information from the program. This research will be considered in this section on children's understanding of television messages. Here the concern is not with what children are looking at and listening to, but what they remember from the TV and what meaning the TV content has for them.

Much of the research which has adopted a cognitive developmental perspective on studies of children and television has examined children's comprehension of television messages. The underlying assumption of these studies is that children bring different cognitive abilities and social experiences to the TV-viewing situation and that these influence how children made sense of the messages. Younger children with more limited inference-making ability are more likely to focus on the consequences of actions rather than the motivations of the actors, and often are shown to construe the television plot line quite differently from children and adults. The way in which children construe meaning from television cannot be directly inferred from cognitive development theory. Cognitive development theory may *aid* us in describing how children make sense of television, but we should examine children's understanding of television directly.

How, then, has cognitive development theory been used to study children's comprehension of television? First, several authors have relied on Piagetian theory to provide evidence of some general cognitive ability, such as the ability to focus on motivations when judging the goodness or badness of an action. These authors attempt to demonstrate through experimental or survey procedures that children of a particular age or stage level accordingly do or do not use television characters' motivations when assessing their behaviors. This is a clear-cut example of directly borrowing developmental theoretical notions and demonstrating their applicability when children are processing television information. In other situations, however, cognitive development theory in general may be less useful in directly describing or predicting age-related changes in children's construction of meaning from television. For instance, we are only beginning to examine children's understanding of various kinds of filmic techniques, such as zooms, camera movements, and montage (see Salomon, 1979).

One researcher in this area, Salomon (1979), argues that these and other sorts of filmic techniques—indeed, the whole symbol system used on television for representing reality—may actually play a role in accelerating or otherwise affecting cognitive developmental changes among child viewers. That is, Salomon argues for a reverse causality, that just as child viewers' level of cognitive development may lead them to interpret television in a certain manner, television viewing may lead to changes in their level of cognitive abilities. This is a relatively new hypothesis in the literature and has seldom been tested.

Television content may pose particular difficulties for children to understand on a number of levels of "understanding." First, children must interpret the social behavior portrayed on television. The typical dramatic program of people engaging in various kinds of interpersonal relationships in usual and unusual circumstances is presented in an abbreviated form on television. Viewers must make inferences regarding motivations of characters and the relationships between characters. Sometimes the cues utilized to enable these inferences are exceedingly complex; sometimes character motives are not explicitly portrayed but must be inferred between scenes. The complexities of interpreting social behavior—even social behavior in day-to-day situations—is heightened on television because of the use of various production techniques. For example, a dissolve from the face of one boyfriend to the other used to illustrate the heroine's ambiguous love relationships could be crucial to the plot. Young children who may not understand such production forms may have more difficulty interpreting the program plotline. Furthermore, use of various production techniques, such as flashbacks, requires that viewers leap back and forth in time and coordinate symbols which may tax and confuse the young child.

On another level, children must develop an understanding of television's reality—Who are those people on television? When is television real and when is it fantasy? The events portrayed on television can represent a "magic window" reality (Hawkins, 1977) showing children places and people beyond their everyday experiences. The characters, however, are "acting," and the programs themselves are drama, not real life. Such understanding about the reality of the events portrayed on television and about the characters on the programs may develop only gradually.

Finally, television has a programming structure which should be understood by the viewers. Programs are distinct from advertisements and other sorts of announcements. Children must come to understand, at the most simplistic level, that advertising content is different from other types of programming and, further, that the motivations of advertisers should be considered when interpreting the advertising message.

In the remainder of this section consideration will be given to each of these issues. First, age-related differences in children's abilities to accurately recognize dramatic plotlines will be discussed. Second, children's perceptions of television characters and developmental changes in such perceptions are reviewed. A brief discussion of the role of various audio-visual filmic techniques in aiding or confusing children's understanding of television messages is then offered. Finally, a brief discussion of various types of understandings children acquire about the medium of television, such as understanding of the economic structure of television, completes this section.

Children's comprehension of television narratives. The traditional dramatic plotline which is used in most narratives, either in print or on television, has a predictable pattern: There is an initiating event where the scene is set, (boy meets girl); events proceed to a crisis (parents intervene to stop the budding love); followed by a resolution of the crisis (boy and girl win over parents to the romance); and the denouement (boy and girl show parents they can live happily ever after). While many television programs involve subplots or other incidental characteristics, adult viewers of a television program can easily bring a new viewer up to date half-way through a program by reiterating the major points of the plotline. Part of the reason we, as adults, are capable of doing this is because we easily recognize plotline structures, and on the basis of both previous experience with television and experience with social relationships we can often predict fairly accurately the progression and outcome of a plot. Thus, as adults, we are capable of recognizing major events central to the plot as they unfold.

There is evidence from research on children's memory for central plotline information that children only gradually develop this kind of understanding of television plotlines. The evidence indicates that (1) young children have difficulty distinguishing essential from nonessential information from a dramatic story, and (2), young children may not be attempting to organize and draw inferences about the behavior or story unfolding on the screen.

Children's abilities to accurately select essential plot information from a dramatic program has been shown to increase with increasing age. Across several studies, Collins (1970, 1973, 1979) and his colleagues have utilized a procedure to examine children's memory for central plot information. This procedure involves showing groups of adults a dramatic or situation comedy program and then interviewing them about the program—specifically, about which scenes they considered essential to understanding the plotline. A series of multiple-choice recognition items are then constructed about the program. Some of the items measure information central to understanding the plot, while others are incidental to the plot. Groups of children of various ages are then shown the television program and after viewing are given the multiple-choice tests.

Across several studies, two findings emerge: first, that, overall, children's memory for the scenes in the program increases substantially with age; and, second, that children's memory for the "essential" information for understanding the plot also increases with age. For instance, in one study where second, fifth, and eight grders were tested on their recognition of essential plot information from a detective program, second graders recognized an average of only 66 percent of the essential scenes; fifth graders 84 percent; and eighth graders 92 percent (or nearly all). Similar age differences were found for children's memory for central information from a situation comedy program (Collins, 1970). Other researchers have noted similar differences in children's memory for central plotline information from television programs (Hale et al., 1968; Hawkins, 1973; Katzman, 1972). Moreover, young children have been found to have difficulty even placing scenes of a plotline into the correct order. Leifer et al. (1971) showed children aged four, seven, and ten a short narrative film. After watching the film, children were shown groups of three, five, seven, or nine photographs and asked to reconstruct the scenes in the correct order. Only four of the 20 four-year-olds tested could correctly order the three photographs, and none were able to order the groups of seven or nine photographs. By contrast, most of the 10-year-old children were consistently able to reproduce even the nine-photo sequence into the correct narrative order.

What are possible reasons for the younger children's rudimentary understanding of narrative information? First, evidence from several studies suggests the younger children may not be focusing their attention on the "essential" information. For instance, in the research by Collins, memory for nonessential information in the programs (such as character's hair color, dress, room furnishings) also tends to increase until junior high school and then decrease. Similar findings were obtained in studies of incidental learning in a variety of specific tasks (Hagen and Hale, 1973). In general, these studies suggest that as children grow older, their ability to know what is important in the plot increases and they acquire greater control in allocating their attention and focusing on what is important. This increased attention control has been found in other types of information-processing tasks. According to Comstock et al. (1978), child viewers have to "learn to learn" what is and what is not important information in a plotline.

In addition to this "learning to learn" hypothesis, it is also likely that as children's general memory capacities increase with age, so too does their ability to remember parts of the program. Collins (1979), however, makes the argument that in addition to memory deficiency, other factors may account for the differences in the younger children's understanding of narrative plot. In a rather ingenious study Collins (1979) examined children's attempts to organize and integrate plotline information as the program proceeds. In this study, Collins showed second-, fifth-, and eighth-grade children a detective show in which the scenes of the plot were randomly ordered or jumbled, or a version in which the scenes were in their original order. When asked questions that required causal inferences about relationships between the scenes of plot, the second graders, even when they had the central information from each discrete scene to do so, correctly answered far fewer of the inference questions than did the older children. Collins argues that the young children not only recall less information from the television shows, but also do not appear to be organizing the information in a meaningful fashion as they watch the program. The fifth and eighth graders, in contrast, appears to be trying to make sense of the programs. While they answered more inference questions than did the younger children, these older children were confused by the jumbled versions of the show and answered far fewer inference questions about the jumbled version than the ordered version—that is, they showed annoyance and poorer comprehension about the less comprehensible program.

In summary, younger children's lesser ability to recognize essential plotline information, to select it, and organize the scenes in a causal fashion has been shown in various manners by several research studies (Collins, 1979; Flapan, 1968). It seems likely that children even as old as seven and eight construe different meanings from a television show than do older children and adults. The difference in meaning will arise from the different cues the younger and older children recollect from the program and piece together to derive plot understanding. Similarly, these younger children appear to view television characters in a different manner.

Children's understanding of television characters. Just as there is evidence that children only gradually acquire adultlike comprehension of narrative forms, research on children's understanding of other people indicates similar age-related trends. As was noted in the first section, general cognitive development research has shown decided age changes in children's understanding about other people—in particular, there is movement from egocentric to nonegocentric views of others occurring about by middle childhood and the development of the concrete operational stage of development. Just as children are developing an understanding of others' points of view, their impressions of other people change in terms of the kinds of characteristics focused on to describe others.

Several studies of children's descriptions of their friends and others have noted age-related changes in the content of these free descriptions (Dornbush et al., 1965; Peevers and Secord, 1973; Scarlett et al., 1971; Lively and Bromley, 1973). The general dimensions of change appear to be that as children grow older they describe others less often in terms of external characteristics, such as overt physical descriptions and appearances, and more in terms of "internal" characteristics, such as personality traits and motivations. Wartella and Alexander (1977) report similar findings for second-, fifth-, and eighth-grade children's descriptions of television characters. They asked children to describe a television father, mother, and child. While the preponderance of descriptions at each age level focused on the actions the characters performed, eighth graders used more personality trait and motivational state descriptors than did fifth or second graders. Second graders, on the other hand, were more likely to describe the characters in terms of physical characteristics, appearances, and possessions. Moreover, the fifth- and eighth-grade children were more likely to attribute causes to the character behaviors they discussed by making references to the character's motivations for the behaviors. Similar findings are reported by Alexander and Wartella (1979) in a replication of this study.

Reeves and Greenberg (1977) and Reeves (1979) report that when children are asked to compare a variety of television characters, third-, fifth-, and seventh-grade children use similar traits in the comparison. In both studies the researchers used a multidimensional scaling system[2] to determine the underlying dimensions children use to differentiate or compare one character with another. They report no age differences in their study. They determined that children at each age level—third, fifth, and seventh grade—utilized four main attributes in differentiating characters: humor, physical strength, attractiveness, and activity. Reeves (1979) attempts to resolve the lack of age differences in these multidimensional scaling studies with age differences found in studies of children's free descriptions of television characters and real people. He argues that differences between the studies may reside in the two methods used or the tasks employed (a comparative versus descriptive task); that is, the differences may be methodological. The two methods may require that children focus on different aspects of people in complying with the researcher's requests. However, if the study differences are not just methodological, Reeves offers an alternative theoretical explanation: Children may learn fairly early (by third grade) that television characters are relatively simple people and only simplified discriminations among them need be made. Thus, while Reeves and his colleagues find no age differences in the underlying dimensions children use to compare television characters, other descriptive studies (as noted above) have found age differences in how children describe TV characters. The difference in findings from these research approaches has not been resolved.

There is support from other research for the finding that children only gradually come to develop an understanding of the motivations and consequences of characters' actions. In a series of studies, Leifer and Roberts (1972) examined kindergarten, third-, sixth-, ninth-, and twelfth-grade children's understanding of the motivations and consequences of aggressive actions. They report that although kindergarteners understood (as measured through a multiple-choice recognition test) only about one-third of the motives asked about, third graders understood about half of the motive cues and the high school seniors understood nearly all of the characters' motivations.

Collins et al. (1974) further examined children's comprehension of the motive-behavior-consequence linkage. They argue that, in keeping with Piaget's research on the developoment of moral judgments in children, the bases of the child's judgments of television acts shift at about age nine or ten from evaluations based on the consequences of the act to more intention-based evaluations of acts. In a nonexperimental procedure they examined whether this might be the case in children's evaluations of television actions. Collins et al. (1974) showed kindergarten, second-, fifth-, and eighth-grade children a specially edited version of an aggressive television program. When the children were asked to recall the aggressive action, kindergarteners mentioned only the action, while second graders mentioned both the action and consequences. Fifth graders mentioned either the motive-behavior linkage or the behavior-consequence linkage, and the majority of eighth graders provided the entire motive-behavior-consequence linkage in their recall of the program. In short, the older children knew that person A killed person B for a certain reason and with a certain consequence; these older children were able to articulate the causal relationships among the action events.

There is some evidence that part of the difficulty young children have in understanding motivations for character behaviors resides in the relatively ambiguous and complex presentation of motivation cues on television. Furthermore, motive cues are often separated in time from the behaviors they elicit. There is evidence that when motives for actions are very explicitly stated and occur contiguous to the actions they elicit, even children as young as seven or eight can recognize them (Berndt and Berndt, 1975). The manner in which these social cues are portrayed, then, may be important for children's understanding of characters and their actions.

In summary, research on children's understanding of television characters suggests that during the elementary school years children have difficulty understanding characters' motivations for actions. Kindergartners seem to be the most deficient at this; high school children the most adept. By fifth grade there is evidence, however, that children begin to describe motivations for why characters behave as they do (Wartella and Alexander, 1977); recognize motive cues in multiple-choice tests about a given television program (Leifer and Roberts, 1972); and offer explanations of motives when describing television plotlines (Collins et al., 1974). However, there may not be developmental differences in the underlying dimensions or traits children use to compare one television character with another, according to Reeves' (1979) research.

Unfortunately, we have relatively little knowledge regarding the effects of various kinds of television production techniques or the audio-visual symbol system on children's comprehension of television messages. While systematic research in this area is only beginning, there are some preliminary indications of age-related growth in children's understanding of filmic techniques. This research will be considered next.

Children's understanding of audio-visual techniques. Various sorts of production techniques, such as cuts, zooms, pans, and montage, are routinely used in television programs. Research on children's understanding of these "formal features," the symbol system of television, is sparse. There is some indication that children's confusion regarding interpretations of television messages may be the result of their misunderstanding of these formal features of television. For instance, Dorr (forthcoming) reports that the five- to seven-year-old children she talked with could not understand how Steve Austin, the "Six Million Dollar Man," could catch the bad guys when he ran so slowly. These children obviously were not interpreting the use of slow motion as an indicator of bionic strength.

Some indication of children's relative lack of understanding of television production features comes from research by Tada (1969), who examined Japanese children's comprehension of film images. He found strong age-related differences in children's understanding of various production techniques and their relationship to theme development. For example, in one study he presented elementary school children with an industrial film about the development of factories along Japan's coastal fishing villages. The film opened with scenes of quiet fishing villages and then cut to groups of factories being built along these shores. Fewer than half of the third-grade children who saw this film were able to predict the effect of the factories on these fishing villages as intended by the producer. Further, these children had difficulty understanding any connection between these two scenes. Tada found that elementary school children had difficulty understanding and predicting the direction of theme development in the film, and that much of the difficulty stemmed from misunderstanding production techniques. His interpretation is that the young children had not yet learned to "read" film images and understand the symbolic meanings of different film techniques such as scenic shifts, rhythym montage, and image symbolism.

Research by Huston-Stein (1977) in the United States and Salomon (1979) in Israel tend to support this interpretation. They find that variations in the use of formal features such as zooms, fades, and pacing affect comprehension of the program. Huston-Stein (1977), for instance, is currently examining the effects of various auditory features which have been found to affect attention on comprehension of the program. Also, Singer and Singer (1979), in reporting current research, argue that some of the production techniques used to capture children's attention such as fast pace may actually hinder young children's learning from television and in the classroom.

The precise nature of children's understanding of various kinds of production techniques has not been detailed. There is some evidence that at least major change points in the structure of television programs are processed by children as early as third grade, even where fancy camera techniques may not be understood. Wartell (1978), for example, reports an examination of the size of units children use to "chunk" a television narrative into different happenings in the program. She found that third graders used smaller units to divide the stream of behavior in the narrative portrayal than did ninth graders or adults. However, major break points in the action, or changes in the direction of the behavior stream, noted by ninth graders and adults were also noted by the third graders. These third graders appeared to have learned at least the basic changes in audio-visuals, such as the use of cuts, to indicate changes in direction of theme development.

Salomon (1979) examined how the symbol system of television may act to "supplant" the child's level of cognitive skills to "cultivate" the development of mental skills. In his research, Salomon has examined the impact of various kinds of camera techniques on comprehension and their relationship to the development of mental skills. For instance, he examined the role of the zoom as a camera movement which relates parts of objects to the whole object and has compared this to the child's ability to relate parts to wholes. His research question is: Can use of zooms aid children's development of an understanding of how parts are related to wholes? He argues that visually the zoom can supplant children's ability to make the connection between parts and wholes on their own. Furthermore, he then asks: Might not television's symbol system aid in the development of other mental skills in children? He suggests that heavy users of television who are working at making sense of the television visuals may acquire various kinds of mental skills more quickly. He reports, for instance, that with the introduction of "Sesame Street" in Israel, second- and third-grade children who viewed the program acquired mastery of various kinds of mental skills, such as relating parts to wholes, as a result of exposure to the symbol system of the program.

Salomon (1979) further reports the results of a cross-cultural study of Israeli and American children's mastery of various kinds of mental skills. In this study fourth- and sixth-grade children were studied. First, he found that Israeli children remembered more of the content of television programs they reported to watch the previous day; that is, Israeli children were more likely to engage in what Salomon calls "literate viewing" than were their American counterparts. Not only did the Israeli children appear to be watching television more "seriously" according to Salomon, but they showed greater mastery of mental skills than did their American counterparts; and in particular the Israeli "literate" viewers showed greater mastery of precisely those mental skills (such as series completion) which correlated with literate viewing, but not of those skills which did not correlate. Salomon argues that the low correlation between viewing and mastery of mental skills among the American sample may be the result of the "less serious" televiewing by the American children; that is, American children may not be trying as hard to make sense of the television programs and extract information from them. Salomon's research represents an unusual hypothesis in the literature and has not been replicated by other studies.

To summarize, our knowledge of children's understanding of the various techniques used in production of television programs is still rudimentary. The research to date suggests that children's understanding of some of the symbols of the audio-visual medium probably does not develop until they acquire mastery of other abstract information-processing abilities—such as relating parts to wholes—and have greater experience with watching television. Unfortunately, we have little evidence pinpointing where confusions arise in interpreting televison messages as a result of the use of particular production techniques.

Children's understanding of the television medium. The content of television can be real-life, as in a news show, and it can be fantasy, as in many comic or dramatic programs. Sometimes television tries to entertain without engaging the viewer's intellect; other times it tries to persuade the viewer to adopt a certain point of view or to buy certain products. How do children understand the nature of television programming? Can they recognize reality from fantasy? Can they distinguish among different kinds of programming? When do they understand that advertising is different from other programming? In short, do they understand the medium of television?

Several studies have reported that as children grow older they are less likely to report that television is "real" or that television people are like people in-real life (Greenberg et al., 1976; Lyle and Hoffman, 1972; Noble, 1975). In particular, preschoolers and kindergartners have been shown to have difficulty understanding that television programs are "make believe" and television characters are actors. These young children are reported to believe that television people live in the television box (Lyle and Hoffman, 1972) and know the viewer just as the viewer knows the characters from television (Noble, 1975).

Furthermore, Noble (1975) argues that young children engage in parasocial interaction with television characters—television characters are viewed as real people and real friends with whom to interact in play and real life. Television seems a very real world indeed to young children, a world in which they become emotionally and cognitively involved. However, evidence of such parasocial interaction is weak and has not been much studied.

While television may not be real in the sense that preschoolers talk to and use it, it does present some events realistically (in a real-life manner). Perceptions of television as real in the sense that television portrays events and people in a real-life manner may be accurate perceptions of the medium. Television does show how people eat, dress, and engage in other sorts of everyday activities. This is not to say tht television does not engage in stereotyped portrayals; television may stereotype different racial and ethnic groups as well as men and women, and yet, at the same time, some aspects of the portrayals are realistic.

Similarly, Hawkins (1977) presents evidence that the construct of perceived reality may have several dimensions and that the general findings that perceived reality decreases as children grow older may refer to only one dimension. In particular, he found that between first and third grade there is a marked increase in understanding that most television programs present fiction or actors playing parts and are not pictures of actual events. That is, between first and third grades children realize that television is not a "magic window" on the world, as the preschoolers and kindergartners are reported to discuss television's reality. Hawkins found a different age pattern, however, for children's perceptions of television people and events being like real life— what he calls the social expectations dimension of perceived reality. There was no age-related decrease in children's perceptions of television characters as similar to people in real life—at least not through the sixth graders he studied.

It seems likely that children's perceptions of television reality are as multiple as the phenomenon would suggest. For example while Archie Bunker is not a "real person" you and I may meet on the street, he may act like "some real people" you and I know. Moreover, "how much" like real-life people we perceive Archie to be depends on our experiences and perceptions of Archie as a stereotype.

The major hurdle may be for children to understand that television people are actors portraying events. This understanding seems to occur between first and second grades. Understanding that television people may be like real people, or that television people may be useful in showing the viewers how to behave, may not decrease with age. This finding may account for the often-cited statistic from Lyle and Hoffman's (1972) study, which found 25 percent of tenth graders interviewed reporting that people on televison were like people in real life. Indeed, television people often act like people in real life, even when the characters are stereotypes. It seems reasonable that children might recognize these similarities.

Just as understanding the reality of television appears to be multidimensional, so too might children's understanding of the structure of television programming. For instance, there is evidence from several studies that between kindergarten and third grade children acquire the knowledge that television advertising content is different from programming because the former tries to sell products (see Adler et al., 1977, for a review). However, comprehension of the relationship between programming, advertising, and audience size (the basic economic structures underlying the television industry) is a more complex notion to understand, one with which many adults might have difficulty. Dorr (forthcoming) reports that none of the elementary school children she spoke with understood the complex economic basis of television programming and advertising. To the best of our knowledge, children have only rudimentary understanding of the business of television.

Summary of children's understanding of television content. The picture which emerges of children's understanding of television is one which indicates that, on a number of dimensions, children in elementary school are not so competent as adults in processing television messages. By kindergarten, when adult-like televiewing begins, children have rudimentary understanding of television characters and actions, probably perceiving television in discrete action bits. Preschooler's interpretations of television programs are probably quite idiosyncratic. Children as old as eight or nine (second or third grade) have been shown to have difficulty in identifying program information which is considered by adults to be central to understanding plotlines. Further, these relatively older children have been shown to have difficulty explaining character motivations for behavior and tend to describe characters in terms of very surface characteristics, such as appearance and behaviors.

Similarly, understanding about the television medium as an economic business is only rudimentary in grade school. In particular, public controversy surrounds the question of children's knowledge and awareness about advertising content on television. In the next section, consideration will be given to several of the research studies regarding when and how children acquire an understanding of advertising content as distinct from other types of programming.

III. CHILDREN'S UNDERSTANDING
OF TELEVISION ADVERTISING

In this last section several pragmatic questions about age-related changes in children's comprehension of television advertising will be discussed. Three major questions will be considered: How do children discriminate between programs and commercials? What is the nature of children's understanding of the concept of television advertising? What is the nature of children's memory for commercials?

Program-commercial separation. Questions of children's awareness of programs as distinct from commercials revolve around the issue of what constitutes awareness. Is evidence of shifts in attention level when commercials come on the screen an indication of "awareness?" Or must the child be able to articulate functional, conceptual explanations of the differences between the two types of content?

Evidence from studies of children's attention to commercials suggests that children as young as three or four shift attention upward at the onset of a commercial (Wartella and Ettema, 1974; Zuckerman et al., 1978). Attention to the screen during the commercial has been found to decrease and then shift upward again at the onset of the second commercial in a sequence. Only Ward and Wackman (1973), who had mothers observe their children watching television in homes rather than utilizing trained observers in a controlled viewing situation, do not find movement toward higher attention for young children at the onset of commercials.

Advertisements, when embedded in programs, seem to represent the kind of "bit changes" Anderson and his colleagues have been studying as mentioned in section II. In one study, Ward and Wackman (1973) found that five- to twelve-year-old children's visual attention to the set decreases at the onset of a commercial—attention went down in the transition from program to commercials. This differentiation in attention was found most strongly for the children at higher cognitive levels (those more than eight). In this study mothers observed their children watching television in the homes and recorded their observations.

However, in two other studies where trained observers recorded children's attention in controlled viewing rooms, an *increase* in attention was found at the onset of a commercial after breaking from a program (Wartella and Ettema, 1974; Zuckerman, et al., 1977, 1978). This is in contradiction to Ward and Wackman. Wartella and Ettema (1974), observing nursery, kindergarten, and second-grade children, found that the youngest age group, in particular, showed variation in attention to commercials depending on the commercials' perceptual activity—the more visual and auditory changes present in the commercial, the more likely it was to elicit full attention by the nursery schoolers. Second graders' attention was less susceptible to variations in perceptual complexity; these children showed uniformly high attention to the commercials.

In contrast to the Wartella and Ettema study, Zuckerman et al. (1977) found second, third, and fourth graders who watched a 15-minute presentation with four commercials embedded in program content to show relatively low mean attention to the commercials. In both studies the pattern of attention to the commercials was comparable: movement toward higher attention at the onset of a commercial with attention falling during the commercials; then again movement toward attention at the onset of a second commercial in the series or at the return to the program.

Two studies which have examined children's attention to clustered commercials, Duffy and Rossiter (1975) and Atkin (1975a) have found that clustering of commercials in blocks does not decrease young children's attention. For instance, Duffy and Rossiter showed groups of first- and fourth-grade children either a clustered commercial/program format or the traditional dispersed commercial/program format in a classroom viewing situation. Observers estimated the percentage of children in the class at "full attention" to each commercial shown. First graders had slightly higher attention to the clustered commercials than to the nonclustered commercials. Fourth graders showed lower attention to the clustered than nonclustered commercials. Atkin (1975a) found higher attention to clustered commercials in his study of preschool through fifth graders, but he reports no age differences.

The recent research on children's patterns of attention to television would suggest an explanation for attentional shifts toward full attention when commercials come on the air. If it is the case that by age five children have acquired adultlike viewing patterns which involve monitoring the screen interspersed with periods of inattention, then any perceptible changes in content should attract viewers' attention. It would seem likely that changes in the visual and audio channels, if even for a split second, are enough to capture an inattentive television watcher. Such changes in television content occur in the movement from programs to commercials and also from one commercial to another. Strong audio and visual shifts (even a blank screen) would appear to be cues even kindergarten children use to note changes in the content of the television and which help them monitor their television-watching. Such cues should result in looking at the television for children who are visually inattentive and perhaps other shifts in attention for children who have been attentive. It would seem to be the shift in content alone, independent of whether the commercials occur in clustered or dispersed formats, which heighted attention.

In addition to shifts in attention at the onset of commercials, children as young as four have been shown to have other sorts of perceptual awareness of program-commercial separation. Gianinno and Zuckerman (1977) have shown that about 50 percent of the four-year-old children they interviewed could correctly pick out a picture of a television commercial character when paired with a TV program character in eight out of 10 comparisons. On the other hand, nearly all of the seven-year-old children they interviewed could recognize the commercial characters when presented with the 10 paired comparisons. Furthermore, when asked to choose the picture of a character who shows products on television, nearly all of the four- and seven-year-old subjects were correct in recognizing the television characters in eight of 10 paired comparisons.

Nevertheless, it is difficult to equate such perceptual discriminations as evidence of conceptual understanding of the functional differences between programs and commercials. While children may be able to recognize perceptual features of commercials, such as characters in commercials, it is an inferential leap to assume this is evidence of understanding the purpose of commercials.

Most tests of conceptual understanding of the distinctions between programs and commercials have relied on verbal measures of children's articulation of differences. For instance, Ward and Wackman (1973) report that 79 percent of five- to eight-year-olds they interviewed distinguished the two types of programming in largely perceptual terms; that is the children recognized that commercials and programs have different characters and are of different lengths. On the other hand, these authors report that 73 percent of nine- to 12-year-olds offered functional differences in making the distinction, such as that commercials tried to sell products and sponsored programs. Even lower estimates of functional discriminations are reported by Giannino and Zuckerman (1977): Only 12 percent of the seven-year-olds and 25 percent of the 10-year-olds they interviewed could articulate that commercials try to sell products.

In summary, awareness of the distinction between programs and commercials appears to proceed from perceptual discrimination (evidenced as early as age four in attentional patterns) through recognition and articulation of perceptual differences by kindergarten and first graders, to higher level understanding of functional differences somewhere between kindergarten and second grade. Depending on the criterion for what constitutes "awareness of the difference between programs and commercials", children of different age levels can be said to be aware. Perceptual discrimination, however, does appear to precede conceptual discrimination.

Children's understanding of the purpose of commercials. Research on children's understanding of the purpose of commercials has relied on verbal measures of children's abilities to articulate the persuasive aspect of advertising. Results of the various survey studies seem to indicate clearly that the vast majority of children below age six (kindergarten) cannot articulate the selling purpose of advertising. Between kindergarten and second grade (between the ages of about six and seven) children have been shown to articulate the selling intent of advertising with various estimates or percentages at each age level. Variations in the percentage of children between kindergarten and second grade who understand the purpose of commercials appear to be the result of the measurement context of question wordings and scoring systems.

Wackman et al. (1979) report estimates that range between one-tenth and one-half of kindergarten-aged children who understand that advertising is trying to sell them products. In a survey study reported in 1977 (Wackman et al., 1977), they interviewed kindergarteners in their homes and asked them several different questions about the purpose of advertisements. In response to the question "What is a commercial?" only 10 percent of the kindergarteners mentioned the persuasive aspect of advertisements. In the same interview, 22 percent of the kindergartners reported that commercials try to get them to buy products in response to the question "What do commercials try to do?" Evidence from their experimental studies in which children are shown commercials and then interviewed about the factual information in the commercials produces even higher estimates of the percentage of kindergartners who understand selling intent. They report that in response to an end-of-interview question, "What does this commercial for (product X) want you to do?" approximately half of the kindergarteners in various viewing conditions (and as high as 62 percent of the kindergarteners in one condition) say that the commercial wants them to buy or try the product.

As children develop beyond kindergarten into late elementary school, more complete understanding develops of the notion of persuasive intent and commercials' role in broadcasting. Several researchers put the demarcation between rudimentary understanding and grasp of the persuasive aspect of advertising at age eight or older (Atkin, 1979; Roberts, 1979; Robertson and Rossiter, 1974). For instance, a slightly different criterion than that used by Ward et al. (1977) and Wackman et al. (1979) is offered by Roberts (1979) for what constitutes understanding of persuasive intent. Roberts argues that just understanding that commercials want someone to buy or try a product is not sufficient evidence of understanding the purpose and persuasive aspect of advertising. From general cognitive developmental notions and research on children's development of role-taking skills, Roberts develops an argument that not until about age nine or 10 can children take the advertiser's motivations into account when considering the advertisement. Children who lack role-taking skills are not able to recognize that because advertisers are trying to sell them products, the presentation of the product information may be biased. Roberts' argument is that children below at least eight years of age cannot be wary consumers of advertising messages. His argument reasons from general cognitive development theory and research, but it has not been put to direct empirical test.

Research supports the notion that as children grow older they acquire a more complete grasp of the notion of advertising, including the idea of sponsorship of programs. It seems likely that, as they grow older, children's understanding of advertising proceeds from rudimentary ideas of commercials trying to sell products to more complete comprehension of the consequences of advertiser motivations in the presentation of product information in commercials.

As the discussion of program-commercial separation and children's understanding of persuasive intent indicates, evidence of "understanding" or "awareness" varies depending on the standards to be used in judging these notions. If evidence of attention shifts when commercials appear on the screen is an acceptable indicator that children "discriminate programs from commercials," then three- and four-year-olds can be said to make such discriminations. However, if other standards are used, such as the ability to articulate the notion that the selling intent of commercials distinguishes them from programs, then only a slim majority of kindergarteners may meet this criterion. On the other hand, most third graders do meet this criterion. And if the criterion of "understanding" is articulation of the total economic relationship between advertising and programming, including the idea of sponsorship, then even most sixth-grade children are deficient.

In summary, children's understanding of advertising proceeds from showing evidence first of perceptual discriminative ability and then rudimentary conceptual distinctions followed by an increasingly better grasp of the concept of advertising through the elementary school years. The beginning of conceptual understanding as articulated verbally by some kindergartners appears to be well articulated by nearly all children by the time they reach third grade. It is difficult to provide evidence of when children begin to take advertiser's motivations into account when assessing any particular advertisement's claims, although there is reason to argue, as Roberts does, that this does not occur until after children understand that advertisements try to sell products. Throughout the elementary school years children build on their understandings of television and advertising to acquire fuller grasps of these concepts.

Memory in advertising information. In this section consideration will be given to research on age-related changes in children's memory for advertising information. Two sorts of measurement procedures have been used: first, measurement of cumulative knowledge about advertising outside of a television-viewing situation and, second, recognition or open-ended recall tests immediately after viewing television advertisements. Both sorts of measurement procedures have yielded essentially similar results: children's recognition and recall of the advertising messages increase as they grow older. Major increases in memory seem to occur between kindergarten and third grade.

Ward (1972) and Ward et al. (1977) report studies of five- to 12-year-old children's recall of their "favorite" television commercial. Measures were taken in the course of an interview outside of a television-viewing situation. The children's responses were content analyzed for the number of commercial elements mentioned, the completeness of the storyline, and mention of brand name and other product features. The general finding from both studies is that children's recall for the commercials becomes more complete, coherent, and unified as they grow older. Whereas the youngest (kindergarten) children tended to recall a single element of the commercial (for example, a girl playing with a doll), the older children tended to recall more product and commercial plotline information, recognized that the information in a sequence was telling a story, and generally gave a more unified multidimensional description of the commercial and the product. The major shift in recall from memory for one dimension to multidimensional memory seems to occur between kindergarten and third grade, according to Ward et al. (1977). The older children recalled both more information about the commercial and more different kinds of information— that is, information about the storyline, brand name, and product attributes.

Studies of children's ability to remember commercials they had just been shown tends to support these findings. For instance, Atkin (1975a) reports several studies of children's memory for product elements in several specially produced commercials. In one study, a cereal commercial was produced which claimed that the cereal had four specific vitamins. Immediately after viewing the commercial, 90 percent of the eight- to 10-year-olds interviewed could recall two or more details from the commercials, while only about two-thirds of the four- to seven-year-old children interviewed could do so. Moreover, about half of the older age group could name all four of the vitamins mentioned in the commercial. One-seventh of the four- to seven-year-old children could name all four vitamins.

Wackman et al. (1979) report three experimental studies of children's information-processing of specially produced television advertisements. Kindergarten and third-grade children were shown groups of television commercials for either candy products or toy products embedded in a half-hour cartoon show in viewing rooms in their schools. A postviewing interview with each child was conducted to measure their recognition and recall of advertisement information. One general finding across studies was that kindergartners performed better on multiple-choice recognition measures than on open-ended recall measures of their memory for the commercials. Kindergartners generally performed at levels above chance on recognition measures (accurate recognition of about 40 percent of the product or commercial storyline elements across recognition measures which offered three choice alternatives). Furthermore, when the information about a relatively simple game product which the kindergartners appeared interested in was presented, they answered three-fourths of the recognition measures accurately. Nevertheless, kindergartners' recognition trailed third graders' recall and recognition memory. Across studies, third graders remembered between two-thirds and three-fourths of the product and commercial elements compared with the kindergarteners' 40 percent.

While the Wackman et al. studies involved children's memory for novel advertisements, there is evidence from other sources that even young children learn particular brand name slogans. For instance, Atkin (1975b, 1975c) reports that memory for slogans is well established by the time children reach grade school. In a survey study he presented three different slogans with the brand name missing. Almost half of the preschool-kindergarten children interviewed and 80 percent of the first to third graders interviewed identified the correct brand referred to in the slogan.

In summary, age-related increases in children's memory for commercials are indicated by the research. In particular, recall of brand name and mention of attributes about the product seems to increase substantially between kindergarten and third grade. There seems to be some indication , also, that young children have an easier time recognizing product information through a multiple-choice test than they do via open-ended measures. In general, kindergartners perform less well in recollecting advertising information, even immediately after watching the ad, than do third grade children. These findings certainly are in keeping with the research on children's memory for television plotlines and narrative information, as discussed in the previous section of this chapter.

IV. SUMMARY AND POSTSCRIPT

In this section the major conclusions presented in the preceding three sections will be summarized. Also, implications of this review of children's understanding of television will be considered in light of current policy concerns.

Section I presented a brief description of cognitive development theory, particularly the work of Jean Piaget and critiques of his approach to examining the development of children's thinking abilities. A major conclusion of this review is that cognitive development theory and research argues strongly for the notion that children's thinking and interpretative abilities change radically as they grow older. Children's attention to and interpretations of the physical and social world follow several dimensions of change. First is the decrease in perceptual boundedness, or the ability to go beyond immediate perception for cues to assess objects as children grow older. A second major dimension of cognitive growth is the development of decentration or the use of multiple dimensions of objects when assessing them. Third, there is evidence that a major dimension of growth in children's interpretations of other people and the social world is the movement from more egocentric ways of perceiving and understanding others to mutual perspective-taking in understanding people's behavior.

Critiques of Piagetian approaches to cognitive development theory also have several implications for approaching research on children's understanding of television. First, one should be wary of making inferences from more theoretical literature on children's general cognitive development to the specific instance of children's responses to television. Second, the particular tasks and measures utilized in television research should be assessed in light of their appropriateness to the children's ability levels. Third, the critiques suggest that stress should be placed on discussions of age-related changes in children's understanding of television as opposed to "stage-related" changes in understanding.

The concept of age-related growth in understanding the medium of television is considered in section II. Evidence from attention research (mainly research on children's television-watching behavior) indicates that attention is influenced by the age of the child, the particular content attended to, and distractions in the viewing situation. First, by about age five, children's patterns of looking and not looking at the television set begin to approximate adult styles of viewing. While at times children may appear glued to the television set (zombie-like), these periods appear to be of relatively short duration—at least in laboratory studies. Second, there is evidence of selective viewing of television. Viewing involves monitoring of the television screen which appears to be elicited and maintained by various kinds of visual and auditory elements on television. In particular, changes in the audio elements appear to have the greatest impact in drawing children's attention back to the set if they are not attending. Finally there is some evidence that the comprehensibility of the television message is important in maintaining the child's attention; when the message is relatively unintelligible for children of a certain age level, continued attention is unlikely. Children appear to be actively and selectively attending to televison. This conclusion is not, however, evidence that television-watching is inherently as "active" or more "active" than other ways in which the child can engage his or her body and mind.

The literature on children's comprehension of television content has found age-related changes in children's understanding of plotlines, perceptions of television characters, perceptions of the reality of television, and comprehension of the economics of the medium. First, children as old as eight and 10 have been shown less proficient than older children in recalling those scenes of a television program adults consider essential to understanding the plotline. Furthermore, there is some evidence that children at this age level also are less proficient at drawing inferences about the relationship between scenes of the plot, and may not be attempting to organize the plotline information in a meaningful fashion as they watch the program.

Similarly, during the elementary school years children have difficulty understanding characters' motivations for actions. Kindergartners through third graders have been found to be less adept at recalling characters' motivations for actions than are older children. There is evidence that by the fifth grade children begin to describe motivations for characters' behaviors when asked to give a description of a television character; children recognize motive cues in multiple-choice tests about a particular television character's actions; and they offer explanations of characters' motives when describing television plotlines. However, there is some evidence that the underlying dimensions or traits children use to compare on television character with another may not change as children grow older; humor, attractiveness, activity, and strength are four dimensions which children of different age levels have been found to use in comparing television characters.

What little research exists on children's understanding of audio-visual techniques and the economics of television as a business suggests that understanding of these aspects of the medium increases as children grow older. Elementary school children appear less adept at understanding various sorts of production techniques, such as flashbacks and slow motion, than older children and adults. Furthermore, children in the elementary grades appear to have little comprehension of the economic relationship among advertising, programming, and viewership or other characteristics of the economics of television.

Further examination of the development of understanding of television advertising is offered in section III. The development of an understanding of the differences between programs and television commercials appears to proceed from perceptual discrimination (as evidenced as early as age four in attentional patterns) through recognition and articulation of perceptual differences between programs and commercials among kindergarten children. Higher level understanding of the functional differences between programs and commercials occurs between kindergarten and third grade. It is during the elementary grades that children develop increasingly better understanding of the purpose of advertising. By about third grade, children have been shown to articulate that advertisers want to sell them products. However, it is difficult to provide evidence that children at this age level take advertisers' motivations into account when assessing any particular advertisement's claims. This may not occur until later than third grade. We have evidence that memory for advertising information, including brand name and attribute claims about products, also appears to increase between kindergarten and third grade. Third graders show more complete, multidimensional, and coherent memory for television advertisements than do younger children.

The major implication of this review for the current policy deliberations concerns the issue of age-specific programming. Is there a need for age-specific programming? On the basis of this review of children's understanding of televison, I think that there *is* a need for age-specific programming. Since children's abilities to interpret and understand television content changes, particularly between preschool and the elementary grades, programming which takes into consideration children's abilities to interpret the messages is needed. Major demarcation points would appear to be between preschool and elementary school-aged children, and, second, between younger and older elementary school children. Major changes in viewing and understanding television occur around third grade (ages eight to ten).

In addition to television programming which represents the child's abilities to interpret and understand the messages, there is also an implication of the need for future attempts to improve children's viewing skills.

Throughout this chapter reference has been made to the notion that children are active cognizers of their world, that they are constantly making sense of objects and events around them. This sense-making occurs within the limits of the child's level of cognitive abilities and set of social experiences. The same appears to be the case with children's interaction with television. The mental and experiential skills children bring to television have an impact in shaping the meanings they construe about the messages in programs and commercials.

Does this mean that the misunderstanding of the seven-year-old child about a program plotline or the rudimentary knowledge about advertising of a five-year-old cannot be changed until the children grow older? Can children be taught or aided to understand more about television earlier than current descriptions of their understanding indicates? Researchers are currently examining this question.

As was pointed out early in the chapter, Piaget's theory and other cognitive developmental research have often been presented as fixed and unchanging descriptions of how children of certain ages think—primarily, the deficits of their way of thinking. However, evidence is mounting that stage guidelines for when children acquire certain cognitive abilities are not fixed, that children can be taught to acquire some cognitive abilities earlier than a given theory's age limit.

Similarly, there is some preliminary evidence that learning environments can be developed to help children acquire better understanding of television earlier. For instance, there is evidence that adults who watch television with young children can help highlight crucial scenes and help interpret the action on the screen (Stevenson, 1972). Furthermore, there is evidence that consumer learning programs can be developed to teach kindergarteners elaborated notions about commercials, advertising, and persuasive intent (Wackman et al., 1979).

Of course, these programs must start with the child's current level of ability and use teaching tools understandable to the child. Appropriate educational materials may help children develop critical viewing skills at earlier ages. Such receivership skills research is currently underway. At this point, it seems likely that appropriate learning materials will be developed to teach children about the medium of television, both its programming and advertising content. Such materials should help children overcome their misunderstandings of television messages. By improving the skills children bring to the viewing situation we may be able to moderate the impact television has on the child.

NOTES

1. The argument advanced here does not mean to imply, however, that children are as "active" when watching television as they are when engaged in athletics or doing other sorts of activities. Activity here is relative.

2. Multidimensional scaling is a statistical technique that looks at how subject's ratings of a variety of variables group together; that is, it seeks to determine underlying dimensions which describe the relationship among a set of variables for a given group of subjects.

REFERENCES

ADLER, R. P. et al. (1977) Research on the Effects of Television Advertising on Children: A Review of Literature and Recommendations for Future Research. Washington, DC: National Science Foundation.

ALEXANDER, A. and E. WARTELLA (1979) "Children's impressions of television characters and real people." Presented to the International Communication Association Annual Conference, Philadelphia.

ANDERSON, D.R. (1977) "Children's attention to television." Presented at the Society for Research in Child Development meeting, New Orleans.

——— and S.R. LEVIN (1976) "Young children's attention to Sesame Street." Child Development 47: 807-811.

ANDERSON, D.R., S.R. LEVIN, and E. PUGZLES LORCH (1977) "The effects of television program pacing on the behavior of preschool children." Audio-Visual Communication Review 25: 159-166.

ANDERSON, D.R., et al. (1979) "Watching children watch television." In G. Hale and M. Lewis (eds.) Attention and the Development of Cognitive Skills. New York: Plenum.

ATKIN, C.K. (1975a) "Effects of television advertising on children: First year experimental evidence." Television Advertising and Children Project, Report No. 1. East Lansing: Michigan State University.

——— (1975b) "Effects of television advertising on children: Survey of preadolescent's responses to television commercials." Television Advertising and Children Project, Report No. 6. East Lansing: Michigan State University.

——— (1975c) "Effects of television advertising on children: Survey of children's and mother's responses to television commercials." Television Advertising and Children Project, Report No. 8. East Lansing: Michigan State University.

——— (1976) "Effects of television advertising on children: Second year experimental evidence." Television Advertising and Children Project, Report No. 2. East Lansing: Michigan State University.

——— (1977) "Effects of campaign advertising and newscasts on children." Journalism Quarterly 54: 503-509.

——— (1979) "Children's response to television advertising." Testimony to Federal Trade Commission Hearings, Washington, D. C.

——— and B. S. GREENBERG (1977) "Parental mediation of children's social behavior learning from television." CASTLE project, Report No. 4. East Lansing/Washington, DC: Department of Communication, Michigan State University/Office of Child Development.

ATKIN, C.K. and G. HEALD (1977) "The content of children's toy and food commercials." Journal of Communication 27: 107-114.

BECHTEL, R.B., C. ACHELPOL, and R. AKERS (1972) "Correlates between observed behavior and questionnaire responses on television viewing." In E.A. Rubinstein, G.A. Comstock, and J. P. Murray (eds.) Television and Social Behavior, Vol. 4. Washington, DC: U.S. Government Printing Office.

BERNDT, T. and E. BERNDT (1975) "Children's use of motives and intentionality in person perception and moral judgments." Child Development 46: 904-912.

BROWN, R. (1976) Children and Television. Beverly Hills, CA: Sage.

BRUNER, J.S. (1966) Studies in Cognitive Growth. New York: John Wiley.

BUCK-MORSS, S. (1975) "Socio-economic bias in Piaget's theory and its implications for cross-cultural studies." Human Development 18: 35-49.

BURR, P. and R.M. BURR (1977) "Product recognition and premium." Journal of Communication 27: 115-117.

BUSS, A.R. (1977) "Piaget, Marx and Buck-Morss on cognitive development." Human Development 20: 118-128.

CASE, R. (1972) "Learning and development: A Neo-Piagetian interpretation." Human Development 15: 339-358.

——— (1974) "Structure and stricture: Some functional limitations on the course of cognitive growth." Cognitive Psychology 6: 544-574.

COLLINS, W.A. (1970) "Learning of media content: A developmental study." Child Development 41: 1133-1142.

——— (1975) "The developing child as a viewer." Journal of Communication 25: 34-44.

——— (1978) "Temporal integration and children's inference about televised social behavior." Address to the Biennial Meeting of the South-Western Society for Research in Human Development, Dallas, Texas.

——— (1979) "Children's comprehension of television content." In E. Wartella (ed.) Children Communicating: Media and Development of Thought, Speech, Understanding. Beverly Hills, CA: Sage.

——— T. BERNDT, and V. HESS (1974) "Observational learning of motives and consequences for television aggression: A developmental study." Child Development 45: 799-802.

COLLINS W.A., H. WELLMAN, A.H. KENISTON, and S.D. WESTBY (1978) " Age related aspects of comprehension and inference from a televised dramatic narrative." Child Development 49: 389-399.

——— (forthcoming) " Age related comprehension and inference from televised dramatic narrative." Child Development.

COMSTOCK, G., S. CHAFFEE, N. KATZMAN, M McCOMBS, and D. ROBERTS (1978) Television and Human Behavior. New York: Columbia University Press.

DASEN, P. [ed.] (1977) Piagetian Psychology: Cross-Cultural Contributions. New York: Gardner Press.

DESMOND, R.J. (1978) "Cognitive development and television comprehension." Communication Research 5: 202-220.

DOOLITTLE, J. and R. PEPPER (1975) "Children's television ad content: 74." Journal of Broadcasting 19: 131-142.

DORNBUSCH, W., A. HASTORF, S. RICHARDSON, R. MUZZY, and R. VREELAND (1965) "The perceiver and the perceived: Their relative influence on the categories of interpersonal cognition." Journal of Personality and Social Psychology 1: 434-440.

DORR, A. (forthcoming) "When I was a child, I thought as a child." In an edited volume by the Committee on Television and Social Behavior of the Social Science Research Council. Washington, Hillsdale, NJ: Lawrence Ehrlbaum.

DUFFY, J. and J.R. ROSSITER (1975) "The Hartford experiment: Children's reactions to television commercials in blocks at the beginning and end of the program." Presented at the Conference on Culture and Communications, Temple University.

ENNIS, R.H. (1976) "An alternative to Piaget's conceptualization of logical competence." Child Development 47: 903-919.

FELDMAN, S., W. ABRAHAM, and D. WARMOUTH (1977) "Parental concern about child-directed commercials." Journal of Communication 27: 125-137.

FIELD, D. (1977) "The importance of the verbal content in the training of Piagetian conservation skills." Child Development 48: 1583-1592.

FLAPAN, D. (1968) Children's understanding of social interaction. New York: Teachers College.

FLAVELL, J.H. (1963) The developmental psychology of Jean Piaget. Princeton: Van Nostrand Reinhold.

——— (1970) "Concept development." In P. H. Mussen (ed.) Carmichael's Manual of Child Psychology, Vol. 1. New York: John Wiley.

——— (1974) "The development of inferences about others." In J. Mischel (ed.) Understanding Other Persons. Oxford: Basil Blackwell.

——— (1977) Cognitive Development. Englewood Cliffs, NJ: Prentice-Hall.

FRIEDLANDER, B.Z., H.S. WETSTONE, and C.S. SCOTT (1974) "Suburban preschool children's comprehension of an age-appropriate informational television program." Child Development 45: 561-566.

FURTH, H.G., M. BAUR, and J.E. SMITH (1976) "Children's conception of social institutions: A Piagetian framework." Human Development 19: 351-374.

GALST, J.P. and M.A. WHITE (1976) "The unhealthy persuader: The reinforcing value of television and children's purchase-influencing attempts at the supermarket." Child Development 47: 1089-1096.

GIANINO, L. J. and P. A. ZUCKERMAN (1977) "Measuring children's responses to television advertising." Presented at the 85th Annual Meeting of the American Psychological Association, San Francisco.

GINSBURG, H. and S. OPPER (1969) Piaget's Theory of Intellectual Development. Englewood Cliffs, NJ: Prentice-Hall.

GREENBURG, B.S. and C.K. ATKIN (1978) "Learning about minorities from television." Presented to the Minorities and Communication Division, Association for Education in Journalism Annual Convention, Seattle, Washington.

——— G. HEALD, J. WAKSHLAG and B. REEVES (1976) "TV character attributes, identification and children's modeling tendencies." Presented to the International Communication Association, Portland, Oregon, April.

GRUBER, H.E. and J.J. VONECHE [eds.] (1977) The essential Piaget. New York: Basic Books.

HAGEN, J.W. and G.A. HALE (1973) "The development of attention in children." In A.D. Pick (ed.) Minnesota Symposium on Child Psychology, Vol. 7. Minneapolis: University of Minnesota.

HALE, G.A., L.K. MILLER, and H.W. STEVENSON (1968) "Incidental learning of film content: A developmental study." Child Development 39: 69-78.

HAWKINS, R.P. (1973) "Learning of peripheral content in films, a developmental study." Child Development 44: 214-217.

——— (1977) "The dimensional structure of children's perceptions of television reality." Communication Research 3: 299-320.

HUSTON-STEIN, A. (1977) "Television and growing up: The media gets equal time." Presented at the 85th Annual Meeting of the American Psychological Association, San Francisco.

——— et al. (1978) "Formal attributes in children's television: How they are organized and how they relate to content and program types." (unpublished)

JAMISON, W. (1977) "Developmental inter-relationships among concrete operational tasks: An investigation of Piaget's stage concept." Journal of Experimental Child Psychology 24: 235-253.

KATZMAN, N. (1972) "Violence and color television: What children of different ages learn." In G. Comstock, E. Rubinstein, and J. Murray (eds.) Television and Social Behavior, Vol. 5. Washington, DC: U.S. Government Printing Office.

KOHLBERG, L. (1969) "Stage and sequence: The cognitive development approach to socialization." In D.A. Goslin (ed.) Handbook of Socialization Theory and Research. Chicago: Rand McNally.

KRULL, R. and W. HUSSON (1979) "Children's attention: The case of television viewing." In E. Wartella (ed.) Children communicating: Media and Development of Thought, Speech, Understanding. Beverly Hills, CA: Sage.

LEIFER, A.D. et al. (1971) "Developmental aspects of variables relevant to observational learning." Child Development 42: 1509-1516.

LEIFER, A. and D. ROBERTS (1972) "Childrens responses to television violence." In J. Murray, E. Rubinstein, and G. Comstock (eds.) Television and social behavior, Vol. 2. Washington, DC: U.S. Government Printing Office.

LESSER, G.S. (1974) Children and Television: Lessons from Sesame Street. New York: Random House.

LEVIN, S. R. and D. R. ANDERSON (1976) "The development of attention." Journal of Communication 26: 126-135.

LIEBERT, D. et al. (1976) "Effects of television commercial disclaimers on the product expectations of children." (unpublished)

——— (1977) "Effects of television commercial disclaimers on the product expectations of children." Journal of Communication 27: 118-124.

LIVESLEY, W. and D. BROMLEY (1973) Person Perception in Childhood and Adolescence. New York: John Wiley.

LYLE, J. and H.R. HOFFMAN (1972) "Children's use of television and other media." In G.A. Comstock, E.A. Rubinstein, and J.B. Murray (eds.) Television and Social Behavior, Vol. 5. Washington, DC: U.S. Government Printing Office.

MOESSINGER, P. (1977) "Piaget on contradiction." Human Development 20: 178-184.

NEWCOMB, A.F. and W.A. COLLINS (1978) "Children's comprehension of family-role portrayals in televised dramas: Effects of SES, ethnicity, and age." Minneapolis: University of Minnesota Institute of Child Development.

NOBLE, G. (1975) Children in Front of the Small Screen. Beverly Hills, CA: Sage.

PALMER, E.L. (1978) "Children's advertising rulemaking comment." (unpublished)

PALMER, E.L. and C.N. McDOWELL (1979) "Program/commercial separators in children's tele-

——— and C.N. McDOWELL (1979) "Program/commercial separators in children's television programming." Davidson, NC: Department of Psychology, Davidson College. (unpublished)

PASCUAL-LEONE, J. (1970) "A mathematical model for the transition rule in Piaget's developmental stages." Acta Psychologica 63: 301-345.

PEEVERS, B. and P. SECORD (1973) "Developmental changes in attribution of descriptive concepts to persons." Journal of Personality and Social Psychology 27: 120-128.

PHILLIPS, D.C. and M.E. KELLY (1975) "Hierarchical theories of development in education and psychology." Harvard Educational Review 45: 351-375.

PIAGET, J. (1923) The Language and Thought of the Child. London: Routledge & Kegan Paul.

——— (1927) The Child's Conception of Physical Causality. London: Routledge & Kegan Paul.

——— (1928) The Child's Conception of the World. New York: Harcourt Brace Jovanovich.

——— (1946) The Child's Conception of Time. London: Routledge & Kegan Paul.

——— (1950) The Psychology of Intelligence. London: Routledge & Kegan Paul.

——— (1952) The Origins of Intelligence in Children. New York: International Universities Press.

——— (1954) The Construction of Reality in the Child. New York: Basic Books.

——— (1975) "The stages of the intellectual development of the child." In P. Mussen, J. Linger, and J. Kagan (eds.) Basic and Contemporary Issues in Developmental Psychology. New York: Harper & Row.

—— and B. INHELDER (1948) The Child's Conception of Space. London: Routledge & Kegan Paul.

PICK, A.D., D.G. FRANKEL, and V.L. HESS (1975) "Children's attention: The development of selectivity." In E.M. Hetherington (ed.) Review of Child Development, Vol. 5. Chicago: University of Chicago Press.

POULOS, R.W., E.A. RUBINSTEIN, and R.M. LIEBERT (1975) "Positive social learning." Journal of Communication 25: 90-97.

PRASAD, K.V., T.R. RAO, and A.A. SHEIKH (1978) "Mothers vs. commercials." Journal of Communication 28: 91-98.

PUGZLES LORCHE, E., D.R. ANDERSON, and S.R. LEVIN (1977) "The relationship of visual attention to children's comprehension of television." Presented at the National Association of Educational Broadcasters' annual meeting, Washington, D.C.

REEVES, B. (1979) "Children's understanding of television people." In E. Wartella (ed.) Children Communicating: Media and Development of Thought, Speech, Understanding. Beverly Hills, CA: Sage.

—— and B.S. GREENBERG (1977) "Children's perception of television characters." Human Communication Research 3: 113-127.

REID, L.N. (1979) "Viewing rules and mediating factors of children's responses to commercials." Journal of Broadcasting 23:15-26.

ROBERTS, D.F. (1973) "Communication and children: A developmental approach." In I. De Sola Pool and W. Schramm (eds.) Handbook of Communication. Chicago: Rand McNally.

—— (1979) "Testimony before the Federal Trade Commission: Child advertising hearings." Washington, D.C.

ROBERTSON, T.S. and J.R. ROSSITER (1974) "Children and commercial persuasion: An attribution theory analysis.: Journal of Consumer Research 1: 13-20.

—— (1977) "Children's responsiveness to commercials." Journal of Communication 27: 101-106.

ROSSITER, J.R. and T.S. ROBERTSON (1974) "Children's TV commercials: Testing the defenses." Journal of Communication 24: 137-144.

SALOMON, G. (1976) "Cognitive skill learning across cultures." Journal of Communication 26: 138-149.

—— (1979) "Shape, not only content: How media symbols partake in the development of abilities." In E. Wartella (ed.) Children Communicating: Media and Development of Thought, Speech, Understanding. Beverly Hills, CA: Sage.

SCARLETT, H., A. PRESS, and W. CROCKETT (1971) "Children's descriptions of peers: A Wernerian developmental analysis." Child Development 42: 439-453.

SCHRAMM, W., J. LYLE, and E.P. PARKER (1961) Television in the Lives of Our Children. Stanford, CA: Stanford University Press.

SELMAN, R. (1971) "Taking another perspective: Role-taking development in early childhood." Child Development 42: 439-453.

SHANTZ, C.U. (1975) "The development of social cognition." In E.M. Hetherington (ed.) Review of Child Development Research, Vol. 5. Chicago: University of Chicago Press.

SHEIKH, A.A. and L.M. MOLESKI (1977) "Conflict in the family over commercials." Journal of Communication 27: 152-157.

SIEGAL, L.S. and C.J. BRAINERD [eds.] (1978) Alternatives to Piaget. New York: Academic Press.

SINGER, J.C. and D.G. SINGER (1979) "Come back, Mister Rogers, come back." Psychology Today.

SPROULL, N. (1973) "Visual attention, modeling behaviors, and other verbal and non-verbal meta-communication of prekindergarten children viewing Sesame Street." American Educational Research Journal 10: 101-114.

STEINER, G. (1974) "On the psychological reality of cognitive structures: A tentative syntheses of Piaget's and Bruner's theories." Child Development 45: 891-899.

STEVENSON, H.W. (1972) "Television and the behavior of preschool children." In J.P. Murray, E.A. Rubinstein, and G.A. Comstock (eds.) Television and Social Behavior, Vol. 2. Washington, DC: U.S. Government Printing Office.

TADA, T. (1969) "Image cognition: A developmental approach." Studies of Broadcasting 7: 105-174.

WACKMAN, D.B., E. WARTELLA, and S. WARD (1977) "Learning to be consumers: The role research and the implication for research on children's responses to television." Communication Research 4: 203-224.

WACKMAN, D.B., E. WARTELLA, and S. WARD (1977) "Learning to be consumers; The role of the family." Journal of Communication 27: 138-151.

——— (1979) Children's Information Processing of Television Advertising. Final report to the National Science Foundation, Grant No. APR 76-20770. Washington, DC: National Science Foundation.

WARD, S. (1972) "Effects of television advertising on children and adolescents." In E.A. Rubinstein et al. (eds.) Television and Social Behavior, Vol. 4. Washington, DC: U.S. Government Printing Office.

——— and D.B. Wackman (1973) "Children's information processing of television advertising." In P. Clarke (ed.), New Models for Communication Research. Beverly Hills, CA: Sage.

WARD, S., D. LEVINSON, and D. WACKMAN (1972) "Children's attention to television advertising." In E.A. Rubinstein et al. (eds.) Television and Social Behavior, Vol. 4. Washington, DC: U.S. Government Printing Office.

WARD, S., D.B. WACKMAN, and E. WARTELLA (1977) How Children Learn to Buy: The Development of Consumer Information-Processing Skills. Beverly Hills, CA: Sage.

WARTELLA, E. (1978) "Children's perceptual unitizing of a televised behavior sequence." Presented to the Association for Education in Journalism Annual Convention, Seattle, Washington.

——— [ed.] (1979) Children Communicating: Media and Development of Thought, Speech, Understanding. Beverly Hills, CA: Sage.

WARTELLA, E. and A. ALEXANDER (1977) "Children's organization of impressions of television characters." Presented at the International Communication Association Conference, Chicago.

WARTELLA, E. and J.S. ETTEMA (1974) "A cognitive developmental study of children's attention to television commercials." Communication Research 1: 46-69.

WARTELLA, E., D.B. WACKMAN, and S. WARD (1977) "Children's consumer information processing: Representation of information from television advertisements." Prepared for the annual meeting of the Association for Consumer Research, Chicago.

WARTELLA, E. et al. (1979) "The young child as consumer." In E. Wartella (ed.) Children Communicating: Media and Development of Thought, Speech, Understanding. Beverly Hills, CA: Sage.

WEISZ, J.R. (1978) "Transcontextual validity in developmental research." Child Development 49: 1-12.

WINN, M. (1977) The Plug-In Drug. New York: Viking.

WOHLWILL, J.F. (1962) "From perception to inference: A dimension of cognitive development." In W. Kessen and C. Kuhlman (eds.), Cognitive Development in Children, Five Monographs of the Society for Research in Child Development. Chicago: University of Chicago Press.

ZUCKERMAN, P.A., M.E. ZIEGLER, and H.W. STEVENSON (1977) "Children's attention to television and memory of commercials." Presented at 85th Annual Meeting of the American Psychological Association, San Francisco.

ZUCKERMAN, P. et al. (1978) "Children's viewing of television and recognition memory of commercials." Child Development 49: 96-104.

Televised violence has led to more research than any other single topic in the history of mass communication research. F. Scott Andison presents a unique analysis of 63 important studies since 1956. His work suggests that altered television viewing patterns over time may have affected experimental results. This harkens to McQuail's point in an earlier chapter about the "historicity" of media research and reinforces the importance to research of the historical-societal context of the media. Andison, a researcher for the Provincial Government of British Columbia, was a graduate student in sociology at the University of Victoria when this report was written.

32

TV VIOLENCE
AND VIEWER AGGRESSION
A Cumulation of Study Results 1956-1976

F. Scott Andison

THE PROBLEM posed by television's violent content and its possible effects on regular television viewers is a critical and pressing one. The need to establish whether a causal link exists between television violence and an increased level of aggression in viewers is urgent because, if such a link exists, then action may be needed if society does not wish an increase in the aggression levels of its members. Studies of the content of television (e.g., Gerbner, 1972; Cater and Strickland, 1975) have consistently found a high degree of violence present in almost all programming. Even though there has been some reduction of the violent content in recent years, there is no doubt that an extensive amount is still present and that violent programs are more popular on the average than nonviolent ones (Clark and Blankenburg, 1972). Moreover, since television is available in almost every American home and is viewed by young and old alike (Arnold, 1969), it is imperative that we find a definitive answer to our study question. Ascertaining whether or not the causal relationship exists is of interest and importance in both the theoretical and practical realms.

Theoretical Framework

Since the mid-1950s, social scientists have attempted to discover a causal link between violence viewed and subsequent aggression. This re-

Abstract   Can watching television violence lead to an increased level of aggression in the viewers of that violence? Using the data cumulation method, the author suggests that the collective findings of previous studies indicate that such a relationship does exist. Further, it is argued that the cumulation linking these two variables should be used as a justification for reducing the amount of violence shown on television.

    F. Scott Andison is a graduate student and Academic Assistant in the Department of Sociology, University of Victoria, B.C., Canada. The author wishes to acknowledge the aid of Dr. R. A. Hedley and Dr. S. D. Webb of the University of Victoria for their assistance in the preparation of this article.

From F. Scott Andison, "TV Violence and Viewer Aggression: A Cumulation of Study Results 1956-1976," *Public Opinion Quarterly* 41 (Fall 1977) 314-331. Reprinted by permission of Elsevier North Holland, Inc.

search was influenced by prior work done on the effect of the cinema on social behavior in the 1930s and 1940s (e.g., Charters, 1933; Dysinger and Duckmick, 1933; Peterson and Thurstone, 1933; Klapper, 1949). Many variables and a multitude of operationalizations have been used in researching the relationship. For example, does class (Wotring and Greenberg, 1973), age (Thomas, 1972), cultural background (Broncato, 1974), or intelligence (Walters and Willows, 1968) affect the level of aggression achieved after viewing television violence; or does the nature of the violence shown, either real or fantasy (Feshback, 1955), against persons or objects (Hanratty et al., 1969) affect the strength and direction of the relationship? Furthermore, how do we measure the effect? We can record the strength and/or duration of shocks given by subjects to confederates before and after violence is viewed (Walters et al., 1962), or we can assess the effect through a questionnaire (Himmelweit et al., 1958), or we can observe overt physical aggression increases or decreases after violence is watched (Bandura et al., 1963), to mention but three in a host of measurement techniques. Over the last 20 years many studies have been conducted using each of the three main research methodologies—the laboratory experiment, the field experiment, and the field survey (Arnold, 1969). The literature contains a mass of individual and collective studies which attempt to ascertain the strength and direction of the relationship between viewing television violence and subsequent levels of aggression manifested by the audience of that violence.

We found that in the literature, there were three schools of thought about the relationship between watching TV violence and subsequent viewer aggression. The first maintains that watching violence will have a cathartic effect on the aggressive levels of the individuals who watch it. A spokesperson for the television industry nicely sums up this attitude: "Human culture is a thin shield superimposed over a violent core. It's better to crack it fictionally than to see it explode in the streets. Exposure to properly presented violence acts as a therapeutic release for anger and self-hatred which are present in almost everybody" (Baldwin and Lewis, 1972:349).

The second feels that watching violent television neither stimulates nor retards the aggressive levels of its viewers. This attitude is characterized by the following statement of psychiatrist Irving Markowitz: "I don't believe that TV violence—repetitive or not—is harmful. Violence in life exists. People have to understand this. But they also have to understand that there are resources for coping with it. They must know their own resources" (Morris, 1971:119).

The third school of thought feels that television violence can stimulate aggression in its viewers. This position is illustrated by the following remarks: "We believe it is reasonable to conclude that a constant diet of violent behavior on television has an adverse effect on human character and attitudes. Violence on television encourages violent forms of behavior and fosters moral and social values about violence in daily life that are unacceptable in a civilized society" (National Commission on the Causes and Prevention of Violence, 1970:169-170).

To ascertain which of these theories is the most tenable, we have systematically collected and recorded results of all available pertinent studies between 1956 and 1976.

In the quest for a valid answer to our stated problem the data cumulation method can be employed as a powerful tool (Feldman, 1971; Freese, 1972; Glaser, 1972; Taveggia, 1974). It is unlikely that we will find consistent error in our cumulative results because of the many methods and individual authors that are in evidence in this study. Also, since the research we will be cumulating covers a 20-year period (1956-1976), it is doubtful that any historical trend that might bias individual study results would pass unidentified. In addition, because our results reflect many studies over a 20-year period, they should be more valid and much more generalizable.

There are, however, inherent problems attached to this method of research, such as selection of studies to be cumulated, indexing, coding and retrieval of the findings they present, analysis of the comparability of the findings, and the analysis of resulting distributions (Taveggia, 1974). These problems are relatively easy to avoid by utilizing a systematic and structured approach and their solutions have been discussed fairly extensively in the literature (Dubin and Taveggia, 1968; Feldman, 1971; Glaser, 1963; Hyman, 1972). However, three main issues remain that deserve additional attention: (1) handling clusters of nonindependent findings, (2) establishing the weight that should be attached to the findings of studies that vary in methodological sophistication (Taveggia, 1974), and (3) dealing with the problem that positive results are generally reported to a greater extent than negative ones. In regard to the first problem, in this article no findings have been reported separately unless they were independent; therefore this issue need not concern us any further. As for the second problem, a stipulated set of criteria had to be met before a study could be included in the cumulation. Once these criteria were met, all collected research findings were given equal weights. The third problem is unfortunately almost impossible to counteract and control for, and leaders of any cumulation must therefore be wary of the possible over-representativeness of positive results. In this particular situation, however, this possible area of bias may not be as pronounced as in others. Three alternative theories are offered to explain the effects of watching television violence on subsequent aggression: (1) acts as a stimulus (positive results), (2) is neither stimulus nor cathartic (neutral results), and (3) acts as a cathartic agent (negative results). Therefore, a null result of any given study is of important significance and hence is as apt to be reported as a positive result.

Procedure

The search for pertinent studies is probably the major difficulty of the data cumulation method, but it is felt that a fairly extensive coverage of the literature has been made. We examined several periodical indexes (including Reader's Guide to Periodical Literature and the Canadian Periodical Index) and a number of Abstract Indexes (including Psychological Abstracts, Sociological Abstracts, and Dissertation Abstracts International). Wherever possible, all materials were looked at from 1956 to early 1976. Additionally, many books on the subject of television violence and subsequent aggression were also given close scrutiny to cover all available leads to further studies. After this preliminary examination of reference, the effect of "data snowballing" quickly led us to the vast majority of the studies used in this article.

In total, 153 referenced studies were scrutinized. Of these, only 67 were accepted for use in the cumulation of results. Most were rejected because their data, procedure, or content were irrelevant. To be accepted a study had to (1) deal with the topic at hand (i.e. research directly on the relationship between TV violence and aggression); (2) present a basic hypothesis which was later rejected or accepted on the grounds of the data collected by the particular study; and (3) use a stimulus (where a stimulus was used) which was shown on a TV screen (in a natural or contrived setting), on a video tape player, or a film projection which had or could have been aired on network television. If all these criteria were met, then the study was added to the list of studies utilized in the cumulation.

Next, we developed a systematic procedure for gathering information from each study on the following:

1. Author and title—used in classification.

2. Study year—to allow a check to see if, over a period of years, any results have become more or less common (historical effects).

3. Number of subjects—to find out the total number of subjects that have been studied over the period this cumulation covers.

4. Age of subjects—to see if there is any significant difference that TV violence has on the aggressive levels of specific age groups.

5. Sex of subjects—these data were collected originally but it was later determined that the results of most studies were applicable only to males. The number of studies reporting separate results for male and female subjects was small and there was only one that dealt entirely with females while many studies dealt exclusively with males. This is an area that requires the further attention of future investigators.

6. Country of study—although most of the studies were done in the United States, this information was collected to ascertain what differences, if any, could be found between various nations.

7. Direction and strength of the reported relationship—these data are paramount in our cumulation and for this reason Table 1 was constructed to aid in the classification of the studies' reported results.

8. Measures of the relationship—to see if any particular measures yield consistent results.

9. Study type—to see if any particular study type yields consistent results. The three main types are defined in this work as (1) Field Survey—the gathering of already existing data in a natural situation; (2) Field Experiment—a contrived data gathering process in a natural setting; and (3) Laboratory Experiment—contrived data gathering in a contrived setting.

The above information was collected for each of the 67 studies, this being the basis of the cumulation (see Appendix).

The Data

Beginning with Table 2 we can see that the modal result of the cumulation is that there is a weak positive relationship between viewing violence on television and subsequent aggressive behavior. One should note, however, that the moderate positive category is for all intents and purposes on par with the weak positive category as far as total results go, lending support to the notion that viewing TV violence can in fact lead to aggressive behavior. The fact that over 30,000 subjects were tested in the 67 studies gives us confidence that the results may indeed be reflective of a great number of individuals and groups. We can probably feel quite comfortable in drawing inferences from the studies we have cumulated.

Table 1. Operational Definitions for Categorizing the Reported Differences Between Aggresssion Levels of Viewing and Nonviewing Subjects of TV Violence

Reporting Device	Strength and Direction Categories				
	Weak Negative	None	Weak Positive	Moderate Positive	Strong Positive
r	−.30 to −.10	−.09 to +.09	+.10 to +.30	+.31 to +.70	+.71 and up
p	≤.1 and ≥.05	Not significant	≤.1 and ≥.05	≤.05 and ≥.01	≤.01
Percent difference between groups	5-25	5	5-25	26-60	61 and over
Words*	Weak	None null insignificant	Weak	Moderate	Strong

* Only a few studies employed such analysis of their data.

Table 2. Summarized Strength and Direction Results of the Data Cumulation by Frequency and Percent

Strength and Direction	(N)	Proportions of Total	Study Numbers (see Appendix)
Weak negative	(3)	4.1%	2,6,57
None	(14)	19.2	3,5,9,26,28,31,35,36,39,43,44,48,49b, 64
Weak positive	(27)	37.0	1,7,14,15,24,25,29,30b,32,33,34,37,38,47, 49c,52,54,56,58,59,60,61a,61b,63,65, 66,67
Moderate positive	(25)	34.2	4,8,10,12,13,16b,17,23,30a,40,41,42,45,46, 49a,50,51,53,55,62a
Strong positive	(4)	5.5	11,16a,27,62b

Historical Trends

The historical trends in the research of television violence and its effects on the aggression levels of individuals are not really that marked (see Table 3). The method (Table 7) seems to account for much of the differences between the four periods. As can be seen in Table 3a, in the two periods when the laboratory experiment method is more numerous than either the field experiment or the field survey the results are skewed to a greater extent to the positive. However, there may be a true time series effect that is reflected in the results tabulated in Table 3. Assuming that the influence of a person's "real life" television viewing affects his or her response to a presented stimulus in a research setting, the point can be made that watching violence on television (aside from the violence any given study shows to its subjects) will have an effect on that study's findings. Therefore, because television has become such an integral part of the average person's life, the increasingly positive results found in the studies in the later periods may be explained by this cumulative, historical effect. In fact, if there is a time-series trend, we can offer three contending hypotheses to explain it (although they are by no means exhaustive and probably not mutually exclusive): (1) improving methods have been better able to evaluate the true strength and direction of the relationship in recent years, (2) altered television viewing experiences have

Table 3. Summarized Results in Five-Year Blocks by Percent

Years	(N)	Results					Study Numbers
		WN	None	WP	MP	SP	
1956-60	(5)	20	40	20	20	0	1-5
1961-65	(13)	7.1	7.1	21.4	50	14.3	6-18
1966-70	(11)	0	18.2	27.3	45.5	9.1	19-29
1971-75	(37)	2.4	21.4	45	28.6	2.4	30-66

Table 3A. Type and Number of Research Methods by Five-Year Blocks

Table 3A. Type and Number of Research Methods by Five-Year Blocks

	Method			
Years	Field Survey	Field Experiment	Laboratory Experiment	N
1956-1960	1	4	0	5
1961-1965	2	3	8	13
1966-1970	2	2	7	11
1971-1975	12	14	11	37

had an effect on the measurement of the relationship, and (3) the varying degrees that researchers have utilized to study the relationship in each time period have altered the cumulated studies' findings. Of the above, the improved research methods hypothesis seems most able to explain the varying results of the five-year blocks and hence leaves us to doubt whether any significant time-series trend exists at all. Only further analysis will resolve this matter.

Age Factors

It is interesting to look at the effects television has on different age groups. The question has often been asked in the literature: are young children more susceptible to the effects of TV violence than older age groups? Many authors have assumed that this is the case, and a number of persons have researched the question. As can be seen in Table 4, the assumption that young children are affected to a greater extent might be unwarranted. In fact, by the results shown in Table 4, the adult age group might be more affected by TV violence than the preschool group.

Table 4. Summary of Studies Dealing with Specific Age Groups* by Percent

	Results						
Age	WN	None	WP	MP	SP	N	Study Numbers
Preschool (to 5 years)	0	0	55.6	33.3	11.1	8	1,7,12,27,33,40,55, 63
Elementary school (6-12 years)	10	30	0	50	10	10	2,8,21,28,31,41,42, 46,48,62b
High school (13-17 years)	0	27.3	36.4	27.3	9.1	10	16,18,29,30a,30b,35, 36,37,53,66
Adult (17 and up)	7.2	7.2	35.7	50	0	14	6,10,13,14,17,19,20, 22,23,24,26,60, 61a,61b

* Studies overlapping age categories not included.

Study by Country

Table 5 gives us the results by country. Even though the vast majority of studies have been conducted in the United States, one can see that when the total results from countries other than the United States are looked at in relation to the summary of the U.S. studies, an interesting trend is apparent. The U.S. studies show a substantially more skewed distribution to the positive. This is shown best in the differences between the Neutral categories of both groups. While only 15.5 percent of the studies of the U.S. group fall into this category, 38.5 percent of the non-U.S studies do. This discrepancy might be a function of methodology, and the possibility of consistent error or bias in either group cannot be ruled out. This area, then, requires further study, ideally of a multinational nature. At the very least it is necessary to explore whether North Americans are more sensitive to television violence or whether a different kind of violence is aired on the networks of other nations. In closing this discussion, it is important to note that Americans are definitely exposed to more violent TV than any other peoples (Gurevitch, 1972) and this could explain why the findings are more positive in the U.S. than in other countries.

Measure of Aggression Employed

Next we come to the question of whether or not a particular measure of violence will bias the results of specific studies. Table 6 shows that this is a distinct possibility. A measure such as degree of shocks is seen to yield consistent, more highly positive skewed results in contrast to the overt physical aggression or questionnaire measures. Of course, we must ask does the degree of shock operationalization overestimate the true relationship or does it more accurately measure the correlation between watching violence and subsequent aggression? In answering we note that the degree of shock technique is perhaps the most scientifically rigorous measurement tool that has been applied to the study of the effect of

Table 5. Results by Country in Percent

| Country | Results | | | | | N | Study Numbers (see Appendix) |
	WN	None	NP	MP	SP		
U.S.A.	5.2	15.5	37.9	37.9	3.4	60	1,2,6,7,8,9,11,12, 13,14,15,17-28, 30a-35,38,40-63, 66,67
All reported countries other than the U.S.A.	0	38.5	30.8	23.1	7.7	13	3,4,5,10,16a,16b, 29,36,37,39,56,64, 65

Table 6. Summary of Results by Measure Utilized in Percent*

| Measures | Results | | | | | N | Study Numbers (see Appendix) |
	WN	None	WP	MP	SP		
Overt physical aggression	0	10	55	25	10	19	1,4,7,11,12,17,25, 27,32,33,34,35,37, 42,55,56,59,64,67
Questionnaire	3.6	35.7	32.1	28.6	0	29	2,3,5,9,13,14,19, 26,28,29,30a,31, 35,36,41,45,48, 49a,49b,49c,51, 52,53,54,58,60, 61a,61b,66
Degree of shocks	9	0	22.2	66.7	11.1	9	10,16a,16b,18,19, 22,23,24,38
Parental or peer rating	0	28.6	42.8	28.6	0	7	15,30a,31,32,35, 47,53
Verbal aggression	0	33.3	16.7	33.3	16.7	6	8,43,44,58,62a, 62b
Other	14.2	14.2	35.8	35.8	0	14	3,6,20,21,30b,39,40, 46, 47, 50, 57, 60, 63,65

* Note that several studies use more than one measure and are therefore included more than once in the table.

watching violent television. This fact leads us to tentatively accepting these studies' findings as more valid than others applying various different types of measurement techniques. However, this assumption may prove to be unfounded as future studies and analyses delve more thoroughly into this problem.

Research Methods Employed

The summary in Table 7 indicates that there are definite differences in the results that various research methods yield. We can see the Laboratory Experiments are more positive than are the two Field methods. Perhaps this is because the laboratory setting is so far removed from reality that it biases the results. This has been argued by several researchers in the field we are exploring (e.g., Hoyt, 1967; Kniveton, 1974) and several have tried to put the "values" of real life into their laboratory experiments; this has resulted in a shift of their findings toward the Neutral category (Bandura, 1963; Lefcourt et al., 1966; etc.). On the other hand, we could just as easily state that the Field methods were not rigorous enough and therefore underestimate the relationship. This argument, however, was not found in the literature. It is essential to note the lesson that Table 7 teaches us, that even a methodology of research can, and does, affect the findings of a study quite substantially. This only reaffirms the argument for using the cumulative research strategy.

Conclusions

Although there do exist several problems with the results cumulated, it seems quite clear that according to the findings of the studies collected there is at least a weak positive relationship between watching violence on television and the subsequent aggression displayed by viewers of that violence. In light of these findings, one would assume that the violence aired on television requires some curtailment, at least until the time that a definite conclusion is reached. Relatively new to the social scene, television and its effects have not really been fully understood. Only now are we able to see what effects growing up with TV have on the mature adult, because only very recently are the children who have known television all their lives starting to have their own families. We have seen that television violence may increase the level of aggression in the viewers of that violence. What we do not know is whether or not its effects are cumulative (e.g. parents developing more lax values on the desirability of nonviolence) or if there are deaths and violence occurring in society today because of what is being shown on the TV screen.

We can conclude on the basis of the present data cumulation that television, as it is shown today, probably does stimulate a higher amount of aggression in individuals within society. Therefore, it seems reasonable to tentatively accept the "TV violence as a stimulant to aggression" theory and to reject the "no-difference" and "cathartic" theories, at least until further, contradictory study is completed concerning this matter.

Table 7. Summary of Results of Studies Employing Specific Research Methods by Percent

| Study Type | Results | | | | | N | Study Numbers (see Appendix) |
	WN	None	WP	MP	SP		
Laboratory experiment	6.5	6.5	32.3	51.6	3.2	31	6,8,10,12,13,14, 16a,16b,17,18, 19,20,21,22,23, 24,26,33,38,40. 45,49a,49b,49c. 50,56,57,58,59, 63,67
Field experiment	4.5	22.7	40.9	18.2	13.6	22	1,2,5,7,11,25,27, 32,34,35,37,42,43, 44,47,48,51,55,60, 62a,62b,64
Field survey	0	30	45	25	0	20	3,4,9,15,28,29,30a, 30b,31,36,39,41, 46,52,53,54,61a, 61b,65,66

Appendix

Summation of Studies and Their Results Concerned with the Relationship Between the Viewing of Violence and Subsequent Aggressive Behavior (by Date)

Study and Year	N	Age of Subjects	Country of Study	Strength and Direction of Relationship					Measuring Techniques and Study Type	
				WN	Zero	WP	MP	SP	Measurement	Study Type
Siegel,[1] 1956	24	4 & 5	U.S.A.				X		Observed overt aggression	Field experiment
Albert,[2] 1957	220	8 & 9	U.S.A.	X					Answers to questionnaire	Field experiment
Himmelweit,[3] 1958	1,854	10-11 & 13-14	England		X				Diary and questionnaire	Field survey
Rudolf,[4] 1958	39	up to 15	England					X	Observed behavior	Field survey
Emery,[5] 1959	43	10-13	Australia	X					Questionnaire	Field experiment
Feshbach,[6] 1961	101	College age	U.S.A.	X					Word assoc'n test	Laboratory experiment
Lövaas,[7] 1961	20	Preschool	U.S.A.				X		Observed overt aggression	Field experiment
Mussen,[8] 1961	36	6 & 7	U.S.A.					X	Verbal aggression	Field experiment
Schramm,[9] 1961	1,708	11 & 15	U.S.A.	X					Questionnaire	Field survey
Walters,[10] 1962	28	Adults	Canada					X	Degree of shocks given	Laboratory experiment
Bandura,[11] 1963	96	3-6	U.S.A.					X	Observed overt aggression	Field experiment
Bandura,[12] 1963	80	3-5	U.S.A.				X		Observed overt aggression	Laboratory experiment
Berkowitz,[13] 1963	90	College age	U.S.A.		X				Questionnaire	Laboratory experiment
Berkowitz,[14] 1963	160	College age	U.S.A.		X				Questionnaire	Laboratory experiment
Eron,[15] 1963	1,211	Children	U.S.A.		X				Parental and peer ratings of aggression	Field survey
Walters,[16] 1963a	24	Average 15	Canada					X	Intensity of shocks given	Laboratory experiment
Walters,[16] 1963b	32	Median 20	Canada				X		Intensity of shocks given	Laboratory experiment
Bandura,[17] 1965	66	4-6	U.S.A.				X		Observed overt aggression	Laboratory experiment
Hartmann,[18] 1965	72	13-16	U.S.A.				X		Intensity of aggression	Laboratory experiment
Berkowitz,[19] 1966	88	College age	U.S.A.				X		Questionnaire and intensity of shocks	Laboratory experiment
Lefcourt,[20] 1966	40	College age	U.S.A.				X		Aggression content of drawings	Laboratory experiment
Meyerson,[21] 1966	90	8	U.S.A.				X		Aggressive performance	Laboratory experiment
Berkowitz,[22] 1967	90	College age	U.S.A.				X		Duration of shocks given	Laboratory experiment
Geen,[23] 1967	108	College age	U.S.A.				X		Intensity of shocks given	Laboratory experiment
Geen,[24] 1968	120	College age	U.S.A.		X				Number of shocks given	Laboratory experiment
Walters,[25] 1968	48	Children	U.S.A.		X				Observed overt aggression	Field experiment
Goranson,[26] 1969	?	College age	U.S.A.	X					Questionnaire	Laboratory experiment
Hanratty,[27] 1969	20	4 & 5	U.S.A.					X	Observed overt aggression	Field experiment
Dominick,[28] 1970	434	9-11	U.S.A.	X					Questionnaire	Field survey
Jones,[29] 1970	228	11,13 & 14	Australia		X				Questionnaire	Field survey
Atkin,[30] 1971 a	473	teens	U.S.A.					X	Questionnaire and interviews with mothers	Field survey
Atkin,[30] 1971 b	151	Adolescents	U.S.A.		X				Self-reports	Field survey

Appendix (Continued)

Study and Year	N	Age of Subjects	Country of Study	WN	Zero	WP	MP	SP	Measurement	Study Type
Benson,[31] 1971	229	11	U.S.A.	X					Questionnaire and rating by teachers	Field survey
Cameron,[32] 1971	254	5	U.S.A.			X			Observed overt aggression and parental rating	Field experiment
Dubanoski,[33] 1971	20	Average 4½	U.S.A.			X			Observed overt aggression	Laboratory experiment
Fechter,[34] 1971	40	?	U.S.A.			X			Observed overt aggression	Field experiment
Feshbach,[35] 1971	395	13-17	U.S.A.	X					Questionnaire Peer rating Observed behavior	Field experiment
Furu,[36] 1971	1,000	15	Japan	X					Questionnaire	Field survey
Heinrich,[37] 1971	2,000	12-16	Germany			X			Observed overt aggression	Field experiment
Johnson,[38] 1971	100	?	U.S.A.			X			Intensity of shocks given	Laboratory experiment
Noble,[39] 1971	74	12-15	England	X					Ability to gauge violence	Field survey
Osborn,[40] 1971	25	4 & 5	U.S.A.					X	Galvanic skin response	Laboratory experiment
Pagel,[41] 1971	442	10 & 11	U.S.A.					X	Questionnaire	Field survey
Steuer,[42] 1971	10	3½-5	U.S.A.					X	Observed overt aggression	Field experiment
Thomas,[43] 1971	143	5½-8½	U.S.A.	X					Verbal aggression	Field experiment
Wotring,[44] 1971	234	12-14	U.S.A.	X					Verbal aggression	Field experiment
Collins,[45] 1972	143	?	U.S.A.					X	Questionnaire	Laboratory experiment
Dominick,[46] 1972	838	9–11	U.S.A.					X	Willingness to be aggressive	Field survey
Eron,[47] 1972	427	Time 1: 8 Time 2: 18	U.S.A.				X		Self-report Peer ratings	Longitudinal field experiment
Feshbach,[48] 1972	129	9-11	U.S.A.	X					Questionnaire	Field experiment
Leifer,[49] 1972 a	271	5-17	U.S.A.					X	Questionnaire	Laboratory experiment
Leifer,[49] 1972 b	132	Preschool, 10, 17	U.S.A.	X					Questionnaire,	Laboratory experiment
Leifer,[49] 1972 c	160	School age	U.S.A.				X		Questionnaire	Laboratory experiment
Liebert,[50] 1972	136	5-9	U.S.A.					X	Willingness to be aggressive	Laboratory experiment
Liebert,[51] 1972	184	Time 1: 8 Time 2: 18	U.S.A.					X	Questionnaire	Longitudinal field experiment
McIntyre,[52] 1972	2,270	12-17	U.S.A.				X		Questionnaire	Field survey
McLeod,[53] 1972	624	Teens	U.S.A.					X	Questionnaire Peer ratings Parent and teacher ratings	Field survey
Robinson,[54] 1972	1,559	Average 19	U.S.A.				X		Questionnaire	Field survey
Stein,[55] 1972	97	3 & 4	U.S.A.					X	Observed overt aggression	Field experiment
Stoessel,[56] 1972	?	3-6	Canada				X		Observed overt aggression	Laboratory experiment
Thomas,[57] 1972	143	5½ & 8½	U.S.A.	X					Intensity of noise punishment given	Laboratory experiment
Collins,[58] 1973	206	8, 11, & 15	U.S.A.				X		Questionnaire Verbal aggression	Laboratory experiment
Friedrich,[59] 1973	97	4-5½	U.S.A.				X		Observed overt aggression	Laboratory experiment
Menzies,[60] 1973	54	18-26	U.S.A.				X		Questionnaire Aggression test	Field experiment
Watt,[61] 1973 a	147	13-17	U.S.A.				X		Questionnaire	Field survey

Appendix (Continued)

Study and Year	N	Age of Subjects	Country of Study	WN	Zero	WP	MP	SP	Measurement	Study Type
Watt,[61] 1973 b	450	13-17	U.S.A.			X			Questionnaire	Field survey
Wotring,[62] 1973 a	242	12-14	U.S.A.				X		Verbal aggression	Field experiment
Wotring,[62] 1973 b	169	9-11	U.S.A.					X	Verbal aggression	Field experiment
Broncato,[63] 1974	60	3 & 4	U.S.A.			X			Aggression tests	Laboratory experiment
Kniveton,[64] 1974	96	?	England	X					Observed overt aggression	Field experiment
Greenberg,[65] 1975	726	9, 12, & 15	England			X			Willingness to be aggressive	Field survey
Hartnagel,[66] 1975	2,128	13-17	U.S.A.			X			Questionnaire	Field survey
Lieberman,[67] 1976	10,000	8-13	U.S.A.			X			Overt aggressive act	Laboratory experiment

NOTE: For two studies the N is unknown, and for four the age of subjects is unknown. Of the 67 studies, several presented more than one set of independent data. Complete bibliographical data for the 67 studies follows the table.

Footnotes to Appendix

[1] A. E. Siegel, "Film-mediated fantasy aggression and strength of aggressive drive." Child Development 27(3), 1956:365-378.

[2] R. S. Albert, "The role of the mass media and the effect of aggressive film content upon children's aggressive responses and identification choices." Genetic Psychological Monographs 55, 1957:221-285.

[3] H. Himmelweit, A. N. Oppenheim, and P. Vince, Television and the Child: An Empirical Study of Television Viewing on the Young. New York: Oxford University Press, 1958.

[4] G. de M. Rudolf, "The effect of children's TV on behavior." Mental Health 17, 1958:55-60.

[5] F. E. Emery, "Psychological effects of the western film: a study in television viewing. II—The experimental study." Human Relations 12(3), 1959:215-232.

[6] S. Feshback, "The stimulating versus cathartic effects of a vicarious aggressive activity." Journal of Abnormal and Social Psychology 63(2), 1961:381-385.

[7] O. I. Lovaas, "Effects of exposure to symbolic aggression on aggressive behavior." Child Development 32, 1961:37-44.

[8] P. Mussen and E. Rutherford, "Effects of aggressive cartoons on children's aggressive play." Journal of Abnormal Social Psychology 62(2), 1961:461-464.

[9] W. Schramm, J. Lyle, and E. B. Parker, Television in the Lives of our Children. Stanford: Stanford University Press, 1961.

[10] R. H. Walters, E. L. Thomas, and C. W. Acker, "Enhancement of punitive behavior by audio-visual displays." Science 136, 1962:872-873.

[11] A. Bandura, D. Ross, and S. A. Ross, "Imitation of film-mediated aggressive models." Journal of Abnormal and Social Psychology 66(1), 1963:3-11.

[12] A. Bandura, D. Ross, and S. A. Ross, "Vicarious reinforcement and imitative learning," Journal of Abnormal and Social Psychology 67(6), 1963:601-607.

[13] L. Berkowitz. "Film violence and subsequent aggressive tendencies," Public Opinion Quarterly 27, 1963:217-229.

[14] L. Berkowitz and E. Rawlings. "Effects of film violence on inhibitions against subsequent aggression." Journal of Abnormal and Social Psychology 66(5), 1963:405-412.

[15] L. D. Eron, "Relationship of television viewing habits and aggressive behavior in children." Journal of Abnormal and Social Psychology 67(2), 1963:193-196.

[16] R. H. Walters and E. L. Thomas, "Enhancement of punitiveness by visual and audio-visual display." Canadian Journal of Psychology 17(2), 1963:244-255.

[17] A. Bandura, "Influence of model's reinforcement contingencies on the acquisition of imitative responses." Journal of Personality and Social Psychology 1(6), 1965:589-595.

[18] D. Hartmann, "The influence of symbolically modeled instrumental aggression and pain cues on the disinhibition of aggressive behavior." Stanford University: Unpublished Doctoral Dissertation, 1965.

[19] L. Berkowitz and R. G. Green. "Film violence and the cue properties of available targets." Journal of Personality and Social Psychology 3(5), 1966:525-530.

[20] H. M. Lefcourt, K. Barnes, R. Parke, and F. Schwartz, "Anticipated social censure and aggression-conflict as mediators of response to aggression induction." Journal of Social Psychology 70, 1966:251-263.

[21] L. J. Meyerson, The Effects of Filmed Aggression on the Aggressive Responses of High and Low Aggressive Subjects. University of Iowa: Doctoral Dissertation, 1966.

[22] L. Berkowitz and R. G. Geen. "Stimulus qualities of the target of aggression." Journal of Personality and Social Psychology 5, 1967:364-368.

[23] R. G. Geen and L. Berkowitz. "Some conditions facilitating the occurrence of aggression after the observation of violence." Journal of Personality 35, 1967:666-676.

[24] R. G. Geen. "Effects of frustration, attack and prior training of aggressiveness upon aggressive behavior." Journal of Personality and Social Psychology 9(4), 1968:316-321.

[25] R. H. Walters and D. C. Willows, "Imitative behavior of disturbed and non-disturbed children following exposure to aggressive and non-aggressive models." Child Development 39(1), 1968:79-89.

[26] R. Goranson, "Observed violence and aggressive behavior: the effects of negative outcomes of observed violence." University of Wisconsin: Unpublished Doctoral Dissertation, 1969.

[27] M. A. Hanratty, R. M. Liebert, L. W. Morris, and L. E. Fernandez, "Imitation of film-mediated aggression against live and inanimate victims." Proceedings of the 77th Annual Convention of the American Psychology Association 4, 1969:457-458.

[28] J. R. Dominick, Jr. The Influence of Social Class, the Family and Exposure to TV Violence on the Socialization of Aggression. Michigan State University: Doctoral Dissertation, 1970.

[29] M. J. Jones, "The effect on television on the socialization of children in Brisbane, Australia," University of Victoria: Unpublished M.A. Thesis, 1970.

[30] C. K. "The relationship between violence viewing patterns and aggressive behavior in two samples of adolescents." University of Wisconsin: Unpublished M.A. Dissertation, 1971.

[31] D. Benson, An Exploration of the Relationship Between TV Habits, Preferences and Aggression in 6th Grade Boys. University of Maryland, 1971.

[32] P. Cameron and C. Janky, "Effects of TV violence on children: a naturalistic experiment." Proceedings of the 79th Annual Convention of the American Psychological Association 6, 1971:233-234.

[33] R. A. Dubanoski and D. A. Parton, "Imitative aggression in children as a function of observing a human model." Developmental Psychology 4(4), 1971:489.

[34] J. V. Fechter, "Modelling and environmental generalization by mentally retarded subjects of televised aggressive or friendly behaviour." American Journal of Mental Deficiency 76(2), 1971:266-267.

[35] S. Feshback and R. D. Singer, Television and Aggression. San Francisco: Jossey-Bass, Inc., 1971.

[36] T. Furu, The Function of Television for Children and Adolescents. Tokyo: Monumenta Nipponica, 1971.

[37] K. Heinrich, "The influence of films of aggression on youngsters." Page 49 in J. L. Singer (ed.), The Control of Aggression and Violence. New York: Academic Press, 1971.

[38] R. C. Johnson, "Seldom tested variables in the effects of televised violence on aggressive behavior." Ohio University: Unpublished Doctoral Dissertation, 1971.

[39] G. Noble, "Discrimination between different forms of televised aggression by delinquent and non-delinquent boys." British Journal of Criminology 11(3), 1971:230-244.

[40] D. K. Osborn and R. C. Endsley, "Emotional reactions of young children to TV violence." Child Development 42, 1971:321-331.

[41] T. F. Pagel, "Choice of violence: a study of values, TV viewing habits and selected socio-psychological characteristics." University of Denver: Unpublished Doctoral Dissertation, 1971.

[42] F. B. Steuer, J. M. Applefield, and R. Smith, "Televised aggression and the inter-

personal aggression of preschool children." Journal of Experimental Child Psychology 11, 1971:442-227.

[43] S. A. W. Thomas, "The role of cognitive style variables in mediating the influence of aggressive TV upon elementary school children." U.C.L.A.: Unpublished Doctoral Dissertation, 1971.

[44] C. E. Wotring, "The effects of exposure to TV violence on adolescent's verbal aggression." Michigan State University: Unpublished Doctoral Dissertation, 1971.

[45] W. A. Collins, "The effect of viewing TV violence with positive versus negative consequences." In G. A. Comstock and E. A. Rubinstein (eds.), Television and Social Behavior-Volume 2, TV and Social Learning. Washington, D.C.: National Institute of Mental Health, 1972.

[46] J. R. Dominick and B. X. Greenberg, "Attitudes toward violence: the interaction of T.V. exposure, family attitudes and social class," in Comstock and Rubinstein (eds.), Television and Social Behavior—Volume 3, TV and Adolescent Aggressiveness. Washington, D.C.: NIMH, 1972.

[47] L. D. Eron, M. M. Lefkowitz, L. R. Huesmann, and L. O. Walder, "Does television violence cause aggression." American Psychologist 27(4), 1972:253-263.

[48] S. Feshbach, "Reality and fantasy in filmed violence." In Comstock and Rubinstein (eds.), Television and Social Behavior—Volume 2. Washington, D.C.: NIMH, 1972.

[49] A. D. Leifer and D. F. Roberts, "Children's responses to television violence." In Comstock and Rubinstein (eds.), TV and Social Behavior—Volume 2. Washington, D.C.: NIMH, 1972.

[50] R. M. Liebert and R. A. Baron, "Short-term effects of televised aggression on children's aggressive behavior." In Comstock and Rubinstein (eds.), TV and Social Behavior—Volume 2. Washington, D.C.: NIMH, 1972.

[51] R. M. Liebert and J. M. Neal, "Television and violence." Current 141, 1972:15-18.

[52] J. J. McIntyre and J. J. Teevan. "Televised and deviant behavior." In Comstock and Rubinstein (eds.), TV and Social Behavior—Volume 3. Washington, D.C.: NIMH, 1972.

[53] J. M. McLeod and S. H. Chaffee, "Adolescents, parents and TV use: adolescent self-report measures from Maryland and Wisconsin samples." In Comstock and Rubinstein (eds.), TV and Social Behavior—Volume 3. Washington, D.C.: NIMH, 1972.

[54] P. R. Robinson and J. G. Backman, "Television viewing habits and aggression." In Comstock and Rubinstein (eds.), TV and Social Behavior—Volume 3. Washington, D.C.: NIMH, 1972.

[55] A. H. Stein and L. K. Friedrick (with F. Vondracek), "TV content and young children's behavior." In Comstock and Rubinstein (eds.), TV and Social Behavior—Volume 2. Washington, D.C.: NIMH, 1972.

[56] R. E. Stoessel, "The effects of aggressive cartoons on children's aggressive behavior." St. John University: Unpublished Doctoral Dissertation, 1972.

[57] S. A. Thomas, "Violent content in TV: effect of cognitive style and age in mediating children's aggressive responses." Proceedings of the 80th Annual Convention of the American Psychological Association 7(1), 1972:97-98.

[58] W. A. Collins, "Effect of temporal separation between motivation, aggression and consequences." Developmental Psychology 8, 1973:215-221.

[59] L. K. Friedrich and A. H. Stein, "Aggressive and pro-social TV programs and the natural behavior of pre-school children." Monographs of the Society for Research in Child Development 38(4), 1973:1-64.

[60] E. S. Menzies, "The effects of repeated exposure to televised violence upon the attitudes towards violence of youthful offenders." Florida State University: Unpublished Doctoral Dissertation, 1973.

[61] J. R. Watt, Jr., "TV viewing and aggression: an examination of the catharsis, facilitation and arousal models." University of Wisconsin: Unpublished Doctoral Dissertation, 1973.

[62] C. E. Wotring and B. S. Greenberg, "Experiments in televised violence and verbal aggression: two exploratory studies." Journal of Communication 23 (December), 1973:466-60.

[63] J. S. Broncato, Jr., "Effects on the aggression of Spanish speaking pre-school children by deliberately contrived television models of violence." Northern Illinois University: Unpublished Doctoral Dissertation, 1974.

[64] B. H. Kniveton, "The very young and television Violence." Journal of Psychosomatic Research 18, 1974:233-237.

[65] B. S. Greenberg, "British children and television violence." Public Opinion Quarterly 38, 1974-5:531-547.

[66] T. F. Hartnagel, J. Teevan, and J. McIntyre, "Television violence and violent behavior." Social Forces 4(2), 1975:341-351.

[67] S. Lieberman, "Television triggers aggression." The Vancouver Sun, 19 March 1976:36.

References

Arnold, A.
1969 Violence and Your Child. New York: Macmillan.

Baldwin, J. F., and C. Lewis
1972 "Violence on TV: the industry looks at itself," in G. A. Comstock and E. A. Rubinstein (eds.), Television and Social Behavior, Vol. 1: Media Content and Control. Washington, D.C.: National Institute of Mental Health.

Bandura, A., D. Ross, and S. A. Ross
1963 "Imitation of film mediated aggressive models." Journal of Abnormal and Social Psychology 2:3-11.

Broncato, J. S.
1974 "Effects on the aggression of Spanish speaking preschool children by deliberately contrived televised models of violence." Northern Illinois University: Unpublished Doctoral Dissertation.

Cater, D., and S. Strickland
1975 TV Violence and the Child. New York: Russel Sage Foundation.

Charters, W. W.
1933 Motion Pictures and Youth. New York: Macmillan.

Clarke, D., and W. Blankenburg
1972 "Trends in violent content in selected mass media." In G. A. Comstock and E. A. Rubinstein (eds.), TV and Social Behavior—Volume 1, Media Content and Control. Washington, D.C.: Government Printing Office.

Dubin, R., and T. C. Taveggia
1968 The Teaching-Learning Paradox: A Comparative Analysis of College Teaching Methods. Eugene, Oregon: Center for the Advanced Study of Educational Administration.

Dysinger, W. S., and C. A. Ruckmick
1933 Emotional Responses of Children to the Motion Picture Situation. New Haven: Yale University Press.

Feldman, K. A.
1971 "Using the work of others: some observations on reviewing and integrating." Sociology of Education 44:86-102.

Feshback, S.
1955 "The drive reducing function of fantasy behavior." Journal of Abnormal and Social Psychology 50:3-11.

Freese, L.
1972 "Cumulative sociological knowledge." American Sociological Review 37:472-482.

Gerbner, G.
1972 "The structure of TV program content in the U.S." In G. A. Comstock and E. A. Rubinstein (eds.), TV and Social Behavior—Volume 1. Washington, D.C.: NIMH, Government Printing Office.

Glaser, B. G.
  1962 "Secondary analysis: a strategy for the use of knowledge from research elsewhere." Social Problems 10:70-74.
  1963 "Retreading research materials: the use of secondary analysis by the independent researcher." American Behavioral Scientist 6:11-14.
Gurevitch, M.
  1972 "The structure and content of television broadcasting in four countries: an overview." In G. A. Comstock and E. A. Rubinstein (eds.), TV and Social Behavior-Volume 1. Washington, D.C.: Government Printing Office.
Hanratty, M. A., R. M. Liebert, L. W. Morris, and L. E. Fernandez
  1969 "Imitation of film-mediated aggression against live and inanimate victims." Proceedings of the 77th Annual Convention of the American Psychological Association 4:457-458.
Himmelweit, H., A. N. Oppenheim, and P. Vince
  1958 Television and the Child: An Empirical Study of Television Viewing on the Young. New York: Oxford University Press.
Hoyt, J.
  1967 "Vengeance and self-defense as justification for filmed aggression." University of Wisconsin: Unpublished Master's Thesis.
Hyman, H.
  1972 Secondary Analysis of Sample Surveys: Principles, Procedures and Potentialities. New York: John Wiley.
Klapper, J. T.
  1949 The Effect of Mass Media. New York: Bureau of Applied Social Research.
Kniveton, B. H.
  1974 "The very young and television violence." Journal of Psychosomatic Research 18:233-237.
Lefcourt, H. M., K. Barnes, P. Parke, and F. Schwartz
  1966 "Anticipated social censure and aggression-conflict as mediators of response to aggression induction." Journal of Social Psychology 70:251-263.
Morris, N. S.
  1971 Television's Child. Boston: Little Brown.
National Commission on the Causes and Prevention of Violence
  1970 "Violence in television entertainment programs," in To Establish Justice, To Insure Domestic Tranquility. New York: Praeger.
Peterson, R. C., and L. L. Thurstone
  1933 Motion Pictures and the Social Attitudes of Children. New York: Macmillan.
Taveggia, R. C.
  1974 "Resolving research controversy through empirical cumulation." Sociological Methods and Research 2:395-407.
Thomas, S. A.
  1972 "Violent content in TV: effect of cognitive style and age in mediating children's aggressive responses." Proceedings of the American Psychological Association's 80th Annual Convention 7:97-98.
Walters, R. H., and D. C. Willows
  1968 "Imitative behavior of disturbed and non-disturbed children following exposure to aggressive and non-aggressive models." Child Development 39:79-89.

Walters, R. H., E. L. Thomas, and C. W. Acker
    1962 "Enhancement of punitive behavior by audio-visual displays." Science
          136:872-873.
Wotring, C. E., and B. X. Greenberg
    1973 "Experiments in televised violence and verbal aggression: two explor-
          atory studies." The Journal of Communication 23:446-460.

The impact of external, social-psychological forces upon research on pornography and media violence is argued in this piece by Thelma McCormack. She points out that most of the research in both areas is only incidentally related to media, and that it contains little communication or social theory. She suggests that the use of a conflict model and reference group theory would show the effects of violence and pornography require social rather than biological explanations. Dr. McCormack is a sociologist at York University, Ontario, Canada.

573

33

MACHISMO IN MEDIA RESEARCH
A Critical Review of Research on
Violence and Pornography

Thelma McCormack

I

Social critics of the mass media of communication have provided abundant documentation of sex biases, stereotypes, and invidious images and themes in our popular culture, but almost no attention has been given to the biases in media research. In the comments that follow, two areas of media research are examined, pornography and violence, drawing on three major investigations: The National Commission on the Causes and Prevention of Violence (1969), the Commission on Obscenity and Pornography (1970) and the Surgeon General's Report on Television and Social Behavior (1972). These reports were selected because they are frequently cited in discussions of social policy and in cases involving censorship, but also because they deal with issues central to the reconstruction of knowledge from a non-sexist perspective. Sexuality and aggression, separately or together, are among the first premises of any social theory.

Currently, the Woman's Movement has become more interested in pornography and more critical of research on the subject (Brownmiller, 1975; Russell, 1977) which supports the view that the effects of pornography are largely innocuous and that censorship is therefore unnecessary and undesirable. One objection commonly made about the studies of pornography is that they do not consider sado-masochistic pornography presenting violence as essential to sexual arousal and satisfaction.

The two violence Commissions similarly avoided this conjunction of violence and sex, but arrived at different conclusions about the social effects of media violence and the desirability of censorship. Censorship in some form was indicated, and subsequent discussions of media violence have accepted the view that media violence leads to anti-social behavior (LaMarsh, 1977).

At the time the contradition between these two sets, pornography and violence, went largely unnoticed. Wills (1977) recently revived and commented on it, accounting for the oversight in terms of a "liberal" perspective which is soft on sexual expression but hard on aggression. Wills attempts to resolve the contradiction by aligning the pornography research with the violence research; he is more critical of the former. Whether he is correct in the direction of realignment is problematic, but he is on firm ground in calling attention to the inconsistency and in expecting that these two sets of findings should point in the same direction.

Our concern is two-fold: to examine each set of research for bias, and to explore the contradiction. Both sets of research show sexist biases in the way the problems were conceptualized and the research designed. An alternative framework for future studies is discussed. Finally, we look at the contradiction as a social fact and suggest that its logic is basically a syndrome of machismo. Although this argument is speculative, it shows the need for studies of machismo

From Thelma McCormack, "Machismo in Media Research: A Critical Review of Research on Violence and Pornography," *Social Problems* 25, 5 (June 1978) 544-555. Reprinted by permission of the Society for the Study of Social Problems.

as a complex phenomenon analogous to the F scale, in incorporating manifestly contradictory attitudes.

The term "sexism" here refers to attitudes and social practices based on the assumption that sexual inequality is a natural, biological, universal phenomenon rather than a social and historical one. This assumption supports a sexual division of labor and a wide range of discriminatory legal, political, and economic practices, policies, and traditions.

Machismo refers to an attitude of male pride in sexual virility, a form of narcissism that condones the sexual use and abuse of women, and, in the extreme, violence as a dimension of sexual gratification or instrumental to sexual goals. Like sexism, machismo is not uniform. It varies in intensity and salience among individuals, cultural groups, and larger social collectivities. While sexism tends to be institutional, a form of structural inequity linked to the discrimination against other disadvantaged groups, machismo tends to be motivational and related specifically to sexual relationships.

II

The catharsis hypothesis. Studies of pornography and studies of media violence have been dominated by controversies over the catharsis hypothesis. More Freudian than Freud, who never used the term catharsis, the hypothesis is usually attributed to him because of his theories of dreams, of wit and fantasy, and of sexuality.

According to the catharsis hypothesis, fantasy, dreams and jokes reveal our tabooed wishes which are, in turn, based on instincts sublimated for the sake of peace and social order. Jokes, for example, constitute a safety valve, reducing the tension created by the imperfectly sublimated anti-social forces in the psyche. Art, literature, religion, ideologies, and other symbolic systems have a similar function by providing vicarious experience. By defusing these volatile forces, they avert the possible destructive outcomes. One way or another, through our own projected fantasies or those presented to us through the media, the delicate balance of our inner psychic economy is maintained. We are saved the pain of neurosis. Indirectly, the equilibrium of the social order is maintained as the sources of subversion are temporarily displaced or dissipated. It is this simplified version of the catharsis hypothesis that social psychologists working in the fields of media violence and pornography have tested, using the most rigorous experimental methods possible.

The assumption that anti-social behavior has its origins in human nature, regardless of any institutional arrangements, is not, of course, confined to Freudian thought. It is logically possible to reject the catharsis hypothesis and retain the assumption, as many conservative thinkers, past and present, have done. But alone, the assumption suggests that children should be shielded from experiences that might elicit feelings of hostility, for example, rather than learning to manage these feelings. Strict surveillance and censorship are necessary to save us from ourselves.

The second assumption is that the reduction of one's drives is socially desirable. "The dominating tendency of mental life, and perhaps of nervous life in general," Freud wrote "is the effort to reduce, to keep constant or to remove internal tension" (1967; 95). And this, too, is politically divisive. Consider Sorel and, more recently, Fanon who argued that the mental health of the oppressed is harmed by apathy and submission, that the wretched of the earth would benefit emotionally from experiences, however abortive pragmatically, that would raise their levels of aggression. The first assumption separates civil libertarians and their opposite numbers; the second differentiates political "left" and "right."

But the third assumption is particularly relevant here. It postulates that men have a different sexual nature from women, that in men (a) sex and aggression are linked; and (b) that men have more difficulty than women in controlling their sexual and aggressive drives. Nature, which made women both powerless and sexually passive, has spared them the need to cope with hostile impulses or erotic energies too great to be satisfied. That is the problem of men, and men constitute the crucial test of the theory.

Evidence: pro and con. Studies of media violence have, by and large, failed to support the catharis hypothesis (Goranson, 1970; Tannenbaum, 1968). A large number of studies indicate that exposure to media violence through the mass media increases tension, and predisposes subjects to aggressive behavior. No one has established a direct, causal connection between media violence and the types or frequencies of violence in real life. Still, the burden of proof has shifted to those who claim there is no connection (Bogart, 1972-73.)

The position that media violence increases the likelihood of normal people engaging in acts of violence is based on a stimulus response model of behavior associated with the work of Leonard Berkowitz on aggression (1962, 1969). Throughout his career, Berkowitz has been more interested in the nature of aggression than in the mass media, and it has been more by chance than design that he used examples from the media in his experiments. Nevertheless, his work is continually cited in discussions of the media as demonstrating strong evidence against the catharsis hypothesis and for the view that exposure to media violence increases aggression and ipso facto, violence.

Supporting the direction of Berkowitz's findings, but based on a different theory, modelling, Bandura and associates demonstrate that we learn patterns of violence from role models in the media (Bandura et. al. 1963). It is not necessary to be frustrated or angry to become highly or irrationally aggressive, for these behavioral predispositions are acquired just as we learn other social habits from examples around us. Like other habits they are absorbed into our permanent repertoire of responses. They can be activated without apparent cause or obvious provocation, just by the presence of subtle, forgotten cues in a situation.

Like Berkowitz's work, Bandura's is more a theory of aggression than of communication; its contribution lies in showing that aggressive behavior is cultural not instinctive. It has had considerable influence in the debates on media violence, particularly the impact of media violence on children.

A third perspective is illustrated by the work of George Gerbner (1974) and is based on content analyses of TV programs and studies of media exposure. Gerbner argues that it is not violence *per se* that is undesirable, but the messages that accompany it. Whether or not people are aroused by media violence as Berkowitz contends, or imitate it as Bandura claims, the programs alter our consciousness by legitimating violence and victimization. The damage is ideological, especially since the excesses of violence are often on the side of the law, the end justifying the means. Repeated exposure to these socio-political messages throughout our lives creates a view of reality as dangerous to the citizen, who becomes increasingly dependent on an authority given extra-legal means to protect the community. Although Gerbner is not able to prove his case—and it may say more about the political mentality of the networks than of the audiences—his statistics of the hours children spend watching television and the number of acts of violence they observe are alarming.

Supporting the catharsis hypothesis is the work of Feshback (1955, 1961, 1969), Singer (1968), Bramel, Taub, and Blum (1968). Milgram and Shotland (1973)—while not supporting it— tend to be reassuring, for they demonstrate that despite arousal and propensities to imitate anti-social behavior there is an intervening, self-inhibiting mechanism which acts as a deterrent. Hyman (1974) suggests that children may learn sympathy from media violence, while Tannenbaum (1970) proposes that other variables present in the situation might account for the results. Several scholars (Ellis, 1974; Howitt and Dembo 1974) have questioned various aspects of the methodology. But they are, for the most part, dissenting voices. Public, as well as considerable professional, opinion is tipped in favour of the views of Berkowtiz, Bandura, and Gerbner, who caution against a permissive policy toward media violence.

Research on pornography is less systematic than research on violence. There are no guiding theories of sexuality comparable to Berkowitz's and Bandura's approaches to violence, but at the conceptual level it is like their's in that the two lines of inquiry share a common weakness, the failure to incorporate any of the literature on communications. For our purposes, the important point is that the pornography findings, based on similar methods of research, are in the opposite direction of those just discussed in connection with media violence.

Exposure to pornographic films creates a mild, short lived erotic response (Byrne and Lamberth, 1970); the sexual acts portrayed are seldom, if ever, imitated in real life (Mann, et. al. 1970). Repeated exposure to erotic stimuli results in satiation rather than increased demand (Mann, et. al. 1974), and there is no evidence that erotic messages have altered our consciousness in any way, positive or negative. On all points,—stimulus-response, modelling, and influence on social thought—the pornography research is inconsistent with the violence research. The catharsis hypothesis is not especially endorsed, but, *tant de mieux*, it has more status here than in the violence work.

Aggressive and erotic humor. One way of resolving the impasse is to examine a related literature where both violence and pornography have been studied, although incidentally to another purpose. Experimental studies of humor offer the opportunity and have the added advantage of having had a similar preoccupation with the pros and cons of the catharsis hypothesis. Indeed, it was in his analysis of wit that Freud (1938) came closest to developing the notion of catharsis. In the humor experiments subjects are aroused by using either aggressive or erotic stimuli. Following that, experimental groups are presented with hostile or erotic jokes, cartoons, or similar material. They are then asked to rate the jokes for funniness. Laughter or ratings of funniness constitute the indices of tension reduction.

Throughout the humor studies, aggressive and sexual humor are used either together or interchangeably, as related or parallel (Prerost, 1975). On the basis of this research, there is no reason to suppose that pornography and media violence are of a qualitatively different order, a notion that might explain the contradictory results.

Separate analyses of sexual (Godkewitsch, 1972) and hostile (Singer, 1968) humor also show that each can and does produce enjoyment, thus adding support for the catharsis model. However, it must be said that many of the humor psychologists are not interested in motivational theory and have been moving in other intellectual directions, for example, cognitive theory. Their findings do not refute the catharsis hypothesis, but to many psychologists the catharsis hypothesis is less parsimonious than some other.

An objection might be that humor can distort and reverse findings. It could be a mistake to rely so heavily on humor studies as a proof. If it were true that humor cancels, alters, or reverses the direction of responses to violence and pornography, the principle should be generally applicable. And it would follow that a distinction should be made, for example, between straight racist propaganda and racist humor, encouraging the latter as a matter of public policy. Implausible as it sounds, this was the position taken by Norman Lear, producer of the popular TV sitcom, "All in the Family" in defense of the bigotted Archie Bunker. Studies of the program, one in Canada and one in the U.S. (Vidmar and Rokeach, 1974) provided no support for Lear's thesis. Too many people, it seems, were laughing with Archie, not at him.

Conflict model and reference group theory. The mystery, then, of why the two sets of findings go in opposite directions remains. But the studies of racist humor are important for another reason. They have not been oriented around the catharsis hypothesis, and are not burdened with its presuppositions concerning sexuality. Instead, they draw on conflict theory—the satisfaction of seeing our enemies humiliated—and reference group theory.

A few examples will illustrate the heuristic value of the model. Jews do not find anti-semitic jokes as funny as non Jews do (Wolff et. al., 1934); blacks are less likely to find anti-Negro humor as funny as whites, although liberal whites—low on the authoritarian scale—

may find anti-negro humor more offensive than conservative blacks high on the scale (Middleton, 1959); Canadians find anti-American jokes funnier than their U.S. counterparts, who are more amused by anti-Canadian jokes (La Fave et. al. 1973); and members of each sex find jokes about the other to be funnier than about their own sex (Priest and Wilhelm, 1974). All of these studies focus on inequality, and inequality whether between two races, sexes, or nations, is presumed to be derivative of the social structure, a social rather than a biological fact. Reference group theory postulates that our perceptions of, and responses to, inequality in life or in art, are structured by our own positions in the social structure, as these are modified by our reference group identification.

III

Applying this perspective to a study of pornography would both conceptualize pornography differently and require a different type of experimental design. Pronography would be seen as an extreme form, almost a travesty, of sexual inequality in which women serve as sex objects to arouse and satisfy men and nothing more. In most pornography—omitting those forms intended for a homosexual market—women are always available, cooperative, eager to please, asking for and expecting nothing in return.

Second, the research design would require subjects of both sexes, just as similar studies of racist content would include both black and white subjects. It is, therefore, significant that the experimental research on pornography has been carried out by men using almost exclusively male subjects.

FIGURE 1

Experimental Studies of Pornography Using Adult Subjects*

Author		Subjects
Amoroso, Donald Brown, Marvin Preusse, Manfred Ware, Edward E. Pilkey, Dennis W.	(a) (b)	60 male 56 male
Byrne, Don Lambeth, John		42 married couples
Davis, Keith E. Braucht, George N.		365 male
Howard, James L. Reifler, Clifford B. Liptzin, Myron B.		32 male
Kutchinsky, Berl		72 "mostly married couples"
Mann, Jay Sidman, Jack Starr, Sheldon		85 married couples
Mosher, Donald L.	(a) (b)	194 single males 183 single females 256 male
Mosher, Donald L. Katz, Harvey		120 male
Tannenbaum, Percy H.		12 male
Katzman, Marshall		285 male

*All studies taken from Technical Reports, Vol. VIII and IX of the *Commission on Obscenity and Pornography*, U.S. Government, 1970.

The few women in these studies are primarily married women viewing pornography in the company of their husbands. Thus the findings which show that women respond to erotica similarly to men, a difference in degree rather than kind, could well be a function of marital status, the compliance of wives to the wishes and tastes of husbands or husband surrogates, the male investigators. One can only speculate on how different the results would have been if the experiments had been conducted by female psychologists using female subjects separately or in groups but with no men, and certainly not spouses, present. In the absence of such research, the literature we now have is biased through omission.

The studies listed in Figure 1 are only the experimental ones, but the Commission on Obscenity and Pornography conducted surveys of the public in which women were, of course, better represented. Commenting on the findings, the investigators expressed both surprise and pleasure in discovering how liberated women are, how far they have travelled from the Victorian stereotype of themselves as prudish and repressed. Clive Barnes (1970) in an introduction to the report draws attention to the remarkable findings about women:

> Perhaps the greatest [surprise]—perfectly evident from the findings—is that women are virtually as interested in erotica as are men.

Using a conflict model, this is tantamount to saying that Blacks are becoming broadminded enough to find some gratifications in racism. For women it may be less of an authentic liberation than a form of what Marcuse (1962) calls "repressive de-sublimiation," a sexual liberation within repressive roles.

In any event, the instruments used by the investigators perpetuate the myth of female sexual passivity. In one survey respondents were asked if they thought that exposure to pronography "makes men want to do new things with their wives." The reversal of this question in which women assume some sexual initiative was not asked. Similarly, the statement that sexual materials "lead people to lose respect for women" was not balanced with "lead people to lose respect for men" (Abelson, et. al. 1970). All things considered, the pornography research is, when examined from a conflict perspective, biased in the way we have defined sexism here.

Experimental studies of media violence have a similar pattern. Again, male investigators have, with few exceptions and excluding studies of children,[1] studied male subjects.

Whether the catharsis hypothesis is accepted or rejected, the sexist premise which assumes men have the problem remains. Alternative hypotheses do not question this assumption.

A more balanced representation of subjects might still be misleading if investigators continued to use the same media materials. In many of the experiments, the researchers use scenes from a motion picture, *Champion,* a story of a boxer; in another, a similar boxing sequence from *Body and Soul*; and in others, knife fights between men. How much credibility does this type of film have for women? We know from studies of media preferences that women have little interest in such films. Women's own experiences of violence tend to be within the household rather than in the ring or on the battlefields (Steinmetz and Straus, 1975). The most common experiences of aggression for women are between husband and wife, father and daughter; that is, cross-sexual occurences in which women do not have a sporting chance. It is interesting to note that in one study (Walters, Thomas 1963) the results were not clear when women were the subjects. The bias of the research is not corrected by merely using more

---

[1] In an unpublished manuscript and in correspondence with the author, Muriel Cantor has argued that the sexist bias can also be found in studies of children. She observes that the definition and measurements of aggression as violence exclude the verbal aggression of women; more generally, Cantor points out that the various theories of aggression used in these studies have ignored sex-role socialization.

FIGURE 2

Experimental Studies of Media Violence Using Adult Subjects[*]

Author	Type of Media Violence	Subjects
Berkowitz, Leonard Corwin, Ronald Heironimus, Mark	*Champion*	Male college students
Berkowitz, Leonard Rawlings	*Champion*	160 male and female students
Berkowitz, Leonard Geen, Russell G.		
1966	*Champion*	88 male students
1967	*Champion*	90 male students
Bramel, Dana Taub, Barry Blum, Barbara		42 male and 48 female students
Doob, Anthony N. Climie, Robert J.	Movie gunfight	40 students "both sexes
Doob, Anthony N. Kirshenbaum, Hershl	"Movie gunfight in which approxi- mately 150 people were shot and killed in 7 minutes"	40 "male and female students"
Feshbach, Seymour	4 TAT Pictures	123 students "Approximately twice as many men as women"
Feshbach, Seymour	Fight sequence in *Body and Soul*	101 male students
Geen, Russell G. Berkowitz, Leonard	*Champion*	108 male students
Geen, Russell G. O'Neal, Edgar C.	*Champion*	48 male students
Meyer, Timothy	3 minute knife fight in *From Here to Eternity* CBS Evening news	200 male students
Speisman, Joseph Lazarus, Richard Mordkoff, Arnold Davison, Les	Documentary film showing "primi- tive ritual involving a crude opera- tion called 'subincision' "	56 students 42 airline executives (sex unspecified)

Walters, Richard
Thomas, Edward
	Knife-fight scene from *Rebel Without
	a Cause*
		(a) 28 male hospital
		        attendants
		
		(b) 24 adolescent males
		
		(c) 32 females "from a
		        hostel for working girls."

Milgram, Stanley Shotland, R. Lance	*Medical Center* with variant endings	(a) 289 (89% male) (b) 488 (82% male) (c) 362 (60% male) (d) 238 unspecified

[*]Sources given in References.

female subjects if the media presentation of violence distances subjects from the start. It is a primary fact of media research that audiences must identify with subjects to be affected by them.

To summarize, by looking at the research on pornography and violence from the perspective of a conflict model and reference group theory, we can see more vividly the sexist bias in the two areas of inquiry. It starts with the catharsis hypothesis, but lingers despite the rejection of the hypothesis. Although many have questioned the validity of the catharsis hypothesis, they have been content with its sexist premises. Indicative of this bias is the use of male subjects, a logic dictated by a notion that for any theory of aggression or sexuality men are the active group; men have the responsibility; and men confront the consequences of their own behavior. Hence, men constitute the test of the theory whatever it is. Any effort to eliminate this bias must go beyond the catharsis principle, which is only one manifestation of a deeper sexist thinking. The conflict model and reference group theory may not be the best alternative approach; but its strength lies in the assumption that social phenomena require social rather than biological explanations.

IV

A sexist bias, however, is not the same as machismo, earlier defined as an attitude idealizing rugged masculinity in response to sexual insecurity (Bergler, 1949). Recall that the problem which initiated this review was the asymetrical findings between the two sets of research, violence and pornography.

Since one side of machismo is male sexual power, it seems obvious that persons, men or women, high on a scale testing machismo would find pornography acceptable, harmless, and inoffensive, an activity as suitable as any other for leisure time. But attitudes toward pornography would not predict anything with respect to violence without some connecting theory.

A theory which links them, as Freud's does, is supported more by literature and folklore than fact. It is a popular belief and richly elaborated by writers like Norman Mailer (Millett, 1970). But the connection is by no means so clear, for more women are seduced than seized, and gifts and flattery are more common than brute force. In other words, it is not enough to assert the relationship; it must be explained and demonstrated.

If a relationship between pornography and violence was found, we would expect consistent findings, but it is their absence that concerns us, the accident of two literatures developing independently. However it happened it remains a conspicuous dilemma.

To understand the research on violence we must ask whether the responses the investigators found were responses to violence as a genre or to a particular type of violence. In addition, we need to know whether the response to the films was aggression, or whether the aggression was itself a response to another, more immediate, but less visible response.

Several studies (Tannenbaum, 1970; Speisman et. al., 1964) suggest that the emotional excitement created by media violence may be more diffuse than the term aggression implies. It may be that stress rather than aggression is experienced by viewers, and that extraneous variables such as mood and style significantly modify responses. Conceivably, the response found by the investigators was anxiety, and the subsequent aggression an attempt to cope with it.

There is good reason to believe that films such as *Champion* create anxiety though they are not, therefore, less entertaining and pleasurable. The anxiety is similar to that experienced by participants or spectators of contact sports. These activities can have a strong homosexual element (Beisser, 1967. Toby, 1975). Subjects were viewing two male boxers slugging it out in the ring, periodically locked in embrace, bare body touching bare body, moving steadily toward a climax in which the loser is subdued and prone on the floor. The complete scenario is seen in the recent film *Rocky*, in which the contender prepares himself by practicing heterosexual abstinence before the big event. War films and Westerns provide similar examples of men made stronger in their aggression when aloof from the society of women.

If we are correct, the other side of machismo is the insecurity men may have about their sexual identity, taking the form of fears of impotence and homosexuality. It is the intervening variable in the violence research and explains why male subjects become more aggressive after viewing media violence between men. The test would be to replicate these studies using punitive attitudes toward sexual impotence and homosexuality as independent or dependent variables; in either way testing the hypothesis that aggression is a way of dealing with the ambivalence created by the film of boxing.

The humiliation of women and insecurity about sexual identity match the two conclusions emerging from the areas of research examined, one condoning pornography as an innocent pleasure without serious social consequences; the other condemning media violence as leading to senseless and brutal acts in everyday life. The contradiction which seemed so puzzling and which we attempted unsuccessfully to resolve in favor of one or the other now turns out to be the central fact. On a deeper level, the contradiction disappears: the unifying variable is machismo. It is similar in this respect to the authoritarian scale (Adorno et. al., 1950) which contains attitudinal contradictions. This suggests an approach to the study of machismo along the same lines.

Finally, in terms of social policy, it implies that the alternative to cultural censorship of either pornography or media violence is a new perspective on the status of women and the normalization of homosexuality, male or female.

REFERENCES

Abelson, H; Cohen R.; Heaton, E.; and Suder, C.
    1970   "National survey of public attitudes toward sex and experience with erotic materials," Technical Report of the Commission on Obscenity and Pornography, Vol. VI., 1-37.
Adorno, T.W.; Frenkel-Brunswick, E.; Levinson, D.J. and Sanford, R.N.
    1950   The Authoritarian Personality, New York, Norton.
Amoroso, Donald M.; Brown, Marvin; Pruesse, Manfred; Ware, Edward and Piley, Dennis W.
    1970   "An investigation of behavioral psychological and physiological reactions to pronographic stimuli" Technical Report of the Commission on Obscenity and Pornography, Vol. VIII, 1-40.
Bandura, Albert; Ross, Dorthea and Ross, Sheila A.
    1963a   "Imitation of a film-mediated aggression model," Journal of Abnormal and Social Psychology, Vol. 66, 1., 3-11.
    1963b   "Vicarious reinforcement and imitative learning," Journal of Abnormal and Social Psychology, 67, no. 6, 601-607.
Barnes, Clive
    1970   "Introduction", Report of the Commission on Obscenity and Pornography, New York, Bantam, p. xiii.
Beisser, Arnold R.
    1967   The Madness in Sports. New York. Appleton-Century-Crofts.
Bergler, Edumund
    1949   "Orality and the Myth of the Superior Male" in The Basic Neurosis, New York, Grune and Stratton.
Berkowitz, Leonard
    1962   Aggression, New York, McGraw-Hill.
    1964   "The effects of observing violence," Scientific American, Vol. 21, No. 2, 35-41.
    1965   "The Concept of Aggressive Drive: Some Additional Considerations," in Leonard Berkowitz, ed. Advances in Experimental Social Psychology, Vol. 2. New York, Academic Press, 301-329.
    1969   "The Frustration-Aggression Hypothesis Revisited" in Leonard Berkowitz, ed. Roots of Aggression, New York, Atherton.
Berkowitz, Leonard; Corwin, Ronald; Heironimus, Mark
    1963   "Film Violence and Subsequent Aggressive Tendencies," The Public Opinion Quarterly, Vol. XXVII, 217-229.
Berkowitz, Leonard and Rawlings, Edna
    1963   "Effects of film violence on inhibitions against subsequent aggression," Journal of Abnormal and Social Psychology, Vol. 66, No. 5, 405-412.
Berkowitz, Leonard; Geen, Russell G.
    1966   "Film violence and cue properties of available targets" Journal of Personality and Social Psychology, Vol. 3, No. 5, 525-530.
    1967   "Stimulus qualities of the target of aggression," Journal of Personality and Social Psychology, Vol. 5, No. 3, 364-368.
Bogart, Leo
    1972-   "Warning: The Surgeon General has determined that T.V. violence is moderately dangerous to
    73   your child's health," The Public Opinion Quarterly, 36, Winter, 491-522.

Bramel, Dana; Taub, Barry and Blum, Barbara
1968   "An Observer's Reaction to the Suffering of his Enemy", Journal of Personality and Social Psychology, Vol. 8, No. 4, 384-392.
Brownmiller, S.
1975   Against our Will. New York. Simon & Schuster.
Bryne, Don and Lamberth, John
1970   "The effect of erotic stimuli on sex arousal, evaluative responses, and subsequent behavior," Technical Report of the Commission on Obscenity and Pornography, Vol. VIII, 170-254.
Davis, Keith E. and Braucht, George N.
1970   "Reactions to viewing films of erotically realistic heterosexual behavior," Technical Report of the Commission on Obscenity and Pornography, Vol. VIII, 68-96.
Doob, Anthony N. and Climie, Robert J.
1972   "Delay of measurement and effects of film violence," Journal of Experimental Social Psychology, Vol. 8, 136-142.
Doob, Anthony and Kirshenbaum, Hershl M.
1973   "The effects on arousal of frustration and aggressive films," Journal of Experimental Social Psychology, Vol. 9 (1) 57-64.
Ellis, Desmond
1974   "Mass media effects on violence in society," York University, Unpublished
Fanon, Frantz
1963   The Wretched of the Earth, New York, Grove.
Feshbach, Seymour
1955   "The drive-reducing function of fantasy behavior," Journal of Abnormal and Social Psychology, Vol. 50, 3-11.
1961   "The stimulating versus cathartic effect of vicarious aggressive activity," Journal of abnormal and Social Psychology, 63, 381 385.
1969   "The catharsis effect: Research and another view," Commission on the Causes and Prevention of Violence, Vol. 9, 461-472.
Freud, Sigmund
1938   "Wit and its relation to the unconscious," Basic Writings of Sigmund Freud, Modern Library.
1967   Beyond the Pleasure Principle. New York. Bantam.
Geen, Russell G. and Berkowitz, Leonard
1969   "Some conditions facilitating the occurrence of aggression after the observation of violence," in Leonard Berkowitz, ed. Roots of Aggression, New York. Atherton, 106-118.
Geen, Russell G. and O'Neal Edgar C.
1969   "Activation of cue-elicited aggression by general arousal," Journal of Personality and Social Psychology Vol. 11, No. 3, 289-292.
Gerbner, George and Gross, Larry
1974   Violence Profile, No. 6, University of Pennsylvania.
Godkewitsch, Michael
1972   "The relationship between arousal potential and funniness in jokes," in Jeffrey H. Goldstein and Paul E. McGhee, eds. The Psychology of Humor, New York, Academic Press.
Goranson, Richard E.
1970   "Media violence and aggressive behavior," in Leonard Berkowitz, ed. Advances in Experimental Social Psychology, Vol. 5, 1970, 1-31.
Howard, James E.; Reifler, Clifford G. and Liptzin, Myron B.
1970   "Effects of exposure to pornography," Technical Report of the Commission on Obscenity and Pornography, Vol. VIII, 97-132.
Howitt, Dennis and Dembo, Richard
1974   "A subcultural account of media effects," Human Relations Vol. 27, No. 1, 25-41.
Hoyt, J.L.
1970   "Effect of media violence 'justification' on aggression," Journal of Broadcasting, 14, 455-464.
Hyman, Herbert H.
1974   "Mass communication and socialization," in W. Phillips Davison and Frederic T.S. Yu eds. Mass Communication Research, New York, Praeger.
Katzman, Marshall
1970   "Relationship of socioeconomic background to judgments of sexual stimulation" Technical Report of the Commission on Obscenity and Pornography, Vol. IX, 1-7.
Kutchinsky, Berl
1970   "The effect of pornography: A pilot experiment on perception, behavior and attitudes," Technical Report Of the Commission on Obscenity and Pronography, Vol. VIII, 133-169.
La Fave, Lawrence
1972   "Humor judgments as a function of reference groups and identification classes," in Jeffrey H. Goldstein and Paul E. McGhee, eds. The Psychology of Humor, New York, Academic Press, 195-210.

La Fave, Lawrence; McCarthy, Kevin and Haddad, Jay.
   1973   "Humor judgment as a function of identification classes: Canadian vs. American," Journal of Psychology, 85, 53–59.
LaMarsh, Judith
   1977   Report of Royal Commission on Violence in Media Industries. Queens Park. Toronto. Canada.
Lear, Norman
   1971   "As I read how Laura saw Archie . . ."New York Times, October 10, 1971. Quoted in Vidmar, Neil and Rokeach, Milton, "Archie Bunker's bigotry," Journal of Communication, 24:1 36–47.
Mann, Jay; Berkowitz, Leonard; Sidman, Jack; Starr, Sheldon and West, Stephen
   1974   "Satiation of the transient stimulating effect of erotic films," Journal of Personality and Social Psychology, Vol. 30, No. 6, 729–735.
Mann, Jay; Sidman, Jack and Starr, Sheldon
   1970   "Effects of erotic films on the sexual behavior of married couples," Technical Report of the Commission on Obscenity and Pornography, Vol. VIII, 170–254.
Marcuse, Herbert
   1962   Eros and Civilization. New York, Vintage.
Meyer, Timothy P.
   1972   "Effects of viewing justified and unjustified real film violence on aggressive behavior," Journal of Personality and Social Psychology, Vol. 23, No. 1, 21–29.
Middleton, Russell
   1959   "Negro and white reactions to racial humor," Sociometry, 22, 175–183.
Millett, Kate
   1970   Sexual Politics. New York. Doubleday.
Millgram S. and Shotland R.L.
   1973   Television and Antisocial Behavior. New York. Academic.
Mosher, Donald L.
   1970   "Psychological reactions to pornographic films," Technical Report of the Commission on Obscenity and Pornography, Vol. VIII, 255–312.
   1970   "Sex callousness toward women," Technical Report of the Commission on Obscenity and Pornography, Vol. VIII, 313–324.
Mosher, Donald and Katz, Harvey
   1970   "Pornographic films, male verbal aggression against women and guilt," Technical Report of Commission on Obscenity and Pornography, Vol. VIII, 357–379.
Prerost, Frank J.
   1975   "The indication of sexual and aggressive similarities through humor appreciation," Journal of Psychology, 91, 283–288.
Priest, Robert F. and Wilhelm, Paul G.
   1974   "Sex, marital status and self-actualization as a factor in the appreciation of sexist jokes." Journal of Social Psychology, 92, 245–249.
Russell, Diana E.H.
   1977   "Pornography: A feminist perspective," in Women Against Violence in Pornography & Media. Berkeley, California.
Singer, David
   1968   "Aggression arousal, hostile humor, catharsis," Journal of Personality and Social Psychology. Monograph Supplement, Vol. 8, No. 1, Part 2, 1–14.
Speisman, Joseph C.; Lazarus, Richard S.; Mordkoff, Arnold and Davison, Les.
   1964   "Experimental reduction of stress based on Ego-defense theory," Journal of Abnormal and Social Psychology, Vol. 68, No. 4, 367–380.
Steinmetz, Suzanne and Straus, Murray A.
   1975   Violence in the Family. New York. Dodd, Mead.
Tannenbaum, Percy H. and Greenberg, Bradley S.
   1968   "Mass communication," in Annual Review of Psychology Vol. 19, 351–386.
Tannenbaum, Percy H. and Gaer, Eleanor P.
   1965   "Mood change as a function of stress of protagonist and degree of identification in a film-viewing situation," Journal of Personality and Social Psychology, Vol. 2, No. 4, 612–616.
Tannenbaum, Percy H.
   1970   "Emotional arousal as a mediator or erotic communnication effects," Technical Report of the Commission on Obscenity and Pornography, Vol. VIII, 326–379.
Toby, Jackson
   1975   "Violence and the masculine ideal" in Steinmetz, S. and Straus, M. eds. Violence in the family, New York, Dodd, Mead. 58–65.
Vidmar, Neil and Rokeach, Milton
   1974   "Archie Bunker's bigotry," Jounal of Communication. 24:1, 36–47.

Walters, Richard and Thomas, Edward Llewellyn
    1963   "Enhancement of punitiveness by visual and audiovisual displays," Canadian Journal of Psychology, 17, 245-255.
Wills, Garry
    1977   "The porno perplex" Psychology Today, 11, No. 3.
Wolff, H.A.; Smith, C.E.; and Murray, H.A.
    1934   "The psychology of humor," Journal of Abnormal and Social Psychology, XXVIII, No. 4. 341-365.

PART VII

INTERNATIONAL AND
COMPARATIVE RESEARCH

Scholarly exchange among mass communication researchers throughout the world has increased dramatically in the last decade. The debates about world news flow and the role of communication in national development both point to an increasing volume of comparative communication research in the future. This section contains research on both European and Asian media systems and news flow.

The first chapter reports major new research that goes to the heart of the arguments about world news flow. Asian wire service and prestige newspapers of the region are analyzed for patterns of international and domestic news circulation.

Two studies of mass communication in China raise important research questions as they describe a highly centralized, low-technology media system.

Dutch television news coverage of foreign lands is studied in the fourth chapter. Questions are raised about the news values of television.

Next, the role of mass media in social change in modern Europe is dealt with. This research suggests the conditions under which the mass media are agents of social change.

The final chapter outlines the role of mass communication in *self*-development, the conception of development that has replaced the notion of national development.

Debate on the Unesco resolutions about Third World news flow has dominated many international conferences and gatherings of researchers in recent years. This report, written by Dr. Wilbur Schramm of the East-West Center at the University of Hawaii especially for this Yearbook, presents empirical data that go to the heart of the Unesco argument. Studying Asian "prestige" newspapers and four wire services in the Orient, the research directed by Schramm shows that Asian papers are essentially local, reflecting the interests and needs of their audiences. They devote about three-quarters of their news to their individual countries and show no greater interest in developmental news than do Western media. Schramm's chapter suggests part of the problem of developmental news hinges upon better education for journalists. Schramm suggests that Asian journalists handle political developmental stories better than economic developmental news. Hence, the implication is that Unesco might well turn more of its energies toward education for journalists.

34

CIRCULATION OF NEWS IN THE THIRD WORLD
A Study of Asia

Wilbur Schramm

This study was intended to throw some light on the topic where there has been mostly heat: the circulation of news through the Third World, and especially the contribution of the international news agencies to that process.[1] It hardly needs saying that the international news agencies have come in for much the same criticism in the Third World as other transnational enterprises. They have been accused of Western bias in their selection and interpretation of news, of ignoring development news and other matters important to the Third World. If Third World governments have been more concerned with the pictures of their countries going *out* on the wires, Third World editors have been more concerned with the pictures of the rest of the world coming *in*. For their part, the international news agencies have been conciliatory, admitting some probable bias because their owners and chief clients are in the West, supporting the idea that the Third World should have a news agency of its own when it can finance and staff it, offering help toward such a service, and insisting only that their sources of news in the Third World should not be closed off.

The dozen or so people who worked on these data have not tried to arbitrate this argument; indeed, they have differed among themselves concerning "media imperialism." But they have realized the importance of the question and the need of hard facts to guide a solution. Therefore, they have tried to keep their own

From Wilbur Schramm, "Circulation of News in the Third World: A Study of Asia," original manuscript.

prejudices out of the report and to ascertain as reliably as they could how much and what kind of news the international wires are carrying to and from the Third World, what news the Third World dailies are publishing, and what news Third World people are reading.

WHAT WE DID

Because we were in Asia, we obtained complete files of the Asia wires of four international news agencies—Reuter, AFP, AP, and UPI[2]—for the week of December 4-10, 1977, and files of several national and regional wires, including Hsinhau (the New China News Agency) of China. Also for the same week, we obtained copies of sixteen daily newspapers from nine Asian countries, selected with a few exceptions as "prestige papers" of their countries.[3] We had hoped to study daily newspaper readership in each of these countries, but our resources limited us to one such study. With the cooperation of the Institute of Mass Communication and its director, Dr. Gloria Feliciano, University of the Philippines, we studied in some detail the readership of Manila's *Bulletin Today*. We also had a number of talks with Asian editors and information officers.[4]

We trained students and secretaries without previous research experience to serve as coders and analysts to prepare material for the hungry computers. And although we regretted how much we wanted to do that we could not afford to do, still we were able to analyze about 2.5 million words of news in 6 languages, to make about 800 interviews, and to perform both content and factor analysis and a number of statistical manipulations. Therefore, I am trying to report on hundreds of tables and hundreds of thousands of measurements. We ask your indulgence for leaving out some of the details and for not answering some of questions we wanted to answer on the ambitious pattern of the study, which was to follow the pattern of news circulation through the complete cycle from (a) what the newspapers published about their own countries, (b) what the news wires picked up and circulated about these countries, (c) what newspapers in *other* Third World countries took from the wires and printed, and finally (d) what readers in these countries read in the news available to them.

THE WEEK WE STUDIED

The week of December 4-10, 1977, was a fairly typical news week in Asia. It began with a shocking event—the crash of a hijacked airplane, killing all its passengers, in Malaysia on its way to the Singapore airport. Particularly in Asia, this generated a vast amount of copy. The full dimensions of an earlier disaster, the overwhelming storm in India that left 8000 dead, were becoming apparent, but this news got surprisingly little coverage. Throughout the world, news was dominated by the Tripoli meeting of Arab states, which was winding down, the President Sadat's peace initiative, which was continuing. This was responsible for more news than usual from the Middle East. There was no news of similar excitement from the industrialized countries. Political violence was occurring in many places in the world from the horn of Africa to the southern Philippines. Politics were heated in a number of Asian countries; these political events were covered locally, but surprisingly seldom in other countries. For example, President Marcos was preparing for a referendum and considering the case of Aquino. President Suharto faced student demonstrations. The new government of Pakistan was deciding what to do with Bhutto. A national commission in India was investigating Indira Gandhi's conduct as prime minister, and Mrs. Gandhi was attacking the commission. Textile-producing nations were negotiating for higher quotas. The King of Thailand was celebrating his fiftieth birthday. China was quiet but apparently restudying its economic policy, looking toward the Fifth Party Congress. A parade of diplomats moved through the region, visiting their opposite numbers. And, appropriately for the timing of this study, a conference sponsored by UNESCO was meeting in Sri Lanka to discuss the need for improving news exchange in the Third World. I am sorry to say that the coverage in Asian papers of this meeting was scant. But it was a week much like all weeks in Asian Third World news.

THE DECLINING GRADIENT OF NEWS FLOW

One of the first outcomes of this study was to attach some hard figures to a phenomenon familiar to anyone who has examined the flow of international news: The amount of news decreases as it moves along the pipeline. That is, more potentially newsworthy events occur in any country than the newspapers of that country can publish. The local newspapers publish more than the international wires can pick up. The wires carry more than their clients can reprint. And these client-newspapers in second countries print more than their readers read. Thus, gatekeepers stand at every point of exchange, and the throughput constantly declines.

The average Asian daily in our sample carried about seventy local and national stories. (This, of course, varied considerably with the papers.) And, even then, the people who lived with those stories doubtless knew of other newsworthy events and wondered why *they* did not make the papers. Of those seventy stories, about four were likely to appear on any one of the four international wires. Thus, four wires might carry sixteen stories from the average country we are talking about, but they would not all be *different* stories: Seven or eight of them would be different. Thus, if any of our prestige papers subscribed to al four wires (and a number of the more prosperous ones did so), they would be likely to receive on average about 10% of the news originally published in any given Third World country. If they subscribed to only one of the international wires, they would have 5% or 6% of the news stories originally carried in the average country.

Of course, the subscribing dailies did not print all the news on the wire. Actually, the average daily in our sample typically carried fewer than two stories per day from each of the other Third World countries in the sample. Thus, something less than one-fourth of the content of the four news wires was likely to be reprinted in the dailies—2% or 3% of what was originally published in the country itself.

How much of this was read by an average reader? Much to our regret, we have only one readership study rather than the 8 or 9 we contemplated, and therefore we do not know how to interpret the fact that average news readership of *Bulletin Today* was under 9%—one story out of 11. Obviously, more work on readership is needed. For a comparison we have to turn to industrialized countries. The largest such example is the Continuing Study of Newspaper Reading, which measured the readership of 130 dailies in the United States in the 1930s and 1940s (Swanson, 1951). For those dailies, the average readership was about twice that of the *Bulletin Today*—20%. It may be that the political situation, the cultural contingencies, and other factors produced a spuriously low average in Manila. But even if we double the estimate we obtained in the Manila study, still we find that less than one story out of 5 published in the second country paper, a fraction of the percentage of the news originally published in another Asian Third World country, would be likely to be read in a second Asian Third World country.

Let us describe this pattern in another way. How many local and national stories would have to appear in one of the chief papers of an Asian Third World country—given a completely average situation—to be sure of reaching a point further along the news pipeline?

It would take ten local and national stories to be sure that one of them appears on at least one international wire.

It would take about forty local and national stories in Country A to be sure that one of them was reprinted in a similar daily in Country B.

It would take between 200 and 400 stories (depending on the reliability of our readership estimate) to be sure that an average reader in Country B reads a story about Country A.

The steepness of this gradient helps explain why some Third World countries know less about each other than some of them think they should.

WHAT ASIAN THIRD WORLD DAILIES PUBLISH
ABOUT THEIR OWN COUNTRIES

Our estimate of 70 local and national stories in the average Asian Daily hides considerable variation between papers. The *Bulletin Today* of Manila printed 70 items of purely Philippine news, plus 23 additional items involving both the Philippine news, plus 23 additional items involving both the Philippines and another country. *The Statesman* of Calcutta published an average of 85 in these categories. On the other hand, *Kompas* of Jakarta carried usually about 50 items on its own country, and the large *Straits Times* of Singapore carried fewer than 50. (The *Straits Times*, serving a tiny state, is almost bound to think of itself as a regional newspaper, and consequently to carry a higher proportion of foreign news than the average Asian newspaper.) Pinch (1978) has reported some figures on the content of 16 Third World newspapers in Africa, the Middle East, Latin

America, and including 4 in Asia, gathered through the cooperation of ICA. He does not say whether these include only stories limited to the newspaper's own country or include news of the country in its relations with others; whichever, his estimate is that they carry between 40 and 50 stories about their own countries.

We have analyzed foreign content for all our sample of dailies, and local content for many of them. However, not all the figures on local content are quite ready to present, so here we are going to give some details on two papers only, one from each of the two main news regions in Asia.

The Statesman of Calcutta and the New Delhi averaged 103 total news items a day: the Bulletin Today of Manila averaged 129. These were divided as follows:

	Bulletin Today		Statesman	
Foreign	36	27.9%	18	17.5%
Both[5]	23	17.8%	8	7.8%
Domestic	70	54.3%	77	74.8%

Indian papers, in general, pay less attention to foreign news than do the papers of East Asia, but even so the proportion of domestic news in these two news-papers is not so far from the proportion in leading U.S. papers during the same period. Pinch (1978) estimates between 70% and 80% U.S. news in the New York Times, Washington Post, Los Angeles Times, and Chicago Tribune.

How much of the content of Third World dailies is concerned with the Third World? The great bulk of it. Pinch (1978) estimates 85% for his sixteen dailies. The Straits Times, despite its wide coverage, devotes about 80% to the Third World. Here are the figures for the two Asian papers we are describing:

	Bulletin Today		Statesman	
Non-Third World	14	10.9%	6	5.5%
Both	32	24.8%	10	10.1%
Third World	83	64.3%	87	84.4%

This represents a striking difference between nations. The four American papers we have just mentioned gave only about 15% of their stories to Third World news.

A newspaper emphasizes its own region. Asian papers concentrate on Asia, African ones on Africa, and so forth. (See Table 1.) A daily like the Washington Post, by contrast, spreads its geographical coverage differently. About 25% of its foreign news in that week dealt with Asia, 17% with the Middle East, 7% with Latin America, 29% with Western Europe, and 11% with Eastern Europe (in-cluding the USSR). Poor Latin America is the orphan of the foreign news editors. It is the least reported region both in the Third World (outside Latin America) and the industrialized nations also.

What categories of news do we find in Third World newspapers? These, too, differ by papers. As the following table will show, the Statesman is preoccupied with domestic politics, as it might well have been in that troubled period follow-

TABLE 1:   Percentages of News Published About Various Regions of the World
            by Two Asian Newspapers

	Bulletin Today		Statesman	
Asia	94	72.9%	92	84.0%
Latin America	2	1.6	– –	– –
Africa	4	3.1	2	2.0
Middle East	7	5.4	2	2.0
North America	13	10.1	4	3.6
Western Europe	8	6.2	6	5.8
Eastern Europe	1	0.8	1	1.1
International Organizations	– –	– –	2	1.5

ing the downfall of Indira Gandhi's government. Both *The Statesman* and the *Bulletin Today,* however, are high in economic news and sports, like newspapers throughout the world. Pinch (1978) estimates that his sixteen papers carried about 18% sports stories. The four American papers carried about 16% sports. Economic coverage is hard to separate from other coverage in his report, but it is generally high, as in the two Asian papers we have been describing. (See Table 2.)

One of the comments most often made about news coverage in industrialized countries is that it emphasizes crime and disaster, and these subjects do seem to bulk larger in American dailies than in Third World ones. Pinch (1978) estimates that the 4 U.S. dailies (New York, Washington, Los Angeles, Chicago) are giving about 17% of their stories to crime and disaster, as compared to 9% of his 16 Third World papers, 10% in *The Statesman,* 5% in the *Bulletin Today.* For *The Statesman* this seems hardly credible, inasmuch as reading it for the week of December 4-10, 1977, gives the impression of a country torn by strife (demonstrations, riots), threatened by crime (criminal proceedings involving many people, including the former prime minister), and stalked by disaster (a flood that killed 8000, a nuclear plant that exploded, train derailments, and the like). This impression is much stronger than any derived from the New York *Times,* which Pinch (1978) calculates gives over 18% of its news to crime and disaster. If we had coded the political investigations of the Gandhi regime as crime rather than domestic politics, the results might have been more nearly comparable to the U.S. figures, but the decision about coding, once made, cannot very well be changed.

Another difference sometimes pointed out between Third World and non-Third World journalism is the greater emphasis by the Third World on economic development. Pinch's figures (1978) do not support that. He calculates that on the average each class of papers gives 18% to 20% to economic and social development news. Our figures support him. The *Straits Times* apparently gives about 20%; the *Bulletin Today,* about 28%; *The Statesman* about 15%. The New York *Times* and the Washington *Post* give that classification 24% or 25%, the Los Angeles *Times* about 16%, the Chicago *Tribune* about 14%.

TABLE 2:   Percentages of News About Various Categories Published in Two
           Asian Newspapers

	Bulletin Today		Statesman	
Military, political violence	4	3.1%	2	2.3%
Foreign Relations	8	6.2	8	7.8
Domestic Political	7	5.4	32	31.3
Economic	46	35.7	26	25.3
Science, Health	7	5.4	1	0.8
Education	8	6.2	2	2.1
Accident, Disaster	2	1.6	4	3.9
Judicial, Crime	5	3.9	6	6.2
Sports	25	19.4	13	12.5
Culture	3	2.3	4	3.5
Human Interest	2	1.6	2	2.3
Other	12	9.3	2	1.9

The picture of Third World newspapers that emerges from this study is less different from non-Third World newspapers than we might have expected. Third World newspapers, like others, are essentially local news media. They reflect the interests and information needs of the people around them. They are greatly interested in the Third World in general and their region in particular. With the exception of a regional newspaper like the *Straits Times,* they devote about three-fourths of their stories to their own country—as do prestige papers in the United States. They carry, on the average, a fewer than one-hundred total stories, of which a little over seventy are likely to be local and national. A high proportion of their coverage is on sports and economic or business news—as is true elsewhere. They have fewer stories on crime and disaster, but development news seems to be just as interesting to the "developed" countries as to the developing ones. Today, development is an issue of worldwide concern.

WHAT THE INTERNATIONAL NEWS WIRES CARRY

Let us now look at the wire news supplied by the international news agencies.

Perhaps the most striking feature of news agency coverage is the amount of Third World news actually flowing over the four Asian wires. This totals about 105,000 words per day, and 408 stories. An average wire therefore carries about 26,000 words per day, although this varies considerably by wire. (See Table 3.)

The best way to categorize the content of the wires is to compare it with what the daily newspapers carry. This will be done in the following section. Suffice it to say here that the largest segment of the international wire news (36%) deals with foreign relations, 15% with economic news, 11.5% with sports, nearly 11% with news of domestic governments, and nearly 7% with military preparations or violent political or international actions throughout the Third World. The attention given accidents and disasters (5%) and crime and court trials (4%) is less

TABLE 3:   Daily Average Number of Stories and Words About the Third World
            in Four Wire Services

	Stories	Words
Wire A	74.8	20,090
Wire B	71.4	20,872
Wire C	129.4	34,222
Wire D	132.2	30,175
Total	407.8	105,352

than one might expect from the criticism of the international agencies, especially
considering that disasters like the crash of the hijacked airplane and the mon-
strous Indian flood, and trials like those of Aquino, Bhutto, and Gandhi were in
the news that week.

What parts of the Third World do the Asian international wires cover? The
bulk of the coverage, as in the newspapers, goes to Asia (58%). Because of the
Tripoli meeting and the hot issue precipitated by President Sadat's overture to
Israel, nearly one quarter of the coverage in our test week was given to the Middle
East. Africa and Latin America get relatively little attention, as in the newspapers
also. (See Table 4).

How much of the total news content of the international wire is devoted to
Third World news? A shade less than one-half. On the average, non-Third World
countries get about 52% of the words, 51% of the stories, on the four international wires in Asia. (See Table 5.)

To sum up, then, about half the news content of these four international wires
available in Asia deals with the Third World, about 60% of that with Asia. This
says nothing about the *quality* of the news; we shall have something to say about
that later. It is a purely *quantitative* measurement. But the quality of Third
World news circulating over these wires is rather impressive. And let us now look
at the content of the wires against that of the newspapers.

WHAT THE ASIAN DAILIES REPORTED
ON OTHER THIRD WORLD COUNTRIES

To put this in perspective, let us here record that the average Asian daily in our
sample carried 23 stories per day about foreign Third World countries, alone or
in terms of their relations to the paper's home country. (This total omits Third
World news dealing exclusively with the home country.) This represented about
12,750 words. Let us recall that the average international wire carried 102 Third
World stories per day, about 26,300 words. All four wires together carried an
average of 408 Third World stories per day, about 105,000 words.

This does not mean, of course, that a subscriber to all the four wires received
408 *different* stories per day. A number of the same stories would be picked up by
more than one wire. Our estimate is that if a daily newspaper had access to all

TABLE 4:   Percentages of Wire News Stories by Region During the Sample Week
            of December 4-10, 1977

	Asia	Latin America	Middle East	Africa
Third World Countries Alone	59.3%	7.0%	22.2%	11.5%
Third World with Other Countries	57.0	7.0	24.7	11.2
All Third World Coverage	58.2	7.0	23.5	11.3

TABLE 5:   Percentages of Wire News About the Third World and Non-Third
            World on a Typical Day

	Stories		Words	
	N	%	N	%
Third World Only	216	(23.5)	49,425	(22.5)
Third and Others	236	(25.7)	56,211	(25.5)
All Third World	452	(49.2)	105,636	(48)
Non-Third World	467	(50.8)	111,246	(52)

four of these international wire services, it probably could choose from about *200* Third World stories per day.

Overall, these daily newspapers received about three-quarters of their foreign Third World news from the four news agencies mentioned here. It was possible to identify the sources of 83% of the foreign stories. Therefore, *three-fourths of the identifiable sources* of Third World news in the fifteen dailies[6] were one or more of the four international agencies. (See Table 6.)

The amount of foreign Third World coverage in the individual papers varied widely—from an average of 56 stories per day in the *Straits Times,* 43 per day in *Nanyang Siang Pao,* 38 in the Hong Kong *Morning Post,* 8 in *Kompas,* 3 in *Pilipino Express,* and 1 in *Ananda Bazar Patrika.*

What about the kinds of foreign Third World news in the dailies as compared with the kinds on the wires? The striking feature of the following table, which makes this comparison, is how similar the general patterns of content were. The wires gave more space proportionately to news of international relations, the newspapers more to domestic government and politics, economic or business stories (we shall speak of economic *development* news later), and human interest stories. But as a whole, the patterns are remarkably similar. And the dailies actually devoted a slightly higher proportion of their news to the highly criticized categories of crime, disasters, and court trials than did the wires. (See Table 7.)

One difference between newspaper and wire emphasis does stand out: The wires devote a significantly higher proportion of their news space to non-Third World countries than do the Asian dailies. We have already said that the wires

TABLE 6:   Number and Percentage of Identifiable Sources of News Stories in
            Fifteen Asian Daily Newspapers During the Sample Week of
            December 4-10, 1977

	Number of Stories	Percentage
International Wire or Wires	1,083	75.7
National or Regional Wire	61	4.3
Paper's Own Correspondent	101	7.1
Local Coverage (of foreign relations)	125	8.7
Special News Service	47	3.3
Reprint	14	1.0
Total	1,431	100.0

TABLE 7:   Number and Percentage of Asian Daily Newspapers and Wire Service
            Foreign Third World News Stories About Various Categories

	Fifteen Newspapers		Four News Wires	
Category	N	%	N	%
Military, political violence	89	5.1	137	6.7
Foreign relations	518	29.9	736	36.1
Domestic government, political	214	12.4	221	10.8
Economic	310	17.9	308	15.1
Science, health	15	0.9	23	1.1
Education	17	1.0	7	0.3
Accidents, disasters	101	6.0	109	5.3
Crime, judicial	83	4.8	82	4.0
Energy, environment	14	0.8	19	0.9
Human rights	26	1.5	55	2.7
Sports	208	12.0	234	11.5
Art, culture	24	1.4	15	0.7
Human interest	77	4.5	42	2.1
Religion	5	0.3	6	0.3
Miscellaneous	26	1.5	45	2.2
Total	1,729	100.0	2,039	100.0

typically used 51% or 52% of their news for non-Third World country events.
Here are the corresponding figures for the newspapers:

	Foreign News Wholly or in Part of Third World Countries		News of Non-Third World Countries	
15 Dailies	433	(61.5%)	271	(38.5%)

In other words, as we might expect, the foreign outlook of the Third World newspapers was toward other Third World countries; the wires were more likely to offer non-Third World news than the dailies were to take it.

We analyzed the number and proportion of stories on twelve selected countries, some in Asia, some not, mostly Third World countries but a few others also, for the fifteen Asian dailies and the four international wires during five days of our sample week. This is an interesting table, both because it shows the imbalance of regional coverage when an exciting news event occurs within the region, and also because it gives us a chance to compare the wire with newspaper coverage of two industrialized countries. (See Table 8.)

During the sample period, a hijacked airplane crashed in Malaysia, on its way to the Singapore airport. Therefore, it is not surprising that about twice as many stories in the Asian dailies as on the international wires were devoted to Malaysia, and about one and a half times as many to Singapore. As we have noted, the very high coverage of Egypt by both newspapers and wires must have represented the effect of the Tripoli protest meeting and the continuing Sadat initiative. The rather surprising thing is that the United States, where ownership of two of the four international wires resides, gets little more coverage on the wires than in the Asian papers. If the wires are giving the United States a disproportionate amount of coverage, it is not greatly at variance with the news judgment of the Asian editors.

One way to estimate the similarity of news selection between the international wires and the dailies is simply to correlate the relative amount of attention each gives to various Third World countries. We were able to do this for 42 Third World countries, 14 Asian dailies (two were excluded because of insufficient

TABLE 8:   Number and Percentage of Foreign News Stories in Asian Daily Newspaper and Wire Services About Twelve Selected Countries

Country	Fifteen Daily Newspapers		Four International News Wires	
	N	%	N	%
China	153	10.6	170	8.7
India	69	4.8	135	6.9
Indonesia	68	4.7	145	7.4
Malaysia	267	18.6	179	9.7
Pakistan	74	5.1	101	5.2
Philippines	82	5.7	189	9.7
Singapore	132	9.2	127	6.5
Thailand	82	5.7	138	7.1
Vietnam	56	3.9	95	4.9
Egypt	229	15.9	288	14.7
Japan	50	3.5	90	4.6
United States	177	12.3	286	14.6
Total	1,439	100.0	1,943	100.0

data), and, of course, the 4 international wires for 5 days in our sample week. These correlations will be published in detail. Here let me merely summarize them. Overall, the correlation (Kendall's tau) between the composite wire and the composite Asian daily was .58. Between the composite wire and 10 English-language dailies it was .57; between the composite wire and 3 Chinese-language dailies it was .63; between the composite wire and 2 Indian papers (excluding *Ananda Bazar Patrika*) it was .40% between the composite wire and 11 non-Indian papers it was .61; and with 8 English-language non-Indian dailies it was .61. In other words, with the exception of some of the Indian papers, the correlations were consistently high. For comparison we also computed correlations with Hsinhua, the news service of the New China News Agency. There is no reason to expect such high correlations with Hsinhua, because the central task of Hsinhua is to carry the news of China, not of 42 Third World countries. And, as we should expect, the tau correlation between Hsinhua and the average Asian daily outside China was about one-third as high as for the international wires; it was .23.

What can we say about these Asian dailies and their relation to the international wires? These newspapers concentrate on their own region and on Third World news. When a special event, like the crash of a hijacked plane, occurs within their own region, they concentrate upon it proportionally more than do the international wires. Like newspapers everywhere, their first interest is in news of their own country, and they do not take a great amount of foreign news. Although 90% of their total content, 60% of their foreign content, deals with the Third World, they take an average of only 23 *foreign* Third World stories a day. What they do take is remarkably similar in category of content and in distribution by country to what the wires carry.

This does not necessarily mean, of course, that they are satisfied with the news they get. Our data do not permit us to say that. They may have few alternatives to the wires from which they take three-fourths of their foreign content. The degree and nature of their satisfaction or dissatisfaction with the wire news is something to be determined, and we are going to suggest some ways to do it. But let us point out here that the wires are delivering a great deal more foreign news, a great deal more Asian and Third World news, than the newspapers are taking. Within the 100,000 words of Third World news and the slightly more than 100,000 words of non-Third World news that arrive on the wires every day, there is ample room for change if the news services and newspapers can agree on what the change should be.

WHAT THE READERS READ

If we had a *series* of readership studies, we could speak with more confidence about news reading in the Third World. Because we have only one such study, we must be cautious about generalizing.

The newspaper whose readers we studied, the *Bulletin Today* of Manila, is one of the most highly respected in the Philippines and also has one of the largest circulations in that country. Like all Philippine dailies, it operates under the restrictions of martial law, but it seems to be regarded neither as pro-nor anti-government. We designed an interview sample of an area basis, with about three-fifths of the interviews in metropolitan Manila and two-fifths outside, corresponding to the circulation of the paper. Interviewers were advanced students of the Institute of Mass Communications, University of the Philippines. They actually completed a total of 481 interviews, 296 in the metropolitan area and 185 outside. Of the respondents, 250 were male, 231 female. All interviews were conducted within 24 hours of the time the paper was printed and circulated.

We have already mentioned the most interesting finding of the study—the low average readership. The average reader read only 8.4% of the news content—11 of 129 items. We suspect that this is lower than the average level of Third World readership, but do not have the figures to prove it. The readers told us they spent about 30 minutes per day on the newspaper—about 5 minutes more for urban readers than for rural. That is a great deal more time than one needs to read 11 news items. What else did they read, then? They spoke of the comics, of the feature materials, of the movie and broadcast columns, and of the classified ads. Much of the use of the *Bulletin Today*, then, must have been for purposes other than news. Whether this is related in any way to government restrictions on official news we do not know, but it would be interesting to find out whether the news reading pattern changes when martial law is ended.

Table 9 shows the average reading by category of news. "Average readership" means the *percentage of available news* of a given kind read by an average reader. "Average number of stories read" refers to the *number* of stories of a given kind read by an average reader on the day of the study. "Proportion of reading" describes *how much* of an average reader's reading was of a given kind of news. Thus, for example, the average reader read 8.1% of the foreign news. He read an average of 2.9 foreign stories, and this constituted 26.9% of his news reading in the paper that day. (See Table 9.)

Some interesting differences show up in the table. Philippine readers seem to be more interested in news of relationships between their country and a foreign country, sometimes a non-Third World one, than in news of their own country or another country alone. Note:

Foreign	8.1%	Non-Third World	6.5%
Both	9.4%	Both	9.6%
Domestic	8.3%	Third World	8.3%

Their interest in foreign news lies more with news of other *Third World* countries than with the industrialized countries (average reading on non-Third World country news is only 6.5%). Of their total reading, 74% is about Asia, but the newspapers publish so much about Asia that they read only 8.6% of Asian news—almost exactly the same percentage as their reading of the paper as a whole. They are obviously highly interested in domestic and political news (they

TABLE 9:   Average Percentage, Number of Stories, and Proportion of Total News Reading of Various Types of News by the Reader of the Manila *Bulletin Today*

Type	Average Readership %	Average Number Stories Read	Proportion of Reading %
Foreign	8.1	2.9	26.6
Both	9.4	2.2	20.2
Domestic	8.3	5.8	53.2
Non-Third World	6.5	0.9	8.3
Both	9.6	3.1	28.4
Third World	8.3	6.9	63.3
Asia	8.6	8.1	74.3
Latin America	15.7	0.3	2.8
Africa	12.7	0.5	4.6
Middle East	14.0	1.0	9.2
North America	5.6	0.7	6.4
Western Europe	3.6	0.3	2.8
Eastern Europe	0.1	– –	– –
Military, political strife	1.0	0.7	6.4
Foreign relations	8.8	0.7	6.4
Domestic, political	25.2	1.8	16.4
Economic	6.6	3.0	27.3
Science, health	4.5	0.3	2.7
Education	5.9	0.5	4.5
Accident, disaster	– –	– –	– –
Judicial, crime	5.3	0.3	2.7
Sports	7.7	1.9	17.3
Culture	– –	0.1	1.0
Human interest	13.7	0.3	2.7
Other	11.3	1.4	12.7
Development news	6.4	2.4	22.0
Not development news	9.3	8.5	78.0
All news	8.4	10.9	100.0

read 25% of it). Of their total news reading, 60% is of economic news, domestic and political news, and sports. One out of every six stories they read is a sports story. And they do not show any great interest in development news.

We have said that the average reader reads 11 news stories of the 129 in the *Bulletin Today*. How were those stories allocated by kinds of news?

Approximately 6 would be domestic news, 3 foreign news, and 2 a combination of domestic and foreign news.

About 7 would be Third World news, 1 non-Third World, and 3 a combination.

About 8 would be news about Asia, 1 about the Middle East, less than 1 about North America.

Another 3 would be economic and business news, 2 on sports and 2 on domestic and political news, and others scattered among other categories.

On the average, a little more than 2 would be development news, while between 8 and 9 would be *not* development news.

Six major interpretable factors among readers according to their news reading emerged in factor analysis of the data.[7] Five of the factors were strongly centered on local and national news—different aspects of it, but still news of the Philippines. The sixth factor contained readers who concentrated on foreign and non-Third World news. Individuals who were separated out by this factor tended to be better educated than the average, higher in occupational status, older, and urban rather than rural. This characteristic of foreign news reading, of course, is not peculiar to the Philippines.

Another way to analyze the results is in terms of the proportion of space devoted to different categories of news as contrasted with the proportion of average reading in those categories. (See Table 10.)

The two columns are not strikingly different except in a few categories. Readers were apparently more interested in domestic and political news than would be expected from the space it got, and they were somewhat more interested in stories of military and political violence than the space allocation would predict. On the other hand, reading was less in proportion to space in the case of economic and business news; newspapers elsewhere have found out that interest in this category is intense among some, but by no means among all of the readers. And readers, as the critics predicted, appeared to be less interested than the space allocation would suggest in news of crime, court trials, accidents, and disasters.

The reading of development news deserves a further word. Of the 129 stories in the *Bulletin Today,* 37 were classifiable as news of economic and social development. These got 32% of the space but only 22% of the reading. Furthermore, with only occasional exceptions, development stories from outside the Philippines, few as they were, drew less reader attention than national and local development stories. Overall, reading of development news was only 6.4% as compared to 8.4% for average news and 9.3% for nondevelopment news. These figures point to the difficulty Third World editors and information policy makers face in trying to accomplish the oft-stated goal of bringing more development news to people and exchanging more of it between countries.

SOME NOTES ON THE QUALITY
OF NEWS COVERAGE

Development News

Let us pick up the topic of development news with which we ended the previous section of this article.

TABLE 10:   Comparison of News Allocation in Asian Daily Newspapers and the
             Percentage of an Average Manila *Bulletin Today* Reader's Daily
             Reading in Each Category

Category of News	Percentage of Space	Percentage of Reading
Military, political violence	3.4	6.4
Foreign relations	7.1	6.4
Domestic, political	5.2	16.4
Economic, business	36.7	27.3
Science, health	3.0	2.7
Education	5.1	4.5
Accident, disaster	2.0	– –
Judicial, crime	4.3	2.7
Sports	18.8	17.3
Culture	1.7	1.0
Human interest	1.0	2.7
Other	11.8	12.7

Third World spokesmen complain of a shortage of "positive" news. For
example, Dilip Mukerjee, a well-known Asian editor, has said:

> Our need is urgent and acute; we belong to societies which are in the process of re-
> structuring and reshaping themselves. In our environment there is and there will be
> for a long time to come, much that is ugly and distasteful. If we follow the western
> norm, we will be playing up only those dark spots, and thus helping unwittingly to
> erode the faith and confidence without which growth and development are im-
> possible [Quoted by Tharoor, 1977: 29].

By development news, Third World spokesmen therefore mean mostly "good"
news. There is no doubt that this kind of news is in short supply on most news
channels in Asia. To find out more about what was actually happening, we
selected thirty stories of "development" from six countries—ten from China, five
from India, three from Sri Lanka, three from South Korea, three from the Philippines, and six from Indonesia. These thirty items were about evenly divided
among science and education (for example, new discoveries in surgery, plans to
revive fourteen academic disciplines in China), agriculture (record harvests in
Korea and elsewhere), and industry and commerce (Shanghai's industries to be
revitalized, Jakarta's harbor to be modernized and enlarged). They range from a
new national economic plan (proposed from Sri Lanka) to one city's opening a
large number of new literacy centers (Delhi). If we had to do it again, we would
ask editors and development agencies in each country to identify, at the time,
what they considered the most significant development events or topics of the
week. But it was impossible to do this after the fact, and so we depended upon the
newspapers and national news wires for the "good" development news originat-

ing in each country. Then we examined the coverage of that news by the wires and by Asian dailies outside the country of origin. (See Figure 1.)

Neither the wires nor the newspapers have any reason to be proud of their record. No development stories were exported from either India or the Philippines. The wires picked up from Sri Lanka only one squib, on one wire only, which was the only negative note (proposed end of free rice ration for families making over $300) in a far-reaching economic plan. The wires thus carried 100 words on the new economic plan, and if the London *Observer's* Overseas News Service (OFNS) had not read the plan and written 800 words on it, which were syndicated and reprinted entirely by the *New Straits Times* and *Amrita* in Calcutta, no Asian readers outside Sri Lanka would have been likely to hear about Sri Lanka's plan at all. Altogether the international news wires carried 6000 words in 5 days on the 30 stories—an average of 1200 words per day, or 300 words per wire per day. The 16 dailies carried a total of 9670 words, an average of 604 per paper, or about 120 words per day. The wires covered 13 of the 30 stories, the dailies 11. Another 4 dailies carried none of the 30 stories at all.

Why such sparse coverage? China did better than other countries in getting its development news reported, and this may be both because China is very interesting to the rest of Asia and because China fills Hsinhua with development news and makes it available to all the international news agencies. But if we look at one of the stories from China that was not covered either by the wires or the dailies, we get another idea why so little development news was being printed. This is a we get another idea why so little development news was being printed. This is the story of China's plans to revitalize fourteen academic disciplines. This is not a "gee whiz" story. It contains no dramatic incidents. It seems to mean little until one looks behind announcement. In other words, this kind of story cannot simone looks behind the announcement. In other words, this kind of story cannot simply be copied off a police blotter or a press release. A reporter has to do some investigating. He has to find out what has been happening to scholarly disciplines in China, what is going to be done about them, what is the political significance of making the change at this particular time, and what is likely to be the effect on China's universities, the careers of its young people, and its economic development.

Many of the stories not covered or covered inadequately were of this kind. The Development Bank loan to Sri Lanka was not much of a story by itself, but it might become one if a reporter found out what it was to accomplish—a large and imaginative irrigation project. The reopening of the chief university in India's capital city is not much of a story in itself unless it is seen in the perspective of the troubled political history of India's universities. The scientist who won the Borlaug award is a local story unless one finds out what his discoveries mean to other agricultural countries in Asia.

In other words, and without going into more detail, the coverage of development news both on the wires and in the newspapers raises questions about how well newsmen are prepared to cover the stories of development. They are trained

	WIRE A	WIRE B	WIRE C	WIRE D	AMRITA ANANDA BAZAR	ANADA BAZAR PATRIKA	BANGKOK POST	CEYLON DAILY NEWS	DONG-A-ILBO	KOMPAS	KOREA TIMES	NANYANG SIANG PAO	NEW STRAITS TIMES	PHILIPPINE DAILY EXPRESS	PILIPINO EXPRESS	SING CHIA JIH PAO	SOUTH CHINA MORNING POST	SING TAO JIH PAO	STATESMAN	STRAITS TIMES
(from China)																				
1. EDUCATION PLANS																				
2. DEVELOPMENT OF ELECTRONICS		x	x	x					x			x	x				x			
3. 450,000 TEXTBOOKS SOLD	x	x		x						x										x
4. NEW DISCOVERY FOR SURGERY				x								x								
5. RECORD HARVESTS			x							x										
6. ELECTRIC SYSTEMS BUILT																				
7. MECHANIZING FARMS		x	x	x	x												x	x		
8. METEOROLOGICAL CONFERENCE	x		x																	
9. DEVELOP SHANGHAI INDUSTRY	x	x		x									x				x			
10. FILMS REHABILITATED	x			x													x	x		
(from India)																				
11. PRIZE TO SCIENTIST																				
12. STIMULUS TO HOUSE BUILDING																				
13. NEW LITERACY CENTERS																				
14. UNIVERSITY OPENS AGAIN																				
15. REGIONAL COMMON MARKET																				
(from Sri Lanka)																				
16. NEW ECONOMIC PACKAGE					x	x							x							
17. IMF GRANT																				
18. DEVELOPMENT BANK LOAN																				
(from South Korea)																				
19. RECORD RICE PRODUCTION	x		x					x									x			
20. FOREIGN CURRENCY LOANS																				
21. NEW CAPITOL CITY																				
(from the Philippines)																				
22. STUDY TOURS TO BARANGAY																				
23. $1.4 BILLION LOANS NEEDED																				
24. NUCLEAR PLANT TO BE BUILT																				
(from Indonesia)																				
25. BRANTAS RIVER REDEVELOPMENT																				
26. TO MODERNIZE HARBOR																				
27. HELP TO FARMERS			x				x													x
28. PROBLEM OF DROUGHT			x				x													
29. WORK-SCHOOL PROBLEM																				
30. OIL FROM THE SEA	x	x																		

Figure 1: Coverage of Thirty Selected Development Stories in the Four Wire Services and Asian Newspapers Outside the Country of Story Origin

to cover politics and to report striking events and feature material. Are they prepared with the economic and social understanding needed to interpret development news in meaningful terms? And is the small amount of development news in Asian dailies due to lack of interest by readers or lack of investigation and interpretation by news staffs?

The regionality of Asia

One can hardly examine a week of news coverage in Asia without concluding that Asia is more than one news region. Therefore, the quality of news coverage depends, at least in part, on where news happens.

An example is the case of Zulfikar Ali Bhutto who had been ousted as prime minister of Pakistan in a 1977 coup. He was imprisoned, and during the week of December 4, 1977, he was appealing a death sentence. The decision came on December 8, and was against Bhutto, but only three countries heard about it— India (250 words in *The Statesman*), Sri Lanka (100 words in the Ceylon *Daily News*), and the Republic of Korea (an incidental mention of 50 words in the Korea *Times*). The wires altogether carried about 150 words on the decision. Wires and papers alike carried more on a hunger strike by journalists in Pakistan going on for several days during the time of the appeal. The Southeast Asia dailies ignored the story entirely, although *Nanyang Siang Pao* of Singapore found space for a story from Pakistan that a wildcat had "made off with a man's ear."

The news from Indonesia got treatment that was a reverse mirror image of the Bhutto story. President Suharto was in trouble with student demonstrations. At the same time, he was appearing at public meetings and defending himself. The wires carried about 1000 words on President Suharto's speeches and 2000 on the student demonstrations. The South China *Morning Post* of Hong Kong printed just under 1300 words during the 5 days on President Suharto and his troubles; the *New Straits Times,* about 650; *Nanyang Siang Pao,* 1400; *Sing Chia Jih Pao* (Kuala Lumpur), just under 2000; and the *Straits Times,* about 1350. Those 5300 words were respectable coverage of the situation, but they all appeared in three Southeast Asian countries—Hong Kong, Malaysia, and Singapore. Except for 300 words in *Dong-a-Ilbo* (Seoul), this was the total Asian coverage of the story.

During the same week, former Senator Benigno S. Aquino, the political rival of President Marcos who had been in jail for five years, was appealing his condemnation to death by a military tribunal. The case had drawn wide attention, particularly in the United States; it therefore got heavy wire coverage, both before and after the decision of the appeal judge. Asian dailies outside the Philippines carried about 7000 words, but four-fifths of the coverage was in the close neighbors of the Philippines—Singapore, Malaysia, and Hong Kong. Altogether, 8 of the 14 non-Philippine papers carried something on the story, but only 5 of the 8 carried their readers as far as the judge's decision. These 5 were all in Southeast Asia. The India papers did not touch the story.

The news from China

It seems only proper to look at the flow of news from the largest country in Asia, the most populous in the world.

The flow of news outward from China is surprisingly large when one considers that the kind of news Chinese journalists call "aberrations" and Western readers think of as exciting events—accidents, disasters, violence, crime, judicial trials— rarely appears in Chinese news coverage, and that many of the most interesting parts of the policy-making process—debates on national and foreign policy, confrontations of political personalities, and election campaigns—are typically conducted away from the public eye and only the results are announced.

The 4 international wires provide about 5000 words a day from China, although the range among wires is large—from 800 to 2500. The 16 Asian dailies in our sample printed a total of about 17,000 words on an average day. Thus the average Asian daily (if there were such a thing) could be thought of as carrying about 1100 words on China, although there is a wide range among newspapers as well as wires—from 0 in *Ananda Bazar Patrika* and 100 per week in *Amirta* to nearly 4000 in *Sing Tao Jih Pao*. Indeed, 40% of all the China news published in the 16 dailies appeared in the 2 large Hong Kong papers, *Sing Tao* and the South China *Morning Post*.

Hsinhua, the official China news agency, carried about 18 stories a day about China on the wire that was made available to Hong Kong bureaus. The 4 international news wires altogether carried an average of 34 stories a day, 12 to 14 being different stories. The "average" daily of our 16 carried 2 or 3 stories, although the South China *Morning Post* averaged 9 a day. Thus we have a pattern much like the general flow described earlier. (See Figure 2.)

About 75% of the news from China reaches Asian daily papers through the four international wires, but Hsinhua should have relatively little objection to the way its news is handled either by the wires or the dailies. Both wires and newspapers follow the Chinese lead in reporting little or no crime or accident news, and a great deal of foreign relations news. The chief difference is that outside observers are more interested in domestic political developments within China than the Chinese media are. The kind of domestic news one finds in Hsinhua or the *People's Daily* tends to be news of development—economic, scientific, and educational. The international wires, the Asian dailies, and Hsinhua all devote somewhere near 40% of their stories on China to domestic, political, economic, scientific, and educational news, although outside China a much higher proportion is concerned with domestic politics, and inside China a higher proportion is economics, science, and education. The cadres read political news in lists of officials who attend a meeting or a ceremony or a banquet, but these names are usually edited out by the international wires. One type of news characteristic of China is the parade of visitors, governmental or nongovernmental, given official attention in Peking, and the parade of Chinese representatives, governmental or nongovernmental, through other countries. The international wires reported the visitors *to* Peking more faithfully than those *from* Peking; the dailies covered

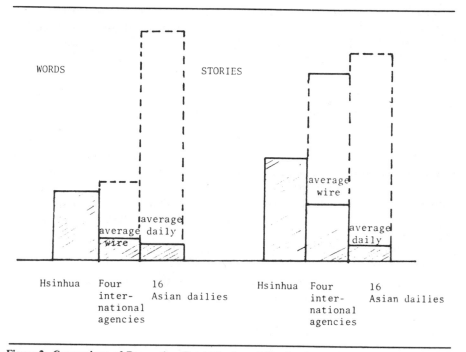

Figure 2: Comparison of Proportion Total Words and Stories Appearing in Asian Newspapers and Wire Services that are About China

neither group very fully, but concentrated on *future* travels—"Teng to visit Burma," "Prime Minister invited to visit Peking."

An example of the kind of editing some Chinese news gets is what happened to Hsinhua's 900-word account of the memorial service for Mr. Wu, who toward the end of a long and distinguished career had become vice president of the National Academy of Science and a member of the Standing Committee of the National People's Congress. The Hsinhua story used almost half of its space to list the national leaders who presented wreaths and attended the memorial service. Wu's career was described briefly, and there were long quotations from the eulogy by Fang Yi. Three international wires picked up the story, carrying a total of about 450 words. Thus the average wire story was about one-sixth the length of Hsinhua's account. Most of the names of dignitaries at the funeral were omitted, Wu's chief titles and positions were briefly listed, and a sentence or so was quoted from Fang's memorial address. Example:

> Fang said Wu "applied himself to science and technology with a strict and down-to-earth approach and passed on his knowledge earnestly. He trained a large number of scientific workers, some of whom have become well-known scientists in China and abroad."

In each of the international wire stories, the name of at least one of China's top leaders was listed as attending the ceremony and/or presenting a wreath, but there were no such long lists as in Hsinhua. The South China *Morning Post* and *Nanyang Siang Pao,* to give examples, used the wire copy with the change of only a few words. The *Post* added a three-column picture.

One type of news story from China more likely to be found in the Asian dailies than in China itself is the general review article on developments in China. This is particularly the case with the dailies in Hong Kong, which sit on the doorstep of China in the midst of a legion of "China watchers." These newspapers, and some others in our sample, have special channels of information on China in addition to the international wires and Hsinhua. The result is articles like "Internal security tightens in Kwangtung," "Freedom of speech in China criticized by Canadian journalist," "Differences erupt in Chinese leadership," "Peking emphasizes educational TV," "Purged leaders back in posts." These headlines are all from Hong Kong papers.

The news from India

The second largest country in Asia got about 3% of the wire service news coverage and a little less in the newspapers. Yet interesting and important things were happening in India at the time.

The country was recovering from the worst storm of the century, which had killed 8000 people; an explosion at the nuclear heavy water plant in Baroda was suspected to be sabotage. Two important commissions were in session, issuing statements and reports which were being discussed and challenged—the Shah Commission, investigating the "national emergency" and consequently the leadership of Indira Gandhi, and the Reddi Commission, investigating illegal acts of former officials including Sanjay Gandhi. Parliament was in session, asking the sometimes newsworthy and embarrassing questions that Indian parliaments ask; politics was hot, with Janata and Mrs. Gandhi's new Congress Party gearing up for important elections. India was playing Australia in cricket at Brisbane; and there were other spicy items, like the arrest of 500 striking teachers, and publications of an allegation that Nehru had asked Mountbatten to take charge of India after partition.

How was this news handled?

The 4 international wires carried 135 stories, about 35,000 words, on India. And 13 Third World newspapers outside India carried 70 stories totaling 24,000 words, an average of 1850 words each. The coverage was uneven: 2 newspapers carried nothing; and 2 other newspapers, the *New Straits Times* and the South China *Morning Post,* actually carried more news than one of the wires. (See Figure 3.)

Since the *New Straits Times* carried the largest amount of copy on India, it may be interesting to review what it told its readers. It reported the Shah Commission at two points during the week: when the Congress Party told its members to boycott the hearings, and when the Commission seemed "headed.

	WIRE A	WIRE B	WIRE C	WIRE D	Bangkok Post	Ceylon Daily News	Dong-A-Ilbo	Kompas	Korean Times	Nanyang Siang Pao	New Straits Times	Philippine Daily Express	Pilipino Express	Sing Chia Jih Pao	Sing Tao Jih Pao	South China Morning Post	Straits Times
SHA Commission	X	X	6X	7X		X					2X	X				2X	X
REDDI Commission		X									X						
BARODA Explosion	X		X	2X		X		X	X		X	X		X			
Mill RIOT	X		2X	2X	X					X	2X	X		X			
P.M. to Nepal	X	X	2X	X													
CRICKET	2X		5X	4X		2X				X	2X					2X	
BASKETBALL	2X	2X	X	X	2X					X				X		X	
STORM Victims	2X	3X	X	X				X							X	X	
TEACHERS Arrested			X			X					X					X	
MURDER Trial				X							X						
India at Sri Lanka MEETING				3X						X							

Figure 3: Coverage of Eleven News Stories from India by Four International News Wires and Thirteen Asian Daily Newspapers[a]

a. Figure preceding X indicates number of stories during the five days.

for a showdown" with Mrs. Gandhi concerning her unwillingness to testify. The Baroda explosion was described as a "setback for India's fuel output." Readers were told about hostages being slain, and workers "dying in riots"; of a crime fancied up by reporters into a "chicken curry murder"; and about the 500 picketing teachers being arrested. The *Times* carried one story on the Reddi Commission: Sanjay Gandhi denied that he exerted any undue influence. It carried one story on Parliament—the Janata Party suffered its first legislative defeat (on a banking reform bill). The cricket match was fully reported; altogether, 43% of the coverage of India was about sports.

As a matter of fact, the cricket match was by far the best covered Indian story of the week on the wires too. No less than 45% of one wire's coverage and 30% of a second wire's coverage were cricket. Together, these two wires carried about 9000 words on the match in Brisbane.

The unevenness of the coverage of political and social news had three results worth noting. In the first place, there was insufficient background for many of the ongoing developments. If readers had heard about the political unrest in Karnataka and Andrha Pradesh, they might have been less surprised to read about the victory of Mrs. Gandhi's new Party in those two elections two months later. India was making a special effort to take care of its storm victims, but readers would hardly have known it, although Billy Graham got several hundred words of wire coverage merely by touring the storm area.

In the second place, readers would not have heard about some events that got attention in India, but little or none outside. One of these was the intended repeal of the Maintenance of Internal Security Act, the chief legislative weapon of Mrs. Gandhi's "emergency." Another was the death of one of India's most famous musicians, Ustad Khan. It was announced that India's budget deficit might be ten times the expected amount. In numerous parts of India, there were violent demonstrations by students, resulting in closing of universities. There was a thoughtful analysis of the results of India's birth control-program. But these were not covered on the wires.

A third result of the uneven coverage was to provide different pictures of India in different places. We were impressed by the relative evenhandedness which both wires and dailies showed in reporting the chief political struggle underway in India—between Mrs. Gandhi and the prime minister, Morarji Desai. They reported both the Shah Commission's accusations and Mrs. Gandhi's replies—when they reported the Commission at all. But we asked a young Chinese scholar to read the three large Chinese dailies in East Asia—*Sing Chia Jih Pao* of Singapore, *Nanyang Siang Pao* of Kuala Lumpur, and *Sing Tao Jih Pao* of Hong Kong—and report to us on the picture of India derived from that experience. He reported with some surprise that the three newspapers had conveyed different impressions.

Sing Chia carried eighteen items concerning India, although only three of them were solely about India and eight mentioned the country only briefly. The bulk of the coverage was on sports. There was one story on crime, two on disasters, two on economic matters, one on domestic government, one on foreign relations. The theme of economic troubles came through clearly—the "Green Revolution" judged a failure, and much of the failure blamed on the caste system; textile workers on strike killing five senior executives; storm victims waiting to be fed, clothed, and sheltered; the former prime minister refusing to testify before the Shah Commission and thus strengthening the suspicion of wrongdoing, and so on. As a whole, he said, the picture of India that emerged from *Sing Chia* was rather grim: its economy hampered by the social structure and stricken by disasters; its lack of political unity in a time of national crisis; a country with little to boast about except basketball.

The sports image also came through in *Nanyang Siang Pao*. Of *Nanyang*'s 33 stories on India, 22 were on sports, along with 3 pictures of her participants in the Asian tournament. The economic troubles also come through: A story reports "50 million people undernourished." But a somewhat different theme also appears—India's international activity. India participates actively in the meeting on news agencies. It is one of the countries negotiating with the EEC for new textile quotas. It is presented as a force to be reckoned with in the future of the Indian Ocean. Thus the general impression is upbeat rather than downbeat. India is active in sports, concerned with economic and political problems, but also active and influential with other nations.

The large Chinese daily, *Sing Tao* in Hong Kong carried only nine stories on India during the week. Three of them were on sports, two on economic matters, one on science, one on human rights, and one apparently written to encourage tourism. Except for the tourism pitch, however, none of the stories is solely about India. India is always mentioned in connection with other countries, sometimes quite casually. Thus, a representative from Hong Kong is attending an international climatology meeting in India; India is one of the countries participating in Hong Kong's present negotiations with the EEC on textiles; the British prime minister is planning a visit to Bangladesh, and India will be his next stop; India is *one* of the countries accused of violating human rights, and so forth. To *Sing Tao*, our reader concluded, India does not seem very important.

Thus, three papers, three pictures.

Two well-covered stories

(1) The plane crash. At about 8:35 in the evening of Sunday, December 4, a Boeing 737 of Malaysia Airlines crashed at Johore, Malaysia. All the one hundred persons aboard were killed. The plane had apparently been hijacked on its way from Kuala Lumpur to Singapore. This was the most spectacular story of the week in Asia, and it provides an opportunity to see how Third World news channels handle a disaster story.

The first bulletin we have seen came at 2140, Sunday the 4th. It came from Singapore and read:

> URGENT: A Malaysia Airlines plane crashed at the Jurong Industrial area here tonight, it was learned here today. It is understood that the plane, from Kuala Lumpur, was carrying about 90 passengers. No further details were available.

That was almost exactly one hour after the crash.

The second report came 40 minutes later. This time, the exact number of passengers (93) and crew members (7) was reported. It was reported also that the plane was a Boeing 737 and "overflew Kuala Lumpur due to a technical fault." No mention of hijacking yet.

Short reports began to come at intervals of a few minutes. A Singapore police rescue squad was rushing to the scene. Then the word "hijack" first appears in the news. It was still in the stage of rumor. It was also reported that the general manager of Malaysia Airlines had left for Singapore to investigate the crash.

The first details on passengers aboard the unfortunate plane came about one and a half hours after the first bulletin. Readers were told that Malaysia's minister of agriculture and the Cuban ambassador to Japan were thought to have been on the plane and to have been killed in the crash.

These preliminary facts about the crash were all reported in takes of one hundred words or less. The first major news-break came two hours after the first report. The wire carried a bulletin saying that according to Malaysia Airline sources, the plane had been hijacked by (Japanese) Red Army men.

About five hours after the crash, it was reported that the site of the crash had been located. Shortly after, integrated stories of the accident began to come out, although still lacking many of the essential details. Rescue workers had reached the crash site. There were no survivors. The rescue team could find only two complete bodies; the rest were torn into bits and pieces. Then the emphasis turned to confirming the names of the victims (among whom were, indeed, the Cuban ambassador, the Malaysian minister, and a high official of the World Bank) and trying to find out reliable details of the cause. Malaysia Airlines denied earlier reports that Red Army guerrillas had been involved, but the pilot was reported to have radioed the tower that he was in distress before the plane disappeared from radar screens.

During the first 24 hours, all the news agencies got correspondents to the site of the crash and carried stories about the scene. One wire warned editors (perhaps thinking of broadcasters who might tear off the copy and read it on the air without editing) that portions of its following report might be objectionable to some readers. The story began:

> There were no groans, no moans and no cries for help at Kampong Tanjung Kutang. . . . There were no survivors. . . . Hideously strewn here and there . . . were a hand, a leg, a head.

Another wire:

> The little fishing village on the Southern tip of Johore where the MAS Boeing 737 exploded in midair never looked like a crash scene at all. . . . I and two other Singapore journalists reached a small clearing that made us wonder if someone had done up the place for the coming Christmas season.

Gradually during the following days, the details were cleared up, and the story was carried through as competent newsmen do.

The wires were really very similar in the coverage they gave the story, and when they diverged it was usually to include feature material (for example, the grief at the homes of victims, or the relief of persons who had almost been passengers on that particular plane). Altogether about 25,000 words moved over the 4 international waves that week. The briefest coverage by an individual wire was about 4000 words; the most extensive, nearly 10,000.

How did the newspapers handle the story? Ten of the sixteen dailies reported it on Monday, December 5. Three more (*Kompas* of Jakarta, the Korea *Times*, and *Dong-a-Ilbo*) caught up with it on Tuesday, December 6. Three papers, two in India, one a native language paper in Manila, did not cover it at all.

The coverage in Singapore and Malaysia was massive. For both these countries, it was practically a local story, and they could use their own reporters and photographers. Here is what appeared during the five days in the two Singapore and the two Kuala Lumpur papers:

Nanyang Siang Pau	1018 column inches of copy, 1206 square inches of photographs
New Straits Times	498 column inches of copy, 706 square inches of photographs
Sing Chia Jih Pao	892 column inches of copy, 767 square inches of photographs
Straits Times	354 column inches of copy, 511 square inches of photographs

This is the equivalent of over 140,000 words, plus 3190 square inches of pictures—more than 10 full pages of pictures.

Coverage elsewhere was less. It depended, except for local angles, on the news agencies. (See Figure 4.)

Despite the extent of the coverage, it was nevertheless uneven throughout Asia. The regionality of news showed up dramatically. The Ceylon *Daily News* carried during the week a total of 26 column inches, no picture; *Dong-a-Ilbo*, 24 column inches, no picture. Of the Indian papers, 2 did not carry anything on it. *The Statesman* had a bulletin, 1½ inches, on Monday. On Thursday it carried 3 inches, mentioning a denial by the Malaysian home minister that the Japanese Red Army had been involved. The total was 4½ inches of copy, no picture. The Malaysian papers carried about 60 times as many words, and the

Newspaper	December					
	5	6	7	8	9	10
South China Morning Post	X	X	X	X	X	X
Sing Tao Jih Pao	X	X	X	X		X
Bangkok Post	X	X	X	X	X	X
Philippine Daily Express	X	X	X	X		
Ceylon Daily News	X	X		X		X
Kompas		X	X			
Korea Times		X	X			
Dong-a-Ilbo		X	X			
Statesman	X				X	

Figure 4: Coverage by Dates of Hijacked Boeing 737 Crash in Newspapers Outside Malaysia and Singapore

Singapore papers about 50 times as many, as the Indian and Sri Lanka papers combined.

Of course, coverage tended to be heavier in countries that were either geographically or psychologically closer to the event. It was also heavier where the newspapers could use their own staffers (as in Singapore and Malaysia), lighter where a newspaper had to depend on the wires, despite the fact that the wires covered the story well and fully. Why no more attention was paid to the story in India we do not know. Perhaps India was preoccupied with its own disasters.

(2) The Tripoli story. The Tripoli meeting of Arab states opposed to President Sadat's initiative began before the week of our study, and almost all the news from it came in the first two days—December 5 and 6 for the wire services, December 6 and 7 for the newspapers. When our week began, therefore, the conference was already winding down, and thereafter the attention of the wires turned back to the continuing confrontation between Sadat and his opponents.

The amount of coverage on Tripoli is even more striking than the raw figures make it seem. In our sample of Asian dailies, it was the most widely covered story, appearing in more papers than did the crash of the hijacked plane. Of the 16 dailies, 14 carried it, all of them with the essential facts. In 2 days the 4 international wires carried nearly 20,000 words, the newspapers nearly 50,000. The average was 4840 per wire, 3430 per paper. The fact that 14 newspapers would average 1700 words per day on a story from a faraway region is little short of phenomenal in view of other coverage we have reported. (See Table 11.)

Why did the story draw so much coverage? It was, of course, the most newsworthy single event in the Third World outside Asia during the early part of that week. Television would provide special competition for newspapers on a story of this kind. Beyond that, it was Third World rather than Big Power news. And there may have been a still more subtle reason: This story, more

TABLE 11: Coverage of Tripoli Arabs States Meeting in Wire Services and Asian Daily Newspapers

Coverage of Tripoli Story (in number of words)			
Wires		Newspapers	
Wire A	5540	Amrita Bazar Patrika	1330
Wire B	3570	Bangkok Post	2040
Wire C	4410	Ceylon Daily	1200
Wire D	5830	Dong-a-Ilbo	4660
Total	19350	Kompas	850
		Korea Times	3720
		Nanyang Siang Pao	9270
		New Straits Times	4110
		Philippine Daily Express	1840
		South China Morning Post	1780
		The Statesman	2750
		Straits Times	910
		Sing Chia Jih Pao	7920
		Sing Tao Jih Pao	5770
		Total	48050

than most others, seemed to provide a reason for interpretation and commentary.

On the wires, for example, the coverage was by no means limited to hard news of events. Several newspapers and commentators were quoted on the meaning of Tripoli. One wire carried almost 1000 words analyzing the rift among the Arab countries, and nearly 900 words of feature material on the meeting after it ended. Other wires carried interpretive and background material. The papers also seemed to feel that the story deserved editorial comment or background articles. No fewer than 5 newspapers published editorials on Tripoli during the 2 days when coverage was high, and 2 others carried general background articles on the Arab situation in general. A distinguished Asian editor remarked recently that Asian readers, unlike Western readers, do not keep up with daily events in the world and therefore need more background in order to understand events as they are reported. This was being provided in the coverage of the Tripoli meeting, and for the most part *not* being provided in the coverage of Asian development news. We return to a question previously asked: Are journalists better trained to analyze and interpret political than economic developments?

SOME MODEST SUGGESTIONS

We fully intend, as we already said, to avoid entanglement in the controversy raging over the international news media. However, on the basis of what we have seen, perhaps we may be permitted to make a few modest suggestions.

(1) We are not the ideal persons to judge the quality and fairness of news in Asia. Any editor or scholar from an Asian country would be better able to say how fairly and perceptively his country is being reported. Is this perhaps a good time to think of repeating in a modernized version what the International Press Institute did in the 1950s? They asked a leading editor from one country, say India, to comment on the coverage of India in some of the leading papers of another country, say Britain, during a one-month period. Would it not be worthwhile to repeat the scheme, bringing together editors from Third World and non-Third World countries, with files of the relevant papers, and files of wire copy also?

(2) Third World countries are not yet ready to do without the international news agencies, from which they get two-thirds of their foreign news. But the enormous amount of unused copy on those wires—7 out of 8 stories for the average Asian daily—suggests that there is plenty of room for negotiation and change if Asia is not satisfied with the wire news coming in. The news agencies are conciliatory. The situation seems to call for a frank exchange of opinion and information on needs and capabilities.

(3) Ultimately, the countries of Asia will want and need a Third World news agency—either regional or global. Few people seem to feel the news pools are working very well as yet. The Third World is not yet ready to staff and finance a full-fledged agency. How can the industrialized countries and the international media help them to get ready? Internships on existing news agencies? Short, intensive workshops on the model of the American Press Institute? Sharing of some experienced wire service newsmen? Sharing of equipment?

(4) In development news, it looks as though both Asian and Western newsmen need help. How can we help them learn enough about economics and social change to cover this kind of news? Seminars? Workshops? Internships in development agencies? Evening courses? A new component in journalism school training in "developed" countries as well as in Asia?

(5) Finally, we hope that nothing we have said about the needs of Third World countries implies that non-Third World countries have any less need to cover the Third World. At this time in history, the industrialized countries of the world have just as much need to understand what is happening in the Third World as Third World countries have to understand what is happening beyond their borders. It would be a very sad day, therefore, if representatives of the international wires or foreign newspapers were restrained from covering news in Third World countries. These news channels are more than channels; they are lifelines.

NOTES

1. This is a summary preview of parts of a book which Dr. Erwin Atwood and I are writing for publication in 1980. The book reports a study done mostly at the Chinese University of Hong Kong

when I was there as Visiting Aw Boon Haw Professor in 1977 and 1978. Dr. Atwood's help was beyond price, especially in the computer analysis, but he should be held blameless for this preliminary report, for which I take sole responsibility.

2. Much to our regret, we were unable to obtain copies of Tass.

3. The dailies were: *Amritabazar Patrika*, Calcutta; *Anandabazar*, Calcutta; Bangkok *Post*, Bangkok; Ceylon *Daily News*, Columbo; *Dong-a-Ilbo*, Seoul; *Nanyang Siang Pao*, Kuala Lumpur; *New Straits Times*, Kuala Lumpur; Philippine *Daily Express*, Manila; *Philipino Express*, Manila; *Sing Chia Jih Pao*, Singapore; *Sing Tao Jih Pao*, Hong Kong; South China *Morning Post*, Hong Kong; *The Statesman*, Calcutta and New Delhi; *Straits Times*, Singapore. For each country, we tried, where feasible, to study one English and one non-English language paper. In addition to these, we studied both content and readership of the *Bulletin Today*, Manila.

4. Chief participants in the study at the Institute of Communication Studies, University of Hong Kong, were Clara King-wah Chan, Mansoon Chow, Mr. and Mrs. Leonard Chu, Paul Siu-nam Lee, Hau-yeung Leung, Chee-kong Yeung, and Mei-fun Ying in addition to Timothy L. M. Yu, director of the Institute. Elsewhere in Hong Kong, Virginia Casino and S. Kamaluddin were involved. At the East-West Center, Dr. Georgette Wang participated. Both in Hong Kong, where he was a visiting professor for one term on leave from Southern Illinois University, and later at his own university, Dr. Erwin Atwood worked on this project. Dr. Atwood was assisted in some of the computer analysis by Mrs. Sunshine Kwang. At the University of the Philippines, Dr. Feliciano, Marilou de Ocamp, and Eleanor Baquiran were participants.

I must say frankly that we had only a few thousand dollars for this entire story, the greater part of which paid for readership interviews in the Philippines. We could never have gathered and analyzed the massive data needed for the study without extraordinary contributions by the participants, many of whom gave time and some of whom contributed cash.

5. I mean, for example, a story about the relations of India and Pakistan—thus of both domestic and foreign interest.

6. It should be explained that these figures are based on 15 rather than 16 dailies. One of the 16 papers in our sample, the *Ananda Bazar Patrika*, the largest newspaper in India, carried that week an average of only *one* foreign Third World story per day. We omitted that daily from the totals, wondering whether its performance that week was representative.

7. Factor analysis was the special province of Professor Erwin Atwood.

REFERENCES

PINCH, EDWARD T. (1978) "A Brief Study of News Patterns in Sixteen Third World Countries." Prepared for presentation April 2, 1978, Cairo, Egypt, and commissioned by the Edward R. Murrow Center of Public Diplomacy, the Fletcher School of Law and Diplomacy, Tufts University, Medford, Massachusetts.
SWANSON, CHARLES E. (1951) "What They Read in 130 Daily Newspapers." Journalism Quarterly, 28: 411-421.
THAROOR, ROGER (1977) "News Flow and Press Freedom." Presented at a conference on the Third World and Press Freedom under the auspices of the Edward R. Murrow Center of Public Diplomacy, May 11-13, New York.

A. Doak Barnett, one of the best-known China scholars, describes how the Chinese use very little technology to achieve striking pervasiveness, penetration, and intensity of mass communication. China has a highly centralized, national system in which messages flow down through the Communist regime's major hierarchies of organization. Great stress is given to interpersonal communication through organizations. Dr. Barnett suggests that much research is needed into the role of communication in conflict resolution in China, especially in light of little apparent upward or lateral communication. Dr. Barnett is Senior Fellow at the Brookings Institution, Washington, D.C.

35

THE COMMUNICATION SYSTEM
IN CHINA
Some Generalizations, Hypotheses, and
Questions for Research

A. Doak Barnett

The revolution in communications in China since 1949 has played a major role in the broader processes of political, economic, and cultural change that have altered profoundly the nature of Chinese society in the past quarter-century. Valuable research has already been done on aspects of China's new system of communication. But there is clearly a need for more.

On the basis of what is now known, what are some of the basic characteristics of this new communication system that need further examination? What are some of the major questions about it that now need to be investigated? Can one formulate hypotheses about the system, its operation, and its effects--in practice as well as in theory--that point to areas for research that should be given priority in the period ahead?

One of the most striking characteristics of the communication system in China today is its pervasiveness, penetration, and intensity, with minimum technology. In relation to its size, China still has only limited communications technology. It is true that the Communists have done a good deal to develop modern media. If one compares the situation of today with that of 25 years ago (to say nothing of that in traditional China), the technology of communication has advanced considerably. Yet if one compares China with societies that are more highly developed, technologically and scientifically, such as Japan, it is clear that the Chinese are still operating with minimum technological facilities for communication. For example, even though the Chinese press has developed substantially, its distribution is still relatively small for the size of its population. The written word obviously has a crucial importance in China today, but its direct impact is greatest on elite groups and those in the bureaucratic structure of power. Television is in its infancy. Of the modern means of mass communication, radio--including the wired rediffusion system that has spread widely throughout the country--probably now has the greatest mass impact. But even in radio communication, if one compares China and Japan, there is no doubt that China's technological capabilities are still limited.

In examining communication media in China, one must look, therefore, at things other than the modern media. A notable characteristic of the present communication system in China is that it incorporates almost every conceivable means of communication, including many traditional ones, such as story telling, old-style "comic books," and popular drama. Nevertheless, even taking these into account,

From A. Doak Barnett, "The Communication System in China: Some Generalizations, Hypotheses, and Questions for Research," *Communication in China: Perspectives and Hypotheses*, Paper 16 of the East-West Communication Institute (March 1978). Reprinted by permission.

the Chinese system appears to be far more pervasive, penetrating, and intense than one would expect simply from an analysis of the media. Why?

One answer is that there is an intimate and crucial link between communication and organization in contemporary China. The Chinese Communists see communication as a means to create new political and social organizations, and they see all political and social organizations as important channels of communication. This makes the system fundamentally different from that in any modern pluralistic society, such as in the United States or Japan, where there is a great outpouring of communications, through many channels, that reach millions of individuals. But no disciplined, organizational structure exists to reinforce them, nor is one desired. In China, a direct link exists between organization and communication. Great stress is placed on face-to-face, oral communication, through organizations. In analyzing how communications are diffused throughout China, it is misleading, therefore, to look simply at what is transmitted via the identifiable media. Even more important are the messages communicated down through the regime's major organizational hierarchies, then out from these hierarchies through organizational channels, and ultimately to the mass of the population.

The following key elements exist in the organizational apparatus in this dual system of communication and organization: at the top, the disciplined Party, state, and military hierarchies are of key importance, as are the organizations for mass campaigns; finally, and perhaps most important, at the bottom levels, Chinese society is organized in a unique way into hsiao-tzu (small groups) of many sorts, including hsüeh-hsi hsiao-tzu (study groups). The organization of the entire population into small overlapping groups is distinctive. Through these groups, intense social pressures of many sorts are exerted on virtually all individuals in Chinese society.

The dividing lines between organization and communication or, more broadly, between state and society are blurred; it is often hard, in fact, to define that line in China. Some scholars argue that this has always been true in Chinese society, at least to some extent: that traditionally the state and society were much more intimately linked than in pluralistic Western societies. Perhaps, but this is even more true now. Since 1949, the state and the society in China have at times seemed to be virtually merged (although in periods when central control has been weakened, as during the Cultural Revolution, it has been evident that the merger is by no means complete).

What are the characteristics of the small groups that play such important roles in the political, social, and communication systems in China today? To start with, normally they are directly linked to higher authorities, which makes them very different from most citizens groups in pluralistic societies. There is almost always a politically-directed hierarchy to which a group is connected. Someone within the group is usually in close touch with the hierarchy, or at least with some group within the leadership sector. Instructions, information, and the definition of acceptable values come from above; they are sent down to these groups by higher authorities. The prime functions of local groups are to mobilize peer pressure and, through propaganda, indoctrination, and "criticism and self-criticism," to achieve acceptance, compliance, commitment, and action--based on the impulses coming

from above. At times, the local groups also express their own interests, but this
is not their primary function (in fact, it is generally not viewed as a legitimate
function).

The intensity with which the system affects different types of people in
China clearly varies. The pressure to submit and conform is greatest with respect
to deviants--for example those in reform-through-labor institutions. However, the
pressure is also great both on all those who work within the bureaucratic hierarchies
of the regime and on intellectuals and students. "Ordinary people," this is, rank
and file workers and peasants, feel the effects of this system, but with less intensity. There are also obvious differences between urban and rural areas; people in
cities are clearly more affected than peasants in the countryside. How great the
differences are is a question that deserves further research.

The communication system in China today is a highly centralized and national system that communicates with speed, as well as intensity, throughout most of
the country. This is very different from what existed in the past. Traditional
China had an effective, but slow, system of communication. Over the decades, and
even centuries, the diffusion of cultural values and social practices through this system was impressive. But it was the result of a very gradual filtering-down process.
Education was of key importance, and various kinds of social pressures reinforced
particular values. But not only was the process extremely slow; there was also a
great deal of regional variation and localism. Today, once the impulses are sent
by the center, they are transmitted very rapidly throughout the entire country.

In order to understand China's present national communication system, it is
necessary to analyze the interrelationships of several elements, some public, some
not. The regime has an elaborate internal structure of bureaucratic communication
(which we have learned something about in recent years from documents that have
filtered out of China) that obviously is a key element in the system. Its messages
are highly differentiated; they are contained in many types of directives, with different levels of authoritativeness and with different degrees of classification. However,
since most of these messages are classified, we know much less about them than we
would like. Ordinary Chinese do not know much about them either.

What we do have is easy access to the open system of public mass communication. Several interesting studies have been made of the mass media in China, and
there is beginning to be a significant literature dealing with them. But much can
still be done to increase our understanding of the media. Finally, a better understanding is needed of the social dynamics of how small groups operate in China,
that is, how social pressure is exerted through them. There have been a few interesting studies of such groups, but much more needs to be done.

In China--in contrast with countries such as Japan or the United States--the
content of communications emanating from the center, and disseminated through the
Party-controlled system, tends to be highly focused, not diffuse. At any particular
time, the top leadership usually focuses attention on a few priority objectives, and
the communication system concentrates on trying to deal with these. This too makes
the system very different from those in pluralistic societies.

The communication system in China today is highly purposeful. Its function is not primarily to inform; rather, it is to stimulate action, to mobilize people, to change values and beliefs, and to change behavior. The Chinese Communists see an intimate link between beliefs and behavior.

By concentrating on a few objectives, Chinese leaders can achieve visible results. But such concentration also has obvious liabilities. The leaders often neglect certain problems while concentrating on priority tasks; the costs of this deserve careful analysis.

Above all, the communication system in China today puts an extraordinary emphasis on normative goals, on values. The leadership stresses what the Chinese call "thought reform," ssu hsiang kai tsao. Because their goal is to create a new "culture," they spend a great deal of time on basic ideological education. This is true in most small groups as well as in the mass media. Great effort is spent on communicating, through repetition, fundamental ideology--simplified, with values usually defined in black and white terms--good and bad. The distinctive scale of values of the late Chairman Mao Tse-tung put enormous stress on the need for ideological transformation, often giving it higher priority than increased production or structural social change, although these are obviously linked. His assumption was that if the mass of people could be induced to accept a new culture, a new set of values, this would automatically set a new framework for thinking and behavior. It would set boundaries on what people could think and do, and make "right thinking" and compliance close to being automatic. The assumption has been that if the people know what the new ground rules of the society are, they will know what patterns of behavior are required and will conform to them.

In China today, the language, per se, is an enormously important transmitter of values. Every revolution introduces a new language, and the Chinese revolution is no exception. The Communists' new terminology carries tremendous freight, introducing new norms and political and social ideas. Language is a tool for change, and the regime's new slogans, symbols, and models, have powerful effects. The use of historical analogy and allusion, as well as of "esoteric communication" (using ideological "code words") requires that members of the society (and outside observers) learn entirely new ways of communicating.

One of the basic functions of the communication system in China today is to control, limit, and restrict information, as well as to diffuse new ideas and values. In certain respects, of course, the system is very effective in transmitting information that the regime wants to spread. One example is the dissemination of simple agricultural information through the regime's extension system, which may well be more effective in China than in any other developing society. The other side of the coin, however, is that the information diffused in China is extremely restricted. The average Chinese today has little knowledge of many aspects of his or her own society, and even less about the rest of the world. These people must spend a great amount of time and effort trying to learn what in another type of society would be in public domain. This raises important questions that deserve further analysis:

What information is disseminated, and what is <u>not</u>, in China? What is the level of knowledge, or <u>lack</u> of knowledge, about key questions among different groups of Chinese?

Finally, it is important to recognize that the present Chinese system is based on a complex mix of persuasion and coercion. Many observers, including myself, have stressed the importance of political persuasion in China. The Chinese put an enormous stress on "voluntarism." Yet much of the persuasion in China is clearly "coercive persuasion." Coercion--sometimes subtle, sometimes not, usually in the background, but at times in the foreground--is essential for the system to work as it does. In the early days of the regime (especially during land reform and the campaign against counter-revolutionaries), there were periods of open violence that demonstrated to everyone the capacity of the regime to deal harshly with its opponents, or deviants, and people did not forget this. Today, everyone is aware of the sanctions that are built into the system to discourage and punish non-conformists. These include extreme penal sanctions, reform-through-labor, and less severe surveillance.

Let me conclude with a few broad judgments, questions, and hypotheses about the strengths and weaknesses of the communication system in China today. Most observers are impressed, rightly, by many of its strengths. Personally, however, I believe that it is most clearly effective in achieving control, compliance, conformity, and submission. How effective it is in achieving basic value change, in bringing about "conversions," and in eliciting real "commitment" is harder to judge. This is not meant to imply that there have not been important changes in values; there obviously have been, although the amount of change doubtless varies, depending on the groups one considers, at what time. For the nation as a whole, however, the changes may be less far-reaching than is sometimes assumed.

It is a reasonable hypothesis, in my opinion, that there is a considerable amount of dissimulation and role playing by large numbers of people in China. Many probably simply do what they feel they must do to get along under the system. Doubtless, many differences exist between public postures and private beliefs. There is unquestionably a great deal of ritualism in political behavior. Clearly, many old values persist, sometimes in new form. But more research is needed if we are to have a better basis for judging both the extent to which the Chinese today accept new values, or old ones, or some complicated mix, and the extent to which their loyalties focus on old social institutions or on the new political groups. At present, we really do not know.

It would also be illuminating to have more research on how much "cognitive dissonance" may exist in China today; that is, how much are people disturbed by the roles they have to play in relation to the realities they see. Perhaps it is easier in Chinese culture than in some others to cope with the differences between the private views that people hold and the public roles that they must play. In any case, more research should be done on this.

Further research is needed on the evolution of the mobilization system in China. This system has been impressively effective in many respects, but there is some evidence that its effectiveness has declined, in part because of a tendency toward routinization. Is this in fact the trend? This too deserves systematic investigation.

Much more research needs to be done on the ways in which traditional forms of communication persist, sub rosa, outside of the official system, transmitting values different from those officially propagated in the Party-controlled system. How and to what extent are information and values, differing from those contained in the official media, disseminated informally through friends, families, factions, cliques, local groups, and the rumor network? There is evidence that a great deal of communication of this sort persists in China, totally outside the official system. But more study is needed on how much there is, on how important it is, and on the extent to which it transmits values that seriously compete with those propagated in the Party's system.

Further research is also needed on other questions concerning possible limitations and costs inherent in China's present communication system, which may counterbalance some of its more obvious advantages. How much does the deliberate restriction of the information disseminated create problems for the regime, retard the development of an efficient economy and social system, and work against real integration of the society? There is little question that it does create problems, but how serious are they? What costs, in terms of utilization of talent, does the system involve? One can argue that in many respects it effectively mobilizes new talent; to a notable degree, it stresses the potentialities of ordinary people and encourages local initiative, creativity, and problem solving, thereby fostering local innovation and change. It is probably equally true, however, that the system, by demanding conformity and perpetuating learning by rote, wastes much talent. It clearly has inhibited the creativity of many of the country's ablest intellectuals. How should one weigh these pluses and minuses?

Still another question deserves careful examination. Although, in theory, the "mass line" demands effective two-way communication, both up and down the regime's hierarchies, in practice does it operate this way? Considerable evidence exists that, although communication downward is usually very effective, there are many inhibitions that make communication upward less effective. The channels for communication upward do exist, but the deep sense of hierarchy and awe of authority held by the Chinese appear to create major obstacles to having effective communication upward to the leadership. It also appears that there is generally relatively little effective lateral communication in Chinese society today. Communication channels focus on the center, and the center seems to discourage lateral communication among different groups and regions. If all this is true, these are obviously flaws in the system. Thus, how serious are they?

Further research also needs to be done on the role of communication in China today as it affects conflict resolution. There is considerable evidence that in some respects the system inhibits social conflicts; it clearly provides controlled outlets for aggressive impulses. However, it is also clear that in some respects the system fosters tensions and conflicts. By stressing contradictions among different groups and classes, the leadership under Mao tried to maintain a state of constant dynamic tension in society. Without doubt, there are many overt, as well as latent, tensions in the society. Periodically, they have come to the fore, either when the leadership has deliberately highlighted them or when the system has temporarily broken down.

The system appeared to operate most effectively during the regime's first few years. Because China's leadership was unified at that time, the regime's propaganda and mass mobilization campaigns generally reflected a consensus at the center, were articulated in a planned way, and were systematically implemented throughout the country, down to the bottom levels of society. In the late 1950s and early 1960s, however, the consensus began to break down. The leadership was doubtless genuinely shocked by the evidence of latent dissidence and tension in Chinese society during the Hundred Flowers period. In the early 1960s, during the post-Great Leap depression, the entire political control system loosened and the intensity and effectiveness of communication from the center temporarily declined, in part because of the adverse impact of economic conditions on the entire political and social system. Then, during the Cultural Revolution, when Mao and his closest followers deliberately attacked the bureaucracies, the system temporarily broke down. As a result, communications from the center no longer originated from a single authoritative source; they emanated from many competitive factional groups. At the end of the Cultural Revolution, steps were taken to restore a centralized system, but in the ongoing struggle among Chinese leaders, conflict was more notable than consensus up until the death of Mao. Without a united leadership to set clear goals and define values, competing groups argued fiercely over priorities and policies. Different bureaucratic and interest groups in the top elite actually debated against one another in the media. A crucial question now is whether, with Mao gone and the radicals purged, China's leadership will be able to restore a more unified system, as they are obviously trying to do.

Many of the observations and judgments made here are tentative hypotheses. All of them are debatable. They all raise questions that deserve further research. More, and better, research needs to be done both on the system in its ideal form and on its strengths and weaknesses in practice.

Much can be done by expanding the kinds of research already completed on the communication system in China, applying old approaches to new questions. However, a need for new approaches also exists. In particular, there needs to be a wider use of two techniques. One is sophisticated content analysis of media output. Much of the research done to date on Chinese media has focused on how the communication system is organized. There should now be more extensive and more sophisticated content analysis to determine the values and information communicated by the system.

Second, in order to understand how the system actually works in practice, a greater effort should be made to combine media research with interviewing. One cannot know how the Chinese system really works, and what effects it has, simply by reading the press or listening to the radio. There needs to be deeper analysis of the actual impact of the system through intensive interviewing of people who have lived under it. Unfortunately, there are not likely--at least in the near future--to be many opportunities for effective interviewing in China itself. However, more systematic efforts can be made to interview both refugees from China and visitors of many kinds who have gone to China--especially overseas Chinese who have returned home, many of whom have had a kind of experience quite different from that of most other visitors.

A great many of the most interesting and important questions that now need to be explored require research that combines in depth interviewing with sophisticated content analysis. Research of this kind is needed to provide greater understanding not just of the surface appearance of China's new communication system but also of its strengths and weaknesses in operation. And it is this kind of understanding of the system that is required to improve our knowledge of the broad political, economic, social , and cultural changes that have occurred, and are still occurring, in the world's most revolutionary and most populous nation.

Scholars such as A. Doak Barnett see the new language of the Chinese revolution as enormously important in the transmission of values in China. Godwin Chu documents some of the changes in the language of mainland China, emphasizing the attempt to use language to shift the traditional view of the universe as static, to a view that it is controllable and conquerable. This is accomplished by replacing archaic terms of classical Chinese with colloquial phrases that contain strong action-oriented connotations. Dr. Chu is Research Associate of the East-West Communication Institute at the University of Hawaii.

36

REVOLUTIONARY LANGUAGE
AND CHINESE COGNITIVE PROCESSES

Godwin C. Chu

China under Communism has been undergoing rather drastic changes.
Beginning with the land reform and the state control of business and industry in the
1950s, the Chinese social and economic structures have been radically altered.
Attempts at ideological reform, as a means to change the traditional Chinese values,
were started in the same period and are still going on today. Beyond the structural
transformation and ideological indoctrination, another trend of a change can be
sensed, one that has a more subtle and less readily perceptible nature. Whether
intentionally or not, the Party leadership over the years has been taking steps that
may some day change the way the Chinese perceive their surroundings and, in
essence, change the Chinese cognitive processes. A major mechanism for initiating
the cognitive change is the popularization of a new, revolutionary language as a
means of communication.

The idea that language is closely related to perception has been discussed by
anthropologists in the West, notably by Edward Sapir and Benjamin Whorf.[1] It is
doubtful, however, that these theoretical discussions were known to the Chinese
Communist leaders. Nevertheless, since the early days of the Communist movement,
the Party leaders have sought to transmit their messages in a language that has its
roots in folksy peasant dialogues, but with a particular ring of its own. This is something that other Chinese revolutionary leaders, like Dr. Sun Yat-sen and his followers, did not do.

The purpose of this section of this publication is to illustrate the possible
impact of the new language on the Chinese cognitive processes, in terms of both continuity with the past and change in the future. It is my hypothesis that the new language both reflects some of the cultural heritage that has been retained, whether
consciously or unconsciously, and at the same time, functions as an agent for cognitive change. In discussing this hypothesis, I shall examine similarities as well as
contrasts between the old and the new. It must be emphasized, however, that these
ideas are highly tentative. They are presented here merely to suggest a topic for
research on communication in China.

COGNITIVE PROCESSES

First, the general concepts of cognitive processes will be briefly discussed.
The American sociologist William I. Thomas once proposed what has come to be

From Godwin C. Chu, "Revolutionary Language and Chinese Cognitive Processes," *Communication in China: Perspectives and Hypotheses*, Paper 16 of the East-West Communication Institute
(March 1978). Reprinted by permission.

known as the Thomas theorem: "If men define situations as real, they are real in their consequences."[2]

The implication is: Human beings do not simply live in a world of reality. Rather, we live in a world of perceived reality that may or may not have full correspondence to reality itself. How individuals behave depends in a large measure on how they have learned to perceive the world around them.

Stated in a different persepctive, we live in a world that in part consists of a physical environment including natural resources, man-made artifacts, and technology. But our world also consists of a social-cultural environment: the individuals around us, with their customs, conventions, beliefs and values, and the social relations among them. Human life is essentially a continuous process of interactions with both our physical environment and social-cultural environment. The point emphasized here is that this interaction is mediated through our cognitive processes, depending, as it were, on what we perceive or do not perceive.

By cognitive processes, we are referring to at least three aspects of perceiving.[3] First, there is the fundamental recognition of our environment, the cognizance of some of its elements that are considered relevant or significant to our life. Both the physical and social-cultural environments are important to our survival and thus need to be dealt with. But the degrees of attention we pay to the various elements in our environment vary from one society to another. We have the familiar example of the Eskimo's recognition of different kinds of snow, which is far more extensive than the differentiations generally noted by other people.[4] In a similar way, the Chinese recognize different aspects of their social environment in terms of kinship relations while the Americans, for instance, generally do not.

Second, whatever we recognize in our environment needs to be classified into categories in order to provide a basis of perceptual clarity. Again, people of different cultural backgrounds follow different patterns. The Chinese, for instance, classify social relations in simulated kinship terms even when no kinship ties exist. Thus friends and acquaintances outside the actual kinship network are placed in the categories of "brothers" or "uncles" depending on age differentiations. A different trend is found among the Americans, who seem to perceive relatives and friends with almost no marked distinction. By the process of classifying and categorizing, we carve our perceptual world into comfortable niches. This process makes it relatively easy for us to recognize and cope with the different aspects of our life.

Finally, we tend to evaluate the individuals and objects that we have perceived and categorized and then structure them into a sort of hierarchical order. We assign greater importance to some elements than to others, that is, certain people and things are closer to our hearts, so to speak. Parallel to the hierarchical order is a relational order, in the sense that the objects and categories are not perceived in isolation, but as related parts of a perceptual whole.

In short, we assume that the elements in our physical and social-cultural environments are perceived, classified, organized, and evaluated in a manner that is somewhat unique to a particular cultural group.

CHINESE COGNITIVE PROCESSES: OLD AND NEW

We shall discuss the Chinese cognitive processes--both their old forms and the new trend the Party is promoting--under three topics: (1) framework of perceiving, (2) nature of classification, and (3) basis of evaluation.

1. Framework of Perceiving.

One noticeable aspect in the traditional Chinese framework of perceiving was a high degree of absolutism. The Chinese tended to see things in an absolute as opposed to relative framework. Things were often seen as all or none, in black and white terms, rather than in different shades of gray. This lack of relativity in perception can be illustrated with traditional sayings from the Chinese language. The following examples emphasized the absolute merit of scholarship:

- "All ten thousand professions are low; only scholarly pursuit is lofty and high. "
- "Of the high ranking officials in the imperial court, all are scholars of learning. "

This tendency seems to have been inherited and even perpetuated under the Communist rule. In China today everything is to be seen in the perspective of the absolute truth of Marxism and Maoism, in a version consistent with the current ideology. Three of the recent campaigns--against Lin Piao and Confucius, against Teng Hsiao-ping, and most recently, against the Gang of Four--are examples. In each campaign, the criticisms have been presented on the same ground of absolute sins even though the targets of condemnation have varied in political ideology.

Another dimension in the framework of perceiving, one in which the old and the new are wide apart, is the degree in which the world around us is seen as potentially changeable. This is a passive versus dynamic dimension. Most cultural groups recognize change as an intrinsic aspect of life. The Chinese in the past certainly recognized the prominence of change, as indicated by the Book of Changes.[5] However, the Chinese seemed to perceive change as something to be adjusted to passively, not as something that they could control with an active effort on their part. To the traditional Chinese, changes were seen as inevitable and unalterable. This passive inevitability is aptly illustrated by the traditional saying: "When the going is rough, adjust compliantly. " The same passive view of the world was reflected in the way the Chinese accepted political disorder with an air of resignation. The Chinese believed, as illustrated by another saying, that "after peace, (there will be) chaos. " In other words, peace and suffering will come in cycles, and one should simply accept them.

The static view of the universe was reflected in many traditional terms in the

Chinese language, which seemed to cover up action with a coat of ambiguity. These
are a few examples (the English translations are approximates):

進行	Proceed
詢問	Enquire
從長計議	Take a long view (meaning disagree)
處理	Deal with
詬病	Note weakness (meaning criticize)
協助	Provide aid

This static view is one aspect that is now being changed. Partly through the
new revolutionary language, and partly through the many campaigns for production,
the universe is presented to the Chinese as controllable and conquerable. The parable
of "The Old Man Who Removed a Mountain," which for centuries was relegated to a
status of obscurity, is now being given national prominence and had the personal endorsement of the late Chairman Mao Tse-tung. The Chinese did have a saying that
"manpower can overcome the will of heaven," but few seemed to have taken it seriously
in the past. Now the whole country has set out to conquer the universe, to do the
impossible.

The vastly different tone of the new language can be illustrated by the revolutionary counterparts of the six obscure phrases from the traditional past (cited
above):

大搞	Vigorously stir up (instead of proceed)
摸底	Feeling the bottom (instead of enquire)
狠批	Ruthlessly criticize (instead of take a long view)
狠抓	Resolutely grasp (instead of deal with)
鬥臭鬥垮	Struggle till it stinks, till it collapses (instead of note weakness)
大力支援	Support mightily (instead of provide aid)

2. Nature of Classification.

Of the many possible ways of classifying the elements in our perceptual world,
the distinction between physical and social-cultural environments will be discussed.
This distinction has been clearly recognized by the Chinese. Confucius, for instance,

16

spoke of ke-wu (distinction of things) and hsiu-shen (cultivation of the whole person). The question is: To what extent does one orientation (for example, the social-cultural) dominate the way the Chinese perceive their world?

In my opinion, the Chinese in the past were oriented primarily toward the social-cultural aspect as a basis of classifying their perceptual elements. The Chinese traditionally tended to see their world as a social world, populated by people having an intricate network of relations, rather than as a world full of material objects to be manipulated. This is indicated by the fact that while the Chinese developed one of the world's most elaborate systems of human relations, for centuries they largely neglected the development of technology and science. It would seem that the adequate utilization of resources was not given full attention by the Chinese.

Indeed, the social orientation was so pronounced that the Chinese tended to create a personal relation between themselves and their material possessions. For instance, there was the popular legend of a scholar who had such a love for the flowering plum trees that he regarded them as his wives. Bamboo acquired such a status of refined dignity among the Chinese that it was said to represent the attributes of a true friend. Inanimate objects were often given names, not in memory of someone who made a large donation (a custom unheard of in olden-day China), but to signify the personal relation between the object and its owner, usually with a moral undertone. For instance, a hut, a pavilion, or even a roadside stone would be appropriately named in a personal manner.

The tendency to personify material objects was reflected in the Chinese religion. Trees, rivers, oceans, mountains, the family residence, the kitchen, the heaven, and the earth--these were personified and deified. A remote but personal relation, exemplified in worship and offerings, was presumed to exist between an individual and the personified deities. In fact, many of the deities were at one time living persons who somehow became symbolized as gods having jurisdiction over some aspect of the physical environment, thus giving it a social orientation.

These tendencies of attributing personal relations to inanimate objects and materials have been condemned by the Communist Party authorities in China. Now far more attention is being directed to the material aspect of life for the sake of development. Even against this background of perceptual change, we can discern a thread of cultural continuity, expressed in a different form of social orientation. From all the pronouncements by the Party leaders, it appears clear that the efforts to seek material development are to be understood not only in physical terms, but also in the perspective of social significance, in terms of their contribution to the establishment of a new social order. The campaign to praise Iron Man Wang Ching-hsi, a deceased oilman at Taching, provides an example. Wang has been glorified as a hero who defied impossible odds in his efforts to develop the Taching Oilfield. His achievements, however, are presented not in terms of physical quantity of production, but in terms of his dedication to the revolution and personal loyalty to Chairman Mao.

3. Basis of Evaluation.

How are the objects and individuals in our perceptual world evaluated? Are they evaluated according to some rigid principles, perhaps on moral grounds, or more flexibly according to empirical evidence? This is a question of flexibility versus rigidity. The Chinese in the past seemed to be bound by a highly rigid evaluative scheme with a moral character. One indication of this tendency is found in the numerous sayings embodied in the Chinese language. For almost every occasion in the life of the Chinese, there was a corresponding saying that told him or her how to view the situation and what the right way was to handle it. For instance, when misfortune would strike, a person should not be depressed, because there was the popular saying that "when old man Sai lost his horse, the loss later brought him luck in return." For centuries, the Chinese peasants accepted their social status compliantly, a reflection of this saying: "If you are blessed, others will serve you; if you are not blessed, you serve others." Another example was when people were in disagreement, do not argue because "harmony is precious." Of all the offenses to an individual's ancestors, the worst was not to have a male child. This was sufficient grounds for a man to dismiss his wife. Extramarital sex could lead to murder because the Chinese character for that term begins with a knife. Many of the sayings contained some element of folk wisdom, but they also tended to limit an individual's perception (and subsequent behavior) to such an extent that empirical reality to the contrary was often ignored.

A similarly high degree of perceptual rigidity appears to be promoted in China today. In place of the old traditional sayings, the Chinese are now urged to follow the quotations of Mao. Every day for years, the People's Daily featured a quotation from him on its front page. Mao's quotations are still prominently placed in this newspaper, although not on a daily basis now. The point is clear. The basis of evaluation, both for personal efforts and state affairs, is whether it does or does not conform to Mao's instructions--according to their current ideological interpretations.

The basis of evaluation has another perspective, namely, the point of reference from which evaluations are made. When speaking of evaluation, we necessarily make a judgment about the desirability, whether it is good or bad, moral, or immoral. The question is: from whose point of view, the individual or the group? The Chinese, in the past as well as the present, have not had a strong orientation toward the individual. Rather, the evaluative aspect of the Chinese cognitive processes has by and large been oriented toward the group. The difference between the past and the present lies in the nature of the group: the kinship groups in the past and the collectives at present. In the past, the Chinese viewed their world not as an arena in which to fight for individual achievement, but as an avenue for advancing the glories of their ancestors. This is illustrated by the traditional saying: "Work for the glories of ancestors and forefathers." This concept was so deeply imbedded in the Chinese mind that many parents named their sons (never daughters) either Kuang-chung (glories for the ancestors) or Yao-chu (splendors for the forefathers). Now the ancestors have faded away. Rather, the Chinese are encouraged to work for the glories of their groups, that is, the collectives. For instance, the young Chinese today are being urged "to think only of workers, peasants and soldiers, and love only their collectivity,"[6] not themselves or their families.

PSYCHOLOGICAL MECHANISMS FOR COGNITIVE CHANGE

The Party authorities have used two major tactics in order to change the cognitive processes of the Chinese people. One, which has been briefly discussed, is language reform in order to change the mode of verbal communication. Many of the archaic terms from classic Chinese have been abandoned. In their places, new colloquial phrases with strong action-oriented connotations have been introduced. If anyone wants to be convinced that the language spoken in China today is different from what it was a quarter-century ago, all they need to do is to read the People's Daily. Phrases such as "feel the bottom" (or find out what is going on) and "walk the socialist road" were previously unheard of, but have now become part of the popular Chinese vernacular. Since our cognitive processes function primarily within the confines of language, changing the language is a fundamental way of changing our cognitive processes.

The other major tactic is the well-known ritual self-criticism. In a self-criticism session, a person is required to make a searching examination of his or her errors not only in overt behavior but also in covert thinking. This self-examination is then verbalized in public in the presence of the individual's own group, either in a production team or in a factory shift. Whether or not coercion has been applied prior to the self-criticism session, it is important to note that the act of self-criticism is done in a manner that is intended to make the person believe that he is doing it voluntarily. Let us assume that the person making a self-criticism is not yet fully convinced by what he himself is saying in front of the group. According to the theory of cognitive dissonance, the individual is caught in between two cognitions that are dissonant with one another: He knows that he holds one kind of belief, and yet he is saying something to the contrary, with an air of deep conviction, and seemingly on a voluntary basis.[7]

There are, among others, two ways of resolving the person's cognitive dissonance. One way is for the individual to change his inner belief to be consistent with his verbal confession, that is, to become genuinely converted. Another way is for him to tell himself that he is merely playing a game for the purpose of survival. In the latter case, the discrepancy between his own belief and his overt verbal performance, and whatever psychological discomfort this discrepancy may cause, is simply a necessary part of the game. As long as he stays out of trouble by periodically putting on his act, he will be rewarded and will continue to play this game. From an article in the People's Daily, it seems that the number of people who take the second course of action is large enough to deserve official attention:

> When a campaign comes, there are people who would prepare themselves
> in every conceivable way. They pretend to be progressive and sincere,
> as if they were really engaged in a relentless struggle against all wrong-
> doings. At a mass meeting for self-criticism, they would cry, moan,
> and confess all their mistakes. After the campaign is over, when the
> "storm has calmed down," they are back to their old selves. Their
> self-criticisms are tossed aside, and they will do whatever they want
> to do.[8]

Because the tactics of self-criticism might be more effective in achieving overt conformity than covert conversion, the function of language reform seems to assume considerable significance. The effects of the new language are more subtle and gradual, and for these reasons it might have some lasting impact in the long run. Because the people who speak the language are not necessarily conscious of the effects, they probably do not make an effort to resist. After they have engaged in the new mode of verbal communication long enough, the Chinese people will probably change some of their cognitive processes accordingly.

This point was brought home to me during a conversation I had recently with a former resident of mainland China. While this person was describing some of the hardships experienced by one of his relatives during the San Fan and Wu Fan[9] campaigns, he did not use terms such as "sufferings" or "physical punishment." He referred to his relative's experience as "having received the impact of waves," a phrase that was not used during the past but that has become popularized in China today. It seems that because he was used to the new language, he began to see things in a different perspective. It may be noted that the conversation took place in private and that he used that term in a completely natural manner without any intention of minimizing the harshness of his relative's experience. To me, however, that phrase gave the impression of someone who had received some unavoidable, and yet justifiable, mild treatment.

SOCIAL IMPLICATIONS OF
OLD AND NEW COGNITIVE PROCESSES

The social implications of the old Chinese cognitive processes can be seen in the perspective of the Thomas theorem referred to earlier: "If men define situations as real, they are real in their consequences."

In terms of social change, this means that if a situation is perceived as unchangeable, then no change is likely to happen. The rigid, passive way the Chinese in the past perceived their world, in which a highly inflexible priority system determined the Chinese evaluation of their alternatives, seemed to be in part responsible for the lack of social change in Chinese history. The traditional cognitive processes appeared to be reinforced by an equally rigid Chinese social structure centered around the kinship system. It was as if because the Chinese social structure remained stable and undisturbed for centuries, the Chinese cognitive processes were able to function adequately despite their rigidity and inflexibility. In a sense, the rigid cognitive processes were a major factor contributing to the structural stability in the Chinese society because the Chinese did not see an active need for change.

This cognitive-structural equilibrium was disrupted during the Nineteenth Century when the guns of European imperialists forced China to open its doors. Even in the face of the necessity for change, however, the rigid Chinese cognitive processes stood in the way of social reforms and cultural adaptation, particularly when the reforms required a reorientation toward the use of material resources, which the Chinese found it difficult to accept. This may explain why the Chinese in the early years of the Twentieth Century resisted the impact of modernization and development.

The Chinese Communist leaders, in their effort to revolutionalize the Chinese society, have not refrained from the use of coercion as a means of changing the Chinese cognitive processes as well as the Chinese social structure. However, the Party leaders seem to be not fully conscious that the new cognitive processes they want to establish may possibly have much in common with the old. Underneath the new emphasis on change and dynamism, a measure of rigidity and absolutism is couched in new ideological terms. It seems that the Party wants changes, but only the kind of changes acceptable to the Party's ideology.

In short, the Party wants the Chinese people today to perceive their world in a new but similarly rigid and inflexible manner, in largely absolute rather than relative terms, with an orientation centered on collective groups rather than kinship groups. The one major difference between the old and the new cognitive processes lies in the dynamic action-orientation of today. Within the Party-directed framework, the Chinese people today must see their world as one calling for continuous actions, not only for class struggle, but also for mobilizing the vast human energy of the Chinese masses for the tasks of development.

NOTES

1.   Edward Sapir, Selected Writings of Edward Sapir (Berkeley, California:
University of California Press, 1949), particularly "The Status of Linguistics of a
Science," pp. 160-166. Also, Benjamin Lee Whorf, Language, Thought, and Reality:
Selected Writings of Benjamin Lee Whorf, edited by John B. Carroll (New York:
Wiley, 1956).

2.   The original idea that led to what is now known as the Thomas theorem in
sociology was first introduced in an almost casual manner by William I. Thomas and
Florian Znaniecki in their discussion of the traditional attitudes of Polish peasants,
in The Polish Peasant in Europe and America (New York: Knopf, 1927), p. 68. The
theorem was restated in its current version by Thomas in a 1938 conference on Polish
peasants. See Herbert Blumer, An Appraisal of Thomas and Znaniecki's "The Polish
Peasant in Europe and America" (New York: Social Science Research Council,
Bulletin 44, 1939), p. 85.

3.   See Noam Chomsky, Language and Mind (New York: Harcourt, Brace and
World, 1968).

4.   Benjamin Lee Whorf, "Language and Stereotype," in Eleanor E. Maccoby,
Theodore M. Newcomb, and Eugene L. Hartley, Readings in Social Psychology, 3rd
edition (New York: Holt, Rinehart and Winston), pp. 1-9.

5.   The Book of Changes, or I Ching, was an ancient Chinese classic of unknown
authors and antiquity. Believed to have existed as early as the Twelfth Century B.C.,
I Ching was one of the classics edited by Confucius. It was a collection of texts dis-
cussing the synchronistic concepts of change and equilibrium in the universe. See
I Ching (the Book of Changes), translated in 1882 by James Legge (New York: Dover
Publications, Inc., 1963).

6.   "School Should be the Instrument for Proletarian Dictatorship," People's
Daily, February 24, 1975.

7.   Leon Festinger, A Theory of Cognitive Dissonance (Stanford University Press,
1957).

8.   An Eze-wen,"To Struggle for Eradication of the Passive Attitude and Unhealthy
Conditions in Party Organizations," official report prepared by the Ministry of Per-
sonnel for the Study Session of the Central Government Cadres on January 7, 1953.
Published in People's Daily, February 12, 1953.

9.   San Fan, or Three Anti, was a movement launched by the Party in December
1951 against corruption, waste, and bureaucratic practices among Party cadres.
Wu Fan, or Five Anti, was a similar movement in 1952 directed at businessmen and
industrialists to stamp out practices such as bribery, tax evasion, pilfering public
property, profiteering, and stealing economic information. For an analysis of these
two movements, see Godwin C. Chu, Communication, Social Structural Change, and
Capital Formation in People's Republic of China, East-West Communication Institute
Paper No. 9 (Honolulu, Hawaii: East-West Center, June 1974).

GLOSSARY

All ten thousand professions are low;
only scholarly pursuit is lofty and high.

萬般皆下品
唯有讀書高

Of the high ranking officials in the imperial court, all are scholars of learning.

滿朝朱紫貴
盡是讀書人

When the going is rough, adjust compliantly.

逆來順受

After peace, (there will be) chaos.

一治一亂

The Old Man Who Removed a Mountain.

愚公移山

Manpower can overcome the will of heaven.

人定勝天

Plum tree wife.

梅妻

Bamboo tree friend.

竹友

When old man Sai lost his horse, the loss later brought him luck in return.	塞翁失馬 馬知非福
If you are blessed, others serve you; if you are not blessed, you serve others.	有福之人人服侍 無福之人服侍人
Harmony is precious.	和為貴
Of the three major offenses to one's ancestors, the worst is not to have a male heir.	不孝有三 無後為大
Extramarital sex leads to murder.	色字頭上一把刀
Work for the glories of ancestors and forefathers.	光宗耀祖
Having received the impact of waves.	受到冲擊

Dutch television news coverge of foreign nations was analyzed by a team of researchers from the University of Amsterdam and the Audience Research Service of the Dutch Broadcasting Foundation. Eighty-five newscasts and public affairs programs from September 1975 and February 1976 were content analyzed to test Galtung's complementarity hypothesis (that the absence of some news values in an event must be compensated for by other news values in order for it to receive news coverage). While the study found that socioculturally distant, less powerful, and poorer nations were more often treated negatively in the news, little support was found for the complementarity hypothesis. Mr. Bergsma is on the faculty of the Institute of the Science of the Press at the University of Amsterdam.

37

NEWS VALUES IN FOREIGN AFFAIRS
ON DUTCH TELEVISION

Frans Bergsma

In 1975 the audience research department of the Dutch public broadcasting organization NOS decided to make a study of the functions of a change in the newscast formula (NOS, 1977). Part of it was to be a content analysis of these newscasts and of the current affairs programs of other TV licentiates in the Dutch broadcasting system (De Brauw, 1974). The NOS researchers suggested the department of mass communication of the University of Amsterdam to take part with a content analysis seminar to accompany the development of hypotheses, variables list, operationalizations and codebook for that side of the project. Next to the variables at the core of the NOS policy problems the seminar introduced a number of variables that were connected with the few hypotheses-testing studies amongst the many descriptive content analysis of news and current affairs, and a number that arose from the few studies of visuals amongst the many text analyses.*

One of these more theoretical topics was the study of *newsworthiness* of foreign news output by the media. Though there are a number of studies dealing with extensivities like number and length of types of news-items, proportions of regions covered, amount of newsflow, etc., intensivities like newsvalues are less analyzed.

As till 1965 newsvalues studied were reviewed by Östgaard (1965) and systematized by Galtung and Holmboe Ruge (1965).

The last authors gave a list of 12 event features which enhance the probability that the event will be reported in the newsmedia. Apart from some general features, they studied specifically *sociocultural proximity* and *wealth or power of the nations*, *saliency of elite people* and *negativity of the event* as conducive to the chances of being recorded. This generalization would hold at least for the media in the 'NW corner of the world'. In this great news-producing area more distant or less powerful nations would draw attention mostly if negativities or political elites were involved, whereas for near or mighty nations positive news and common people would be also covered.

Next to these Norwegian data, there is some evidence in such direction more recently supplied on Irish, Swedish and Nigerian television by Golding and Eliott (1977) and on the British press by McQuail (1977).

* The present study would not have been possible without the computer files, computing assistance and the videotapes which the NOS audience research department made accessible to us. Paul Hendriksen and Harold de Bock supervised the entire project. Michiel van 't Hoff was project leader of the content-analysis. A number of M.A. students developed ideas at the seminars, supervised by the author and carried them out at the NOS research department.

From Frans Bergsma, "News Values in Foreign Affairs on Dutch Television," *Gazette: International Journal for Mass Communication Studies* 24, 3 (1978) 207-222. Reprinted by permission of Van Loghum Slaterus.

Yet a generalization should be limited to a 'middle principle' (Mannheim, 1949) or a 'theory of the middle range' (Merton, 1949), for Galtung and Ruge surmise that, elsewhere, underdog nations, structural interests or positive orientations might prevail in gatekeeping. To some extent this was corroborated, at least from news agency data, when Robinson (1977) signalled that Tanjug was less person- and more structure-oriented and like Tass less negativity-focused than AP.

Some methodological problems

Now Galtung and Ruge, like their colleague Sande (1969) in a later follow-up on Norwegian media, start with hypotheses on the relation between event features and media coverage, but are well aware of the fact that they studied only the dependent variable, the media output. Several authors, Rosengren (1970, 1974), Ultee and Van Wijngaarden (1972) objected to this procedure and maintained, that extra-media baseline data should and can be brought into the picture as the independent variables. In their studies they refer to very specific facts, however: election results and health data respectively. Galtung (1974) rightly replies that in such cases extra media data are welcome of course, but not to be expected in the case of general news reports. One could add, that such things as 'event lists' at best could result in a coverage comparison of different *kinds* of media, more and less reliable or balanced ones, in as far as one cannot station participant observers anywhere and has to rely on other written sources. Even Breed (1958) in his study of non-coverage had to compare sources: case studies vs.newspapers and did not get at the event.

Moreover the objections would only be valid, if we knew next to nothing about the distribution in 'the real world' of the event-features called news values. But we could try at least to make some rudimentary model of these distributions and compare it with some common sense gatekeeper formulae, as in figure 1.

Figure 1. Inversion of feature proportions by gatekeepers.

Independent variables		→ *Intervening variable*
World model: N(A)	< M(not-A)	Gatekeeper formulae:
N elite nations	< M other nations	Huge winds blow on high hills.
N kindred nations	< M other nations	Close is my shirt, closer my skin.
N elite persons	< M other persons	The highest tree, the greatest fall.
N negative events	< M other events	No news is good news.
↓		↓
Non-mediated variables		*Dependent variables*
Random coverage:		Media coverage:
prob(A)	< prob(not-A)	n(A) > m(not-A)

In other words than figure 1: the media cover elite countries and persons, socioculturally near countries and negative events beyond chance. Thus we would not need to test the relations between independent baseline data and dependent media output, but the fit of a gatekeeper model as intervening variable on that media output, assuming some knowledge of the outside world.

With these common sense assumptions it does not seem necessary to compensate, as Galtung *et al.* seem to have it (1970, p. 271) and Rosengren (1974) understood it, for the lack of baseline data by two further assumptions: The additivity and the complementarity hypotheses.

The first states: The more newsvalues an event satisfies, the higher the chance it will be reported (*e.g.* the Lockheed affair: negative news of political elites in a near, elite country).

The second: If an event is low on some features, it will have to be high on other newsvalues to make news (*e.g.* corruption and coups in the third world – the more distant and poorer the country, the more news on negativities and political elites).

With Rosengren (1974), we cannot find much of a compensation for baseline data in these and similar assumptions, though they are interesting in themselves. However, plausible as they may seem, there is a rather puzzling measurement model behind them in as far as arbitrariness in adding unrelated things is to be avoided.

The additivity hypothesis and the accompanying assumption of some fundamental newsworthiness dimension, common to separate event features, might suggest an implicit factor-analytic or scalogram model. In such a model these features, for unweighted adding, would have to show close intercorrelations in one direction and so corresponding loadings on a common factor (or positive contributions to a scale) explaining more of the variance than the separate features.

Now, possible interrelations between *e.g.* proximity and wealth of countries are certainly dependent on the place on the globe of the nations studied, but do not require us to believe in an intersecting cluster of a close wealthy clique of powerful sodoms and gomorrahs with an overload of elites struck by the wrath of fate and nature, which would be the corollary of positive intercorrelations of the features mentioned in the beginning.

Rosengren (1974) suggested on the contrary, that wealth and power might have inverse, negative correlations with negativities like poverty, misery, illness and crime.

This contention and the scarceness of such 'real world data' lead us to assume that there are elite countries in the three worlds, that all countries have some kindreds and some elites and that negative events from nature, mishaps, mischief or conflicts are rather widely, if not haphazardly distributed, in other words that the mentioned features are if at all, only weakly related, in different directions.

In that case a factor-analytic model might not produce the newsworthiness factor from 'real world' event features. Then such a factor needs another basis and, as we did with frequencies of the newsvalues, we could probe the gatekeepers. Skipping the unlikelihood that a majority of them worked with a world picture like the sketched sodom-cluster, we may hypothesize that gatekeepers give positively correlating adhesion scores to the mentioned newsvalues. Such a pattern might also result in a common factor of newsworthiness. Lastly the additivity could be based on the correlations of newsvalues within the mediacontent. But then the founding of the additivity hypothesis would be the same as testing the complementarity hypothesis, by means of the same ambiguous resultant from 'real world' clusters as well as gatekeepers preference clusters.

Now little was done to either found or validate the additivity hypothesis. Rosengren (1974) with different variables took a different road by using multiple regresssions to predict coverage of specific events from specific world data. Sande at least validated the additivity hypothesis by showing positive associations between the number of newsvalues in newsstories and their space percentage in newspapers or amount of display in radio newscasts in Norway.

But he summed positively and negatively correlated newsvalues and did not make clear whether the associations of the sumscore with space and display were stronger than those of separate newsvalues with these coverage measures.

The complementarity hypothesis got more attention. Galtung *et al.* tested the *general* version, stating that absence of some newsvalues in an event have to be compensated by others to make it newsworthy, by simplified *special* versions of it, stating that any pair of newsvalues in media newsstories will be negatively associated.

Their reasoning is: If there were two dichotomous newsvalues A1 and A2, events low in both A1 and A2 would hardly appear as news (table 0, quantity d in the media) and the chance of having either one high (quantity b or c) will not stay behind that of having both high (quantity a). Therefore news will in the majority of cases be high on either one of these A's, which pro-

Table 0. Crossing of two dichotomous news values.

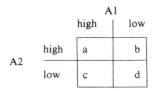

duces a negative association between them. Yules $Q = \dfrac{ad - bc}{ad + bc}$ $e.g.$ will be negative; or the more A1, the less A2 $v.v.$

Two objections can be made: First, as Rosengren (1973) put it, a negative correlation of newsvalues in newsreports might come from a possible negative correlation in the world between say social status of persons (high) and illness, misery, crime and such negativities (low). In such cases a negative association is no sign of compensatory selectivity of distortion. Galtung (1974) admits it, but continues, that the point is that even if the newsvalues were positively correlated in the world, they could still easily end up with negative correlations in media coverage, through selectivity. But all the same he cannot maintain then, that a negative association of some newsvalues is a final test of *general* selective complementarity.

But one could admit that if a large majority of negative correlations appeared between the newsvalues in news reports there would be some ground for confirming it.

Secondly one can wonder with Galtung, to what extent the complementarity hypothesis would hold for not just two, but any two of the five, not to speak of the twelve newsvalues suggested by Galtung *et al.* Can one expect that if one is low, all others have to be high? For that is assumed if one tests binary correlations between any one of the newsvalues and each of the others seperately. Now suppose one controls for the other three: If these are low, the two newsvalues studied may both need to be high, or if the other three are high both studied are allowed to be low and a positive correlation would result over these subgroups. Then the remaining subgroups had to compensate this positive part correlation by a stronger negative one to produce a negative correlation for the whole.

So it is remarkable, that Galtung and Ruge reported four out of five special complementarity hypotheses to be confirmed and Sande three out of four, which would leave the general complementarity hypothesis on its feet. But some doubts may remain: no tests of statistical significance were presented and not all presented tables were self evident as to that. Some exceptions were explained away and not all pairs of used newsvalues explored.

Sande excluded two positively correlated pairs from the complementarity test (though he included these opposite items in the newsvalue sumscore).

Taking additivity and complementarity hypotheses together, it is possible, that uncorrelated or weakly and diversely related event features in the 'real world' and positively correlated newsvalue appreciations by gatekeepers, supporting newsvalue-additivity, through some ceiling effect of time pressures in the media, produce negatively correlating newsvalues in the media content. In that case a kind of 'utility model' might be supposed behind the journalistic flair, routine and pressures in gatekeepers implicit choices. There are many other possibilities of course, because for any set of newsvalues there are three correlation signs: positive, zero and negative, at three levels: event features, gatekeeper appreciations and media content, which give 3^3 combinations, not to speak of subsets of newsvalues with opposite correlations within the same level.

The study

Having neither world data, nor gatekeeper ratings, but only some content data and a few doubts we can in the following only retest the binary negative complementarity hypotheses of Galtung etc., though gatekeeper studies or multiple and partial correlation analysis seem the most urgent at present. In a secondary analysis of the computerfiles on two months of videotaped TV newscasts and current affairs programs by Dutch broadcasting organizations we retested the following hypotheses about foreign news.

1. The more distant socioculturally the nations, the more negative the events.
2. The less powerful the nations the more negative the events.
3. The poorer the nations the more negative the events.
4. The more distant the nations the more elite actions.
5. The less powerful the nations the more elite actions.
6. The poorer the nations the more elite actions.
7. The more elite actions, the less negative events.

We explored some other relations with other variables. Altogether we find difficulty in specifying how many should be confirmed to save the general complementarity hypothesis.

The sample

The NOS research department intended the sample used for a somewhat different purpose: A before-after analysis of the effects of a change in the newscast formula on the audience and on the formulae of current affairs programs of other TV licentiates in the Dutch broadcasting system (NOS, 1977). So it consisted of two time clusters of TV newscasts and current affairs programs in September 1975 and February 1976. Apart from some events these clusters were on inspection not severely dominated by preponderant events.

From this sample we took all available 20-minute main newscasts (daily 8 p.m.) and the regular current affairs programs (except some one-item specials) of the five largest licentiates. Altogether there were 42 newscasts and 43 current affairs programs of the working days. The unit of analysis was the program item or topic. Excluding weatherforecasts, trailers and summaries, there were 625 items, of which 320 dealt with foreign sources. Because of an ambiguity of source-country vs. subject-country codings, we had to limit ourselves mainly to 268 items which presented locations and or pictures from identified foreign countries. For reasons of classification- or scoring problems 47 of these had to be largely excluded, 28 because they dealt with combinations of very different countries, 19 because of other ambiguities.[1]

The 221 remaining items included 86 dealing with foreign politics proper, 16 with foreign economics, 24 with war and revolts, 95 with other topics in foreign countries. 102 covered W.Europe, 5 E.Europe, 27 N.America, 28 M.East and N.Africa, 30 rest of Africa, 13 Asia, 16 Latin America.[2]

The variables

Over one hundred variables were coded for each item under supervision of the NOS research department by students participating in a related seminar at the department of mass communication of the University of Amsterdam. The seminar also covered the variable list, the operationalizations and

1. A somewhat dominating topic in September 1975 was the independence of Surinam. Also the large variance in the judgements on its sociocultural distance led us to exclude these items from the analysis. Other events in september '75: military disengagement in the Sinai; Cyprus summit; Lebanon armistices; Ulster intransigence; end of 7th UN assembly on new economic order; PLO speaker in UN; assault on Gerald Ford; Timor; Angola. In February '76: US primaries; Nixon invited by China; Iceland-Britain fishing conflicts; EC on MPLA siege in Angola; Lockheed affair; Castro on party-congress in Moscou; etc.

2. Number of items, categories of proximity, GNP, GNP/Cap. per country, region.

	n	*Prox.*	*GNP*	*GNP/Cap.*	
Fed. Rep. Germany	8	I	II	II	
France	10	I	II	II	
Gr. Britain	13	I	II	III	
Belgium	14	I	IV	II	
Luxemburg	1	I	VI	II	
Denmark	1	II	IV	II	
Sweden	4	II	IV	I	
Italy	4	II	II	III	
Switzerland	5	II	IV	I	
Austria	10	II	IV	III	
USA	25	III	I	I	
Ireland	5	IV	VI	IV	
Spain	13	IV	III	IV	
Portugal	14	IV	VI	IV	
Canada	2	IV	III	I	
S. Africa	3	IV	III	V	
Russia	3	V	I	III	
E. Europe	2	V	IV	III	mean country
Japan	3	V	I	III	
M. East, N. Africa	28	V	V	V	mean country
China	3	VI	I	V	
Rest Asia	3	VI	VI	VI	mean country
Rest Africa	27	VI	VI	VI	mean country
Lat. America	16	V	V	V	mean country
Rest S. hemisph.	4	VI	VI	VI	mean country

In tables 2 thr. 7, groups I and II, III and IV, V and VI were merged.

hypotheses. From the variable list we took:

1. A recode of the countries or regions as to *socio-cultural distance*, as rankordered by a jury of 9 MA students in mass communications. The countries and regions were subsequently divided into six groups: I, the nearest group that was in the first quartile for every judge; II, countries that were in the first or second quartile; III, those in the first, second or third but mainly in the second; IV, those in the second or third; V, those in the third or fourth; VI, the farthest countries, exclusively in the fourth quartile for every judge.

2. *Involvement of the Netherlands* in the foreign issue, a three–place variable: Not involved, indirectly so, directly involved. This variable became a substitute for Galtung's 'relevance' which was defined in a more complex way. McQuail used similarly involvement of Britain.

3. *Economic power* of the countries or regions, as measured by gross national product. Again 6 groups were conceived, but we had difficulties with data for regions that were filed according to subcontinent instead of per country (E.Europe excl. Russia, Lat.America, N.Africa and the Middle East, Black Africa, SE Asia excl. Japan and China). We had to group them according to the estimated mean for the countries of the region.

4. *Wealth* of these entities as measured by GNP per capita. Here of course the same problem appeared, but mitigated in as far as the intercountry variance within the region will be less than with GNP per country.

5. *Status of persons* making statements or referred to. We had to delete rather ambiguous values of the status variable like: employees-employers-union staff, civil servants-technicians-scientists, nobilities-artists-sportsmen to distil a clearcut status-variable: political elites (Statesmen, MP's) versus ordinary people.

6. '*Negativity*' of the event. Crime, disasters, war or revolts each accounted for only 6% of the topics and were hardly feasible as dichotomous variables with abt. 94% in the remainder. As variables we had:
Amount of conflict: no conflict; unarmed conflict; armed conflict.
Violence display: no violence; demolished objects on screen; fights on screen; victims on screen.
Direction of comment: positive; mixed or neutral; negative. This variable was included, because Galtung (1965) remarked, that their negativity judgements were sometimes influenced by the manner of reporting.
Sensationalism of topic: Very sensational; rather sensational; not so. This is a rather imponderable global newsvalue often mentioned in this negative nexus. It was designed as a jury judgement, but as yet only filed as a two-judge rating, with a reliability of 86% agreement.

7. As a newsvalue peculiar to visual media we included *spectacularity* of the visuals, in the same way as sensationalism of topic, with a reliability of 92% agreement.

The last three variables are close to McQuails two of direction and drama.

Results

In order to test the hypothesized negative correlations of these newsvalues we calculated the Kendall Tau rank correlations for any pair.

Table 1. Matrix of Kendall Tau rank correlations between news values.*

	range	1	2	3	4	5	6	7	8	9
1. Soc. Cult. prox imity	6									
2. Involvement Netherlands	3	25···								
3. Nat. Power (GNP)	6	54···	12·							
4. Nat. Wealth GNP/Cap.	6	69···	23···	71····						
5. Personal Status	2	–03	–12″	–04	–07					
6. Spectacularity	3	–17″	–01	–11··	–13″	–21″″				
7. Comment negativity	3	–01	–12′	01	02	05	11			
8. Conflict in topic	3	–18‴	–24″″	–28″″	–29″″	01	06	11		
9. Violence on screen	4	–10″	–07′	–08′	–10	–10″	23···	11··	15··	
10. Topic sensationalism	3	02	–01	15··	08	–08	33···	10	00	10···
		1	2	3	4	5	6	7	8	9
		Prox.	Invt.	GNP.	GNP. Cap.	Status.	Spect.	Neg. Comm.	Confl. topic	Viol. screen

* The varying n's, different ranges of variables, diverse formats of cross tables and consequent alternating Tau bêta and gamma, make that level of significance is more indicative than value of tau; for negative taus one-tailed. for positive ones two-tailed:

′ signif. at .05 level, ″ at .01, ‴ at .001, ″″ at .0001 level 1-tailed. 2-tailed.

Before giving somewhat more detailed tables on the hypothesized negative correlations that were significantly confirmed, we can globally remark, that in the matrix of table 1 there are two evident clusters of countervailing, positive correlations: the top left and the bottom right triangles.

The first one reflects the fact that proximity, status and relevance of a country and by consequence their intercorrelation are largely determined by their position on the globe relative to the monitoring country, in this case the Netherlands. These variables could for any W.European country hardly be correlated negatively, in so far as their kins and neighbours, in which they will be involved, are largely in the wealthy group.

The bottom right triangle also shows plausible, though weaker positive correlations. The strongest ones are spectacularity of visuals with sensationalism of topic and violence on screen, followed by those of conflict in topic with negativity of comment and violence on screen. Together dramatism and negativities seem to go loosely hand in hand.

Looking to the inner rectangle of the matrix in table 1 we see the intercorrelations between the nations features, the negativities, the drama variables and personal status. Taking them together we can state that of the 29 possible correlations only 15 were statistically significant in the expected direction: 7 were in the wrong direction, of which one significantly so.

In the columns we can see that sociocultural proximity, power and wealth of nations give about the same pattern of significant negative correlations with two of the four negativity variables (conflict and visual violence) and with spectacularity of visuals. Involvement of the Netherlands deviates a bit from this pattern because it is also negative with negative comment and with personal status, but not so with spectacularity.

The personal status variable worked only with one negativity variable (visual violence), with one nation variable (involvement of the Netherlands) and with spectacularity. Hypothesis 4, 5 and 6 would have to be rejected from this evidence: There are not significantly more elite actions reported in more distant, less powerful or less wealthy nations. Of the newly introduced variables spectacularity was positive with the negativity variables, but it did work negatively with the nation variables. In the rows we can see that of the two others, negativity of comment and sensationalism did hardly work negatively.

For the significant negative correlations of Table 1 we will give some more details, but for reasons of space we will give them in a very condensed format. Having found that only two of our negativity measures worked as expected we will also enter some percentages on disasters and crime, war and revolts.

The *socioculturally near* countries in Table 2 consist of eight EC countries plus Scandinavia, Austria and Switzerland. They have lower proportions of all negativity values mentioned in the table than the rows marginal (20%). The middle group consisting of all other Western nations in the sample also has them below or about the rows marginal percentage (28%). The far group includes E.Europe and all of Asia, Africa and Latin America and is amply above the marginal (40%). Also disasters and crime, war and revolts share in this abundance of negative news values in the items on socioculturally far countries and in their relative sparseness in those of the near countries.

So hypothesis 1 might be considered as confirmed for once, though negativity of comment and sensationalism did not corroborate it.

But negativity of comment cannot be said to be a news value and sensa-

Table 2. Negativity features by sociocultural proximity.*

Soc. Cult. Proximity		Common total	Conflict in topic	Visual violence	Crime + disasters	War + revolts
Near	abs.	70	24	8	7	1
	%	32	24	19	29	03
Mid	abs.	62	29	11	4	4
	%	28	30	26	16	16
Far	abs.	89	46	23	14	19
	%	40	47	55	56	79
n		221	99	42	25	24
		100	100	100	100	100

* The totals and percentages in the left margin are common to the tables of these newsvalues of which only the presence alternatives are given in the columns.

tionalism of topic is not necessarily negative, so they need not weaken this hypothesis. (Nevertheless sensationalism is a news value that did not work at all).

This inverse relation between sociocultural proximity and negativity of event was held undecided by Galtung and Ruge (1965), while Sande (1969) just stated it was an important newsvalue but did away with it because of some technical problem. Rosengren (1973) reduced sociocultural distance to either geographical distance which hardly worked at all, or to trade relations which did remarkably well. The latter variable is not yet coded and filed by us, but we do have another dimension of distance, which might be akin also to Galtungs "relevance" of the item: the involvement of the Netherlands in the specific foreign issue.

With this *involvement of the Netherlands* in Table 3 a somewhat larger n appears in the common totals, because the uncodable countries and combinations were included and the coding was not restricted to items with

Table 3. Negativity features by involvement of the Netherlands.*

Involvement		Common total	Conflict in topic	Visual violence	Crime + disaster	War + revolts	Negative comment	Comment total
Netherlands directly involved	abs.	63	18	6	2	0	12	40
	%	20	12	11	6	0	21	25
Indirectly involved	abs.	43	11	5	6	1	7	25
	%	14	07	09	18	33	13	15
Not involved	abs.	213	121	44	26	31	37	96
	%	67	81	80	77	97	66	60
n		319	150	55	34	32	56	161
		100	100	100	100	100	100	100

* Arrangement as in Table 2, but larger n and common totals because of inclusion of ambiguous nation combinations, etc. Comment total smaller on the base of presence of comments.

(foreign) locations and pictures. Here we see for once an excess proportion of negative comment when the Netherlands are not involved, in comparison to the marginal total of comments percentage (60% righthand total). The other negativity features in the toprow also fall behind the common total percentage (20% lefthand marginal) when the Netherlands are directly involved, and in the bottom row exceed the marginal (67%) when the Netherlands are not involved. Again, as we saw earlier, sensationalism of topic did not work. The involvement dimension was not treated often by the other researchers so we did not hypothesize these inverse relations explicitly, but they seem to give an indirect corroboration of hypothesis 1.

Table 4. Negativity features by national power (GNP).*

GNP		Common total		Conflict in topic		Visual violence		Crime + disasters		War + revolts	
High	abs.	74		22		11		8		3	
	%		34		22		26		32		13
Mid	abs.	48		18		5		1		0	
	%		22		19		12		4		0
Low	abs.	98		58		26		16		21	
	%		44		59		42		64		88
n		220		98		42		23		24	
			100		100		100		100		100

* Arrangement as in Table 2.

Table 5. Negativity features by national wealth (GNP/Cap).*

GNP per capita		Common total		Conflict in topic		Visual violence		Crime + disasters		War + revolts	
High	abs.	70		21		10		8		0	
	%		32		22		24		32		0
Mid	abs.	67		30		99		3		3	
	%		30		31		21		12		13
Low	abs.	84		47		23		14		21	
	%		38		48		55		56		87
n		221		98		132		25		24	
			100		100		100		100		100

* Arrangement as in Table 2.

Tables 4 and 5 on *power and wealth of nations* resemble each other even more than Tables 2 and 3 did on proximity and Dutch involvement. We see in the top rows that mighty and rich countries get fewer negativity proportions than the marginal (34%), and weak and poor countries in the bottom row get more than the marginal (44%).

So hypothesis 2 and 3 can be considered as confirmed: The less powerfull or the poorer the nation the more negative events are covered. But again negativity of comment and sensationality of topic are not implied.

As to the *status of the persons* being discussed or making statements in the newsitems we see in Table 6 that in the subsample of items with or about political leaders or ordinary people, the poli⌐ ⌐l leaders are underrepresen-

Table 6. Negativity features, spectacularity and Dutch involvement by personal status of subjects or staters.*

Personal status		Common total	Visual violence	Crime + disaster	War + revolts	Spectacu-larity	Netherl. involved
Foreign pol.	abs.	140	18	5	2	27	33
leaders	%		87	72	46	14	66	77
Foreign ord.	abs.	21	7	6	12	14	10
people	%	13	28	55	86	34	23
n		161	25	11	14	41	43
		100	100	100	100	100	100

* Reduced n because of deleted ambiguous status values.

ted and the ordinary people overrepresented compared with the marginal percentages in three of the original 6 negativity aspects. Of the three others conflict mostly worked but failed to do so here. So it is hard to confirm hypothesis 7 'The more elite actions the less negative events are reported' on this basis and we have to leave it undecided. In this table we also see the only relation which is in tune with the rejected hypothesis 4: If the Netherlands are involved (the closer), the ordinary people are overrepresented and the political leaders underrepresented compared with the marginal percentages.

The introduced newsvalue of *spectacularity* of visuals is in Table 6 negatively associated with personal status: foreign ordinary people are more often spectacular and foreign political leaders less than the marginals. In Table 7 we see how spectacular items are also overrepresented among the farther, weaker and poorer nations.

So here complementarity may have worked again, but it may also be the

Table 7. Spectacularity by nation's proximity and level.

		Common total	Soc.-Cult. prox.			Power (GNP)			Wealth (GNP/Cap)		
			near	mid	far	high	mid	low	high	mid	low
Spectacular	abs.	76	16	19	41	22	13	41	17	21	38
or rather sp.	%		34	23	31	46	30	27	42	24	31	45
Not	abs.	145	54	43	48	52	36	57	53	46	46
spectacular	%	66	77	69	54	70	73	58	76	69	55
n		221	70	62	89	74	49	98	70	67	84
		100	100	100	100	100	100	100	100	100	100

case, that locations and pictures of far, poor countries and of ordinary people are in themselves more spectacular than Western locations and the inevitable officials. In Table 1 we saw that the involvement of the Netherlands was not associated with spectacularity, though for that visually rather neutral involvement the complementarity mechanism might have worked at least. In Table 1 spectacularity was seen to be not complementary to the negativity features, but to be rather positively associated with them, as well as with sensationality of topic.

Altogether we cannot say that spectacularity is complementary to other newsvalues except perhaps to a nation's nearness or status.

Discussion

Three out of seven complementarity hypotheses from the original Galtung frame were confirmed (H. 1, 2, 3), one was undecidable (H. 7), three were rejected (H. 4, 5, 6). Of the four newly introduced features only one worked complementarily (involvement of the Netherlands), one is undecided (spectacularity) and two did not work at all (negativity of comment and sensationalism of topic). All confirmed hypotheses involved inverse relations of the nations proximity or status with negativity of the events. But even these need not result from compensating mechanisms and could result from a larger share of disasters, revolts etc. in the more distant and poorer group of nations. Besides, not all negativity aspects suggested a compensating mechanism: sensationalism of topic and negativity of comment were mostly not negatively, or even positively related to proximity and status of nation.

Moreover, it should be mentioned and stressed here, that the proportion of comments, background news and explications did not differ significantly for the several groups of nations. Nor did the average length of items. In these respects there was no selectivity.

Now the fact that sociocultural proximity, involvement of the Netherlands, GNP and GNP per capita are so similar, reflects that at least these newsvalues are strongly positively correlated in our sample.

In fact all of the near countries were in the richer half of GNP per capita and all of the development countries in the far half, though not inversely so. Moreover the high GNP group relied for about 50% of items on countries of the nearest group, the low GNP group for 79% of items on the most distant group. The few items on far but high-GNP countries (Japan 3, China 3, Russia 3) could not counterbalance this. In the positive correlation of sociocultural proximity and involvement of the Netherlands we can see at the same time a corollary of Galtung's similar rejection of complementarity between proximity and relevance.

It is safe to assume that Rosengren's (1974) trade relations would also figure positively in this matrix and might play the role of a common factor.

Another not complementary, but positive relation appeared between negativity features and spectacularity, which we deemed plausible already. This positive correlation is in agreement with the fact that spectacularity of visuals seemed to have about the same inverse relations with proximity and status of nations as did the negativity features. Finally personal status was complementary only to one of the nation variables (involvement of the Netherlands) and half of the negativities.

Altogether the general complementarity hypothesis seems rather shattered by this score of absent or even positive correlations.

Unfortunately our material does not allow for further explorations by means of multivariate analysis as Galtung suggested and Rosengren did. The sample of foreign items is too small, the variables are too rough and too many and the distributions too skewed to expect much from 3-dimensional tables and ternary partial rank correlations, which hardly could save some more complementarity hypotheses.

So we cannot answer the question whether perhaps the items were already too saturated with negativities (45% dealt with conflict, 20% showed violence results, 26% dealt with war, revolts, crime, accidents or disasters) to give the personal status news value much of a chance. Therefore we would have to control for all negativities. Then in the positive news group a negative correlation between nationstatus or proximity and personal status might appear as yet.

Another question we abstained from is the problem of the additivity hypothesis, partly for the same reason that our data do not allow for multiple correlations. But also, because our data hardly give a firmer basis with their core of rather weak and sometimes conflicting correlations, than would the hypothetical model we suggested before: Western Gatekeepers giving correlating ratings to the diverse news values among several unrelated event features and acting according to some utility model in spreading their odds instead of waiting for the ideal-typical big story or risking the loss of readers' interest.

But the pattern of these flair- and routine-choices seems less clear-cut than the Galtung frame suggests and less clear than the likely accumulation of newsvalues in the big stories, which be it Serajewo 1914, Watergate or Lockheed-affair seem to be loaded with negativities, political elites and socially near, elite countries. Whether non-advertising good news, non-graphic structural treatment and non-touristic distant countries can be made interesting for a larger audience than that of quality magazines, remains an open question.

Summary

In a content analysis of two months of Dutch TV newscasts and current affairs programs during 1975-76 the items with foreign locations were analyzed as to news values stipulated by Galtung *et al.* They suggested hypotheses on the complementarity of news values within the media stating, that features like sociocultural proximity, wealth and power of the foreign nations, status of persons in the news, negativities of events etc. compensated for each other when absent. After a discussion of some fundamental problems in testing such hypotheses a retest of them was tried in the form of negative rank correlations between these news values in the items of the said programs.

The inverse relations between negativity of the news and the foreign nations's sociocultural proximity, wealth or power were confirmed. Spectacularity of visuals worked like negativity, involvement of the Netherlands like proximity. For the status of persons in the news no clear pattern emerged.

Altogether too many exceptions seem to shatter the generality of the compementarity hypothesis with regard to all newsvalues.

The inverse correlation of the nation's status and proximity with the negativities might be due to such a relation in the 'real world', instead of resulting from compensating gatekeepers.

References

Brauw, C. de (1974); Broadcasting in the Netherlands. *Journal of Broadcasting* 18/4, p. 453-465.
Breed, W. (1958); Mass communication and sociocultural integration. *Social Forces* 37, p. 109-116.
Galtung, J. (1974); A rejoinder to K. Rosengren. *Journal of peace research* 11, p. 156-160.
Galtung, J., and M. Holmboe Ruge (1965); The structure of foreign news. *Journal of peace research* 2, p. 64-91. Idem (1970) in: Tunstall, J.; Media sociology, p. 259-98.
Golding, P., and P. Elliott (1977); *Making the news*, Chs. 4 and 6.
Mannheim, K (1949); *Man and society*, p. 177-187.
McQuail, D. (1977); *Analysis of newspaper content*, p. 245-277.
Merton, R.K. (1949); *Social theory and social structure*, p. 5-10.
NOS (1977); *Journaal 1975-76*, vol. 4: Inhoudsanalyse. Report 160.
Östgaard, E. (1965); Factors influencing the flow of news. *Journal of peace research* 2. p. 39-63.
Robinson, G.J. (1977); *Tito's maverick media; the politics of mass communication in Yugoslavia*, p. 164-182.
Rosengren, K.E. (1970); International news: intra- and extra media data. *Acta sociologica* 13, p. 96-109.
Rosengren, K.E. (1974); International news: methods, data, theory. *Journal of peace research* 11, p.
Sande, O. (1969); The perception of foreign news. *Journal of peace research* 8, p. 223-237.
Ultee, W., and P.J. van Wijngaarden (1972); Enkele methodologische opmerkingen over de bruikbaarheid van inhoudsanalyse als vorm van toetsend onderzoek. *Sociologische Gids* XIX/4, p. 239-49.

Elisabeth Noelle-Neumann, Director of the Institute of Communication Research at the University of Mainz, Federal Republic of Germany, uses cross-national, longitudinal survey and media content data to address the role of mass media in modern Europe. First presented at the International Sociological Association's World Congress in Uppsala, Sweden, in the summer of 1978, this chapter is a revised and updated version of Dr. Noelle-Neumann's work. The chapter presents data supporting both agenda-setting and opinion-molding functions of the mass media.

38

MASS MEDIA AND SOCIAL CHANGE IN DEVELOPED SOCIETIES

Elisabeth Noelle-Neumann

In 1972, at the International Congress of Psychology in Tokyo, I presented a paper entitled "Return to the Concept of Powerful Mass Media" (1973). As a point of departure, the theses I developed at the time will be introduced here. Today as then, the rules of selective perception and a regained conception of public opinion seem to me to be indispensable for the understanding of the effect of mass media. From the one as from the other, there arise consequences for methods of effects research.

This article summarizes the studies about media effects from the Institute for Communication Research at the University of Mainz and the Institut fuer Demoskopie Allensbach. It is easy to criticize their deficiencies, but it is more useful to take them as a stimulus to conduct similar and, wherever possible, improved investigations so that the number of such studies will eventually increase. Even though media practitioners have plainly declared that they are not interested in successful investigations of media effects, communication researchers must support each other in penetrating into this field. The mass media are too important for a working democracy to be left in the dark as to their effects.

THE POSITION OF 1972

At the time of the Tokyo Congress of Psychology, a fierce dispute about selective perception had been waged for well over a decade (Freedman and Sears,

From Elisabeth Noelle-Neumann, "Mass Media and Social Change in Developed Societies," original manuscript.

1965). Evidence with which Lazarsfeld, Berelson, Gaudet had presented selective perception in "The People's Choice" was reanalyzed. New interpretations were offered under the heading "de facto selectivity" (Sears and Freedman, 1967). Selective perception was replaced by the concept of selective avoidance. Contradictory laboratory experiments which revealed no consistent selective perception were reported (Abelson et al., 1968). The refutation was born from *laboratory* experiments, but selective perception was actually found in the *field* investigation of Erie County, and in field research selective perception was *incontestably confirmed* in the 1970s (Noelle-Neumann, 1973).

All of the interest, all the effort, was justified, for, with the principle that people look for supportive communication and avoid that which contradicts their opinions, the authors of the Erie County study explained unexpected findings, the fact that the mass media had no attitude-changing effect. Only for confirmation, for reinforcement, do people use the media. This finding had for a long time, almost up to the end of the 1960s, supported the dogma of the ineffectiveness of the mass media, the so-called "reinforcement hypothesis," but only because the rule had remained incomplete. It lacked the addition which had to read: The more a medium or a media system makes selective perception difficult, the greater its effect will be—that is to say, in both directions: It reinforces when it supports predominantly existing attitudes; it changes when it contradicts predominantly existing attitudes (Noelle-Neumann, 1971).

A series of observations—which will be dealt with later in the main part of the article—suggests that we reconsider the power of the mass media to change attitudes. This was connected above all with the innovation of television, which makes selective opinion-supporting perception more difficult than does the traditional print media. TV is also superior to print in its forcefulness and directness of picture and sound.

With the rule of selective perception now complete, two factors shifted further into the foreground of interest: the cumulation resulting from the periodical publication of media; and consonance, that is, unanimous illumination, unanimous argumentation with regard to events, people, and problems. Consonance appears not only where the media are state controlled, but also under the conditions of Western parliamentary democracy. The report of 1972 was concerned in detail with the origin of consonance. Consonance and cumulation were drawn together, because it is their common characteristic to prevent selective perception. It was tersely stated: "The thesis that mass media do not change attitudes but only reinforce them cannot be upheld under conditions of consonance and cumulation" (Noelle-Neumann, 1973: 109).

A third factor about media influence that was emphasized in the 1972 report is the effect of being *public*. Hardly any importance had been attached to this element in the effects research of the past decades; the design of most investigations has failed to simulate a public situation. The concern with the phenomenon of "public opinion" was said to be necessary, "because otherwise it would not be possible to gain an impression of the opinion-forming power of the mass media" (Noelle-Neumann, 1973: 88).

The process of an interaction between individual and environment, where dominant opinion is defended and new opinion is established, was termed "spiral of silence" (Noelle-Neumann, 1974b). People, so the thesis claimed, by nature social beings, live in perpetual fear of isolating themselves and carefully observe their environment to see which opinions increase and which ones decrease. If they find that their views predominate or increase, then they express themselves freely in public; if they find that their views are losing supporters, then they become fearful, conceal their convictions in public, and fall silent. Because the one group express themselves with self-confidence whereas the others remain silent, the former appear to be stronger in public, the latter weaker than their numbers suggest. This encourages others to express themselves or to fall silent, and a spiral process comes into play. Public opinion is understood as opinion within a field of tension which one may express openly, without danger of isolating oneself. This describes only one of two aspects of the social psychological phenomenon of public opinion. The second aspect concerns the defense of norms. The individual *must* display a certain behavior in public if he does not want to isolate himself. This refers to public opinion as the "punishing angel of morality" ("Zuchmeisterin des Sittlichen"), as the German jurist Rudolph Jhering called it. Public opinion, the assessment of the environment by the individual, has, according to this conception, two sources: the content of the mass media and the original observation which the individual makes within his environment. To the individually oriented concept of effects research an element of collectivity is added—formation of opinion climate by mass media.

This approach has consequences for the choice of the research method: "It is especially important to investigate the combination of the three elements— consonance, cumulation, public character—as an effective factor of mass media. This presumably powerful combination can hardly be simulated realistically in a laboratory experiment. The study of media effectiveness therefore demands a shift in emphasis to field research" (Noelle-Neumann, 1973).

This has been done in the ensuing years, and the results are now to be reported. In addition to the emphasis on field research in place of laboratory experimentation, still a second methodological principle is to be stressed as characteristic for effect research: the multimethod approach, particularly the combination of content analysis and panel research as well as the synchronized examination of different target groups, particularly communicators and the public.

FAVORABLE CONDITIONS FOR THE RESEARCH OF MASS MEDIA EFFECTS

In the debate about whether mass media act as agents of change or as reinforcers of status quo, it has never been assumed that there was no effect if and when, with a high degree of concordance, a change is advocated in the mass media. It has been hypothesized that primarily affirmative media contents result from the ownership structure and that therefore the media only fortify any existing control. The workings of selective perception and the quest for confirmation that was found within the public led to the assumption that reinforcement of status quo always sells better and that, therefore, the culture industry "unswervingly and unconceptually redoubles the existing structure and its power over people" (Schmidt, 1978: 19). It has not been taken into account in this context that a situation could arise which, for various reasons, creates a demand for social change in developed societies, in which the satisfaction of elementary needs no longer absorbs the individual's energies. In the long run, energies are released for the search of new goals, new orientations. In the short run, something similar to the situation described by Donohew and Tipton (1973) will happen. In the case of a low activation level or the feeling of monotony, a willingness to take in variety instead of consistency develops, a quest for the "curiosity value." Much as this holds true for the population at large under certain circumstances, it is even more distinctive with journalists who, due to their occupation, look for the new, for surprise, for change—the designation "newsperson" bears witness to this—and they give preference to it whenever the power conditions permit.

In terms of research results, we know very little about what determines the direction of social change and value orientation advocated by journalists in a peculiar kind of consensus. What kind of consensus do they want? We are using the term consensus from now on in the sense not of complete concordance but of distinct predominance, i.e., where opposing opinions and opposing tendencies are considered to be deviant. How does this consensus come about? Ever since the publication of the pioneer study made by Lang and Lang (1953), well-founded findings by David Manning White (1950), Walter Gieber (1956), Einar Östgaard (1965), Johan Galtung (1965), James D. Halloran et al. (1970), and Winfried Schulz (1976) have indicated that "news values" in everyday journalistic work evoke a remarkable consonance of media contents.

The Federal Republic of Germany has, in the 1960s and 1970s, furnished very favorable conditions for the investigation of the connection between mass media and social change. The reason is the great gulf that apparently separated journalists and population after the end of World War II and the reconstruction of press and broadcasting. It is true that content analyses and surveys among journalists did not begin before the mid-1960s, and, likewise, it is not before the mid-1960s that, with the help of opinion research, we observe a remarkably strong change of attitudes among the population. But there are indications that the value orientation of journalists diverged from the prevailing mood of the population as early as the 1950s.

The constellation, a gulf between the attitudes of journalists and population and the emergence of great changes in the attitudes of the population, is described as favorable for communication research because the temporal relationship may thus be clarified: Have the media come closer to the attitude of the population or has the attitude of the population come closer to the consonant general mood of the media? The results—and this is rare in communication research—are unequivocal: media content and journalists' attitudes were always ahead of the changes in the attitudes of the population (see Kepplinger and Mathias, 1976).

Nevertheless, in various cases the population has come closer to the majority attitude of the journalists but then moved away from it again. Thus the relationship is really more complicated. Even if the media transmit a consonant message, an unlimited moldability of the attitudes of the population does not exist.

The point of departure with regard to the attitude-changing power of mass media was, as so often is the case in scientific work, a puzzling finding. A question regularly included in representative surveys conducted since 1952 by the Institut fuer Demoskopie Allensbach ("Generally speaking, what do you consider to be the best qualities of the Germans?") showed proof of a peculiar and constant decrease in positive replies and at the same time a continual increase in answers such as: "I don't know of any positive qualities." This trend did not reverse itself until 1976 (see Table 1).

No clear reasons for the increasing deterioration of the nation's self-esteem during a successful phase of recovery after 1945 were discernible. We asked, therefore, if it could be the outcome of a consonant and mostly negative presentation of the German character by the mass media. As the first stage of our investigation, conducted during the seminar on "media diversity" at the Institute for Communication Research of the University of Mainz in the summer term of 1968 under the direction of this author, we carried out a content analysis on the basis of videotape recordings of the regular political programs televised by the German ARD network (i.e., German television channel I: "Monitor," "Report," "Panorama," "Perspektiven") between February 1 and April 24, 1968, and also of the right-wing newspaper, the *Bild-Zeitung* (four million circulation, tabloid type, therefore low prestige), which is generally characterized as nationalistic, during the same period. We took into account every reference to the German character or German manners and behavior which by content or formulation implied a generalization. The television programs were chosen on account of their large audiences (embracing altogether about half of the population), their markedly public character in the sense of an omnipresence of television, and also because it was assumed that it is much more difficult for a television than for a print medium audience to avoid communication that does not support but which undermines self-esteem (Noelle-Neumann 1977a: 143-144). The *Bild-Zeitung*, on the other hand, was included not merely because of its mass circulation and corresponding omnipresence (it is read by about half the population each week), but because such a newspaper would show whether a supposed nagative stereotype of the German character permeated the entire media system or whether this paper would produce a favorable stereotype in keeping with its nationalistic character.

TABLE 1: German Respondents' Perceptions of the Qualities of the German People, 1952-1976 (in percentages)

QUESTION: "Quite generally, what would you say are the Germans' best qualities?"

	July 1952	Aug. 1962	Oct. 1963	Sept. 1970	May 1972	April 1973	April 1975	June 1976	Representative journalists' sample Summer 1976
Favorable replies	96	86	84	81	80	78	78	86	78
"Don't know of any favorable qualities"	4	14	16	19	20	22	22	14	22
Total %	100	100	100	100	100	100	100	100	100
Total n =	1058	2086	970	1003	908	1037	1026	489	100

SOURCE: Allensbach Archives, IfD-Surveys, Nos. 052, 1059, 1081, 2065, 2082, 2093, 3014, 3031/I-2187.

The content analysis of the TV programs confirmed our expectations. Of 39 references to the German character which implied a generalization, 32 were negative stereotype of the German character permeated the entire media system of 82 evaluating references, 51 were negative, 31 positive.

The first content analysis in which a possible connection between mass media and change in opinions about the national self-image was sought was not undertaken until 1968. And it was not until 1976 that the first journalists' survey was conducted: "Generally speaking, what do you consider to be the best qualities of the Germans?" There is only weak empirical support of the hypothesis that the constant decrease of national self-esteem in the fifties and sixties could be explained to be an effect of mass media influences. There are no contradictory explanations for this "enigma," and there are no explanations that are better substantiated empirically.

A CLASSICAL CASE OF PUBLIC OPINION PROCESS

A different example of the change in the population's attitudes in the direction suggested by preceding media consonance is the German Ostpolitik. The 1968 content analysis, again in the Mainz seminar of the summer term of 1968, started here with the same model that had been used for the national self-image study, and again the results of content analyses were connected with survey results. A different type of opinion-formation process takes place:

(1) Not a long-term process over decades, but new, pushed up to a high degree of saliency after the Social Democrats entered into government in 1966.

(2) The subject: no fundamental value orientation but a political program with the concrete goal of decision and action, recognition of the new East German border that was established after World War II.

(3) Media consonance in opposition to the majority opinion of the population.

According to the content analysis of the two German TV channels, fifteen of the twenty arguments broadcast between February 1 and April 24, 1968, in connection with the subject, "recognition of the new Eastern border," fifteen were for and five were against. Table 2 shows how the opinion of the population changed in the direction of media consonance over a period of two and a half years.

The data suggest that mass media act as "agents of change," however, on the specific condition that media consonance and proclaimed government policies influence the population in the same direction. The basis of empirical data obtained from the content analysis is small. This does not impair its value because there is no difficulty in widening the base by conducting content analyses of the press of the second half of the 1960s.

Whether the conditions of consonance and cumulation—under which a changing effect of mass media is assumed—really existed here, was only incompletely evidenced between 1968 and 1972. There was the above-mentioned, rather small content analysis of political TV broadcasts over a period of only six weeks. There were, in addition, two surveys among a representative cross-section of newspaper journalists, which showed, for 1969 and 1973, that, unlike the population at large, three-quarters of the journalists were adherents of the government parties Social Democrats and Liberals (the parties which supported the new Ostpolitik; see Table 3). Table 4 lists the survey results with regard to the party preference of journalists up to the summer of the election year, 1976. For the last of these surveys, there are also results concerning TV and radio

TABLE 2:   German Respondents' Opinions on Accepting or Rejecting New Eastern Border with Poland at the Oder-Neisse Line (in percentages)

QUESTION: "Should we formally recognize the Oder-Neisse Line, the present German-Polish frontier, as Germany's definitive Eastern border, or do you think we should not do so?"

	November 1967	September 1968	May 1969	May 1970
Recognize	31	34	37	50
Not recognize	50	43	37	26
Undecided	19	23	26	24
Total %	100	100	100	100
Total n =	519	2104	1048	977

SOURCE: Allensbach Archives, IfD-Surveys Nos. 2033, 2044, 2052, 2963/III.

TABLE 3: Trends in the Electoral Preference of Journalists and Population (in percentages)

	November 1969		September 1973		Summer 1976	
	Total population	Daily newspaper journalists	Total population	Daily newspaper journalists	Total population	Daily newspaper journalists
Party Preference (where concrete statements were made):						
Christian Democrats	46	24	44	22	49	26
Social Democrats	47	63	43	48	42	45
Liberals	4	12	11	30	8	29
No party preference indicated	3	1	2	x	1	x
Total %	100	100	100	100	100	100
Total n =	1485	93	1368	86	1590	41

NOTE: x = less than 0.5%. The selection of the journalists' sample was made in consideration of the papers' circulation. Thus the journalists represented, as it were, the circulation of the daily press. More detailed information on the 1969 and 1973 sampling design may be found in: Elisabeth Noelle-Neumann Umfragen zur inneren Pressefreiheit. Das Verhältnis Verlag -Redaktion. Droste, Düsseldorf 1977 (Journalismus, Band 7). The same procedure was applied in 1976. SOURCE: Allensbach Archives, IfD-Surveys 2058, 1185, 2097, 1235, 3032, 2187.

journalists which show a far-reaching homogeneity of political attitudes in the whole media system and, at the same time, a distinct disparity from the population.

What follows after a violent process of opinion changes, as could be observed in the case of Ostpolitik in the Federal Republic of Germany of the late 1960s and early 1970s? This situation of "thereafter" has hardly been analyzed and, also, has not been theoretically clarified. In the case of Ostpolitik, the journalists who popularized the policy of detente originally were avant-garde at the end of the 1960s. After 1973, however, the journalists retained their position toward detente policy and their liberal attitude toward communism, while the majority of the population returned to its original distrust (see Table 5). The result was a deep gulf in the summer of 1976 between the attitudes of the journalists and those of the population (see Tables 6 and 7). There is a widespread assumption that the views of journalists and population always differ a great deal. In such simple terms, this is not true. And it was even less true for the Federal republic of, say, the early 1970s than it is for the Federal Republic today.

As a theoretical tool to deal with such results, the theory of public opinion, sketched at the beginning of this article, is used. Public opinion in this connection—in the realm of controversy, that which one is able to express without risk of isolating oneself—has two sources: mass media and the immediate observation of the environment, of what other people think and of what they dare say publicly.

TABLE 4: Party Preference of Broadcast and Print Journalists and of the Total Population (in percentages)

	Summer 1976			
	TV and radio journalists	Journalists with daily newspapers, magazines	Journalists total	Total population (for comparison)
Party Preference (where concrete statements were made):				
Christian Democrats	19	26	21	49
Social Democrats	62	50	55	42
Liberals	19	24	24	8
No party preference indicated	x	x	x	1
Total %	100	100	100	100
Total n =	32	55	87	1590

NOTE: x = less than 0.5%. The selection of the journalists' sample was made in consideration of the papers' circulation. Thus the journalists represented, as it were, the circulation of the daily press. More detailed information may be found in: Elisabeth Noelle-Neumann: Umfragen zur inneren Pressefreiheit. op. cit. The same procedure was applied in 1976.
SOURCE: Allensbach Archives, IfD-Surveys 2187, 3032.

TABLE 5: German Population Feeling About Whether Menaced by the Soviet Union, 1952-1976 (in percentages)

QUESTION: "Do you feel we are menaced by Russia, or not?"

	July 1952	March 1958	November 1964	September 1969	April 1971	August 1976
Menaced	66	51	39	33	28	47
Not Menaced	15	27	37	55	46	38
Undecided	19	22	24	12	26	16
Total %	100	100	100	100	100	100
Total n =	2116	1997	1079	994	987	961

SOURCE: Allensbach Archives, IfD-Surveys 052, 1017, 1094, 2056, 2071, 3032/I.

In direct environmental observation and debate, the mistrust of the East prevailed once more and was openly expressed, even without the majority support of the mass media. We do not yet know, however, what the impact of a constant gulf between the convictions of the journalists and those of the population is. Such a gulf can originate from the fact that journalists adhere to a particular point of view once it has been presented, whilst—contrary to the

TABLE 6:   Comparison of Journalist and German Population Attitudes Toward
            Foreign Policy Issues (in percentages)

Contrasts between journalists and population

QUESTION: "Here is a list of political demands. Which of them do you find especially
            important? Could you lay down the pertinent cards? (Interviewer presents
            deck of cards)

	July 1976 Population over 18	Summer 1976 Journalists
—Excerpt from the replies—		
Found *especially important*		
Not to be too lenient toward the East, no under- taking without getting something in return	55	20
Prevent communist influences from advancing in Europe	51	26
No cooperation with communist groups in the Federal Republic	46	14
Stengthen NATO and the Bundeswehr (federal army) so that the Russians do not get an ever- growing military lead over the West	40	15
Total n =	1265	100

SOURCE: Allensbach Archives, IfD-Surveys 2185, 2187.

TABLE 7:   German Opinions About Ostpolitik (in percentages)

Opinions about Ostpolitik

QUESTION: "In this picture, two men are talking about Russia. With whom would you
            rather agree, with the first one or with the second?" (Interviewer presents
            graphic picture)

	June 1976 Population over 16	Summer 1976 Journalists
Agreeing to:		
"I think that the Russians abuse our goodwill to reconcile with the East. They make use of our willingness to come to terms in order to expand their power in the world"	62	37
"I think that the Russians are serious about detente policy. They do not abuse our confidence in order to expand their power in the world"	19	32
Undecided, no reply	19	31
Total %	100	100
Total n =	1000	100

SOURCE: Allensbach Archives, IfD-Surveys, 3030/I, 2187.

predominant argumentation in the media—the population turns away from it once again. It could be that the influence of mass media upon the process of public opinion is thus weakened on the whole. It is not without danger for a democracy if a larger portion of its population finds its emotional convictions seldom or never articulated in the mass media. Convictions thus remain intellectually unclarified and, being emotionally charged, they have the potential for being radicalized in times of crisis.

Theoretically there are two possible predictions of journalistic behavior on this point. Research results, such as those of Kelley and Volkart (1952) in the United States, suggest a reduced tendency to change attitudes when one has committed oneself in public, since the flaw of fickleness is inherent in the change of attitude. It could also be that journalistic self-esteem requires journalists to make "correct" forecasts, which again would make a change of attitude difficult. Nevertheless, the hypothesis that journalists may change their opinion would certainly have suggested itself, because mass media thrive when they have something new to offer. Apparently, however, journalists look for new things in quite a different way and not by changing their convictions.

The question stemming from nineteenth-century discussions about freedom of the press and twentieth-century communication research—whether mass media are a mirror or a molder of prevailing opinion—will, according to the present research results, certainly not be answered in terms of the mirror idea. This is even contradicted by the very assumption that the mass media are one of two sources of public opinion: When mass media mold public opinion in this sense, then they cannot be a mirror at the same time—in any case, not predominantly. The assumption that public opinion has two sources, or, rather, not the mass media exclusively—a hypothesis which is supported by the development of opinions about Ostpolitik after 1973—makes understandable why consonant media opinion and opinion of the population can diverge to such an extent, and thereby makes the very idea of a "mirror" simply out of the question (Deutsche UNESCO-Kommission, 1972).

MODEL OF AN EFFECT STUDY

It seems, however, as if there would be a tendency among journalists to refrain from expressing attitudes for which they find no support at all among larger groups of the population, suggesting that they are not utterly insensitive when a gulf opens between themselves and the population. In this direction points a model for the investigation of mass media effects, applied in 1976 within the framework of an international research project sponsored by UNESCO (Noelle-Neumann and Kepplinger, forthcoming).

As this is an investigation with multimethod, multilevel designs, a model which has been rare in hitherto published empirical research, I present excerpts from its results here. It was conducted by the Institut fuer Publizistik at the University of Mainz in cooperation with the Institut fuer Demoskopie Allensbach, sponsored by the German National Science Foundation (Deutsche Forschungsgemeinschaft).

In each of the eight participating European countries, the investigation concentrated geographically on one big city with more than 100,000 inhabitants. This was designed to improve international comparability. In Germany, the city of Mainz was chosen for this purpose. The period of the investigation in the Federal Republic of Germany was January to December 1976.

In its subject matter, the cross-national, longitudinal investigation dealt with problems, concerns, and difficulties on a local, a national, and an international level. In the case of such problems on these three levels that were named spontaneously, it was inquired where, in particular, the difficulties were ("problem dimensions"), what had created the problem, and how the problem should be solved. In order to introduce a certain element of international comparability, two problems were expressly broached: unemployment and overpopulation of the world.

In order to find out the perspectives of the population, of the journalists, and of experts on the respective questions, four different groups of people, each chosen representatively, were interviewed. Of the population, two groups composed of the lower and upper ends of the social scale (both workers and local elites) were selected. The third group was composed of journalists working in the city of Mainz, including those who worked elsewhere but whose work circulated widely in Mainz, from supraregional newspapers, magazines, television, and radio. The fourth group was formed by experts on all the problems dealt with.

Panel interviews of workers and local elite in the middle and end of 1976 were combined with one-time interviews of journalists and experts in mid-1976. Content analyses were conducted for the media circulated in Mainz (press, television, radio): for the local newspaper from January to December 1976, and for the remaining media only in those parts that referred to the problems investigated, from April to December 1976. (A more detailed description as well as a definition of the respondent groups and information about the same may be found in Noelle-Neumann and Kepplinger, forthcoming.)

CLOSE-UP VIEW OF AGENDA-SETTING FUNCTION
OF MASS MEDIA

The results of such a study are demonstrated by the example of the unemployment problem, more specifically by several problem dimensions which the journalists emphasize more than the population, as well as several dimensions with which the journalists are less concerned than the population (see Table 8). Two results stand out: First, there is a concordance of conviction of the journalists and the media content, limited only whenever the journalists stand alone with their convictions and thus detect no support, neither from the workers nor from the elite. One may conclude that arguments which are emphasized in the

TABLE 8: Assessment of Problem Dimensions of Unemployment by Workers, Members of the Elite Group, and Journalists in Such Cases where Journalists are at Variance with the Other Categories, May/June 1976 (7 out of 16 response alternatives, in percentages)

QUESTION: "Here on these cards we have put down some arguments we have heard about unemployment. Would you, please, read them. What, in your opinion, is the worst about unemployment? Could you accordingly select the respective cards, but only the most important arguments. (Presentation of cards with 16 response alternatives)

—Excerpt from answers—	Workers	Elite	Journalists	Prestige Newspapers and both TV Networks* 9 months: April-December 1976
Problem dimensions more frequently mentioned by journalists:				
Job difficulties for women	19	22	44	61
Job difficulties for the untrained	45	46	52	34
Job difficulties for older people	51	54	57	27
Problem dimensions not so frequently mentioned by journalists:				
Trade unions being responsible	14	22	4	4
Radicalization of the unemployed	32	48	12	1
Unwillingness of many unemployed to work	37	20	5	3
Demoralization of the unemployed	27	15	4	6
Total n =	219	46	81	

*Number of published arguments.
SOURCE: UNESCO investigation of the Institute für Publizistik der Universität Mainz in conjunction with the Institut für Demoskopie Allensbach, IfD-No. 1261, 1976.

media according to the content analysis reflect the actual convictions of journalists. Concerns with which the population is occupied, but not the journalists, are seldom dealt with in the media (see Table 9). The finding contradicts the mirror hypothesis. Second, the arguments emphasized in the media within half a year (July to December 1976) clearly gained ground with the population; the unemphasized arguments lost ground, especially with the workers. The finding confirms the molder hypothesis.

If the first example—national self-image—referred to a long-term process of attitude change and the second one to a short and impetuous process pressing for action, the third example—unemployment—can perhaps be understood as an illustration of how the normal agenda-setting function of the mass media works: by determining where the main difficulties of an unsatisfactory situation must be seen and, derived from that, priorities of political action.

TABLE 9: 　Increase and Decrease in the Emphasis of Problem Dimensions of Unemployment Between July and December 1976, with Workers and Members of the Elite Group Interviewed Twice (in percentages)

	Development of opinions between July and December 1976	
	Male workers (n=131)	Male elite (n=37)
Problem dimensions more frequently emphasized by journalists:		
Job difficulties for women	+6	± 0
Job difficulties for the untrained	+9	+ 3
Job difficulties for the older people	+4	+11
Problem dimensions less frequently emphasized by journalists:		
Trade unions being responsible	−3	± 0
Radicalization of the unemployed	−9	− 8
Unwillingness of many unemployed to work	−3	+ 5
Demoralization of the unemployed	−3	+ 5

SOURCE: UNESCO investigation of the Institut für Publizistik der Universität Mainz in conjunction with the Institut für Demoskopie Allensbach, IfD-No. 1261, 1976.

HOW MEDIA EFFECTS BECOME PERCEPTIBLE

In contrast to formerly held assumptions that the relationship between mass media and changing attitudes cannot be traced with the help of statistical means, this type of panel research seemed suitable to uncover the influence of mass media. This is even more surprising, as the original application of this research technique in the Erie County study resulted in not finding effects of change to be related to mass media. There are—the enumeration is certainly not complete—at least three reasons which may explain why panel research, today, makes media effects visible:

(1) Through the spread of television, the influence of mass media has become stronger. Selective, supporting perception—the defensive mechanism by means of which people protect themselves against the change of their own attitudes—is more easily overcome. A direct connection between the use of the media and a change in attitude has thus become easier to measure, easier to bring to light.

(2) Change of attitude is no longer measured where attitudes are most deep-rooted and thus least subject to change (e.g., party preference) but, rather, where it occurs with more ease (e.g., attitude toward persons or perception of the climate of opinion).

(3) Surveys of the population are combined with surveys of journalists and content analyses. Thus it can be determined more accurately where con-

sonant views are presented by the media and, particularly for these areas, the change of attitudes can be observed.

The indication—based on this combination of methods—that, above all, television changes attitudes, has been conveyed in an earlier publication (Noelle-Neumann, 1978). The most interesting finding, ascertained with the help of a panel survey and interviews of journalists, concerned a reversal in the climate of opinion in the election year of 1976 as to who would win the forthcoming federal election. The reversal was detected first only among persons who were much exposed to political broadcasts, then, later (in accordance with the rule of the two-step flow of communication) among the rest of the population. The evaluation of the opinion climate changed in the direction of the Grand Coalition, which the journalists favored (Noelle-Neumann, 1977c).

A BROADER PERSPECTIVE

The most conspicuous social change in the Federal Republic of Germany has taken place, within the past fifteen years, in the field of moral convictions. Content analyses and surveys among journalists that might show the influence of the mass media in this development do not yet exist. This case reveals the extent to which the evidence hinges on the hazard of subject matter in those investigations on which I rely here, but which, originally, served quite different purposes.

In a certain respect, the subject "mass media and social change" is, in any case, dealt with too narrowly in the context of this article. This holds true in two directions: First, the treatment is virtually fixed on the occurrence of an influence upon attitudes by opinions that are consonantly spread by the media. In fact, an important part of the changing effects of mass media results from the fact that, under the influence of mass media, *reality* changes. A case in point is the prediction by the mass media of a shortage of goods which leads to an actual shortage, and then to a chain of measures and to changed attitudes. Second, mass media have a changing effect not only because of their content but because of their mere existence. This can be shown in the case of television (see the conclusion of this article).

Combination of Field Experiment and Population Surveys to Observe Effects of TV

We are relying on a field experiment, conducted in 1966-1967 by the Allensbach Institute in order to observe what actually changes after people buy their first television set. The investigation was supported by two broadcasting stations, the Seuddeutscher Rundfunk in Stuttgart and the Suedwestfunk in Baden-Baden (Institute fuer Demoskopie Allensbach, 1968). When the investigation started, 71% of the households in the Federal Republic of Germany already owned a TV set. In representative population surveys, the addresses of households that planned to buy a TV set shortly were ascertained. These households formed the test group. The control group was formed according to the selection principle of statistical twins: pertaining to each household of the test group, another household without a TV set and also without buying intentions and with the same number of adults in the same age and same professional groups was chosen. Before the TV set was bought by the test group, both groups were interviewed with an identical questionnaire. One year later, a second interview with largely identical questions was conducted both in those households that had meanwhile bought a TV set and in the statistically comparable control group. As expected, in the beginning, test group and control group differed somewhat in their interest and in their attitudes, in spite of their statistical equalization. Wherever test group and control group already differed to a larger extent, the development between the first and the second interview was measured with index numbers (the situation in the first interview equalling 100 (see Table 10).

Some results of this investigation are reported here.

First, the field experiment showed that after a TV set had been bought, the interest in politics increased substantially. The following long-term observation corresponds with this finding: In the ten years between 1952 and 1962, the interest in politics remained almost unchanged in the population; the number of those who described themselves as politically interested oscillated between 27% and 31%. In the following ten years—a period of time that coincided with the spread of television, which in the early 1960s was installed in a little less than half of all households and in the early 1970s in practically all households—the proportion of politically interested persons rose to some 50%. Further empirical findings that were presented elsewhere support the asssumption that television effected the great increase of interest in politics (Blumler and McQuail, 1968; Blumler, 1977).

Family life changed after the first TV set had been bought (Robinson, 1972; Szalai, 1972). Conversations between married couples were reduced. This was

TABLE 10: Changes in Interest in Politics, 1966 and 1967, Between Groups with TV and Those Without (in percentages)

QUESTION: "Quite generally speaking, are you interested in politics?"

	Test group before and after TV sets were bought (n=167)		Control group without a TV set (n=169)		Index 1966=100%	
	1966 (before)	1967 (after)	1966	1967	Test group	Control group
Yes	36	44	51	48	122	94
Not particularly	40	40	40	40	100	100
Not at all, no reply	24	16	9	12	38	133
Total %	100	100	100	100		

SOURCE: Allensbach Archives, IfD-Surveys 551, 552.

TABLE 11: Increase in Interest in Politics, 1952-1973 (in percentages)

QUESTION: "Quite generally speaking, are you interested in politics?"

	Interested
June 1952	27
January 1960	30
April 1961	31
August 1962	30
April 1965	31
September 1965	39
November 1965	35
June 1967	39
November 1967	38
August 1969	45
September 1969	41
January 1971	43
September 1972	46
June 1973	49

NOTE: Some 2000 adult persons were interviewed in each case (exceptions: June 1952 and September 1969, some 1000 adults in each case).
SOURCE: Allensbach Archives, IfD-Surveys 051, 1039, 1052, 1069, 2001, 2006, 2008, 2029, 2033, 2054, 2055, 2068, 2085, 2095.

measured with the question posed to husbands: "Some men talk much with their wives about their job and about what happens at work, and others hardly talk about it. What about you in this respect: Do you often talk about your job with your wife, or do you rather not want to think of your work at home?" Wives, in turn, were asked: "What about your husband: Does he often talk about his job with you, or does he rather not want to think of his work at home?" (see Table 12). Again, a long-term change that was ascertained by surveys of the Allensbach institute between 1963 and 1978 corresponds with this result of the field experiment. American long-term studies arrived at the same results (Robinson, 1972). The data in Table 13 certainly indicate other influences as well, but one cannot mistake the long-term trend that the frequency of discussions between married couples about the husband's job has decreased in the subjective judgment of both men and women.

Third, the enjoyment of work decreased after the first TV set had been bought. Again, there are indications that this effect was not a short-term phenomenon that occurred after the first TV set had been bought. A decreased enjoyment of work, as compared with 1962, stands out with the gainfully employed persons at the end of the 1960s and in the 1970s (see Table 14).

These are only three examples of a greater number of observations that short-term changes which were made visible by the field experiment corresponded

TABLE 12:   Conversations about Work Reported by Married Men and Married
            Women in TV and Non-TV Households (in percentages)

QUESTION to men:
    "Some men talk much with their wives about their job and about what happens at work,
    and others hardly talk about it. What about you in this respect: Do you often talk about
    your job with your wife, or do you rather not want to think of your work at home?"

| Married Men | Test group before and after TV sets were bought (n=80) | | Control group without a TV set (n=79) | | Index 1966=100% | |
	1966 (before)	1967 (after)	1966	1967	Test group	Control group
"Often talk about job, work"	40	39	36	62	97	172
"From time to time"	45	31	47	22	69	47
"Never, almost never"	15	30	17	16	200	94
Total %	100	100	100	100		

QUESTION to women:
    "Some men talk much with their wives about their job and about what happens at work,
    and others hardly talk about. What about your husband in this respect: Does he often
    talk about his job with you, or does he rather not want to think of his work at home?"

| Married Women | Test group before and after TV sets were bought (n=57) | | Control group without a TV set (n=54) | | Index 1966=100% | |
	1966 (before)	1967 (after)	1966	1967	Test group	Control group
"Often talks about job, work"	54	46	43	54	85	126
"From time to time"	25	33	45	35	132	78
"Never, almost never"	21	21	12	11	100	92
Total %	100	100	100	100		

SOURCE: Allensbach Archives, IfD-Surveys 551, 552.

with long-term changes that evolved within the population in the 1960s and
1970s. It can be assumed that considerable changes of social and individual
reality take place through the television medium (see Table 15).

    Increased difficulties in reading or changes of thinking habits, like diminish-
ment of reflectiveness can also be linked to the mere existence of TV, quite apart
from effects of content. But this leads to quite another research realm.

TABLE 13: Changes in Conversational Frequency Reported by Married Men and
Married Women, 1963 and 1978 (in percentages)

QUESTION to married men:
"Do you sometimes talk about your job with your wife?"

QUESTION to married women:
"Does your husband sometimes talk with you about his work?"

	Aug./Sept. 1963	April 1978
Married Men:		
Talk about everything with her	34	19
Often talk about it with her	30	34
Not so often	36	47
Total %	100	100
Total n =	351	661
Married Women:		
Talks about everything with me	38	19
Often talks about it	31	41
Not so often	31	40
Total %	100	100
Total n =	347	664

SOURCE: Allensbach Archives, IfD-Surveys 256/M, 1263, 3056, 256/F, 1259, 3056.

TABLE 14: Differences in Work and Leisure Hour Enjoyment Reported by TV
and Non-TV Households, 1966 and 1967 (in percentages)

QUESTION: "Which hours of the day do you generally like most: the hours at work or the
hours during which you do not work or do you like both?"

	Test group before and after TV sets were bought (n=167)		Control group without a TV set (n=169)		Index 1966=100%	
	1966 (before)	1967 (after)	1966	1967	Test group	Control group
When I don't work	24	30	21	21	125	100
The hours at work, like both	70	65	68	72	93	106
Undecided	6	5	11	7	83	64
Total %	100	100	100	100		

SOURCE: Allensbach Archives, IfD-Surveys 551, 552.

TABLE 15:   Changes in Reported Work and Leisure Hour Enjoyment, 1962-1978
             (in percentages)

QUESTION: "Which hours of the day do you generally like most: the hours at work or the
             hours during which you do not work or do you like both?"

| | Employed persons between 16 and 59 | | | | | | | |
	Aug. 1962	June 1967	Aug. 1972	Sept. 1975	June/July 1976	Nov. 1976	Oct. 1977	April 1978
When I don't work	33	38	38	42	45	49	46	46
The hours at work, like both	58	54	58	54	50	46	50	51
Undecided	9	8	4	4	5	5	4	3
Total %	100	100	100	100	100	100	100	100

SOURCE: Allensbach Archives, IfD-Surveys, 253, 2029, 2123, 3018, 3031, 3036, 3048, 3056.

SUMMARY

The question of whether mass media contribute to the reinforcement of status quo or whether they act as agents of change is linked with the question—raised as early as in the nineteenth century—whether the mass media should be considered as a mirror or a molder of the attitudes of a population. Results of empirical studies from the last decade in the Federal Republic of Germany show the media rather as agents of change, show their molding influence, although only under certain conditions, the most important of which is a majority agreement of argumentation and representation in the media, "media consonance." This influence, however, does not appear to be unlimited. Therefore, a considerable gulf between media consonance and attitude of the population can arise.

Not only through its content, but also through the mere existence of a medium, is social change effected. This is shown by the example of television.

As a method of effect research, the combination of panel surveys, surveys of journalists, content analyses, and field experiment has proven its value. The method provides us, in increasing number, findings which complement each other and which allow us to check the famous "middlerange theories" in the realm of mass communication.

REFERENCES

Abelson, Robert P., Elliot Aronson, William J. McGuire, Theodore M. Newcomb, Milton J. Rosenberg, and Percy H. Tannenbaum [eds.] (1968) Theories of Cognitive Consistency: A Sourcebook. Rand McNally, Skokie, IL.

Blumer, Jay G. (1977) "The Intervention of Television in British Politics." In: Lord Annan: Report of the Committee on the Future of Broadcasting. Appendices E-I Her Majesty's Stationery Office, London, Cmnd. 6753-1, pp. 1-28.

Blumler, Jay G. and Denis McQuail (1968) Television in Politics: Its Uses and Influences. Faber & Faber, London.

Deutsche UNESCO-Kommission (ed.) (1972) Forschung und Massenmedien. Bericht ueber ein internationales Seminar, das die Deutsche UNESCO-Kommission vom 7. bis 9. September 1970 in Konstanz veranstaltete. Verlag Dokumentation, Muenchen.

Donohew, Lewis and Leonard Tipton (1973) A Conceptual Model of Information Seeking, Avoiding and Processing. In: Peter Clarke (ed.): New Models for Mass Communications Research. Sage Publications, Beverly Hills, CA, pp. 243-268.

Freedman, Jonathan L. and David O. Sears (1965) "Selective Exposure." In: Leonard Berkowitz (ed.): Advances in Experimental Social Psychology, Vol. 2, Academic Press, New York, pp. 57-97.

Galtung, Johan and Mari Holmboe Ruge (1965) "The Structure of Foreign News: The Presentation of the Congo, Cuba and Cyprus Crisis in Four Foreign Newspapers." Journal of International Peace Research 1, pp. 64-90.

Gieber, Walter (1956) "Across the Desk: A Study of 16 Telegraph Editors." Journalism Quarterly 33, pp. 423-432.

Halloran, James D., Philip Elliot, and Graham Murdock (1970) Demonstrations and Communication: A Case Study. Penguin Books Ltd, Harmondsworth, England.

Horkheimer, Max and Theodor W. Adorno (1969) Dialektik der Aufkaerung. Philosophische Fragmente. S. Fischer, Frankfurt/Main. English translation: Dialectic of Enlightenment, trans. John Cumming. Allen Lane, London, 1973.

Institut fuer Demoskopie Allensbach (1968) Auswirkungen des Fernsehens in Deutschland. Lebensgewohnheiten, Interessen und Bild der Politik vor und nach der Anschaffung eines Fernsehgeraets. Allensbacher Archiv, IfD-Bericht 1489, August.

Kelley, Harold H. and Edmund H. Volkart (1952) The Resistance to Change of Group-Anchored Attitudes. American Sociological Review 17, pp. 453-465.

Kepplinger, Hans Mathias (1976) "The Quality of Listening." Presented to the "Meeting of Experts on Interpretation of Experiments by and through the Mass Media," Department of Philosophy, UNESCO, Paris (SHC-76/CONF. 621.6).

Lang, Kurt and Gladys Engel Lang (1953) "The Unique Perspective of Television and Its Effect: A Pilot Study." American Sociological Review 18 (February), pp. 3-12.

Noelle-Neumann, Elisabeth (1971) "Wirkung der Massenmedien." In: Elisabeth Noelle-Neumann and Winfried Schulz (eds.): Publizistik. Das Fischer Lexikon. Fischer Taschenbuch Verlag, Frankfurt/Main, pp. 316-350.

——— (1973) Kumulation, Konsonanz und Oeffentlichkeitseffekt. Ein neuer Ansatz zur Analyse der Wirkung der Massenmedien.[11] In: Publizistik, 18. Jg., Hft 1 (Januar-Marz 1973), pp. 26-55. English translation: "Return to the Concept of Powerful Mass Media." Studies of Broadcasting 9 (March 1973): pp. 67-112.

——— (1974a) "Die Schweigespirale. Ueber die Entstehung der oepffentlichen Meinung. In: Ernst Forsthoff and Reinhard Hoerstel (eds.): Standorte im Zeitstrom. Festschrift fuer Arnold Gehlen zum 70. Geburtstag. Athenaeum, Frankfurt/Main, pp. 299-330. English translation (abridged version): "The Spiral of Silence." Journal of Communication, 24 (Spring 1974): pp. 43-51.

——— (1974b) "Wahlentscheidung in der Fernsehdemokratie. Eine sozialpsychologische Interpretation der Bundestagswahl." In: Dieter Just and Lothar Romain (eds.): Auf der Suche nach dem muendigen Waehler. Die Wahlentscheidung 1972 und ihre Konsequenzen. Koeln (Schriftenreihe der Bundeszentrale fuer politische Bildung, Heft 101), pp. 161-205.

——— (1977a) "Das doppelte Meinungsklima. Der Einfluss des Fernsehens im Wahlkampt 1976." Politische Vierteljahresschrift, 18. Jg., Heft 2-3, pp. 408-451. English translation: "The Dual Climate of Opinion: The Influence of Television in the 1976 West German Federal Election." In: Klaus von Beyme and Max Kaase (eds.): German Political Studies. Vol. 3: Elections and Parties. Sage, Beverly Hills, CA, pp. 137-169.

——— (1977b) "Oeffentlichkeit als Bedrohung." In: Oeffentlichkeit als Bedrohung. Beitraege zur empirischen Kommunikationsforschung. (Alber-Broschur Kommunikation, Vol. 6) Karl Alber, Freiburg, Muenchen, pp. 204-233.

———— (1977c) Umfragen zur inneren Pressefreiheit. Das Verhaeltnis Verlag. Radaktion: Droste, Duesseldorf (Journalismus, Band 7).

———— (1978) "The Dual Climate of Opinion: The Influence of Television in the 1976 West German Federal Election." In: Klause von Beyme and Max Kaase (eds.): German Political Studies, Vol. 3, Sage, Beverly Hills, CA, pp. 137-169.

Noelle-Neumann, Elisabeth and Hans Mathias Kepplinger (forthcoming) "A report on the German section of an international research project." In: James D. Halloran (ed.): Communication in the Community. UNESCO, Paris.

Oestgaard, Einar (1965) "Factors influencing the Flow of News." Journal of Peace Research 1, pp. 39 ff.

Robinson, John P (1972) "Television's Impact on Everyday Life: Some Cross-national Evidence." In: Eli A. Rubinstein, George A. Comstock, and John P. Murray (eds.): Television and Social Behavior. Vol. 4: Television in Day-to-Day Life: Patterns of Use. U.S. Government Printing Office, Washington, D.C., pp. 410-431.

Schmidt, Alfred (1978) Der Uebergang zur verwalteten Welt. Wiedergelesen: "Dialektik der Aufklaerung" von Max Horkheimer und Theodor W. Adorno. In: Frankfurter Allgemeine Zeitung 158 (26 July), p. 19.

Schulz, Winfried (1976) Die Konstruktion von Realitaet in den Nachrichtenmedien. Eine Analyse der aktuellen Berichterstattung. Karl Alber, Freiburg (Alber-Broschur Kommunikation, Vol. 4).

Sears, David O. and Jonathan L. Freedman (1967) "Selective Exposure to Information: A Critical Review." Public Opinion Quarterly 31, pp. 194-213.

Szalai, Alexander (ed.) (1972) "The Use of Time: Daily Activities of Urban and Suburban Populations in Twelve Countries." Mouton and Co., The Hague.

White, David Manning (1950) "The 'Gate Keeper': A case study in the selection of news." Journalism Quarterly 27, pp. 383-390.

World events and severe intellectual criticism have eclipsed the old paradigm of communication and national development which implied a primarily one-way flow of messages from government development agencies to the people. The new paradigm of self-development, described here by Everett M. Rogers, suggests two main roles for mass communication: (1) answering requests for technical information by local constituencies, and (2) disseminating information about the self-development accomplishments of local groups. Rogers concludes that the passing of the old paradigm is an example of a move to a more international behavioral science. Dr. Rogers is Janet M. Peck Professor of International Communication at Stanford University.

39

THE RISE AND FALL OF
THE DOMINANT PARADIGM

Everett M. Rogers

"Self development implies a different
role for communication than the usual
top-down development approach of the past."

Through the late 1960s, a dominant paradigm ruled intellectual definitions and discussions of development. This concept of development grew out of certain historical events, such as the Industrial Revolution in Europe and the United States; the colonial experience in Latin America, Africa, and Asia; the quantitative empiricism of North American social science; and capitalistic economic-political philosophy. Implicit in the ruling paradigm were numerous assumptions that were generally thought to be valid, or at least were not widely questioned, until the early 1970s. Let us examine each of these influences on the older conception of development.

The Industrial Revolution. During the later 1800s, it was usually accompanied by foreign colonization and domestic urbanization. The older paradigm stressed economic growth (through industrialization) as the key to development. At the heart of industrialization were technology and capital, which substituted for labor. This simple synthesis of development may have been a correct lesson based on the experience of the Industrial Revolution in Western Europe and North America. But now we know that what happened in Western nations while on their pathways to development is not necessarily an accurate predictor of the process in non-Western states. For instance, European nations were often greatly aided in their socioeconomic transformation by their exploitation of colonies.

Reprinted from "The Rise and Fall of the Dominant Paradigm" by Everett M. Rogers in the JOURNAL OF COMMUNICATION 28 (Winter 1978) 64-69. Copyright 1978 by the Annenberg School of Communications.

The causes were thought to be (1) of an individual-blame nature (peasants were traditional, fatalistic, and generally unresponsive to technological innovation), or (2) of a social-structural nature within the nation (for example, a tangled government bureaucracy, a top-heavy land-tenure system).

Western intellectual models of development, and Euro-American technical assistance programs based on such models, were less likely to recognize the importance to a nation's development of external constraints such as international terms of trade, the economic imperialism of international corporations, and the vulnerability and dependence of the recipients of technical assistance programs.

In the late 1960s and the 1970s world events,
combined with intellectual critiques, began to
crack the credibility of the dominant paradigm.

The ecological disgust with environmental pollution in the developed nations led to their questioning whether they were, after all, such ideal models for development. Population pressures on available resources helped create doubts about whether unending economic growth was possible or desirable, and whether high technology was the most appropriate engine for development.

The world oil crises demonstrated that certain developing countries could make their own rules of the international game, and also produced some suddenly rich developing nations. Their escape from national poverty, even though in part at the expense of other developed countries, was a lesson to their neighbors in Latin America, Asia, and Africa. No longer were these nations willing to accept prior assumptions that the causes of underdevelopment were mainly internal.

In addition, the sudden opening of international relations with the People's Republic of China allowed the rest of the world to learn details of her pathway to development. Here was one of the poorest countries, and the largest, that in two decades created a public health and family planning system that was envied by the richest nations; well-fed and well-clothed citizens; increasing equality; and an enviable status for women. All this was accomplished with very little foreign assistance and presumably without much capitalistic competition. China, and to a lesser extent, Cuba, Tanzania, and Chile (in the early 1970s) suggested that there were alternatives to the dominant paradigm.

Finally, and perhaps most convincing of all, was the discouraging realization that development was not going very well in the developing countries that had closely followed the paradigm. However one measured development in most of the nations of Latin America, Africa, and Asia in the past twenty-five years, not much of it had occurred. Instead, most "development" efforts had brought further stagnation, a greater concentration of income and power, high unemployment, and food shortages in these nations. If these past development programs represented any kind of test of the intellectual paradigm on which they were based, the model had been found rather seriously wanting.

Capital-intensive technology. More-developed nations possessed such technology. Less-developed nations had less of it. So the implication seemed plain: Introduce the technology in the less-developed countries and they would become relatively more developed too.

When the needed social structures did not always materialize in less-developed countries, the fault was accorded to "traditional" ways of thinking, beliefs, and social values. Social science research was aimed at identifying the individual variables on which rapid change was needed, and the modernization of these traditional attitudes become a priority task of various government agencies, an activity in which the mass media were widely utilized.

Economic growth. It was assumed that "man" was economic, that he would respond rationally to economic incentives, that the profit motive would be sufficient to motivate the widespread and large-scale behavior changes required for development to occur. Economists were firmly in the driver's seat of development programs. They defined the problem of underdevelopment largely in economic terms, and in turn this perception of the problem as predominantly economic in nature helped to put, and to keep, economists in charge.

The focus on economic growth carried with it an "aggregate bias" about development: It had to be planned and executed by national governments. Local communities, of course, would be changed eventually by such development, but their advance was thought to depend upon the provision of information and resource inputs from higher levels. Autonomous self-development was considered unlikely or impossible. In any event, it seemed too slow.

Further, growth was thought to be infinite. Those rare observers who pointed out that known supplies of coal or oil or some other resource would run out in so many years were considered alarmists, and they were told that new technology would be invented to compensate for future shortages.

Quantification. One reason for reliance on per capita income as the main index of development was its deceitful simplicity of measurement. The expression "quality of life" was seldom heard until the very late 1960s.

Further, the quantification of development invoked a very short-range perspective of the past ten or twenty or twenty-five years at most. It was easy to forget the old centers of civilization, whose rich cultures had in fact provided the basis for Western cultures. Such old cultures were now poor (in a cash sense), and, even if their family life displayed a warmer intimacy and their artistic triumphs were greater, *that* was not development. It could not be measured in dollars.

Further, what was quantified about development was usually just growth, measured in the aggregate or on a per capita basis. Development policies of the 1950s and 1960s paid little attention to the equality of development benefits. The growth-first-and-let-equality-come-later mentality often was justified by the "trickle-down" theory: Leading sectors, once advanced, would then spread their advantage to the lagging sectors. It was not until the 1970s that the focus of quantification began to shift to measures of the equality of distribution.

Western models of development assumed that the main causes of underdevelopment lay within the underdeveloped nation rather than external to it.

in each locale. The integration of Chinese medicine with Western scientific medicine in contemporary China is an example of this approach to development. Acupuncture and antibiotics mix quite well.

I can summarize these newer conceptions by defining development as a widely participatory process of social change in a society, intended to bring about both social and material advancement (including greater equality, freedom, and other valued qualities) for the majority of the people through their gaining greater control over their environment.[1]

The rise of alternatives to the old paradigm of development implies that the role of communication in development must also change.

A decade or so ago, mass communication was often thought to be a very powerful and direct force for development. This period was characterized by considerable optimism about the potential contribution of communication, one that was consistent with the generally upbeat opinion about the possibilities for rapid development.[2] Certainly, the media were expanding during the 1950s and 1960s. Literacy was becoming more widespread in most developing nations, leading to greater print media exposure. Transistor radios were penetrating every village. A predominantly one-way flow of communication from government development agencies to the people was implied by the dominant paradigm. And the mass media seemed ideally suited to this role. They could rapidly reach large audiences with informative and persuasive messages about the details of development.

In the early 1960s, the relative power of the mass media in bringing about development was mainly assumed rather than proven. Gradually, it was realized that the role of mass communication in facilitating development was often indirect and only contributory to other social factors rather than direct and independently powerful.

Self-development implies a different role for communication than the usual top-down development approach of the past. Technical information about development problems and possibilities and about appropriate innovations is sought by local systems from the central government. The role of government development agencies, then, is mainly to communicate in answer to these locally-initiated requests, rather than to design and conduct top-down communication campaigns.

---

[1] As a commentary on how the present author's conception of development has changed, compare this definition with one that I proposed a decade ago: "*Development* is a type of social change in which new ideas are introduced into a social system in order to produce higher per-capita incomes and levels of living through more modern production methods and improved social organization" (3).

[2] The major change in conceptions of the role of communication in development from the 1960s to the 1970s is illustrated by comparing the two books edited by Lerner and Schramm in 1967 (1) and in 1976 (4).

Robert Gwathmey

From these events grew the conclusion that there are many alternative pathways to development. While their exact combination would be somewhat different in every nation, some of the main elements in this newer conception began to emerge:

The equality of distribution of information, socioeconomic benefits, etc. This new emphasis in development led to the realization that villagers and urban poor should be the priority audience for development programs and, more generally, that the closing of socioeconomic gaps by bringing up the lagging sectors was a priority task in many nations.

Popular participation in self-development planning and execution, usually accompanied by the decentralization of certain of these activities to the village level. Development came to be less a mere function of what national governments did to villagers, although it was recognized that government assistance was necessary even in local self-development.

Self-reliance and independence in development, with an emphasis upon the potential of local resources. Not only may international and binational technical assistance be rejected, but so, too, are most external models of development—leading to a viewpoint that every nation, and perhaps each village, may develop in its own way. If this occurs, of course, standardized indices of the rate of development become inappropriate and largely irrelevant.

Integration of traditional with modern systems so that modernization is a syncretization of old and new ideas, with the exact mixture somewhat different

Key elements in self-development approaches are participation, mass mobilization, and group efficacy, with the main responsibility for development planning and execution being at the local level. The main roles of mass communication in self-development may be summarized as (1) providing technical information about development problems and possibilities and about appropriate innovations, in answer to local requests, and (2) circulating information about the self-development accomplishments of local groups so that other such groups may profit from their experience and perhaps be challenged to achieve a similar performance.

Further, after a decade or more of enthusiasm for "big media" (like instructional television, satellite broadcasting, and computers) in seeking to achieve development in Latin America, Africa, and Asia, the 1970s marked a return to the use of radio and "little media." These lower-cost communication channels (especially radio) reach wide audiences in most developing countries, including villages and urban poor. Such media seem uniquely able to close the communication effects gap between elites and the masses, or at least not to widen it further. These "little media" are often used in development campaigns as one part of a communication system in which the audience is organized into small listening and discussion groups to facilitate feedback to the communicators.

The fall of the dominant paradigm of development is an example of a shift to a more international behavioral science, in which Western thought is but one ingredient.

REFERENCES

1. Lerner, Daniel and Wilbur Schramm (Eds.) *Communication and Change in the Developing Countries.* Honolulu: University Press of Hawaii, 1967.
2. Rogers, Everett M. "Communication and Development: The Passing of the Dominant Paradigm." *Communication Research* 3, 1976, pp. 213–240.
3. Rogers, Everett M. with Lynne Svenning. *Modernization Among Peasants: The Impact of Communication.* New York: Holt, Rinehart and Winston, 1969.
4. Schramm, Wilbur and Daniel Lerner (Eds.) *Communication and Change: The Last Ten Years— and the Next.* Honolulu: University Press of Hawaii, 1976.

PART VIII

POLICY RESEARCH

Growing importance of mass media systems and their sometimes troubled relationships with government have led to increasing involvement of mass communication scholars in policy research. Although the problems raised in policy research are not particularly new to mass communication research, the debate about policy research is unrestrained.

In this section, two major party cases are considered. The first is a proposal for cooperative research with British broadcasters. The second is a report on research that recommends changes of televised election coverage in Great Britain.

Debate by both American and European scholars is contained in this section. The major issues are whether robust intellectual questions are possible within an institutional policy research setting, and whether the independence of the researcher can be maintained under the conditions of policy research.

After fifteen months as a resident scholar with the British Broadcasting Company, Elihu Katz pro-
posed a program of policy research involving independent scholars and broadcasters. In a BBC
lunchtime lecture in February 1977, Dr. Katz summarized the ideas contained in a longer report
to the BBC, Social Research on Broadcasting: Proposals for Further Development. *In the abridged*
version of the lecture reprinted here, Dr. Katz argues that British researchers are much closer to
broadcasters than are their American colleagues. British researchers are members of the same elites
as broadcasters, and they are listened to. In Katz's view, there should be more than this "common
ground" between researchers and broadcasters. He argues that a "better shelter" is needed for co-
operative research on institutional, audience, and societal questions. Following the Katz chapter are
three responses by other scholars. James D. Halloran stridently takes issue with most of the Katz
chapter. He sees the report's statement of research priorities as asociological and atheoretical, and
he argues that the report is framed primarily in the broadcasters' terms of reference. Furthermore, he
fears that attempts to formalize researcher-broadcaster cooperation will not be productive and that
only research which supported broadcasters' positions would be accepted. James W. Carey argues
that the Katz proposal highlights the basic problem of policy research, the scholar's independence.
He argues that significant intellectual questions are unlikely to emerge from the cooperative setting
proposed and that it is only compelling intellectual questions which will attract the best minds to
mass communication research. Herbert J. Gans is highly supportive of the Katz report, but he has
suggestions for improving mass communication research generally. He argues that our work is too
media centered in that it often ignores the macro-social processes that surround mass communica-
tion. Dr. Katz has the last word here, with his comments on some of the arguments raised above.
He contends that policy research can be intellectually challenging and that diverse financial support
should be provided for the collaborative experiment he envisions. (The articles reprinted here are
from a symposium published in the Journal of Communication. *Because of limited space, not all the*
articles can be included. In Dr. Katz's rebuttal, points by Dr. Gaye Tuchman are quoted. For her
excellent comments, see "Professionalism as an Agent of Legitimation," in the Journal of Communication, *Spring 1978, pp. 106-119.) Dr. Katz is Professor and Director of the Communications*
Institute, Hebrew University of Jerusalem. Dr. Carey is Dean of the College of Communications,
University of Illinois. Dr. Halloran is Director of the Centre for Mass Communication Research
at the University of Leicester, England. Dr. Gans is Professor of Sociology at Columbia University.

686

40

LOOKING FOR TROUBLE

Elihu Katz

A liason between broadcasters and academics
proposes areas where social research
can help improve media products and policy.

The BBC invited me to consider the state of social research on broadcasting and to propose an agenda for further development which would take account of the needs of policy and program-making. The hint of a new deal in broadcaster-researcher relationships seemed unmistakable—and irresistible. I spent the better part of 15 months, intermittently, doing the two sorts of things. I made the rounds of the broadcasters trying to identify problems which might lead to useful research, and I made the rounds of academic research trying to specify points of contact between the interests of researchers and broadcasters.

Manifestly, part of the job was to look for trouble, the sort to which applied social research might lend a hand. For example, during my tenure as sociologist-in-residence, debate was raging over the proposition that television news in its present form constitutes a "bias against understanding." Now the question of what viewers understand—however you may wish to define understand—is an empirical one and only the viewers can answer it. It is eminently accessible to research, even if the debaters, in their zeal, overlook this.

Other researchable problems which arose include the perennial allegations that broadcasting is overstepping the boundaries of mores and tastes, that the sub-cultures of the regions are being overlooked, that the treatment of industrial or religious or racial strife is biased towards one side or the other, or even worse, is exacerbating the conflict. Some of these questions are easier to answer than others, but in principle, social research can help. Indeed, looking for trouble is one of the ways of defining social research. Its job is to understand how, and

Elihu Katz is Director of the Communications Institute at the Hebrew University of Jerusalem. He is the first recipient of the "In Medias Res" award of DM 25,000 given for distinguished achievement in communications research by the Burda publishing group of the Federal Republic of Germany. Part of this article is taken from a lecture entitled "Looking for Trouble: Social Research on Broadcasting," delivered in the eleventh series of BBC lunch-time lectures, February 25, 1977.

Reprinted from "Looking for Trouble: by Elihu Katz in the JOURNAL OF COMMUNICATION 28 (Spring 1978) 90-95. Copyright 1978 by the Annenberg School of Communications.

how well, social arrangements are working, even if we find that things are not as simple as they seem.

For a related reason, journalism—electronic and print—is also on the lookout for trouble. Indeed it would be difficult to describe the underlying scenario of the news without reference to the notion of conflict. Broadcast news and current affairs, like the rest of journalism, is a running chronicle of troubles, giving a nice twist to the sociological definition of a professional as a person whose job it is to make routine of other people's emergencies.

Given this shared orientation, one might have expected the relationship between broadcasters and researchers to be smoother than it has been. When I visited American universities and told colleagues about my mandate from the BBC, the unanimous reaction was—what an enlightened organization! But the fact is that the history of the broadcaster–researcher relationship in Britain is strewn with conflict. Broadcasters do not much appreciate the inclination of social research to make ostensibly simple things complex and the researchers do not much appreciate the inclination of broadcasters to make complex things simple. More important, however, broadcasters do not like the idea that researchers want to study them. From the broadcasters' point of view, the researchers seem bent on finding fault and ignoring achievement. From their point of view, the researchers are only going about their business. Speaking to American journalists, my teacher, the late Paul Lazarsfeld remarked 30 years ago: "If there is one institutional disease to which the media of mass communications seem particularly subject it is a nervous reaction to criticism. As a student of the mass media, I have been continually struck and occasionally puzzled by this reaction, for it is the media themselves which so vigorously defend principles guaranteeing the right to criticize."

> *It gradually dawned on me that I ought to be*
> *asking myself why the BBC invited me in?*

Why this gesture of interest in the possibility of a major expansion of social research on broadcasting? Wasn't this looking for more trouble? You may be surprised, but I shall be asking the same question about broadcasting research. Ostensibly, broadcasting is an attractive area for students of society. The media of mass communication were thought to hold the key to the study of social control in modern societies. But the unadorned truth is that this research has not gone very well. The media have not yet been shown to be the omnipotent source of all influence and, what is more, the problems of conceptualizing and isolating the effects of the media have long defied the conventional tools.

To this frustration, add the marked lack of enthusiasm with which broadcasters have greeted proposals to permit themselves to be studied. When the broadcaster finds a receptive researcher with whom to share his troubles, the results are often good. But when the researcher insists on the right to define a problem in his own terms, and unrelentingly petitions for access to tape recordings and to the meeting rooms and studios where decisions are taken, the broadcaster is reluctant, even adamant. The researchers are convinced, rightly I would say, that there is no use just studying audiences; one must have access to producers and content as well. Faced with methodological pitfalls, theoretical heartbreaks, and lack of willing hospitality, why go on? Why look for more trouble?

My exploits of the last months, however, lead me to think that things may be changing. I don't mean that all trouble will disappear, but that we may be beginning on a new phase of better understanding. I bring you news that British broadcasters are indeed determined to get more good out of social research. Researchers, for their part, are overcoming some of the frustrations of their own discipline and, while they may be no less critical, there is renewed vigor and affirmation in their work.

> *The first signs of revival of media research came
> to America in the 1960s, when the assasinations,
> the black revolt, the youth revolt, women's liberation,
> the Vietnam War, and, ultimately, Watergate,
> led to second thoughts about television.*

Television was a convenient scapegoat for politicians, in thwarting criticism directed at themselves and in explaining the eruptions of all of the demographic variables: age, sex, class, and race. Serious attention was directed to the violent and sensational content of American television, and a number of researchers began to look again. At the behest of a Committee of the U.S. Senate, the Surgeon–General appointed a Scientific Advisory Committee on Television and Violence. The committee, consisting of researchers from academia and the media, invited research proposals and commissioned some 25 studies at the cost of one million dollars. It published four volumes of research reports and its own conclusions inspired work elsewhere, including the BBC.

The "politicization" of academic research led to the call for a reunion of the fields of media research and opinion research. From Germany, from the United States and elsewhere, senior researchers were arguing for a "return to the concept of powerful mass media" based on the idea that the media are emitting homogenous and powerful messages and that their effect is empirically discernible not in changes of opinion but in modes of thinking or what is called "consciousness." whether reinforcement of pre-existing attitudes—the dubious effect conceded in the golden age of media research—is as innocent as it sounds.

Another important stimulus to the revival of media research came from the writings of Marshall McLuhan. It is easy enough to try and dismiss his technological theory of society. But the fact is that McLuhan, more than anybody, caused researchers to broaden their definition of effect to include the effects of media on styles of perception and cognition. McLuhan argues that these cognitive styles are transformed into social arrangements (print-linear, thinking-assembly lines). The idea of "media effects" independent of messages rose again.

Still another stimulus to media research comes from the success of "Sesame Street." A three-cornered team of producers, educational psychologist, and researchers joined forces and in the context of a foundation-sponsored production company (and a lot of money) created a program that revolutionized children's television. I am not arguing the merits of this program but rather the lesson of what has come to be called "formative research" where producers and researchers join together in an alliance based, ultimately, on the channelling of audience reaction into the creative process.

Institutional studies have taken a great leap forward as well. More self-confident than heretofore, communications researchers have followed the lead of their colleagues in fields such as the sociology of medicine: sociologists are now regularly installed in clinics and hospitals observing processes of inter-action, decision-making, and consulting on the well-known problems of a bureaucratic organization staffed by professionals. Media researchers are not yet as welcome, but they have usually (not always) emerged unscathed from obser-vational studies in television and radio newsrooms and studios. Considering how few such studies there were previously, and the interest and controversy that has been aroused by the newer studies, there is hope that such observational work will gain ground.

> *The American media, however, do not take*
> *much notice of the researchers.*

Their role in the U.S. is to *get* attention. The kind of attention given by media, government and other elites in Britain to the work of James Halloran, Jay Blumler, Stuart Hall, Andrew Ehrenberg and their groups, Tom Burns, Richard Hoggart, Hilde Himmelweit, the Glasgow group—to name only some of the names which have been mentioned recently—is rare in the United States.

Also in contrast with the Americans, I daresay that most British research-ers—even those with strong political commitments—feel much closer to broad-casting. They are fully aware that the BBC takes note of what they have to say, and takes them seriously, sometimes to the point of a duel. By virtue of their own membership in the same elites, they know they have influence on the broadcasters. The younger researchers know the younger producers, and the older researchers know the managers. And they have mutual friends in the political elite. In the United States, academics and broadcasters tend to belong to different networks; in Britain, access of broadcasters and researchers to each other is easier. Despite the suspiciousness, the ideals of public service broad-casting, and the legitimacy of debate over its implementation, makes for much firmer common ground. But broadcasting research needs more than common ground; it needs better shelter.

The broadcasters' curiosity about the media extends far beyond the prob-lems of attracting and pleasing audiences, and if I have interpreted them correctly, their interests often coincide with those of social research. As we have seen, the research horizon extends far beyond the traditional conceptions of audience research or media effects. It is not particulary difficult, therefore, to draw up an agenda for further research which reflects these areas of mutual interest. This I have done in *Social Research on Broadcasting*, my report to the BBC. Substantively, what I have suggested consists of six sets of proposals roughly divisible into problems of "media" and problems of "message."

1. *The Media: Impact of Broadcasting.* This group of proposals deals primarily with the communications policy problems of society. It addresses the impact of broadcasting on leisure time, on other media and other social institutions, on cognitive processes, and on social interaction. Specific areas of focus include comparative study of the cognitive processing of the media—their implications for perception, styles of thought, memory, affectivity, reporting; problems of translation from one medium to another; the effect of the social and physical contexts in which media are contacted; public perceptions of the functions of the media; and the interaction of media institutions with other social institutions such as education and politics.

2. *The Nature of the Audience.* Proposals in this section are aimed at describing the nature of the audiences for broadcasting. Gaps in the area of research on the nature of the audience as individual and as mass are outlined, with emphasis on the need to arrive at accurate assessments of the degree of audience participation and level of sophistication. Areas of proposed investigation include questions of how the audience classifies different program types, viewers' knowledge of the genres of television, and degree of connoisseurship. Further research into the "mass dynamics" of audiences—about the loyalties, switching, inheritance, popularity, days of the week, etc. is proposed, with the suggestion that passive or selective viewing patterns then be looked at in terms of the individual differences in uses and gratifications from programs.

3. *The Organization: Management of Creativity.* The major focus of research proposed in this area is the formulation and testing of hypotheses about the relationship between organizational conditions and creativity in the BBC at this time. A first proposal is to review what has been learned from organizational studies of the management of other types of professional and creative organizations, followed by sociological reconstruction of the organizational conditions which produced great programs or radical new departures at the BBC in the past. These reviews are expected to feed a series of experimental studies of the organizational conditions said to be linked to creativity. This program of experimentation is to focus equally on the structure of social contacts within the organization and contacts between producers and the audience.

4. *News, Information and Current Affairs: Programming Reality.* The proposals in this section are policy-oriented. The most elementary ones treat comprehension and motivations in the audience. Several of them deal with possible uses of research to innovate in the field of news and current affairs. Several others relate to the "theories" used by journalists in the definitions of news and it is asked whether audiences can be trained to understand and to participate more actively in broadcasting and in public affairs by understanding these theories. Two proposals ask about the effects on society and on the participants themselves of certain kinds of people and certain kinds of stories which appear in the news.

5. *Entertainment: Programming Pleasure.* Starting with the assumption that entertainment is the primary function of television for most people, the first set

of proposals in this section considers the little known area of the psychology of being entertained, or the dynamics of experiencing catharsis. Other proposals focus on changing boundaries of taste, with particular emphasis on generational and cultural differences. The question of what values are implicit in entertainment programming is also raised. Finally, it is proposed that researchers be encouraged to have access not just to newsrooms but to the production meetings and studios of the producers of comedy, drama, and other entertainments.

6. *Social Differentiation: Programming Identity.* Proposals in this group deal with programs and channels serving minority interests and issues arising over the axes along which some minorities are to be defined, the resources to be allocated to each (channels, programs), and the anxiety over contributing to the further fragmentation of the society. Proposals focusing on the basis of differentiation inquire into the subjective salience of boundaries such as age, sex, class, geographical region, etc., for those who have objective membership within them, and interest that exists in giving cultural expression to such membership. Types of differentiation are then dealt with which are based less on demographic or geographic considerations and more on special interests which create social networks—such as hobbies, social and religious beliefs, etc. A final set of proposals relates to the organization of broadcasting to serve differentiation and with the functions (and dysfunctions) of such recognition for the groups themselves and for society as a whole.

An obvious question is, "Who will pay for all this?" It is a question about which I have some ideas but no answers, except for a story which gives additional proof, if any is needed, of the aptness of the title of this paper. My story is about a potential patron of broadcasting research. He is an executive of a leading foundation, and I was consulting him, as part of this project, about the funding of communication studies. He confided to me—though I am not sworn to secrecy—that British social science, preoccupied as it is with class, frames its research proposals in terms of the study of underdogs—the new immigrant, the welfare client, the lower classes, the indigent patient. "If you people only had an underdog," he said, "you might find more support for your work." I assured him that we would immediately begin looking for one.

41

FURTHER DEVELOPMENT—
OR TURNING THE CLOCK BACK?

James D. Halloran

*"It is no exaggeration to say that in Britain some people
see Katz as castrating critical research—or at least as
fulfilling a useful alibi function for the broadcasting
establishment and keeping the situation cool."*

The presentation of the Katz report is clear, the treatment is systematic, and Katz deserves credit for producing some order and direction from material from two general sources (i.e., broadcasters and researchers) which—despite the fact that Katz now feels they have many interests in common—have not always been noted for their agreement and compatibility. Although priorities are not stated, there are clear recommendations and enough suggestions about possible research development to keep the hundred or so researchers (mentioned by Katz as occupying the mass communication research field in Britain) busy and perhaps even happy for years to come. That is, of course, provided that the necessary financial support, cooperation and facilities are made available. But one must presume that the BBC would never have commissioned such a report had it not intended to do something in this connection.

It is no exaggeration to say that in Britain some people see Katz as castrating critical research—or at least as fulfilling a useful alibi function for the broadcasting establishment and keeping the situation cool. Is this then a report that all hard-pressed, impoverished mass communication researchers in Britain should welcome with open arms? Should they see it as their great opportunity— perhaps even as their charter for the future? Should they react with enthusiasm to this apparent interest and involvement on the part of the BBC, an institution not hitherto well known for its dedication to independent, systematic, social scientific inquiries into broadcasting in general or into its own operation in particular?

James D. Halloran is Director of the Centre for Mass Communication Research at the University of Leicester, England.

Reprinted from "Further Development—or Turning the Clock Back?" by James D. Halloran in the JOURNAL OF COMMUNICATION 28 (Spring 1978) 120-132. Copyright 1978 by the Annenberg School of Communications.

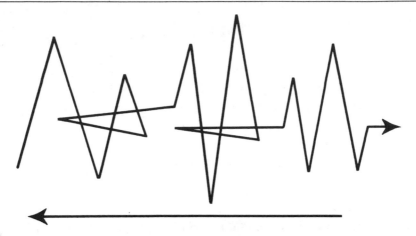

Reactions so far have been predictably mixed. Some researchers (chauvinistic and vested interests apart) were suspicious from the start, seeing the whole exercise as a typical BBC ploy, an attempt at window dressing for the Annan Committee. It was impressive and respectable, but safe as houses. Some people have welcomed the report, genuinely accepting and agreeing with it. But others, equally accepting and perhaps attracted by the hidden and as yet unfulfilled promises of access and financial support, have apparently not recognized, glossed over, or chosen to ignore its weaknesses and shortcomings.

Unfortunately, as it happens there are clear indications that the BBC is already writing and talking in terms of the Katz concepts, categories, functions, and programs. The overall framework of the report seems to have been accepted by the Corporation apparently without much critical discussion, and decisions about future research have already been made within this framework. None of this augurs well for the future.

Cooperation is important, but it is the basis of the cooperation that matters. The most important aspect of research is the quality of the questions asked in the first place. Conceptualize the problem inadequately, ask the wrong questions, get your directions and priorities wrong—and no matter how sophisticated your methods, no matter how much effort you expend, what facilities are available, what cooperation you obtain, you will still do little or nothing to increase knowledge, to further understanding, or to be of practical assistance to those working in the media. It is this that worries me about the implications of the Katz report for mass communication research in Britain.

> *For those reasonably familiar with mass communication research*
> *in Britain over the past ten years or so, a first reaction*
> *to the Katz publication might well be, "What does it tell us*
> *that we did not know already and that has not already been said?"*

On further consideration this question might be extended to, "What has Katz missed—what areas, directions, approaches or questions has he neglected that some researchers in Britain have thought important and worthy of consideration and research effort?" *In essence,* despite the elaborations, there is little or nothing in the Katz report that has not been suggested before—and this often more specifically, in greater detail, and with more intellectual support. It may impress, but it fails to convince. As far as Britain is concerned in terms of research ideas it doesn't really break new ground. One is bound to ask "Was it really necessary?" or perhaps "What is behind it all?" Incidentally, it puzzles me why the *Journal of Communication* has decided to make a mountain out of a molehill.

In fairness to Katz, he readily admits that his inventory is not meant to be comprehensive, and he accepts that it represents only a sample of the research that might be done. He writes that he would be satisfied if his report and his proposals led to other proposals and even evoked counter-proposals. Interestingly enough, it is possible to regard *his* proposals as "safe" counter-proposals to some of those that have been put forward by other researchers in Britain in recent years. There is no real challenge here. In terms of radical criticisms there is nothing to match what has already been attempted and achieved. In fact it has been suggested that we have been presented with the "Katztration" of research.

Taken together, the first working paper of the Television Research Committee (set up by the British Government in 1963)—*The Effects of Mass Communication* (3), the first progress report of the same Committee—*Problems of Television Research* (12), its final report and recommendations (13), and a policy statement of the Centre for Mass Communication Research, University of Leicester (established by the TVRC in 1966)—*Mass Media and Society: The Challenge of Research* (5), represent far more comprehensive, radical and challenging approaches to the study of media and mass communication than can be found in the Katz report. Moreover, much of the research carried out in Britain in the last ten years (some of it but not necessarily the most important projects mentioned with approval by Katz) stemmed from these reports and, with other work from other sources, form the base for some of Katz's proposals. Katz recognizes the Television Research Committee as being the springboard for this work, and considers that its most important achievement was to set up the Leicester Centre. Perhaps I should not disagree with that, but I am surprised that he appears to miss completely what I consider to be the most important achievement of that Committee—and that is its thinking, its research strategy and policy, and its overall approach.

As I see it, and I admit to my involvements, vested interest, and possible prejudice, this Committee, as far as Britain was concerned, was more or less treading virgin territory. Its work represented one of the first attempts to formulate a policy and strategy for mass communication research. Fortunately, it was not shackled by the historical, political, commercial, and institutional impediments of American communication research. In fact, its aim and hopefully its achievement was to break (although not by any means completely) and reject the North American connection. There was a conscious attempt to do this and a determination to start afresh. In the early days of its deliberations the Committee reviewed existing research, most of it from the U.S. Although not sure what to do, the Committee became convinced of what *not* to do, namely, not to repeat the American experience. It was recognized that we ought to benefit from that experience and learn from the trials and errors of others. This interpretation of the American scene and the decisions that stemmed from it were reflected in some of the major research projects that were carried out in Britain in the sixties.

> *Katz, although fully familiar with this work and making many favorable comments about it, would not appear to recognize this fundamental change in direction.*

Yet this was undoubtedly the main contribution of the Television Research Committee to developments in mass communication research. Incidentally, it is perhaps worth noting that the Committee risked, and in fact received, criticism for not accepting the most "obvious" interpretation of its remit, namely, to study exclusively the alleged media-crime/violence relationship. The Committee decided to work through its terms thoroughly and scientifically, and went on to produce a systematic, social scientific strategy for a comprehensive study of mass media and mass communications. We might ask why Katz did not do the same with his terms of reference. One doesn't know the full circumstances, but he seems to have settled too easily and too readily for unnecessary circumscriptions.

We have argued for years that one of the main tasks of the mass communication researcher is to redefine the problems put by the broadcaster rather than accept them at face value. One of the main weaknesses in the Katz report is its excessive broadcaster orientation. Katz has failed to make a clear distinction between the very legitimate tasks of communicating and working with broadcasters on the one hand, and the not-so-acceptable one of serving them on their terms on the other.

For far too long in Britain there has been a tendency to equate the needs or the good of the broadcasting institution with the needs or the good of society. For example, it seemed to be implicitly assumed that what was good for the BBC was obviously good for the country at large. Often the debate about the future of broadcasting at base has been in terms of how can we deal, say, with new developments in communication technology and maintain existing institutional structures. We would suggest that it would be more appropriate if the debate were couched in terms of communication needs, difficult though these may be to identify in the plural society. Should we not be asking such questions as "What organization and structures will make it possible for media potential to be realized in such a way as to maximize the satisfaction of social needs?" Ideally, communication research should be geared to this but these questions do not appear on the Katz agenda, which is perhaps not surprising for the agenda was really set by broadcasters and apparently accepted at face value.

The many references to American work in Katz's overview of research developments are more a reflection of his own past experience than a contribution to an understanding of research developments in Britain. The "withering away of broadcasting research" referred to by Katz was essentially an American phenomenon—at that time there was no flower to wither away in Britain. The flowers that bloomed in Britain in the sixties had their main roots on this side of the Atlantic, where many new approaches were pioneered. The pruning may have been guided by the American experience, and a little fertilizer may also have been added. But there were also imports from continental Europe—a productive area (particularly Scandinavia) which is clearly undervalued by Katz.

In addition to the reports of the Television Research Committee, two UNESCO publications—*Mass Media in Society: The Need of Research* (14) first presented in 1968 and published in 1970, and *Proposals for an International Programme of Communication Research* (15) in 1971 which are both related to and in some senses spring from the British works—do two things not attempted by Katz: (a) develop and illustrate a sociological approach to media and communication studies and (b) look at the question of media and development in the Third World (which is, incidentally, an important part of the current research program at Leicester and elsewhere). This prompts one to ask why Katz chose to ignore the extensive BBC overseas operation from Bush House and why he had so little to say about the international connections of the BBC with regard to co-productions, the import and export of fictional and non-fictional material, advice to Third World broadcasting institutions, training, and so on? Are these not questions for social research? Have they no policy implications for broadcasting?

These sorts of concerns are not adequately reflected in the Katz report. At the risk of over-simplification, the essence of this "British approach" is sociological and critical. Admittedly, to some, the term "sociological" begs at least as many questions as it answers (there are different sociological approaches) but in general, despite the differences, it is an approach which focuses on the study of mass communications as a social process and the mass media as social institutions, both process and institutions being studied within the appropriate wider historical, economic, political and social contexts. In our case it is also critical and problem and policy-oriented, although not "critical" in the emasculated and misleading way in which Katz uses the term.

Katz, as a sociologist, would probably not wish to dissociate himself from this position, and it must be admitted that in his report he does in fact recognize the need for a multidisciplinary approach to the study of broadcasting, and he also accepts that media institutions should be studied not in isolation but in relation to other institutions. However, his specific proposals, whilst not entirely ignoring other institutions or the production side of broadcasting, fall far short of the sociological minimum that might be expected in a "key work" which seeks to map out the path for further research developments. These shortcomings, this regression, become even more obvious when one bears in mind research developments in Britain in recent years.

Katz appears to make the same mistake as McQuail (9) in seeing the main characteristic of the "sixties revival" in mass communication research as the return to a "theory of powerful media." Without rejecting this return as one of several developments, I see the main characteristic of the revival as the development of a sociological perspective, hitherto lacking, which, *inter alia*, set out to examine the total communication process and looked at the concept of influence in ways other than those that depended on such processes as imitation and attitude change. Association, legitimation, amplification, and related processes spring to mind, but there is no mention by Katz of the work of Cohen (1), Young (19), or Wilkins (18) who, to name but a few, made important contributions in the exploration of these processes. Here as elsewhere, Katz is either not aware of the work, which I would find surprising, or does not regard it as relevant, which I would find regrettable.

> *In fact, the general orientation of the Katz work is curiously both asociological and atheoretical.*

It does little to counter the all-too-prevalent *ad hoc*, piecemeal, fragmented approach which many of us have found it necessary to criticize in the past. The section in the book on recent advances in theory and method is particularly disappointing and leaves one wondering what Katz really means by theory. Contending positions, say, the pluralist and Marxist, often at the heart of the current debate about the role of media in society, are not examined at all. In fact, they are not even mentioned. Neither is McCron's (8) interesting and nonconventional (in terms of traditional mass communication research) approach to the media and socialization, or Hartmann and Husband's (7) and Halloran's (4) critical studies of the media and attitudes, or the attempts of several others to tease out the relationship between mediated culture and situated culture. Moreover, these serious omissions are in a book which is predominantly geared to audience, effects, influence, uses, gratifications, etc. The theoretical aspects of the study of what governs what appears on our screens are not covered in any way, and there is no reference to theories of mass communication (if indeed they exist), let alone to a relevant theory of society.

> *It would appear that the differences between the research approaches are not as obvious to some as they are to me.*

In his report, Katz writes that "the Noble (TVRC) Committee in Britain, like the Surgeon General's Committee in the United States, accounted for a great spurt of work at a number of different centres." True, but the comparisons should not stop at that, as they tend to do with Katz, for the differences between these two Committees—both generally and in their approach to the media/violence problem—are far more important than any of the relatively superficial similarities referred to by Katz. The whole problem is conceptualized (explicitly in one case, implicitly in the other) in entirely different ways. Moreover, these differences are not just confined to the media/violence question.

Two years ago I had the opportunity to attend a Joint Conference on Television Research Priorities at Reston, Virginia.* I found the experience most

* *Editor's note:* See a summary report of this conference in the *Journal of Communication*, Spring 1976.

rewarding, primarily because it enabled me to focus more sharply on—and get a clearer picture of—the differences in research approaches to which I have just referred. After the conference I wrote that some years earlier, together with one or two other mass communication researchers in Europe (Kaarle Nordenstreng for example), I had suggested that a general criticism of mass communication research in the U.S. was that it was concerned more with doing than with thinking. This was rather a crude way of drawing attention to a fragmented approach and a theoretical paucity which some of us felt had characterized mass communication research for so many years. To me, the Surgeon General's work (16), the recent Pool-Schramm *Handbook* (11), the *Television and Human Behavior* series (particularly the volume on *The Research Horizon Future and Present*) (2), and the general content of the exchanges at Reston, competent and stimulating although all of these are in their own way, may still be seen as manifestations of the same malaise.

At the risk of oversimplification, it seems to me that the question "What research can we do next about television?" is more frequently asked than such questions as "What is the most appropriate way of studying mass communications as a social process?", "How can we best study media institutions or media experiences in relation to other institutions and experiences?", "What is the relationship between mediated culture and situational culture?", "What functions are served by the media at both macro and micro levels?", "What are the most suitable structures for maximizing media potential and for meeting communication needs?" Yet it is this type of question rather than the narrower one on the effects of television that in the long run will prove to be both more critical and more practical, and that are much more likely to bring us to a full and proper understanding of the role of television and the other media in our society.

These were my thoughts after Reston. These, *mutatis mutandis*, are still very much my thoughts after Katz. The general overall approach remains more or less the same, and it is difficult to avoid the déjà vu feeling after reading Katz. Again we need not be surprised, although one is bound to be disappointed— particularly on this side of the Atlantic where we thought there had been some steady progress in other directions over the last twelve years or so. Should the Katz report be used as a guidebook there is certainly a danger that it could turn the clock back for us.

> *From a social scientific standpoint, the major weaknesses in the Katz work clearly stem from the terms of reference which were formulated by the BBC and apparently uncritically accepted by Katz.*

The weight of research evidence and social scientific thinking in Britain over the last decade argues quite convincingly for a broader approach, an approach where television and radio (and for that matter the other media) are removed from the center of the research stage and allowed to take their appropriate places alongside other social institutions in a research strategy which reflects, as indeed it should, an appropriate sociological model of society.

It needs to be stressed here that to take this position is not to deny either that mass communication research is a legitimate field of study or that it is necessary to have specialized studies and specialized institutions. Moreover, I would maintain that the approach outlined above is the most appropriate and economical way of supplying the basic information which is the *sine qua non* of intelligent policy formulation and practical decision-making.

In Britain over the last year or so we have had the unfortunate experience of the Royal Commission on the Press and the Annan Committee of Enquiry into the Future of Broadcasting both ploughing their own unrelated furrows of investigation and both making their own medium-centered recommendations. Both their investigations and recommendations would appear to largely ignore, first, the inter-media and wider social implications of the prevailing trends in media ownership, control, organization, and traffic, internationally as well as nationally; second, that the development of new communication technologies tends to blur the conventional distinctions between print and electronic media; and third—and perhaps the most important of all—that our primary concern is not to serve broadcasting but to serve society.

I would think that Katz might accept, or at least not explicitly disagree with this position. However, if this assumption is correct, then surely we ought to expect him (a) to focus on social or at least mass communication research (as we define it), not just broadcasting research; (b) to seek to further communication research policies, not just broadcasting research policies, and (c) to lean toward communication research trusts rather than broadcasting trusts. But we do not find this, although we would maintain that in the long run this would all be in the best interests of broadcasting. There is no need for research to follow blindly the existing paths or to accept and work within frameworks determined by the current divisions and institutional arrangements in society. Let research lead, not follow.

The Katz report is certainly not without merit. Among other things it outlines projects which, if competently executed, effectively communicated, and intelligently applied, would undoubtedly be of considerable benefit to both broadcasters and to society at large. Interesting points are made, implying quite correctly that all broadcasting research should not be grouped together under one heading, or organized in the same way. And there are interesting recommendations that different types of research should be carried out at different "distances" from the broadcasting institutions.

> *Katz has a striking ability to give order and meaning*
> *to complex and potentially confusing material*
> *by his use of typologies and classification systems.*

But he over-indulges a little and, as I hope to illustrate, I find his grouping of research tasks and specification of "distances" vis-a-vis different research institutions somewhat restrictive and removed from reality as I see it.

Some of the points about the crucial relationship between broadcasters and researchers, although open to dispute, are well made by Katz, but his experience and knowledge of the British and European scene appear to be so limited as to

seriously reduce the value of his interpretations, conclusions, and recommendations.

At first glance I find it strange that in discussing the relationship between
broadcasters and researchers, Katz makes no references to the UNESCO-spon-
sored international seminar on this topic which was held in Leicester in 1970.
This was attended by nearly one hundred top level broadcasters and researchers
from many different countries. Elihu Katz was there, as was the Director-
General of the BBC and some of his colleagues. On second thoughts, however,
perhaps the omission is not so strange for many of those attending the seminar,
including several senior European broadcasters and even some from the BBC,
felt that the Corporation was somewhat different from other broadcasting
institutions in that it appeared distinctly suspicious about independent research.
There was a defensiveness which to some seemed at times to border on hostility.

Sir Charles Curran, the Director-General of the BBC, steadfastly refused to
regard research as an integral part of the broadcasting operation, maintaining
that the Corporation would be quite wrong to use the license fee provided by
viewers and listeners "for basic research," or "to look into viewers' heads." As
far as access to the Corporation to study aspects of the broadcasting operation
and general co-operation were concerned, Sir Charles was a little more forthcoming: "Certain sensitive areas" must be barred to the researcher, but "in
other areas we are perfectly open to propositions." It can only be assumed that
some of the propositions put to the BBC in recent years must have been in
sensitive areas. Access (funds were not requested) was not granted, even after
Sir Michael Swann (Chairman of the BBC Board of Governors) had emphasized
the need for research.

In the report, Katz tells us of the many interests that researchers and
broadcasters have in common in Britain, and he writes of a growing awareness
and recognition on the part of broadcasters of the importance and social
usefulness of research. He admits that he gives more attention to the positive
reactions of broadcasters than to the negative ones, but he still feels his optimism is justified and concludes that all is set well for future cooperation and that
we "may be at the threshold of a major expansion."

> *In carrying out institutional research it is*
> *possible and normally desirable to direct*
> *questions (the same questions) at different*
> *levels of the operation within the institution.*

For example, we might seek information about (a) what the institution is
legally or formally charged to do; (b) what it officially and formally states as its
aims and objectives and what it claims with regard to the achievement of these
(studying annual reports, etc.); (c) what those who work in the institution (at
different levels) claim to be doing; (d) what is *actually* being done (say through
participant observation) and what has really been achieved; and possibly (e)
how others, external to the operation, evaluate all this.

After conducting some eighty interviews and attending several other meetings, etc., over a fifteen-month period, Katz was on the whole favorably im-

pressed by the attitudes towards research of broadcasters within the BBC. He based his conclusions on *what they told him.* No one was really put to the test.

I base my less enthusiastic conclusions about the same issue on over ten years' experience in Britain and elsewhere which has included (in addition to many interviews and numerous informal meetings) specific requests for access and general research facilities. Not all the requests were rejected by any means, but some were, and I think this is very much a situation where actions speak louder than words. Katz may be correct in thinking that all augurs well for the future as far as researcher/broadcaster cooperation is concerned, and I hope he is, but in terms of genuine cooperation on specific projects it still remains to be proved—perhaps more so with the BBC than elsewhere.

Let me make it clear that we have cooperated, most fruitfully in fact, with the BBC in several research exercises, but most of these (and indeed all the major ones) were in the early days of our operations. Our first working research contacts with the BBC were made with individuals, mostly departmental heads, and usually in the first instance at the European Broadcasting Union or Prix Jeunesse (Munich) meetings. It is worth mentioning here that the policies and programs of Prix Jeunesse International, have led directly or indirectly to more research projects involving broadcaster/researcher cooperation than any others of which I am aware. These research activities have embraced many countries (including Britain and the BBC) and have led to the production of several research reports. Moreover, the results contained in these reports, in addition to providing the basis for stimulating exchanges in fruitful researcher/broadcaster seminars, have also been used in policy formulation and in practical decision-making at program level in more than one broadcasting institution.

Neither Prix Jeunesse nor any of its several publications which describe the nature, extent, and results of researcher/broadcaster cooperation are mentioned by Katz. Yet they are crucial to an understanding of what has *actually happened* over the last ten years in this area of cooperative relationships, an area at the heart of the Katz report. The same may also be said about those Council of Europe-sponsored research activities which have been characterized by close cooperation between researcher and broadcaster in several countries over the last few years.

> *I have argued for many years that broadcasting and other media*
> *institutions have an obligation to support independent mass*
> *communication research financially, by granting access*
> *to their operations and by providing other essential facilities.*

I think that in the case of bona fide researchers this cooperation might even be formally required of the institution. The recommendations of Annan to the contrary, accountability of broadcasters through independent research must be seriously considered. In fact, I feel it ought to be regarded as an essential requirement.

But having said that and firmly believing that broadcasting institutions should not be allowed to place obstacles in the way of research or to agree to cooperate only on their own terms, I also know that no amount of legislation, formal requirements, or the setting up of official bodies will automatically lead to the fruitful, cooperative working relationships that social scientists and, according to Katz, the broadcasters at the BBC so earnestly seek. In fact, my experience suggests that the more formal, the more centralized, and perhaps the more categorized (in Katzian terms) the arrangements become, the less rewarding and less fruitful will be the outcome.

In our early work on news and current affairs (6) and our study of the BBC Local Radio experiment (17), we received all the necessary cooperation in the planning and execution stages. But the results of both these projects were not exactly greeted with enthusiasm. Of course, it would be naive to expect enthusiasm from those for whom the results were perceived as a challenge to their professional values, a threat to their basic assumptions, a criticism of their modus operandi, a questioning of their policies, or (in the case of local radio) a contradiction of their claims. If the research results threaten, then the first cooperative research venture may well be the last.

It could be pure coincidence, of course, or it may have to do with the way we presented our results, but there was a distinct cooling off from this point onwards. It would also be possible to trace from this point a growing critical, and at times hostile, reaction on the part of broadcasters to the works of the new band of intruders, "the media sociologists." It appears that it was the emergence of this new strange questioning band that began to cause the trouble. Prior to this it was taken for granted, particularly after Pilkington (10), that "academics" would always be on the side of the angels, but the research revival of the sixties changed all this.

The criticism and hostility to research by broadcasters, irrespective of its merits, has continued to the present day.

Broadcasters may tell Katz that they are aware of the need for research and that they wish to cooperate in research exercises, and he may believe them and feel that we are all on the threshold of great developments. Again, I hope he is correct. But when we move forward to deeds, and from promises to actual cooperation and application, I still require more evidence before I am convinced of the change in heart that Katz claims to have detected. My fear still is that broadcasters may be willing to accept research only when they see it as reinforcing their position or serving their interests in some way or other. "Bad" research is research that produces results that they don't like.

The proposal to set up a Broadcasting Research Trust is an interesting one, and in one way could possibly mark a step forward (long overdue) on the part of the BBC. We are told that one of its advantages will be to guarantee the cooperation of broadcasters. But there is a danger here, for projects which win financial support may be confined to those which broadcasters approve. Should ever such a Trust be established, the further removed it is from broadcasting institutions the better.

When it comes to the organization of research and the development of research centers, I share with Katz his reservation (albeit for different reasons) about the creation of a Central Institute for Mass Communication Research. However, I do not agree with him about the expansion and lines of development he suggests for internal audience research departments. In fact, I see no need to depart in any way from the recommendations made by the Television Research Committee as long ago as February 1969 (13). The Committee recommended that the BBC, ITA, independent television companies, publishing, cinema, advertising and other media interests should provide financial support in the shape of research grants, fellowships, scholarships etc., to enable independent research to be carried out in universities and other institutions of higher education, along the lines indicated in their Report (which are similar to those referred to in this article).

The Committee also called for "full cooperation by the media in all aspects of the research effort," including "the provision of 'research services' over and above what the media need for their own day-to-day purposes. For example, in broadcasting, sound tapes records, videotapes and films should be preserved, indexed and, together with playback facilities, made freely available to researchers," and "the provision of greater opportunities and facilities for research with regard not only to effects studies, but also to studies of the production process and decision-making at all levels within the media industry." The Television Research Committee recognized the need to preserve the freedom and autonomy of broadcasters and other media practitioners, but emphasized that this freedom carried with it heavy responsibilities. Cooperation with research in this way was regarded as one aspect of broadcaster accountability.

It is worth noting that the above recommendations were accepted by the Social Science Research Council panel specially set up to study the matter.

The panel maintained that the agencies of the mass media ought to contribute to the cost of research and training along the lines suggested by the Television Research Committee, and it was also felt that these organizations, quite apart from providing financial support, should contribute more directly to the expanding knowledge of mass communication processes. There were references to an obligation on the part of the broadcasting agencies both to initiate and support programs which will contribute to collaborative research, and it was suggested that the other agencies of mass communication, such as the press and the cinema, should follow a similar course.

It was further recommended that, because of the special importance of collaborative research in this field one or several special centers for mass communication research should be encouraged. Specialized research centers, it was hoped, would come to serve as focal points for research where training, consultation, research expertise, and knowledge about a special topic would be readily available. It was argued that research centers were able, to a degree not possible for individual investigators, to work out long-range research programs and carry them through systematically and efficiently by virtue of the fact that they enjoyed the advantages of permanent specialized research facilities and administration. It was further recommended that it was to centers such as these to which the Government and others could initially look for the development of the research necessary for the establishment of a sound basis for public policy in the development and use of mass communication media.

Really we need go no further than these recommendations of almost ten years ago. Katz merely nibbles at the edges of the real problem. As far as Britain is concerned, his report is no advance on the thinking of ten years ago; in fact it clearly falls far short in almost every possible way of what was recommended at that time.

However, we must be prepared to accept the possibility that despite all its inadequacies the Katz report may well lead to an increase in research support, activity, and involvement, particularly as far as the BBC is concerned. This need not be a bad thing. In fact, it could be welcomed as long as the activity which might stem from the report is not unduly influenced by its underlying principles.

REFERENCES

1. Cohen, S. *Folk Devils and Moral Panics*. London: MacGibbon and Kee, 1972.
2. Comstock, G. A. and G. Lindsey. *Television and Human Behavior*, Vol. I: *A Guide to the Pertinent Scienctific Literature;* Vol. II: *The Key Studies;* Vol. III: *The Research Horizon, Future and Present*. Santa Monica: Rand, June 1975.
3. Halloran, J. D. *The Effects of Mass Communication, with Special Reference to Television* (fifth edition). Leicester, England: Leicester University Press, 1971.
4. Halloran, J. D. "Mass Media and Race—A Research Approach." Introduction to *Race as News*. Paris: UNESCO, 1974, pp. 9-34.
5. Halloran, J. D. "Mass Media and Society: The Challenge of Research." An inaugural lecture delivered in the University of Leicester, Leicester University Press, 1974.
6. Halloran, J. D., P. Elliott, and G. Murdock. *Demonstrations and Communication: A Case Study.* Harmondsworth, England: Penguin, 1970.
7. Hartmann, P. and C. Husband. *Racism and the Mass Media*. London: Davis-Poynter, 1974.
8. McCron, R. "Changing Perspectives in the Study of Mass Media and Socialization." In J. D. Halloran (Ed.) *Mass Media and Socialization*. International Association for Mass Communication Research, 1976.
9. McQuail, D. "The Influence and Effects of Mass Media." In J. Curran, M. Gurevitch, and J. Woollacott (Eds.) *Mass Communication and Society*. London: Edward Arnold in association with The Open University Press, 1977.
10. Pilkington Committee, 1962. *Report of the Committee on Broadcasting*. London: HMSO, 1960.
11. Pool, I. de S., W. Schramm, *et al.* (Eds.). *Handbook of Communication*. Chicago: Rand McNally, 1973.
12. Television Research Committee. *Problems of Television Research* (First Progress Report). Leicester, England: Leicester University Press, 1966.
13. Television Research Committee. *Second Progress Report and Recommendations*. Leicester, England: Leicester University Press, 1969.
14. UNESCO. *Reports and Papers on Mass Communication, No. 59: Mass Media in Society: The Need of Research*. Paris: UNESCO, 1970.
15. UNESCO. *Com/MD/20: Proposals for an International Programme of Communication Research*. Paris: UNESCO, September 10, 1971.
16. U.S. Surgeon General's Report. *Television and Social Behavior*, 5 volumes. G. A. Comstock, J. P. Murray, and Eli A. Rubinstein (Eds). Washington: Government Printing Office, 1971.
17. Wells, A. "Study of the BBC Local Radio Experiment." Mimeographed report, 1976.
18. Wilkins, L. *Social Deviance*. London: Tavistock Publications, 1964.
19. Young, J. *The Drugtakers*. London: MacGibbon and Kee, 1971.

42

THE AMBIGUITY OF
POLICY RESEARCH

James W. Carey

*"The oft-felt danger [is] that research itself
has become a menace, . . . a semantic crucifix warding off
modern vampires of public and political pressure."*

The publication of Elihu Katz's report for the BBC on priorities in broadcasting research is an important though ambiguous event. The importance is easy enough to state. First, Katz is among the most distinguished senior scholars in communications and his attempt to shape the contours of the field while advising the BBC merits serious attention. Second, the BBC is perhaps the most distinguished broadcasting organization in the world. Its willingness to support Katz's inquiry and to encourage and support basic research signals a new period of cooperation between broadcasters and researchers: a movement beyond deténte or the partnership in an official estrangement toward active cooperation and mutual support. Third, the report itself proposes a number of important lines of investigation, some of which we have long recognized but delayed because of short funds, the absence of sponsorship, and a failure of nerve and method. Many of the proposals are, however, quite novel and will be mined by students and researchers for years to come and with quite productive results. Finally, the report is peppered, and I can't emphasize this too strongly, with sharp observations concerning broadcasting, communications, and the research process.

Yet there are ambiguities in the argument presented and dangers in the report itself. Rather than concentrate on the individual proposals, I would like to present some reactions to the report as a whole: to the directions it seems to impel the field, to the underlying assumptions in the argument, and to the circumstances of its creation. While I have exceptional respect and admiration for Professor Katz, I think it is necessary to dwell on the problems the report creates rather than on the more obvious opportunities it presents.

James W. Carey is George H. Gallup Professor of Journalism at the University of Iowa.

Reprinted from "The Ambiguity of Policy Research" by James W. Carey in the JOURNAL OF COMMUNICATION 28 (Spring 1978) 114-119. Copyright 1978 by the Annenberg School of Communications.

There is a danger, first of all, that the report will be taken as definitive rather than merely suggestive, a statement of fact rather than an invitation to argument. Katz clearly states throughout that the proposals represent one man's vision of the needs of the field, albeit a vision shaped by extensive conversation with BBC personnel and British and American researchers. While Katz is an unusually gifted and sympathetic interpreter of the work of others, they remain his interpretations of what was said and his statement of priorities. And, as I hope to show, some of the interpretations are quite arguable.

The danger is that in an intellectual community hungry for ideas, in which an oversupply of researchers chases an undersupply of researchable notions, the Katz proposals are likely to have an impact which, if not definitive, is nonetheless powerful. His own reputation plus the sponsorship of the BBC might shortcut the careful and sustained argument that will be necessary if the research community, like a collective character from a Stephen Leacock poem, is not to leap upon its horse and set off simultaneously in several directions. Of course, this says more about a persistent quality of the field than about the proposals.

The arguable assumptions of the Katz report center on three areas: the nature of policy research and of the BBC assignment, the history of mass communication research implicit in the report which provides the background to the proposals, and the isolation of the proposals from any informing social theory, that is, the decision to make the report theoretically eclectic. Let me take each in turn.

> *The proposals were developed to meet criteria*
> *stated in advance by the BBC: "to take account of*
> *past and ongoing work in Britain and elsewhere, and*
> *have policy and/or editorial implications for the BBC."*

While Katz interpreted this charge as broadly as possible, the necessity of recommending research that had policy implications for the BBC is felt throughout the report in the definition of problems and in the details of the proposals. It was possible for him to accept the charge from the BBC because he assumes that "what the broadcaster would like to know . . . is not so different from what the social scientist would like to know." We need not necessarily agree with that assumption or with the parallel assumption that the active cooperation of professional broadcasters and researchers will benefit both broadcasting and scholarship.

By accepting the policy framework, the Katz report is not an encouragement to "re-think" television or a call for scholarship about it—it is a call for research on it. That call must pretty much assume the existing social structure and political arrangements and the existing role television plays in our personal, political, and cultural life. We are back in the bind of administrative and critical research. Policy research must assume that TV is a policy problem, that we need to know how to get television to operate more effectively and with less danger and abrasion. It cannot, for example, raise, even in fantasy, the question of whether television should be abolished or that the trouble is not in the messages or in the institutions but in the medium itself. Nor can the proposals start from the far less radical notion that, at the very least, the role television plays in social life has to be decisively cut back. Similarly, the specific research proposals developed within a policy framework must pretty much study television directly. However, we have learned that it is often best when studying television to ignore the medium in order to concentrate on the leisure behavior, states of consciousness, social structures, and political phenomena with which television intersects.

Let me be fair. Katz realizes this more than most and his restless imagination and intelligence keep expanding beyond the limits of his assignment. Many of his most important proposals concern the study of ordinary conversation, conventional conceptions of time, and the structure of differentiation in modern societies. But the ·policy stipulation does lead to a real danger: the policy priorities are not the same as the intellectual priorities and when the actual research is funded, it will be the latter that will be abandoned. Such action, in turn, augments the oft felt danger that research itself has become a menace, that it functions merely as symbol and talisman: not an attempt to get real understanding but a symbol of an organization's rectitude and progressiveness and simultaneously a semantic crucifix warding off modern vampires of public and political pressure.

But the policy framework bespeaks a deeper problem. It is possible, as the report shows, to frame theoretical speculation and empirical inquiry in terms congenial to both professional broadcasters and communications researchers. This is because a silent embrace has been growing up between these two communities. But is this embrace beneficial to scholarship and society? I do not think it produces any necessary or potential benefits for scholarship.

*In fact, I think a better case can be made that
scholarship, like many of the arts, flourishes when
it stands in determined opposition to the established order.*

If you are in opposition, you have to work very much harder to get a hearing at all and that extra effort makes the critical difference. But, more importantly, to attract and hold major scholars, the field of communications must formulate puzzles and dilemmas that are intellectually challenging and provocative. While questions of policy research can at times also be intellectually interesting, that is not necessarily the case. In economics there was such a happy moment with the simultaneous failure of classicial theory to account for unemployment and the policy questions surrounding "the great depression." No such happy moment has yet occurred in communications. It is not so much, as Bernard Berelson once charged, that the field·has lost its major figures but that it has not attracted enough people of unusual ability. To attract such people major intellectual questions must be on the agenda.

Formulating research priorities in terms of policy research is not likely to improve the situation for the research is grounded in institutional needs, not in the theoretical dispute or persistent intellectual dilemmas. While there are some intellectually interesting proposals in the Katz volume, much of the research called for, even if of value to a broadcasting organization, is intellectually trivial, in the precise sense that it does not address as the first order of business theoretical dispute or intellectual puzzles.

If the embrace of the research and broadcasting community places limitations on scholarship, it may also be socially damaging. There is an often conscious struggle in modern societies over who is to control broadcasting: the state, the public, commercial institutions, professional broadcasters. Social scientists have become one of the status groups in the fray. There are shifting coalitions among these groups depending upon time, place and circumstance. The status interests of broadcasters and researchers are often in sharp conflict and those interests in turn lead to sharp differences in research priorities and, above all, in the interpretation and application of data. The Katz report tends to fudge those conflicts in order to produce a marriage. But that fudging in turn leads to a devitalizing of research questions. Were Katz successful it would rob society of the one useful role scholars can perform: the statement of problems, issues, and solutions in terms that are outside and opposed to the established center of power and authority. That scholars have been badly corrupted on this matter is no argument to extend the corruption.

The second problem derives from the history of mass communication research that Katz assumes as background and occasionally moves to the center of focus.

The history, which I must strip down to the point of burlesque, goes something like this. Early work on mass communications concentrated on the question of effects and built a model of the powerful influences of the media. Subsequent research, in the forties and fifties, systematically cut this model down to size, hedging in and modifying the claims for powerful effects, with empirical data showing the relative ineffectiveness of the media in producing fundamental changes: in short, building a model of "limited effects." At this point Katz felt the field was, in a well-known phrase, "withering away." Subsequently, attention shifted to the needs of the audience leading to a growth in uses and gratifications research. Then in the sixties the image of the powerful mass media returned because of the impact of McLuhan and other scholars and the rejoining of communication research to the problem of public opinion.

There is nothing startling in this history and it is correct as far as it goes. But it omits two critical elements. The history of mass communication research is more than the history of "findings," the history of the autonomous processes of theoretical and empirical development. The history of mass communication research must include, as a parallel, a history of the changing world of mass communications: of the purposes to which these institutions are put, the audiences that gather to them, the social structures they more or less shape. In terms of this latter history, it can be argued that the basic reason behind the shift in the argument about effects from a powerul to a limited to a more powerful model is that the social world was being transformed over this period, transformed by a series of cycles moving around a linear trend. That is, the basic model for studying communication effects is that of business cycles: the inflation and deflation of effects around a linear historical movement. Powerful effects of communication were sensed in the thirties because the Depression and the political currents surrounding the entrance into war created a fertile bed for the production of certain kinds of effects. Similarly, the normalcy of the fifties and sixties led to a limited effects model. In the late sixties a period of war, political discord and inflation again conspired to expose the social structure in fundamental ways and to make it permeable by the media of communication. These cyclical movements occurred around a fundamental social process, however: the progressively deeper penetration of the media into the social structure and its constitutent institutions. One need only look at the role of popular culture and the media in the schools, for example.

> *The history of communication effects, however,*
> *intersects at every point with the history*
> *of communication researchers: their*
> *interests and implicit ideological position.*

When I say the "interests" of researchers, I mean that often maligned word in a dual sense: the problems which interest researchers and the self-interest, particularly the status interests of researchers. I elsewhere argued, with a colleague, Albert Kreiling, that the shift from a powerful effects model to a limited effects model paralleled a shift in the outlook of social scientists from a prophetic to a priestly class: from a group of outsiders hurling barbs at established society to a group of insiders. Researchers were joined to the establishment and research underwent what Kenneth Burke called a "bureaucratization of the imaginative." This incorporation in turn paralleled a de-politicization of the social structure, a declaration of the end of ideology and a convergence of status interests between university researchers and other powerful elements within society. In turn the re-politicalization of the social structure in the late sixties was marked by the decided tension between these groups, a slight but significant radicalization of faculties, a re-attentiveness to propaganda and manipulation, and the growing necessity within universities under the force of students (and the drying up of federal funds) of adopting critical and prophetic stances. But researchers retained certain status interests however realigned: look, for example, at the differing tones and conclusions of the commission reports on pornography and violence.

The point is a simple one: the problem of communications effects is a diachronic not a synchronic one. The failure to grasp this leads to a deeper theoretical weakness. Katz continues to press for a natural science of communi-

cation, a science wedded to causal and functional models, revealing universal
needs of persons and societies, stating invariant laws. That this model has pretty
much exhausted its usefulness is, I think, clear. As I tried to briefly exemplify
above, we need a model that is throughly historical and reflexive: a model in
which the history and intentions of the observer are part of the history and
meaning of the observed.

> *Finally, these weaknesses come down to*
> *one overriding consideration: the*
> *absence in the volume of any informing*
> *relation between communication and social theory.*

The proposals themselves can only be described as eclectic, despite Katz's
efforts to categorically order them. Eclecticism can be a virtue and it never is the
worst of intellectual sins. Yet the decision to draw proposals out of a wide variety
of theoretical positions—structuralism, phenomenology, functionalism, organization theory, etc.—inevitably has given the work a sense of inconsistent
backgrounds, a gnawing uncertainty as to what the program, if rigorously
pursued, would add up to, if anything, in intellectual terms. The inconsistency
of backgrounds is masked by Katz's rhetorical transformation of proposals into
categories. But this also masks the fact that the proposals as a whole contain a
social theory, a theory which is never exposed and therefore cannot be critiqued.
I suppose we could call it a BBC view of the world, a form of democratic
meliorism. But the insinuation rather than the statement of this theory makes an
important point: any adequate theory of communication or any set of proposals
must derive from an underlying theory of society.

There are only two directions to go in this matter. One can develop a theory
of communication and a program of research from a theory of society or one can
develop a theory of communications that is explicitly a theory of society. You
can start from Marx or Kenneth Burke. But the point is that powerful and
fundamental work in this field, as in the other social sciences, will only proceed
under the reflexive guidance and criticism of such theory. Without such a theory
the proposals in the Katz volume will fragment into so many atomized investigations which never produce an informing vision of the relation of broadcasting
to society, to social stratification and group psychology, to, most importantly,
the growth of a human culture. And that consequence is itself a theoretically
guided political intervention.

Lastly, the proposals as put forward will fail to capture in research the major
currents of contemporary life and the involvement of broadcasting in them. In
failing to do this they will also fail to meet the minimal demand on scholarship:
that it attach the life of the citizen and scholar to the fundamental currents of
social change of which broadcasting is such an important part. I do not think
this set of proposals, taken as a whole, as an imaginative program, will attach
history to biography or produce an informing and reliable knowledge of mass
communication.

43

SOME ADDITIONAL PROPOSALS

Herbert J. Gans

*Suggestions for "decentering" the media,
studying the effects of society on the media,
and looking at what researchers do to, for,
and against television and its viewers.*

Elihu Katz's report to the BBC is the latest example of a recently revived genre in the mass communications literature; a research program for the future. Asked by the BBC to prepare "an agenda for new projects of social research in the field of broadcasting which would ... have policy/editorial implications for the BBC" (p. 1), and given autonomy to pursue this broad assignment his own way, Katz developed a methodology that can fruitfully be copied by agenda-setters in other fields of study. He made an informal study of the BBC and its problems, spoke with broadcasters and researchers in several countries, reviewed the media literature, and drew on his own ideas and past studies. The result is a thoughtful analysis of the BBC and an excellent set of research proposals, covering both the timeless and "frontier" issues of our field; it should be an extremely useful guide for the BBC and for mass communications researchers in all Western societies.

I shall not review his analysis or proposals, for I find little with which I disagree. Instead, I want to write an addendum to his report, further emphasizing parts of some proposals, elaborating on others, and suggesting additional ones. My addendum extends the agenda-setting effort beyond the parameters in which Katz worked, and is thus also free of the restraint under which he worked: to produce a report of policy relevance for a broadcasting organization. I should add, however, that my addendum is also evoked by my own current research on the national news of television and the news magazines, and the questions I raise below have come up as I have pondered my own data and that of other media researchers. My addendum consists of seven items, four having to do with the media and three with media research itself.

Herbert J. Gans is Professor of Sociology, Columbia University and Senior Research Associate, Center for Policy Research.

1. *"Decentering" the media.* Many media researchers "center" the media; like practitioners and researchers in all fields, they assign their subject central importance. As a result, society too often seems to revolve around the media in our research, and audience studies treat people as if being an audience was their central role in life. If the impact and uses of the media are to be properly understood, however, they also have to be placed off-center at times, where they exist for the audience. We must remember that for most people other than media addicts, the print and electronic media are tools for leisure time rather than for navigating around society. This applies, I think, even to most news media, for they can rarely provide the individually-tailored information people need to navigate around the micro-society in which they actually live.

Having just reviewed a large number of audience studies, I am once more struck by how shallow an impression television and print messages, if not media, make on their audiences. Viewers seemingly exert little effort to comprehend what is broadcast and, as a result, they have difficulty recalling and reacting in detail to what they have seen. Television may take up a major slice of people's time budget, but it does not seem to take up much of their attention or involvement. The same viewers who enjoy the vicarious fantasy the media supply are far more deeply immersed in the reality and fantasy of their own personal and social lives.

For audiences, the media are near the margins of the society in which they live and which they construct. Consequently, audience studies must incorporate that perspective. More important, they must also be complemented by other research, such as community studies, which try to trace people's public and private lives in order to determine the interplay between their roles as persons, family members, workers, neighbors, citizens etc., and their media usage. I would begin by studying people in terms of the roles and relationships that are most central in their lives, and then try to determine (1) how these are affected by media usage, and (2) how media usage is affected by them. Understanding the interplay between the reality and fantasy in people's own lives, and the reality and fantasy of the media, is, as Katz suggests, still beyond the ability of our research methodologies, although I also wonder about our willingness. Few researchers, of the media or any other topic, can live comfortably with the knowledge that the phenomena they work so hard to study make only a shallow impression on most people.

2. *Decentering media fare.* In centering the media, researchers also have, to my mind, sometimes looked at social phenomena too much through the eyes of broadcasters (and editors), giving them the same undue attention as the media. Political news provides one example. As I was reading Katz's book, I was also reading about a poll, taken in New York City just before its 1977 mayoralty primary election, in which 60 percent of the respondents indicated, rightly I think, that New York City's fate would not be significantly altered by whoever was elected as mayor. Broadcasters and media researchers alike, however, have paid a lot of attention to elections of all kinds, without sufficiently realizing that they play only a minor part in shaping the fate of the polity, nation, or society. Similarly, while American journalists have performed effectively as watchdogs, most recently in exposing the Watergate scandals, researchers who have studied

the audience reaction to their exposés have not always been sufficiently aware of the limited political consequences of this form of journalism. Individual rascals are thrown out, but overall political and policy processes change little.

I am not suggesting an end to studies of the media's role in elections, but an additional perspective which pays more attention to the political functions of elections. For example, presidential election studies should not begin with the primaries, but with the macro- and micro-political processes, and their agents, that "recruit" the candidates and issues, not to mention the images in which both are clothed. Some candidates are helped, and even shaped, by the media, but others are not. I suspect the explanation has less to do with the media than with political and social conditions within which specific elections take place.

Conversely, media research should pay more attention to studying the role that the media play (and do not play) in more significant aspects of the political process, including the everyday, and often barely visible, forms of pressure politics, and the macro political and economic processes that help shape day-to-day politics. To illustrate: while Katz makes several useful proposals for the incorporation of social trends into television news (pp. 66–68), I would add, using Britain as a case, the trends of economic crisis and heightened class conflict which were taking place in Britain while he worked at the BBC, as well as the larger trends that are altering Britain's position in the world economy and power structure. The news deals with instances and incidents in all of these trends, but less often with the trends themselves. Nevertheless, media researchers must be aware that they have media ramifications, for the economic and political future of the media organizations themselves, for audiences as workers, citizens, etc., and therefore perhaps even for what viewers want or will accept in the way of information and entertainment.

Let me take another, less directly political, example. In the last decade, the media and media researchers have been preoccupied with media violence and, thanks in part to the research done by the editor of this *Journal*, we now know a great deal about who does what to whom and how in television violence. Concurrently, we know very little about the same questions in real world violence, or about the effect of that violence on television and its viewers. Media researchers have worried about television's impact on crime and violence, but not enough about the impact of crime and violence on television.

We cannot become criminologists, but we must broaden our perspective beyond the television set in order to determine whether and how the rising rates of crime and violence, both by the powerful and the powerless, have affected people in their centrally important public and private roles, and therefore as viewers as well. Many poor viewers are forced to live in areas with a good deal of real crime and violence; perhaps for them, television violence is realistic even if it is nothing like what they encounter in their own neighborhoods. Similarly, more affluent fans of television violence, equally powerless to defend themselves against real crime, perhaps therefore draw some measure of satisfaction and revenge from seeing criminals get their just deserts on the small screen.

3. *The media as institutions.* In both of the previous proposals, I have suggested that media researchers must decenter the media and look at the larger societal context in which the media operate. But we ought to look further at the media themselves, both intra-organizationally and inter-organizationally as Katz proposes, and also as national institutions. Paul Hirsch and others have shown that the mass media are oligopolistic producers of symbolic consumer goods; at the same time, they are elite institutions, run by an elite. Marxist scholars have long asserted this point, but they have not gone far beyond assertion, and there is much to explore.

For one thing, we need to study what kinds of elites are recruited into the mass media. In Britain, Oxbridge is still well-represented, as is the Ivy League in the U.S., at the high echelons of the media organization. But people born into lower strata have long been influential in America and are coming to be so in Britain. In the process, prestigious liberally-educated amateurs have been replaced by professionals, who are, however, part of another elite. Even so, it is equally possible that who runs the media or who produces the media fare does not matter, for the media are themselves elite organizations, funded by or through the economically powerful, and in close touch with the centers of political power, albeit sometimes as adversaries. Thus, media professionals become an elite even if they began life as proletarians.

To be sure, the media are also popular institutions, creating fare that seems to be wanted by, or at least acceptable to, most of their non-elite audiences; clearly, even BBC 2 and America's public television produce only a modicum of elite culture, however defined. Still, one can usefully ask what happens to popular media fare when it is produced by an organization run by an economic or social elite, or by professionals producing for a lay audience, or by an organization which is elite by being close to the centers of power. For example, Archie Bunker is not really a working-class character, but an upper-middle class professional's conception of a working-class character. Likewise, most news is about the routine activities of the political elite, and ordinary people get into the news mainly when they engage in individual deviance or social protest. Or as Katz puts it, "Elites make news by speaking up; non-elites by acting up" (p. 66).

4. *Alternative media organizations.* Research on media organizations should also be complemented by studies that investigate the possibilities and consequences of alternative media organizations. What I have in mind is not only pay TV or cassettes which are the media's own alternatives, but vastly different models. Although I do not believe that small is beautiful, it is worth considering the effects of smaller media organizations, decentralized not by region but by other criteria, including audience tastes, as well as of non-elite organizations, in which media fare is produced by laypersons. I do not want to argue that these are either feasible or desirable, but I think they provide perspectives that can enrich both empirical and policy-oriented research. Moreover, media research is almost always policy-oriented, if not in intent, then in its implications. Media researchers wanting to limit themselves to basic research have every right to do

so, but research agendas, which are idealistic statements in any case, should include some reference to "far out" alternatives. In the same vein, although we should continue to try to study how society has changed since the mass media came on the scene, it might also be useful, even for that study, to speculate systematically how society would change if the mass media were now abolished.

My remaining proposals have to do with ourselves, the media researchers. Researchers have never been overly enthusiastic about studying themselves, and self-study is a methodologically and otherwise hazardous venture. But a sociology of sociology has come into being in the last decade, with some worthwhile results; consequently, a sociology of media research is now equally relevant.

5. *Media researchers as employees.* Katz's review of the current media research scene serves as a reminder that most media researchers work either for the media themselves, or for universities which get grants and contracts from them, or from government and foundations. Ever since Karl Mannheim asked "who plans the planners?" we should have been asking an equivalent question about researchers, i.e., "who hires the hired," to consider the impact of those who give us grants on the research problems we investigate and ignore.

I do not mean here to suggest conspiracies, but rather a need to understand the context in which we work and how it affects our product, much as media researchers have studied organizational effects on the form and substance of entertainment and news. For example, most media research is done for the suppliers of media fare, or for agencies that regulate or seek to influence the suppliers. Few researchers are hired, or work for, the audience or for non-audiences; while some researchers think of themselves as representing the audience, they are also self-appointed and not accountable to it. The organizational effects on any product are inevitable; they can neither be wished away nor are they necessarily bad. But they exist for us, as for everyone else in the symbolic products industries, and they ought to be studied.

6. *The researcher and practitioner.* Katz's report on his research within the BBC, in noting the anxieties of broadcasters about their audience, alludes also to their fear of audience research (pp. 14–19). This raises the question of the effects of media research on the media, and on broadcasters and other practitioners in them. While one can ask about the effects of organizational research on the organization (I shall be curious about the impact of Katz's study on the BBC itself), I want to limit the discussion to audience research.

Katz's findings at the BBC duplicate my own in studying television and magazine journalists; many are highly ambivalent or hostile toward audience research, even if they often ponder questions which could be answered by such research, including that already available in-house. Their ambivalence is not hard to understand, however, for they are professionals with a professional mission, which they sometimes practice with missionary zeal. But they deal with a distant, large, fickle, and often not very interested audience. As a result, audience research can be a threat, especially since in American media organizations, research departments report not to the producers of media fare, but to management. Management, however, is hired to maintain and enlarge profits, and therefore usually audience size as well. To make a long story short, the journalists are not only nervous about the audience and about researchers, but also about management's possible use of audience research to alter the news in search of larger audiences and, in the process, to cut down the autonomy of the journalists.

Media researchers usually believe that more research is a Good Thing and, in the abstract, it probably is. Still, in concrete practice, it can help some and can hurt others, and we must be aware of the consequences.

7. *The researcher as citizen.* Some years ago, Howard M. Becker asked sociologists of deviance "Whose Side Are We On?" The previous two proposals have already raised the same question about media researchers in two different ways. It must, however, be asked in yet a third way—about ourselves and our own research interests. As researchers, our overt research agendas are shaped by our own curiosities, by the paradigms in our fields, and, perhaps less overtly, by the usual desire for fame and immortality, not to mention tenure and promotion.

I am, however, curious about an even less overt agenda. What else are we after in doing media research, particularly as persons and citizens? Do we want our media research to improve media fare and, if so, how, for whom, and why? My hunch is that some television researchers would like to extend, not necessarily consciously, what I call the upper-middle-class taste culture of public television to the commercial networks, perhaps to improve the overall societal culture or perhaps also to have more of the programming they prefer. Likewise, what do media researchers want to do to and for television when they study television violence? I do not doubt their genuine abhorrence of real or symbolic violence, but I have a hunch that they are also doing their bit in the upper-middle-class's struggle against the "dangerous classes," as well as promoting the spread of upper-middle-class taste culture, which shuns violence. (I get this feeling especially when media researchers begin to treat television violence and sex as equivalent evils, and then cannot help but note that public television, in the U.S. at least, is virtually sexless.)

Finally, I wonder what we have in mind when we study the news. Given that journalism and the social sciences are both devoted to the empirical analysis of society and are in that sense competitive occupations, do we want to extend the sociological or psychological construction of society to the news, and thus knock, convert, or coopt a competitor? Or do we want, like journalists, a more informed citizenry, in order to increase citizen participation and enhance democracy? If so, why have we, again like journalists, often failed to see that informing the citizenry does not necessarily increase its participation, its power, or democracy? Or is an informed citizenry supposed to be informed on the issues and values which media researchers (and journalists) themselves prefer; if so, is the desire to inform the citizenry a search for political allies—and in support of what issues and causes?

I do not mean to suggest conspiracies. Nor do I want to impugn motives or suggest that self-interest is necessarily a bad motive. Still, we are persons and citizens as well as researchers, and we should be thinking about what motivates us, consciously and otherwise, and about how it affects our research.

44

OF MUTUAL INTEREST

Elihu Katz

In which the author of the report
to the BBC reflects on the issues
raised by contributors to this colloquy.

I will be forgiven, I hope, if I see the brighter side of things. "The BBC is already writing and talking in terms of the Katz concepts" writes Halloran. Carey comments on the persuasive impact of my proposals on the "oversupply of researchers chasing an undersupply of researchable notions." That can't all be bad.

Admittedly, I think the BBC's groping toward an organizational framework appropriate to the implementation of the report would have been enriched by earlier discussions with British researchers, and I said so. But the time is still ripe. I also think—and said—that I hoped that my selection of proposals would invoke additional proposals, counterproposals and argument. They have.

Four issues stand out. First, I am criticized for forfeiting the researcher's duty to formulate his own questions. The policy concerns of broadcasters, it is alleged, narrowed the scope of my thinking and there is danger that my proposals will likewise contaminate those who may wish to implement them. Policy research is here contrasted with what is called, very loosely, critical research. In reply, I shall try to argue that critical research is itself a kind of policy research.

A second, and related, issue has to do with the professionalism of broadcasting. I am criticised for naively assuming that an ethic of public service is implicit in the concept of professionalism or that the concept, so defined, applies at all to broadcasting, even public broadcasting. Professionalism, we are told, is a peer-oriented ethic, grounded in self-defense, and the public is very poorly served by it. Social science would do better to concentrate on exposing the workings of the professions rather than viewing them, anachronistically, as sharing some of its own commitments.

The question of theory in communications research is the third big issue. The Katz Report is theoretically eclectic, says one critic, and another says it is hopelessly atheoretical. Without a unifying theory, the various proposals are so many fragments which will not fit together, and which can only please those dark powers who prefer to keep things that way.

Finally, there is the question of the organizational framework in which these—or other—proposals might be carried out. What should be the broadcasters' involvement in this framework? Can—or should—broadcasters and researchers try to work together, and if so, in what ways?

The argument against policy research is that true social scientists ought not to let interested parties set their agendas.

"Were Katz successful," says Carey, "it would rob society of the one useful role scholars can perform: the statement of problems, issues and solutions in terms that are outside and opposed to the established centers of power and authority." Halloran, in his best bedside manner, says that "some people see Katz as castrating critical research." In a letter to me about the report, Hilde Himmelweit says, more generously, that both "its values and limitations stem from the fact that you were asked to look at the questions that broadcasters pose."

It is easy enough to agree that the report is selective: its proposals simply are projects which I think are of mutual interest, given the state of the art and the needs of policy. It is also easy to persuade most people that the BBC's public expression of interest is worth having both for its own sake and for the discussions it triggered in broadcasting organizations around the world. But must we agree with these critics that the price of it all is the exclusion of the most interesting people and problems in the field? The answer is no.

Carey says that had I been truly free I would have permitted myself to ask, at least in fantasy, whether TV ought to be abolished or "cut back." Halloran feels that I could not ask how communications structures might be re-tailored "to maximize the satisfaction of social needs in a pluralist society." Both men are certain that I had to take the media as given, together with the institutional contexts in which they are embedded.

I firmly believe that had I wished to propose studies to consider the proposition that television be abolished, I could have done so. In fact, I did, if Carey means—as perhaps he does—that it is important to study whether television may be doing harm to the disciplined patterns of thought and speech or to the uses of leisure, which are basic to the functioning of democratic society. Curiously, the report will show that BBC people put such questions to me!

Similarly, for the relationship between broadcasting and other institutions, consider Proposal 1f, "The Interaction of Media and other Institutions," "The Latent Structure of News and Public Affairs Programmes" (Proposal 4b), and "The Broadcasting of Conflict" (Proposal 4c).

Restructuring media to serve social needs? See Proposal 6d, "The Dilemma of Organizing Broadcasting to Serve Differentiation" and "The Comprehension of Broadcasting Information" (Proposal 4a). Indeed, if I now were choosing a label to describe the report, I would incline toward Halloran's "to maximize the satisfaction of social needs in a pluralist society."

Of course, these proposals and the problems to which they are addressed can be formulated in different ways. Mine are "safe" formulations, says Halloran, in another of his contraceptive metaphors. Perhaps they are safe, but I must insist on the recognition that they are not hiding or missing.

By the same token, the report does not contain proposals to study problems which I regard as conceptually uninteresting, despite their administrative relevance. Thus, I do not propose the further study of the effects of televised violence, or the relative popularity of male vs. female news presenters.

Admittedly, there is a kind of critical research which is so far removed from "the established centres of power and authority" that it is absent here. A classic example would be the Frankfurt School's insistence that mass communication and mechanical reproduction have transformed the arts into products, and connoisseurship into consumption. But most critical research is of a "middle range" which betrays an interest in affecting policy and, as such, definitely belongs on my research agenda. Thus, the academic search for a latent theory of the news—though it aims at the very heart of the Liberal theory of the press—belongs here, as does research on the hypothesis that certain groups are unwittingly victimized in television entertainment. So do analyses of the latent message of the news: legitimation, reassurance, parliamentarism, mystification, status conferral, racialism, and the like. Research findings from studies of this kind are negotiable, I think, within extant broadcasting institutions. In Britain, at least, I would venture that the broadcasting organization is the right place to begin, even if such things have not always ended well.

> *Critical research, by definition, is engaged; it is not to be confused with basic research.*

It is applied as administrative research even when differing in its conception of who is to be served and what must be changed. Rightly, it regards the object needing change as an unlikely sponsor. And yet, government ministries and public service organizations in a democracy may sponsor research "unwillingly" because they are constrained to do so under the rules of accountability. Ministeries of Education which have opted for programs of racial and ethnic integration are not always eager to have hard facts about whether the policy is succeeding, just as broadcasting organizations may not be eager to learn that "reality" is a social construction or that treatment of a certain issue may be biased. But, sometimes they "have" to want to know. And sometimes, as I found, they may even "want" to want to know. The report explains why.

I am arguing, then, that critical research is a form of policy research. Carey may be right that, in the crunch, the more critical projects will be less likely to find support. But if support is sought and obtained, it need not be carried out at the BBC television center under the supervision of a member of middle management. Not at all! I tried to classify types of research in terms of their needed "proximity" to the production process and duly announced that "critical research"—in the language of the report—should be "far" from the organization rather than "near."

I am also arguing that policy research is interesting and contains, I think, some of the sorts of puzzles which might attract Carey. For example, if the audience is non-selective in its viewing behavior, why does a gratifications model fit so much of the attitudinal data? Or, if a majority of the audience is exposed daily to information on political issues, why is so little retained or understood? Why do politicians and advertisers act as if the media were more effective than they are? How does one explain the apparent appetite for repetition, not only of fairy tales? The answers to each of these have immediate policy implications, not alone for the broadcaster but "to maximize the satisfaction of social needs."

Nevertheless, I would not want to persuade anyone that research is best done "inside." Nor would I disagree, in principle, that there is often a struggle over research agendas in policy research, and that the researcher may often lose, knowingly or not. Nor would I want to do policy research for an organization of whose goals I disapproved. But more of this under the heading of "professionalism."

*Tuchman rightly notes that I have attempted to apply
to public broadcasting that aspect of the model of professionalism
which asserts that the client is its prime beneficiary.*

She berates me for being out of touch with the sociology of the professions where peers have long since replaced clients as the reference group to be satisfied, and where peer judgments have tended to supply only consensual validation rather than effective mutual criticism. Far from serving the public, she argues, the public is deprived of the service it requires.

What is true of medicine, she proposes, is true of journalism: professional practice is designed to establish the legitimacy of the profession by brandishing the elementary methodology of objectivity and impartiality. The result is that no one is held accountable for social problems, and that the pros and cons of any story are presented from well within the establishment. The overall effect, she argues, is to reify the status quo.

In his recent book on the BBC, Tom Burns takes a related stance. He considers professionalism a retreat from public service into a private world. Professionalism is peer-oriented and autistic; it has little interest in the audience. Halloran, too, calls for liberation from the monopoly of professional broadcasters.

These authors fail to distinguish, I feel, between institutional goals and practices. The *norms* of professionalism speak of public service. To the extent that journalism is striving toward professionalization, the notion of orientation toward clients becomes more salient, whether in the gatekeeper stance or the advocacy stance. The problem in journalism as in medicine is that there are also institutionalized departures from the norms. But the norms are there, and they make a difference. Indeed, they are what make it possible, in my opinion, for social scientists and (public) broadcasters to share so many concerns.

In my interviews at the BBC, I repeatedly heard affirmations of the norm of public service, not just at the managerial level, but at the producer level as well. If the norms are there, the aim of research is to point out the disparity between doctrine and practice and to reason why. Only if the norms have changed, or were never there, would Tuchman be right in asserting that the aim of research on news-making should not be to help strengthen journalism as a profession but rather to debunk it.

I am criticized for naively believing broadcasters' pronouncements about public service, accountability, and interest in research. I agree that this ostensible change of heart remains to be tested. But it is quite different, I repeat, if one is dealing with an organization which is committed to public service—even if it wanders away from its commitment. It is just as Halloran says: the goals which society invests in an institution, the institution's own formulation of its goals, and the actual behavior of the members may all be quite different. But it is a lot more scientific, as a start, to study the constraints which cause individuals or groups to depart from their own norms than to brand them as lackeys touting the legitimacy of the capitalist industrial order.

As a matter of fact, Tuchman and her colleagues have gone some distance in showing how the rules of procedure in the gathering and editing of TV news may contribute to an affirmation of the status quo and lull the "consciousness" of the viewer. But it is no less interesting that these procedures are probably unwitting. The methods of programming reality by means of the reporting of discrete events culled from a limited number of established beats and presented with the voice of authority and the picture of authenticity all conspire to mystify, say Tuchman and others.

The production and consumption of news are
one of the central foci of my report.

I insist on the confrontation of the latent-message analysis with the question of what gets through to the viewer. Even if the message that all is very well is being sent and received, it does not mean that broadcast journalism is part of a conspiracy. Indeed, to the extent that journalism is a profession—in my sense—it will be occupied with what is getting through to the audience. And the appropriateness of the alliance with academic research will become more apparent as the theories underlying the gathering and production of news become better established. But not every latent function—not even the latent function of legitimation—is automatically evil or a betrayal of the public trust. Thus, if journalists' treatment of Watergate revealed that the system of checks and balances—Congress, the courts, and the press—was in working order, despite the high crime, what is inaccurate about that? Making this latent function manifest does not yet prove that the media are "serving as the cultural arms of the industrial order."

Social science has good reason to support journalism. Ultimately, it is the set of academic disciplines in which journalism ought to be grounded. The problem of how to observe society, and from what vantage points, is no less that of social science than of journalism. The anguish over the concept of objectivity is as great—even if it takes a different form—in social science as in journalism. Nor is social science exempt from some of the very charges—paradigmatic perceptions, latent ideological functions—that have been levelled against journalism. Let us look to our own problems as well, while studying other people's.

There is yet another—and more important—reason to support the professionalization of journalism and broadcasting through alliance with social science research. However much the governors and controllers of broadcasting organizations can protect their producers and editors against external pressures, the ultimate source of countervailing power must come from the organization of journalism as a profession and the internalization of professional ethics by its members. It is therefore in the common interest to strengthen the profession in its classical sense and to bolster the primacy of society as the client. I cannot foresee the day in which broadcasting will be removed from the hands of professionals and redistributed among the people. I cannot foresee the displacement of the broadcast media by the telephone and conversation, although I fear the displacement of the latter by the former. Access will be mediated by professionals, as far as I can see, and community television will probably not be much more popular than home movies.

> *As to the question of theory, the*
> *object of my report was obviously not to*
> *propose a grand theory of communications to the BBC.*

If I knew one to which I could subscribe, I might have found a way to use it. I do not have such a theory. Neither has Halloran, I dare say. Many of the proposals are informed by theoretical perspectives, however, albeit of several different kinds, as Carey notes. Halloran finds no trace of theory.

I made no effort to label the theoretical orientations which guide the report. Considering the audience to whom the report was addressed, there would have been little point in writing in the multi-disciplinary argot of the trade. I think it is obvious, nevertheless, that a functional perspective pervades the report. Its starting point, as noted earlier, is with the social and psychological needs of audiences, not with the needs of broadcasters. It accepts parliamentary democracy, social stratification, sex and age differentiation, etc., as both given and problematic, and asks about the ways in which broadcasting is affected by, and influential for, the needs arising from these social arrangements. It pays particular attention to the role of the media in promoting participation in the role of citizen, and the barriers of access to this role. It contrasts the conventional and emergent bases of identity in modern society, and proposes inquiry into the relative importance of these identities and the extent to which the media support them.

Two of the areas may be said to be more media-centered—one sociological, the other psychological. Thus, one set of problems considers the management of creativity and seeks to explore the conditions under which broadcasting—or, indeed, other creative organizations—can maximize creative potential. The other deals with the experience itself—the aesthetics of listening and viewing.

Although no grand theory underlies the proposals—and Carey is right that such a theory would help hold the pieces together—there is implicit an "accounting scheme" which calls for study of (1) external constraints on what the media say; (2) the process of production and the values implicit therein; (3) the manifest and latent messages as encoded; (4) audience behavior in decoding, absorbing, and applying these messages; and (5) the process of feedback to other institutions.

If Halloran finds this familiar, it is because there is broad agreement on this research agenda, not only in Britain and in Europe (which, alas, is seriously under-represented in my report) but even in America. Perhaps the bulk of American research is as unchanged as Halloran asserts, but that surely excludes the present contributors and all of those with whom I talked. For some ten years now, the frontiers of communications research everywhere have focused on patterns of ownership and control; media transformations of reality; journalists' routines and values; media agendas and public agendas; gaps of knowledge and understanding, and their implications for identity and consciousness; latent messages about the legitimacy of the social order and the rules of decorum; witting and unwitting bias in matters of race, sex, political minorities, trade unions; cognitive processing of the media; and so on.

> *The search for powerful effects*
> *implicit here is still on.*

In the report, I suggest that the anxiety over this quest is an important component of theory-making in communications. If effects are as limited as they seem, why go on? One answer is that the study of mass communications is interesting and important as a sociology and aesthetics of popular art. Humanists and linguists of many ilks have joined the quest. Another answer is evident in the examination of new types of effects, and thus, implicitly, that the powerful effects of the media have yet to be uncovered. Hence agenda setting, knowledge gap, legitimation, false consciousness, mild arousal, spiral of silence, and others. The difference between these functions and effects and those of 30 years ago is that theory has taken the lead over method, and that some progress has been made in devising methods appropriate to the study of these concepts. But, parenthetically, it is a mistake to disparage the value of the negative findings of the forties and fifties.

There may be the germs of a grand theory in all of this which may win over skeptics like Herbert Gans and myself to a new sociology of mass communications, or, if Carey is right, to a historically-situated theory. The theory draws liberally on Marxism, functionalism, mass society theory, and organization theory. It appears to argue that (1) the message of the media is highly homogeneous, because of (2) the interlocking directorates which control them, and/or because of (3) the professional huddling together of communicators, which produces (4) an agreed-on view of reality, legitimating an elite and a system of stratification (5) before the eyes of the ubiquitous audience, (6) looking to the media as the monolithic reference group. Note the disappearance of the primary group and other membership and reference groups, i.e., all the institutions which were thought to mediate between the individual and the media; the qualitative difference assigned to television as compared with other media; and the consolidation of communicators through ownership and professionalization. This is a theory of mass society, not just of powerful media.

To reiterate: while the report does not pretend to derive from grand theory, it does attempt to call attention to theoretical developments, past and present. Indeed, some of its proposals permit testing of propositions associated with different—often opposing—viewpoints.

Clearly, the need for theory development continues to be acute, and there is no reason at all to be complacent about the development noted above. It has a long way to go to prove itself, and it would be well to encourage competing formulations. Is this the theory that has come to substitute for the classical conception of the relationship between government and public opinion, where government initiates, the press diffuses, the cafes and salons buzz with conversation, opinion is formed and segmented, and fed back to government? Probably not. In any case, it is clear that we have only the vaguest idea about the connection between mass communication and democratic participation. It is also clear that to do this—and other things—the net must be widened to include representatives of disciplines not much concerned, these days, with communications research.

The BBC wished to set up a Trust (foundation) financed
by broadcasters and others to promote initiative in this area.

The Trust would act as matchmaker and chaperone to broadcasters and researchers, respecting the need of critical research for independence and smoothing the way for evaluative, formative, etc., research. The Trust would also seek to make possible access to broadcasting organizations, to tape recordings, etc.

Halloran rightly emphasizes that the security and independence of broadcasting research cannot be vested exclusively in *ad hoc* funding, certainly not the kind over which broadcasters have direct or indirect control. One false or unpopular move, and an entire research organization may become *non grata*. He insists—as do I, in the report—that the first requisite of communications research in Britain is in the sustained endowment of university research centers and groups. For this reason it is also important—as Hilde Himmelweit emphasizes—that a Broadcasting Research Trust, if established, not draw off money from foundations already supporting such research, nor presume to act as go-between in the relations of researchers and foundations.

I also argue strongly for the strengthening and re-orientation of audience research within the broadcasting organizations themselves. Most of the energies of audience research go into ratings and it often distracts attention from the other research projects. The BBC, for example, has a major resource in its Daily Survey of Listening and Viewing which it should itself exploit for secondary analysis of audience behavior and for other survey research. Its status within the organization as gatekeepers of the ratings and as colleagues make for innumerable opportunities for cooperative research with producers and managers.

Thus, my proposals are not monolithic. First of all, I see four different kinds of support: endowed centers strong enough to carry on even when project support is absent; foundation supported projects; Broadcasting Trust projects; and audience research departments. Secondly, even within the Trust, I urge the orchestration of different kinds of broadcaster-researcher relations.

Thus, on a "distance" scale, formative research—such as "Sesame Street"—must be an integral part of the production process; evaluative research needs to be "near"; critical research needs distance.

It is ironic, in the light of this discussion, that I see "nearness"—that is, active collaboration with broadcasters—as less likely of fruition than critical research at a distance. The report strongly advocates experimentation with closer alliances between broadcasters and researchers, on the assumption that the shared values of public broadcasting and social science may find creative and public-serving expression in collaborative effort. But those are the things we have been arguing about.

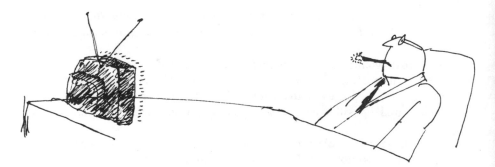

This symposium contains spirited debate about major policy research conducted in Britain by a distinguished research team at the University of Leeds. Jay G. Blumler, Michael Gurevitch, and Julian Ives were invited in 1975 by the major political parties, the BBC, and the Independent Broadcasting Authority to examine the strengths and problems of the British system of election broadcasting. With financial support from the Rowntree Social Service Trust and British broadcasters, the team conducted hundreds of interviews with experts and participants in the political campaign process. Content analysis of political coverage and secondary analysis of election surveys complemented elite interviews. The first chapter in the symposium is reprinted from The Challenge of Election Broadcasting, *the official report of the Blumler team's research. In their report, the Blumler team called for a series of programs called "Election Access," whereby the political parties would have unbridled party advocacy followed by broadcaster-controlled journalistic scrutiny. As a complement to this approach, broadcast news would be relieved of its obligations to provide precisely equal time and would assume a more journalistic, reportorial view of the campaign, reporting only what was newsworthy in the broadcaster's conception. Third, a "Campaign Review" program would periodically air the parties' reactions to the news. In the chapter reprinted here from the Blumler team's report, the underlying assumptions of the team's research are outlined. Briefly, they assume that television has a formative influence on political campaigning and that there should be a clear division of labor between the televised political advocacy of the parties and journalistic scrutiny of the parties. In the second piece, Nicholas Garnham writes a strident criticism of the Blumler report, arguing that its recommendations were pro-broadcaster and likely to accelerate the decline of political parties. Blumler and his colleagues cogently respond to the criticism and extend the debate to the crucial problem of policy research: To whom or what does the policy researcher owe allegiance? Dr. Blumler is Director of the Centre for Television Research, University of Leeds, England. Dr. Garnham is Managing Editor of the journal* Media, Culture & Society *published at Polytechnic of Central London.*

45

FIRST PRINCIPLES LAST

Jay G. Blumler, Michael Gurevitch, and Julian Ives

What were the ultimate principles which guided us while we were working our way through these ideas? We assumed from the outset that television exerts a formative influence in shaping election campaigns, certainly in affecting politicians' behaviour, and possibly in guiding voters' perceptions and reactions as well. It delivers to the parties — at one go and in an endless succession of such 'goes' — a bigger audience than they could ever secure by their own unaided efforts and than they ever secured in the days before broadcasting came on the scene. Television is also the one information source which invariably receives more mentions than does any other when people are asked — not just in Britain but in many other countries as well — which medium they depend on most for following an election. Its massive presence has stimulated a host of party publicity adaptations — in rhetorical manner, in the length, content and style of messages, and in the organisation and tactical conduct of campaigning. What is more, its potential for influencing the outlook of viewers is no longer so heavily discounted by scholars of political communication effects as was the case some fifteen years ago. Partly this is because television has demonstrated its power to override formerly effective defensive barriers — such as selective exposure patterns. Partly it is because it can penetrate with political materials formerly impervious and possibly persuasible electoral circles — such as individuals weak in political interest and floating voters.[41]

For all these reasons, the design of television's election role is vital. In the end, it should be helping to involve citizens in their society's political affairs, providing materials from which informed choices can be made, and strengthening confidence that political broadcasting exists to serve voters' needs. But in order to advance these objectives, two operating principles, each equally legitimate and indispensable, have to be related effectively to each other.

---

[41]For a sustained discussion of recent developments in academic perspectives on the effects-potential of broadcasting, see Blumler, Jay G. 'The Intervention of Television in British Politics', an essay submitted to the Annan Committee (*Report of the Committee on the Future of Broadcasting*, Appendix E, Cmnd. 6753-1, HMSO, London, 1977).

From Jay G. Blumler et al., "First Principles Last," *The Challenge of Election Broadcasting*, Chapter 6 67-69, Leeds, U.K.: Leeds University Press. Reprinted by permission.

One such principle has already been enunciated many times in the foregoing pages. It stems from the fact that it is the political parties which pose the terms of the choice that the electorate has to make. Therefore, *there must be sufficient outlets in broadcasting to enable the parties to state their views on the campaign issues fully and in their own way without interference from other elements.* Yet this principle alone cannot be relied on to give shape to the argument, to ensure that the discussion is joined, or to clarify for voters what they most want to find out. Realism dictates, and experience demonstrates, that at campaign time the top priority of the parties is to conquer power not to disseminate enlightenment. Left to their own devices, they may side-step awkward issues, fail to give an ordered picture of the issue agenda, slant facts and figures in their own favour, declaim in high generalities, and try to deflect attention away from their own policies to their opponents' shortcomings. After all, an election campaign involves them, not in a seminar, but in a winner-take-all fight. There follows a need for a second operating principle which is that in a public service election broadcasting system, *broadcasters should act as trustees for the voters' campaign information needs.* It then becomes necessary to find a way of inter-relating these principles, so that justice is done to each without loss of integrity to either, and so that voters' requirements are served as fully and effectively as possible.

Even a cursory glance round the democratic world will show that these principles have been combined in different ways in different election broadcasting systems:

(1) Where television mainly provides a platform for the parties — i.e. the party advocacy principle strongly predominates over the broadcasting trusteeship principle. Typically, such a system is found where television has recently appeared on the political scene, or where the parties constitutionally have a big say in the machinery of broadcasting organisation. Some examples of such 'platform' systems might include Britain in the 1950s, Israel since the introduction of broadcasting in the 1960s, and Spain very recently.

(2) Where exactly the reverse obtains, television in some sense or other almost 'belongs' to the broadcasters, and there is little formal acknowledgement of the parties' entitlement to free advocacy outlets. In a sense, the American system exemplifies such a case, since to gain unfettered access to the electorate, candidates must pay for air time instead of receiving it as of right.

(3) Where a segregated division of labour is supposed to prevail —
i.e. there are separate party programmes and broadcasters'
programmes, each have their own tasks to perform, they come
under distinct forms of control, and they are not mixed in any way.
This is essentially the kind of election broadcasting system which
Britain has supposedly been operating since the early 1960s.

On the face of it, the third alternative respects both operating principles
fully and gives them plenty of scope to function within their allotted
spheres. Nevertheless, in modern conditions, the boundaries between the
separate compartments seem ever in danger of erosion. Party broadcasts are
weak advocacy tools. Media styles are frequently imported into them. The
main thrust of party campaigning is increasingly directed towards news
outlets, where it becomes increasingly difficult clearly to preserve the
distinction between journalistic reporting and propaganda projection. Even
current affairs planning is sometimes bedevilled by prolonged hassling,
mutual second-guessing and eventual compromise. Yet the voter is left to
suppose that the regime of segregated division of labour remains in force
intact.

When the alternatives are laid out in this way, another perspective on our
'options for change' comes into view. What we are proposing for
consideration is: neither a reassertion of party supremacy, which would be
unthinkable in these less partisan times; nor a celebration of broadcaster
sovereignty, which would improperly downgrade the place of party
competition in defining the terms of electoral choice; nor even a call to
everyone to march back into the simple compartments of a fully segregated
division of labour, which would be unrealistic. Instead we are suggesting
that thought be given to the advantages of a fourth kind of system, one that
is based on a *coordinated division of labour* between the major operating
principles and the elements involved in applying them. In such a system, the
functions of party advocacy and broadcaster scrutiny would not be
compromised in any way, but at strategic points they would be harnessed to
each other so as to perform their tasks in complementary interaction rather
than in difficult-to-sustain isolation.

46

POLITICS AND THE MASS MEDIA IN BRITAIN
The Strange Case of Dr. Blumler

Nicholas Garnham

The occasion of this essay is the appearance of *The Challenge of Election Broadcasting* [1] by Blumler, Gurevitch and Ives (1978). This is a report of an enquiry commissioned by nominees of the Conservative, Labour and Liberal Parties, the BBC and the IBA. This study merits close attention for a number of reasons, firstly because of the importance of its specific subject matter.

In the words of the authors, it 'raises for public discussion a number of fundamental issues about the role of television in British election campaigns'. There was a time when to be concerned with such issues was itself considered to be a sign that one was tarred with the empiricist and liberal-pluralist brush. But given the increased attention being given within historical materialism to Gramscian theories of hegemony and given the developments covered by the term Eurocommunism, it now seems that Marxist or Marxian mass media researchers can no longer afford to take such a dismissive attitude, whether they regard the mechanisms of bourgeois democracy as a repressive ideological and political mechanism or whether they regard them as important democratic gains won by popular political struggle and to be developed and extended rather than overthrown.

Within the next year a General Election will have taken place in Britain and the familiar debate will start again concerning the role of the media in general and of television in particular, for as all students of the subject now agree, the role of TV, in what A. Smith (1978) has dubbed 'A maturing telocracy', is central to our political process. Was there too much coverage or too little? Did the coverage influence the result? Was there bias as between the political parties? etc. In that debate the proposals for changing the modes of election broadcasting contained in CEB are likely to be influential, both because of the nature of its sponsorship and because of Dr Blumler's unique status in this field. Since in my view these recommendations for change are fundamentally misguided, I believe that there is a political duty to explain why with some care. And in order to do so it will be necessary to examine Dr Blumler's other recent work in this general field.

This work raises two general questions. One is methodological, namely the status of empirical investigation within the study of mass-communication and the relation of that empirical investigation to what Blumler calls 'grand theory', a term referring in the context of current debates within British media studies to a range of Marxist or Marxist-influenced positions. The other question concerns the relationship between research and researchers on the one hand and communications policy on the other.

I do not raise these questions at random in connection with CEB, for they are explicitly foregrounded in the text itself:

* School of Communication, Polytechnic of Central London, UK.

[1] Hereinafter referred to as CEB.

With permission from *Media, Culture and Society* 1 (January 1979) 23-34. Copyright by Academic Press Inc. (London) Ltd.

In assembling its results first priority was given to the production of this report, to be focused centrally on *policy* concerns (p. 7, italics in original).

We hoped to produce a report that would be enjoyable to read and could engage interest in its ideas. It was composed as a policy document for public action and not as a learned treatise (p. 12).

We have no wish to become known as the Don Quixotes of election broadcasting policy— as visionaries 'inspired by lofty and chivalrous but unrealisable ideals' (p. 9).

and these explicit policy aims are linked to the methodological question, because Blumler *et al.* put forward as one of their means of overcoming possible resistance to their proposals, the placing of their 'diagnosis within the context of a realistic analysis of recent political trends affecting the audience reception of election messages' (p. 12). That is to say they are involved not only in an ideological operation, namely the use of the prestige or the supposed scientificity of empirical research to gain acceptance for normative policy proposals, but they are also guilty in the report, and this is characteristic, as we shall see, of the thrust of all Blumler's recent work, of at least a sneaking positivism in believing that their proposals in some way naturally flow from this empirical evidence. The use here of the word 'realistic' is revealing.

Dr Blumler has been consistent recently in condemning radical critics of the media for mere negativism, for failing to couple their criticisms with alternative concrete policy proposals. He has made this critique even when these critics, as in the case of *Bad News* (Glasgow University Media Group, 1976), use empirical methods. In general I share this position and applaud the resolutely practical and relevant tone of CEB. I support Blumler's desire to relate research to the actual hurly-burly of policy, against either those who would see their science as a value-free positivistic activity which merely accurately describes a world progressing independently beyond the confines of their ivory towers or, on the other hand, those Marxists who are so arrogantly secure within their self-justifying socio-political theories that the workings of the actual society in which they live is reduced to triviality by the march of history. It is important to stress this because I wish to argue that Blumler's own view of what policy research amounts to is narrowly circumscribed with potentially dangerous ideological and policy results and because I also wish to argue that the specific policies he advocates do not follow from his own empirical data. That is, I would wish to question the 'realism' of his analysis.

A critique of the Blumler position is important because it illuminates the nature of the dispute in which Blumler has been engaged with the 'grand theorists'. Blumler's most complete statement of his position appears in a course unit on *The Political Effects of the Mass Media* which he wrote for the Open University course on Mass Communication and Society. There he writes:

Some sociologists of mass-communication are not all that enamoured of mass-media effects research; they have given the systematic attempt, empirically and quantitatively, to measure the impact on audience members' ideas of the flow of mass-communicated messages what can only be termed a 'bad name'. In fact, effects research is virtually treated in some quarters as the brothel of media studies: the 'madam' rather than the 'queen' of our science. The critics, then, have variously portrayed such research as arid and trivial in outcome: tarnished with the discredited promises of atomistic mass-society theory; obsessively preoccupied with issues of technique and method; wedded to naïve and atheoretical versions of positivism and empiricism; and (most damning indictment of all) as essentially supportive of the *status quo* . . . one reason for doubting the validity of more extreme lines of criticism arises from the very fact that political communication effects research is still being actively pursued today and is even enjoying a vigorous renaissance. Indeed it is difficult to see how this field could dispense entirely with some kind of effects research—unless, that is, its devotees really do want all their observations about the relationship between mass-media systems and social and political orders to remain on the realm of high-pitched polemic and high-flown (and unsubstantiated) speculation (Open University, 1977: 6).

It is tempting when reading CEB to respond that Blumler is involved in low-pitched polemic and low-flying and equally unsubstantiated speculation. What Blumler is engaged in is a dual enterprise. He is presenting political effects studies in general, and his work in particular, as a testing ground for the validity or otherwise of the effects research tradition. And he is at the same time claiming extra validity for his policy proposals, because they are based upon effects research. What I will attempt to show, while accepting the value of empirical 'effects' research, is that Blumler's own work is susceptible to the criticisms levelled against effects research in general and that the empirical evidence, when interpreted from a different theoretical position, leads to quite other policy conclusions to those arrived at by Blumler and his colleagues.

He argues that the 'methodological individualism' of effects research must be distinguished from 'social atomism':

In media effects research, 'the main object of attention is the individual and his relationship to the mass media', but the adoption of such a form of investigation does not entail any particular view of how the individual is related to other members of society—and certainly not an atomistic one (Open University, 1977: 6).

However, Blumler does in fact adopt an essentially atomistic political theory in which individual voters make political decisions issue by issue and he is led to this position by data which does indeed reflect a society in which, for reasons that we will examine, people are being driven into a position of social atomism and into a politics that results from that atomism. This general line of thought starts with Blumler and McQuail in *TV in Politics* (1967) in which they argue on the basis of their audience research for a shift away from broadcasting as a platform for party rhetoric and more towards its use as a window through which the voter can get a true view of the political arena. This position was then further developed by Katz in his famous essay *Platforms and Windows* where he argued that 'Again and again, one is led to the conclusion that election campaigns are better designed to serve the political parties, particularly the dominant ones, than to serve society or the voter—if the liberal desiderata of optimizing rationality and participation are accepted' (Katz, 1972: 369–370).

While, in CEB, Katz's extreme anti-party, pro-broadcaster position is explicitly rejected, perhaps, as the authors half admit, out of a pragmatic policy need to win party support for their proposals, there is little question that a consistent theme in the Blumler position is a negative valuation of the political party, and a corresponding positive valuation of the non-partisan individual voter who, in Katz's words, 'wants, in return for his investment of time, the feeling that he has fulfilled his duty as a citizen by orienting and updating himself to the political situation. He wants to be able to identify the candidates and the issues; he wants the issues clearly and interestingly explained; he wants to know where parties stand with respect to the issues and how these stands are likely to effect him' (Katz, 1972: 363).

Paralleling this positive vision of the rational individual voter, supposedly constructed from empirical research in the Uses and Gratifications tradition, is placed an equally consistent negative valuation of politicians and the political party.

Realism dictates, and experience demonstrates, that at campaign time the top priority of the parties is to conquer power not to disseminate enlightenment. Left to their own devices, they may side-step awkward issues, fail to give an ordered picture of the issue agenda, slant facts and figures in their favour, declaim in high generalities, and try to deflect attention away from their own policies to their opponents short-comings (CEB, p. 68).

Since large scale industrial societies have found no substitute for representation as the mechanism of democratic participation; since, that is to say, political action cannot be carried out by direct citizen participation and since also coherent political action in a world of interconnections cannot be carried out either on the basis of single issues and isolated yes/no decisions or without organized support, any withdrawal of the political party as the organizing instrument requires the substitution of an alternative mechanism of representation, which in the Katz/Blumler model is to be found explicitly in public service broadcasting. As CEB puts it, 'Broadcasters should act as trustees of the voters campaign information needs' (CEB, p. 68).

Blumler and Gurevitch indeed explicitly contrast the broadcaster to the political party in a way which, within their liberal theory, clearly endorses the broadcaster's role as opposed to the politician's: 'The centrality of the service function in the behaviour of media professionals is reflected in the claim commonly made by them to be concerned primarily to serve the audience members' "right to know", as distinct from the primary concern of the politician to persuade them in the course of political and partisan goals' (Blumler and Gurevitch, 1977). There is no inkling here that politicians and political parties exercise a representative function and that they are not primarily persuaders but spokesmen for and articulators of group or class interests, while broadcasters, as the empirical evidence shows, represent none but themselves. Although as we shall see, Blumler recognizes this problem, he ultimately endorses the Katz view of the broadcaster's role on the grounds that it is consonant with available evidence as to what voters want.

But how should the attempt of the BBC current affairs producers to contribute to election broadcasting policy in 1966 be evaluated? This observer found it acceptable, for the overriding aim was to use television to achieve a more revealing campaign than the political parties were likely to provide through their unaided efforts. And that is consistent with a function which viewers themselves wish television to discharge in its coverage of an election campaign (Blumler, 1970).

Before reviewing the general empirical evidence in this field and Blumler's interpretation of this evidence, let us first examine the claim made above. It and similar claims in CEB are based upon work within a Uses and Gratifications framework carried out by Blumler and McQuail in the UK and McLeod and Becker in the USA. This research was concerned to find out not what effect political broadcasting had on viewers but, on the contrary, why viewers watched political broadcasting. Viewers' responses to this line of enquiry were then gathered into four audience role clusters; the monitor, the spectator, the partisan and the liberal citizen.[2] In brief, the monitor wants to see what politicians are, or are likely to be, up to. In Katz's words 'they want to know "what will happen" to them and/or their country (Katz, 1972: 360). The spectator wants to watch a good fight, the partisan 'to use the information as ammunition in arguments with others' and the liberal citizen (a phrase of significant valuation) wants help in making up his mind how to vote. The evidence showed that monitors and liberal citizens, that is to say those in search of neutral information, were in a clear majority and that partisans 'comprised a distinctive and possibly declining minority' (Blumler, 1977: 15). On the assumption that viewers are

[2] For a review of this research, see Blumler (1977).

rational in these role choices, Blumler then consistently argues that broadcast political communication must be designed to appeal to this vast majority of monitors and liberal citizens who want information, a new version in fact of 'giving the people what they want'. The first question Blumler's evidence raises is what kind of rationality does this viewer wish for what Blumler has dubbed 'surveillance' express? In my view it can best be explained as the rational response to perceived powerlessness. It is essentially defensive and protective and is closely allied to the increased disenchantment with politics reflected in the decline of voter turn-out and surveys of viewers' attitudes to political communication. As we shall see this measured viewer response is a crucial symptom of the kind of coverage given to politics in particular and to views of the world in general by TV, that is to say it is a distant, strange and threatening world out there which one confronts as a relatively isolated and powerless individual. It is, in fact, an expression of an internalized rational response to the reality of TV agenda setting. But Blumler never asks why people use TV in this way. He accepts it as a *fait accompli*. But the failure to ask this question leads to an acceptance of the surface evidence as a validation of a process that then becomes self-justifying and self-reinforcing.

Moreover if one raises an even more central question, what is politics about?, one can, I think, reasonably claim that the responses of individual viewers as expressed to the Users and Gratification researchers are irrational, an expression precisely of false consciousness. In a revealing phrase Blumler describes politics as 'the competition-through-communication that is waged in a democratic pluralist society' (Blumler, 1977: 18). But nowhere in his work is there any hint of what this competition might be about. This lack is most clearly expressed in his essay with Gurevitch, 'Linkages between Mass-Media and Politics', in which they enunciate a so-called systems approach to political communication research which is totally devoid of any political content. Given Blumler's career, with its long, close and honourable connection with the British Labour movement, this remains to me a surprising and inexplicable lacuna, perhaps related precisely to the value-free biases of the effects research tradition. Be that as it may, if one undertakes work on political communication from the assumption that politics is a process concerned with the preservation or elimination of systematic and structured inequalities, in short, that it is about class conflict, however such conflict may be mediated and disguised, one is then led to interpret Blumler's data as the perfectly explicable expression of a familiar ideological formation, that social atomism and its related 'possessive individualism', which is objectively against the class interests of those expressing it and which is, as we have seen, also one of the principal methodological biases of which effects research has been accused. When we now come to examine other available evidence we will see the crucial role that TV appears to play in the development and maintenance of that very ideological formation, a formation that is undoubtedly concretely there and that therefore is measured by Blumler's effects research.

In Blumler's presentation of the argument, not only in CEB but also in Appendix E of the Annan Report, it is very difficult to tell at times, in a characteristic positivistic ideological operation, where presentation of the evidence ends and theoretical and normative interpretation comes into play. In his defence of empiricism and attack on 'grand theory' Blumler states:

Although effects investigators are still committed to the task of finding out how people actually react to mass communication . . . such investigators now fully accept that (a) the media constitute but one factor in society among a host of other influential variables, (b) the exertion of their influence may depend upon the presence of other facilitating circumstances and (c) the extent and direction of media influence may vary across different groups and individuals.

They are not innocent of theory, though they do tend to assign it a more modest role than the rather ambitious task given it by more wide ranging thinkers . . . In their eyes the accumulation of knowledge is more like a step-by-step venture than the attainment of some comprehensive illuminating weltanschauung all at once . . . secure gains are more likely to be won by working within the bounds of some carefully delineated territory . . . It may even be suspected that those who protest so vociferously about the limitations of empiricism only manifest thereby their own determination to keep out of the way of awkward facts (Open University, 1977: 6–8).

But in effect, as I hope to demonstrate, Blumler is himself guilty, in his interpretation of the available data, of neglecting the wider context that he claims effects investigators now take into account and as a result he neglects 'awkward facts'. This neglect stems precisely from a too careful delineation of his territory and the granting of too modest a role to theory. Whether this neglect stems from intellectual conviction or from the tactical necessities of his version of policy research it is difficult to say. But the result is that in CEB he overlooks or suppresses interpretations that he shows elsewhere he knows exist and so ends up involved in a self-fulfilling prophecy of profound political significance, because by positivistically interpreting his effects data, he may in fact be contributing to the creation of those very effects. That is to say that many of the voter characteristics upon which he calls as support for his position that the broadcasters should play a greater role in the electoral process and the political parties a lesser role (for this is in effect what his proposals amount to), while no doubt flattering to the broadcasters who commission his research, may be reinforcing the very trends he is measuring.

Let us then look at the available evidence and how it can be interpreted. The earlier tradition of empirical political effects studies came to the conclusion that party loyalties stemmed from family and class, that they were relatively stable, that the mass media during election campaigns served to activate voters, i.e. it effected turn-out rather than attitudes and reinforced existing political loyalties through the phenomenon of selective perception. As Blumler himself puts it, 'a key lynch pin of this edifice of interpretation . . . concerned the role of party loyalty in mass electoral psychology' (Blumler, 1977: 3). The 'new look in political communication research' thus stems from the growing evidence across a range of established bourgeois democracies of electoral volatility. This volatility not only makes election campaigns more crucial, since there are more 'floating voters' to be won, but evidence also shows that in those election campaigns the influence of the media, especially television, is independently important. In the past, evidence showed that floating voters, because they also possessed low political motivation, were those least likely to be reached by political communication via the mass media, whereas evidence now shows that floating voters may also be high consumers of political communication, especially on TV. Indeed, TV seems to have played a key role in this, because 'large numbers of people are watching election broadcasts not because they are interested in politics, but because they like viewing television' (Katz, 1972: 359). However, there has also developed, over recent elections, a clear trend of declining turn-out and a growing antipathy to all political communication and indeed to the politics about which that communication attempts to talk.[3]

Blumler's response to this evidence is not just to recognize it, but to give it normative endorsement, as we have seen. That is to say, since the evidence points to an

[3] See Blumler (1977), CEB and Open University (1977) for details of this evidence.

increasingly non-partisan, issue oriented public, since the public says that, in general, it wishes to use television to gather political information and to monitor the political process, then policy proposals must aim to give them what they apparently want and this will be good for democracy. Since party loyalty is on the wane, the role of the parties in political communication must be diminished and in their place must be put the broadcasters who, working with their inherited traditions of neutrality, impartiality and fairness, will hold the political ring, and make sure the issues are presented and clarified so that individual voters can reach a rational decision on the issues.

That this is not a necessary interpretation of the available data, even from within a shared liberal-pluralist perspective, can be seen if we turn to the work of Seymour-Ure, who advocates a diametrically opposed solution to the problem of election broadcasting, one with the general trend of which I agree, namely that the decline of direct party access to TV should be massively reversed and that in order to balance any increased freedom for the broadcasters in their watchdog role, regular current affairs time throughout the year with matching resources should be handed over to the political parties (Seymour-Ure, 1974, chs 6, 7 and 8).

Seymour-Ure arrives at this diametrically opposed conclusion for three crucially important reasons: (a) he regards the political party and not the individual voter as central to the political system, (b) he also considers the relationship between broadcasting and newspapers and (c) because he approaches the problem historically. In brief, Seymour-Ure argues that historically there is a close and important relationship between political parties and the press; that what evidence there is shows both that parties of change have a greater need for what he calls a parallel press, i.e. a press with which the party has some degree of ideological convergence if not actual control over, and that at the same time in advanced industrial democracies left-wing parties have less than their fair share of press parallelism: that there is a tendency towards conflict politics where you find press parallelism and towards consensus politics where you don't: that there has been a steady decline in press partisanship in Britain ever since the so-called Northcliffe revolution, a shift in the nature of the press the consequences of which he describes as 'overwhelmingly conservative': that possibly with a cause and effect relationship the press and statutorily non-partisan broadcasting have converged in this respect. He foresees further convergence and, so far as broadcasting is concerned, the symptoms of such a convergence are remarkably close to what Blumler actively advocates, namely 'broadcast programmes increasingly free of rules imposed from outside about party balance at election time: and an orientation in current affairs broadcasting that was similar to what has been called positive criticism in the press'. But his judgment on the effects of such a convergence are harsh:

Such convergence could cause serious dislocation in the political system. It is debatable whether political parties can effectively sustain mass support without the opportunity for their leaders to project themselves and their policies as they themselves wish, and whether general elections can operate as an instrument of effective representation in the absence of well organised and coherent parties (Seymour-Ure, 1974: 237).

This is part of the answer to a challenge that Blumler has made to the 'grand theorists'. After reviewing (Open University, 1977: 37–41) the evidence presented by Lang and Lang (1966), by Robinson (1976) and by Miller et al. (1976), that the domination of television has contributed to the citizens' general distrust of politics, Blumler asks,

How do these conclusions contrast with the views of Murdoch and Golding that the mass media are essentially agents of legitimation, that is, forces that maintain 'the central assumptions and values of the ruling or core ideology, which in turn sustain the prevailing social and political order' (Open University, 1977: 41).

Blumler assumes that the answer to his question is that the empirical evidence conflicts with this more Marxist view, when he goes on to answer himself:

Perhaps this provides an illustration of the confrontation between 'grand theory' untested by effects research designs and empirical work, which strives so to operationalize speculative hypotheses that their validity can be independently checked against a set of relevant facts (Open University, 1977: 41).

But Murdoch and Golding and those who think like them cannot so easily be driven from the field. In the first place, as Seymour-Ure shows, the effect of this delegitimation has a differential effect on rival political forces and parties. It is a delegitimation that acts precisely to reinforce consensus. It is the parties of change that are worst affected. Moreover, it can be plausibly hypothesized that this general distrust of politics stems, at least in part, from the way in which television sets, not only the content agenda, but also the form agenda, the way in which it approaches politics in general. Its tendency to break politics down issue by issue rather than on a basis of coherent ideologies, the fact that it reaches people individually or in small groups in their homes rather than at work. The inherent ideology of non-partisanship then reinforces the general professional anti-government ideology of media practitioners based upon notions of the Fourth Estate. If then one looks at the growing evidence that it is the control of these practitioners over the long term issue agenda which is politically crucial; it can be plausibly argued that TV in both its form and its content reinforces a general political theory or ideology that sees the State as separate from and inferior to civil society and so both reinforces the existing power structure of economic inequality in civil society and at the political level supports those parties or those elements within parties who favour less State intervention. And I think it is clear in contemporary British politics which side that favours.

It is within an analytical context of this sort that one needs to look at the tension between the Labour Party and the BBC. As both Grace Wyndham-Goldie (1977) from within, and Butler and Stokes (1966) from without, recognize, the Labour Party looked upon party access to broadcasting as a means of counteracting the general bias against them in the press. As the evidence marshalled by Seymour-Ure shows, they were not wrong so to do. Indeed one of the key results of Blumler's own study of a group of Leeds first time voters was to show the crucial effect of press partisanship upon voter turn-out. In that study it was the partisanship of those papers that supported Labour which helped to stop potential Conservative voters actually voting (Blumler and McLeod, 1974). But since that study was done the crucial partisanship change has been that of the *Sun*, which, on Blumler's evidence, should act as a potent motivator of abstention among potential working-class labour voters. So not only were the Labour Party not wrong, their need for this counterweight has grown stronger as their effective access to TV has declined. Where they were wrong, however, was in believing that public service broadcasting as at present structured could fulfil this function, for it is the very non-partisan nature of broadcasting that works against the Labour Party's necessary ideological commitment to social change. Blumler is himself honest and perceptive enough to recognize this, when he is not writing specifically for broadcaster consumption, as he avowedly is in CEB. Elsewhere he writes:

Since broadcasting may not support individual parties, it is obliged to adhere to such non-partisan—perhaps even anti-partisan—standards as fairness, impartiality, neutrality and measured choice—at the expense, then, of such alternative values as commitment, consistent loyalty and a forthright readiness to take sides. Thus television may tend to put staunch partisans on the defensive and help to legitimate the less certain attitudes of those who feel that a conditional and wary commitment is the outlook most appropriate to a model citizen (Blumler, 1977: 13).

Blumler's avoidance in CEB of his own 'awkward question' is symptomatic both of his general attitude to broadcasters and of the limitations of his version of policy research. That is to say he has for a long time largely endorsed the broadcasters' own view of their role, both out of a personal sympathy and because it chimes in both with his general liberal-pluralist political theory and with his resulting interpretation of the empirical evidence. This is clear in his 1966 study of 'Producers' Attitudes Towards Television Coverage of an Election Campaign', in Appendix E to the Annan Report an d even more clearly in CEB. But there it is in part tactical and his adoption of it does, I think, well illustrate the dangers of attempting to narrow research policy research to those areas of policy and those policy recommendations the broadcasters can accept. This is an issue of wide general importance in the political struggle to make broadcasting more accountable. Blumler himself recommended, in his evidence to Annan, the setting up of a Broadcasting Centre to carry out independent research as part of the accountability structure of British Broadcasting. Annan rejected this and similar proposals on the extraordinary grounds that they were 'sceptical whether research which is not commissioned by those responsible for decision taking is likely to be of direct use in making policy decisions' (Report of the Committee on the Future of Broadcasting, 1977, para 6.25, p. 63). The recent Government White Paper follows this lead. There seems little doubt that the kind of policy research exemplified by CEB reinforces this entrenchment of broadcaster autonomy and of the persistence of closed government in our broadcasting system. This point relates to the criticism levelled at Katz's recent report on broadcasting research by Professor Halloran, among others (*Journal of Communication*, 1978). And it is perhaps not without significance that Blumler was the only British researcher to be favoured with a commission among those projects set up by the BBC following the publication of the Katz report. Perhaps the core of Blumler's position on this matter is expressed in his Annan Appendix, where having reviewed research evidence that, as he puts it, 'casts fundamental doubts on the viability of a philosophy that pins its faith on the development of a sense of responsibility among mass media executives and staff communicators themselves to ensure that higher expectations of public service are met', he then goes on to argue that 'the attitudes of television and radio journalists matter, . . . because no proposal for change could possibly succeed in the teeth of professional resistance' (Blumler, 1977: 22).

But what I would wish to argue is that the Blumler strategy and the reading of the empirical evidence that stems from it is excessively concerned to avoid such resistance. This is particularly damaging in the policy context under discussion where, as we have seen, much of the evidence points precisely to broadcasters, or the present structure and behaviour of broadcasting institutions, as being a central part of the problem. Now of course neither Blumler or the broadcasters would deny this. But they would and do define the problem, as a result of their position, in a particular way and in a way which leads Blumler in his role as policy researcher to ignore important evidence which, from other contexts, one knows he recognizes to be important.

Thus, in his Annan Appendix, he recognizes the need to see broadcasting in relation to the press, but as we have seen, fails, when advising the broadcasters, to pursue the logic of that recognition. But, above all, there he also recognizes the increasing importance within 'new look' political communication research of the 'cognitive approach', an approach which clearly leads to conclusions opposed to those advocated in CEB. In brief, this 'cognitive approach' has shifted the attention of effects researchers away from persuasion and attitude change and towards information perception. This new trend demonstrates not the opposition between empirical effects research and 'grand theory', but its increasing convergence for it is, within a different intellectual tradition, really just another version of the general study of ideology.

As Becker, McCombs and McLeod have pointed out, 'Most of the resources of newspapers and news-staffs of television and radio stations are devoted to information transmittal, not persuasion, (quoted in Blumler, 1977: 7). That is to say, the media help, by providing the informational building blocks, to structure views of the world, views towards which people may have a variety of attitudes and from which may stem a range of actions. But, nonetheless, these structured views of the world, or ideologies, do lay certain limits upon the range of attitudes that people can adopt.

Within this tradition emphasis has been placed upon the agenda-setting function of the mass media: 'Thus more emphasis is now being placed on how the media project definitions of the situation that political actors must cope with than on attitudes towards those actors themselves' (Becker, McCombs and McLeod, 1975). As Blumler himself puts it:

Newsmen in the several mass media are engaged in propagating images of political reality that few people can challenge for lack of first-hand experience. And in so far as reporting of news topics achieves a consonance that excludes alternative perspectives, to that extent is the chance increased that an influence will be exerted on how audience members think about them' (Blumler, 1977: 8).

So we have a situation in which current empirical research seems to be consonant with the study of ideology within the 'grand theory' tradition in putting forward the following explanation of how political communication in Britain is actually working.

(a) Because of increased electoral volatility, itself in part created by the dominance of TV, the mass media possess an increased potential for political influence.

(b) This influence is exerted, as much between as during elections by the media setting their own issue agenda.

(c) This agenda is in part mediated via 'news values' that are a highly artificial social construct and are in general supportive of the *status quo*.

(d) The agenda is also set by the very non-partisan nature of TV itself, which not only projects a consensus, socially atomized view of the world, but also leads to a sense of trust that reinforces this influence. As Blumler puts it, 'Where overt persuasion is recognized, its [the audiences'] guard may tend to be raised. But mass media content may be received in a less sceptical spirit if it purports to shed an informative light on political events and how these could impinge on voters 'personal circumstances' (Blumler, 1977: 13).

(e) Broadcasters have little real idea of the needs and values of their audience, but construct their agenda under the influence of institutional, peer-group and class pressures (Blumler, 1977: 7).[4]

All this evidence would seem to point to the conclusion that since the role of the agenda set by TV is crucial, the setting of that agenda must be brought more squarely into the political arena. And yet Blumler proposes the opposite, an even more autonomous role for the broadcasters in setting the issue agenda during election

[4] See especially Tracy (1977), McQuail (1969), Elliott (1972) and Burns (1977).

campaigns. They will, for instance, if his reforms are carried out, immediately be allowed to challenge the parties' own statement of their case. 'Normal' news values will operate in campaign reporting rather than the present strict 'balance'. I imagine that there are no other serious mass communication researchers, with the possible exception of Katz, who would at this time and on the available evidence join Blumler, Gurevitch and Ives in their call for greater broadcaster autonomy in this field. Interestingly, Grace Wyndham-Goldie, the doyen of BBC political coverage, who might have been expected to share Blumler's views, in fact argues consistently and cogently against them and warns broadcasters that they will take over more power from the politicians at their peril. But then she has a proper respect for the calling of politics and is clear that broadcasting is there at its sufferance to serve it, not vice-versa. Unfortunately, her solution to the dilemmas of political communication, the television coverage of Parliament, seems inadequate to the problem.

To criticize Blumler is not to deny that there is a serious problem. Anthony Smith has pointed out the extent to which TV is now a crucial institution within the political process; 'the broadcasting environment of a society is an element in the political environment and has responsibilities to it, not merely to reflect it but to sustain it' (Smith, 1978: 96) and this because it provides 'the basic structure by which politicians communicate with people' (Smith, 1978: 98). But a recognition of this leads to a major challenge to broadcasting institutions, to their present relationship to the political system and to the whole liberal-pluralist theory within which Blumler (and indeed Anthony Smith) works. That Blumler avoids the most reasonable approach to solution of the problem because of this theoretical disposition is clear from his Annan Appendix where he writes: 'It is extremely difficult to conceive a promising strategy for raising journalistic standards in the news media. We lack confidence in policies of authoritative intervention into mass-media affairs and in the likely consequences of supporting an unfettered exercise of media freedom. The former runs unacceptable political risks and is at odds with long-established liberal tradition' (Blumler, 1977: 22). He thus in effect puts his name to proposals that would lead us further down the road to unfettered media freedom.

So, in short, the lessons that I would like to draw from this examination of Dr Blumler's recent work are the following.

(a) The conflict within British mass media research should not be defined, as Blumler attempts to define it, as one between empiricism and theory, but as one between different political and social theories and their differing interpretations of the empirical evidence. Judgment between those theories should be based both upon their normative presuppositions and upon the cogency of their differing interpretations.

(b) Mass-media researchers do indeed have policy responsibilities. Not only are they examining the workings of an important contemporary social institution with social consequences, but their findings will be used, often unscrupulously, in the battles over policy, whether they wish it or not. However, a commitment to the policy implications of their research must not lead them to define policy research in such a way as to allow the vested interests to define their questions or their area of inquiry or in such a way as to see 'realistic' policy proposals as those which will be acceptable to their vested interests in the short term and without a struggle. It is always dangerous in such an undertaking to try and guess what will be acceptable and it can act as a distraction from the very real difficulties of working out and then fighting for what you believe to be true.

As Morris Janowitz wrote in his introduction to a book which ironically also con-

3

tains one of Blumler's most important recent studies: 'Social policy-making is enriched by an admixture of the search for broad hypotheses and a recognition of the concrete and specific context. The assessment of the causal patterns and sequences in a particular social setting investigated by survey research, supplies no mechanical guidelines to other circumstances; each application must involve reasoned judgments beyond the findings of social research. In fact to isolate patterns of influence does not necessarily indicate the likeliest and most legitimate approach for social intervention and social policy, which requires political imagination, moral conviction and the ability to create new solutions and build institutions without being confined to the patterns of influence which have operated in the past. But the essential component of survey research findings, grounded in some elements of sociological theory, is that they offer alternative explanations as a basis for estimating the consequences of various social policies' (see Blumler and McLeod, 1974: 12).

Bibliography

BECKER, L. B., MCCOMBS, M. E. and MCLEOD, J. M. (1975). In Chaffee, S. H., Ed., *The Development of Political Communication*, Sage, London

BLUMLER, J. (1970). Producers' attitudes towards coverage of an election campaign, in Tunstall, J., Ed., *Media Sociology*, Constable, London, p. 418

BLUMLER, J. (1977). The intervention of TV in British politics, *Report of the Committee on Broadcasting*, Cmnd 6753-1, Appendix E

BLUMLER, J. and GUREVITCH, M. (1977). Linkages between mass media and politics, in Curran, J., Gurevitch, M. and Woollacott, J., Eds, *Mass Communication and Society*, Arnold, London, p. 281

BLUMLER, J., GUREVITCH, M. and IVES, J. (1978). *The Challenge of Election Broadcasting*, Leeds University Press

BLUMLER, J. and MCLEOD, J. M. (1974). Communication and voter turn-out in Britain, in Leggatt, T., Ed., *Sociological Theory and Survey Research*, Sage, London

BLUMLER, J. and MCQUAIL, O. (1967). *TV in Politics*, Faber and Faber, London

BURNS, T. (1977). *The BBC: Public Institution and Private World*, Macmillan, London

BUTLER, D. E. and KING, A. (1966). *The British General Election of 1966*, Macmillan, London

ELLIOTT, P. (1972). *The Making of a TV Series*, Constable, London

GLASGOW UNIVERSITY MEDIA GROUP (1976). *Bad News*, Routledge and Kegan Paul, London

Journal of Communication (1978). Vol. 28, no. 2, Spring

KATZ, E. (1972). Platforms and windows, in McQuail, D., Ed., *Sociology of Mass-Communication*, Penguin, Harmondsworth

LANG, K. and LANG, G. (1966). The mass media and voting, in Berelson, B. and Janowitz, M., Eds, *Reader in Public Opinion and Communication*, The Free Press, New York

MCQUAIL, D. (1969). Uncertainty about the audience and the organisation of mass-communication, in Halmos, P., Ed., *The Sociology of Mass Media Communicators*, University of Keele Press

MILLER, A. H., ERBRING, L. and GOLDENBURG, E. (1976). Type-set politics: impact of newspapers on issue salience and public confidence, paper presented to the Annual Meeting of the American Political Science Association

OPEN UNIVERSITY (1977). *Mass Communication and Society, Unit Eight*

Report of the Committee on the Future of Broadcasting (1977). Cmnd 6753

ROBINSON, M. J. (1976). American political legitimacy in an era of electronic journalism, in Cater, D. and Adler, R., Eds, *Television as a Social Force*, Martin Robertson, London

SEYMOUR-URE, C. (1974). *The Impact of the Mass Media*, Constable, London

SMITH, A. (1978). *The Politics of Information*, Macmillan, London

TRACY, M. (1977). The absent framework: the audience–communicator relationship, in *The Production of Political TV*, RKP, Ch. 7

WYNDHAM-GOLDIE, G. (1977). *Facing the Nation. TV and Politics 1936–76*, The Bodley Head, London

47

THE REFORM OF ELECTION BROADCASTING
A Reply to Nicholas Garnham

Jay G. Blumler and Michael Gurevitch

When writing *The Challenge of Election Broadcasting*,[1] which was criticized by Nicholas Garnham in the previous issue of this journal, we (together with our co-author, Julian Ives) were guided by three underlying assumptions.

One was that merely cosmetic tinkering—introducing an extra programme idea here or a new form of debate there—would not suffice to overcome the deep-seated dilemmas and problems surrounding the role of television in British election campaigns. Fundamental reforms, including some re-structuring of relationships between politicians and professional broadcasters, were required. A second assumption was that academic researchers should play a constructive part in proposing lines of change. They should not merely criticize existing practices but should also recommend new measures that stood some chance of being adopted. And thirdly, we were influenced by an assumption about the *inter-connectedness* of political communication patterns. Election broadcasting forms part of a wider system, including at least party spokesmen, professional mass media personnel, and audience members, the traditional programme formats and communication styles to which they have become accustomed, the form of political system to which these are related, as well as influential ideas about the functions that political communications do and should serve in our society. In our view, this last assumption rules out what might be termed single-minded approaches to reform—ones that disregard how change at one point in the system may provoke reactions elsewhere, or that ignore the need for change to be accepted by all the elements which are inevitably involved in operating the system.[2]

So far as we can tell, Nicholas Garnham accepts the first two of our assumptions but completely rejects—even fails to *notice*—the third. Single-mindedly, he supposes that all our political broadcasting ills can be cured by giving the political parties massive grants of free air time, while firmly subordinating professional broadcasters to politicians' dictates. In contrast, we say that a reformed system of election broadcasting should be designed to solve many problems, meet many needs, and satisfy many interests.

Nevertheless, we welcome Nicholas Garnham's attempted critique of CEB. However else they differ, most media scholars in this country are in some sense committed and engaged—are prepared, that is, to mix their academic and civic roles. More open debate amongst ourselves, especially when focused on such a crucial test

* Centre for Television Research, The University of Leeds, Leeds LS2 9JT.
† Faculty of Social Sciences, The Open University, England.
[1] Hereinafter referred to as CEB.
[2] Previous writings in which the authors have developed their perspective on political communication at length include Gurevitch and Blumler (1977) and Blumler and Gurevitch (1975).

case as election television, should clarify the opportunities and pitfalls we face when struggling to influence broadcasting policy. This reply—which aims to advance the dialogue as well—will be developed in three parts. First, since Garnham has grossly misrepresented our own position, we wish to show how, and ask why, he has managed to state it so falsely. Second, we argue that Garnham has misunderstood the problem of election broadcasting reform, a central issue here turning on the fabric of interests that political television should serve and how they can be most usefully related to each other. Finally, we conclude with some observations on the strategy of policy research.

I

According to Garnham, CEB is an anti-party manifesto. Its point of departure, he maintains, is a preoccupation with the audience, and particularly with the recent growth within it of large numbers of volatile and sceptical voters, who find the main partisan power-contenders singularly uninspiring. CEB, then, not only treats their existence as a fact of political life (it is said), but also regards their outlook as a positive source of value to be respected and catered for. Consequently, CEB is alleged to take their side against the political parties—for example, by recommending a sharp curtailment of the parties' rights of access to broadcasting, while elevating the role of professional broadcasters, regarded as defenders of the interests of the new breed of disgruntled and anti-political citizens, at the parties' expense. CEB is also said to rest on dubious appeals to 'realism' (about what many viewers expect from and dislike about political programmes), almost proposing to give the detached voters merely 'what they want'. Finally, we are accused of having allowed both the questions we raised and the solutions we recommended to be determined and limited by what broadcasters would find acceptable.

As Garnham puts it, 'a constant theme in the Blumler position is a negative valuation of the political party and a corresponding positive valuation of the non-partisan individual voter'. He claims that we recommend a 'withdrawal of the political party as the organising instrument' of political communication and the installation of 'public service broadcasting' as 'an alternative medium of representation'. We want broadcasters 'to play a greater role in the electoral process and the parties a lesser role'. Again, 'since party loyalty is on the wane, the role of the parties in political communication must be diminished in setting the issue agenda during election campaigns', leading us, as a result, 'further down the road to unfettered media freedom'.

Yet this account is a travesty of CEB's position. It is at least as selective and distorted as is the picture of trade union activity that broadcasters are often accused of propagating in their news and current affairs programmes! It is true that we urge both politicians and broadcasters to take full account of the declining power of inherited party loyalties to determine how people vote, feel about major issues, and react to political messages. Of that form of 'realism', we are unashamedly 'guilty'. But even this stance involves no pandering to *anti*-political instincts. As one of us put it in an essay published three years ago, '. . . there is no easy way out of our present communication difficulties unless politicians learn to address their listeners not so much as committed loyalists, nor so much as manipulable floaters, but more as would-be "problem solvers" instead' (Blumler, 1975).

In any case, CEB tackled at least three major problems that the political parties face when presenting their ideas to the public on television. Because Garnham has not faced up to them, he cannot begin to offer a way out of the parties' current communication predicaments.

One of our concerns was *to revitalize the principle of free party access to broadcasting*. Although lip service is often paid to this principle, little enthusiasm and much contempt is shown for the particular genre in which it is clothed in Britain, namely the ten-minute party broadcast. In CEB we cite this as 'the political advocacy dilemma', which we define in the following terms:

As the seekers of electoral support, what the parties wish to tell voters in their own way deserves pride of place in a public service broadcasting system. Yet the format through which this principle has traditionally been applied seems at best to have earned a grudging tolerance and at worst to have invited much ridicule and disbelief (p. 42).

Does Garnham deny the existence of such a dilemma? If not, how exactly would he resolve it? For all his professed regard for practical policy prescriptions, we can find no answer in what he has written.

A second concern was to ensure that *political talk on TV will be heeded by those for whom it is intended*. Does Garnham agree that this is at risk nowadays, and if so, what does he think should be done about it? It is solely in this context that CEB adopts the language of realism, as the following passage patently demonstrates:

. . . we decided to place our diagnosis within the context of a realistic analysis of recent political trends affecting the audience's reception of election messages. In that way we hoped to lend urgency to the campaign reform quest. The public mood about political talk has become so ambivalent in recent years that we cannot afford to be complacent about any of its less appetising features (p. 12).

Thirdly, we sought to protect the integrity of political messages from inexorable '*trivialisation due to pressures to adapt to the demands of television* [*news*]' (p. 7). This too is a problem that Garnham appears to ignore—unless he imagines that it can somehow be by-passed by giving the political parties yet longer broadcasts. But the parties are not asking for longer programmes, would not know how to use the extra time if it was granted, and have more often sought permission to transmit *shorter* broadcasts (five-minute ones). Meanwhile, the trivialization process is deeply embedded, not only in how newscasters work, but also in the parties' responses to the public dislike of unadulterated propaganda. This point is aptly illustrated by the remark of the leading politician we interviewed, who, after pointing out that viewers heavily discount party broadcasts, went on:

That is why I believe in getting your message into the news, providing in your speech or whatever it may be you can get across this one point you are trying to make (p. 31).

Our approach to these problems was at no stage animated by an anti-party or anti-political spirit. As we clearly state on p. 21:

In principle, it is between the rival parties and their candidates that voters must choose at election time. If their contribution to campaigning is unsatisfactory, then the first priority of reform must be to seek ways of changing *that*. It is no solution to that particular problem to tilt the balance of communication activity yet further towards a body of electorally non-responsible middle men.

Later on (p. 68) we argue that election broadcasting should be shaped by two operating principles, both equally legitimate and indispensable. And although the second of these holds broadcasters responsible for serving certain viewer needs, the first maintains that, '. . . there must be sufficient outlets in broadcasting to enable the parties to state their views on the campaign issues fully and in their own way without interference from other elements'. That is why we claim in numerous other passages that our proposals are 'in the best interests of politicians and broadcasters alike' (p. 9) and 'in line with the enlightened long-term interests of the politicians and the broadcasters themselves' (p. 13).

Similarly, many of our practical proposals were deliberately fashioned to help the political parties. Of course there is room for argument over whether they would achieve this end and would satisfactorily meet the parties' needs. That is why we hoped that a pilot test could be given to some of our ideas in advance of the next election campaign. But it is simply not possible to contend that we were trying to do the parties down. On the contrary, we wished to restore their position through such suggestions as the following:

(1) Each passage of party broadcasting should immediately be followed by some form of scrutiny of the case developed in it, which, though organized under broadcasters' editorial control, would include representatives of the party concerned. This proposal was intended not only to ensure that party programmes have 'something for everyone' in the TV audience and that party arguments are taken as serious points of departure for further discussion. It also aimed to harness the producers' current affairs efforts more closely than hitherto to the election issues as initially defined by the parties.

(2) Election reporting in news bulletins should be drastically reduced. Instead, the bulk of election news coverage should appear in a nightly programme of campaign analysis. This proposal was not only designed to combat the sterile repetitiousness of much snippety news reporting. It also aimed to relieve the pressure on the political parties to plant a series of 'golden nuggets' each and every night into the news within the time constraints imposed by a maximum item length of about two minutes.

(3) Such a news analysis programme should regularly (perhaps three to five times in a campaign) provide a home for a *Campaign Review* item, in which party representatives, under a moderator, would discuss those events of election relevance that had broken into the news in the preceding few days. This recommendation would give the parties a guaranteed slot, in which they could react in a considered way to those dramatic happenings that habitually disrupt a campaign and throw one or another of the parties off balance.

(4) The BBC should give far more generous production assistance to the political parties for making their broadcasts. These should be given a new title— *Election Access*—to highlight the analogy with the broadcasting rights of other groups in such programmes as *Open Door*.

What is strange, then, is not CEB's point of view, but how comprehensively it has been misconstrued by Garnham. This is because he has read our book through his own ideological spectacles instead of trying to grasp our position in its own terms. Garnham classifies us (correctly) as upholders of a liberal-democratic/pluralist position, so far as media involvement in politics is concerned. *A priori* he considers that such a position is bound to favour broadcaster autonomy and to devalue and diminish the role of the political parties. He then looks for evidence to support this interpretation. Yet he has attacked us on false grounds, for, as we have tried to illustrate above, we agree with Garnham that broadcaster autonomy should not be entrenched at the expense of the parties' interests. It is true that we defend broadcaster autonomy and that we think political communication should have something to offer undecided voters when making up their minds how to cast a ballot. But it does not follow that because we are 'for' such interests, we must be 'against' party interests. On the contrary, we are looking for ways of bringing all legitimate political communication interests into line with each other. This leads us to the second stage of our argument.

II

How should the policy-minded researcher approach the task of election broadcasting reform? Garnham's answer seems to reflect the slogan, 'You cannot serve two communication masters at once'. The interests of party politicians and professional broadcasters are wholly opposed, and the researcher must choose between them. Garnham sides with the parties against the broadcasters for a curious mixture of 'realistic' and 'normative' reasons. Realistically, he believes that broadcast output serves political ends, and he wants this to be made manifest. Yet he also wants the broadcasters to be brought even more effectively under political party control than at present, since, unlike the politicians, broadcasters are not representative of any interest other than that of their own professional aggrandizement. Meanwhile, the interests of information-seeking viewers are disregarded as if of no significant account. Their concerns simply betray the powerlessness of their position. Insofar as they aspire to a more meaningful part in the public information process, they are deluded—struggling in the mists of 'false consciousness'. In our view, however, a democratic political communication system is essentially a three-legged stool. And it can be improved only if *all* the interests at stake—those of the political parties, the broadcasters, and the voters—are better served.

Since we have already outlined our attitude to the political parties in the preceding section of this article, it remains to consider the place of the other two groups in a sound political broadcasting system—starting with the voters. In so blithely dismissing voters' informational needs, Garnham not only reveals a breathtakingly élitist outlook. He also ignores the necessary mutuality of communication relationships (involving those who receive as well as those who send) and adopts a short-sighted view so far as political party requirements are concerned. If the audience for political broadcasting is not being properly served, then the political parties cannot be adequately served in turn. Unless voters and viewers feel that there is something of value for them in the exchange that inheres in any communicator-audience member relationship, the political parties will always be fighting an uphill battle—and losing it. That way indeed signposts the road towards yet deeper voter scepticism and lower turnout at the polls.

So there is nothing anti-political about our form of concern for the electoral audience. A pro-audience orientation would be anti-political only if, in developing it, we had limited ourselves to recommending a big cut-back in campaign programming so as to stop imposing it on an unwilling public. But that is not our position. We regard the typical audience member as a political animal and as having certain serious (though not necessarily solemn) needs to be met when election campaigns are unleashed. We recognize that the same audience member may be ambivalent about or highly mistrustful of much political talk. Our concern, however, has not been to validate or reinforce his anti-political streak but rather, through a more adventurous approach to political broadcasting, to bring him back into the political fold. That is why we stress in CEB the 'need to find ways of enabling the political parties to talk effectively over television to the body of floating, uncertain and potentially volatile voters who form such a large part of the electorate nowadays'—individuals who, we say, want above all 'to be treated as intelligent citizens' (p. 47).

Now according to Garnham, 'Blumler never asks why people use TV in this way', why, that is, they chiefly seek information about what politicians might do if elected to power and other forms of help in deciding how to vote. As answer, he depicts such motives as a 'rational response to perceived powerlessness'. On both counts Garnham is wrong. Research on political efficacy shows that voters who regard themselves as powerless tend to turn away from political communication altogether. Despite their mixed feelings, the surveillance-seeking 'monitor' of political news and the guidance-seeking 'liberal citizen' are rather more hopeful about their place in the political process. In any case, 'Blumler' did enquire about the source of these uses of television when they originally surfaced in the 1964 survey that was reported in Blumler and McQuail (1968). Despite its obvious lack of sophistication, the authors noted, 'There is a sense in which the approach of these voters to propaganda might be said to be guided by rationality'. They were probably interested 'in forming some impression of how political developments might affect the tangible circumstances of their own lives in the near future'. So 'if trying to plan one's life in the light of information about the various circumstances that can affect it . . . is rational, then this should count as a rational basis for following political television' (p. 84).

Such a concern was allied, the authors of *Television in Politics* also observed, to a 'debate model of political campaigning'. According to such a model, the rational citizen is 'someone who is prepared to follow political materials as if a debate were being conducted of which he was trying to make sense'. This did not imply, however, a quite vacuous state of open-mindedness:

An assessment of the rational potential in the audience of electors would turn . . . on whether they could respond appropriately to such a campaign . . . not necessarily by wearing their votes on their sleeves, but by trying to grasp what has been proposed and to sift some of the main arguments in light of their own experiences and values (Blumler and McQuail, 1968; 84–85).

Clearly, this passage proclaims a normative ideal. But it corresponds with many people's expectations of political television and with how they actually use it when given the chance. The large amount of policy knowledge which American watchers absorbed from even the much maligned Carter–Ford debates in 1976 points impressively to the educative potential of such uses of election TV (see Sears and Chaffee, forthcoming).

Some readers of this journal might be willing to concede the claims to respect of voters' needs but be highly doubtful about those of the third leg of the political communication stool, namely the broadcasters. 'Representativeness' justifies Garnham's heavy weighting of partisan against broadcaster interests. The former possess while the latter lack this supposedly crucial characteristic. It seems strange, perhaps, that Garnham should so extol the representativeness of the major political parties, which are often criticized by other Marxists for neglecting many vital interests and masking the real issues that society faces. We even venture to suggest that if broadcasters enjoyed more freedom than at present, they might be able to give a fuller hearing to radical voices and minority views on controversial issues. Certainly one force which inhibits the airing of unorthodox opinions is fear of major party displeasure. In this connection it should be noted that it was the BBC and the IBA who championed the claims of the Scottish and Welsh Nationalists to more generous party broadcasting time in the 1974 elections than the major parties were initially inclined to concede.

If the major parties are incompletely representative, we accept that the broadcasters are not at all representative. But neither are they supposed to be, nor are they unique in failing to be. Many social functions are performed by groups whose legitimacy does not depend on their representativeness—including academics (of whom Garnham is one). University and polytechnic scholars are entrusted with resources to carry out a production and dissemination of knowledge function (similar to that of the broadcasters), not because society elected them to their chairs and lectureships, but because their training, mode of operation and experience are geared to the services that academics are supposed to provide.

So what is the task that gives broadcasters a rightful place in political communication? The answer eludes Garnham because he conflates two different communication functions which all free societies strive to distinguish. Of course there is the advocacy function, which the political parties (and many other bodies) perform, promoting particular ideas, causes and interests and thus periodically defining a polity's main lines of ideological cleavage. And of course it is vital for audience members to hear what the spokesmen of such causes have to say. But there is another communication function to be discharged, that of surveying the wider socio-political environment so as to report developments that may condition the success prospects of advocates' proposals or impinge more directly on the welfare of citizens themselves. Moreover, the various journalistic media that carry out this function must be sufficiently independent of the advocates to be able, when necessary, to relay news that the latter would regard as 'bad'. Their utility to audience members and their credibility turns on their autonomy.

We recognize that in the world of real institutions, functional boundary lines are untidy and tensions abound. Through its commitment to public service, broadcasting, for example, supposedly epitomizes the second communication function defined above. Yet it also stands in danger of being compromised by its subservience to organs of the state and the market. It is also true, as media sociologists have repeatedly found, that journalistic accounts of certain portions of the environment often assume a highly patterned and uni-directional form. Yet those are precisely the tendencies that all of us agree should be exposed by research, should be criticized when documented, and should be put right so far as possible. From a policy point of view, the question is what should be done about this and which course is better: One that says that the mass media should explicitly recognize their subservience to dominant power forces and draw the conclusion that they can do no better than knuckle under to the major political parties? Or one that attempts to open the eyes of the media professionals and others to what is happening, so as to encourage them to seek ways of improving their performance and bringing it more in line with their professed fourth-estate values?

It is in this area, we feel, that policy research has much to offer. CEB exemplified this type of contribution, when it pointed out that broadcast election news had virtually become a propaganda mill, uncritically passing on to viewers daily (and equally measured-out) doses of party-originated materials. From this standpoint, we agree with Katz's recent observation: '... critical research is a form of policy research' (Katz, 1978). And so it is to some problematics of policy research strategy, implicit in Garnham's critique, that we now briefly turn.

III

Who is the policy researcher's client? This is probably the most difficult question of all for 'engaged' scholars to answer. The problems stem from the conflicting appeals of integrity and influence. On the one hand, the academic wants to be his own man—to develop his theories, methodologies, findings and critiques according to his own standards and judgments, undiluted by regard for vested media interests. On the other hand, he does not wish to be confined merely to an ivory tower; he wants to have an impact on decisions made in the world of affairs. We consider that only one form of answer is capable of reconciling these divergent demands: The policy researcher's 'client' is an abstract set of values, which media institutions are supposed to serve, but which they often fail to live up to in practice. If the researcher shares those values, then his integrity will not be in jeopardy, and he can strive to exert influence by proposing ways of closing the gap between institutional norms and practices. But if the very values of the system leave him cold, then he has no business fishing in policy waters at all.

We are uncertain whether Garnham has fully worked out his own answer to the core question posed here. It appears to be less value-oriented and more oppositional than our own. Media organization, he implies, embraces a conflict of irreconcilable interests, which the researcher cannot transcend; rather must he take sides. But surely such a perspective defeats the object of policy research itself. If the researcher makes recommendations on behalf of one side (whether political parties or broadcasters), then they must be at the expense of the other—and would, almost by definition, be rejected by the other side. In that case, there could only be a continuing struggle and little hope of winning a considered hearing for the researcher's ideas.

Consistent with his oppositional perspective, Garnham has accused us of writing 'specifically for broadcaster consumption', of allowing 'the vested interests to define the questions' we asked, and of narrowing our recommendations to those that 'the broadcasters can accept'. We categorically refute these charges. First, it is untrue that we were writing solely for broadcaster consumption. Our report was intended for everyone who is likely to be significantly affected by the organization and output of political broadcasting. Second, a false logic underlies this line of criticism. While we freely admit that we have attempted to take account of the ability of the broadcasters (as well as the political parties) to act on our recommendations, it does not follow that we are bound to accept either side's definition of the problems to be addressed. Indeed, one of the main challenges confronting those engaged in policy research—and one we accepted throughout our enquiry—is to seek a redefinition of the problem, one which would encourage the parties involved to view and think afresh about the outstanding issues. When redefinitions are successfully promulgated, they often contain the seeds of their own solutions. Third, any fair-minded reader of CEB must realize how dissatisfied we were with certain entrenched approaches to election programming—e.g. the application of conventional news reporting and presentation routines to campaign coverage (see pp. 25–31). Finally, the allegation that we trimmed our policy sails to broadcasters' views presupposes a monolithicity of broadcaster opinion about TV's election role that is simply not supported by the interviews we held with more than 125 producers, reporters and executives. 'The broadcasters' showed no common front to us. Their evaluations of past election programming patterns ranged from keen enthusiasm to wholesale condemnation, and their ideas about how to improve the system were equally diverse (for chapter and verse see Appendix B of CEB).

We take our stand, then, not with 'the broadcasters' but with the values of public service broadcasting. These are precious and should not be cavalierly dismissed as mere myths and shams. Because they are often neglected or twisted does not mean that they lack beneficial impact. Insofar as they are applied, they confer fairness, reason and dignity on the struggle for votes through campaign communication. We are not blind to what is sordid and imperfect in the workings either of competitive democracy or of political broadcasting. But that is exactly why public service standards are so vital—to serve as spurs to improvement and guides to correction. Without their influence, political communication arrangements would stand for nothing better than domination by the loudest voice. And it is difficult to imagine how in such a system any leg-room at all could be found for constructive policy research.

Bibliography

BLUMLER, J. G. (1975). Impact of TV on public opinion, *View*, no. 2, November

BLUMLER, J. G. and GUREVITCH, M. (1975). Towards a comparative framework for political communication research, in Chaffee, Steven H. (ed.), *Political Communication: Issues and Strategies for Research*, Sage, Beverley Hills and London

BLUMLER, J. G. and MCQUAIL, D. (1968). *Television in Politics: Its Uses and Influence*, Faber and Faber, London

GUREVITCH, M. and BLUMLER, J. G. (1977). Linkages between the mass media and politics: a model for the analysis of political communication systems, in Curran, J., Gurevitch, M. and Wollacott, J. (eds), *Mass Communication and Society*, Edward Arnold, London

KATZ, E. (1978). Of mutual interest, *Journal of Communication*, vol. 28, no. 2, pp. 133–141

SEARS, D. O. and CHAFFEE, S. H. (forthcoming). Uses and effects of the 1976 debates: an overview of empirical studies, in Kraus, S. (ed.), *The Great Debates, 1976: Ford vs. Carter*, Indiana University Press, Indianapolis